Database Explorations

Essays on *The Third Manifesto* and related topics

C. J. Date
and Hugh Darwen

Order this book online at www.trafford.com
or email orders@trafford.com

Most Trafford titles are also available at major online book retailers.

Printed in the United States of America.

ISBN: 978-1-4269-3723-1 (sc)
ISBN: 978-1-4269-3724-8 (e-b)

Library of Congress Control Number: 2010909190

Our mission is to efficiently provide the world's finest, most comprehensive book publishing service, enabling every author to experience success. To find out how to publish your book, your way, and have it available worldwide, visit us online at www.trafford.com

Trafford rev. 07/05/2010

www.trafford.com

North America & international
toll-free: 1 888 232 4444 (USA & Canada)
phone: 250 383 6864 • fax: 812 355 4082

There are two ways of constructing a software design:
One way is to make it so simple that there are obviously no deficiencies,
and the other way is to make it so complicated
that there are obviously no deficiencies.

—C. A. R. Hoare

———♦♦♦♦♦———

In science it often happens that scientists say, "You know, that's a really good argument, my position is mistaken," and then they actually change their minds, and you never hear that old view from them again. They really do it. It doesn't happen as often as it should, because scientists are human and change is sometimes painful. But it happens every day. I cannot recall the last time something like that happened in politics or religion.

—Carl Sagan

———♦♦♦♦♦———

Experience is what allows us to recognize a mistake
when we make it the second time.

—Anon.

———♦♦♦♦♦———

To all those who have contributed, and continue to contribute,
to our efforts to make *The Third Manifesto*
the best it can possibly be

Contents

Preface

This book consists of a collection of exploratory essays on database management—more specifically, on issues arising from and related to *The Third Manifesto,* which is a proposal by the authors for a foundation for data and database management systems (DBMSs). Like Codd's original papers on the relational model, *The Third Manifesto*—"the *Manifesto*" for short—can be seen as a blueprint for the design of a DBMS. It consists in essence of a rigorous set of principles, stated in the form of a series of prescriptions and proscriptions, that we require adherence to on the part of a hypothetical database programming language that we call **D**. We've described those prescriptions and proscriptions in detail in our book *Databases, Types, and the Relational Model: The Third Manifesto,* 3rd edition (Addison-Wesley, 2006)—referred to throughout the present book as "the *Manifesto* book" for short. *Note:* More information relating to the *Manifesto* can be found on the website *www.thethirdmanifesto.com*. In particular, information can be found on that website regarding a number of experimental—and, in at least one case, commercial—implementations of the *Manifesto* ideas (see later in this preface).

The present book is arranged into five parts, as follows:

I. Foundations

II. Language Design

III. Type Inheritance

IV. Missing Information

V. Miscellaneous Topics

Each part has its own introduction, and further details of individual chapters are left to those introductions. Most of the chapters were originally meant to stand alone; as a result, some of them contain references and examples—sometimes even appendixes—whose numbering is unique only within the chapter in question. To a large extent, we've preserved the independence of individual chapters; thus, all references within a given chapter to, say, Example 3 or Appendix A are to be taken as references to the indicated example or appendix within the chapter in question. Also, some of the chapters overlap each other a little; we apologize for this fact, but we felt it was better, as already indicated, to preserve the independence of individual chapters as far as possible.

Note: Most of the chapters started out in life as single-author papers, which explains the use in certain cases of the first person singular. However, the first person singular can always be interpreted to mean both of us, barring explicit statements to the contrary. For the record, Chris was the original author for Chapters 3-4, 7-8, 10, 12-15, 17-18, 22, and 27-31; Hugh was the original author for Chapters 2, 5-6, 9, and 23-26; and Chapters 1, 11, 16, and 19-21 were joint productions.

Examples throughout the book are expressed in a language called **Tutorial D,** which is the language used for examples in the *Manifesto* book. The specific version of that language used herein—the most recent version, in fact, which differs in certain important respects from earlier versions—is defined in Chapter 11 of the present book. (The differences with respect to those earlier versions are also explained in that chapter.)

Prerequisites

Our target audience is database professionals. Thus, we assume you're somewhat familiar with both the relational model and the SQL language (though certain relational and/or SQL concepts are reviewed briefly here and there—basically wherever we felt such explanations might be helpful). Prior familiarity with *The Third Manifesto* would also be advantageous.

Projects Related to The Third Manifesto

For interest we give here a brief summary of projects related to *The Third Manifesto* (abbreviated *TTM*) that have come to our attention. As previously noted, further information regarding these projects is available at *www.thethirdmanifesto.com*, including in each case an essay by the project author(s) on the motivation for the project in question and the relevance of *TTM* to it.

- Rel (*dbappbuilder.sourceforge.net/Rel.html*)

  By Dave Voorhis. A faithful implementation of **Tutorial D**.

- Duro (*duro.sourceforge.net*)

  By René Hartmann. A relational database library based on *TTM,* written in C; comes with an interpreter that supports **Tutorial D** statements.

- D4 (*www.alphora.com*)

  The first known attempt at a commercial implementation of *TTM.* Syntax similar to **Tutorial D**.

- Muldis Rosetta (*www.muldis.com*)

  By Darren Duncan. Work in progress on a complete implementation of *TTM* for Perl users.

- Opus

  By David Cauz. In the syntactic style of C, claiming conformance to *TTM.* Work in progress.

- CsiDB

  A C++ library developed internally by an international corporation; used in a general bookkeeping and accounting application.

- MighTyD (*sourceforge.net/projects/mightyd*)

  A final year project by undergraduate students at the University of Warwick (2005-2006). A prototype implementation of **Tutorial D** with some of the extensions proposed for temporal database support by Date, Darwen, and Lorentzos (see *Temporal Data and the Relational Model,* Morgan Kaufmann, 2003).

- Web Relational Blocks (*services.alphaworks.ibm.com/webrb*)

  By researchers at IBM. A visual language for constructing enterprise applications, influenced by *TTM.*

- Dee (*www.quicksort.co.uk*)

  From the developers of ThinkSQL. An implementation of a **D** as an extension to Python.

- TclRAL (*tclral.sourceforge.net*)

  An implementation of the relational algebra concepts in *TTM* as an extension of the Tcl language.

- Open Database Project, University of Northumbria (*computing.unn.ac.uk/openDBproject/*)

  A proposed proof of concept of *TTM* using RAQUEL, a language devised prior to the first publication of *TTM.*

- Ingres D (*community.ingres.com/wiki/Project_D*)

A project to add support for **Tutorial D** to Ingres Database Server.

- SIRA_PRISE (*shark.armchair.mb.ca/~erwin*)

  By Erwin Smout. An effort to build a usable "true relational" DBMS based on *TTM,* including support for temporal extensions.

A Note on the Diagrams

This book contains numerous tabular pictures of relations. Double underlining in such pictures is to be interpreted as follows:

- *Case 1* (the relation depicted is a sample value for some relvar *R*): In this case, double underlining indicates that a primary key *PK* has been declared for *R* and the pertinent attribute is part of *PK*.

- *Case 2* (the relation depicted is a sample value for some relational expression *rx*, where *rx* is something other than a simple relvar reference): In this case, *rx* can be thought of as defining some temporary relvar *R,* and double underlining indicates that a primary key *PK* could in principle be declared for *R* and the pertinent attribute is part of *PK*.

Acknowledgments

Each chapter includes specific thanks to reviewers and other parties who helped in one way or another with the chapter in question. In addition, we would once again like to thank our wives Lindy Date and Lindsay Darwen for their support throughout the production of this book and all of its predecessors. We would particularly like to thank Lindy for allowing us to reproduce a piece of her artwork ("Mount St. Helena") on the front cover.

Publishing History

A few of the chapters in this book are based on earlier published writings, as indicated below.

- "*The Third Manifesto*" (Chapter 1), "**Tutorial D**" (Chapter 11), and "The Inheritance Model" (Chapter 19): Based on Chapters 4, 5, and 13, respectively, of *Databases, Types, and the Relational Model: The Third Manifesto* (3rd edition, Addison-Wesley, 2006); revised versions published by permission of Pearson Education, Inc.

- "Setting the Record Straight, Parts 1-6" (Chapters 4-9): Based on a series of articles appearing in *DB/M Magazine* (Array Publications, Netherlands, 2007-2008); revised versions published by permission of Array Publications b.v. (Netherlands).

- "Orthogonal Language Design: How Not to Do It" (Chapter 18): Based on an article of the same name that appeared in *Business Rules Journal* on the website *www.BRCommunity.com* (2007); this version published by permission of Business Rule Solutions, Inc.

- "A Critique of *Nulls, Three-Valued Logic, and Ambiguity in SQL: Critiquing Date's Critique*" (Chapter 28): Based on an earlier paper of the same name in *ACM SIGMOD Record 37,* No. 3 (September 2008); this version published by permission of ACM.

- "Nothing to Worry About" (Chapter 29): Based on an article of the same name that appeared on the website *www.dbdebunk.com* (December 2004) and elsewhere; this version published by permission of Fabian Pascal.

C. J. Date / Hugh Darwen *Healdsburg, California / Shrewley, England*
2010

About the Authors

C. J. Date is an independent author, lecturer, researcher, and consultant, specializing in relational database technology. He is best known for his book *An Introduction to Database Systems* (8th edition, Addison-Wesley, 2004), which has sold over 825,000 copies at the time of writing and is used by several hundred colleges and universities worldwide. He is also the author of many other books on database management, including most recently *Logic and Databases: The Roots of Relational Theory* (Trafford, 2007); *The Relational Database Dictionary, Extended Edition* (Apress, 2008); and *SQL and Relational Theory: How to Write Accurate SQL Code* (O'Reilly, 2009). He was inducted into the Computing Industry Hall of Fame in 2004.

Hugh Darwen was employed in IBM's software development divisions from 1967 to 2004. In the early part of his career, he was involved in DBMS development; from 1978 to 1982, he was one of the chief architects of an IBM product called Business System 12, a product that faithfully embraced the principles of the relational model. He was an active participant in the development of the international standard for SQL (and related standards) from 1988 to 2004. Based in the U.K., he currently teaches relational database theory at Warwick University and is a tutor and course development consultant for the Open University. His book *An Introduction to Relational Database Theory,* based on his lectures at Warwick, was published in 2009 as a free download at *http://bookboon.com/uk/student/it.*

Part I

FOUNDATIONS

This part of the book consists of ten chapters. Chapter 1 is a self-contained and updated definition of *The Third Manifesto* as such ("the *Manifesto*" for short). Chapter 2 is an investigation into a question that underpins the *Manifesto,* as well as just about everything else in the book: viz., what exactly is a predicate? Chapters 3-9 are detailed responses to certain criticisms of the *Manifesto* that have appeared in the literature in the past couple of years. Chapter 10 consists of an extended argument in support of the position that, contrary to popular belief, there's no such thing as a view that's intrinsically nonupdatable.

Chapter 1

The Third Manifesto

... the powerful plain third manifesto
—with apologies to Stephen Spender

These principles are eternal, and will remain eternal
—unidentified politician, quoted in a recent news item

This chapter provides a precise and succinct definition of the various components that go to make up *The Third Manifesto* ("the *Manifesto*" for short). The bulk of the chapter consists of a revised version of Chapter 4 from the book *Databases, Types, and the Relational Model: The Third Manifesto,* 3rd edition, by C. J. Date and Hugh Darwen, Addison-Wesley, 2006 ("the *Manifesto* book" for short). The principal revisions are as follows:

- This introductory section has been added. Its purpose is to make the chapter more self-contained by providing definitions and explanations of terms used in the rest of the chapter.
- Numerous changes have been made at the detail level.
- The final section ("Recent *Manifesto* Changes") has been completely rewritten. In the *Manifesto* book, it served to summarize differences between the *Manifesto* as defined therein and the version defined in that book's predecessor (viz., *Foundation for Future Database Systems: The Third Manifesto,* 2nd edition, by C. J. Date and Hugh Darwen, Addison-Wesley, 2000); now it summarizes differences between the *Manifesto* as defined in the present chapter and the version defined in the *Manifesto* book.

Here now are the promised definitions and explanations of terms (extracted, mostly, from earlier chapters of the *Manifesto* book but reworded somewhat here):

- ***D:*** The *Manifesto* makes repeated reference to a hypothetical language it calls **D**. However, the name **D** is merely a useful generic label; any language that conforms to the principles laid down in the *Manifesto* is a valid **D** (and any language that fails so to conform is not a valid **D**).
- ***Tutorial D:*** The *Manifesto* book includes a fairly formal (though certainly not rigorous) definition of a particular **D** it calls **Tutorial D**. **Tutorial D** is a computationally complete programming language with fully integrated database functionality. However, it's deliberately not meant to be industrial strength; rather, it's a "toy" language, whose principal purpose is to serve as a teaching vehicle. Thus, many features that would be required in an industrial strength language are intentionally omitted; in particular, it includes no exception handling, no I/O facilities, and no authorization features of any kind.
- *"RM" and "OO":* The *Manifesto* defines a number of prescriptions and proscriptions that **D** is required to adhere to. Prescriptions that arise from the relational model are called *Relational Model Prescriptions* (*RM Prescriptions*). Prescriptions that do not arise from the relational model are called *Other Orthogonal Prescriptions* (*OO Prescriptions*). Proscriptions are similarly divided into RM and OO categories. The *Manifesto* also includes a series of *Very Strong Suggestions,* likewise divided into RM and OO categories.
- *Expression:* The term *expression* refers to the representation in concrete syntactic form of a read-only operator invocation. Observe in particular that variable references are regarded as expressions in exactly this sense; so too are constant references (see RM Prescription 19). *Note:* Two important examples of the

latter, not explicitly referenced in the *Manifesto* as such but supported by **Tutorial D,** are TABLE_DUM and TABLE_DEE. TABLE_DEE is the unique relation with no attributes and just one tuple—the empty tuple, of course—and TABLE_DUM is the unique relation with no attributes and no tuples at all.

- *Literal:* A literal is an expression denoting a selector operator invocation (see RM Prescriptions 4, 9, and 10) in which every argument expression is a literal in turn. In other words, a literal is, loosely, what's sometimes called a *self-defining symbol;* i.e., it's a symbol that denotes a value that's fixed and determined by the symbol in question, and hence can be determined at compile time (and the type of that value is therefore also fixed and determined by the symbol in question, and can also be determined at compile time). Observe that there's a logical difference between a literal as such and the value it denotes.

- *Argument and argument expression:* An argument is what's substituted for a parameter when an operator is invoked; it's denoted by an argument expression, which is part of the representation in concrete syntactic form of the operator invocation in question. An argument is either a value or a variable. To be specific, if the parameter in question is subject to update (see RM Prescription 3), the argument must be a variable (and the corresponding argument expression must be a variable reference specifically, denoting the variable in question); otherwise it must be a value (though the corresponding argument expression might still be just a variable reference, denoting in this case the current value of the variable in question).

- *Scalar:* Loosely, a type is *scalar* if and only if it has no user visible components, and *nonscalar* if and only if it's not scalar; and values, variables, attributes, operators, parameters, and expressions of some type *T* are scalar or nonscalar according as type *T* itself is scalar or nonscalar. But these definitions are only informal, and the *Manifesto* doesn't rely on the scalar vs. nonscalar distinction in any formal sense. For the purposes of the *Manifesto,* in fact, the term *scalar type* can be taken to mean a type that's neither a tuple type nor a relation type, and the term *nonscalar type* can be taken to mean a type that is either a tuple type or a relation type. The terms *scalar value, nonscalar value, scalar operator, nonscalar operator,* etc., can be interpreted analogously.

- *Ordered type:* An ordered type is a type for which a total ordering is defined. Thus, if *T* is such a type and *v1* and *v2* are values of type *T,* then (with respect to that ordering) exactly one of the following comparisons returns TRUE and the other two return FALSE:

```
v1 < v2        v1 = v2        v1 > v2
```

One last point: The *Manifesto* book also includes a detailed proposal for a model of type inheritance. However, everything to do with that inheritance model is ignored in the *Manifesto* per se, except for very brief mentions in RM Prescription 1, OO Prescription 2, and OO Very Strong Suggestion 1. The concepts of the inheritance model extend, but do not otherwise invalidate, the concepts of the *Manifesto* per se.

RM PRESCRIPTIONS

1. A **scalar data type** (**scalar type** for short) is a named, finite set of scalar values (**scalars** for short). Given an arbitrary pair of distinct scalar types named *T1* and *T2,* respectively, with corresponding sets of scalar values *S1* and *S2,* respectively, the names *T1* and *T2* shall be distinct and the sets *S1* and *S2* shall be disjoint; in other words, two scalar types shall be equal—i.e., the same type—if and only if they have the same name (and therefore the same set of values). **D** shall provide facilities for users to define their own scalar types (*user defined* scalar types); other scalar types shall be provided by the system (*built in* or *system defined* scalar types). With the sole exception of the system defined empty type *omega* (which is defined only if type inheritance is supported—see OO Prescription 2), the definition of any given scalar type *T* shall be accompanied by a specification of an **example value** of that type. **D** shall also provide

facilities for users to destroy user defined scalar types. The system defined scalar types shall include type **boolean** (containing just two values, here denoted TRUE and FALSE), and **D** shall support all four monadic and 16 dyadic logical operators, directly or indirectly, for this type.

2. All scalar values shall be **typed**—i.e., such values shall always carry with them, at least conceptually, some identification of the type to which they belong.

3. A **scalar operator** is an operator that, when invoked, returns a scalar value (the **result** of that invocation). **D** shall provide facilities for users to define and destroy their own scalar operators (*user defined* scalar operators). Other scalar operators shall be provided by the system (*built in* or *system defined* scalar operators). Let *Op* be a scalar operator. Then:

    a. *Op* shall be **read-only,** in the sense that invoking it shall cause no variables to be updated other than ones local to the code that implements *Op*.

    b. Every invocation of *Op* shall denote a value ("produce a result") of the same type, the **result type**—also called the **declared type**—of *Op* (as well as of that invocation of *Op* in particular). The definition of *Op* shall include a specification of that declared type.

    c. The definition of *Op* shall include a specification of the type of each parameter to *Op,* the **declared type** of that parameter. If parameter *P* is of declared type *T,* then, in every invocation of *Op,* the expression that denotes the argument corresponding to *P* in that invocation shall also be of type *T,* and the value denoted by that expression shall be **effectively assigned** to *P*. *Note:* The prescriptions of this paragraph c. shall also apply if *Op* is an update operator instead of a read-only operator (see below).

    It is convenient to deal with update operators here as well, despite the fact that such operators are not scalar (nor are they nonscalar—in fact, they are not typed at all). An **update operator** is an operator that, when invoked, is allowed to update at least one variable that is not local to the code that implements that operator. Let *V* be such a variable. If the operator accesses *V* via some parameter *P,* then that parameter *P* is **subject to update**. **D** shall provide facilities for users to define and destroy their own update operators (*user defined* update operators). Other update operators shall be provided by the system (*built in* or *system defined* update operators). Let *Op* be an update operator. Then:

    d. No invocation of *Op* shall denote a value ("produce a result").

    e. The definition of *Op* shall include a specification of which parameters to *Op* are subject to update. If parameter *P* is subject to update, then, in every invocation of *Op,* the expression that denotes the argument corresponding to *P* in that invocation shall be a variable reference specifically, and, on completion of the execution of *Op* caused by that invocation, the final value assigned to *P* during that execution shall be **effectively assigned** to that variable.

4. Let *T* be a scalar type, and let *v* be an appearance in some context of some value of type *T*. By definition, *v* has exactly one **physical representation** and one or more **possible representations** (at least one, because there is obviously always one that is the same as the physical representation). Physical representations for values of type *T* shall be specified by means of some kind of *storage structure definition language* and shall not be visible in **D**. As for possible representations:

    a. If *T* is user defined, then at least one possible representation for values of type *T* shall be declared and thus made visible in **D**. For each possible representation *PR* for values of type *T* that is visible in **D,** exactly one **selector** operator *S,* of declared type *T,* shall be provided. That operator *S* shall have all of the following properties:

1. There shall be a one to one correspondence between the parameters of *S* and the components of *PR* (see RM Prescription 5). Each parameter of *S* shall have the same declared type as the corresponding component of *PR*.

2. Every value of type *T* shall be produced by some invocation of *S* in which every argument expression is a literal.

3. Every successful invocation of *S* shall produce some value of type *T*.

b. If *T* is system defined, then zero or more possible representations for values of type *T* shall be declared and thus made visible in **D**. A possible representation *PR* for values of type *T* that is visible in **D** shall behave in all respects as if *T* were user defined and *PR* were a declared possible representation for values of type *T*. If no possible representation for values of type *T* is visible in **D,** then at least one **selector** operator *S*, of declared type *T*, shall be provided. Each such selector operator shall have all of the following properties:

1. Every argument expression in every invocation of *S* shall be a literal.

2. Every value of type *T* shall be produced by some invocation of *S*.

3. Every successful invocation of *S* shall produce some value of type *T*.

5. Let some declared possible representation *PR* for values of scalar type *T* be defined in terms of components *C1, C2, ..., Cn* ($n \geqslant 0$), each of which has a name and a declared type. Let *v* be a value of type *T*, and let *PR*(*v*) denote the possible representation corresponding to *PR* for that value *v*. Then *PR*(*v*) shall be **exposed**—i.e., a set of read-only and update operators shall be provided such that:

a. For all such values *v* and for all *i* ($i = 1, 2, ..., n$), it shall be possible to "retrieve" (i.e., read the value of) the *Ci* component of *PR*(*v*). The read-only operator that provides this functionality shall have declared type the same as that of *Ci*.

b. For all variables *V* of declared type *T* and for all *i* ($i = 1, 2, ..., n$), it shall be possible to update *V* in such a way that if the values of *V* before and after the update are *v* and *v'* respectively, then the possible representations corresponding to *PR* for *v* and *v'* (i.e., *PR*(*v*) and *PR*(*v'*), respectively) differ in their *Ci* components.

Such a set of operators shall be provided for each possible representation declared for values of type *T*.

6. **D** shall support the **TUPLE** type generator. That is, given some heading {*H*} (see RM Prescription 9), **D** shall support use of the **generated type** TUPLE {*H*} as a basis for defining (or, in the case of values, selecting):

a. Values of that type (see RM Prescription 9)

b. Variables of that type (see RM Prescription 12)

c. Attributes of that type (see RM Prescriptions 9 and 10)

d. Components of that type within declared possible representations (see RM Prescription 5)

e. Read-only operators of that type (see RM Prescription 20)

f. Parameters of that type to user defined operators (see RM Prescriptions 3 and 20)

The generated type TUPLE {*H*} shall be referred to as a **tuple type,** and the name of that type shall be, precisely, TUPLE {*H*}. The terminology of **degree, attributes,** and **heading** introduced in RM

Prescription 9 shall apply, mutatis mutandis, to that type, as well as to values and variables of that type (see RM Prescription 12). Tuple types TUPLE {*H1*} and TUPLE {*H2*} shall be equal if and only if {*H1*} = {*H2*}. The applicable operators shall include operators analogous to the RENAME, *project,* EXTEND, and JOIN operators of the relational algebra (see RM Prescription 18), together with tuple assignment (see RM Prescription 21) and tuple comparisons (see RM Prescription 22); they shall also include (a) a tuple selector operator (see RM Prescription 9), (b) an operator for extracting a specified attribute value from a specified tuple (the tuple in question might be required to be of degree one—see RM Prescription 9), and (c) operators for performing tuple "nesting" and "unnesting."

Note: When we say "the name of [a certain tuple type] shall be, precisely, TUPLE {*H*}," we do not mean to prescribe specific syntax. The *Manifesto* does not prescribe syntax. Rather, what we mean is that the type in question shall have a name that does both of the following, no more and no less: First, it shall specify that the type is indeed a tuple type; second, it shall specify the pertinent heading. Syntax of the form "TUPLE {*H*}" satisfies these requirements, and we therefore use it as a convenient shorthand; however, all appearances of that syntax throughout this *Manifesto* are to be interpreted in the light of these remarks.

7. **D** shall support the **RELATION** type generator. That is, given some heading {*H*} (see RM Prescription 9), **D** shall support use of the **generated type** RELATION {*H*} as the basis for defining (or, in the case of values, selecting):

   a. Values of that type (see RM Prescription 10)

   b. Variables of that type (see RM Prescription 13)

   c. Attributes of that type (see RM Prescriptions 9 and 10)

   d. Components of that type within declared possible representations (see RM Prescription 5)

   e. Read-only operators of that type (see RM Prescription 20)

   f. Parameters of that type to user defined operators (see RM Prescriptions 3 and 20)

   The generated type RELATION {*H*} shall be referred to as a **relation type,** and the name of that type shall be, precisely, RELATION {*H*}. The terminology of **degree, attributes,** and **heading** introduced in RM Prescription 9 shall apply, mutatis mutandis, to that type, as well as to values and variables of that type (see RM Prescription 13). Relation types RELATION {*H1*} and RELATION {*H2*} shall be equal if and only if {*H1*} = {*H2*}. The applicable operators shall include the usual operators of the relational algebra (see RM Prescription 18), together with relational assignment (see RM Prescription 21) and relational comparisons (see RM Prescription 22); they shall also include (a) a relation selector operator (see RM Prescription 10), (b) an operator for extracting the sole tuple from a specified relation of cardinality one (see RM Prescription 10), and (c) operators for performing relational "nesting" and "unnesting."

   Note: When we say "the name of [a certain relation type] shall be, precisely, RELATION {*H*}," we do not mean to prescribe specific syntax. The *Manifesto* does not prescribe syntax. Rather, what we mean is that the type in question shall have a name that does both of the following, no more and no less: First, it shall specify that the type is indeed a relation type; second, it shall specify the pertinent heading. Syntax of the form "RELATION {*H*}" satisfies these requirements, and we therefore use it as a convenient shorthand; however, all appearances of that syntax throughout this *Manifesto* are to be interpreted in the light of these remarks.

8. **D** shall support the **equality** comparison operator "=" for every type *T*. Let *Op* be a read-only operator (other than "=" itself) with a parameter *P*, let *P* be of declared type *T*, and let *v1* and *v2* be values of type *T*. Then *v1* = *v2* shall evaluate to TRUE if and only if, for all such operators *Op*, two successful invocations

of *Op* that are identical in all respects except that the argument corresponding to *P* is *v1* in one invocation and *v2* in the other are indistinguishable in their effect.

9. A **heading** {*H*} is a set of ordered pairs or **attributes** of the form <*A,T*>, where:

   a. *A* is the name of an **attribute** of {*H*}. No two distinct pairs in {*H*} shall have the same attribute name.

   b. *T* is the name of the **declared type** of attribute *A* of {*H*}.

   The number of pairs in {*H*}—equivalently, the number of attributes of {*H*}—is the **degree** of {*H*}.

   Now let *t* be a set of ordered triples <*A,T,v*>, obtained from {*H*} by extending each ordered pair <*A,T*> to include an arbitrary value *v* of type *T,* called the **attribute value** for attribute *A* of *t*. Then *t* is a **tuple value** (**tuple** for short) that **conforms** to heading {*H*}; equivalently, *t* is of the corresponding tuple type (see RM Prescription 6). The degree of that heading {*H*} shall be the **degree** of *t,* and the attributes and corresponding types of that heading {*H*} shall be the **attributes** and corresponding **declared attribute types** of *t*.

   Given a heading {*H*}, exactly one **selector** operator *S,* of declared type TUPLE {*H*}, shall be provided for selecting an arbitrary tuple conforming to {*H*}. That operator *S* shall have all of the following properties:

   1. There shall be a one to one correspondence between the parameters of *S* and the attributes of {*H*}. Each parameter of *S* shall have the same declared type as the corresponding attribute of {*H*}.

   2. Every tuple of type TUPLE {*H*} shall be produced by some invocation of *S* in which every argument expression is a literal.

   3. Every successful invocation of *S* shall produce some tuple of type TUPLE {*H*}.

10. A **relation value** *r* (**relation** for short) consists of a *heading* and a *body,* where:

    a. The **heading** of *r* shall be a heading {*H*} as defined in RM Prescription 9; *r* **conforms** to that heading; equivalently, *r* is of the corresponding relation type (see RM Prescription 7). The degree of that heading {*H*} shall be the **degree** of *r,* and the attributes and corresponding types of that heading {*H*} shall be the **attributes** and corresponding **declared attribute types** of *r*.

    b. The **body** of *r* shall be a set {*b*} of tuples, all having that same heading {*H*}. The cardinality of that body shall be the **cardinality** of *r*. *Note:* Relation *r* is an *empty relation* if and only if the set {*b*} is empty.

    Given a heading {*H*}, exactly one **selector** operator *S,* of declared type RELATION {*H*}, shall be provided for selecting an arbitrary relation conforming to {*H*}. That operator *S* shall have all of the following properties:

    1. The sole argument to any given invocation of *S* shall be a set {*b*} of tuples, each of which shall be denoted by a tuple expression of declared type TUPLE {*H*}.

    2. Every relation of type RELATION {*H*} shall be produced by some invocation of *S* for which the tuple expressions that together denote the argument to that invocation are all literals.

    3. Every successful invocation of *S* shall produce some relation of type RELATION {*H*}: to be specific, the relation of type RELATION {*H*} with body {*b*}.

11. **D** shall provide facilities for users to define **scalar variables**. Each scalar variable shall be named and

shall have a specified (scalar) **declared type**. Let scalar variable *V* be of declared type *T;* for so long as variable *V* exists, it shall have a value that is of type *T*. Defining *V* shall have the effect of initializing *V* to some value—either a value specified explicitly as part of the operation that defines *V,* or some implementation defined value otherwise. *Note:* Omitting an explicit initialization value does not preclude the implementation from checking that no reference is made to scalar variable *V* until an explicit assignment to *V* has occurred. Analogous remarks apply to tuple variables (see RM Prescription 12), real relvars (see RM Prescription 14), and private relvars (again, see RM Prescription 14).

12. **D** shall provide facilities for users to define **tuple variables**. Each tuple variable shall be named and shall have a specified **declared type** of the form TUPLE {*H*} for some heading {*H*}. Let variable *V* be of declared type TUPLE {*H*}; then the degree of that heading {*H*} shall be the **degree** of *V,* and the attributes and corresponding types of that heading {*H*} shall be the **attributes** and corresponding **declared attribute types** of *V*. For so long as variable *V* exists, it shall have a value that is of type TUPLE {*H*}. Defining *V* shall have the effect of initializing *V* to some value—either a value specified explicitly as part of the operation that defines *V,* or some implementation defined value otherwise.

13. **D** shall provide facilities for users to define **relation variables** (**relvars** for short)—both database relvars (i.e., relvars that are part of some database) and application relvars (i.e., relvars that are local to some application). **D** shall also provide facilities for users to destroy database relvars. Each relvar shall be named and shall have a specified **declared type** of the form RELATION {*H*} for some heading {*H*}. Let variable *V* be of declared type RELATION {*H*}; then the degree of that heading {*H*} shall be the **degree** of *V,* and the attributes and corresponding types of that heading {*H*} shall be the **attributes** and corresponding **declared attribute types** of *V*. For so long as variable *V* exists, it shall have a value that is of type RELATION {*H*}.

14. Database relvars shall be either *real* or *virtual*. A **virtual relvar** *V* shall be a database relvar whose value at any given time is the result of evaluating a certain relational expression at that time; the relational expression in question shall be specified when *V* is defined and shall mention at least one database relvar other than *V*. A **real relvar** (also known as a **base relvar**) shall be a database relvar that is not virtual. Defining a real relvar *V* shall have the effect of initializing *V* to some value—either a value specified explicitly as part of the operation that defines *V,* or the empty relation of type RELATION {*H*} otherwise (where RELATION {*H*} is the type of relvar *V*).

    Application relvars shall be either *public* or *private*. A **public relvar** shall be an application relvar that constitutes the perception on the part of the application in question of some portion of some database. A **private relvar** shall be an application relvar that is completely private to the application in question and is not part of any database. Defining a private relvar *V* shall have the effect of initializing *V* to some value—either a value specified explicitly as part of the operation that defines *V,* or the empty relation of type RELATION {*H*} otherwise (where RELATION {*H*} is the type of relvar *V*).

15. Every relvar shall have at least one **candidate key**. At least one such key shall be defined, explicitly or implicitly, at the time the relvar in question is defined, and it shall not be possible to destroy all of the candidate keys of a given relvar other than by destroying the relvar itself.

16. A **database** shall be a named container for relvars; the content of a given database at any given time shall be a set of database relvars. The necessary operators for defining and destroying databases shall not be part of **D** (in other words, defining and destroying databases shall be done "outside the **D** environment").

17. Each **transaction** shall interact with exactly one database. However, distinct transactions shall be allowed to interact with distinct databases, and distinct databases shall not necessarily be disjoint. Also, **D** shall provide facilities for a transaction to define new relvars, or destroy existing ones, within its associated

database (see RM Prescription 13). Every execution of every **statement** (other than a "begin transaction" statement—see OO Prescription 4) shall be performed within the context of some transaction. Every statement execution shall be **semantically atomic** (i.e., it shall be as if either the statement executes in its entirety or it fails to execute at all), unless either of the following is the case:

a. The statement in question is not syntactically atomic (i.e., it contains another statement nested inside itself).

b. The statement in question represents the invocation of a user defined update operator.

18. **D** shall support the usual operators of the **relational algebra** (or some logical equivalent thereof). All such operators shall be expressible without excessive circumlocution. **D** shall support **type inference** for relation types, whereby the type of the result of evaluating an arbitrary relational expression shall be well defined and known to both the system and the user. *Note:* It follows from this prescription that **D** shall also support type inference for tuple types, whereby the type of the result of evaluating an arbitrary tuple expression shall be well defined and known to both the system and the user.

19. **Variable references** and **constant references** shall be valid expressions. The expression *V*, where *V* is a variable reference, shall be regarded as an invocation of a read-only operator that returns the current value of variable *V*. The expression *C*, where *C* is a constant reference, shall be regarded as an invocation of a read-only operator that returns the value of constant *C*.

20. **D** shall provide facilities for users to define and destroy their own **tuple operators** (*user defined* tuple operators) and **relational operators** (*user defined* relational operators), and paragraphs a.-c. from RM Prescription 3 shall apply, mutatis mutandis. **Recursion** shall be permitted in operator definitions.

21. **D** shall support the **assignment** operator ":=" for every type *T*. The assignment shall be referred to as a scalar, tuple, or relation (or relational) assignment according as *T* is a scalar, tuple, or relation type. Let *V* and *v* be a variable and a value, respectively, of the same type. After assignment of *v* to *V* (the "target variable"), the equality comparison *V* = *v* shall evaluate to TRUE (see RM Prescription 8). Furthermore, all variables other than *V* shall remain unchanged, apart possibly from variables *V'* in terms of which *V* is defined or variables defined, directly or indirectly, in terms of such variables *V'*.

D shall also support a **multiple** form of assignment, in which several individual assignments shall be performed as a single semantically atomic operation. Let *MA* be the multiple assignment

```
A1 , A2 , ... , An ;
```

(where *A1, A2, ..., An* are individual assignments, each assigning to exactly one target variable, and the semicolon marks the overall end of the operation). Then the semantics of *MA* shall be defined by the following pseudocode (Steps a.-d.):

a. For *i* := 1 to *n*, expand any syntactic shorthands involved in *Ai*. After all such expansions, let *MA* take the form

```
V1 := X1 , V2 := X2 , ... , Vz := Xz ;
```

for some $z \geqslant n$, where *Vi* is the name of some variable not defined in terms of any others and *Xi* is an expression of declared type the same as that of *Vi*.

b. Let *p* and *q* ($1 \leqslant p < q \leqslant z$) be such that *Vp* and *Vq* are identical and there is no *r* ($r < p$ or $p < r < q$) such that *Vp* and *Vr* are identical. Replace *Aq* in *MA* by an assignment of the form

```
Vq := WITH ( Vq := Xp ) : Xq
```

and remove *Ap* from *MA*. Repeat this process until no such pair *p* and *q* remains. Let *MA* now consist of the sequence

```
U1 := Y1 , U2 := Y2 , ... , Um := Ym ;
```

where each Ui is some Vj ($1 \leqslant i \leqslant j \leqslant m \leqslant z$).

c. For *i* := 1 to *m*, evaluate *Yi*. Let the result be *yi*.

d. For *i* := 1 to *m*, assign *yi* to *Ui*.

Note: Step b. of the foregoing pseudocode makes use of the WITH construct of **Tutorial D**. For further explanation, see Chapter 11 of the present book (or Chapter 5 of the Manifesto book).

22. **D** shall support certain **comparison operators,** as follows:

    a. The operators for comparing scalars shall include "=", "≠", and (for ordered types) "<", ">", etc.

    b. The operators for comparing tuples shall include "=" and "≠" and shall not include "<", ">", etc.

    c. The operators for comparing relations shall include "=", "≠", "⊆" ("is a subset of"), and "⊇" ("is a superset of") and shall not include "<", ">", etc.

    d. The operator "∈" for testing membership of a tuple in a relation shall be supported.

    In every case mentioned except "∈" the comparands shall be of the same type; in the case of "∈" they shall have the same heading. *Note:* Support for "=" for every type is in fact required by RM Prescription 8.

23. **D** shall provide facilities for defining and destroying **integrity constraints** (**constraints** for short). Let *C* be a constraint. Then *C* can be thought of as a boolean expression (though it might not be explicitly formulated as such); it shall be **satisfied** if and only if that boolean expression evaluates to TRUE, and **violated** if and only if it is not satisfied. No user shall ever see a state of affairs in which *C* is violated. There shall be two kinds of constraints:

    a. A **type** constraint shall specify the set of values that constitute a given type.

    b. A **database** constraint shall specify that, at all times, values of a given set of database relvars taken in combination shall be such that a given boolean expression (which shall mention no variables other than the database relvars in question) evaluates to TRUE. Insofar as feasible, **D** shall support **constraint inference** for database constraints, whereby the constraints that apply to the result of evaluating an arbitrary relational expression shall be well defined and known to both the system and the user.

24. Let *DB* be a database; let *DBC1, DBC2, ..., DBCn* be all of the database constraints defined for *DB* (see RM Prescription 23); and let *DBC* be any boolean expression that is logically equivalent to

    ```
    ( DBC1 ) AND ( DBC2 ) AND ... AND ( DBCn ) AND TRUE
    ```

    Then *DBC* shall be the **total database constraint** for *DB*.

25. Every database shall include a set of database relvars that constitute the **catalog** for that database. **D** shall provide facilities for assigning to relvars in the catalog. *Note:* Since assignments in general are allowed to be multiple assignments in particular (see RM Prescription 21), it follows that **D** shall permit any number of operations of a definitional nature—defining and destroying types, operators, variables, constraints, and so on—all to be performed as a single semantically atomic operation.

26. **D** shall be constructed according to well established principles of **good language design**.

RM PROSCRIPTIONS

1. **D** shall include no concept of a "relation" whose attributes are distinguishable by ordinal position. Instead, for every relation *r* expressible in **D,** the attributes of *r* shall be distinguishable by *name.*
2. **D** shall include no concept of a "relation" whose tuples are distinguishable by ordinal position. Instead, for every relation *r* expressible in **D,** the tuples of *r* shall be distinguishable by *value.*
3. **D** shall include no concept of a "relation" containing two distinct tuples *t1* and *t2* such that the comparison "*t1* = *t2*" evaluates to TRUE. It follows that (as already stated in RM Proscription 2), for every relation *r* expressible in **D,** the tuples of *r* shall be distinguishable by value.
4. **D** shall include no concept of a "relation" in which some "tuple" includes some "attribute" that does not have a value.
5. **D** shall not forget that relations with no attributes are respectable and interesting, nor that candidate keys with no components are likewise respectable and interesting.
6. **D** shall include no constructs that relate to, or are logically affected by, the "physical" or "storage" or "internal" levels of the system.
7. **D** shall support no tuple level operations on relvars or relations.
8. **D** shall not include any specific support for "composite" or "compound" attributes, since such functionality can more cleanly be achieved, if desired, through the type support already prescribed.
9. **D** shall include no "domain check override" operators, since such operators are both ad hoc and unnecessary.
10. **D** shall not be called SQL.

OO PRESCRIPTIONS

1. **D** shall permit **compile time type checking.**
2. If **D** supports **type inheritance,** then such support shall conform to the inheritance model defined in Part IV of the *Manifesto* book (and revised in Chapter 19 of the present book).
3. **D** shall be **computationally complete**. **D** may support, but shall not require, invocation from "host programs" written in languages other than **D**. **D** may also support, but shall not require, the use of other languages for implementation of user defined operators.
4. **D** shall provide **explicit transaction** support, according to which:

    - Transaction initiation shall be performed only by means of an explicit **"begin transaction"** statement.
    - Transaction termination shall be performed only by means of a **"commit"** or **"rollback"** statement; commit must always be explicit, but rollback can be implicit (if and only if the transaction fails through no fault of its own).

    If transaction *TX* terminates with commit ("normal termination"), changes made by *TX* to the applicable database shall be committed. If transaction *TX* terminates with rollback ("abnormal termination"), changes made by *TX* to the applicable database shall be rolled back.

Optionally, **D** shall also provide **implicit** transaction support, according to which any request to execute some statement *S* (other than a "begin transaction," "commit," or "rollback" statement) while no transaction is in progress shall be treated as if that statement *S* is immediately preceded by a "begin transaction" statement and immediately followed by either a "commit" statement (if statement *S* executes successfully) or a "rollback" statement (otherwise).

5. **D** shall support **nested transactions**—i.e., it shall permit a parent transaction *TX* to initiate a child transaction *TX'* before *TX* itself has terminated, in which case:

   a. *TX* and *TX'* shall interact with the same database (as is in fact required by RM Prescription 17).

   b. Whether *TX* shall be required to suspend execution while *TX'* executes shall be implementation defined. However, *TX* shall not be allowed to terminate before *TX'* terminates; in other words, *TX'* shall be wholly contained within *TX*.

   c. Rollback of *TX* shall include the rolling back of *TX'* even if *TX'* has terminated with commit. In other words, "commit" is always interpreted within the parent context (if such exists) and is subject to override by the parent transaction (again, if such exists).

6. Let *AggOp* be an **aggregate** operator, such as SUM, and let *r* be the relation over which the aggregation is to be done in some given invocation of *AggOp*. If *r* happens to be empty, then:

   a. If *AggOp* is essentially just shorthand for some iterated dyadic operator *Op* (the dyadic operator is "+" in the case of SUM), and if an identity value exists for *Op* (the identity value is 0 in the case of "+"), then the result of that invocation of *AggOp* shall be that identity value.

   b. Otherwise, the result of that invocation of *AggOp* shall be undefined.

OO PROSCRIPTIONS

1. Relvars are not domains.

2. No database relvar shall include an attribute of type *pointer*.

RM VERY STRONG SUGGESTIONS

1. **D** should provide a mechanism according to which values of some specified candidate key (or certain components thereof) for some specified relvar are **supplied by the system**. It should also provide a mechanism according to which an arbitrary relation can be extended to include an attribute whose values (a) are unique within that relation (or within certain partitions of that relation), and (b) are once again **supplied by the system**.

2. Let *RX* be a relational expression. By definition, *RX* can be thought of as designating a relvar, *R* say—either a user defined relvar (if *RX* is just a relvar name) or a system defined relvar (otherwise). It is desirable, though perhaps not always feasible, for the system to be able to **infer the candidate keys** of *R*, such that (among other things):

   a. If *RX* constitutes the defining expression for some virtual relvar *R'*, then those inferred candidate keys can be checked for consistency with the candidate keys explicitly defined for *R'* (if any) and—assuming no conflict—become candidate keys for *R'*.

   b. Those inferred candidate keys can be included in the information about *R* that is made available (in response to a "metaquery") to a user of **D**.

D should provide such functionality, but without any guarantee (a) that such inferred candidate keys are not proper supersets of actual candidate keys ("proper superkeys") or (b) that such an inferred candidate key is discovered for every actual candidate key.

3. **D** should support **transition constraints**—i.e., constraints on the transitions that a given database can make from one value to another.

4. **D** should provide some shorthand for expressing **quota queries**. It should not be necessary to convert the relation concerned into (e.g.) an array in order to formulate such a query.

5. **D** should provide some shorthand for expressing the **generalized transitive closure** operation, including the ability to specify generalized *concatenate* and *aggregate* operations.

6. **D** should provide some means for users to define their own generic **operators,** including in particular generic **relational** operators.

7. **SQL** should be implementable in **D**—not because such implementation is desirable in itself, but so that a painless migration route might be available for current SQL users. To this same end, existing SQL databases should be convertible to a form that **D** programs can operate on without error.

OO VERY STRONG SUGGESTIONS

1. Some level of **type inheritance** should be supported (in which case, see OO Prescription 2).

2. Operator definitions should be **logically distinct** from the definitions of the types of their parameters and results, not "bundled in" with those latter definitions (though the operators required by RM Prescriptions 4, 5, 8, and 21 might be exceptions in this regard).

3. **D** should support the concept of **single level storage**.

RECENT *MANIFESTO* CHANGES

As indicated in the introduction to this chapter, there are several differences between the *Manifesto* as defined herein and the version defined in Chapter 4 of the *Manifesto* book. For the benefit of readers who might be familiar with that earlier version, we summarize the main differences here. Of course, wherever there's a discrepancy, the present chapter should be taken as superseding.

- RM Prescription 1 has been extended to require that all scalar types, system or user defined, have an associated *example value* (except for the special case of the empty scalar type *omega,* which is part of our inheritance model—see Chapters 19 and 20 of the present book). Note that it's a logical consequence of this new requirement that scalar types are always nonempty (again, except for the special case of type *omega*).[1]

- Several other prescriptions have been revised to drop the explicit requirement that some type be nonempty, since that requirement is now satisfied implicitly.

- Several RM Prescriptions, including RM Prescription 3 in particular, have been reworded slightly to take

---

[1] Thanks to Alfredo Novoa for suggesting the idea of example values. *Note:* We might be persuaded to make specification of such values optional if it can be shown there's a serious requirement for user defined empty types.

account of the logical difference between arguments and argument expressions.

- RM Prescription 10 has been corrected (in fact, the version published in the *Manifesto* book—which was an attempt to clarify the version in the second edition of that book—was seriously in error). It has also been extended slightly to include an explicit definition of the term *empty relation.*

- Bowing to inevitability, RM Prescription 14 has been expanded to allow real relvars to be referred to alternatively as base relvars.

- RM Prescription 17 has been extended to make it clear that (a) statements are generally executed within the context of some transaction and (b) such statement executions are always semantically atomic, unless either (a) the statement in question isn't syntactically atomic (e.g., it's a CASE statement or an IF statement), or (b) it's the invocation of some user defined update operator (i.e., it's a CALL statement, or something equivalent to a CALL statement, that causes such an operator to be invoked). Loosely speaking, in other words, if we assume statements terminate in semicolons, then the unit of "semantic atomicity" is what comes between consecutive semicolons is (with the sole exception already noted).

- RM Prescription 18 has been extended to include a note pointing out that the requirement that relation type inference be supported applies to tuple types as well, mutatis mutandis. Also, a sentence listing certain relational algebra operators that **D** was required to "support, directly or indirectly" has been deleted, since it added nothing.

- RM Prescription 19 has been completely replaced. Previously it read as follows:

  > **Relvar names** and **relation selector invocations** shall both be valid relational expressions. **Recursion** shall be permitted in relational expressions.

  The part about relvar names has been generalized to cover names of variables (and constants) of all types. The part about relation selector invocations is and always was implicit in other prescriptions (RM Prescription 10 in particular). Finally, the part about recursion was, frankly, always a trifle confused; however, the original intent has been preserved in the revised version of RM Prescription 20.

- The term *ordinal type* (mentioned in RM Prescription 22) has been replaced by the more appropriate term *ordered type*. An ordered type is, as the introduction to this chapter indicates, a type for which a total ordering is defined—implying that if *T* is such a type, then the expression "*v1* < *v2*" is defined for all pairs of values *v1* and *v2* of type *T*, returning TRUE if and only if *v1* precedes *v2* with respect to the applicable ordering. An ordinal type is an ordered type for which certain additional operators are required: *first, last, next, prior,* and possibly others. In **Tutorial D,** for example, type INTEGER is an ordinal type; type RATIONAL, by contrast, is an ordered type but not an ordinal one. (The rationale here is that if *p*/*q* is a rational number, then—in mathematics at least, if not in computer arithmetic—there is no rational number that can be said to be the "next" rational number, immediately following *p*/*q*.)

- RM Prescription 23 has been clarified. It has also been extended slightly to include an explicit definition of what it means for a constraint to be violated.

- A note has been added to RM Prescription 25 to point out an important implication that might not be immediately obvious.

- OO Prescription 4 has been extended to allow **D** to support "implicit transactions." *Note:* In practice, we would expect use of this feature to be limited to the use of **D** in an interactive environment.

- RM Very Strong Suggestion 2 ("foreign key shorthand") has been deleted, and RM Very Strong

Suggestions 3-8 have been renumbered accordingly. Arguments supporting this change can be found in Chapter 13 of the present book; in a nutshell, however, we feel that (a) foreign keys as usually understood are unnecessarily limited in their applicability, and (b) the usual shorthand formulation is often longer than its longhand equivalent, anyway.

In addition to all of the foregoing, many of the prescriptions, proscriptions, and very strong suggestions have been reworded (in some cases extensively). However, those rewordings in themselves are not intended to induce any changes in what's being described.

Chapter 2

What's a Predicate?

No! No! Sentence first—verdict afterwards.
—Lewis Carroll: *Alice's Adventures in Wonderland*

This sentence no verb
—Douglas Hofstadter

This chapter was prompted by, and is a kind of postscript to, reference [1], which includes the following:

> Hugh [Darwen] raised an interesting question: What does it mean for two predicates to be equal? Or equivalent? For example, the predicates "$a < b$" and "$x < y$" are clearly not identical, but they do "mean the same thing"; what's more, their extensions are equal, both consisting as they do of all possible true instantiations—1 < 2, 2 < 3, 1 < 3, and so forth—of the corresponding predicate. Can we say the intensions are equal as well? These are issues that deserve careful discussion—probably in a follow-on paper.

This chapter is offered as that "careful discussion." *Note:* In case you're not familiar with the term, I should explain that the *intension*—note the spelling—of a given predicate is, loosely, what that predicate means; it's what's sometimes called the "intended interpretation" of the predicate in question. Hence, to ask whether the intensions of predicates *p* and *q* are equal is indeed to ask whether *p* and *q* themselves are equal, or perhaps equivalent.

The first thing I need to say is that (as I'm sure you've realized already) the question that forms the title of this chapter—what's a predicate?—isn't quite the same as the question that reference [1] originally asked. In fact, however, I take the questions to be equivalent (!), in the sense that the answer to either will surely follow immediately from the answer to the other.

Now, I dare say you might be surprised to hear that such questions even need to be asked; surely any decent book on logic will answer them? In fact, however, it turns out to be quite difficult to find a book that even bothers to defines the term (*predicate,* that is), let alone two that give the same definition—despite the fact that the concept, however it's defined, lies at the very heart of the subject. In fact, we're touching here on an area in which there seems to be very little consensus, and possibly a certain amount of confusion, in the literature in general. Before I start getting into the substance of the chapter, therefore, I'd like to take a few moments to examine this lack of consensus. *Note:* I said there might be "a certain amount of confusion" on these matters, so perhaps I should state explicitly that what confusion there is has to do (I assume) with terms, not concepts. It goes without saying that I'm not accusing the logic community of confusion over the underlying concepts.

TERMS USED IN THE LITERATURE

Observe first of all that the opening quote from reference [1] does assume that "$a < b$" is a predicate. But many logicians (not all) would disagree right away; they would say rather that "<" by itself is the predicate, and "*a*" and "*b*" are parameters to that predicate. Well ... that's not really true, either; I mean, they probably wouldn't say quite what I've just said they'd say. Instead:

- Most logicians would say, not that "<" is a predicate, but rather that it's a *predicate letter* or *predicate symbol.* As noted earlier, very few writers ever say exactly what a predicate, as such, is; and as for the (to me, slightly strange) terms *predicate letter* and *predicate symbol,* I've found only one writer—see the section "Overlooking the Distinction," later—who uses what's surely the most obvious term, *predicate name* (always understanding that such names can be arbitrarily complex, of course). Then whatever's referred to by such a name would be the predicate as such. For example, we might say that the thing that's identified by the name "<" is, precisely, the predicate whose intension is "is less than."

- Most logicians wouldn't say "*a*" and "*b*" are parameters (or parameter names, perhaps?), either. Rather, they would say we're dealing with a predicate that's *two-place,* or *dyadic,* or of *degree* two, or of *arity* two—and all of these terms mean, as far as the logicians are concerned, that (a) the predicate has exactly two parameters and (b) those parameters are distinguished by ordinal position (so there's a first parameter and a second). Since parameters are identified by ordinal position in this way, they don't have to have names. (Sometimes they're given names anyway, but, to repeat, they don't have to be.)

- Logicians usually assume they're dealing with what's called *unsorted logic.* In the database world, by contrast, we deal with its opposite, *sorted* logic, which means the values we're interested in—in particular, the values represented by parameters like *a* and *b* in the "<" example—are divided into *sorts,* where "sorts" in turn is the logician's term for what we would call *types* (or data types). In "*a* < *b*," for example, we might require *a* and *b* to be of "sort," or type, integer. In unsorted logic, the assumption is effectively that everything is of the same type (often referred to as "the universe, or domain, of discourse"); and if everything is of the same type, then there's obviously no need to specify the types of parameters in particular. For the logician, therefore, parameters have no name and no explicit type, and so there's no need to include parameter specifications in the definition of a predicate; all the logician has to do is specify the name of the predicate and its degree.

- Well, actually, most logicians don't talk about *parameters,* as such, anyway. Rather, they talk about *arguments,* or *variables,* or *individual variables,* or *free variables,* or *predicate variables,* or occasionally *placeholders*. I'd like to elaborate briefly on each of these terms:

  1. *Argument:* Normal usage in the database and programming languages communities, which is the usage I want to stay with in this chapter as much as possible, is for (a) *parameter* to mean a formal operand in terms of which some operator is defined and (b) *argument* to mean an actual operand that replaces that formal operand when the operator in question is invoked. I really don't know why so many logicians use *argument* to mean a parameter; in fact, the usage seems a little odd, given that *argument* has another (totally unrelated, but very important) meaning in logic—viz., as a sequence of propositions, the last of which is supposed to follow logically from its predecessors. *Note:* I'll have more to say about propositions later. For the time being, you can take a proposition to be anything that's unequivocally either true or false—for example, "William Shakespeare wrote *Pride and Prejudice*" (a false proposition, as it happens).

  2. *Variable:* Again we have a different meaning for this term in the database and programming language communities, so I prefer to avoid the logician's usage here too. (For the record, I take the term *variable* to mean, in essence, anything that's updatable. In other words, to be a variable is to be assignable to, and to be assignable to is to be a variable.)

  3. *Individual variable:* Logicians use the term *individual* to mean what we would call simply a *value.*[1] Hence, an *individual variable,* to the logician, is just a variable (a variable whose value is an "individual," if you like).

  4. *Free variable:* Individual variables in logic are either *free* or *bound.* A bound variable is a variable that's bound by a quantifier such as EXISTS or FORALL (and is thus definitely not a parameter, in

[1] Perhaps more specifically a value that isn't a predicate (see the remarks in paragraph 5 regarding the term *predicate variable*).

our sense); a free variable is a variable that isn't bound. So if the "variable" terminology is to be used at all, using the "free" and "bound" qualifiers as and when appropriate is probably a good idea, for clarity. On the other hand, I feel bound to add (pun intended) that the "free vs. bound variables" terminology isn't very good, because the terms really apply not to variables as such, but rather to variable *references* or *occurrences*. For example, in the expression

```
FORALL x ( x > 0 ) AND x > 3
```

there are three references to *x*, of which the last is free and the first two are bound. Equivalently, we might say there are two distinct variables here, both called *x*, one of which is free and one bound.[2]

5. *Predicate variable:* In the programming languages world, a "type *T* variable" is a variable whose values are values of type *T*. For example, an integer variable is a variable of type INTEGER, and its values are integer values, or just integers for short. Therefore, programmers at least would surely expect a predicate variable to be a variable of type PREDICATE, whose values are predicates per se. *Note:* As a matter of fact, some of the logic texts I consulted do use the term *predicate variable* in exactly this sense. Those same texts also use the term *predicate constant* to mean a predicate per se, a usage with which I have no quarrel. However, other writers apparently use the term *predicate constant* to mean what I would greatly prefer to call a predicate name (again, see the section "Overlooking the Distinction," later, regarding this latter term).

6. *Placeholder:* I have no argument (pun intended) with this term, except for the fact that we already have a perfectly good term, *parameter,* for the concept.

As you can see, then, there's certainly, as claimed, a considerable lack of consensus in the logic literature over the use of terms. But perhaps more important is the fact that we in the database community have certain requirements that the logicians don't have, of which the most significant, here, is the need to be able to specify names and types for the parameters in terms of which a given predicate is defined. Given this state of affairs, I think it's reasonable for us to adopt our own terms and definitions where necessary (just so long as we don't do violence to the underlying logical concepts, of course). More specifically, in this chapter I intend to use terms and definitions that accord as much as possible with those used in reference [2]. *Note:* For interest, the appendix to this chapter contains some additional discussion of the various terms and definitions to be found in the logic literature.

PREDICATES AND SENTENCES

What does it mean for two predicates to be equal? Well, obviously enough, they're equal if and only if they're actually one and the same predicate. So if "$a < b$" and "$x < y$" are predicates—and let's assume for the moment that they are—and if they're equal, then they must be one and the same. And if they're one and the same, then wherever one of them appears it must be possible to replace it by the other without any significant effect. But now consider the following expression, which under my assumption is another predicate:

```
a < b AND x < y
```

Observe now that this latter predicate is tetradic, whereas

---

[2] But the following quote from reference [6] shows that logicians wouldn't always say there are two distinct variables, either, in examples like this one: "A variable is **free in a formula** if and only if at least one occurrence of it is free, and a variable is **bound in a formula** if and only if at least one occurrence of it is bound. A variable may be both free and bound in a formula."

```
a < b AND a < b
```

and

```
x < y AND x < y
```

are both dyadic.[3] (I'm appealing here (a) to the fact that every appearance of a given parameter name within a given predicate is understood to refer to the same parameter, and also (b) to the fact that if *p* is a predicate, then *p* AND *p* is also a predicate, and it reduces to just *p*.) It follows that either "*a* < *b*" and "*x* < *y*" are different predicates, or else they're not predicates at all but something different.

So are they predicates? I say *no*—I say they're *sentences* that *denote* predicates. Note carefully: *denote,* not *are*. Rather than say that certain sentences (namely, declarative ones) are predicates and others aren't, I prefer to say that certain sentences denote predicates and others don't. Contrast this with my willingness to say that certain rectangles *are* squares and others aren't. I regard sentences as *syntactic* constructs, predicates as *semantic* ones.

I should say immediately that here, again, we're running into an area where there's little terminological agreement in the literature. Some writers do use the term *sentence* but take it to mean what I think of as a predicate. Others take it to be synonymous with *proposition.* Some distinguish between open and closed sentences, using *closed* to refer to a proposition and *open* to refer to a predicate that's not a proposition. Some use *statement* or *formula* in place of *sentence,* with any of the foregoing meanings. Most important of all, most writers don't even seem to mention what I regard as the crucial logical difference here: viz., the logical difference between what we say (the sentence) and what we mean (the predicate)—in other words, the logical difference between syntax and semantics. The textbook I find closest to my own position in this connection is reference [3], which says this:

> A proposition is what is expressed by a sentence ... Logic ... is primarily about propositions, and only secondarily about sentences.

Even here, I would prefer to replace *A proposition* and *propositions* by *A predicate* and *predicates,* respectively.

To be fair, I should now say that perhaps those books on logic don't need to mention that "crucial logical difference" explicitly, and perhaps they don't need to lay as much stress on it as I think I do. After all, the books are filled with examples like the following (chosen more or less at random from reference [6]):

> Let *C* be "Today is clear," *R* be "It is raining today," *S* be "It is snowing today," and *Y* be "Yesterday was cloudy." Translate into acceptable English the following: [*Here follows a series of formal expressions involving C, R, S, and Y.*]

In other words, the books are all about using certain formal expressions (i.e., *syntactic* constructs—my *sentences*) to represent certain less formal utterances (i.e., *semantic* constructs—my *predicates*), and then manipulating those formal expressions according to certain formal laws for various purposes (e.g., to check an argument for validity). That's why logic—at least, logic as we understand it for our purposes in the database world—is often called, more specifically, *formal* logic (sometimes *symbolic* or *mathematical* logic). The following excerpt from the *Oxford English Dictionary* is enlightening in this regard:

> **logic** ... The branch of philosophy that treats of the forms of thinking in general, and more especially of inference and of scientific method ... Also, since the work of Gottlob Frege (1848-1925), a formal system using symbolic techniques and mathematical methods to establish truth-values in the physical sciences, in language, and in philosophical argument. The proper scope of this department of study has been and is much controverted, and books on "logic" differ widely in the range of subjects which they include. The definition formerly most commonly accepted is "the art

---

[3] As far as I'm concerned, to say some predicate is *n*-adic for some $n \geqslant 0$ just means the predicate in question has *n* parameters; it doesn't mean those parameters are distinguished by ordinal position.

of reasoning"; for various modern definitions see [*some of the more recent of a set of quotations that I omit here*]. At all times the vulgar notion of "logic" has been largely that it is a system of rules for convincing or confounding an opponent by argument. [*Incidentally, I can just see in my mind's eye the satisfaction on the writer's face as he or she concocted this last sentence.*]

Be all that as it may, let me now explain my own justification for the position I'm taking. Consider the English sentence "*a* is less than *b*" and the French sentence "*a* est moins que *b*." If a predicate *is* a sentence, then these two aren't the same predicate, nor is either of them the same predicate as "$a < b$." But that English sentence is exactly the way an English speaking person pronounces "$a < b$"; likewise, the French one is exactly the way a French speaking person pronounces it. It follows that what we're dealing with is different sentences that happen to mean the same thing. I wish to use the term *predicate* for that "same thing."[4]

Now, you might be thinking I'm leading up to a position where "$a < b$" and "$x < y$" are different sentences but nevertheless denote the same predicate. I'm not. If they did, then the predicates denoted by "$a < b$ AND $x < y$" and "$a < b$ AND $a < b$" would also be the same, which they clearly aren't. (The argument that shows they aren't is essentially the same as the one I used to show that "$a < b$" and "$x < y$" aren't predicates in the first place: The sentence "$a < b$ AND $x < y$" denotes a tetradic predicate, the sentence "$a < b$ AND $a < b$" denotes a dyadic one.) In fact, I don't even need to use logical connectives to make this point. For if parameter names are to be ignored, so that "$a < b$" and "$x < y$" denote the same predicate after all, then presumably the dyadic "$a < b$" and the monadic "$a < a$" also denote the same predicate! Clearly, however, predicates with different numbers of parameters can't possibly be equal.

OVERLOOKING THE DISTINCTION

I've gone to great lengths to stress the logical difference between a sentence and a predicate, but now I have to admit that it's often convenient to ignore it, at least in less formal contexts.[5] That is, once we're sure we properly understand that difference, we can and typically do agree—for reasons of simplicity and convenience—to overlook it and to revert to saying a sentence just *is* a predicate after all. For example, we would probably say "Consider the predicate $a < b$" rather than the slightly fussy "Consider the predicate denoted by the sentence $a < b$." Likewise, we would probably say "*a* is less than *b*" and "*a* est moins que *b*" are the same predicate—but now we know we really mean they *denote* the same predicate. In fact, now we understand exactly what *equivalence relation* we're appealing to when we say two sentences "are the same predicate"—just as we know what we mean when we say we're reading "the same book" at the same time. (I'll explain later what I mean by the term *equivalence relation* here.)

As a matter of fact, however (and as I've already said), logicians typically don't just agree to overlook the distinction as a matter of convenience; typically, rather, they don't even mention it. Here for example is the definition of *predicate* given in reference [4] (one of the few texts I consulted that did actually contain a definition!)—and let me say that in spite of its obvious weaknesses, this definition does accord quite well with what I want the term to mean:

> [A] predicate is defined to be a string of English words and individual variables, such that if the individual variables are replaced by appropriate designators, then the whole becomes a declarative sentence with these designators as constituents.

---

[4] To repeat, different sentences can denote the same predicate; for completeness, I should add that the converse is true too—i.e., the same sentence can denote different predicates. Consider, for example, the sentence "I love you." Obviously, the meaning of this sentence depends on who "I" and "you" are! In a more formal treatment, therefore (more formal, that is, than the one I'm attempting here), we would have to be careful over the definition of the term *sentence,* too.

[5] And we do ignore it, almost universally, elsewhere in this book.

So much for "*a* est moins que *b,*" then! To be fair, however, the author of reference [4] does make it pretty clear in his opening chapter that for convenience he assumes English to be the human language to which he relates his formal discourse. More to the point, observe that his definition says a predicate *is* "a string of ... words ..." (from the context, clearly a string of words that form a sentence); as far as he's concerned, therefore, a predicate is indeed a sentence.[6] *Note:* The term *designator* refers to an expression that identifies some specific object (some "individual," in logic parlance). For example, in the sentence "The Queen of England is married to the Duke of Edinburgh," "The Queen of England" and "the Duke of Edinburgh" are designators. So are "1" and "2" in the sentence "1 < 2," and so is "Relvar S" in the sentence "Relvar S must not be empty." (Thus, a designator too is basically just a name—a name for an "individual value," in fact.)

Now, the foregoing definition does imply that "$a < b$" and "$x < y$" are distinct. Unfortunately, it also implies that "$a < b$" and "*a* is less than *b*" are distinct as well ... Perhaps we should look for another definition. I tried reference [5]. That book doesn't actually give a definition, but on page 179—of the 188 that constitute the main body of the book—I did find the following (lightly edited here):

> If we select a sentence and drop from it a proper name, we obtain a predicate. For example, if we drop the proper name "oxygen" from "oxygen is an element," we obtain the predicate "... is an element."

Again, then, we have an assertion to the effect that a predicate is a sentence, albeit one that's allowed to contain "holes," as it were. But notice the sleight of hand in the example: We've haven't just dropped the proper name "oxygen," we've put a "hole" (an ellipsis) in its place. Now, reference [5] does go on to explain that dropping two or more proper names in like manner yields a dyadic (or, more generally, polyadic) predicate. Presumably, therefore, neither "$a < b$" nor just "<" alone is a predicate according to that reference. Rather, the following is:

```
... < ...
```

But if parameters are to be represented by "holes" in this manner, how can we ever represent the fact that the same parameter is supposed to appear in two distinct "holes"—i.e., at two distinct positions? For example, consider what's involved in representing the predicate "$x^2 = x + 1$" (which is monadic but would presumably have to involve two "holes").

Here's one more quote (from the *Oxford English Dictionary* again):

> **1973** H. Hermes *Introd. Math. Logic* i. 40 In the statement *The crown jewels are kept in the Tower of London, The crown jewels* and *the Tower of London* can be understood as names for individuals and *are kept in* as a name for a predicate ...

I would prefer *values* or *arguments* in place of *individuals* here, but otherwise I rather like this quote. The nested sentence in italics is (more precisely, denotes) a proposition; that proposition is an instantiation of a predicate named *are kept in;* and the phrases *The crown jewels* and *the Tower of London* are designators, or in other words names for the actual arguments to that proposition. In particular, as I've already mentioned, I like the idea that things like *are kept in* (and "<" and "is less than" and so on) are predicate *names*—though I'd prefer to distinguish between what we might call abstract names and concrete ones, so that, e.g., *are kept in* and *is kept in* and *se tiennent à* (and so on) are all concrete forms of the same abstract name.

---

[6] He also says elsewhere that he'll use *declarative sentence* to mean a proposition, thereby defining a proposition too to be a sentence as such, instead of something denoted by a sentence.

EQUAL PREDICATES

I've said I'm going to overlook the distinction between a predicate *P* and a sentence *S* that denotes it, and simply say, in effect, that predicate *P is* sentence *S* (or the other way around). But I still haven't pinned down exactly what *kind* of sentence a predicate "is." As we've seen, there's no consensus on this matter in the literature: It might be just a name (like *are kept in*—which isn't much of a sentence, of course, but I'll ignore that point); or it might be such a name accompanied by "holes"; or it might be such a name accompanied by explicit parameter specifications. So I'm going to set a stake in the ground and state categorically that as far as I'm concerned, it's the last of these three (as in fact I suggested earlier, in connection with that definition from reference [4]).

If we accept this position, then it follows that two predicates will be equal only if they have the same predicate name and involve the same parameter specifications. But I want that predicate name to be a semantic construct rather than a syntactic one, so that (to repeat my earlier example) the concrete names "<", "is less than," and "est moins que" are all understood as denoting the same abstract name.

Just having the same parameter specifications (the same parameters, for short) and the same abstract name is still inadequate, however—for if those were the only requirements, then "*a* < *b*" and "*b* < *a*" would be, or would denote, the same predicate. Clearly, when there are two or more parameters, we need to know which one is which—i.e., we need to know which *role* is being played by which parameter (where, of course, the roles played by distinct parameters are themselves distinct). Syntactically, we can specify those roles by writing the parameter names in the appropriate places in a sentence that denotes the predicate. (In particular, we can write the same name in more than one place if we need to.) Once again, however, I don't want to depend on syntax; so let me define two predicates to be equal if and only if they have the same name and same parameters *and* each parameter plays the same role in each predicate.

Given this definition, the following sentences do all denote the same predicate:

```
a < b

a is less than b

a est moins que b
```

By contrast, the following sentences all denote different predicates:

```
a < b

x < y

b < a

a < a
```

What's more, I think the sentences "*a* < *b*" and "*b* > *a*" denote different predicates, too. However, you might unkindly point out that "<" and ">" could be considered distinct concrete forms of the same abstract name and *a* and *b* could be considered to be playing the same roles in both "*a* < *b*" and "*b* > *a*," in which case I would have to suppose you were right. In any case, "*a* < *b*" and "*b* > *a*" certainly have something very interesting in common, even if "<" and ">" don't denote the same abstract name. And that observation brings me to the second question posed in the text I cited from reference [1] at the very beginning of this chapter.

EQUIVALENT PREDICATES

What does it mean for two predicates to be equivalent, as opposed to equal? Well, actually it can mean whatever we want it to mean, so long as we understand exactly what *equivalence relation* we're appealing to. For example, we might—though I don't want to—define an equivalence relation on predicates that makes predicates *p1* and *p2* equivalent if and only if they have the same abstract predicate name. In that sense the predicates denoted by

“$a < b$” and “$x < y$” would certainly be equivalent. In any case (and regardless of whether they’re equivalent or not), those two predicates certainly have the same *extension,* or set of true instantiations.[7] For example, the sentence “$1 < 2$” denotes a proposition that’s a true instantiation of both—because we’ve replaced the parameters by certain specific arguments, thereby losing the parameter names that made the predicates distinct.

By the way—I haven’t stated this fact explicitly yet in the present chapter, but I’ve done so in numerous previous writings—a proposition can be regarded as a special case of a predicate. To be precise, it’s a predicate for which the set of parameters happens to be empty.[8] As a direct consequence of this fact, we can say that, e.g., “$1 < 2$” and “1 is less than 2” both denote the same proposition. In other words, a proposition, like a predicate, is necessarily a semantic construct rather than a syntactic one. As with predicates in general, however, we often say for simplicity that a proposition *is* a sentence, rather than something that’s denoted by a sentence (where, of course, the sentence in question must be one that’s either unequivocally true or unequivocally false).

Anyway, to get back to the example from the end of the previous section: Is there some pleasing sense in which we can say that predicates “$a < b$” and “$b > a$” are equivalent? Well, if we decide that “$<$” and “$>$” are distinct names, then those predicates certainly don’t have the same extension. For example, the proposition “$1 < 2$” appears in the extension of “$a < b$” (only) and the proposition “$2 > 1$” appears in the extension of “$b > a$” (only). And while these two propositions are both true and, loosely, “have the same meaning,” the fact remains that they’re distinct; thus, even substituting the same arguments for corresponding parameters fails to yield the same proposition. But, of course, it’s easy to define a notion of equivalence between the two predicates. To be specific, we can say the predicates are equivalent in the following precise sense: There’s a one to one mapping between them according to which the proposition “$A < B$” appears in the extension of one of the predicates if and only if the proposition “$B > A$” appears in the extension of the other. Using the symbol “$\equiv$” to denote “is equivalent to,” we could write this equivalence as follows:

$$a < b \quad \equiv \quad b > a$$

More generally, we could define an equivalence relation on dyadic predicates in general according to which—to adopt an obvious notation—predicates $p1(a,b)$ and $p2(b,a)$ are equivalent if and only if $p1(A,B)$ appears in the extension of $p1(a,b)$ just when $p2(B,A)$ appears in the extension of $p2(b,a)$; and then “$a < b$” and “$b > a$” would be equivalent as a special case. And if we wanted “$a < b$” and “$x < y$” to be equivalent (though, again, I’ve already said I don’t), then we could define another equivalence relation: Predicates $p1(a,b)$ and $p2(x,y)$ are equivalent if and only if $p1(A,B)$ appears in the extension of $p1(a,b)$ just when $p2(A,B)$ appears in the extension of $p2(x,y)$—i.e., when they have the same extension, loosely speaking. But now we’re getting into rather deep water ... In fact, this whole issue appears to be something that logicians themselves have partly given up on! Here’s a quote from reference [3] (edited fairly heavily, however, partly due to a desire to make it accord with our own terminology):

> How do we know when predicates are identical and when they’re different? ... For example, suppose $A(x)$ is “x is less than 3 and even” and $B(x)$ is “x is less than 50,000 and an even factor of 110,158.” It so happens that the only true instantiations of these predicates both have $x = 2$. Does this fact mean that $A(x)$ and $B(x)$ are identical? This question raises the very difficult problem of specifying exactly when predicates are identical. Certainly a *necessary* condition is that they be true of the same set of objects [*i.e., they have the same extension* (?)] ... But the question of what would

[7] The term *extension* is also sometimes used to refer to the body of a relation, since the tuples of such a body correspond in a certain precisely specified way to the true instantiations of a certain predicate. In the formalism of reference [2], however, the relations corresponding to “$a < b$” and “$x < y$” would have different extensions in this sense, because the tuples concerned would presumably have attribute names A and B in the one case and X and Y in the other.

[8] Note that we have here a good reason for adopting the position that the predicate notion does include the parameters: If we were to take a predicate to be just a name like *are kept in,* then we couldn't say a proposition was a special case after all.

> constitute a sufficient condition is one to which there is at present no universally accepted answer. The one which commands the greatest following takes the necessary condition as a sufficient one also. That is, two predicates are identical if and only if they're true of the same set of objects. This last statement is a version of the *axiom of extensionality,* and it's embodied in most systems of higher order logic ... The acceptance of this axiom allows us to treat the notions of *predicate* and *set* as equivalent from a logical point of view.

Observe that this extract suggests that if two predicates have the same extension, then they're not just equivalent but *identical* (in other words, equal)—even though the concrete predicate names in the example, "is less than 3 and even" and "is less than 50,000 and an even factor of 110,158," are certainly distinct.

And on that note—not wanting to get any further out of my depth than I probably already am—I'll stop, except to offer by way of a little light relief the following famous, and pertinent, extract from *Through the Looking-Glass and What Alice Found There,* by Lewis Carroll:

> "The name of the song is called '*Haddocks' Eyes.*'"
>
> "Oh, that's the name of the song, is it?" Alice said, trying to feel interested.
>
> "No, you don't understand," the Knight said, looking a little vexed. "That's what the name is *called.* The name really *is 'The Aged Aged Man.'*"
>
> "Then I ought to have said 'That's what the *song* is called'?" Alice corrected herself.
>
> "No, you oughtn't; that's quite another thing! The *song* is called *'Ways and Means':* but that's only what it's *called,* you know!"
>
> "Well, what *is* the song, then?" said Alice, who was by this time completely bewildered.
>
> "I was coming to that," the Knight said. "The song really is *'A-sitting On A Gate':* and the tune's my own invention."

REFERENCES AND BIBLIOGRAPHY

1. C. J. Date: "Some Operators Are More Equal than Others," in *Logic and Databases: The Roots of Relational Theory.* Victoria, B.C.: Trafford Publishing (2007). See *www.trafford.com/07-0690.*

2. C. J. Date and Hugh Darwen: *Databases, Types, and the Relational Model: The Third Manifesto* (3rd edition). Boston, Mass.: Addison-Wesley (2006).

3. Howard DeLong: *A Profile of Mathematical Logic.* Mineola, N.Y.: Dover Publications (2004).

4. Wilfrid Hodges: *Logic.* London, U.K.: Penguin Books (1977).

5. E. J. Lemmon: *Beginning Logic.* London, U.K.: Thomas Nelson and Sons Ltd. (1965).

6. Robert R. Stoll: *Sets, Logic, and Axiomatic Theories.* San Francisco, Calif.: W. H. Freeman and Company (1961).

APPENDIX A: A SURVEY OF THE LITERATURE

As promised, in this appendix I offer, purely for interest, more examples to illustrate the lack of consensus on terminology in the logic literature. I'll start with the following from the *Oxford English Dictionary:*

> **1950** tr. [David] Hilbert and [Wilhelm] Ackermann's Princ. Math. Logic iii. 57 To the formula $x + y = z$ there corresponds a triadic predicate $S(x,y,z)$. The truth of $S(x,y,z)$ means that x, y, and z are connected by the relation $x + y = z$. [*Note*] Hitherto it has been customary in logic to call only functions with one argument place predicates, while functions with more than one place were called relations. Here we use the word "predicate" in a quite general sense.

This text, in its original German version, is in fact the source of the term *predicate* in its modern sense—whatever that sense might be, I suppose I should add! But the major point is that, apparently for the first time in the literature, it does include the notion that predicates can be *n*-adic for some $n \geqslant 2$. It's interesting to see, therefore, that it appears to agree with our own preferred definition in that a predicate does include its parameters (note the phrase "a triadic predicate $S(x,y,z)$"). And the reference to functions suggests agreement with our sentence vs. predicate distinction, too, inasmuch as exactly the same kind of distinction applies to functions as well (of course, a function is basically just a special case of a predicate). Note the use of another term (*argument place*) for parameter, though.

By way of contrast, here's an excerpt, from Johan Kerstens, Eddy Ruys, and Joost Zwarts (eds.): *Lexicon of Linguistics* (Utrecht, Netherlands: *http://www2.let.uu.nl/UiL-OTS/Lexicon*, 1996-2001), that illustrates what we might call the pre Hilbert definition of *predicate* (and much else besides):

> **Predicate**
>
> **SEMANTICS:** traditionally, an expression which takes a subject to form a sentence. The predicate ascribes a property to the subject.
>
> **EXAMPLE:** *Socrates* is the subject in the sentence *Socrates is mortal* and *is mortal* is the predicate. In predicate logic, a predicate designates a property or a relation. P in P(a) and R in R(b,c) are called predicates. P in P(a) assigns a property to a and R in R(b,c) designates a relation between b and c. The expressions a, b and c are called the arguments of the predicates P and R.
>
> **Predicate constant**
>
> **SEMANTICS:** a basic expression in predicate logic denoting properties of or relations between individuals. One-place predicate constants combine with one individual term: P(a), two-place predicates with two individual terms: R(b,c), etcetera [*sic*]. One-place predicates are interpreted as sets, n-place predicates with n > 1 as sets of ordered pairs. In "higher-order" predicate logic and in type logic, it is also possible for a predicate to take another predicate as an argument. Predicates which take other predicates as their argument are called second-order predicates.

These definitions tacitly make the terms *predicate* and *predicate constant* synonymous, a position I agree with (see the body of the chapter); indeed, the second uses them interchangeably. I disagree with the definitions in other respects, however; in particular, I disagree with the idea that a predicate is, in effect, just a name. (The very next definition after the ones just given reads as follows: "Predicate letter: see Predicate constant.") It's also somewhat surprising to learn that, e.g., triadic predicates are "interpreted as sets of ordered pairs," rather than as sets of ordered triples.

Now another quote from the *OED:*

> **1969** D. J. Foulis *Fund. Concepts Math.* i. 14 Suppose that *P*(*x*) ... becomes a proposition whenever *x* takes on any particular value in *U*. Then *P*(*x*) is called a predicate or a propositional function, and the object variable *x* is called its argument.

Observe that this quote (a) supports the position that a proposition is a special case of a predicate (or more precisely, perhaps, that a predicate is a generalized proposition), and (b) mentions the rather attractive term *propositional function* as a synonym for *predicate*. I say "rather attractive" because, after all, a predicate can certainly be thought of as a proposition valued, or propositional, function: It returns a proposition when arguments are substituted for its parameters (just as, e.g., an integer valued function returns an integer when arguments are substituted for *its* parameters).[9] But I still prefer *parameter* to *argument* (and note that the quote gives yet another term for parameter, viz., *object variable*).

One more quote from the *OED:*

> **1965** Hughes & Londey *Elem. Formal Logic* xxxix. 270 We shall ... speak of the expressions, such as "greater than" and "between", which stand for two-place, three-place, etc., relations, as two-place, three-place, etc., predicates respectively.

---

[9] And in fact, since a proposition in turn has a truth value, we often define a predicate simply, though a trifle informally, to be a *truth valued function:* Substituting arguments for its parameters yields a truth value, albeit indirectly. I've given such a definition in numerous other writings.

As you can see, this extract departs from Hilbert (or my own understanding of what Hilbert was saying, at any rate) in that it defines a predicate to be what I would prefer to regard as just the predicate name. As a matter of fact, the majority of the texts I consulted agree with Hughes and Londey here (or sometimes, possibly, they take a predicate to be whatever such a name denotes). Texts that adopt this position include:

- Rudolf Carnap: *Introduction to Symbolic Logic and its Applications.* New York, N.Y.: Dover Publications (1958).
- J. N. Crossley et al: *What Is Mathematical Logic?* Mineola, N.Y.: Dover Publications (1990).
- G. T. Kneebone: *Mathematical Logic and the Foundations of Mathematics.* Mineola, N.Y.: Dover Publications (2001).
- Moshé Machover: *Set Theory, Logic, and their Limitations.* Cambridge, U.K.: Cambridge University Press (1996).
- Zohar Manna and Richard Waldinger: *The Logical Basis for Computer Programming. Volume 1: Deductive Reasoning.* Reading, Mass.: Addison-Wesley (1985). *Volume 2: Deductive Systems.* Reading, Mass.: Addison-Wesley (1990).
- James D. McCawley: *Everything that Linguists Have Always Wanted to Know about Logic (but were ashamed to ask).* Chicago, Ill.: University of Chicago Press (1981).
- Howard Pospesel: *Introduction to Logic: Predicate Logic.* Englewood Cliffs, N.J.: Prentice-Hall (1976).
- Steve Reeves and Michael Clarke: *Logic for Computer Science.* Reading, Mass.: Addison-Wesley (1990).
- Raymond Reiter: "Towards a Logical Reconstruction of Relational Database Theory," in Michael L. Brodie, John Mylopoulos, and Joachim W. Schmidt (eds.), *On Conceptual Modelling: Perspectives from Artificial Intelligence, Databases, and Programming Languages.* New York, N.Y.: Springer-Verlag (1984).
- Tom Richards: *Clausal Form Logic: An Introduction to the Logic of Computer Reasoning.* Reading, Mass.: Addison-Wesley (1989).
- Raymond M. Smullyan: *First-Order Logic.* Mineola, N.Y.: Dover Publications (1995).
- Patrick Suppes: *Introduction to Logic.* Princeton, N.J.: Van Nostrand (1957).
- Paul Teller: *A Modern Formal Logic Primer. Volume I: Sentence Logic; Volume II: Predicate Logic and Metatheory.* Englewood Cliffs, N.J.: Prentice-Hall (1989).

Some texts seem to adopt the same position, more or less, but don't use the term *predicate,* unqualified, at all; instead, they use terms such as *predicate letter* or *predicate symbol,* or sometimes *predicate expression* (another new term!). Examples of such texts include:

- John L. Bell, David DeVidi, and Graham Solomon: *Logical Options: An Introduction to Classical and Alternative Logics.* Orchard Park, N.Y.: Broadview Press (2001).
- Samuel Guttenplan: *The Languages of Logic.* Oxford, U.K.: Blackwell (1986).

A few of the texts I consulted did come a little closer to my own preferred definitions, however. Examples here include the following:

- Howard DeLong: *A Profile of Mathematical Logic.* Mineola, N.Y.: Dover Publications (2004).
- Peter M. D. Gray: *Logic, Algebra and Databases.* Chichester, England: Ellis Horwood Ltd. (1984).
- Wilfrid Hodges: *Logic.* London, U.K.: Penguin Books (1977).
- David McGoveran: "Nothing from Nothing" (in four parts), in C. J. Date, Hugh Darwen, and David McGoveran, *Relational Database Writings 1994-1997.* Reading, Mass.: Addison-Wesley (1998).
- Sybil P. Parker (ed.): *The McGraw-Hill Dictionary of Mathematics.* New York, N.Y.: McGraw-Hill (1994).
- Robert R. Stoll: *Sets, Logic, and Axiomatic Theories.* San Francisco, Calif.: W. H. Freeman and Company (1961).

However, these latter texts still assume, almost universally, that parameters are identified by ordinal position and are more or less typeless; thus, they still avoid at least some of the issues I've been discussing in the body of the chapter, regarding (e.g.) whether predicates that differ only in the naming of their parameters are identical or not. And the last book in particular (Stoll), although I've said it adheres more closely to my own position, is, to be frank, not entirely clear on the matter:

> An *n*-place predicate is a statement function of *n* variables ... e.g., $P(x,y)$ [stands] for some ... two-place predicate ... We shall call the given predicates **predicate letters** ... From [the predicate letters] we generate ... formulas ... [*Later:*] The denotation **predicate symbol** indicates a predicate letter which is intended to stand for a *fixed* predicate.

I should add that elsewhere Stoll makes it clear that what he calls the predicate letter above does include the parameters. For example, on page 156 he refers to "the predicate letter $P(x1,x2,...,xn)$."

I note too that at least one of the books listed above (Richards) uses *predicate* to mean a predicate name and *predicate schema* to mean such a name plus the parameters. And at least one (Guttenplan) uses *predicate frame* where Richards uses *predicate schema.*

Let me say a little more regarding the term *propositional function.* The book by McCawley is another that uses that term. Here's an extract:

> Such notions as "being a man" are generally dealt with in logic in the form of PROPOSITIONAL FUNCTIONS such as "*x* is a man." A simple propositional function consists of one or more VARIABLES (here, the *x*) and a PREDICATE (here, *man*).[10] Let us assume that the *is* and the *a* of "*x* is a man" are simply meaningless syllables that are forced on us by quirks of English grammar and accordingly shift to a notation in which only the predicate and the variables appear: "man *x*". A propositional function is something that yields a proposition when specific entities are substituted for the variables. For example, if you substitute *Socrates* for *x* in "man *x*", you get "man Socrates", which expresses the proposition that Socrates is a man.

DeLong uses *propositional function* too, but unlike McCawley he equates it with the term *predicate:*

> The central notion is that of a propositional function or predicate ... An *n*-place predicate is a function of *n* individual variables ... When each variable in a predicate has assigned to it an individual, the result is a proposition ... For example, *x* is a prime, $x < y$, $(x < y)$ OR $(y < x)$ are examples of predicates ... We shall use 'A^n', 'B^n', 'C^n', etc., to represent *n*-place predicate constants, which in a given context stand for fixed (though perhaps unknown) predicates ... If all individual variables in a predicate are replaced by individual constants, the result is a *substitution instance*.

As an aside, I note that we apparently now have another term for *proposition* (or for an instantiation, perhaps): viz., *substitution instance.* (It's tempting to ask, therefore, whether a predicate might be called a

---

[10] It appears from that "one or more" that McCawley doesn't regard a proposition as a special case of a propositional function.

substitution instance function.)

The term *propositional function* also appears in the book by Pospesel:

> [Things like] "is greedy" are predicates ... We call the letters that abbreviate English predicates *predicate letters* (or just *predicates*) ... A propositional function is a formula which results when zero or more (contiguous) quantifiers are deleted from the front of a formula which is a wff.

Frankly, I can't tell from this quote whether a propositional function and a predicate are to be regarded as the same thing or not (or indeed whether one is to be regarded as a special case of the other).

I'll close with a lightly edited extract from the book by Carnap:

> To form sentences we need designations for the properties and relations predicated of the individuals—we call these *predicates* ... For *predicates* we use the letters '*P*', '*Q*', '*R*', '*S*', '*T*'. For example, '*P*' might designate the property Spherical ... Now suppose we take '*a*' to designate the sun ... We write the sentence '*P*(*a*)' for "the sun is spherical" ... '*P*(*a*)' is a sentence and *a* is an *argument-expression* ... '*P*' is a one-place (or monadic) predicate ... Generally, a predicate is said to be *n*-adic (or *n*-place, or of degree *n*) in case it has *n* argument-positions ... We say that '*P*(*a*)' is a *sentence-completion* or *full-sentence* of the predicate '*P*'.

Well, it's very tempting to close with the well known folk saying *If you're not confused by all this, you can't have been paying attention.* But that would be very naughty of me, so I won't.

Chapter 3

The Naming of Types

The Naming of Types is a difficult matter,
It isn't just one of your everyday games;
You may think at first I'm as mad as a hatter
When I tell you, a type has N DIFFERENT NAMES.
—with apologies to T. S. Eliot

The Third Manifesto [2]—"the *Manifesto*" for short—has been criticized on the grounds that it doesn't explicitly require a given type to have exactly one name but frequently talks as if it did. Clarification is needed. Such is my purpose in this brief chapter.

In essence, what I propose is that (a) a given type shall have exactly one name, together with zero or more *synonyms* (these latter shall be usable interchangeably with the name in most situations, though possibly not in all), and (b) no name or synonym shall apply to two or more distinct types. The remainder of the chapter elaborates on these ideas. *Note:* Inheritance and subtyping considerations have little effect on these proposals and are therefore ignored throughout (except for a few remarks in passing).

SCALAR TYPES

In this section I limit my attention to scalar types, which for present purposes can be taken to mean any type that's neither a tuple type nor a relation type. By way of example, consider the type "character string," which isn't in fact prescribed by the *Manifesto* but is supported, as a system defined type, by **Tutorial D** [3]. **Tutorial D** allows this type to be referred to, more or less interchangeably, as either CHARACTER or CHAR.[1] As far as **Tutorial D** is concerned, however, these two keywords are both (like the type itself) system defined; the *Manifesto* currently prescribes, and **Tutorial D** currently supports, no means by which users can introduce names of their own for a system defined type.

As for user defined types, the *Manifesto* currently prescribes, and **Tutorial D** currently supports, no means by which users can assign more than one name to a user defined type.

Now, I don't dispute the usefulness of being able, e.g., to refer to type "character string" as either type CHARACTER or type CHAR or both, depending on circumstances; however, any such feature must be very carefully designed and specified. The SQL standard [4] provides an example of the kind of difficulties such a feature can lead to otherwise. For example, that standard states that FLOAT and REAL both denote the data type "approximate numeric, with [*some implicit or explicit*] precision." The comma here strongly suggests that the precision and the type are regarded by SQL as two different things (i.e., the type per se is just "approximate numeric"); if so, then the names FLOAT and REAL apparently both refer to the same type. Alternatively—i.e., if the precision is considered to be part of the type, so that, e.g., FLOAT(6) and FLOAT(16) are regarded as different types—the default precision for FLOAT can nevertheless still be the same as the implied precision for REAL, implying again that the names FLOAT and REAL might both refer to the same type. So are there two (or perhaps more than two) types here, or is there just one? And either way, what appears in the system catalog when a reference to the type is required?

---

[1] *Interchangeably* might be a small overclaim here. In particular, the system catalog will presumably have to refer to types by their names as such, not by synonyms, and so users accessing the catalog—or pertinent portions thereof, at any rate—will probably have to know those names.

For scalar types, therefore, I propose the following:

- **Proposal:** A given scalar type shall have exactly one name, which shall be assigned to it when the type in question is defined and shall remain in effect for as long as the type is available for use. It shall also have zero or more synonyms, distinct from each other and from the corresponding type name; for example, CHARACTER and CHAR might be, respectively, the name and a synonym for the scalar type "character string." Whether synonyms must be defined when the type in question is defined or can be defined at some later time is deliberately left unspecified, as is the matter of whether synonyms can be dropped without dropping the type in question. No type name shall apply to more than one type (scalar or otherwise). Likewise, no synonym shall apply to more than one type (scalar or otherwise), and no type name shall be the same as any synonym.

Implications for the Manifesto: The *Manifesto* might need to be revised—see later—to make it clear that every scalar type has exactly one name, and further that the name in question is unique. Regarding synonyms for such types, however, my feeling is that the *Manifesto* should neither prescribe nor proscribe, nor even "very strongly suggest," synonym support. Since it currently does none of these things anyway, I believe the concept of synonyms has no implication for the *Manifesto* at all.

Implications for ***Tutorial D:*** **Tutorial D** does already support synonyms for system defined scalar types, inasmuch as it does at least allow both CHARACTER and CHAR to be used to refer to the type "character string." (Just to be definite, I propose, a trifle arbitrarily, that CHARACTER should be the type name and CHAR a synonym. I also propose that we introduce INT, RAT, and BOOL as system defined synonyms for INTEGER, RATIONAL, and BOOLEAN, respectively.) However, I propose that we not add a facility at this time for users to define their own synonyms for system defined types, pending further study of the issue. As for user defined types, I propose that we not add a facility at this time for users to define synonyms for such types either, again pending further study.

RELATION TYPES

I now turn my attention to nonscalar types, which (as previously indicated) for present purposes can be taken to mean any type that's either a tuple type or a relation type. For simplicity, I concentrate on relation types specifically; everything I have to say regarding such types applies to tuple types also, mutatis mutandis. *Note:* An analogous remark applies to relation values vs. tuple values (see the section "Relation Values," later).

According to the *Manifesto,* something—*RT,* say—is a relation type if and only if it's obtained by invoking the RELATION type generator with some specified heading {*H*}.[2] Note, therefore, that as far as the *Manifesto* is concerned all relation types are, specifically, generated types. Moreover, the *Manifesto* prescribes a unique name for such a type, of the form RELATION {*H*}, where {*H*} is the heading in question.[3] Here's an example of such a type name:

```
RELATION { S# S# , SNAME NAME , STATUS INTEGER , CITY CHARACTER }
```

---

[2] For the "if" part of this definition, see the *Manifesto,* RM Prescription 7; for the "only if" part, see the *Manifesto,* RM Prescriptions 10 and 13.

[3] The following lightly edited text from the *Manifesto,* RM Prescription 7, is relevant here: "When we say the name of a certain relation type shall be RELATION {*H*}, we do not mean to prescribe specific syntax. The *Manifesto* does not prescribe syntax. Rather, what we mean is that the type in question shall have a name that does both of the following, no more and no less: First, it shall specify that the type is indeed a relation type; second, it shall specify the pertinent heading. Syntax of the form RELATION {*H*} satisfies these requirements, and we therefore use it as a convenient shorthand; however, all appearances of that syntax throughout this *Manifesto* are to be interpreted in the light of these remarks."

This name can be regarded as—and is in fact the written text form of—an invocation of the RELATION type generator with an argument consisting of the heading {S# S#, SNAME NAME, STATUS INTEGER, CITY CHARACTER}. One context in which this name might appear is the definition of the base relvar S ("suppliers"), which would typically look like this in **Tutorial D** (except that for simplicity I've chosen to omit the keyword BASE—or its synonym, REAL—that **Tutorial D** would actually require):

```
VAR S RELATION
  { S# S# , SNAME NAME , STATUS INTEGER , CITY CHARACTER }
    KEY { S# } ;
```

In general, of course, a relation type name can be represented in text form in several different ways, owing to the fact that sets have to be represented in text form by means of commalists (i.e., sequences, possibly even with repeated elements). For example, the following are all equally valid text representations of the relation type name shown above:

```
RELATION { STATUS INTEGER , SNAME NAME , S# S# , CITY CHARACTER }

RELATION { SNAME NAME , STATUS INTEGER , CITY CHARACTER , S# S# }

RELATION { S# S# , CITY CHARACTER , SNAME NAME ,
           STATUS INTEGER , CITY CHARACTER , STATUS INTEGER }

RELATION { S# S# , SNAME NAME , STATUS INTEGER , CITY CHARACTER ,
           S# S# , SNAME NAME , STATUS INTEGER , CITY CHARACTER }
```

And so on. To repeat, however, these examples don't represent different names for the same type; rather, they merely represent different spellings of the same name.[4] The type as such has (to say it one more time) just the one name, unique to the type in question. *Note:* The *Manifesto* doesn't state explicitly that relation types are the only types with names of the form RELATION {*H*}—but it doesn't need to, either, given that every name of that form is a relation type name by definition.

> *Aside:* Incidentally, one consequence of the fact that relation types in the *Manifesto* are always generated types (and, more specifically, have names of the form RELATION {*H*} for some heading {*H*}) is that there's no such thing as an empty relation type. That's because any such type always has at least one value—viz., the empty relation of that type. (Tuple types, by contrast, can be empty. To be specific, a given tuple type is empty if and only if at least one of its attributes is itself of some empty type.) *End of aside.*

Now, the main reason the *Manifesto* prescribes the foregoing approach to relation type naming is that it allows us to specify, simply and straightforwardly, what the type of the result of an arbitrary relational expression is; in other words, it helps with the important issue of *relation type inference*. (Of course, it goes without saying that a workable type system does require the system to know the type of the result of every relational expression; that is, the type inference problem does need to be addressed.) By way of example, consider the following **Tutorial D** expression, which denotes the projection of the current value of the suppliers relvar S over S# and CITY:

```
S { S# , CITY }
```

The type of the result of this expression—and hence, by definition, the type of the expression per se—has

---

[4] Note that the same can't be said of (e.g.) CHARACTER and CHAR—these aren't different spellings of the same name, they're a name and a synonym for that name.

the following name:

```
RELATION { S# S# , CITY CHARACTER }
```

Observe in particular that the result type here does have a name of the prescribed form: namely, RELATION {*H*}, where {*H*} is the pertinent heading. The example thus illustrates the *Manifesto*'s rule for determining the type of the result of an arbitrary projection operation: If *r* is a relation and {*X*} is a subset of the attributes of *r*, then the projection of *r* over {*X*}—*r*{*X*}, in **Tutorial D**—has type RELATION{*X*}. Since the *Manifesto* defines such rules for all of the relational operators for which it prescribes support, it follows that the type of the result of every conforming relational expression is well defined and understood by both the user and the system.

The advantages of the foregoing scheme are best appreciated by considering what would happen if it weren't in effect—in particular, if relation types (like scalar types) could have names that were arbitrary text strings. Suppose, for example, that users could introduce such names, perhaps as indicated in this example (patterned after **Tutorial D**'s existing TYPE statement, which is used to define scalar types):

```
TYPE S_RELTYPE RELATION { S# S# , SNAME NAME ,
                          STATUS INTEGER , CITY CHARACTER } ... ;
```

Now we could presumably define the suppliers relvar S like this:

```
VAR S S_RELTYPE KEY { S# } ;
```

One disadvantage of this scheme is obvious immediately: The relvar definer effectively has to know what the name S_RELTYPE "stands for," as it were, in order to know what attributes can legally be mentioned in the KEY specification. In other words, the relvar definer, at least, does effectively have to know the "true" name of the relation type anyway. What's more, the same goes for anyone who wishes to make use of the relvar in question for any purpose (for example, to formulate queries against it); for otherwise how would such a user know that, e.g., the expression S{S#,CITY} is legal?

Moreover, what can we say about that expression S{S#,CITY}? What's the type of its result? (Equivalently, what's the type of the expression itself?) It seems to me there are two possibilities:

- We could define the result type to be RELATION {S# S#, CITY CHARACTER}, exactly as the *Manifesto* currently prescribes.

- We could require the user to introduce an explicit name for that type, perhaps like this:

```
TYPE S#_CITY_RELTYPE RELATION { S# S# , CITY CHARACTER } ... ;
```

If we were to adopt the first possibility, the entire user defined relation type name scheme would merely "live alongside" the *Manifesto* scheme, as it were, and would in fact be wholly redundant (not to mention the complications it would doubtless cause for the system catalog). If we were to adopt the second possibility, users would have to define names of their own, ahead of time, for every possible relation type (i.e., for every possible relational expression): a scheme that seems to me completely unworkable. In other words, it's my position that the idea of allowing relation types to have arbitrary names leads to redundant naming at best and is unworkable at worst. For relation types, therefore, I propose the following:

- **Proposal** (tentative): A given relation type shall have exactly one name, as currently prescribed. It shall have no synonyms, except as discussed in the section "Relation Values," later. No type name shall apply to more than one type (scalar or otherwise).

  *Implications for the Manifesto and **Tutorial D**:* None.
  Note: One idea I haven't discussed so far is the possibility of permitting synonyms for the RELATION

type generator itself (as opposed to synonyms for relation types as such). For example, we might define REL to be a synonym for RELATION; then REL {*H*} would be a synonym for RELATION {*H*}, for all possible headings {*H*}. Such a scheme appears to have no serious consequences for relation type inference, so I see no reason to outlaw it; in fact, Chapter 11 of the present book, q.v., proposes the introduction of exactly such a scheme into **Tutorial D**.

Net of the discussions so far: A type does have *N* different names, but *N* is always equal to one.

SCALAR VALUES

The *Manifesto* states (in RM Prescription 2) that "scalar values shall ... carry with them, at least conceptually, some identification of the type to which they belong." In other words, the underlying model looks something like this:

1. There exists an underlying set of objects which I'll refer to for present purposes as *individuals*.[5]

2. Defining a scalar type involves specifying some subset of the set of individuals and assigning a unique name to that subset. Such definitions are provided either by some user (via the TYPE statement, in **Tutorial D**) or by the system. Note that the provisions of this paragraph allow the same individual to be specified as belonging to more than one scalar type—but see paragraph 8 below.

3. A scalar type can thus be formalized as an ordered pair *<T,{I}>*, where *T* is the type name and {*I*} is a set of individuals. The scalar type in question is referred to in less formal contexts as "type *T*." Observe that this nomenclature is unambiguous, because (in accordance with paragraph 2 and the proposals discussed in the section "Scalar Types," earlier) type names are unique—no two distinct types, scalar or otherwise, have the same name.

4. A value of scalar type *T* can be formalized as an ordered pair *<T,i>*, where *i* is an individual from the applicable set {*I*}. Such values are called scalar values (scalars for short).

5. Scalar value *<T,i>* is said to have, or be of, type *T*.

6. Scalar types *<T1,{I1}>* and *<T2,{I2}>* are equal—i.e., they're the same type—if and only if the names *T1* and *T2* are the same (in which case the corresponding sets of individuals {*I1*} and {*I2*} are the same too, necessarily). *Note:* This paragraph and the next two will need some slight refinement if type inheritance is supported.

7. Scalar values *<T1,i1>* and *<T2,i2>* are equal—i.e., they're the same value—if and only if the names *T1* and *T2* are the same and the individuals *i1* and *i2* are the same. It follows that if scalar types *<T1,{I1}>* and *<T2,{I2}>* are distinct, then they're disjoint (i.e., no scalar value is of both type *T1* and type *T2*).

8. Let *T1* and *T2* be distinct scalar types, and let *<T1,i1>* and *<T2,i2>* be values of those types. Then it might be the case that the individuals *i1* and *i2* are one and the same, *i* say—but if so, this fact has no significance whatsoever as far as the model is concerned. In particular, there's no sense in which the scalar values *<T1,i>* and *<T2,i>* are "the same" as far as the model is concerned.

9. In fact, if *T1* and *T2* are distinct scalar types, it could even be the case that the corresponding sets of individuals {*I1*} and {*I2*} are identical. In particular, this state of affairs could arise if the sets {*I1*} and {*I2*} are specified by distinct but equivalent predicates;[6] as a simple example, suppose {*I1*} is defined as

---

[5] Taking a leaf here out of the logicians' book (see Chapter 2).

[6] See Chapter 2 regarding what it might mean for distinct predicates to be equivalent.

"integers divisible by 10" and {*I2*} is defined as "even integers divisible by 5." *Note:* These two types are, to repeat, distinct; but (of course) there's nothing in the *Manifesto* to prevent a CAST operator from being defined for mapping values of one type to values of the other.

10. A particular case of the situation described in paragraph 9 occurs when the sets {*I1*} and {*I2*} are both empty. The formalism so far described would therefore allow any number of empty scalar types (where an empty scalar type is a scalar type <*T*, {*I*}> for which the set of individuals {*I*} is empty), and those types would be all be logically distinct. However, it turns out to be desirable:

    a. To prohibit empty scalar types entirely if type inheritance is not supported

    b. To support exactly one empty scalar type (usable only in certain limited contexts) if type inheritance is supported[7]

RELATION VALUES

A relation value *r* is an ordered pair <{*H*},{*b*}> where (a) {*H*} is a heading, (b) {*b*} is a set of tuples, and (c) each tuple in {*b*} has heading {*H*}. It follows that relation values effectively carry their type around with them, just like scalar values. (At least, they carry their heading around, and the heading in turn implies the type.) However, there's one point that needs some clarification: What exactly is a heading? According to the *Manifesto* (RM Prescription 9), it's a set of ordered pairs of the form <*A*,*T*>, where *A* is an attribute name and *T* is a type name—a type name, observe, not a synonym. So the following—

```
RELATION { S# S# , SNAME NAME , STATUS INTEGER , CITY CHAR }
```

—is strictly invalid as a relation type name, if CHAR is (as suggested earlier) just a synonym and not the actual name for the scalar type "character string." Now, we could presumably allow the foregoing example in concrete syntax as shorthand for the actual relation type name; but if we did, it would follow that relation types must be allowed to have synonyms after all. So I suggest the following modified form of my earlier proposal regarding relation type names:

- **Proposal** (revised): A given relation type shall have exactly one name, as currently prescribed. It shall have no synonyms, other than those arising from synonyms if any for the types in terms of which it is, directly or indirectly, defined. No type name shall apply to more than one type (scalar or otherwise). Likewise, no synonym shall apply to more than one type (scalar or otherwise), and no type name shall be the same as any synonym.

Implications for the Manifesto and ***Tutorial D:*** None, apart from those already discussed earlier in the section "Scalar Types."

REVISING THE *MANIFESTO* (?)

RM Prescription 1 is the only one in the *Manifesto* that prescribes anything having to do with the names of scalar types. Here's the current text of that prescription, repeated from Chapter 1:

> A **scalar data type** (**scalar type** for short) is a named, finite set of scalar values (**scalars** for short). Given an arbitrary pair of distinct scalar types named *T1* and *T2*, respectively, with corresponding sets of scalar values *S1* and *S2*, respectively, the names *T1* and *T2* shall be distinct and the sets *S1* and *S2* shall be disjoint; in other words, two scalar types shall be equal—i.e., the same type—if and only if they have the same name (and therefore the same set of

---

[7] The slight lack of orthogonality implied by the parenthetical remark here is a trifle unfortunate but seems to be unavoidable.

> values). **D** shall provide facilities for users to define their own scalar types (*user defined* scalar types); other scalar types shall be provided by the system (*built in* or *system defined* scalar types). With the sole exception of the system defined empty type *omega* (which is defined only if type inheritance is supported—see OO Prescription 2—and is not permitted as the declared type of anything), the definition of any given scalar type *T* shall be accompanied by a specification of an **example value** of that type. **D** shall also provide facilities for users to destroy user defined scalar types. The system defined scalar types shall include type **boolean** (containing just two values, here denoted TRUE and FALSE), and **D** shall support all four monadic and 16 dyadic logical operators, directly or indirectly, for this type.

Let's examine this text sentence by sentence.

- A **scalar data type** (**scalar type** for short) is a named, finite set of scalar values (**scalars** for short).

  This sentence is correct as it stands. I don't believe the terminology of "named sets" requires any further explanation, or apology. It might help to state explicitly that a scalar type name can't take the form TUPLE {*H*} or the form RELATION {*H*}, though as indicated earlier in this chapter this fact is at least implicit in the *Manifesto* (in RM Prescriptions 6 and 7, respectively).

- Given an arbitrary pair of distinct scalar types named *T1* and *T2,* respectively, with corresponding sets of scalar values *S1* and *S2,* respectively, the names *T1* and *T2* shall be distinct and the sets *S1* and *S2* shall be disjoint; in other words, two scalar types shall be equal—i.e., the same type—if and only if they have the same name (and therefore the same set of values).

  This sentence is also correct as it stands, so long as it's clearly understood that there's a logical difference between a scalar value and what earlier in this chapter I referred to as an "individual." *Note:* Use of the phrase "in other words" in this sentence has been criticized on the grounds of inexactitude (possibly other grounds as well), but I see nothing wrong with it.

- **D** shall provide facilities for users to define their own scalar types (*user defined* scalar types); other scalar types shall be provided by the system (*built in* or *system defined* scalar types).

  This sentence is obviously still correct.

- With the sole exception of the system defined empty type *omega* (which is defined only if type inheritance is supported—see OO Prescription 2—and is not permitted as the declared type of anything), the definition of any given scalar type *T* shall be accompanied by a specification of an **example value** of that type.

  This sentence is obviously still correct.

- **D** shall also provide facilities for users to destroy user defined scalar types.

  This sentence is obviously still correct.

- The system defined scalar types shall include type **boolean** (containing just two values, here denoted TRUE and FALSE), and **D** shall support all four monadic and 16 dyadic logical operators, directly or indirectly, for this type.

  This sentence is obviously still correct.

The net of all this as I see it is that neither the *Manifesto* as a whole, nor RM Prescription 1 in particular, need any revision at all in order to conform to the proposals of the present chapter.

REFERENCES AND BIBLIOGRAPHY

1. C. J. Date and Hugh Darwen: *Databases, Types, and the Relational Model: The Third Manifesto* (3rd edition). Boston, Mass.: Addison-Wesley (2006).

2. C. J. Date and Hugh Darwen: *The Third Manifesto* (Chapter 4 of reference [1]; see also the revised version, Chapter 1 of the present book).

3. C. J. Date and Hugh Darwen: **Tutorial D** (Chapter 5 of reference [1]; see also the revised version, Chapter 11 of the present book).

4. International Organization for Standardization (ISO): *Database Language SQL,* Document ISO/IEC 9075:2008 (2008).

Chapter 4

Setting the Record Straight

(Part 1 of 6):

The Two Great Blunders

The Third Manifesto—"the *Manifesto*" for short—is a formal proposal by the present writers for a solid foundation for database management systems and the language interface to such systems. We've described it in (among other things) a series of books, the most recent of which is reference [1]. Here's a lightly edited extract from the opening chapter of that reference:

> The *Manifesto* rests squarely in the classical relational tradition ... The ideas are in no way intended to supersede those of the relational model, nor do they do so; rather, they use the ideas of the relational model as a base on which to build. The relational model is still highly relevant to database theory and practice and will remain so for as far out as anyone can see. Thus, we see our *Manifesto* as being very much in the spirit of Codd's original work and continuing along the path he originally laid down. We are interested in evolution, not revolution.

The *Manifesto* has had its critics, of course—many writers have commented on it over the years, some favorably, others less so. As a general rule we welcome such commentaries; peer review is part of the mechanism by which progress is made in scientific endeavors, and serious and informed discussion of the issues can only be beneficial. Indeed, those commentaries have sometimes caused us to make changes to our proposal (though only at the level of detail, we hasten to add—we've never changed our overall direction).

The latest such commentary is a paper by Maurice Gittens [2].[1] It deals with six somewhat separate issues, each of which (it claims) constitutes a significant defect in the *Manifesto* in its present form. Unfortunately, however, it does not, in our opinion, offer "serious and informed discussion" of those issues. Rather, it appears to be based on a series of misconceptions and misunderstandings of our ideas; at least, it certainly misrepresents those ideas in a variety of ways. Given this state of affairs, we feel obliged to respond to Gittens's criticisms, and such is the purpose of this series of chapters (i.e., the present chapter and the next five).

Gittens's issues are as follows (verbatim):

1. No more **Great Blunders**
2. Treating operations as relations without rigor
3. No adherence to the principle of semantic compositionality
4. No semantic integrity in the presence of relational assignment
5. Undermining issues with relation valued attributes
6. No sound substantiation for the rejection of unknown values

Our response is divided into six parts accordingly. *Note:* In order to allow our response to stand on its own as much as possible, we've included certain portions of Gittens's text here and there in the various chapters. The portions in question are basically as provided to us by Gittens in various English language versions of his paper, but we've edited them slightly for reasons of flow and continuity. Of course, it goes without saying that

[1] Our responses are based on various English language versions of this paper. A Dutch version appeared in *DB/M Magazine* (Array Publications, Netherlands, April 2007). For an online version, see reference [2].

we've done our best to retain the original sense in every case.

Our response on the first of the six issues follows immediately.

THE TWO GREAT BLUNDERS

Here's the relevant text from Gittens's paper:

> Relative to the second edition of *The Third Manifesto,* the third edition has changed, on many points. This edition gives a better impression of Date and Darwen's position on databases, types and the relational model than the previous version. There is no longer much ado about the so called *great blunders,* so prominently present in the second edition of *The Third Manifesto.*

Before responding to the substance of this criticism, we'd like to clarify something—a small (?) matter of terminology. The fact is, there's a logical difference between (a) *The Third Manifesto* as such, on the one hand, and (b) reference [1], which is a book that describes that *Manifesto,* on the other. The latter is a much bigger deal than the former!—in fact, the *Manifesto* as such is just one chapter (out of 16, not to mention ten appendixes) in the book. But Gittens's phrases "the second edition" and "the third edition" (of *The Third Manifesto* in each case) in the extract just quoted clearly refer to editions of the book rather than to editions of the *Manifesto* as such. Well, critics do often use the term *The Third Manifesto* as if it referred to the book as a whole (and Gittens does so repeatedly throughout his paper)—but we prefer to be a little more precise. However, we won't mention this matter again in this series of chapters (except briefly in the next one), letting this one comment do duty for all.

To respond now to Gittens's criticism: Gittens seems to be under a misconception here. It's true that we no longer refer to the errors in question as "Great Blunders"; however, it shouldn't be concluded that we have in any way changed our position regarding the errors as such. We simply wanted to make the book a little more suitable for an academic audience. The two OO Proscriptions arising from the Great Blunders still remain, as does most of the original discussion. Here are the proscriptions in question:

- **OO Proscription 1: Relvars Are Not Domains**

  Relvars are not domains.

- **OO Proscription 2: No Object Ids**

  No database relvar shall include an attribute of type *pointer*.

These proscriptions are supported by the same lengthy discussion as appeared in previous editions of the book (though part of that discussion has been moved to a different chapter, Chapter 9). OO Proscription 1 is motivated by the common confusion between types (which Codd called domains) and relvars (which Codd called time-varying relations)—a confusion exhibited by, for example, SQL's "typed tables." (Such a table is meant as the SQL counterpart to what the object world calls the "extent" of a type, which is essentially just the set of all values of the type in question.) OO Proscription 2 is merely a reiteration of one of Codd's own motivations for his relational model; we felt it needed to be restated in view of, for example, SQL's support for "REF types" (for object identifiers). *Note:* "Typed tables" and REF types were both added to SQL in the 1999 edition of the standard.

LOGICAL INCONSISTENCIES (?)

Following on from the previous criticism, Gittens continues:

> Still, there remain issues with the logical consistency of the dissertation presented in the third edition of *The Third Manifesto.* In my opinion, the standard set by the maxim *All logical differences are big differences* and its corollary *All logical mistakes are big mistakes* that Date and Darwen present as a guiding principle in their work has not yet been met by *The Third Manifesto.*

Well, of course we can't be sure our work is 100 percent consistent, but—as noted earlier in the present chapter—whenever we're shown it isn't, we do our best to correct it; in particular, an errata list for reference [1] is maintained and available at *www.thethirdmanifesto.com.* As for the specific inconsistencies that Gittens accuses us of, however, we believe he's mistaken, and in this series of chapters we'll try to show why. We'll also provide some in depth discussion of each of the issues he raises, including in particular the justifications he asks for in connection with the last two (relation valued attributes and "unknown values"). We'll also explain why some of his observations about our book are factually incorrect.

REFERENCES AND BIBLIOGRAPHY

1. C. J. Date and Hugh Darwen: *Databases, Types, and the Relational Model: The Third Manifesto* (3rd edition). Boston, Mass.: Addison-Wesley (2006).

2. Maurice Gittens: "The Third Manifesto Revisited," *www.gittens.nl/TheTTMRevisited.pdf* (March 25th, 2007).

Chapter 5

Setting the Record Straight (Part 2 of 6): Treating Operators as Relations

Gittens asserts in his paper [4] that *The Third Manifesto* "[treats] operators as relations without rigor." The pertinent section of that paper is quite brief, and we cite it here in its entirety:

> In Appendix A of *The Third Manifesto,* Date and Darwen repeatedly make the unqualified statement that operators can be treated as relations. This idea, which they claim as their own, is used as grounds for dispensing with a few operators from Codd's algebra as can be read in the following quote taken from Appendix A.
>
> > We now claim that, given the fact that operators can be treated as relations, and given also the availability of the **A** operators AND, REMOVE, and RENAME (the latter two still to be discussed), it is indeed the case that we can dispense with *restrict,* EXTEND, and SUMMARIZE. We will justify this claim in the next section but one.
>
> First, it seems fair to assume that many people familiar with, for example, truth tables as they are known in the context of boolean algebra, have for many years appreciated the fact that *commutative* operators can be treated as relations. So, Date and Darwen seem to have discovered hot water here. Second and more significantly, while making claims about operators in general, Date and Darwen attempted to motivate their dispensing of specific operators from Codd's algebra based on an example involving the *commutative* operator PLUS. Rigor would require them to show that pertinent operators from Codd's algebra are also commutative. Alternatively, rigor would require an elaboration on noncommutative operators such as SUBTRACT as well. Attempting to view noncommutative operators as relations one soon encounters the problem that it is necessary not only to identify the operands of noncommutative operators but it is also necessary to designate their respective roles. Information about the roles of operands is lacking in the relational representation of *noncommutative* operators and Date and Darwen would need to illustrate how this information could be catered for without violating their proscriptions and prescriptions.

Note: Gittens's phrase "Appendix A of *The Third Manifesto*" refers to Appendix A of reference [1], which isn't *The Third Manifesto* as such but is, rather, a book that describes it (*The Third Manifesto* as such [2] is just one chapter, Chapter 4, in that book). As noted in the previous chapter, however, the phrase *The Third Manifesto* is often used, incorrectly, to mean reference [1] in its entirety.

Anyway, our overall reaction to the foregoing extract from Gittens's paper is threefold:

1. First of all, Gittens seems not to have understood what we were trying to do when we claimed in "Appendix A of *The Third Manifesto*"—i.e., the present chapter's reference [3]—that we could dispense with certain operators. We certainly weren't saying the operators in question should be removed from the user language, as even a cursory examination of our own language **Tutorial D** should make clear. Rather, we were saying those operators weren't primitive, and so could be removed from the *foundations* for such a language without any loss of functionality. In other words, we were trying to provide a solid basis for defining those operators. That's all.

2. Gittens asserts that our treatment of such matters "lacks rigor" and/or is otherwise incomplete (with respect to commutativity in particular). Part at least of what he says here is simply incorrect, as we will show.

3. What's more, we believe our treatment *is* rigorous as far as it goes—but we can certainly make it more so,

and we'll do that later in the present chapter. (We didn't do so in reference [3] because we didn't think it necessary. After all, Gittens himself says that we've only "discovered hot water here," implying that the material in question is already familiar to everyone anyway.)

In what follows we first explain in more detail just what we were trying to do when we claimed that certain operators (*restrict,* EXTEND, and SUMMARIZE, to be specific) could be dispensed with. We then provide a blow by blow response to certain specific points in Gittens's text. Third and most important, we elaborate on the whole question of operators as relations.

Note: This part of our response to Gittens has been revised considerably since it was first published. However, the revisions are meant as clarifications only; the substance of the original remains unchanged.

WHAT WE WERE TRYING TO DO

Before we explain what we were trying to do in reference [3], we would like to comment on a possible confusion in Gittens's text. What we showed in reference [3] was that certain *nonrelational* operators (e.g., PLUS) could be treated as relations, and hence that certain *relational* operators (e.g., EXTEND) could be defined in terms of others (e.g., JOIN). However, Gittens asserts that (a) we "attempted to motivate [our] dispensing of specific operators from Codd's algebra based on an example involving the *commutative* operator PLUS," but that (b) rigor "would require [us] to show that pertinent operators from Codd's algebra are also commutative." Observe that part (a) of this quote refers to the fact that the *nonrelational* operator PLUS is commutative, while part (b) refers to the possibility that certain *relational* operators might not be. Now, perhaps the writer isn't confused here, but the reader could certainly be forgiven for thinking otherwise.

Be that as it may, we stand by our claim—indeed, it's a widely recognized fact—that conventional operators such as PLUS and MINUS can be treated as relations, and hence by our claim that certain operators of the relational algebra can be defined in terms of others. On the strength of these claims, we define (in reference [3]) a new and fairly abstract relational algebra that we call **A**. **A** is agreeably small, in that it involves a very small number of primitive operators—arguably as few as two—and yet is still relationally complete. Our idea was that **A** could be used as a basis for defining the semantics of a relational language; we use it for that purpose ourselves in reference [3] for **Tutorial D** in particular, and we offer it for consideration by other database language designers for use in connection with their own languages. Please note, however, that it was never our intention that **A** be used for direct computation purposes. Please note too that *The Third Manifesto* as such doesn't depend on it at all. **Tutorial D** does, as already noted, but **Tutorial D** isn't part of the *Manifesto*—it's merely a language we use to illustrate the ideas of the *Manifesto* (the *Manifesto* per se isn't a language, of course, but rather a set of proposals for a language).

RESPONSES TO SPECIFIC CRITICISMS

All otherwise unattributed quotes in this section are taken from Gittens's paper [4].

- "This idea, which they claim as their own, ...": On page 366 of reference [3] we wrote: "In this section we elaborate on our idea of treating operators as relations." We did not mean to give the impression that we were the first to think of this idea; the concept is well established and has been so for many years, and any good book on logic explains it. In fact, the team who worked on IS/1—one of the very first, if not *the* first, of the relational prototypes developed in the early 1970s—even attempted to embrace the idea in their language ISBL; however, they found it led to excessively complicated expressions and so invented the EXTEND and SUMMARIZE operators instead (not using those particular names, however). See reference [5] for further discussion.

- "This idea ... is used as grounds for dispensing with a few operators from Codd's algebra": Not all of the operators we propose "dispensing with" are in Codd's algebra. To be specific, Codd's algebra does include restriction (of course), but nothing in any of Codd's publications suggests that it might also include anything analogous to EXTEND or SUMMARIZE.

- "[Many] people familiar with ... truth tables [have] appreciated the fact that *commutative* operators can be treated as relations": The reason why operators can be represented as relations has nothing to do with commutativity. If the "many people" Gittens mentions think otherwise, they're mistaken. In fact, however, it's very hard to believe they do, given that one of the most familiar truth tables of all—namely, the one for implication—quite clearly defines an operator that's not commutative.

- "Rigor would require [Date and Darwen] to show that pertinent operators from Codd's algebra are also commutative": Whatever Gittens might mean by "pertinent operators" here (see the previous section), there's no need for us to show that any operators are commutative, because our treatment has nothing to with commutativity.

- "Alternatively, rigor would require an elaboration on noncommutative operators such as SUBTRACT as well": The treatment described on pages 366-369 of reference [3] makes absolutely no distinction between commutative and noncommutative operators. Furthermore, we explicitly go to the trouble of pointing out, in the middle of page 367, that the relation named PLUS that we use to represent the predicate $a + b = c$ might just as well be called MINUS, since it represents the predicates $c - a = b$ and $c - b = a$ equally well. *Note:* Actually, reference [3] uses *x, y,* and *z* in place of *a, b,* and *c,* respectively; we've changed the symbols here in order to avoid certain confusions that might otherwise arise later in the present chapter. We also use A, B, and C in place of X, Y, and Z, respectively (see the paragraph immediately following), for the same reason.

- "Attempting to view noncommutative operators as relations one soon encounters the problem that it is necessary not only to identify the operands of noncommutative operators but it is also necessary to designate their respective roles": By "roles" here, Gittens presumably means whatever is needed to distinguish, for example, the subtrahend from the minuend in subtraction. In conventional mathematics such roles are designated by the positioning of the operands. In database theory they're designated by attribute names; the attribute names of a database relation correspond to the parameter names in whatever predicate that relation represents. In the case of PLUS and MINUS, for example, the parameter names are *a, b,* and *c* and the attribute names are A, B, and C.[1] For PLUS, where the predicate is $a + b = c$, C designates the result of an invocation and A and B designate the operands. We could perhaps say that A designates the "first" operand and B the "second," but we could equally well go the other way, precisely because addition *is* commutative. When we wish the relation to represent $c - a = b$, B takes on the role of the result, C that of the minuend, and A that of the subtrahend. When instead it represents $c - b = a$, A becomes the result, C stays as the minuend, and B becomes the subtrahend.

- "Date and Darwen would need to illustrate how [information about the roles of operands] could be catered for without violating their proscriptions and prescriptions": The prescriptions and proscriptions Gittens refers to here are those of *The Third Manifesto* [2]. The relevant prescriptions are those that collectively define what a relation is (RM Prescriptions 6, 7, 9, and 10). The only *pro*scription that might be relevant to the present issue is RM Proscription 1, which reads as follows:

> **D** shall include no concept of a "relation" whose attributes are distinguishable by ordinal position. Instead, for

[1] As this example suggests, we use lowercase italics for parameter names in predicates, uppercase Roman for the corresponding attribute names.

every relation *r* expressible in **D,** the attributes of *r* shall be distinguishable by *name*.

The relations we conceive of as representing operators satisfy those prescriptions and that proscription. More to the point, we believe we have shown in reference [3] exactly how they do so. Nevertheless, we now proceed to give a more detailed explanation.

MATHEMATICAL RELATIONS vs. DATABASE RELATIONS

The remainder of this chapter consists of a more rigorous treatment of the idea that operators can be represented by relations, and hence that invocations of such operators can be represented by relational expressions. The present section lays some groundwork for that treatment by clarifying what we mean by the term *relation* and elaborating somewhat on the relationship between relations and predicates.

First of all, then, here's a definition of the term *relation* as that term is used in mathematics:

- **Definition (mathematical relation):** Given a collection of *n* sets *X, Y, ..., Z,* not necessarily distinct, *r* is a (mathematical) relation on those sets if and only if it's a set of ordered *n*-tuples <*x,y,...,z*>, each of which has its first element *x* from *X,* its second element *y* from *Y,* ..., and its *n*th element *z* from *Z.*

In practice, however, the term *relation* is usually taken in mathematics to mean a binary relation specifically. Here's an edited version of the foregoing definition that reflects this fact:

- **Definition (mathematical binary relation):** Given sets *X* and *Y,* not necessarily distinct, *r* is a (mathematical, binary) relation on those sets if and only if it's a set of ordered pairs <*x,y*>, each of which has its first element *x* from *X* and its second element *y* from *Y.*

What we call a binary relation in database theory (in *The Third Manifesto* in particular) is merely an alternative way of representing this latter concept; the main difference is that a binary relation in database theory is a set of *un*ordered pairs of elements, the elements in question being identified not by ordinal position but by attribute name. Indeed, it's surely obvious that a mapping can be defined—a rather trivial one at that—that shows that, for any given binary mathematical relation, there exists at least one corresponding binary database relation that represents the same predicate (and vice versa). We'll go into details of such mappings later; for now, we'll just assume they can indeed be defined. *Note:* For clarity, let's agree until further notice to refer to mathematical relations as *m*-relations and database relations as *TTM*-relations (*TTM* for *The Third Manifesto,* of course).

Let *r* be a binary relation. Regardless of whether *r* is an *m*-relation or a *TTM*-relation, then, it necessarily represents some predicate, by providing a set whose elements represent the true instantiations, or true invocations, of that predicate. (Note, however, that the elements referred to here are *pairs,* where each such pair <*x,y*> has its first element *x* from some underlying set *X* and its second element *y* from some underlying set *Y.*) For example, consider the predicate $y = x^2$, where *X* is the set {–9,–8,...,0,1,...,9} and *Y* is the set {0,1,2,...,99}. Clearly, the corresponding *m*-relation contains the ordered pairs <–9,81>, <–8,64>, ..., <9,81>, and the corresponding *TTM*-relation contains the *un*ordered tuples {X –9, Y 81}, {X –8, Y 64}, ..., {X 9, Y 81}. *Note:* We'll explain what we mean by the term *unordered tuples,* and this notation for them, in the next section.

Now, the predicate $y = x^2$ is in fact a mathematical *function.* Here's a definition (refer to Fig. 1 opposite for a pictorial illustration of the concepts involved):

- **Definition (function):** Given two sets *X* and *Y,* not necessarily distinct, *f* is a function from *X* to *Y* if and only if it's a rule—also known as a map or mapping—pairing each element of *X* (the domain) with exactly one element of *Y* (the codomain); equivalently, *f* is just that pairing itself (i.e., the set of ordered pairs <*x,y*> that constitute that pairing). The unique element *y* of the codomain corresponding to the element *x* of the domain is the *image* of x under f, and the set of all such images is the *range* Z of f. Note that the range is a subset (often a proper subset) of the codomain,[2] and the function can be regarded as a many to one correspondence from the domain to the range. Moreover, if the range is equal to the codomain, the function is said to be *onto* the codomain; otherwise it's said to be *into* the codomain.

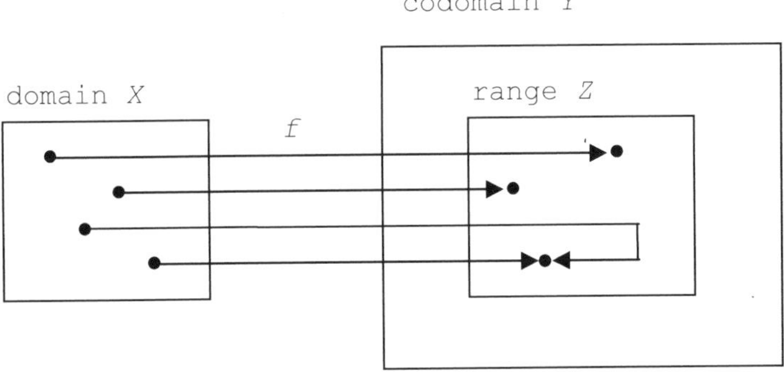

Function *f* maps elements of *X* to *image* elements in *Z;* every element of *X* maps to exactly one element of *Z;* every element of *Z* is the image of at least one element in *X;* if *Z* = *Y*, *f* is *onto,* else *into,* *Y.*

Fig. 1: Function terminology

Now, it's immediate from the foregoing definition that a function is a special case of a binary *m*-relation. To spell the point out (and with reference to the definition we gave earlier for this latter concept), it's a binary *m*-relation that contains exactly one pair for each element x of the set X. And the predicate that's represented by an *m*-relation that happens to be a function is a predicate of the generic form $y = f(x)$, where f denotes the function in question and x and y are parameters; the parameter x denotes the argument to an invocation of f and the parameter y denotes the result of that invocation.[3] Thus, the mathematical view of a function is as a binary *m*-relation, representing a dyadic predicate.

Observe now, however, that what we've just referred to as "the" argument (to some invocation of some function) is, in general, composite; for example, an invocation of the function PLUS takes an argument that consists of a pair of numbers. In other words, we can certainly regard PLUS as a function as defined above, just so long as we understand that the domain of that function is a set of pairs of numbers and not just (e.g.) a set of numbers as such. And here's as good a place as any to state explicitly that the operators we want to discuss in this chapter—the operators, that is, that we claim can be treated as relations—are indeed all functions in the same sense that PLUS is a function. (In the terminology of *The Third Manifesto,* they're *read-only* operators, and *read-only operator* is just another term for function.)

In practice, of course, we don't usually say PLUS "takes a composite argument"; rather, we say it takes two arguments, or is dyadic—but now the term *dyadic* refers not to the number of parameters in the corresponding predicate, but to the number of parameters in that predicate not counting the one denoting the result. The predicate per se is triadic: $a + b = c$. To obtain a binary *m*-relation representing this predicate, therefore, the

---

[2] The $y = x^2$ example illustrates this point: The codomain is the integers from 0 to 99 (i.e., the set {0,1,2,...,99}), but the range is just the perfect squares (i.e., the set {0,1,4,...,81}).

[3] Note that f itself is not a parameter; it is, rather, a *name* for the predicate (or function)—e.g., "square of," perhaps, in the case of $y = x^2$.

mathematician has to "wrap" the a and b together to form the ordered pair <*a,b*>.[4] (And yes, it does need to be an *ordered* pair, even for a commutative operator like PLUS, for otherwise we wouldn't be able to investigate the commutativity of such an operator in the first place!) More generally, in fact, the x in $y = f(x)$ can stand for an ordered n-tuple of arbitrary degree n (so for that matter can the y, though this latter fact is mostly irrelevant to our purpose in this chapter).

Of course, a *TTM*-relation can directly represent an n-adic operator for arbitrary nonnegative integer n—i.e., the operator in question doesn't have to be dyadic specifically. In the database context, in other words, we have no compelling need to do any "wrapping" at all; we can do so if we like, but usually there'll be good reasons not to. See the further remarks on this point at the end of the next section.

MAPPING BINARY *m*-RELATIONS TO *TTM*-RELATIONS

A function is a binary m-relation, and thus a set of ordered pairs; by contrast, a *TTM*-relation is a set of unordered n-tuples (more precisely, the body of such a relation is a set of such n-tuples), where n is the degree of the *TTM*-relation. If we can show how to map an arbitrary ordered pair to an unordered n-tuple, therefore, we will have shown how to map an arbitrary function to an n-ary *TTM*-relation. Such is the aim of the present section.

We begin with the fact that the elements of an ordered pair might themselves be ordered pairs, or more generally ordered n-tuples for arbitrary degree n. For example, in the case of the function PLUS, the fact that 2 + 3 is equal to 5 is represented by the ordered pair <<2,3>,5>, in which the first element is itself an ordered pair in turn. Now, the ordered triple <2,3,5> can clearly be interpreted to convey exactly the same information as that ordered pair <<2,3>,5>, just so long as we "remember" how we obtained the triple from the pair, so to speak. To be specific:

- The first element of the triple, 2, is the first element of the first element of the ordered pair <<2,3>,5>; i.e., it's what denotes the first argument to the PLUS invocation in question.

- The second element of the triple, 3, is the second element of the first element of the ordered pair <<2,3>,5>; i.e., it's what denotes the second argument to the PLUS invocation in question.

- The third element of the triple, 5, is the second element of the ordered pair <<2,3>,5>; i.e., it's what denotes the result of the PLUS invocation in question.

By analogy with the term *wrapping* previously discussed, the process of replacing the element <2,3>, within the ordered pair <<2,3>,5>, by its constituent elements 2 and 3 in that order (thereby obtaining the ordered triple <2,3,5>) is known as *unwrapping*.

More generally, if either element of some ordered pair is itself an ordered n-tuple ($n \geqslant 0$), we can unwrap it if we wish (i.e., replace it by its constituent n elements, retaining their order) to yield an ordered (n+1)-tuple. And if some element of that ordered (n+1)-tuple is yet another ordered tuple, we can go on and unwrap that tuple, if we want to ... and so on. Applying this process, repeated as often as necessary, to all of the pairs constituting the function in question, we will wind up with an m-relation of degree n for some $n \geqslant 0$; and, of course, that m-relation of degree n will still be a legitimate representation of the function we started with.

The next step is to assign a name to each position in that m-relation, making sure no such name is assigned to more than one such position. In our PLUS example, we assign the names A, B, and C to positions 1, 2, and 3, respectively. Using these names, the ordered triple corresponding to 2 + 3 = 5 becomes <A 2, B 3, C 5>, where "A 2" can be read as "the first element has name A and value 2," "B 3" can be read as "the second element has

---

[4] The term *wrap* is taken from reference [1]—though there it's applied to sets, not sequences, of elements. Similar remarks apply to the term *unwrap* (see later).

name B and value 3," and so on. But of course we now no longer need to refer to elements by their position—the names are sufficient. So we can write, instead, {A 2, B 3, C 5} (or, equivalently, {B 3, C 5, A 2}, say), where the braces signify that the elements they enclose denote those of a *set*. The original ordered triple has become an unordered 3-tuple—i.e., a set of cardinality three. And the set of all such unordered 3-tuples constitutes (the body of) a *TTM*-relation: more precisely, a *TTM*-relation that conveys exactly the same information as the original *m*-relation. And so we have demonstrated a mapping from the original function PLUS to an *n*-ary *TTM*-relation, as required: a mapping for which $n = 3$, as it happens.

We remark in passing that, starting with the very same function or binary *m*-relation, we can obtain a *TTM*-relation representing $a - b = c$ by assigning the name A to position 3, the name B to position 2 (or 1), and the name C to position 1 (or 2), respectively. (And "–" is noncommutative, of course; *pace* Gittens, therefore, we can obviously represent noncommutative operators, as well as commutative ones, as *TTM*-relations.) We remark also that the *TTM*-relation for $a + b = c$ is also the *TTM*-relation for both $c - b = a$ and $c - a = b$ (as well as for $b + a = c$).

Note: In practice, we will be guided in the foregoing process—the process, that is, of mapping some function to an *n*-ary *TTM*-relation—by the specific predicate we wish to represent. Our ultimate goal will be to come up with a *TTM*-relation whose attributes are in one to one correspondence with the parameters of that predicate. For example, with reference to the function PLUS and the ordered pair <<2,3>,5>, we could conceivably have decided not to unwrap the element <2,3> after all—in which case the corresponding unordered 2-tuple might have looked like this: {AB <2,3>, C 5}. And then we could have gone a step further to obtain, say, {AB {A 2, B 3}, C 5} (i.e., an unordered 2-tuple one of whose elements is an unordered 2-tuple in turn). However, we chose to unwrap the element <2,3> for the very good psychological reason that we normally write the predicate for PLUS as $a + b = c$, and hence we prefer to have a *TTM*-relation with three attributes A, B, and C.

MAPPING *TTM*-RELATIONS TO BINARY *m*-RELATIONS

We have shown that for every binary *m*-relation there's at least one *TTM*-relation that represents the same predicate; in fact, a given binary *m*-relation usually has several corresponding *TTM*-relations.[5] But what about the inverse question? That is, could there exist *TTM*-relations that have no corresponding binary *m*-relation?

Well, the process described in the previous section can clearly be applied in the inverse direction (as it were), implying that any *TTM*-relation of degree two or more can certainly be mapped to some binary *m*-relation. But what about *TTM*-relations of degree one or zero? Could it be that such *TTM*-relations have no corresponding binary *m*-relation?

Consider the case of a *TTM*-relation of degree one. Let *r* be such a relation; let its sole attribute be named A; and suppose (just to be definite) that {A 42} is a tuple in *r*. Now consider the ordered tuple <42,<>>, where the symbol "<>" denotes the ordered (!) 0-tuple, or in other words the "ordered" tuple that contains no elements at all. Clearly, unwrapping that 0-tuple yields no elements at all; so if we replace the tuple <42,<>> by the tuple obtained by unwrapping its second element, we obtain the "ordered" 1-tuple <42>. From such considerations, it follows immediately that the *TTM*-relation *r* can be mapped to a binary *m*-relation containing (a) an ordered pair <*a*,<>> for every tuple {A *a*} in *r* and (b) no other ordered pairs. What's more, that binary *m*-relation is in fact a function, albeit a somewhat degenerate one. To be specific, it's a function that returns the empty ordered tuple <> (or equivalently the empty unordered tuple {}), no matter what its argument happens to be; in other words, it's a function whose range *Y* is a singleton set whose sole element is the empty set.

Suppose now that our *TTM*-relation *r* of degree one is also of cardinality one; i.e., suppose it contains just one tuple, say the tuple {A 42}. By the argument of the previous paragraph, then, *r* maps to a binary *m*-relation

---

[5] The differences between distinct *TTM*-relations that correspond to the same binary *m*-relation can lie in the attribute names, the amount of unwrapping, or both.

containing just the ordered pair <42,<>>. By an essentially similar argument, however, it can alternatively be considered as mapping to a binary *m*-relation containing just the ordered pair <<>,42>—and this latter *m*-relation is (by definition) precisely the *m*-relation that is the niladic function that returns the value 42 whenever it's invoked.[6] So not only can the special case of a *TTM*-relation of degree one and cardinality one be mapped to some binary *m*-relation, but it can be mapped to a binary *m*-relation that represents, very specifically, a niladic function (its domain *X* and range *Y* are both singleton sets; the sole element of *X* is the empty set, and the sole element of *Y* is the value the function returns whenever it's invoked—42, in the example).

Going one step further, consider now the ordered pair <<>,<>>, which pairs the ordered 0-tuple with itself. The set whose sole element is this ordered pair is a function once again: namely, the function that has, as both its domain *X* and its range *Y*, the singleton set whose sole element is the empty set. If we unwrap both elements of the only ordered pair in this function, <<>,<>>, we obtain the empty ordered tuple <>, which, as we already know, is logically equivalent to the empty unordered tuple {} (and note that this latter tuple, since it has no attributes, obviously has no attribute names either).

Now, the *TTM*-relation that contains just the empty unordered tuple is TABLE_DEE (the sole *TTM*-relation of degree zero and cardinality one). So a *TTM*-relation of degree zero certainly has a corresponding binary *m*-relation if the *TTM*-relation in question is TABLE_DEE, meaning it contains just one tuple. But what if it's TABLE_DUM, which is the *TTM*-relation of degree zero that contains no tuples at all? (TABLE_DEE and TABLE_DUM are, of course, the only *TTM*-relations of degree zero.) Well, any empty *TTM*-relation, including TABLE_DUM in particular, clearly corresponds to an empty binary *m*-relation. Such an *m*-relation represents a function whose domain *X* and range *Y* are both the empty set (in other words, a function for which the pertinent set of ordered pairs is itself empty).

OPERATOR INVOCATION

In this, the final section of the chapter, we take the term *relation* to mean a *TTM*-relation specifically. We also take the name PLUS to refer to the relation (with attributes A, B, and C) that represents the operator usually denoted "+". To invoke that operator (as in 2 + 3, for example), we must provide a value for A and a value for B, and the result of the invocation will be the unique corresponding value for C. We need to show that such an invocation can be represented by some relational expression.

Now, we've claimed that treating operators as relations allows us to dispense with the operator *restrict* in particular. For that reason, we mustn't use that operator in our attempt to represent an invocation of "+". In other words, we can't begin our attempt to compute 2 + 3 like this:

```
PLUS WHERE A = 2 AND B = 3
```

But nor do we need to; instead, we can *join* the relation PLUS and the relation that contains just the 2-tuple {A 2, B 3}. In **Tutorial D,** that join can be expressed thus:

```
PLUS JOIN RELATION { TUPLE { A 2 , B 3 } }
```

This expression evaluates to the following relation of cardinality one:

```
RELATION { TUPLE { A 2 , B 3 , C 5 } }
```

The desired result is in sight now, but we have to "extract" it from the tuple in which it occurs as the C value, and in order to do that we must first "extract" that tuple from the relation that contains just that tuple. The **Tutorial D** operator TUPLE FROM lets us do the tuple extraction:

---

[6] A niladic function is a function that takes no arguments and hence returns the same result on every invocation.

```
TUPLE FROM ( RELATION { TUPLE { A 2 , B 3 , C 5 } } )
```

This expression yields (surprise, surprise):

```
TUPLE { A 2 , B 3 , C 5 }
```

And then the **Tutorial D** operator *<attribute name>* FROM lets us do the attribute value extraction:

```
C FROM ( TUPLE { A 2 , B 3 , C 5 } )
```

This step completes the desired computation (it yields the result value 5). Putting it all together, then (and using WITH to show the steps clearly), then, we have:

```
WITH ( T1 := PLUS JOIN RELATION { TUPLE { A 2 , B 3 } } ,
       T2 := TUPLE FROM T1 ) :
C FROM T2
```

As for the noncommutative operator "–", as in (e.g.) 2 – 3, we can just use PLUS again, substituting 2 for C and 3 for either A or B. E.g.:

```
WITH ( T1 := PLUS JOIN RELATION { TUPLE { C 2 , B 3 } } ,
       T2 := TUPLE FROM T1 ) :
A FROM T2
```

Now, the **Tutorial D** operators TUPLE FROM and *<attribute name>* FROM aren't relational operators as such, because they return a result that isn't a relation.[7] For that reason, the relational algebra **A** doesn't include them, nor anything like them. But it doesn't need to, precisely because it does always produce results that are relations. For example, it never produces a scalar result like the integer 5; but it can certainly produce a result that's a relation that contains such a scalar value (or, more precisely, a result that's a relation of degree and cardinality both one that contains a tuple that contains such a scalar value). And it can certainly make use of operators (or relations) such as PLUS in computing those results. For example, suppose we're given a relation—let's call it EMP—with attributes EMP#, SALARY, and BONUS, and we wish to obtain the total pay (salary plus bonus) for each employee. In **Tutorial D:**

```
( EXTEND EMP : { PAY := SALARY + BONUS } ) { EMP# , PAY }
```

If the operator "+" is unavailable to us but the relation PLUS is available, we can write:

```
( EMP JOIN
    ( PLUS RENAME
         { A AS SALARY , B AS BONUS , C AS PAY } ) ) { EMP# , PAY }
```

We can also save ourselves from having to write out that final projection explicitly by using COMPOSE instead of JOIN, thus:

```
EMP COMPOSE ( PLUS RENAME { A AS SALARY , B AS BONUS , C AS PAY } )
```

These last two **Tutorial D** expressions both have a direct analog in **A**. For example, here's an **A** version of the second one:

---

[7] Actually, the expression *A* FROM *t* does return a relation in the special case in which attribute *A* of tuple *t* is relation valued, but this point is irrelevant to the overall message of the chapter.

```
EMP ◄COMPOSE► ( ( ( PLUS ◄RENAME► ( A , SALARY ) )
                         ◄RENAME► ( B , BONUS ) )
                         ◄RENAME► ( C , PAY ) )
```

REFERENCES AND BIBLIOGRAPHY

1. C. J. Date and Hugh Darwen: *Databases, Types, and the Relational Model: The Third Manifesto* (3rd edition). Boston, Mass.: Addison-Wesley (2006).

2. C. J. Date and Hugh Darwen: "*The Third Manifesto*" (Chapter 4 of reference [1]); see also the revised version, Chapter 1 of the present book).

3. C. J. Date and Hugh Darwen: "A New Relational Algebra" (Appendix A of reference [1]).

4. Maurice Gittens: "The Third Manifesto Revisited," *www.gittens.nl/TheTTMRevisited.pdf* (March 25th, 2007).

5. Patrick Hall, Peter Hitchcock, and Stephen Todd: "An Algebra of Relations for Machine Computation," Conf. Record of the 2nd ACM Symposium on Principles of Programming Languages, Palo Alto, Calif. (January 1975).

Chapter 6

Setting the Record Straight (Part 3 of 6): "Semantic Compositionality"

Gittens asserts in his paper [3] that *The Third Manifesto* displays "no adherence to the principle of semantic compositionality." The pertinent section of that paper is quite brief, and we cite it here in its entirety:

> It is a general principle of language design that the substitution of variables for their corresponding values should not change the meaning of expressions containing them. In the third edition of *The Third Manifesto* Date and Darwen are in violation of this principle. Consider that the type of a relvar is determined by the header of the relvar. The candidate keys associated with a relvar are *not* part of their type according to *The Third Manifesto*. This choice by Date and Darwen, represents a serious logical error because it causes variables and values of the *same* type to not be interchangeable. This is evident when one considers that a relation value *C* of type *T* may not be assignable to a relational variable *V* of type *T*. More specifically, the assignment of *C* to *V* is not allowed when there are candidate key constraints defined on *V* to which *C* is not in adherence. Put another way, even though *V* and *C* share the same type, the assignment *V* = *C* may or may not be allowed depending on whether or not *C* is in adherence with all candidate key constraints defined for *V*.
>
> Similarly, nested relation *values* and non nested relation *values,* cannot play the role of *parent* in foreign key relations using facilities provided by *The Third Manifesto.* This is obviously true because according to *The Third Manifesto,* relation *values* have no associated candidate keys and foreign keys are defined in terms of candidate keys of the parent relation *variable*. Thus, [in] *The Third Manifesto,* relvars cannot be in general replaced by their values and are consequentially not *referentially transparent*. Finally, it can also be noted that Date and Darwen are in violation of the principle of *conceptual integrity* and of their own RM Prescription number 21. This is obvious because the assignment of a value *v* to a variable *V* denoted *V* := *v,* where both *V* and *v* share the same type *T,* does not *in general* imply that the equality expression *V* = *v* yields true. Again the reason for this inconsistency is because the type of relation variables does not include their associated candidate keys.

To be frank, we find this text quite hard to follow (though we strongly dispute the allegations in the parts we do understand). Because of this state of affairs, the best we can do in response is to offer a kind of blow by blow deconstruction of Gittens's text—which we now proceed to do, starting with the section title. We've numbered the points for purposes of subsequent reference.

DETAILED RESPONSES

1. No adherence to the principle of semantic compositionality.

Wikipedia [4] defines *The Principle of Compositionality*—not *semantic* compositionality as such, but it's clear from other sources that this principle is indeed the one to which Gittens refers—as "the principle that the meaning of a complex expression is determined by the meanings of its constituent expressions and the rules used to combine them." And it goes on to say:

> This principle is sometimes called **Frege's Principle,** because Frege is widely credited for the first modern formulation of it. However, the idea appears already among Indian philosophers of grammar such as Yaska, and also in Plato's work such as in *Theaetetus* ... [It] also exists in a similar form in the compositionality of programming languages.

Well, a database language that failed to conform to this principle would certainly fail to conform to *The Third Manifesto,* thanks to RM Prescription 26 at least (which requires a conforming language to be constructed according to well established principles of good language design). Nothing in *The Third Manifesto* is in conflict with the principle. That said, however, we have to say too that the connection between (a) Gittens's claim in the title of the pertinent section of his paper (i.e., that we fail to adhere to the principle), on the one hand, and (b) his claims in the body of that section, on the other, is far from clear to us. We therefore simply have to assume that an acceptable refutation of the claims in the body of that section is equally acceptable as a refutation of the claim in the title as well.

2. ***It is a general principle of language design that the substitution of variables for their corresponding values should not change the meaning of expressions containing them.***

First of all, we assume that by "expressions containing them" here, Gittens means expressions containing variables, not expressions containing values—but perhaps the point is irrelevant, because expressions as such don't contain either! Rather, an expression can contain (among other things):

- Variable references, which denote variables and hence—in the context under discussion, at least—denote, indirectly, the values of the variables in question
- Literals, which directly denote values as such

By way of example, consider this expression:

```
x - y
```

This expression contains two variable references, *x* and *y,* and it denotes the subtraction of the current value of *y* from the current value of *x*—where the term *current* refers to the time at which the expression is evaluated. From the text of the expression alone we can't say any more about it than that, because the values assigned to *x* and *y* vary over time, more or less by definition (i.e., to say something is a variable is to say, more or less by definition, that it has different values assigned to it at different times).

Now suppose the values assigned to *x* and *y* at some particular time are 5 and 2, respectively. Substituting the literals 5 and 2 for the variable references *x* and *y,* respectively, yields the expression 5–2, which denotes the subtraction of 2 from 5 (and hence denotes the value 3, under the accepted meaning of the term "subtraction"). *At that time,* then, the meaning of *x–y* is the same as that of 5–2. And all of this is in full accordance with our normal understanding of the semantics of expressions in programming languages, of course.

However, in the text quoted above, Gittens isn't talking about what happens when we substitute values for variables; rather, he's talking about what happens if we go the other way, as it were, and substitute variables for values. Well, if we start with the expression 5–2 and then substitute *x* for 5 and *y* for 2, we're certainly changing the meaning! As we've already said, the expression *x–y* denotes the subtraction of the current value of *y* from the current value of *x*—which is the same as the subtraction of 2 from 5 only in the very special case in which 5 and 2 happen to be the current values of *x* and *y,* respectively.

So we freely admit we don't really understand what Gittens is getting at in this particular criticism. However, it seems to have little bearing on his subsequent text, so perhaps the point isn't very important.

3. ***In the third edition of* The Third Manifesto *Date and Darwen are in violation of this principle.***

To repeat, we don't understand what principle it is that we're accused of violating here. However, we can assert most definitely that under *The Third Manifesto,* the expression *x–y* does denote the subtraction of the current value of *y* from the current value of *x* and 5–2 does denote the subtraction of 2 from 5. A similar observation applies to all expressions containing references to variables, including relation variables (relvars) in particular. For example, if *R1* and *R2* are relvars of the same type—say type RELATION {X INTEGER}—then the expression *R1* UNION *R2* denotes the union of the relations that are the current values of *R1* and *R2*. If those current values are RELATION {TUPLE {X 1}} and RELATION {TUPLE {X 2}}, respectively—more precisely, if those current values are *denoted by the literals* RELATION {TUPLE {X 1}} and RELATION {TUPLE {X 2}}, respectively—the expression *R1* UNION *R2* effectively becomes:

```
RELATION { TUPLE { X 1 } } UNION RELATION { TUPLE { X 2 } }
```

And this expression denotes the union of those current values of those variables *R1* and *R2*.

4. ***Consider that the type of a relvar is determined by the header of the relvar.***

Correct, except that the term is *heading,* not header. Also, for clarity (as well as other reasons, beyond the scope of the present chapter), we normally use the term *declared type* instead of just *type,* unqualified, for the type of a variable. Specifically, if the heading of the relvar is {*H*}, where *H* is a commalist of attribute-name/type-name pairs, then the declared type of that variable is RELATION {*H*}, meaning that only values of type RELATION {*H*} can be assigned to that variable. We call the variable a relation variable, or relvar, precisely because its declared type is a relation type, meaning its permitted values are relation values of that type.

5. ***The candidate keys associated with a relvar are not part of their type according to The Third Manifesto.***

By definition, a key *K* for relvar *R* is some subset of the heading of *R* (note that we usually abbreviate the term *candidate key* to just *key*); more precisely, it's a subset that satisfies the properties of *uniqueness* and *irreducibility*. In a certain sense, then, we might say *K* is "part of" the declared type of *R,* because it's part of the heading and the heading is part of the declared type. Almost certainly, however, Gittens is referring here not to keys per se, but rather to the constraints implied by the definitions of such keys: that is to say, to the corresponding key *constraints*. Now, the set of relations constituting the declared type of *R* will be a superset, probably a proper superset,[1] of the set of relations of that type that satisfy that relvar's key constraints. In other words, there'll almost certainly be relations of the declared type of *R* that fail to satisfy the key constraints for *R* (and/or any other constraints that apply to *R,* come to that)—and any attempt to assign such a relation to *R* will fail at run time on a violation of the pertinent constraint. (By contrast, any attempt to assign a relation to *R* that isn't of the declared type of *R* will fail at compile time.)

6. ***This choice by Date and Darwen, represents a serious logical error because it causes variables and values of the same type to not be interchangeable.***

We don't understand what Gittens means by interchanging a value and a variable. Under point 2—which we also didn't understand!—he talked about *substituting* a variable for its value: in other words, *replacing* one by the other (actually, we suspect he might have meant replacing a variable by its value and not the other way around, but it's not what he said). But when two things are interchanged, each takes the other's place; i.e., each replaces the other (?).

7. ***This is evident when one considers that a relation value C of type T may not be assignable to a relational variable V of type T.***

"This" here presumably refers to Gittens's previous point, although assignment isn't interchange. Nor is it substitution, though it might perhaps be said to "substitute" some "new" value of the variable in question for the "old" value (better: *replace* the "old" value by some "new" value). Note, however, that—to use Gittens's example—the assignment of relation *C* to relvar *V* is certainly legal from a syntactic point of view, precisely because *C* and *V* are of the same type *T*. As previously explained, however, it will fail at run time if it would

---

[1] It will fail to be a proper superset only in the special case where the entire heading is the only key.

cause any constraint to be violated otherwise.

Now, we do understand why some people might (wrongly) think of key constraints as being part of the pertinent type definition. However, integrity constraints in general can't possibly be so perceived. One obvious reason is that some constraints refer to more than one relvar (for example, foreign key constraints usually do), and the notion of some *type* being defined in terms of some *variable* clearly makes no sense. In fact, it's well known (not to say obvious) that—precisely because constraints do refer to variables—certain relational assignments will succeed at some times and fail at others, depending on the values of the variables in question at the time in question.

Perhaps we should say a little more about types and database constraints. The purpose of a type is to determine the operators that are available for operating on values and variables of that type. The purpose of a database constraint is to preserve the logical integrity, in the face of updates, of the collection of interrelated variables that constitute a database. There's a logical difference between the two!—and any attempt to muddle them should be resisted, firmly.

8. ***More specifically, the assignment of C to V is not allowed when there are candidate key constraints defined on V to which C is not in adherence.***

We repeat: Such an assignment is syntactically legal but fails at run time. Also, as we've already said, other constraints might also cause it to fail at run time. It isn't a logical error (see point 6) to enforce a constraint. It *is* a logical error not to.

9. ***Put another way, even though V and C share the same type, the assignment V = C may or may not be allowed depending on whether or not C is in adherence with all candidate key constraints defined for V.***

Correct, except that (a) the syntax is *V* := *C* (the expression *V* = *C* denotes an equality comparison, not an assignment) and (b) as we've said before, the assignment can fail on violation of *any* constraint, not just key constraints specifically.

10. ***Similarly, nested relation*** **values** ***and non nested relation*** **values*****, cannot play the role of parent in foreign key relations using facilities provided by The Third Manifesto.***

The Third Manifesto does not "provide facilities." Rather, it provides a set of prescriptions that (we propose) a relational database language should conform to. Moreover, we don't understand the repeated use of the emphasized term *values* here. A foreign key involves two relation *variables,* usually distinct. The two are normally called the referencing relvar (to which the foreign key belongs) and the referenced relvar (to which the referenced key belongs). *Note:* As Gittens suggests, the referenced relvar is sometimes called the parent, but we don't use that term (and in fact regard it as deprecated, for more reasons than we have room to go into here).

Now, *The Third Manifesto* certainly requires a conforming language to support the expression of every constraint that can be stated in terms of a **Tutorial D** expression of the form IS_EMPTY(*rx*), where *rx* is a relational expression of arbitrary complexity. In particular, suppose the definition for relvar *R2* includes the following (hypothetical) **Tutorial D** specification:[2]

```
FOREIGN KEY { A } REFERENCES R1
```

(Of course, *R1* here is another relvar, and {*A*} is a set of attributes that are common to *R1* and *R2*.) This specification is defined to be shorthand for the following expression:

```
IS_EMPTY ( R2 { A } NOT MATCHING R1 { A } )
```

[2] Hypothetical, because **Tutorial D** doesn't currently support such specifications; nor does *The Third Manifesto* require such support. Proposals to add such support to **Tutorial D** are under active consideration, however [1].

As the foregoing equivalence shows, *The Third Manifesto* does indeed require the constraint to be expressible. (What's more, it does so even in the case where the declared type of one or more of the attributes in the set of attributes {*A*} is some relation type. We make this point in case it's relevant to Gittens's criticisms regarding "nested" and "non nested" relations, which we don't understand at all.)

To sum up, point 10 seems to be saying that certain constraints would not be expressible in a conforming language. If so, then point 10 is quite simply, and badly, wrong.

11. ***This is obviously true because according to The Third Manifesto, relation values have no associated candidate keys and foreign keys are defined in terms of candidate keys of the parent relation* variable.**

We don't understand what Gittens is driving at. Nor, because of our failure to understand point 10, do we know exactly what it is that he claims to be "obviously true."

As an aside, we remark that a relation that satisfies a key constraint might be said, loosely, to "have" the key that implies that constraint—but the term "key" is much better reserved for relvars. In any case, the term *superkey* would be more appropriate.[3] For example, consider the fact that a relation containing no more than one tuple satisfies every key constraint that could possibly be defined for a relvar of its type; in particular, it "has" the empty set as a key, implying that all other keys it might be said to "have" are really proper superkeys. Note too that relvars to which it might be assigned would typically have nonempty keys.

12. ***Thus, [in] The Third Manifesto, relvars cannot be in general replaced by their values and are consequentially not* referentially transparent.**

We had to look up *referentially transparent*. From Wikipedia [4]: "An expression is said to be referentially transparent if it can be replaced with its value without changing the program (in other words, yielding a program that has the same effects and output on the same input)." This definition is a bit loose—a value isn't a piece of program text!—but we get the gist. In fact, "referential transparency" doesn't seem to be anything more than a rather grand term for the notion that a variable reference in an expression denotes the current value of the variable in question (and if so, then it's something we've always just taken for granted). In particular, and contrary to Gittens's complaints, it certainly doesn't seem to require every value of type *T* to be legally assignable at all times to an arbitrary variable of declared type *T*.

13. ***Finally, it can also be noted that Date and Darwen are in violation of the principle of* conceptual integrity *and of their own RM Prescription number 21.***

Conceptual integrity is being true to one's chosen concepts. We believe we've achieved that, and we're relieved to have been able to refute Gittens's attempted demonstrations to the contrary. As for RM Prescription 21, see the point immediately following.

14. ***This is obvious because the assignment of a value v to a variable V denoted V := v, where both V and v share the same type T, does not in general imply that the equality expression V = v yields true.***

Here Gittens is invoking RM Prescription 21 directly, which reads as follows (in part):

> After assignment of *v* to *V*, the equality comparison *V* = *v* shall evaluate to TRUE.

Gittens has failed to demonstrate in his critique that there's anything in *The Third Manifesto* that violates this prescription.

At this point we would like to offer a piece of advice to anyone wishing to criticize, question, or just discuss aspects of computer language design or some particular computer language: Wherever appropriate,

---

[3] A superkey for relvar *R* is a subset of the heading of *R* that possesses the uniqueness property but not necessarily the irreducibility property.

illustrate your points by *examples,* preferably using concrete syntax. After all, in the case of *The Third Manifesto* in particular, we provided **Tutorial D** for that very purpose! With respect to the topic at hand ("semantic compositionality"), we believe we've refuted Gittens's criticisms, but we've also admitted to not fully understanding all of the points he wanted to make. For all we know he does have a valid issue for us to consider after all—in which case we warmly invite him to resubmit, but with examples to demonstrate the inconsistencies he perceives.

15. Again the reason for this inconsistency is because the type of relation variables does not include their associated candidate keys.

And if it did, exactly which assignments $V := v$ would then result in $V = v$ evaluating to TRUE that don't have the same effect under *The Third Manifesto?*

REFERENCES AND BIBLIOGRAPHY

1. C. J. Date: "Inclusion Dependencies and Foreign Keys" (Chapter 13 of the present book).
2. C. J. Date and Hugh Darwen: *Databases, Types, and the Relational Model: The Third Manifesto* (3rd edition). Boston, Mass.: Addison-Wesley (2006).
3. Maurice Gittens: "The Third Manifesto Revisited," *www.gittens.nl/TheTTMRevisited.pdf* (March 25th, 2007).
4. Various authors: Wikipedia, http://en.wikipedia.org.

Chapter 7

Setting the Record Straight (Part 4 of 6): Integrity and Assignment

In his paper [2], Gittens gives an example in which a relvar AUTHOR with key {SURNAME} and current value as follows—

SURNAME	FIRST_NAME
Date	Chris
Darwen	Hugh

—is updated so that its value becomes:

SURNAME	FIRST_NAME
Darwen	Chris
Date	Hugh

The update is carried out by means of the following "double UPDATE" statement:

```
UPDATE AUTHOR WHERE SURNAME = 'Date'   : { SURNAME := 'Darwen' } ,
UPDATE AUTHOR WHERE SURNAME = 'Darwen' : { SURNAME := 'Date'   } ;
```

This statement is a multiple assignment and the two single assignments (i.e., the individual UPDATEs) it immediately contains are relational assignments.[30] We mention these facts because:

- The title of the pertinent section of Gittens's paper is "No semantic integrity in the presence of relational assignment," implying that it's, specifically, *relational* assignment that he wants to criticize.
- By contrast, text in that same section—"since integrity checking is postponed [until the entire multiple assignment has been performed]"—implies that it's *multiple* assignment that he's criticizing instead.

Whichever it is, Gittens then goes on to say:

> Given the relation values of the AUTHOR relvar before and after this single assignment [*sic*] and the knowledge that only one assignment has taken place [*sic*], consider a forensic application which needs to find out what was changed

[30] As is well known, the familiar INSERT, DELETE, and UPDATE operators are all just shorthand for, and therefore logically equivalent to, certain relational assignments.

by this assignment statement. Not appreciating this fundamental breach of integrity facilitated by *The Third Manifesto* will likely lead to seriously erroneous conclusions like:

The first name of the AUTHOR with surname "Date" was changed to "Hugh"

and

The first name of the AUTHOR with surname "Darwen" was changed to "Chris."

Well, there seems to be some confusion here. In what follows, we take Gittens's points one at a time.

WHAT WAS CHANGED?

Gittens says: "Consider a forensic application which needs to find out what was changed by [the double UPDATE shown in the previous section]." Well, the change, as such, is perfectly clear—the original value of the relvar was changed to (better: *replaced by*) a different value, and both the original value and the replacement value are completely explicit.

WHAT BREACH OF INTEGRITY?

Gittens refers to a "fundamental breach of integrity." There is no breach of integrity. After the update, the relvar still satisfies the only integrity constraint mentioned (namely, the key constraint to the effect that surnames are unique); indeed, if it didn't, the update would be rejected.

We note in passing, incidentally, that one reason multiple assignment is useful is in connection with examples very similar to the one under discussion. Consider the problem of interchanging the values of two variables X and Y. The "obvious" way to achieve this result without multiple assignment involves a temporary variable Z, thus:

```
Z := X ;   X := Y ;   Y := Z ;
```

With multiple assignment, however, the desired effect can be achieved more simply (and more intuitively) thus:

```
X := Y , Y := X ;
```

WHAT ERRONEOUS CONCLUSIONS?

Gittens refers to certain "conclusions" that he claims are "seriously erroneous." In what sense exactly are the conclusions in question "seriously erroneous"? Some clarification is required. In fact, we suspect there might be some muddle over realms here. To elaborate:

- Elsewhere in the same section of his paper, Gittens refers to the double UPDATE as "swapping the key values for the two tuples" (rewording slightly). But tuples are *values* and thus can't be changed, by definition. (Note that the phrase "swapping the key values" certainly implies that the tuples in question are being changed.)

- We might, however, guess that what Gittens is getting at is something along the following lines:

  1. Each tuple in the AUTHOR relvar represents an author in the real world. More specifically, the SURNAME value in such a tuple identifies the author in question in the obvious way (since Gittens says the relvar has "key SURNAME," and we must therefore understand SURNAME values to be unique).

  2. Let tuple *t* in the AUTHOR relvar represent author *x* (i.e., the real world author with surname *x*).

3. Updating the AUTHOR relvar such that (a) its value after the update differs from its previous value only in that tuple *t* is replaced by tuple *t1,* and (b) tuple *t1* differs from tuple *t* only in that it has a different FIRST_NAME component, can be regarded as reflecting a change to the first name of author *x*.

4. Under such an interpretation, however, we probably wouldn't want to permit keys to be updated (apologies for the sloppy phrasing, but we hope our meaning is clear). For suppose we were to update the AUTHOR relvar such that (a) its value after the update differs from its previous value only in that tuple *t* is replaced by tuple *t2,* and (b) tuple *t2* differs from tuple *t* only in that it has a different SURNAME component (*y,* say, instead of *x*). Then we could hardly regard that update as reflecting a change to the surname of author *x*—because authors are *identified* by surname, and after the update the phrase "author *x*" apparently doesn't denote any real world author at all. Certainly it doesn't denote any real world author now represented in the AUTHOR relvar.

5. So we might want to introduce a convention according to which certain attributes—certain key attributes in particular—are explicitly defined to be nonupdatable (apologies for the sloppy phrasing once again). Suppose SURNAME is such an attribute in the case at hand. Then it would appear that an UPDATE statement such as

   ```
   UPDATE AUTHOR WHERE SURNAME = x : { SURNAME := y } ;
   ```

   would be illegal. (Note that if our interpretation of Gittens's criticism is correct, there doesn't seem to be any need to drag multiple assignment into the picture at all. For simplicity, therefore, we limit ourselves to single assignments only in the remainder of this discussion.)

6. Gittens might then complain that relational assignment (which is the sole relational update operator actually prescribed by the *Manifesto*) just isn't fine grained enough for rules like "Attribute *A* is nonupdatable" to make sense, because it simply replaces the entire value of a target relvar by another such value lock, stock, and barrel. Certainly it would be hard to state precisely which assignments would be illegal under such a rule.

7. Accordingly, Gittens might further complain that an explicit UPDATE statement must be supported (instead of being just an optional shorthand form of assignment as it is in the *Manifesto*), in order for rules like "Attribute *A* is nonupdatable" to make sense.

8. But even if we accept the argument of the previous paragraph, defining an attribute to be nonupdatable actually achieves nothing! Let the tuple with SURNAME value *x* have FIRST_NAME value *z*. Then the effect of the UPDATE

   ```
   UPDATE AUTHOR WHERE SURNAME = x : { SURNAME := y } ;
   ```

   (which will presumably fail under the proposed nonupdatability rule) can clearly be obtained by the following entirely legal DELETE / INSERT sequence:

   ```
   DELETE AUTHOR WHERE SURNAME = x ;

   INSERT AUTHOR
          RELATION { TUPLE { SURNAME y , FIRST_NAME z } } ;
   ```

   (Or by a logically equivalent pair of explicit relational assignments, of course.)

A POSSIBLE DISCIPLINE

Gittens continues: "The problem is that assignment lacks facilities for keeping track of specific tuples, because Date and Darwen have chosen to reject the concept of tuple identity" (somewhat reworded once again). On its face this sentence does not make sense; more precisely, the phrase "keeping track of specific tuples" does not make sense. To paraphrase Gertrude Stein, a tuple is a tuple is a tuple; it's a value; and, like all values, it simply *is*—it has no location in time and space, and the question of "keeping track of it" simply doesn't arise. What Gittens really wants, we believe, is a means of keeping track of the history of values of tuple *variables*. But we agree with Codd in not permitting any kind of variable in the database except *relation* variables, and we therefore reject such a requirement.

All of that being said, there's absolutely nothing in the *Manifesto* to prevent the adoption of a convention, or discipline, that does achieve something like what Gittens seems to want. In terms of his example:

1. We could adopt the convention that all tuples that have ever appeared, appear right now, or ever will appear within the AUTHOR relvar having the same specific SURNAME value *x* all refer to "the same" real world author (or, more accurately, the convention that *we interpret* all such tuples as referring to the same real world author).

2. We could keep a log showing when such tuples appear in and disappear from the relvar.

3. That log could additionally indicate the values of the other attributes of those tuples. (Of course, there's just one such "other attribute," FIRST_NAME, in the example.)

4. That log could also show who and what caused those appearances and disappearances.

5. Alternatively, we could add a surrogate key to the AUTHOR relvar and reinterpret Steps 1-4 above in terms of values of that key instead of SURNAME values. (Although the *Manifesto* doesn't actually require support for surrogate keys, it does strongly suggest that they be supported—see reference [1], RM Very Strong Suggestion 1.) Then a given real world author could remain "the same author" even if his or her surname changes: a realistically desirable state of affairs, in fact, since people do change their surname from time to time.

What's more, not only do we believe a convention like the foregoing could easily be adopted, we also believe it would often be a good idea to do so. What we don't believe, however, is that the *Manifesto* can or should legislate on such matters; by definition, such matters are beyond its purview.

REFERENCES AND BIBLIOGRAPHY

1. C. J. Date and Hugh Darwen: *Databases, Types, and the Relational Model: The Third Manifesto* (3rd edition). Boston, Mass.: Addison-Wesley (2006).

2. Maurice Gittens: "The Third Manifesto Revisited," *www.gittens.nl/TheTTMRevisited.pdf* (March 25th, 2007).

Chapter 8

Setting the Record Straight

(Part 5 of 6):

Relation Valued Attributes

Gittens is very critical of the fact that the *Manifesto* permits (in fact, requires) support for relation valued attributes. His comments on this topic in reference [13] begin as follows:

> Contrary to Codd, Date and Darwen allow relation valued attributes. Please consider the following questions.
>
> - What problem is solved by support for these attributes that could not be solved otherwise?
> - What propositions can be represented by relvars including relation valued attributes? Can these propositions not be represented by other relational means?
> - What positive traits of alternative solutions are not available to solutions based on relation valued attributes?

The first few sections of this chapter address themselves to these opening remarks. *Note:* Arguments in support of our position on this topic were first articulated in reference [3]. This chapter can be seen, in part, as an elaboration on those original arguments.

A SIMPLE EXAMPLE

Of course, Gittens is quite right when he says we allow relation valued attributes (hereinafter abbreviated RVAs). Fig. 1 overleaf shows an example of a relation with such an attribute, which we'll refer to (the relation, that is, not the attribute) formally as *spq* but informally as "shipments." Relation *spq* has two attributes, S# and PQ; S# values are supplier numbers and PQ values are relations, and so attribute PQ is an RVA. Those PQ values (i.e., relations) in turn also have two attributes, P# and QTY, where P# values are part numbers and QTY values are quantities. The intended interpretation, or meaning, of relation *spq*—i.e., the *relation predicate* for that relation—is:

> *The specified supplier supplies the specified parts in the specified quantities.*

For example, the tuple in Fig. 1 for supplier S4 represents the proposition: *Supplier S4 supplies part P2 in quantity 200, part P4 in quantity 300, and part P5 in quantity 400.*

Please note, however, that our formulations of the foregoing predicate and sample proposition are deliberately both quite loose. In the case of the predicate, a more precise formulation is:

> *For a given supplier, represented by supplier number (S#), the set of parts supplied by that supplier, together with the corresponding quantities, is represented by the corresponding PQ value; each such part is represented by part number (P#), and the corresponding quantity is represented by the corresponding QTY value.*

Our reason for giving this somewhat more precise formulation—"somewhat," because as a matter of fact it could still do with some tightening up—will become apparent in the section immediately following.

<table>
<tr><th>S#</th><th>PQ</th></tr>
<tr><td>S3</td><td><table><tr><th>P#</th><th>QTY</th></tr><tr><td>P2</td><td>200</td></tr></table></td></tr>
<tr><td>S4</td><td><table><tr><th>P#</th><th>QTY</th></tr><tr><td>P2
P4
P5</td><td>200
300
400</td></tr></table></td></tr>
<tr><td>S5</td><td><table><tr><th>P#</th><th>QTY</th></tr><tr><td></td><td></td></tr></table></td></tr>
</table>

Fig. 1: Relation *spq* ("shipments" with an RVA)

REPRESENTING PROPOSITIONS (I)

Now we turn to Gittens's questions. We choose to address them in reverse order. The last one is:

- What positive traits of alternative solutions are not available to solutions based on relation valued attributes?

We address this question first in order to dismiss it. The fact is, the question can't be answered in any absolute sense—sometimes solutions based on RVAs are better, sometimes alternative ones are. The remainder of this chapter can be seen as an extensive elaboration on this position!

Gittens's second question (or pair of questions, rather) is:

- What propositions can be represented by relations including relation valued attributes? Can these propositions not be represented by other relational means?

Note: Actually, Gittens frames these questions in terms of relvars, not relations, but relvars are a red herring here; his question can be discussed in terms of relations without having to drag relvars in at all. We'll come back to relvars, as such, later.

Consider the tuple shown in Fig. 1 for supplier S5. Appealing to the more precise form of the predicate, it's clear that that tuple represents the proposition:

For supplier S5, the set of part-number/quantity pairs for parts supplied by that supplier is empty.

Or more idiomatically: *Supplier S5 supplies no parts at all.*

> *Aside:* Actually this latter "more idiomatic" formulation is a trifle sloppy. Abstracting a little, if we know only that no *y-z* pairs exist for a given *x,* we can't logically infer that no *y*'s exist for that *x;* we can only infer that either no *y*'s exist or no *z*'s exist (or both) for that *x*. Taking *x*'s, *y*'s, and *z*'s to be supplier numbers, part numbers, and quantities, respectively, however, we can appeal to a certain real world fact—namely, the fact that if a supplier supplies a part, it must do so in some quantity—to infer that if there are

no part-number/quantity pairs for a given supplier number, then there aren't any parts for that supplier. *End of aside.*

Now suppose we were to choose (as in practice we normally would) to represent shipments, not by a relation like *spq* with an RVA, but rather by a relation—let's call it *sp*—like the one shown in Fig. 2, with no RVA. The predicate is: *Supplier S# supplies part P# in quantity QTY.* Then we observe that such a relation cannot explicitly represent a proposition like that just given for supplier S5 ("Supplier S5 supplies no parts at all"). Why not? Because, for such a supplier (*s#,* say), there is no part *p#* and no quantity *q* for which the predicate *Supplier s# supplies part p# in quantity q* evaluates to TRUE, and hence no tuple that can logically appear in the relation.

S#	P#	QTY
S3	P2	200
S4	P2	200
S4	P4	300
S4	P5	400

Fig. 2: Relation *sp* ("shipments" without an RVA)

So now we've provided a partial answer to Gittens's question; to be precise, we've shown a proposition that can be explicitly represented by a relation with an RVA and can't be explicitly represented by a relation without an RVA. However, note the repeated use of the qualifier *explicitly* in the foregoing sentence. The point is, it can be argued that relation *sp* (the one without an RVA) does at least represent the proposition in question implicitly. To be specific, relations are conventionally interpreted in accordance with what's called *The Closed World Assumption;* and *The Closed World Assumption* says, among other things, that if some tuple *t* could appear in relation *r* but doesn't, then the proposition represented by that tuple *t* is false. (For more details regarding *The Closed World Assumption,* see reference [6].) In the case at hand, therefore, we might argue as follows:

- Relation *sp* contains no tuple for supplier S5.
- Therefore, the predicate *Supplier S5 supplies part P# in quantity QTY* evaluates to FALSE for all possible part/quantity pairs.
- Therefore, there is no part/quantity pair for which the predicate *Supplier S5 supplies part P# in quantity QTY* evaluates to TRUE.
- Therefore, there is no part that supplier S5 supplies.
- Therefore, supplier S5 supplies no parts at all.
- Therefore, relation *sp* does indeed represent the pertinent proposition as claimed—it just doesn't do so explicitly.

REPRESENTING PROPOSITIONS (II)

The arguments of the previous section notwithstanding, the question remains: Can the proposition *Supplier S5 supplies no parts at all* be represented *explicitly* without using an RVA? And of course the answer is yes. All we need to do is have, in addition to relation *sp* (which shows which suppliers supply which parts), another relation *snp* showing which suppliers supply no parts at all. See Fig. 3.

S#	P#	QTY
S3	P2	200
S4	P2	200
S4	P4	300
S4	P5	400

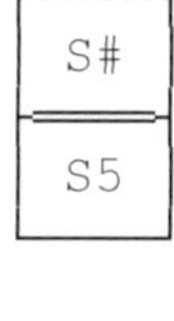

S#
S5

Fig. 3: Relations *sp* and *snp*

Figs. 1 and 3 are logically equivalent, of course, in the sense that the relations in Fig. 3 can be derived from the relation in Fig. 1 (and vice versa) by means of appropriate expressions of the relational algebra. However, situations do exist where no such equivalence applies; that is, relations with RVAs do exist that have no exact equivalent in terms of relations without RVAs. An example, relation *sibs* (taken from reference [5]), is shown in Fig. 4. The intended meaning of that relation is that the persons represented within any given PERSONS value are all siblings of one another (and have no other siblings). Thus, Amy and Bob are siblings; Cal, Don, and Eve are siblings; and Fay is an only child. The sole attribute of relation *sibs* (viz., PERSONS) is an RVA.

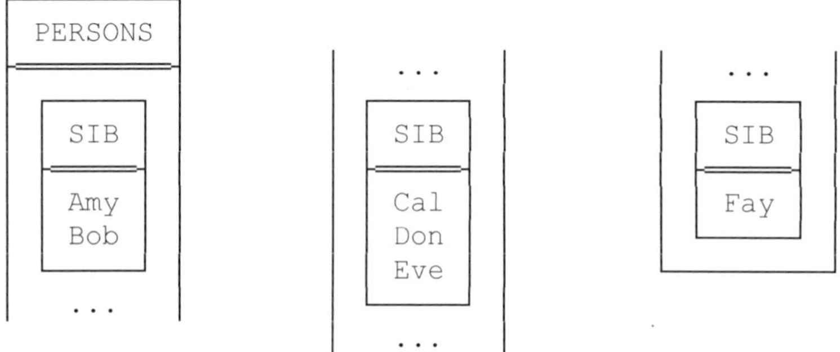

Fig. 4: Relation *sibs*

To repeat, there's no relation without an RVA that's logically equivalent to (i.e., carries exactly the same information as) relation *sibs*. In particular, if we ungroup relation *sibs* on attribute PERSONS, thus—

```
sibs UNGROUP ( PERSONS )
```

—we obtain the relation shown in Fig. 5 opposite, a relation that clearly fails to show who is a sibling of whom. In other words, the ungrouping has "lost information," in a certain (rather fuzzy!) sense.

Of course, it's possible to come up with a relation not involving RVAs that does represent the same information, more or less, as relation *sibs* does. Fig. 6 opposite shows such a relation. But note that "more or less"! The fact is, the relations in Figs. 4 and 6 really represent different things; to be specific, the relation in Fig. 6 really means the specified person *belongs to the specified family,* a concept that isn't represented in the relation of Fig. 4 at all. More precisely, there's no relational expression (in general) by which a relation like that in Fig. 6 can be derived from one like that in Fig. 4.

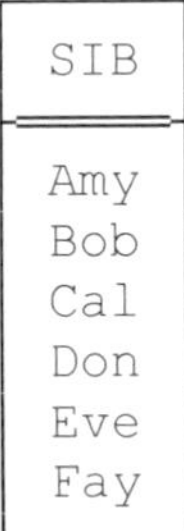

SIB
Amy
Bob
Cal
Don
Eve
Fay

Fig. 5: Ungrouping relation *sibs* on attribute PERSONS

FAMILY	SIB
Mozart	Amy
Mozart	Bob
Walton	Cal
Walton	Don
Walton	Eve
Dvorak	Fay

Fig. 6: A relation showing family memberships

So now we've answered another of Gittens's questions: "Can these propositions not be represented by other relational means?" The answer is: Yes, they can, but not always in a precisely equivalent fashion. (In any case, we observe that a given proposition can typically be represented in many different relational forms even without using RVAs—that's why different designers come up with different database designs for the same information—and so this particular question is perhaps not a very important one.)

DISPENSING WITH OUTER JOIN

Gittens's first question is:

- What problem is solved by support for [RVAs] that could not be solved otherwise?

Well, we believe we've now given at least one good answer to this question, inasmuch as we've given an example of a relation with an RVA that has no exact equivalent in terms of relations without RVAs. But there's quite a lot more that can usefully be said on the matter.

Suppose we were to agree that it's a good idea to try to avoid RVAs, at least in base relvars (a discipline we happen to subscribe to, incidentally, and one we'll have a little more to say about later). In accordance with this discipline, we might come up with a design for suppliers and shipments that looks as suggested by the sample values in Fig. 7 overleaf. Note that there's no explicit representation in that figure of the fact that supplier S5 supplies no parts; instead, we appeal—as indeed we normally do—to *The Closed World Assumption* to infer that fact, implicitly.

S

S#	CITY
S3	Paris
S4	London
S5	Athens

SP

S#	P#	QTY
S3	P2	200
S4	P2	200
S4	P4	300
S4	P5	400

Fig. 7: Suppliers and shipments (conventional design)—sample values

Now consider the query: "For each supplier, get supplier number, city, parts supplied, and corresponding quantities." The most immediately obvious formulation of this query involves a join: S JOIN SP. But this formulation doesn't do the job, of course, because, in terms of the sample values in Fig. 7, it misses supplier S5 (see Fig. 8).

S#	CITY	P#	QTY
S3	Paris	P2	200
S4	London	P2	200
S4	London	P4	300
S4	London	P5	400

Fig. 8: Join of relations from Fig. 7

Precisely for that reason, a user familiar with SQL would probably try to formulate the query in terms of *outer join,* perhaps as follows:

```
SELECT * FROM S NATURAL LEFT OUTER JOIN SP
```

This SQL expression yields the result shown in Fig. 9 (note the nulls in that result in particular).

S#	CITY	P#	QTY	
S3	Paris	P2	200	
S4	London	P2	200	
S4	London	P4	300	
S4	London	P5	400	
S5	Athens			⇐ *nulls*

Fig. 9: Outer join of relations from Fig. 7

Observe, however, that the object depicted in Fig. 9 *isn't a relation*—and we don't refer to it as such—precisely because of those nulls. (See reference [4] for detailed arguments in support of the position that a "relation" that "contains a null" isn't truly a relation at all.) Here by contrast is a formulation of the query that does yield a result that's a relation—to be specific, the relation shown in Fig. 10, with an RVA:[1]

```
WITH ( xyz := SP RENAME { S# AS SNO } ) :
EXTEND S : { PQ := ( xyz WHERE SNO = S# ) { P# , QTY } }
```

<table>
<tr><th>S#</th><th>CITY</th><th>PQ</th></tr>
<tr><td>S3</td><td>Paris</td><td><table><tr><th>P#</th><th>QTY</th></tr><tr><td>P2</td><td>200</td></tr></table></td></tr>
<tr><td>S4</td><td>London</td><td><table><tr><th>P#</th><th>QTY</th></tr><tr><td>P2
P4
P5</td><td>200
300
400</td></tr></table></td></tr>
<tr><td>S5</td><td>Athens</td><td><table><tr><th>P#</th><th>QTY</th></tr><tr><td></td><td></td></tr></table></td></tr>
</table>

Fig. 10: Relational analog of Fig. 9

Explanation: The first step (involving WITH) introduces a temporary name *xyz* in order to avoid a naming clash that would otherwise arise in the second step; the name *xyz* denotes a relation that's identical to SP, except that attribute S# is renamed SNO. The second step then extends each tuple of S with an additional attribute, called PQ, whose value in any given tuple *t* is a relation, derived from *xyz* (in effect, from SP) and containing part-number/quantity pairs for all shipments corresponding to the supplier number in that tuple *t*. We stress the point that the expression (*xyz* WHERE SNO = S#) {P#, QTY}, and hence the "introduced" attribute PQ, are both relation valued.

Observe now that, in the relation shown in Fig. 10, the empty set of part-number/quantity pairs corresponding to supplier S5 is represented by an empty set—not by some weird "null" construct as in Fig. 9. To represent an empty set by an empty set seems like such an obviously good idea! In fact, as the example suggests, *there would be no need for outer join at all* if RVAs were supported—a fact that can be seen as another strong argument in favor of RVAs.

DATABASE DESIGN ISSUES

On the basis of examples like the foregoing, we claim that RVAs are certainly useful for query purposes; in other words, derived relations, at least, should be allowed to have RVAs. But what about base relations? More precisely, when we design a database, and in particular when we decide what base relvars that database is to contain, should those base relvars be allowed to have RVAs?

---

[1] A much simpler formulation uses an *image relation*, thus: EXTEND S : {PQ := !!SP}. See reference [10].

The short answer to the question is *yes*—in accordance with *The Principle of Interchangeability* [11], if relations in general are allowed to have RVAs, then base relations (and hence base relvars) in particular must certainly be *allowed* to have RVAs as well. But note the italics here: Although RVAs must indeed be allowed in base relvars, we should immediately add that in our opinion such RVAs are usually contraindicated; that is, RVAs in base relvars are usually a bad idea. Detailed arguments in support of this position can be found in reference [5]. Note, however, that we're talking here about database *design* issues: Whether RVAs should be allowed in base relvars is a database design question, not a question of what's allowed according to the underlying theory (or model). Database design issues are important, of course, but they're beyond the scope of *The Third Manifesto* as such; the *Manifesto* is concerned with database *language* design issues (and hence DBMS design issues also), not database design issues.

Despite the foregoing, there's a little more we'd like to say regarding the specific database design issue under consideration. As we've already said, we think such database designs are usually not a good idea (and there's nothing in the *Manifesto* to suggest otherwise). But we must make it clear that this position is only a guideline—it's not an inviolable rule. In fact, we've found at least one fairly compelling example where a base relvar with an RVA seems to be exactly the right design. The example (taken from reference [5] once again) involves a catalog relvar KEYS that documents the relvars in the database and their keys. A sample value for that catalog relvar is shown in Fig. 11 below; we assume in that figure that (a) one of the relvars in the database is called MARRIAGE, and it has attributes SPOUSE1, SPOUSE2, and wedding DATE, and (b) relvar MARRIAGE has three distinct keys, each consisting of two of those three attributes.

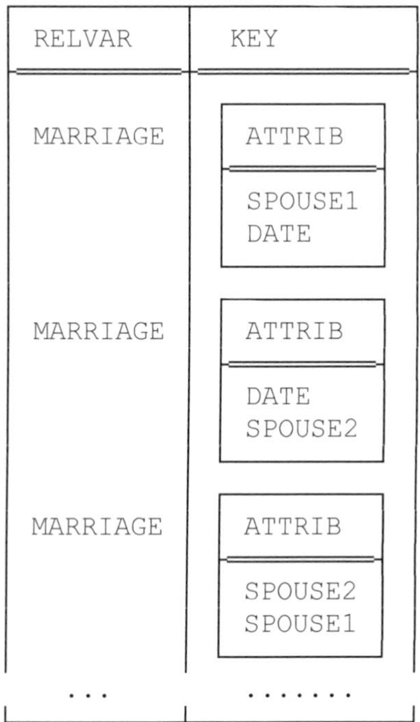

Fig. 11: The catalog relvar KEYS—sample (and partial) value

We close this section with one final observation. Suppose for the sake of argument that we decide to adopt a database design discipline according to which we prohibit RVAs in base relvars but permit them in derived ones. Then that position is analogous to one adopted by many designers today, according to which base relvars are required to satisfy the constraints of, say, Boyce/Codd normal form but the results of queries aren't, and often don't.

SUMMARIZATION QUERIES

We have one further answer to Gittens's question "What problem is solved by support for [RVAs] that could not be solved otherwise?" In a word, our answer is: Summarization. By way of example, consider the following query against the conventional design for suppliers and shipments as illustrated in Fig. 7:

```
SUMMARIZE SP PER ( S { S# } ) : { TQ := SUM ( QTY ) }
```

This expression represents the query: "For each supplier, get the supplier number and total shipment quantity." The result, given the sample values in Fig. 7, is shown in Fig. 12.

S#	TQ
S3	200
S4	900
S5	0

Fig. 12: Supplier numbers and total shipment quantities

It should be intuitively clear that the semantics of the foregoing SUMMARIZE expression can be defined as follows (in outline):

- From S and SP, derive an intermediate result *r* with attributes S# and PQ, where PQ is an RVA. (That result might look like relation *spq* as shown in Fig. 1.)
- From that intermediate result *r*, derive the desired final result by evaluating the expression SUM(SP, QTY) for each of the relations that happen to be values of the relation valued attribute PQ.

In other words, the SUMMARIZE operator is fundamentally defined in terms of RVAs.[2]

Note: Reference [12], by Nikos Lorentzos and the present authors, contains a detailed set of proposals for applying the relational model to the problem of temporal data. A crucial aspect of those proposals is the definition of two new relational operators called PACK and UNPACK. We mention this point here because, like SUMMARIZE, those operators too are fundamentally defined in terms of RVAs.

IS OUR POSITION "CONTRARY TO CODD"?

Gittens opens his criticism of our position of allowing RVAs by claiming that it's "contrary to Codd." Actually this claim is not correct; Codd changed his mind on the matter over the course of time. In his first paper [1], he did allow RVAs. In his second [2], he said the possibility of eliminating them "appears worth investigating," but he didn't actually insist on such elimination. In later writings, of course, he did prohibit RVAs; however, we believe his reasons for doing so were based on a misconception—namely, that the notion of "data value atomicity" has some kind of absolute meaning. We reject those reasons, and we do support RVAs. For further

---

[2] You might think SQL manages to do summarization without involving RVAs, but it doesn't—not really. However, to discuss SQL's approach to the problem would take us further afield than we wish to go here. A detailed discussion can be found in Chapter 7 of reference [9].

discussion of these matters, see reference [5].

A REMARK ON CONSTRAINTS

Following his list of questions as quoted near the beginning of the present chapter, Gittens continues:

> [The foregoing] questions are ... pertinent in the light of the fact that [values of] these relation valued attributes are [relations] and as such they lack associated candidate keys. In addition relation valued attributes cannot play any role in foreign key constraints given the facilities provided by *The Third Manifesto*. Which is to say that alternatives to relation valued attributes have more facilities to accurately constrain databases to adhere to requirements of business and other applications.

We respond to these comments as follows. First of all, of course it's true—by definition!—that RVA values are relations (i.e., relation *values*) and not relvars, and hence that, as Gittens says, they have no candidate keys (keys for short). To say that something—*R,* say—has a key is to say that (a) that *R* is a *variable* (again by definition) and (b) updates to *R* are constrained in a certain way (they will fail if they attempt to assign a value to *R* that fails to satisfy the associated key constraint). So a relation—meaning, to repeat, a relation value—has no key, by definition. However, it does at least make sense to say of some given relation that it either does or does not satisfy some key constraint; we might even go further and say, a trifle sloppily, that if the relation in question does satisfy the key constraint in question, then that relation actually "has" that key—though such a manner of speaking is likely to cause confusion, and we wouldn't recommend it.

Now, *The Third Manifesto* certainly requires support for any constraint that can be stated in terms of a **Tutorial D** expression of the form IS_EMPTY(*rx*), where *rx* is a relational expression of arbitrary complexity, and the constraints that Gittens is concerned about in the passage quoted above can certainly be so expressed, even if RVAs are involved; so his concerns in this connection are groundless. (It's true that **Tutorial D** provides no syntactic shorthands to simplify the task of expressing those particular constraints, but that's because we believe, as mentioned earlier, that base relvars with RVAs should be discouraged. But the *Manifesto* doesn't prohibit the provision of such shorthands, just so long as they're logically and psychologically well designed; as a matter of fact, a possible shorthand is suggested, albeit very tentatively, in Chapter 26 of the present book.)

ARE WE COMPLICATING THE RELATIONAL MODEL?

Gittens continues:

> So, the question remains, why should the relational model be complicated for dubious gain relative to Codd's alternative? Appendix B of *The Third Manifesto* represents an elaboration of sorts on this topic. This [appendix] digresses much but provides little that is of substance. I quote:
>
> > What then is the criterion for making something a type and not a relvar? In our opinion this question is still somewhat open.
>
> Put another way, Date and Darwen do not seem to know (!), in any definite sense, what the advantages of relation valued attributes are relative to alternative solutions. The disadvantages, however, are clear: The employment of relation valued attributes as introduced by *The Third Manifesto* provides less opportunity for the expression of candidate key and foreign key constraints in databases, relative to alternatives not involving relation valued attributes.
>
> Is it not up to Date and Darwen to provide proper arguments for adding relation valued attributes to the relational model? Until logically valid advantages of relation valued attributes can be illustrated, relative to alternatives, support for such attributes, as defined by *The Third Manifesto,* seem[s] not only a solution in search of a problem but also a needless and pointless complication. Consequently, given the current state of affairs on this issue, I maintain that support for relation valued attributes as defined by *The Third Manifesto* represents a violation of at least the parsimony requirement of RM Prescription 26.

We respond to these criticisms as follows. First of all, it could be argued that permitting RVAs not only fails to complicate the relational model, it actually simplifies it, by removing a restriction on the permitted types of attributes. (And in any case, we've already observed that Codd's rule to the effect that attribute types must be "atomic" doesn't stand up, in our opinion, because the notion of "data value atomicity" fails to stand up in turn.) As for "dubious gain," we believe we've demonstrated some of the advantages of permitting RVAs in preceding sections of the present chapter.

Second, Gittens's reference to "Appendix B of *The Third Manifesto*" is completely out of left field! That appendix has nothing to do with RVAs as such. Its title is "A Design Dilemma," and it has to do with questions of the following nature (this is a lightly edited quote from the opening to that appendix):

> Suppose we need to deal with employees, where every employee has an employee number (EMP#), a name (ENAME), a department number (DEPT#), and a salary (SALARY) ... Clearly, we could define an EMP *type* ("Design T") or an EMP *relvar* ("Design R"). The question we address in this appendix is: Which approach is better? In other words, are there any grounds for choosing one over the other?

So, although it might indeed be claimed that the appendix "provides little that is of substance" (we would dispute any such claim, of course), Gittens's conclusion that "Date and Darwen do not seem to know ... what the advantages of [RVAs] are" simply doesn't follow. We do know, and we've documented them in the present chapter. What's more, we've also shown that Gittens's claimed disadvantages are specious.

Gittens continues: "The employment of relation valued attributes as introduced by *The Third Manifesto* provides less opportunity for the expression of candidate key and foreign key constraints in databases, relative to alternatives not involving relation valued attributes." As we've already shown, this claim is also false.

Gittens continues: "Is it not up to Date and Darwen to provide proper arguments for adding [RVAs] to the relational model?" Well:

- First, we aren't adding them. The relational model originally included them; it's true they were subsequently removed, but only for what we consider to be invalid reasons.

- Second, we gave "proper arguments" in favor of RVAs years ago, in reference [3]. It's not our intent to repeat such arguments in the *Manifesto* as such; the *Manifesto* is a detailed proposal for database language and DBMS externals design, based on principles and positions that have been adequately articulated elsewhere, and it's meant to be judged on its own merits. If we had to justify every aspect of that proposal within the *Manifesto* itself, the document would be orders of magnitude bigger than it already is.

Finally, Gittens says: "I maintain that support for relation valued attributes as defined by *The Third Manifesto* represents a violation of at least the parsimony requirement of RM Prescription 26." No, it doesn't, for reasons adequately documented in the present chapter and elsewhere.

IMPLICATIONS FOR RELATIONAL ALGEBRA

Appendix A of reference [11] contains a formal definition of a relational algebra called **A** (described in reference [7], slightly tongue in cheek, as "the one true relational algebra"). Our aim in defining that algebra was to provide a rigorous foundation for the design of relational languages; reference [11] itself uses it as a basis for defining **Tutorial D,** and it's our hope that designers of other relational languages will use it for analogous purposes. But Gittens's criticisms of RVAs include some remarks on **A** that suggest some misunderstandings of that algebra and our intent with respect to it:

> [The] algebra **A** appears to have no operators which allow [values of] relation valued attributes to be singled out for manipulation. This entails that from the perspective of *The Third Manifesto*'s algebra **A,** [values of] relation valued attributes are not relation values at all. This is obviously true because [values of] these relation valued attributes cannot be manipulated by the set of relational operators specifically designed to accommodate the transformation of relation values. Consequently, from the perspective of the transformations facilitated by **A,** relation valued attributes seem a purpose unto themselves. So from the perspective of the algebra **A** questions like the following can be asked:

- In what way would the algebra **A** be logically different if the GROUP operator produced an XML value?
- More generally, in what way is support for relation valued attributes logically different from, for example, built in support for XML valued attributes?

The most serious claim here, and the one we want to deal with first, seems to be that relations that happen to be values of RVAs are somehow special, inasmuch as operators that apply to relations in general don't apply to such relations in particular. This claim is false. Consider the following example:

```
spq WHERE TUPLE { P# P#('P2') } ∈ PQ { P# }
```

This expression has the effect of restricting relation *spq* (see Fig. 1) to just those tuples in which the PQ value—a relation, of course—contains a tuple for part P2. The expression PQ{P#} denotes the projection of the PQ value over P#; in other words, it's an example of the application of a conventional relational operator—viz., projection—to a relation that happens to be the value of an RVA within (some tuple within) some relation. More generally, in fact, reference [11] explicitly states on page 155 that "the *Manifesto* requires support for relations with relation valued attributes, and *all* ... operators that apply to relations in general are available for values of the attributes in question" (emphasis added).

Of course, relations are values, and so "operators that apply to relations in general" are read-only operators by definition. In particular, the operators of **A** are all read-only, since **A** is an algebra and therefore has no notion (nor any need for a notion) of either variables or update operators, relational or otherwise. But there's nothing to prevent a relational language from providing convenient shorthand update operators for updating relvars with RVAs. **Tutorial D** in particular provides such shorthands. Here are a couple of examples (also taken from reference [11], page 155):

```
UPDATE SPQ WHERE S# = S#('S2') :
 { UPDATE PQ WHERE P# = P#('P3') : { QTY := QTY * 2 } } ;

UPDATE SPQ WHERE S# = S#('S2') :
 { INSERT PQ RELATION { TUPLE { P# P#('P5') , QTY QTY(500) } } } ;
```

(We assume in these examples that SPQ is a relvar of the same type as relation *spq* from Fig. 1.)

There are a few more things we want to say in connection with Gittens's criticisms of **A** and related matters. First, we don't really understand what it would mean for [values of] RVAs "to be singled out for manipulation." We can certainly "single out" individual RVA values if we want to. For example, the following expression "singles out" the relation that's the PQ value for supplier S4 within relation *spq:*

```
PQ FROM ( TUPLE FROM ( spq WHERE S# = S#('S4') ) )
```

What's more, in accordance with the well known language design principle called orthogonality, this expression can be used to denote the specified relation in any context where the rules of the language require a relation of the appropriate type: for example, within an expression calling for the join of that relation with some other relation. So if that's what Gittens means by "singling out for manipulation" some value of some RVA, well, we can certainly do it. In other words, RVA values certainly can be "manipulated by the set of relational operators specifically designed to accommodate the transformation of relation values," contrary to Gittens's claim.

Or perhaps by "manipulation" Gittens really means update? (The term *manipulation* is often used in this sense; it isn't a very apt term, but it has become sanctified, somewhat, by usage.) Well, we've already shown how syntactic shorthands can be defined that give the illusion of directly updating an RVA.[3] So we can do this one, too.

Gittens also asks: "In what way would the algebra **A** be logically different if the GROUP operator produced an XML value?" It's very tempting here to answer with another question: "In what way would a cat be different if it were a dog?" More politely, perhaps, we should admit that we simply don't understand the significance of the question. If we allow relation valued attributes, we clearly need operators for mapping between relations that contain such attributes and relations that don't. That's what GROUP and UNGROUP do—GROUP transforms a relation without an RVA into one with one, and UNGROUP does the opposite (speaking rather loosely in both cases).

All of that being said, we now add that, *pace* Gittens's claim, the algebra **A** doesn't include explicit GROUP and UNGROUP operators anyway! Part of the point of Appendix A of reference [11] is precisely to show that, while such operators are very useful in a concrete relational language, they are in the final analysis just shorthand for certain combinations of other operators.

We would like to say too that there's nothing wrong in principle with the idea of defining an operator that transforms a relation into an XML document. However, (a) such an operator couldn't be part of any relational algebra as such, precisely because it yields something that's not a relation; (b) it would probably not be a good idea to call that operator "GROUP," because the name "GROUP" is already spoken for, as it were.

Finally, Gittens asks: "More generally, in what way is support for relation valued attributes logically different from, for example, built in support for XML valued attributes?" Again we have to admit that we don't really understand the significance of this question. Part of the point of the *Manifesto* is to define a theory of types: one that accompanies, but is orthogonal to, the theory that is the relational model. And part of the point of that theory of types is to say, in effect, that relational attributes can be of any type whatsoever.[4] So attributes "of type XML" (more accurately, of type XML *document*) are certainly not prohibited. Whether support for that type is built in or user defined makes no difference as far as we're concerned. By contrast, we do require support for RVAs to be built in, insofar as relation types are themselves built in.

Note: Actually the last sentence of the foregoing paragraph is a little oversimplifed: Relation types aren't, in general, built in—at least, not exactly. However, we can treat them as if they were, at least to a first approximation, and that's good enough for present purposes. (The complete story is a little complicated, and to explain it fully would take us further afield than we wish to go in the present chapter. More specifics can be found in Chapter 2 of reference [9].)

CONCLUDING REMARKS

Gittens is not the first writer to criticize *The Third Manifesto*'s support for RVAs. Curiously enough, however, most previous critics have limited their criticisms to one or both of the following two issues, neither of which Gittens mentions in reference [13] (at least, not explicitly):

- Don't RVAs violate first normal form?
- Don't RVAs take us into the realms of second order logic?

Since Gittens didn't ask these questions explicitly, we choose not to respond to them in detail here. For the

---

[3] Perhaps we should remind the reader that *all* shorthands that allow "direct updating" of attributes (relation valued or otherwise) are in fact illusory, in a sense. See Chapter 5 of reference [9] for further discussion.

[4] With two small exceptions, which we mention here for completeness: First, we don't allow recursively defined types (i.e., types that are defined in terms of themselves); second, the relational model doesn't allow relations to have attributes of type pointer (where by "type pointer" we mean a type with associated referencing and dereferencing operators).

record, however, the answer to the first question is *no;* the answer to the second is *maybe,* with the rider that we're not sure it's the right question to ask, anyway. Detailed discussions of these issues can be found in references [5] and [8].

REFERENCES AND BIBLIOGRAPHY

1. E. F. Codd: "Derivability, Redundancy, and Consistency of Relations Stored in Large Data Banks," IBM Research Report RJ599 (August 19th, 1969).

2. E. F. Codd: "A Relational Model of Data for Large Shared Data Banks," *CACM 13,* No. 6 (June 1970). Republished in "Milestones of Research," *CACM 26,* No. 1 (January 1982).

3. Hugh Darwen: "Relation Valued Attributes; *or,* Will the Real First Normal Form Please Stand Up?", in C. J. Date and Hugh Darwen, *Relational Database Writings 1989-1991.* Reading, Mass.: Addison-Wesley (1992).

4. C. J. Date: "Missing Information," in *An Introduction to Database Systems* (8th edition). Boston, Mass.: Addison-Wesley (2004).

5. C. J. Date: "What First Normal Form Really Means," in *Date on Database: Writings 2000-2006.* Berkeley, Calif.: Apress (2006).

6. C. J. Date: "The Closed World Assumption," in *Logic and Databases: The Roots of Relational Theory.* Victoria, B.C.: Trafford Publishing (2007). See *www.trafford.com/07-0690.*

7. C. J. Date: "Why Is It Called Relational Algebra?", in *Logic and Databases: The Roots of Relational Theory.* Victoria, B.C.: Trafford Publishing (2007). See *www.trafford.com/07-0690.*

8. C. J. Date: "Frequently Asked Questions," in *Logic and Databases: The Roots of Relational Theory.* Victoria, B.C.: Trafford Publishing (2007). See *www.trafford.com/07-0690.*

9. C. J. Date: *SQL and Relational Theory: How to Write Accurate SQL Code.* Sebastopol, Calif.: O'Reilly Media, Inc. (2009).

10. C. J. Date: "Image Relations" (Chapter 14 of the present book).

11. C. J. Date and Hugh Darwen: *Databases, Types, and the Relational Model: The Third Manifesto* (3rd edition). Boston, Mass.: Addison-Wesley (2006).

12. C. J. Date, Hugh Darwen, and Nikos A. Lorentzos: *Temporal Data and the Relational Model.* San Francisco, Calif.: Morgan Kaufmann (2003).

13. Maurice Gittens: "The Third Manifesto Revisited," *www.gittens.nl/TheTTMRevisited.pdf* (March 25th, 2007).

Chapter 9

Setting the Record Straight (Part 6 of 6): Nulls and Three-Valued Logic

Gittens asserts in his paper [8] that *The Third Manifesto* displays "no sound substantiation for [its] rejection of unknown values." The implicit reference is to RM Proscription 4 ("No Nulls") of reference [7], which reads as follows:

> **D** shall include no concept of a "relation" in which some "tuple" includes some "attribute" that does not have a value.

The name **D** here refers generically to any language that conforms to the prescriptions of *The Third Manifesto*. The *pro*scriptions (RM Proscription 4 in particular) are included in the *Manifesto* for purposes of clarification and emphasis only—they all follow logically from the prescriptions (in fact, most of them are included precisely because SQL violates the relevant prescription, as is the case here).

Further discussion of the RM Proscriptions appears in Chapter 7 of reference [7]. The discussion of RM Proscription 4 is brief:

> By definition, tuples, and therefore relations, do not contain nulls (nulls are not values!). SQL, however, does permit nulls in its tables—yet another reason why SQL tables are not true relations. In the *Manifesto*, by contrast, nulls are absolutely, categorically, and unequivocally outlawed (and so too therefore is n-valued logic for any $n > 2$).

Note: The reason for the remark in parentheses is that, as is well known, SQL's support for nulls is based on three-valued logic specifically (hereinafter abbreviated 3VL).

There's one important point to be made before we elaborate on our rejection of nulls and 3VL and respond to Gittens's criticisms in connection with this issue. The fact is, the problem that nulls are supposed to address has been shown (e.g., in reference [4]) to be solvable without them, and indeed without recourse even to "special values" (which were suggested in earlier editions of reference [7] but were dropped from the third edition). So it's certainly not the case that a problem that might be perceived as solvable using nulls and 3VL can't be solved using a **D**.

GENERAL OBSERVATIONS

We find Gittens's criticisms on this topic quite hard to follow. Throughout reference [8] he appears to agree with Codd—in particular, with reference [1], which we refer to throughout the present chapter as "Codd's 1979 proposal"—and he does note in Section 6 of his paper that Codd himself proposed a form of support for nulls in reference [1] that's very similar to what we find in SQL. On the other hand, he also appears to agree with our rejection of 3VL and with our outlawing what he calls "instances" of null (we prefer the term *appearances*):

> Date and Darwen seem to have rejected the concept of *the unknown* based on issues with nulls encountered in SQL. For *example,* since many agree that nulls are not values, it just might be possible that a language with consistent semantics can be designed that accommodates the *concept* of the unknown in databases while, at the same time, the same language would have no notion of an *instance* of a null value. Such a language would accommodate Codd's concept of an attribute whose value is not known without mandating three valued logic.

After some elaboration of the foregoing idea (which we refer to hereinafter as "Gittens's suggestion"), he concludes with the following question, in italics:

- *Is it a matter of fact that Date and Darwen have provided proper substantiation for the rejection of nulls?*

The apparent contradictions in these extracts from reference [8] make it a little difficult for us to know how to respond and, indeed, what to respond to. It's clear that Gittens wants to see our justification for rejecting something. The question in italics explicitly calls that something "nulls," but the earlier text appears to be asking why we reject some other approach ("Gittens's suggestion") that doesn't involve either nulls or 3VL. Then again, however, the idea that such an approach "would accommodate Codd's concept" doesn't make sense to us, because "Codd's concept" certainly did involve both nulls and 3VL.

Be that as it may, we fully agree that the *Manifesto* includes no justification for our rejection of nulls and 3VL. We justify the omission by observing that (a) the *Manifesto* is a proposal, meant to be judged on its own merits (note that reference [7] is already over 500 pages long), and (b) we've already given detailed justifications elsewhere for rejecting various aspects of SQL in general, and nulls in particular, on many occasions and in many publications. *Note:* In the case of nulls in particular, such justifications are to be found in 18 (!) separate chapters in the books listed under reference [5], also in reference [6].

We also agree that the *Manifesto* includes no justification for rejecting Gittens's suggestion—but it's surely unreasonable to expect any such justification. Why should we give a justification, anywhere, for rejecting something that as far as we know has never been properly spelled out?[1]

In this chapter we first respond to Gittens's italicized question by summarizing the justifications we've given previously for rejecting SQL-style (and Codd-1979-style) nulls and 3VL. Then we comment on Gittens's suggestion—viz., that we might be able to avoid appearances of anything like null and stay with two-valued logic (2VL) and yet still "accommodate the *concept* of the unknown," as Gittens puts it.

WHAT'S WRONG WITH NULLS AND 3VL?

As already noted, we've answered the question that forms the title of this section elsewhere in numerous publications and on numerous occasions. For completeness, however, we give below a succinct summary of our position on the matter. But first we want to offer a preliminary observation. Here again is Gittens's question:

- *Is it a matter of fact that Date and Darwen have provided proper substantiation for the rejection of nulls?*

We want to comment on Gittens's use of the phrase "rejection of nulls." In our opinion, that phrase is quite misleading. We would prefer to say rather that *The Third Manifesto* proposes a scheme based on the mathematical theory of *n*-ary relations, as Codd did in 1969. That mathematical theory is based in turn on the well established first order predicate calculus, which includes the propositional calculus that's been with us, arguably, for some 2300 years, and whose logic is two-valued. The main aim of *The Third Manifesto* was to clarify what it takes to make a truly relational DBMS. We didn't think it either necessary or appropriate to explain yet again why relational databases might be preferred over databases based on other ideas, such as hierarchies, or networks, or variables of absolutely any kind (as in the object oriented approach), or the kind of structures Gittens appears to be contemplating. We could argue, therefore, that Gittens's question could be paraphrased thus: *Is it a matter of fact that Date and Darwen have provided proper substantiation for rejecting structures other than relations?* And then we could respond in kind by asking whether Gittens has provided proper substantiation for rejecting relations.

---

[1] Actually, reference [9], by the late Adrian Larner, might be seen as an attempt to spell out something similar to Gittens's suggestion; but that paper has received little attention, and in any case it appears to us not to stand up to careful analysis.

Anyway, here yet one more time is our position on three-valued logic. We begin by summarizing certain salient features of the propositional and predicate calculus (i.e., features of *two*-valued logic) that lie at the very heart of our foundation:

1. There are just two truth values, TRUE and FALSE.

2. Because there are just two truth values, the number of monadic operators that can be defined to operate on a truth value and return a truth value is four (2 to the power 2); and the number of dyadic operators that are similarly closed over truth values is 16 (2 to the power 2 squared—i.e., 2 to the power 4).

3. Of the total set of 20 logical operators (so called) mentioned in point 2, several proper subsets have been identified as being *truth functionally complete.* A set of logical operators is truth functionally complete (with respect to 2VL) if and only if all 20 operators can be defined in terms of those in that set. Well known examples of such sets, using the familiar English names of the operators, are {AND,NOT}, {OR,NOT}, {NAND}, and {NOR}.[2] The set usually chosen for its practicality and usefulness is of course {AND,OR,NOT}. If and only if a set of operators is truth functionally complete, then every proposition that's theoretically expressible using the logic in question can be expressed using just the operators of that set (in particular, there's no theoretical need to give any other operators explicit names of their own).

4. The truth functional completeness of AND, OR, and NOT notwithstanding, several other operators are so useful in practice that they *are* given names of their own. By way of example, (p AND q) OR (NOT(p) AND NOT (q))—i.e., "p has the same truth value as q"—is called *logical equivalence,* often written $p \Leftrightarrow q$ or $p \equiv q$. By way of another example, NOT(p) OR q is called *logical implication,* often written $p \Rightarrow q$, and pronounced "p implies q" or "if p then q." Note that $p \Leftrightarrow q$ is equivalent to ($p \Rightarrow q$) AND ($q \Rightarrow p$).

5. Based on the aforementioned operators we have certain well defined *rules of inference* by which further propositions can be derived from a given set of propositions. Such a derivation is called a *proof* and such derived propositions are called *theorems*. Moreover, if the given propositions are true and the rules of inference are valid, it follows that those derived propositions (i.e., those theorems) are also true. The rules of inference include, for example, *modus ponens* (given $p \Rightarrow q$ and p, we can conclude q) and *modus tollens* (given $p \Rightarrow q$ and NOT(q), we can conclude NOT(p)). One important application of these rules in the database context is the use of *modus tollens* in checking integrity constraints: When the database is updated, the proposed new value of that database is checked against declared constraints; if the proposition expressed by some constraint is false, then it follows that the result of applying the update also represents falsehood, and so the update is rejected.

6. Two-valued logic is known to be both *sound* and *complete,* where soundness means that every proposition that can be derived by a proof is true (in other words, every theorem is a tautology), and completeness means that every expressible proposition that is true can be proved to be true (in other words, every tautology is a theorem). *Note:* For present purposes, a tautology can be defined as a proposition that's necessarily true, regardless of the truth values of any component propositions it might contain. For example, let p be some arbitrary proposition; then p OR NOT(p) is clearly true and thus a tautology, regardless of whether p itself is true.

7. Let P be an n-adic predicate and let t be an n-ary tuple whose n components are in one to one correspondence with the parameters of P. Then t *satisfies* P if and only if—to use an obvious notation—

---

[2] In fact, these particular sets aren't just truth functionally complete, they're *primitive,* in the sense that removing an operator from any of them would result in the set in question being truth functionally complete no longer.

$P(t)$ is true. The body of the n-ary relation r that represents P is the set of tuples that satisfy P. The n-ary relation r' that represents NOT(P) is the *complement* of r; its body is the set of n-ary tuples t' such that the components of t' are in one to one correspondence with the parameters of P but t' doesn't satisfy P (i.e., $P(t')$ is false).

8. One particular relation—the *identity* relation—is of paramount importance. It corresponds to what's sometimes called *The Axiom of Equality* and hence to the comparison operator *equals* ("="). Its body consists of every 2-tuple that pairs something with itself;[3] the body of its complement therefore consists of every 2-tuple that pairs something with something other than itself. The operators of the relational algebra depend for their definition on the identity relation.

In Codd's 1979 proposal, by contrast, none of the foregoing properties holds. Instead:

1. There are three truth values, TRUE, FALSE, and UNKNOWN.

2. Because there are three truth values, the number of monadic operators that can be defined to operate on a truth value and return a truth value is 27 (3 to the power 3), and the number of dyadic operators that are similarly closed over truth values is 19,683 (3 to the power 3 squared—i.e., 3 to the power 9).

3. 3VL counterparts of AND, OR, and NOT are proposed that reduce to their 2VL counterparts when applied to just TRUE and FALSE. However, this set of three operators is patently not truth functionally complete (i.e., in the 3VL sense of that term, which would require all 19,710 operators to be definable in terms of those three). In other words, there exist 3VL operators that can't be defined in terms of the proposed 3VL counterparts of AND, OR, and NOT. For example, there's no way, using just AND, OR, and NOT, to define the monadic operator whose result is UNKNOWN for every possible input. In fact, reference [1] doesn't even address the pragmatically important question of defining a (desirably small!) proper subset of the 19,710 operators in total that would be truth functionally complete.[4]

4. Further interesting operators are also not discussed in reference [1]. We observe, however, that the operator meaning "p has the same truth value as q" isn't equivalent to (p AND q) OR (NOT(p) AND NOT(q)), because if p and q are both UNKNOWN, the result is UNKNOWN instead of TRUE. Moreover, no counterpart of 2VL's *implication* ($p \Rightarrow q$) is proposed. Note in particular that its 2VL definition, as being equivalent to NOT(p) OR q, would fail under 3VL to satisfy our intuitive requirement that $p \Rightarrow p$ is a tautology.

5. No counterparts of 2VL's rules of inference have been proposed. It follows that no proof procedure has been proposed either. Furthermore, several familiar 2VL tautologies aren't tautologies in 3VL—leading to many traps for the unwary. An example is p OR NOT(p), which is a tautology in 2VL as we know, but not in 3VL. One possibly surprising consequence of this fact, for SQL in particular, is that the SQL expressions

```
CASE
   WHEN p THEN a
   ELSE b
END
```

[3] There's a question here you might like to ponder: In the formalism of reference [7], attributes of relations have types; so what type are the attributes of the identity relation?

[4] A fortiori, therefore, it doesn't address the question of defining a primitive subset either.

and

```
CASE
   WHEN NOT(p) THEN b
   ELSE a
END
```

aren't logically equivalent.

6. Because no rules of inference have been proposed, we have no concept of what either soundness or completeness might mean in this system.

7. It's not clear what it might mean for a tuple to satisfy a predicate. In SQL in particular, the criterion used for evaluating restriction (WHERE) is different from the one used for checking constraints. Also in SQL (and in Codd's 1979 proposal), although the comparison $x = y$ doesn't yield TRUE when x and y are both null, two or more appearances of null are regarded as equal in the treatment of operators such as DISTINCT, GROUP BY, and UNION.

8. 3VL doesn't seem to have a proper counterpart of the identity relation. As noted in the previous paragraph, in both SQL and Codd's 1979 proposal there are two distinct *equals* operators. In one of them null isn't considered to be the same thing as itself;[5] in the other it is. For psychological reasons we might refer to the first of these operators as *horizontal equals,* the second as *vertical equals;* horizontal equals is used in restriction and extension, vertical equals in projection and grouping. The fact that the comparison $x = x$ can yield TRUE in some contexts and not in others doesn't seem to offer a sound basis for consistency (to put it mildly).

Actually, Codd later rejected his own 1979 proposal in favor of a different one, based on four truth values and four-valued logic (4VL). He first briefly mentioned this possibility in reference [2]; he then went on to publish two different sets of 4VL truth tables, the first in reference [3] and the second, to supersede the first, in a July 1991 reprinting of that reference. Further details are given in reference [6], which describes yet another subsequent revision by Codd (and it's worth noting that this latest revision is strictly incompatible with his own 3VL, which is why we say Codd "later rejected" his original 3VL proposal). It seems, then, that people in favor of either 3VL or 4VL should be very wary of citing Codd in support of their position.

In any case, our commentary on Codd's 3VL applies with even more force, mutatis mutandis, to each of Codd's 4VLs.[6] As for nulls, support for nulls implies support for 3VL *by definition,* so rejecting 3VL implies rejection of nulls as well. 4VL arises when two different (but equally malignant) varieties of null are supported.

Gittens poses a second question that we need to respond to:

- *Is it a matter of fact that The Third Manifesto has provided evidence of properly researching the issue of nulls?*

The answer is "No, it isn't." *The Third Manifesto* is a proposal, not a criticism of other proposals. We don't consider it the *Manifesto*'s responsibility to include arguments against everything it doesn't include. It should be judged on its own merits.

---

[5] Nor is it considered to be not the same thing as itself (!).

[6] More generally, our position on n-valued logic (nVL) for any $n > 3$ is similar but stronger. The more truth values, the worse it gets, we say.

GITTENS'S SUGGESTION

We turn now to Gittens's suggestion:

> [Many] agree that nulls are not values, [so] it just might be possible that a language with consistent semantics can be designed that accommodates the *concept* of the unknown in databases while, at the same time, the same language would have no notion of an *instance* of a null value. Such a language would accommodate Codd's concept of an attribute whose value is not known without mandating three valued logic.

Before examining the substance of this suggestion, we would like to comment on the specific phrase *no notion of an instance of a null value.* Since we all seem to agree that null isn't a value (in part because it doesn't compare equal to itself), we take this phrase to be synonymous with *no notion of an appearance of null.*[7] But can something be meaningfully said to exist if it can't appear anywhere? We think not. So we assume Gittens really means *no notion of null.* But then he goes on to illustrate his idea by saying "Please consider the following Codd styled relation *s*," which he depicts thus:[8]

SUPPLIERID	Name	City (possibly null)
S1	John	
S2	Jane	Paris
S3	Judy	

Now, "Codd styled" here presumably refers to Codd's 1979 proposal—in which case the blank cells in the table definitely do represent "appearances of null" (and the column heading for the pertinent column appears to confirm this interpretation). So we're already confused; but matters get worse when Gittens—who elsewhere in his paper [8] criticizes us for a certain "lack of rigor" he perceives in our *Manifesto*—continues thus:

> As long as a language can *guarantee* that operators in the language would allow *no* relation values to be derived from our example relation *s*, which refer to the unknown, all would be well. Which in our example is to say that the statement:
>
> ```
> select * from s
> ```
>
> would produce an error.

Well, if there's any such thing as a "relation" that "refer[s] to the unknown," then there must be at least one operator that can be used to denote it—because *every* relation must be the result of some expression denoting it! We strongly suspect that what Gittens really means here is that the "example relation *s*" is the current value of some relation *variable,* say S. In that case *s* must somehow have been assigned to S. The expression denoting *s* in that assignment is, by definition (but see further discussion below), an invocation of some operator—even if the assignment is done by means of one of the familiar shorthands INSERT, DELETE, or UPDATE. For example, the DELETE statement

---

[7] When we're talking about *values,* at least (i.e., as opposed to nulls), we pay attention to the logical difference between (a) values as such, on the one hand, and (b) appearances of those values, on the other. For example, variables *V1* and *V2* might both have the same current value *v*—in which case we would say there's just one value as such, but two appearances of that value.

[8] Gittens refers to this "Codd styled" relation as *R,* not *s*. Our reasons for changing his text slightly here will shortly become clear.

```
DELETE S WHERE City = 'Paris' ;
```

is shorthand for the following assignment:

```
S := S MINUS ( S WHERE City = 'Paris' ) ;
```

The expression on the right side of this assignment is an invocation of an operator, MINUS, that's normally defined as operating on two relations to yield a relation. Gittens wants to distinguish between "relations" that somehow "refer to the unknown" (for convenience, let's call them RTRTUs) and relations that don't (which we'll continue to call relations). Now, the invocation of MINUS shown above can certainly be said to derive something from *s,* where *s* is the current value of the variable S that's referred to twice in the invocation. Furthermore, the second argument to that invocation is obtained by invoking the operator WHERE, and this latter invocation also derives something from *s*. What about the first argument, which is represented by just the expression S? That expression is a variable reference; when evaluated, it yields the current value of S. But a variable reference is just a special case of an operator invocation, logically speaking (the operator is "return the current value of"). And if the operator in question isn't allowed to yield an RTRTU, and yet the current value of S is an RTRTU and not a relation, then the expression S is illegal under Gittens's suggestion, and so a fortiori are the expressions S WHERE City = 'Paris' and S MINUS (S WHERE City = 'Paris').

Note, incidentally, that the conclusions of the previous paragraph are entirely consistent with Gittens's suggestion that the SQL expression "select * from S" (or "select * from *s,*" rather) should "produce an error." In fact, "select * from S" is just SQL's idiosyncratic longhand for what in most languages would be written simply "S".

We spare Gittens, and the reader, further painful deconstruction of his suggestion. More constructively, we suggest that if a language is to recognize the distinction Gittens seems to have in mind (i.e., between RTRTUs and relations), then that language needs at a minimum all of the following:

- Operators that when invoked yield relations
- Operators that when invoked yield RTRTUs
- Operators (including some of the above) that operate on relations
- Operators (including some of the above) that operate on RTRTUs
- Support for relation variables, and operators to update such variables (including assignment)
- Support for RTRTU variables, and operators to update such variables (including assignment)
- Comparison operators for relations
- Comparison operators for RTRTUs

By providing *The Third Manifesto,* together with the language **Tutorial D** to illustrate its proposals, we've given the database community something that can be evaluated, criticized, and accepted or rejected. If Gittens had likewise provided us with a definition of a model based on his suggestions and an example of a language embracing them, then we would likewise have been able to evaluate them and criticize them and accept them or reject them. As a matter of fact, we think it might be a very good idea to attempt to define such a model and language, if only for evaluation purposes.[9] But until that's been done we can have no more to say on the matter.

---

[9] In fact we've made such an attempt ourselves. See Chapter 24 of the present book.

REFERENCES AND BIBLIOGRAPHY

1. E. F. Codd: "Extending the Database Relational Model to Capture More Meaning," *ACM TODS 4,* No. 4 (December 1979).

2. E. F. Codd: "Missing Information (Applicable and Inapplicable) in Relational Databases," *ACM SIGMOD Record 15,* No. 4 (December 1986).

3. E. F. Codd: *The Relational Model for Database Management Version 2.* Reading, Mass.: Addison-Wesley (1990).

4. Hugh Darwen: "How to Handle Missing Information Without Using Nulls" (presentation slides), *www.thethirdmanifesto.com* (May 9th, 2003; revised May 16th, 2005). See also Chapter 23 of the present book.

5. C. J. Date: *Relational Database: Selected Writings* (Reading, Mass.: Addison-Wesley, 1986); *Relational Database Writings 1985-1989* (Reading, Mass.: Addison-Wesley, 1990); (with Hugh Darwen) *Relational Database Writings 1989-1991* (Reading, Mass.: Addison-Wesley, 1992); *Relational Database Writings 1991-1994* (Reading, Mass.: Addison-Wesley, 1995); (with Hugh Darwen and David McGoveran) *Relational Database Writings 1994-1997* (Reading, Mass.: Addison-Wesley, 1998).

6. C. J. Date: "Why Three- and Four-Valued Logic Don't Work," in *Date on Database: Writings 2000-2006.* Berkeley, Calif.: Apress (2006).

7. C. J. Date and Hugh Darwen: *Databases, Types, and the Relational Model: The Third Manifesto* (3rd edition). Boston, Mass.: Addison-Wesley (2006).

8. Maurice Gittens: "The Third Manifesto Revisited," *www.gittens.nl/TheTTMRevisited.pdf* (March 25th, 2007).

9. Adrian Larner: "A New Model of Data," *http://www.btinternet.com/~adrian.larner/ database.htm* (undated).

Chapter 10

How to Update Views

The duke of Ormond took a view yesterday of his troop,
and ordered all that had bay or grey horses to change them for black.

—earliest known example (1693) of view updating,
quoted in the Oxford English Dictionary from
"A Brief Historical Relation of State Affairs 1678-1714,"
by Narcissus Luttrell (1857)

Conventional database wisdom has it that some views, at least, are intrinsically nonupdatable. I disagree with this position, and in this chapter I want to show why.[1] It'll take me quite a while to get to my main point, however, because I need to build up to it gradually (there are some important preliminary matters I need to get out of the way first), so please bear with me. *Note:* I've written on these matters before, in references [1] and [3] in particular, but certain recent experiences have made me realize I need to try to explain my position yet one more time. Apologies if you've heard this all before.

THE RUNNING EXAMPLE

I'll base my examples as usual on the familiar suppliers-and-parts database, with definition as follows:[2]

```
VAR S BASE RELATION    /* supplier is under contract */
  { S# S# , SNAME NAME , STATUS INTEGER , CITY CHAR }
    KEY { S# } ;

VAR P BASE RELATION    /* part is of interest */
  { P# P# , PNAME NAME , COLOR COLOR , WEIGHT WEIGHT , CITY CHAR }
    KEY { P# } ;

VAR SP BASE RELATION   /* supplier supplies (or ships) part */
  { S# S# , P# P# , QTY QTY }
    KEY { S# , P# }
    FOREIGN KEY { S# } REFERENCES S
    FOREIGN KEY { P# } REFERENCES P ;
```

Sample values are shown in Fig. 1 overleaf (and I'll assume these particular values in examples throughout the chapter, barring explicit statements to the contrary).

---

[1] The first person singular in this chapter refers to Chris Date specifically.

[2] The definition is expressed in **Tutorial D** (more precisely, a dialect of **Tutorial D** that includes explicit foreign key support). **Tutorial D** is the language used in reference [7] to illustrate the ideas of *The Third Manifesto.* I assume you're reasonably familiar with that language, though in fact it's more or less self-explanatory.

S

S#	SNAME	STATUS	CITY
S1	Smith	20	London
S2	Jones	10	Paris
S3	Blake	30	Paris
S4	Clark	20	London
S5	Adams	30	Athens

P

P#	PNAME	COLOR	WEIGHT	CITY
P1	Nut	Red	12.0	London
P2	Bolt	Green	17.0	Paris
P3	Screw	Blue	17.0	Oslo
P4	Screw	Red	14.0	London
P5	Cam	Blue	12.0	Paris
P6	Cog	Red	19.0	London

SP

S#	P#	QTY
S1	P1	300
S1	P2	200
S1	P3	400
S1	P4	200
S1	P5	100
S1	P6	100
S2	P1	300
S2	P2	400
S3	P2	200
S4	P2	200
S4	P4	300
S4	P5	400

Fig. 1: The suppliers-and-parts database—sample values

UPDATING IS SET AT A TIME

Although I'm supposed to be talking about views, I want to forget about views entirely until further notice—relvars S, P, and SP in the running example are all base relvars, and my discussion and examples will all be framed in terms of those base relvars specifically, until further notice. From this point forward, therefore, you can take the term *relvar* to mean a base relvar specifically (again, until further notice)—though it's only fair to warn you that almost everything I'll be saying about base relvars will turn out to apply to views as well, as we'll see.

The first point I need to stress, then, is that updating is *set at a time*—more precisely, relation at a time—in the relational model. (In fact, all operations in the relational model are set at a time, meaning they take entire relations or entire relvars as operands, not just individual tuples.) Thus, INSERT inserts a set of tuples into the target relvar; DELETE deletes a set of tuples from the target relvar; and UPDATE updates a set of tuples in the target relvar. Now, it's true that we often talk in terms of (for example) updating some individual tuple as such—indeed, I'll often talk in such terms in the rest of the chapter, since it does save a lot of circumlocution—but you need to understand that:

- Such talk really means the set of tuples we're updating just happens to have cardinality one.
- What's more, updating a set of tuples of cardinality one sometimes isn't possible anyway.

For example, suppose relvar S is subject to an integrity constraint to the effect that suppliers S1 and S4 must always be in the same city. Then any "single tuple update" that tries to change the city for just one of those two suppliers will necessarily fail. Instead, we must change them both at the same time, perhaps like this:

```
UPDATE S WHERE S# = S#('S1')
            OR S# = S#('S4') : { CITY := 'New York' } ;
```

What's being updated here, given the sample values shown in Fig. 1, is a set of two tuples.

I remark in passing that those who think view updating is, in general, impossible often overlook the point I'm making here: viz., that updating is set at a time. Instead, they assume updating can always be done at the level of individual tuples, and then they point out certain anomalies that arise from this assumption if certain view updates are permitted. Be that as it may, the fact that updating is set at a time has certain important implications:

- First, integrity checking mustn't be done until all of the updating has been done (see the next section for further discussion of this point).
- Second, "cascade delete" and other such actions—see later in this chapter—also mustn't be done until all of the updating has been done.[3]

In other words, a set level update mustn't be treated as a sequence of individual tuple level updates. Rather, update operations—in fact, all operations—in the relational model are always *semantically atomic;* that is, either they execute in their entirety or they have no effect (except possibly for returning a status code or something of that nature). Thus, although we do sometimes think of a set level operation, informally, as if it were shorthand for a sequence of tuple level operations, it's important to understand that such a way of thinking isn't really accurate but is, at best, only an approximation to the truth.

THE GOLDEN RULE

Every relvar is subject to a number of integrity constraints, or just constraints for short. For example, relvar SP is subject to the following constraints:

- A key constraint, defined by the specification KEY {S#,P#}
- A foreign key constraint, defined by the specification FOREIGN KEY {S#} REFERENCES S
- And another foreign key constraint, defined by the specification FOREIGN KEY {P#} REFERENCES P

As it happens, these three are the only database constraints, as such, explicitly specified for relvar SP in our running example, but in practice there could be any number of others; for example, there could be one to the effect that QTY values lie in a certain range. What's more, each of the three relvars is additionally subject to a number of what I'll refer to here as *attribute* constraints, which specify that each specific attribute is of some specific type (for example, there's an attribute constraint to the effect that attribute SNAME is of type NAME); however, such constraints are irrelevant for the purposes of this chapter, and I'll ignore them from this point forward.

Tutorial D supports a CONSTRAINT statement that allows the expression of database constraints of arbitrary complexity. (In fact, KEY and FOREIGN KEY specifications like those in the example are, in the final analysis, just shorthand for constraints that can alternatively be expressed by means of a suitable CONSTRAINT statement.) The general format is:

```
CONSTRAINT <constraint name> <boolean expression> ;
```

For example:

```
CONSTRAINT CX1
   IS_EMPTY ( ( S JOIN SP ) WHERE STATUS < 20 AND P# = P#('P6') ) ;
```

---

[3] In fact, there's a third implication too: Since updating is set at a time, it follows that there's nothing in the relational model corresponding to SQL's "positioned updates"—i.e., UPDATE or DELETE "WHERE CURRENT OF cursor"—because those operations are tuple at a time (or row at a time, rather), not set at a time, by definition.

This constraint says: No supplier with status less than 20 can supply part P6. Observe that it mentions, and thus affects updates on, two distinct relvars, S and SP. In general, of course, a given constraint can mention any number of relvars. So let *R* be a relvar, and let *C1, C2, ..., Cm* (*m* ⩾ 0) be all of the constraints that mention *R* (and let's assume that each *Ci* is just a boolean expression—i.e., let's ignore the "CONSTRAINT <*constraint name*>" specifications, for simplicity). Then the boolean expression

```
( C1 ) AND ( C2 ) AND ... AND ( Cm ) AND TRUE
```

is the *total* constraint for relvar *R,* or just *the* constraint for *R* for short. Clearly, *R* must never be allowed to have a value that causes its total constraint to evaluate to FALSE. Hence we have **The Golden Rule** (or the first version of that rule, to be more precise):

No update on relvar R must ever cause the constraint for R to evaluate to FALSE.

Now let *DB* be a database, and let *R1, R2, ..., Rn* (*n* ⩾ 0) be all of the relvars in *DB*. Let the (total) constraints for those relvars be *C1, C2, ..., Cn,* respectively. Then the boolean expression

```
( C1 ) AND ( C2 ) AND ... AND ( Cn ) AND TRUE
```

is the total constraint for database *DB,* or just *the* constraint for *DB* for short. And so we can extend **The Golden Rule** accordingly:

No update on database DB must ever cause the constraint for DB to evaluate to FALSE.

Here's a simple example of an update that fails on a violation of **The Golden Rule:**

```
INSERT SP
   RELATION { TUPLE { S# S#('S1') , P# P#('P1') , QTY QTY(50) } } ;
```

This update fails (given the sample values shown in Fig. 1) because it violates the key constraint on relvar SP.

THE ASSIGNMENT PRINCIPLE

Like **The Golden Rule,** *The Assignment Principle* too is extremely simple; in fact, it's little more than common sense, which is perhaps why it isn't often spelled out explicitly. Here it is:

After assignment of value v to variable V, the comparison (i.e., the boolean expression) V = v must evaluate to TRUE.

For example, suppose X is a variable of type INTEGER, and suppose we assign the value 3 to X. After that assignment, then, we would be very surprised if the comparison X = 3 didn't evaluate to TRUE.

Now, *The Assignment Principle* is so obvious—in effect, it's just a definition of what the operation of assignment means—that it's no wonder (you might think) that it isn't often spelled out explicitly. Unfortunately, however, it's often violated in the database world, owing to a variety of idiosyncrasies (or rather, to be a little less mealy mouthed about the matter, logical errors) in the design of the language SQL. Here are some illustrations of this point:

- Let C3 be an SQL variable of type CHAR(3) and let the string 'AB' (which is of length two, not three, observe) be assigned to it. This assignment succeeds. After the assignment, however, if NO PAD applies to C3, then the comparison C3 = 'AB' evaluates to FALSE, not TRUE.

- Again let C3 be an SQL variable of type CHAR(3) and let the string 'AB ' (which is of length four—note the two trailing spaces) be assigned to it. This assignment succeeds. After the assignment, however, if NO

PAD applies to C3, then the comparison C3 = 'AB ' evaluates to FALSE, not TRUE.

- Let X be an SQL variable of any type, let *x* be assigned to it, and let *x* be null. After the assignment, then, the comparison X = *x* evaluates to UNKNOWN, not TRUE.

- Let T be an SQL table and let *t* be the value assigned to it via some SQL update operation (INSERT, DELETE, or UPDATE).[4] Then after the assignment the comparison T = *t* can't even be done, because SQL doesn't support comparison operators on tables; the comparison thus certainly doesn't (and can't) evaluate to TRUE.

And so on (this isn't an exhaustive list). *Note:* I hope it goes without saying that no similar anomalies occur in **Tutorial D**.

Now, it's easy to come up with examples of updates that fail on a violation of **The Golden Rule;** it's a little harder to come up with examples—other than SQL examples, that is—that fail on a violation of *The Assignment Principle*. Probably the easiest way to do so is to start with the realization that the entire database is actually a single variable (perhaps a rather large one): a database variable, to be precise, and its values are database values. (See reference [7] if you want to see these claims elaborated.) After all, when we perform an update on the database, conceptually what we're doing is replacing one value of the database by another—and this state of affairs means the database is a variable, by definition. (To be a variable is to be updatable; conversely, to be updatable is to be a variable.)

So let's consider the variable that's the suppliers-and-parts database in particular. More specifically, let's consider the following update on that variable:

```
DELETE S WHERE S# = S#('S1') ;
```

Now, if this update were to do (or were to try to do, rather) exactly what it says, no more and no less, it would fail on a violation of **The Golden Rule;** to be specific, it would fail on a violation of the foreign key constraint from relvar SP to relvar S. Precisely for that reason, the DBMS might very well "cascade" the operation under the covers to delete the shipments for supplier S1 as well; integrity will thereby be preserved, and the operation will succeed. But note what's happened if that "cascade delete" does in fact occur:

1. The user has requested a rather simple assignment on the suppliers-and-parts database variable: namely, an assignment that has the effect of merely removing one tuple, the S tuple for supplier S1.

2. That request has apparently succeeded.

3. After the assignment, however, the value of the suppliers-and-parts database variable is *not* equal to its previous value minus just the S tuple for supplier S1.

By rights, therefore, the original delete ought to have failed on a violation of *The Assignment Principle*. It didn't, of course; but why not, exactly? I discuss this question in the section immediately following.

THE CASCADE DELETE RULE

I said in the previous section that the DBMS might cascade the delete *under the covers*. But what does "under the covers" mean? In order for that cascade to happen at all, an appropriate *cascade delete rule* must be in effect and must therefore have been stated somewhere. (Typically, of course, it will have been stated as part of the pertinent foreign key specification, but I want to ignore this detail for the time being.) Now there are two possibilities:

---

[4] Of course, *update* is just another term for assignment. In particular, INSERT, DELETE, and UPDATE are all fundamentally just shorthand for certain relational assignments (though SQL as such doesn't explicitly support any such operation).

1. The user requesting deletion of the S tuple for supplier S1 is aware of that cascade delete rule.
2. The user is unaware of that rule.

Well, if the user is unaware of the rule (possibility 2), then, as I've already explained, the user will perceive a violation of *The Assignment Principle*—and that fact in itself is a strong argument in favor of the position that the user *mustn't* be unaware of the rule. (Of course, I'm assuming here that the user is at least aware that relvar SP exists; i.e., I'm assuming that relvar SP is part of the database as seen by the user. If it isn't, then the user won't perceive a violation of *The Assignment Principle* after all. But this possibility seems unlikely in practice; it doesn't seem reasonable to give the user the authority to perform deletes on relvar S without that user being aware that such deletes will cascade to perform deletes on relvar SP as well. We surely don't want data to be deleted "by accident," after all.)

Note, incidentally, that if the cascade delete rule weren't in effect and the delete therefore did fail, the very fact that it failed—or the exception code associated with that failure, perhaps—would tell the user that a certain foreign key constraint had been violated. The user would therefore be aware that at least one relvar with a foreign key referencing relvar S did exist. Again, therefore, it seems reasonable to assume that a user holding delete authority on relvar S would be aware of any such referencing relvars, and aware also of any corresponding cascade delete rules.

I conclude, therefore, that the user must be aware of the rule (possibility 1)—in which case, the cascading isn't exactly "under the covers" after all. In other words, the user must be aware that his or her original request—

```
DELETE S WHERE S# = S#('S1') ;
```

—is really shorthand for the following double delete (note the comma separator, which indicates syntactically that the end of the overall statement hasn't yet been reached):[5]

```
DELETE S  WHERE S# = S#('S1') ,
DELETE SP WHERE S# = S#('S1') ;
```

In practice, of course, it's virtually certain that the user will indeed be aware of the cascade delete rule, because as I mentioned earlier it's probably stated explicitly as part of the pertinent foreign key specification, perhaps like this:

```
VAR SP BASE RELATION ...
    FOREIGN KEY { S# } REFERENCES S ON DELETE CASCADE ... ;
```

I observe, however, that although it is indeed what's typically done in practice, this placement for the rule isn't very logical, because it defines what's supposed to happen when a delete is performed on relvar S, not relvar SP, and yet it's specified as part of the definition of relvar SP, not relvar S. In what follows, therefore, I'll define such rules by means of a hypothetical new standalone statement as suggested by the following example:[6]

```
ON DELETE s FROM S : DELETE ( SP MATCHING s ) FROM SP ;
```

---

[5] A double delete is really a double assignment, of course; I'm appealing here to the fact that *The Third Manifesto* requires support for a multiple form of assignment, according to which any number of individual assignments can all be performed as a single operation, without any integrity checking being done until the entire operation has completed. See reference [8] for detailed discussions and further explanation.

[6] If the rule really does have to be bundled with some other definition, then the logical place is the definition of the pertinent integrity constraint. Given current practice, however, there are at least two problems with this idea. First, in the example under consideration, the "pertinent constraint" is a foreign key constraint, and foreign key constraints in particular are already bundled (perhaps unfortunately) with the definition of the pertinent referencing relvar. Second, in the case of views (see the section "More on Compensatory Actions" later), the "pertinent constraint" is stated only implicitly anyway!

Note: My syntax is deliberately verbose. Obviously some language design work will need to be done in this area, but I don't want to get into such issues here;[7] rather, I just want to be sure the semantics are clear. The example at hand can be read as follows: On deletion of relation *s* from relvar S, the delete should cascade to delete relation *sp* from relvar SP, where *sp* = (SP MATCHING *s*).[8]

One last point to close this section: In reference [5], I've proposed "no cascade" as an alternative—the only sensible alternative by my current way of thinking, though I reserve the right to change my opinion at a later time—to "cascade." However, I've concentrated on "cascade" in this section because it's the interesting case, in a sense, and I'll continue to do so throughout the rest of this chapter. Of course, specifying "no cascade" is essentially equivalent to specifying no rule at all.

COMPENSATORY ACTIONS

Now let me abstract a little from the discussions of the previous section. Cascading an update is a typical example of a *compensatory action.* Here's a definition of this concept (taken from reference [2]):

- **Definition (compensatory action):** An update performed automatically by the system in addition to some requested update, with the aim of avoiding some integrity violation that might otherwise occur. Cascading a delete operation is a typical example. Such actions should be specified declaratively, and users should generally be aware of them; that is, users should generally know when their update requests are shorthand for some more extensive set of actions, for otherwise they might perceive an apparent violation of *The Assignment Principle,* q.v.

Of course, we can't do much in the way of specifying such actions in SQL products today (with the sole exception of foreign key constraints, where we've been able to define such actions, in the standard at least, ever since 1992).[9] But the point is, such actions aren't a new idea; it's just that, as so often, practice has lagged behind theory somewhat. What's more, it's clear from the definition that the concept of compensatory actions applies to much more than just foreign key constraints—it ought logically to be available in connection with constraints of all kinds. I'll illustrate this latter point with another simple example.

Suppose we extend the suppliers-and-parts database to include the following additional relvar LS ("London suppliers"):

```
VAR LS BASE RELATION    /* London suppliers */
  { S# S# , SNAME NAME , STATUS INTEGER , CITY CHAR }
    KEY { S# } ;
```

Let's also assign it a value:

```
LS := S WHERE CITY = 'London' ;
```

As this assignment suggests, relvar LS is supposed to contain a tuple for each London supplier (and no other tuples). Given the sample values in Fig. 1, LS now looks like this:

---

[7] With one possible exception: If my arguments regarding view updating are accepted (and in accordance with *The Principle of Interchangeability*—see the next section but one), then I think we should consider the possibility of revising the syntax of relvar definitions to drop the distinguishing keywords BASE and VIRTUAL (among other things).

[8] In case you're not familiar with **Tutorial D**'s MATCHING operator, here's a definition: The expression *r1* MATCHING *r2* is shorthand for the expression (*r1* JOIN *r2*){*X*}, where {*X*} is all of the attributes of *r1*. In the example, therefore, the expression SP MATCHING *s* denotes the shipments for suppliers whose supplier number is one of those mentioned in relation *s*.

[9] I don't count "triggers," for reasons to be discussed in the section "What about Triggers?" later in this chapter.

LS

S#	SNAME	STATUS	CITY
S1	Smith	20	London
S4	Clark	20	London

By the way, it could certainly now be argued that the database isn't very well designed, for at least two reasons. First, there's not much point in retaining the CITY attribute in relvar LS, since its value is the same, London, in every tuple. Second, we now have some redundancy, since all of the information represented by relvar LS is already represented in relvar S anyway. However, I'm going to ask you to overlook these objections until further notice; I'll come back and address them in the section "Concluding Remarks," later.

Like all relvars, relvar LS is subject to a variety of constraints. First of all, there's the key constraint, which is stated explicitly in the relvar definition. Second, as I just mentioned, there's the constraint that the CITY value must be London in every tuple. Well ... to be more precise about the matter, there's the constraint that a tuple appears in LS if and only if it appears in S and its CITY value is London. Let's state that constraint explicitly:

```
CONSTRAINT CX2 LS = S WHERE CITY = 'London' ;
```

Note, incidentally, that there's also a foreign key constraint from LS to S—but that constraint is in fact implied by constraint CX2, so there's no need to state it explicitly.

Now consider the following update request once again:

```
DELETE S WHERE S# = S#('S1') ;
```

Clearly, there are two possibilities: The request can fail on a violation of **The Golden Rule** (more specifically, a violation of constraint CX2), or it can succeed and cascade to relvar LS, in which case it's really shorthand for the following double update:

```
DELETE S  WHERE S# = S#('S1') ,
DELETE LS WHERE S# = S#('S1') ;
```

In the latter case, of course, the cascade rule must have been specified somewhere, perhaps like this:

```
ON DELETE s FROM S : DELETE ( s WHERE CITY = 'London' ) FROM LS ;
```

As an aside, I remark that, on the assumption that an attempt to delete a nonexistent tuple has no effect, we could replace the expression in parentheses here by just *s*. However, the expression in parentheses is perhaps preferable, in that it's at least more specific. Be that as it may, suppose now that the original update request had been directed not at relvar S but at relvar LS instead:

```
DELETE LS WHERE S# = S#('S1') ;
```

Again there are two possibilities (though they're very similar to the previous ones): The request can fail on a violation of **The Golden Rule,** or it can cascade to relvar S, in which case it's really shorthand for this double update (actually the same double update as before):[10]

[10] The order in which individual updates are specified in a multiple update (equivalently, in a multiple assignment) is essentially irrelevant. Again, see reference [8] for more explanation.

```
DELETE LS WHERE S# = S#('S1') ,
DELETE S  WHERE S# = S#('S1') ;
```

In the latter case, again, an appropriate cascade rule must have been specified:

```
ON DELETE ls FROM LS : DELETE ls FROM S ;
```

Given the two proposed ON DELETE specifications, then, deletes on either of the two relvars will now cascade appropriately to the other,[11] and integrity will be preserved (in other words, **The Golden Rule** will be satisfied). But note too that, to repeat, users must be aware of those ON DELETE specifications, for otherwise they might perceive violations of *The Assignment Principle.*

THE PRINCIPLE OF INTERCHANGEABILITY

Now (at last) let's get back to views. First let's make relvar LS a view instead of a base relvar:

```
VAR LS VIRTUAL ( S WHERE CITY = 'London' )
    KEY { S# } ;   /* London suppliers */
```

Note: Views are called *virtual relvars* in **Tutorial D,** and the syntax for defining a view is

```
VAR <view name> VIRTUAL ( <relational expression> ) ... ;
```

The *<relational expression>* is, of course, the expression that defines the views in terms of other relvars—in other words, it's the *view defining expression.* Observe that **Tutorial D,** unlike SQL, allows view definitions to include key and foreign key specifications, as the example suggests.

The first point I need to stress is that views, or virtual relvars, are indeed relvars; as such, they have all of the properties of relvars in general (such as having keys in particular, which is why **Tutorial D** allows key specifications to appear in view definitions). And it follows right away from this first point that we *must* be able to update views (i.e., views *must* be updatable), and it's tempting just to say "I rest my case." But I won't; rather, I want to present a series of more detailed, and I hope more convincing, arguments in support of my position.

First of all, then, let me extend the example to introduce a second view, NLS ("non London suppliers"):

```
VAR NLS VIRTUAL ( S WHERE CITY ≠ 'London' )
    KEY { S# } ;   /* non London suppliers */
```

Given the sample values in Fig. 1, NLS looks like this:

---

[11] Note that cascading the delete from LS to S will presumably cause the cascade delete rule from S to LS to be invoked in turn. In the case at hand this second cascade won't have any effect; however, it does raise the interesting question of when cascading has to stop in general. I believe this issue deserves more investigation; for the purposes of this chapter, I'll adopt the pragmatic position that it should certainly stop if it reaches a relvar that's already been updated during execution of the same update request. However, I realize this simple rule is likely to be inadequate if certain cyclic constraints are in effect—for example, if there's a referential cycle, or in other words a cycle of foreign key constraints [2].

NLS

S#	SNAME	STATUS	CITY
S2	Jones	10	Paris
S3	Blake	30	Paris
S5	Adams	30	Athens

As I've defined them here, then, S is a base relvar and LS and NLS are views. *But it could have been the other way around.* That is, I could have made LS and NLS base relvars and S a view, like this:

```
VAR LS BASE RELATION
  { S# S# , SNAME NAME , STATUS INTEGER , CITY CHAR }
    KEY { S# } ;

VAR NLS BASE RELATION
  { S# S# , SNAME NAME , STATUS INTEGER , CITY CHAR }
    KEY { S# } ;

VAR S VIRTUAL ( LS D_UNION NLS )
    KEY { S# } ;
```

Note: **Tutorial D**'s D_UNION operator—"disjoint union"—is a version of the regular relational union operator that requires its operands to have no tuples in common. More important, note that in order to guarantee that the foregoing design is indeed logically equivalent to the previous one, the following constraints need to be stated and enforced:

```
CONSTRAINT CX3 IS_EMPTY ( LS WHERE CITY ≠ 'London' ) ;

CONSTRAINT CX4 IS_EMPTY ( NLS WHERE CITY = 'London' ) ;
```

In general, therefore, we see that which relvars are base ones and which virtual is arbitrary (at least from a formal point of view). In the case at hand, we could design the database in at least two different ways: two different ways, that is, that are logically distinct but information equivalent. (By *information equivalent* here, I mean, loosely, that the two designs represent the same information. See the next section for further details.) And *The Principle of Interchangeability* follows logically from such considerations:

- **Definition (*The Principle of Interchangeability* of base and virtual relvars):** There must be no arbitrary and unnecessary distinctions between base and virtual relvars; i.e., virtual relvars should "look and feel" just like base relvars so far as users are concerned.

And it follows immediately from this principle that we must be able to update views—because if we can't, then that fact in itself would constitute the clearest possible violation of the principle. Certainly the updatability of the database mustn't depend on the arbitrary choice as to which relvars we decide to make base ones and which relvars we decide to make views.

MORE ON INFORMATION EQUIVALENCE

Let *DBD1* and *DBD2* be logical database designs. In what sense might we say these two designs are information equivalent? Well:

- Let *db1* and *db2* be database values that conform to *DBD1* and *DBD2,* respectively.

- Let *M12* and *M21* be mappings that transform *db1* into *db2* and *db2* into *db1,* respectively.

Then the existence of those mappings *M12* and *M21* clearly implies that *db1* and *db2* are information equivalent, in the sense that for every query on *db1* there's a logically equivalent query on *db2* that yields the same result, and vice versa. *Note:* We can also say that (a) mappings *M12* and *M21* are *invertible;* (b) each is the *inverse* of the other; and (c) each is in fact a *bijection* (see reference [2] for a definition of this latter concept).

Now suppose the following are both true:

- For every possible database value *db1* conforming to *DBD1,* applying mapping *M12* to *db1* yields an information equivalent database value *db2* conforming to *DBD2*

- For every possible database value *db2* conforming to *DBD2,* applying mapping *M21* to *db2* yields an information equivalent database value *db1* conforming to *DBD1*

Then we can clearly extend the notion of information equivalence to say that designs *DBD1* and *DBD2* per se are information equivalent. And, of course, it's this extended notion that's the really important one. To be specific, when we say two databases are information equivalent, we're usually being a little sloppy; what we usually mean is that the corresponding *designs* are information equivalent.

Now let *DBD1* and *DBD2* be two information equivalent designs; let *DB1* and *DB2* be databases (meaning, specifically, database *variables*) that conform to *DBD1* and *DBD2,* respectively; and let the current values of *DB1* and *DB2* be *db1* and *db2,* respectively. By definition, those database values *db1* and *db2* are information equivalent. Now let *U1* be some update on *DB1* that replaces that value *db1* by some other value *db1'*. Then there must exist an update *U2* on *DB2* that transforms that value *db2* into some other value *db2',* such that *db1'* and *db2'* are information equivalent in turn—for if not, then *DBD1* and *DBD2* can't have been information equivalent in the first place. In other words, if two designs are information equivalent, they must be what we might call *isomorphic with respect to update.* In particular, therefore, if *DB1* consists solely of base relvars and *DB2* solely of views of those base relvars, then those views must be updatable.

By contrast, if *DBD1* and *DBD2* aren't information equivalent, then there'll be some updates on *DB1* that have no counterpart on *DB2* or the other way around. I'll give some examples of this state of affairs in Appendix A, also in the section "Summarization and Aggregation."

THE PRINCIPLE OF DATABASE RELATIVITY

Suppose we're given a database design in which all of the relvars mentioned are base ones, not views. Let's agree to call the set consisting of all of those base relvars "the real database." In general, however, the user interacts not with that real database but rather with what might be called an "expressible" database, consisting of some mixture of base relvars and views. Now, we can assume that none of the relvars in that expressible database can be derived from the rest, because such a relvar could be dropped without loss of information. From the user's point of view, therefore, those relvars are, by definition, all base relvars!—precisely because (to repeat) none of them is defined in terms of any of the others. It follows that if any of those relvars is in fact a view, it must still "look and feel" just like a base relvar to the user—which is, of course, what *The Principle of Interchangeability* is all about.

What's more, considerations similar to those articulated in the foregoing paragraph apply at the database level as well. That is to say, which database is considered the "real" one and which ones are considered merely "expressible" are arbitrary decisions too!—just so long as the choices are all information equivalent, of course. This interchangeability at the database level is sometimes referred to, a trifle grandly, as *The Principle of Database Relativity.*

MORE ON COMPENSATORY ACTIONS

Now I want to take a closer look at the example of London vs. non London suppliers. To repeat, we have three relvars:

```
VAR S ... KEY { S# } ;

VAR LS ... KEY { S# } ;

VAR NLS ... KEY { S# } ;
```

Now, some of these relvars are base relvars and some of them are views; however, *The Principle of Interchangeability* implies that the user shouldn't need to know, or care, which ones are which (it might even be that all three are base relvars or all three are views). It follows that, no matter which relvars are of which kind, the following constraints need to be understood by the user:

```
CONSTRAINT CX3 IS_EMPTY ( LS WHERE CITY ≠ 'London' ) ;

CONSTRAINT CX4 IS_EMPTY ( NLS WHERE CITY = 'London' ) ;

CONSTRAINT CX5 S = LS D_UNION NLS ;
```

Aside: Perhaps I should elaborate a little on constraint CX5. In general, a boolean expression of the form *X* = *Y* D_UNION *Z* won't just give FALSE if *Y* and *Z* are not disjoint; rather, it will raise a run time error. Run time errors during constraint checking are probably best avoided. In practice, therefore, it might be better to state the constraint in a slightly different form, thus:

```
CONSTRAINT CX5 DISJOINT {LS,NLS} AND S = LS UNION NLS ;
```

The expression DISJOINT {LS,NLS} returns TRUE if and only if LS and NLS are indeed disjoint at the time of evaluation. See Chapter 16 of the present book. *End of aside.*

Be that as it may, the significant point is that these three constraints need to be specified *in all cases*. Of course, we typically don't state such constraints in all cases in practice; in the example under discussion, we don't state them in the specific case in which S is a base relvar and LS and NLS are views, precisely because in that case the constraints are implied by the view definitions. In my opinion, however, this state of affairs derives from a conceptual mistake—a mistake to be found in all of today's SQL systems (and in **Tutorial D** as well, as a matter of fact). The mistake is this: The syntax of view definitions is such that the mapping between any given view and the relvar(s) in terms of which it's defined is explicitly stated as part of the view definition, and is thus explicitly visible to users of the view in question. As a consequence, users of the view in question certainly do know among other things that the view is indeed a view.

To repeat, the mistake is that view definitions explicitly reveal the mapping information. As a consequence, they certainly make it difficult to hide that information from the user, and (more important, perhaps) they make it difficult to hide from the user just which relvars are base ones and which ones are views—despite the fact that, conceptually speaking, hiding such information is precisely what needs to be done.[12] But here I'm trying to explain how systems ought to work, not how they actually do; so let me continue with my conceptual explanations.

Consider the following delete request once again:

---

[12] Ironically enough, the structure of the view, which the user does need to be aware of, *isn't* defined explicitly but is merely inferred from the mapping! (By *structure* here, I really mean the virtual relvar heading—i.e., the names of the attributes of the view and their corresponding attribute types.)

```
DELETE S WHERE S# = S#('S1') ;
```

Now, I've already explained what happens with this delete if S and LS are both base relvars: Assuming an appropriate compensatory action has been specified (from S to LS), it will cascade from base relvar S to base relvar LS. In accordance with *The Principle of Interchangeability,* therefore, exactly the same should be the case if S is still a base relvar but LS is a view. Of course, if LS is a view, the delete *will* cascade, precisely because LS *is* a view. So what I'm saying is that, in order to explain that cascade to the user without the user having to know which relvars are base relvars and which ones are views, *an appropriate compensatory action should be specified,* even though the cascade in question happens "automatically," as it were:

```
ON DELETE s FROM S : DELETE ( s WHERE CITY = 'London' ) FROM LS ;
```

Now consider this delete request:

```
DELETE LS WHERE S# = S#('S1') ;
```

Again, we've already seen what this delete involves if LS and S are both base relvars: Assuming an appropriate compensatory action has been specified (from LS to S this time), it will cascade from base relvar LS to base relvar S. In accordance with *The Principle of Interchangeability,* therefore, exactly the same should be the case if, again, S is a base relvar and LS is a view. Of course, if LS is a view, the delete will cascade "automatically" (though I should immediately add that we don't normally think of it as "cascading," as such, precisely because LS *is* a view; rather, we think of the delete on LS as "really" being a delete on S, and thus having the effect of implicitly deleting tuples from LS as a kind of side effect). However, what I'm trying to suggest here is that, in accordance with *The Principle of Interchangeability,* thinking of it as cascading is the logically correct way to understand what's going on. Again, therefore, an appropriate compensatory action really needs to be specified, in order to explain that cascade—even though, to repeat, the cascade does happen "automatically" if LS is a view:[13]

```
ON DELETE ls FROM LS : DELETE ls FROM S ;
```

Considerations precisely analogous to the foregoing apply if the roles are reversed (i.e., if LS is a base relvar and S is a view), or even if LS and S are both views of some other relvar(s). So the net of the argument is that regardless of which relvars if any are base ones and which relvars if any are views—and now bringing relvar NLS back into the picture—we wind up, or should wind up, with compensatory actions that look like this:

```
ON DELETE s FROM S : DELETE ( s WHERE CITY = 'London' ) FROM LS ,
                     DELETE ( s WHERE CITY ≠ 'London' ) FROM NLS ;

ON DELETE ls FROM LS : DELETE ls FROM S ;

ON DELETE nls FROM NLS : DELETE nls FROM S ;
```

INSERT Rules

So far I've concentrated on deletes because delete is, in a sense, the easy case. But what about inserts? Well, let me continue with the example of relvars S, LS, and NLS. Let me also remind you of the pertinent constraints, which (loosely speaking) are as follows:

---

[13] Note that if it's legal to specify compensatory actions for base relvars, it must be legal to specify them for views (*The Principle of Interchangeability* at work again). As a matter of fact, in the example, if a compensatory action could be specified from LS to S when LS was a base relvar but not when it was a view, then that very state of affairs would constitute a violation of *The Principle of Interchangeability.* In general, in fact (though not in the particular case at hand, as it happens), such a state of affairs would also mean that certain updates would succeed in the one case and fail in the other.

- Key constraints: {S#} is a key for each of S, LS, and NLS.
- CX3: Every tuple in LS has CITY value London.
- CX4: No tuple in NLS has CITY value London.
- CX5: S is the disjoint union of LS and NLS.

Then we have the following:

- Inserting tuple *t* into S, if it succeeds, must cause *t* to be inserted into LS as well if the CITY value in *t* is London and into NLS otherwise.[14] It will fail if it violates the key constraint on S.
- Inserting tuple *t* into LS, if it succeeds, must cause *t* to be inserted into S as well. It will fail if it violates constraint CX3 or the key constraint on LS or S.
- Inserting tuple *t* into NLS, if it succeeds, must cause *t* to be inserted into S as well. It will fail if it violates constraint CX4 or the key constraint on NLS or S.

Note that I haven't said anything here as to which relvars are base ones and which ones are views—the foregoing observations apply in all cases. So we need some more compensatory actions, perhaps as follows:

```
ON INSERT s INTO S : INSERT ( s WHERE CITY = 'London' ) INTO LS ,
                     INSERT ( s WHERE CITY ≠ 'London' ) INTO NLS ;

ON INSERT ls INTO LS : INSERT ls INTO S ;

ON INSERT nls INTO NLS : INSERT nls INTO S ;
```

Incidentally, I said above, among other things, that inserting a tuple into relvar LS will fail if it violates constraint CX3. If it does, and if relvar LS is in fact a view, then obviously we have an example of a view update failing—but note that it fails *because it violates* ***The Golden Rule***.[15] In other words, it's true that certain updates will fail on certain views; however, just as with base relvars, such failures occur *not* because the relvar (i.e., the view) is intrinsically nonupdatable, but rather because the updates in question cause some integrity constraint to be violated. (However, view updates should never violate *The Assignment Principle,* just so long as all pertinent compensatory actions are properly defined.)[16]

UPDATE Rules

Let *U* be an update on relvar *R* that has the effect of replacing *r1* (i.e., some subset of the tuples currently appearing in *R*) by *r2* (i.e., another set of tuples of the same type). Then the effect of update *U* can be achieved by first deleting *r1* from *R* and then inserting *r2* into *R,* and the following statement has exactly that effect:

```
INSERT r2 INTO ( R MINUS r1 ) ;
```

---

[14] I remind you that I shouldn't really be talking about inserting or deleting individual tuples like this—the relational INSERT and DELETE operators insert or delete entire sets of tuples (i.e., relations, not just single tuples) into or from their target relvar. As noted earlier in this chapter, however, it's convenient to overlook this point in informal contexts.

[15] A logically equivalent statement—and this is the way we've tended to look at the matter historically, though I'm trying to argue in this chapter that it's a logically inferior way—is this: It fails because otherwise it would cause LS to violate its own view defining expression.

[16] And here I must confess that I was a little confused myself on this particular issue when I wrote reference [1]. Reference [3], which was written later, is clearer, and more correct.

(The expression *R* MINUS *r1* has the effect of deleting *r1* from *R,* loosely speaking.) A conservative position regarding compensatory actions for UPDATE would thus be just to say they're a combination of those for DELETE and INSERT. Let's see how this position works out in practice. With reference to relvars S, LS, and NLS once again, consider the following examples (observe yet again, incidentally, that I don't specify which relvars are base ones and which ones are views):

- ```
  UPDATE S WHERE S# = S#('S1') : { STATUS := 10 } ;
  ```

  In this example, what happens is this, conceptually (and rather loosely) speaking:

  1. The existing tuple for supplier S1 is deleted from relvar S and (thanks to the cascade delete rule from S to LS) from relvar LS also.
  2. Another tuple for supplier S1, with STATUS value 10, is inserted into relvar S and (thanks to the cascade insert rule from S to LS) into relvar LS also.

- ```
  UPDATE S WHERE S# = S#('S1') : { CITY := 'Oslo' } ;
  ```

  In this example, conceptually what happens is this:

  1. The existing tuple for supplier S1 is deleted from relvar S and (thanks to the cascade delete rule from S to LS) from relvar LS also.
  2. Another tuple for supplier S1, with CITY value Oslo, is inserted into relvar S and (thanks to the cascade insert rule from S to NLS) into relvar NLS also. In other words, the tuple for supplier S1 has moved from one relvar to another!—now speaking *very* loosely, of course. Observe in particular that this effect occurs (and correctly occurs) even in the case in which S is a view and LS and NLS are base relvars: "The tuple moves" from one relvar to another (in this case, from one *base* relvar to another).

- ```
  UPDATE LS WHERE S# = S#('S1') : { CITY := 'Oslo' } ;
  ```

  Note that this update, if successful (but it won't be), would violate constraint CX3 on relvar LS. Conceptually, in fact, what happens is this:

  1. The existing tuple for supplier S1 is deleted from relvar LS and (thanks to the cascade delete rule from LS to S) from relvar S also.
  2. An attempt is made to insert another tuple for supplier S1, with CITY value Oslo, into relvar LS. This attempt fails, however, because it violates constraint CX3. So the update fails overall; the first step (viz., deleting the original tuple for supplier S1 from LS and S) is therefore undone, and the net effect is that the database remains unchanged.

So far, then, treating UPDATE operations as a DELETE followed by an INSERT seems to work just fine. But now consider suppliers and shipments (i.e., base relvars S and SP) once again. Earlier I defined the following delete compensatory action from S to SP:

```
ON DELETE s FROM S : DELETE ( SP MATCHING s ) FROM SP ;
```

However, I didn't define any corresponding insert compensatory action.[17] So now consider the following UPDATE operation on S:

---

[17] The reason I didn't is because (as should be obvious, if you think about it) there's no action that makes any sense, in this particular example.
```

```
UPDATE S WHERE S# = S#('S1') : { S# := S#('S6') } ;
```

Apparently, then, what happens is this:

1. The existing tuple for supplier S1 is deleted from relvar S. Thanks to the cascade delete rule from S to SP, the existing tuples for supplier S1 are deleted from relvar SP also.

2. A tuple for supplier S6 (identical except for the S# value to the tuple deleted from relvar S in the first step) is inserted into relvar S.

However, this second step has no effect on relvar SP at all, and so the net result is that some shipments are lost. This result is clearly unacceptable. On the face of it, then, it looks as if some kind of explicit UPDATE rule is needed in this example—perhaps as follows:

```
ON UPDATE s { S# := s# } IN S :
   UPDATE ( SP MATCHING s ) { S# := s# } IN SP ;
```

In what follows, therefore, I'll assume that UPDATE is treated as a delete followed by an insert unless an explicit UPDATE rule is in effect.

Relational Assignment

I've concentrated to this point on updates that are expressed by means of explicit INSERT and DELETE (and UPDATE) operations specifically. But what about updates that are expressed directly in terms of relational assignment? Do we need to specify a separate set of compensatory actions for such updates? The answer is: I don't think so. Reference [1] shows that a relational assignment of the form

```
R := exp ;
```

(where *R* is a relvar and *exp* is a relational expression of the same type as *R*) is logically equivalent to, and can therefore be replaced by, a relational assignment of the form—

```
R := ( r MINUS d ) UNION i ;
```

—where:

- The symbols *r, d,* and *i* denote the value of *R* before the assignment, the set of tuples to be deleted from *R,* and the set of tuples to be inserted into *R* after that deletion has been done, respectively.

- The set *d* is a subset of the set *r;* the sets *r* and *i* are disjoint; and the sets *d* and *i* are disjoint.

- The sets *d* and *i* are well defined and unique.

It follows that the original assignment can be expressed as follows (pseudocode once again):

```
INSERT i INTO ( R MINUS d ) ;
```

Or equivalently:

```
DELETE d FROM ( R UNION i ) ;
```

Or possibly even:

```
UPDATE R : { d := i } ;
```

Note, however, that this last "expansion" isn't meant to be genuine **Tutorial D** syntax—it's just meant to show that the original assignment can be thought of as an explicit UPDATE operation if desired (though I observe that the UPDATE operation in question includes a nested relational assignment, so we need to be careful over the possibility of infinite regress here). Overall, however, I think the foregoing discussion shows that other discussions in this chapter are directly applicable.

Rule Inference

One final point to close this section: I've suggested in the foregoing subsections (though I haven't said as much outright) that the various compensatory actions need to be specified explicitly. From the user's perspective, that's true. But in case you're thinking that specifying such actions explicitly looks like yet another administrative burden on the already overworked DBA, let me now point out that in many cases (not all) the system ought to be able to work out those actions for itself. In particular, I suggest that such will often, though perhaps not always, be the case in the situation that's our primary concern in this chapter: viz., when some of the relvars involved are views of others.

Consider the London vs. non London suppliers example once again. Suppose now, just to be specific, that S is a base relvar and LS and NLS are views of that base relvar (restriction views, to be precise). Then the system is, obviously, aware of the corresponding view definitions:

```
VAR LS VIRTUAL ( S WHERE CITY = 'London' ) ... ;

VAR NLS VIRTUAL ( S WHERE CITY ≠ 'London' ) ... ;
```

From these definitions, it seems to me that the system should be able to determine, "automatically," *all* of the compensatory actions that apply, in both directions (as it were). Those actions are as follows (and here I bring together all of the rules I've introduced earlier in this section for this example):

```
ON INSERT s INTO S : INSERT ( s WHERE CITY = 'London' ) INTO LS ,
                     INSERT ( s WHERE CITY ≠ 'London' ) INTO NLS ;

ON DELETE s FROM S : DELETE ( s WHERE CITY = 'London' ) FROM LS ,
                     DELETE ( s WHERE CITY ≠ 'London' ) FROM NLS ;

ON INSERT ls INTO LS : INSERT ls INTO S ;

ON DELETE ls FROM LS : DELETE ls FROM S ;

ON INSERT nls INTO NLS : INSERT nls INTO S ;

ON DELETE nls FROM NLS : DELETE nls FROM S ;
```

And so the task of stating them explicitly for the benefit of the user can and should be performed by the system, not the DBA.

WHAT ABOUT TRIGGERS?

At this point I'd like to digress for a moment to head off at the pass, as it were, another objection that might have occurred to you—viz., isn't this whole idea of compensatory actions just SQL-style triggers by another name? In other words, is there really anything new in what I've been saying?

Well, obviously there are some points of similarity between the two concepts; it might even be possible to use triggers to implement compensatory actions, if the system provides no direct support for this latter concept. But there are lots of differences too. Here are some of them:

- Triggers can and often do involve procedural code. (As a matter of fact, I checked several textbooks in this connection—books on both SQL products and the SQL standard—and found the universal assumption to be that, in practice, triggers generally do involve procedural code.) By contrast, the compensatory actions I propose in this chapter are all purely declarative in nature.

- With triggers in general, there's no notion that the system ought to be able to determine for itself what actions are to be performed (indeed, if it could, then triggers wouldn't be necessary!). With compensatory actions, by contrast, I've already said that in many cases the system should be able to work out for itself just what actions are required.
- Details of the operation, and possibly even the existence, of triggers in general are typically concealed from the user. As a consequence, therefore, it's likely from the user's perspective that triggers will lead to violations of *The Assignment Principle*. Again, contrast the situation with compensatory actions.
- In SQL in particular, triggers can and often do violate the set level nature of the relational model. As we saw earlier in this chapter, relational updates—which are set level, by definition—mustn't be treated as a sequence of individual tuple level updates (or row level updates, in SQL); in particular, integrity constraints mustn't be checked, and compensatory actions mustn't be performed, until the entire set level update has been done. Yet SQL supports what are called *row level triggers,* which certainly have the potential to violate these relational prescriptions.
- Finally (and again unlike triggers in general), the specific compensatory actions I propose are all in fact logically required, thanks to *The Principle of Interchangeability*.

MANY TO MANY JOINS

Of course, the London vs. non London suppliers example is very simple, and you might be a little skeptical as to whether the ideas illustrated by that example extend gracefully—or at all!—to more complicated situations. For that reason, I'd like to consider a couple of examples that are indeed a little more complicated. In this section, I'll discuss views that are defined as a many to many join of two base relvars. *Note:* The discussion that follows partly duplicates one in reference [1], but I think it's worth including here nevertheless (in fact, it corrects that earlier discussion in certain respects).

Again I'll begin by considering the situation in which all of the relvars involved are base ones. So let's assume again, then, that relvars S (suppliers) and P (parts) are both base relvars; for simplicity, however, let's agree to ignore all attributes except S# and CITY (for S) and P# and CITY (for P). Thus, the relvars might look like this (and I'll assume these particular sample values throughout the present section):

S

S#	CITY
S1	London
S2	Paris
S3	Paris
S4	London

P

P#	CITY
P1	London
P2	Paris
P4	London
P5	Paris
P6	London

Now let me now define another base relvar:

```
VAR SCP BASE RELATION { S# S# , CITY CHAR , P# P# }
    KEY { S# , P# } ;
```

Let's also assign it a value:

```
SCP := S JOIN P ;
```

The join here is a many to many join; the expression S JOIN P represents the join of S and P on {CITY}. Given the sample values shown above for relvars S and P, relvar SCP now looks like this:

SCP

S#	CITY	P#
S1	London	P1
S1	London	P4
S1	London	P6
S2	Paris	P2
S2	Paris	P5
S3	Paris	P2
S3	Paris	P5
S4	London	P1
S4	London	P4
S4	London	P6

Assume now that we want relvar SCP to have a value at all times that's the join on {CITY} of the current values of relvars S and P at the time in question. By definition, then, the relvars satisfy the following constraint:

```
CONSTRAINT CX6 SCP = S JOIN P ;
```

What's more, relvar SCP in particular satisfies the following additional constraint:

```
CONSTRAINT CX7 SCP = SCP { S# , CITY } JOIN SCP { P# , CITY } ;
```

In other words, and adopting an obvious shorthand notation for tuples, if tuples *<sx,c,px>* and *<sy,c,py>* appear in SCP, then tuples *<sx,c,py>* and *<sy,c,px>* appear in SCP also (which means, incidentally, that SCP is not in fourth normal form). Note that this constraint is indeed satisfied by the sample SCP value shown above.

Now let me jump ahead of myself for a moment. Clearly, I'm going to consider, later, the case in which SCP is a base relvar and S and P are views (actually projection views) of that base relvar:

```
VAR SCP BASE RELATION { S# S# , CITY CHAR , P# P# }
    KEY { S# , P# } ... ;

VAR S VIRTUAL ( SCP { S# , CITY } )
    KEY { S# } ... ;

VAR P VIRTUAL ( SCP { P# , CITY } )
    KEY { P# } ... ;
```

Now, constraints CX6 and CX7 must still apply to this revised design, for otherwise the designs wouldn't be equivalent; in particular, constraint CX7 must apply to the base relvar version of SCP. What's more, the following additional constraint clearly applies to the view versions of S and P:

```
CONSTRAINT CX8 S { CITY } = P { CITY } ;
```

This constraint says: No CITY value can appear in either S or P that doesn't appear in the other. And since it applies when S and P are views, it must also apply when they're base relvars—for otherwise, again, the designs wouldn't be equivalent. (In case you're wondering, it was because of this constraint that I dropped the tuples for supplier S5 and part P3 from the sample values I gave above.)[18]

Now let's get back to our original assumption (i.e., that S, P, and SCP are all base relvars), and let's consider some update operations. I'll use a kind of pseudocode syntax for simplicity. First of all, then, here's an example of an insert on relvar SCP:

```
INSERT <S9,London,P8> INTO SCP ;
```

If this insert were to do exactly what it says, no more and no less, then it would violate both constraint CX6 and constraint CX7. Can we avoid those violations by defining an appropriate set of compensatory actions? Well, the answer is clearly *yes*. The obvious actions are as follows:

```
ON INSERT scp INTO SCP :
   INSERT scp { S# , CITY } INTO S ,
   INSERT scp { P# , CITY } INTO P ;

ON INSERT s INTO S : INSERT ( s JOIN P ) INTO SCP ;

ON INSERT p INTO P : INSERT ( p JOIN S ) INTO SCP ;
```

Given all of these actions, the original insert now succeeds. To be specific, it has the following effect:

- It inserts the tuple <S9,London> into S.
- It inserts the tuple <P8,London> into P.
- It inserts the following six tuples into SCP:

```
<S9,London,P1>  <S9,London,P8>
<S9,London,P4>  <S1,London,P8>
<S9,London,P6>  <S4,London,P8>
```

Here now is a delete on relvar SCP:

```
DELETE <S1,London,P1> FROM SCP ;
```

Without an appropriate set of compensatory actions, this delete will also fail on a violation of constraints CX6 and CX7. Here are the actions we need:

```
ON DELETE scp FROM SCP :
   DELETE scp { S# , CITY } FROM S ,
   DELETE scp { P# , CITY } FROM P ;

ON DELETE s FROM S : DELETE ( s JOIN P ) FROM SCP ;

ON DELETE p FROM P : DELETE ( p JOIN S ) FROM SCP ;
```

Now the original delete succeeds. To be specific, it has the following effect:

- It deletes the tuple <S1,London> from S.
- It deletes the tuple <P1,London> from P.

---

[18] If S and P are base relvars and SCP is a view, however, then it might be the case that constraints CX6 and CX7 apply but constraint CX8 doesn't. I'll examine this possibility in Appendix A.

- It deletes the following four tuples from SCP:

```
<S1,London,P1>  <S4,London,P1>
<S1,London,P4>
<S1,London,P6>
```

So much for updates on relvar SCP; what about updates on relvars S and P? Consider first the following insert on base relvar S:

```
INSERT <S5,Athens> INTO S ;
```

This insert fails on a violation of constraint CX8. What's more, the idea of avoiding such failures by means of a compensatory action that inserts some appropriate tuple into base relvar P clearly isn't going to work, because there's no P# value available that would let us define such a tuple. In fact, the existence of constraint CX8 strongly suggests that relvars S and P will sometimes have to be updated simultaneously, by means of an explicit multiple assignment. For example:

```
INSERT <S5,Athens> INTO S ,
INSERT <P7,Athens> INTO P ;
```

This double insert succeeds and has the following effect:

- It inserts the tuple <S5,Athens> into S.
- It inserts the tuple <P7,Athens> into P.
- Thanks to the cascade insert rules from S and P to SCP, it inserts the tuple <S5,Athens,P7> into SCP.

Note: By contrast, the following insert on S succeeds even though it isn't a double insert—

```
INSERT <S6,Paris> INTO S ;
```

—because relvar P already contains at least one tuple with CITY value Paris. It has the following effect:

- It inserts the tuple <S6,Paris> into S.
- It inserts the tuples <S6,Paris,P2> and <S6,Paris,P5> into SCP.

Turning now to delete operations on relvars S and P, I think it's clear without going into a lot of detail that, given compensatory actions as defined above, a delete such as the following—

```
DELETE <S2,Paris> , <S3,Paris> FROM S ;
```

—succeeds and has the following effect:

- It deletes the tuples <S2,Paris> and <S3,Paris> from S.
- It deletes the tuples <S2,Paris,P2>, <S2,Paris,P5>, <S3,Paris,P2>, and <S3,Paris,P5> from SCP.
- It deletes the tuples <P2,Paris> and <P5,Paris> from P.

By contrast, the following delete fails on a violation of constraints CX6 and CX8:

```
DELETE <S2,Paris> FROM S ;
```

Now I remind you that I've been assuming so far that all three relvars (S, P, and SCP) are base relvars. However, as I hope you've come to expect, it makes essentially no difference—i.e., the very same compensatory actions are needed—if S and P are base relvars but SCP is a view:

```
VAR S BASE ... ;

VAR P BASE ... ;

VAR SCP VIRTUAL ( S JOIN P ) KEY { S# , P# } ;
```

Here then is the complete set of actions, listed now all in one place for ease of reference:

```
ON INSERT s INTO S : INSERT ( s JOIN P ) INTO SCP ;

ON INSERT p INTO P : INSERT ( p JOIN S ) INTO SCP ;

ON INSERT scp INTO SCP :
   INSERT scp { S# , CITY } INTO S ,
   INSERT scp { P# , CITY } INTO P ;

ON DELETE s FROM S : DELETE ( s JOIN P ) FROM SCP ;

ON DELETE p FROM P : DELETE ( p JOIN S ) FROM SCP ;

ON DELETE scp FROM SCP :
   DELETE scp { S# , CITY } FROM S ,
   DELETE scp { P# , CITY } FROM P ;
```

To sum up, then: As I hope the foregoing example suggests, updating a many to many join is reasonably straightforward; as a matter of fact, the rules for updating a many to many join are exactly the same as the rules for updating a one to one or one to many join, as reference [1] shows.[19] (It's true, though, that updates are more likely to fail in the many to many case. But the reason is *not,* to say it one more time, because such views are intrinsically nonupdatable—rather, it's just that updates on such views are more likely to lead to violations of **The Golden Rule**.)

Note finally that although the present section was supposed to be about updating many to many join views, I've actually shown how to update certain projection views as well. However, I should perhaps stress the point that, thanks to the existence of constraints like constraint CX8, sometimes it won't be possible to update individual projection views in isolation; sometimes it will be necessary to update two or more such views simultaneously, using multiple assignment—though I hasten to add that such a situation arises only when the very same is true if the relvars in question are in fact base relvars instead of views.

SUMMARIZATION AND AGGREGATION

The other "more complicated" example I want to discuss in this chapter involves summarization and aggregation. Once again I'll begin by considering the situation in which all of the relvars involved are base ones. So let's agree once again that relvars S, P, and SP are base relvars (and let's also revert to the original sample values as given in Fig. 1), and let me now define another base relvar:

```
VAR STQ BASE RELATION { S# S# , TQ QTY } KEY { S# } ;
```

Now let's assign it a value:

```
STQ := SUMMARIZE SP PER ( S { S# } ) : { TQ := SUM ( QTY ) } ;
```

---

[19] I don't mean to suggest that I've described those rules in full detail here, however—I haven't. See reference [1] for further specifics.

As this assignment suggests, relvar STQ is supposed to contain a tuple for each supplier, giving the pertinent supplier number and the sum of shipment quantities for that supplier, and no other tuples.[20] Given the sample values in Fig. 1, STQ now looks like this:

STQ

S#	TQ
S1	1300
S2	700
S3	200
S4	900
S5	0

If the foregoing interpretation of STQ is indeed the intended one, then we'll need a constraint that says as much:

```
CONSTRAINT CX9
   STQ = SUMMARIZE SP PER ( S { S# } ) : { TQ := SUM ( QTY ) } ;
```

Observe, incidentally, that constraint CX9, together with the explicitly stated key constraints for relvars S and STQ, implies that:

- {S#} in relvar STQ is a foreign key referencing relvar S.
- {S#} in relvar S is a foreign key referencing relvar STQ.[21]

Now consider the following update request:

```
DELETE STQ WHERE S# = S#('S1') ;
```

This request fails, of course, because it would cause constraint CX9 to be violated if it didn't. But we could define a suitable compensatory action that would allow it to succeed:

```
ON DELETE stq FROM STQ : DELETE ( S MATCHING stq ) FROM S ;
```

Of course, we'll also need some rules for relvars S and SP:

```
ON DELETE s FROM S :
   DELETE ( SP MATCHING s ) FROM SP ,
   DELETE ( STQ MATCHING s ) FROM STQ ;
```

---

[20] I'm assuming here, reasonably enough, that summing values of type QTY returns a result that's also of type QTY. *Note:* A proposal to replace **Tutorial D**'s SUMMARIZE by an extended version of EXTEND is under active consideration at the time of writing (see reference [6]). For present purposes, however, I'm assuming, obviously enough, that SUMMARIZE is supported.

[21] Alternatively, instead of saying that each of S and STQ has a foreign key referencing the other, we might say, following reference [5], that there's a certain *equality dependency* (EQD) between the two. (In fact, of the various constraints already discussed in this chapter, all except CX1, CX3, and CX4 are EQDs.)

```
ON DELETE sp FROM SP :
   DELETE ( STQ MATCHING sp ) FROM STQ ,
   INSERT ( SUMMARIZE SP PER ( ( S MATCHING sp ) { S# } ) :
                            { TQ := SUM ( QTY ) } ) INTO STQ ;
```

Clearly, these three delete rules merit further discussion. Let me refer to them, just for the moment, as the STQ rule, the S rule, and the SP rule, respectively. Then:

- The S rule says two things. First, it says that deletes on S cascade to SP; this rule is basically just the conventional cascade delete rule for the foreign key from SP to S. *Note:* It follows that the STQ rule, which says that deletes on STQ cascade to S, indirectly causes deletes on STQ to cascade to SP as well, and so there's no need to define an explicit cascade delete rule from STQ to SP (though presumably it wouldn't be wrong to do so).

- Second, the S rule also says that deletes on S cascade to STQ. This rule is basically a conventional cascade delete rule for the foreign key from STQ to S.

- The STQ rule, which as already noted says that deletes on STQ cascade to S, is also basically a conventional cascade delete rule (this time for the foreign key from S to STQ).

- But, of course, it's the SP rule that's the interesting one. Note in particular that it's the first example we've seen that doesn't just cascade a delete to a delete or an insert to an insert.[22] Let me explain it on the assumption that the delete on SP is deleting just one tuple (the extension to more than one is essentially straightforward). Basically, then, what the rule says is this: If the tuple deleted from SP is *t,* then (a) the existing tuple for the supplier mentioned in *t* must be deleted from STQ, and (b) the remaining SP tuples (if any) for that supplier must be resummarized and the resulting (single tuple) relation inserted into STQ.

  Let me illustrate this last point. Suppose we delete the tuple for supplier S1 and part P1 from relvar SP:

  ```
  DELETE SP WHERE S# = S#('S1') AND P# = P#('P1') ;
  ```

Then *sp,* the relation being deleted from SP, contains just the SP tuple for supplier S1 and part P1, and the expression S MATCHING *sp* evaluates to a relation containing just the S tuple for supplier S1. The system therefore (a) deletes the existing tuple for supplier S1 from STQ and then (b) inserts the relation resulting from evaluation of the following expression into STQ—

```
SUMMARIZE s1p BY { S# } : { TQ := SUM ( QTY ) }
```

—where *s1p* denotes the restriction of SP to just the tuples for supplier S1. The net effect, with our usual sample values, is to replace the tuple for supplier S1 previously existing in relvar STQ—viz., the tuple <S1,1300>—by the tuple <S1,1000>.

So much for deletes; what about inserts? Without going into a lot of detail, I think it should be clear that:

- Inserting a tuple into S (necessarily for a new supplier) will require a corresponding tuple, with total quantity zero, to be inserted into STQ. *Note:* I'm relying here on the fact that the sum of an empty set is zero, not (as SQL would have it) "null."

- Inserting a tuple into SP (necessarily for a supplier for whom a tuple already exists in STQ) will require the corresponding sum to be recomputed and the corresponding tuple in STQ to be replaced accordingly.

---

[22] In fact, it might be possible to define it in terms of an explicit UPDATE instead of a combination of DELETE and INSERT.

- Inserting a tuple into STQ has no obvious compensatory action; such inserts will thus probably fail on a violation of **The Golden Rule** (most likely on a violation of constraint CX9). *Note:* The reason there's no compensatory action in this case is, of course, that the database consisting of relvars S and SP and the database consisting of just relvar STQ aren't information equivalent: The latter can be derived from the former, but the former can't be derived from the latter. The example thus violates *The Principle of Database Relativity,* and it's only to be expected that there'll be updates on relvar STQ that have no counterpart on relvars S and SP.

  Overall, therefore, the insert compensatory actions in this example look like this:

```
ON INSERT s INTO S :
   INSERT ( EXTEND s { S# } : { TQ := QTY ( 0 ) } ) INTO STQ ;

ON INSERT sp INTO SP :
   DELETE ( STQ MATCHING sp ) FROM STQ ,
   INSERT ( SUMMARIZE SP PER ( ( S MATCHING sp ) { S# } ) :
                             { TQ := SUM ( QTY ) } ) INTO STQ ;
```

To sum up so far, then (and I remind you that I'm still talking about base relvars only—no views yet): If the foregoing compensatory actions aren't specified, many updates on relvars S, SP, and STQ will fail (though perhaps I should also remind you that we might be able to use multiple assignment to ensure that certain updates succeed that would fail otherwise—i.e., if we tried to perform them one individual assignment at a time). But if appropriate compensatory actions are specified, then many more updates can succeed.

Well, by now I hope it's clear that defining STQ as a view instead of as a base relvar doesn't really change the picture at all. Here first is that view definition:

```
VAR STQ VIRTUAL
  ( SUMMARIZE SP PER ( S { S# } ) : { TQ := SUM ( QTY ) } )
   KEY { S# } ;
```

Now, updates on S and SP *will* cause updates to be made on STQ, precisely because STQ is now a view, and so the following compensatory actions definitely apply:

```
ON INSERT s INTO S :
   INSERT ( EXTEND s { S# } : { TQ := QTY ( 0 ) } ) INTO STQ ;

ON DELETE s FROM S : DELETE ( SP MATCHING s ) FROM SP ,
                     DELETE ( STQ MATCHING s ) FROM STQ ;

ON INSERT sp INTO SP :
   DELETE ( STQ MATCHING sp ) FROM STQ ,
   INSERT ( SUMMARIZE SP PER ( ( S MATCHING sp ) { S# } ) :
                             { TQ := SUM ( QTY ) } ) INTO STQ ;

ON DELETE sp FROM SP :
   DELETE ( STQ MATCHING sp ) FROM STQ ,
   INSERT ( SUMMARIZE SP PER ( ( S MATCHING sp ) { S# } ) :
                             { TQ := SUM ( QTY ) } ) INTO STQ ;
```

However, the system is clearly capable of determining these compensatory actions for itself, since (even in today's SQL products) it applies them "automatically." But what about other compensatory actions? To be specific, what about compensatory actions in connection with updates on view STQ? Here I see the situation as being exactly the same as it was when STQ was a base relvar:

- The DBA (or some suitably skilled user) can define the following delete rule explicitly, in which case deletes, at least, can be performed on view STQ:

  ```
  ON DELETE stq FROM STQ : DELETE ( S MATCHING stq ) FROM S ;
  ```

  If no such rule is defined, then deletes on STQ won't be supported. (I don't know whether it would be possible for the system to determine such a rule for itself. Doing so doesn't look all that difficult to me, but I'm not an implementer, and I'm probably overlooking something important.)

- As noted previously, inserting a tuple into STQ has no obvious compensatory action (though this isn't to say that the DBA or some suitably skilled user couldn't define one). Thus, if no insert rule is defined, inserts on STQ will fail on a violation of **The Golden Rule**.

OTHER RELATIONAL OPERATIONS

I've now discussed the updating of views defined in terms of restriction (the London vs. non London suppliers examples), many to many join (the SCP examples), projection (the SCP examples again), and summarization (the STQ example). And I've claimed that most if not all of the appropriate compensatory actions can be determined by the system itself, "automatically," from the pertinent view definition(s). More generally, in fact, I've shown—or tried to show, at any rate—in one or both of references [1] and [3] how the system can determine for itself the appropriate compensatory actions for views involving any of the following relational operations:

- restriction
- projection
- union (disjoint or otherwise)
- intersection
- difference
- join (one to one, one to many, or many to many)
- cartesian product
- extension

Observe in particular that several of these operations are such that views defined in terms of them are usually regarded as nonupdatable—but I've tried to explain why I reject that position.

CONCLUDING REMARKS

I have a small piece of unfinished business to attend to. I suggested earlier, in the section "Compensatory Actions," that if the suppliers-and-parts database were to contain both relvar S ("suppliers") and relvar LS ("London suppliers"), then the database wouldn't be very well designed for at least the following two reasons:

- First, there isn't much point in retaining the CITY attribute in relvar LS, since its value is London in every tuple.

- Second, the design is redundant, since all of the information represented by relvar LS is already represented in relvar S anyway.

The first of these objections is probably valid; I retained the CITY attribute in relvar S in my examples purely to make those examples and accompanying discussions easier to follow, but I fully accept that we'd probably want to project that attribute away in practice (in which case the rules for updating projections would come into play, of course). The second objection, however, is I think less valid. It's true that the design involves some redundancy; but redundancy in logical design is harmless, just so long as it's *controlled.* To quote reference [2]:

> Redundancy is controlled if it does exist (and the user is aware of it), but the task of "propagating updates" to ensure that it never leads to any inconsistencies is managed by the DBMS, not the user. Uncontrolled redundancy can be a problem, but controlled redundancy shouldn't be. As a general rule, databases shouldn't include any uncontrolled redundancy.

The whole point—or a large part of the point, at any rate—of the notion of compensatory updates in general is to ensure that redundancy is indeed controlled and doesn't lead to inconsistencies (which are just integrity constraint violations by another name, of course).

Let me try to summarize what I've covered in this chapter. The fundamental point, as I see it, is that *views are no more intrinsically nonupdatable than base relvars are*—or, to put it equally correctly but a little more positively, views are no less intrinsically updatable than base relvars are. In my opinion, the key to understanding this whole issue—the key, that is, to determining how updates should work on any given view *V*—is to consider what would happen if that view *V* were defined as a base relvar instead, living alongside (as it were) the base relvars in terms of which it's defined. Thinking about the issue in this way shows clearly that (a) updates on views, just like updates on base relvars, will fail if they violate **The Golden Rule** but will succeed otherwise; (b) updates on views, just like updates on base relvars, will fail if appropriate compensatory actions aren't in effect but will succeed otherwise. And for views (as opposed to base relvars) suitable compensatory actions can often, though not always, be determined "automatically" by the system.

One last point: I know from experience that even when they're presented with examples like the ones discussed in this chapter, many people continue to doubt whether view updating in its full generality will ever be possible. Well, I certainly make no claim that the treatment in this chapter has been exhaustive; there are numerous loose ends, and the devil is always in the details. But I remain optimistic; I don't believe there are any showstoppers, and at the very least I think the ideas described herein deserve further, and careful, investigation.

ACKNOWLEDGMENTS

I'd like to thank David McGoveran for helpful comments on an earlier draft of this chapter and much technical discussion. In fact, I'd like to acknowledge David's major contributions in this entire area. In particular, it was David who first got me to think about the issue in the way I've tried to present it in this chapter, in which I consider what would happen if the view in question were defined as a base relvar instead, living alongside the base relvar(s) in terms of which it's defined. David's own view updating proposals are described in detail in reference [9].

REFERENCES AND BIBLIOGRAPHY

1. C. J. Date: "View Updating," in reference [7].

2. C. J. Date: *The Relational Database Dictionary, Extended Edition.* Berkeley, Calif.: Apress (2008).

3. C. J. Date: "The Logic of View Updating," in *Logic and Databases: The Roots of Relational Theory.* Victoria, B.C.: Trafford Publishing (2007). See *www.trafford.com/07-0690.*

4. C. J. Date: *SQL and Relational Theory: How to Write Accurate SQL Code.* Sebastopol, Calif.: O'Reilly Media, Inc. (2009).

5. C. J. Date: "Inclusion Dependencies and Foreign Keys" (Chapter 13 of the present book).

6. C. J. Date: "Image Relations" (Chapter 14 of the present book).

7. C. J. Date and Hugh Darwen: *Databases, Types, and the Relational Model: The Third Manifesto* (3rd edition). Boston,

Mass.: Addison-Wesley (2006).

8. C. J. Date and Hugh Darwen: "Multiple Assignment," in C. J. Date: *Date on Database: Writings 2000-2006.* Berkeley, Calif.: Apress (2006).

9. U.S. Patent and Trademark Office: "Accessing and Updating Views and Relations in a Relational Database." U.S. Patent No. 7,263,512 (August 28th, 2007).

APPENDIX A: MORE ON MANY TO MANY JOINS

In a footnote in the section "Many to Many Joins," I mentioned the fact that if relvars S and P are base relvars and relvar SCP is a view defined as follows—

```
VAR SCP VIRTUAL ( S JOIN P ) KEY { S# , P# } ;
```

—then constraints CX6 and CX7 would still apply but constraint CX8 might not. Let me remind you of the specifics of that example:

- For simplicity, we're ignoring all attributes except S# and CITY (for S) and P# and CITY (for P).
- Sample values are as follows:

S

S#	CITY
S1	London
S2	Paris
S3	Paris
S4	London

P

P#	CITY
P1	London
P2	Paris
P4	London
P5	Paris
P6	London

SCP

S#	CITY	P#
S1	London	P1
S1	London	P4
S1	London	P6
S2	Paris	P2
S2	Paris	P5
S3	Paris	P2
S3	Paris	P5
S4	London	P1
S4	London	P4
S4	London	P6

- Constraints CX6 and CX7 are as follows:

```
CONSTRAINT CX6 SCP = S JOIN P ;

CONSTRAINT CX7 SCP = SCP { S# , CITY } JOIN SCP { P# , CITY } ;
```

  These two constraints obviously do still apply if S and P are base relvars and SCP is a view.

- Constraint CX8 is as follows:

```
CONSTRAINT CX8 S { CITY } = P { CITY } ;
```

  Clearly, this constraint won't be satisfied if we allow tuples to appear in either S or P that have no match in the other—for example, if we allow the following insert to succeed:

```
INSERT <S5,Athens> INTO S ;
```

  If we do allow this insert to succeed, however, it won't have any effect on view SCP, because relvar P has no tuples with CITY value Athens. Of course, allowing the insert to succeed means that constraint CX8 isn't being enforced; indeed, it obviously can't even be stated.

As a matter of fact, the state of affairs illustrated by this example is typical of what people usually assume as soon as the issue of updating join views is raised: They take it for granted that constraints like constraint CX8 don't apply, and then they point out certain anomalies that arise from this assumption if certain view updates are permitted. Here's a very simple example to illustrate the point. Suppose relvars S, P, and SCP contain just one tuple each, as follows:

S

S#	CITY
S1	London

P

P#	CITY
P1	London

SCP

S#	CITY	P#
S1	London	P1

Now consider the following update on view SCP:

```
DELETE <S1,London,P1> FROM SCP ;
```

The claim now is that the effect of this delete can be achieved by deleting the tuple for supplier S1 from base relvar S, or by deleting the tuple for part P1 from base relvar P, or by deleting both. The further claim is that there's no good reason for choosing any particular one of these options over the others; the original view update is thus inherently ambiguous, and so it should be rejected.

Well, observe now that if we allow, say, the tuple to be deleted from S and not P, then:

- We're rejecting the idea—discussed in detail in the body of the chapter—that the design under discussion, with S and P as base relvars and SCP a join view, should be information equivalent to the design with SCP as a base relvar and S and P projection views. (In the example, information equivalence is clearly lost. As a simple example, the query "How many cities are there altogether?" gives different answers, after the update, depending on which of relvars S and P we apply it to. Such is not the case, and could not be the case, if information equivalence is preserved.)
- We're also rejecting *The Principle of Interchangeability:* Base relvars and views now have different properties, and users now need to know which are which (in general).
- We're therefore also rejecting *The Principle of Database Relativity.*

Now, I've discussed such matters before in reference [3], but I think it's worth repeating the essence of that discussion here. First I need to introduce a couple of terms. I'll say the mapping from base relvars S and P to view SCP is *total* if every tuple in either S or P contributes to a tuple in SCP; otherwise I'll say the mapping is *partial*. In the body of the chapter, the mapping from S and P to SCP was total (and the two designs were information equivalent). By contrast, in the example above (in which relvar S is allowed to contain the tuple <S5,Athens> without there being a corresponding tuple in relvar P), the mapping is partial; to be specific, that tuple <S5,Athens> contributes nothing to SCP.

Now consider the following delete example again:

```
DELETE <S1,London,P1> FROM SCP ;
```

The rule I gave in the body of the chapter for deleting through a join would cause the S tuple for S1 *and* the P tuple for P1 both to be deleted. Such behavior is clearly required if the mapping from S and P to SCP is total; but in the case at hand, of course, it isn't—that's the whole point—and hence (as I've already said) the desired effect could be achieved by deleting the S1 tuple from S or just the P1 tuple from P. Nevertheless, I now want to argue that we should still delete from both, for at least the following reasons:

- Deleting from both has the advantage of symmetry. *Note:* Reference [3] has more to say regarding the virtues of symmetry, but I'll omit those additional arguments here.
- In particular, symmetry allows us to avoid an arbitrary choice (regarding which of S and P to delete from). Note that one consequence of *not* appealing to symmetry could be that the expressions S JOIN P and P JOIN S might have different semantics—surely an undesirable state of affairs.
- Deleting from both also means we have one universal rule for deleting through join, instead of having to deal with possibly many different rules for possibly many different cases. *Note:* I don't mean to suggest that the brief characterization "delete from both" captures the essence of that universal rule—deleting from both just happens to be the degenerate form of the rule that applies in the many to many case. See reference [1] for further discussion.
- It's intuitively obvious that inserting a tuple into SCP must cause a tuple to be inserted, in general, into both S and P, even if the mapping isn't total (for otherwise the new tuple wouldn't appear in the join, as required).[23] Thus, deleting from both in the case under discussion means not only that the delete rule is symmetric in itself, but also that it's symmetric with respect to the insert rule.
- Finally, we can of course avoid deleting from both, if we want to, by not deleting from SCP in the first place—in particular, by not giving the user delete rights over that view.

I want to offer one additional argument. In the example under discussion, it would indeed be safe for the system to delete just the S1 tuple from S or just the P1 tuple from P, as we've seen. However, it would be safe *only because the mapping is partial;* it would definitely be unsafe, and in fact incorrect, otherwise. So the question is: Is the system aware of this fact—the fact, that is, that the mapping in question is partial?[24] More generally, does the system know which mappings are partial and which total?

Well, if constraint CX8 had been stated (and of course enforced), then it seems to me the system would, or at least could, know that the mapping is total. In the case at hand, however, that constraint *isn't* stated—that's the whole point. But not stating the constraint doesn't mean the mapping must be partial!—users might be following some discipline that amounts to enforcing the constraint for themselves, independently of the system. It seems to me, therefore, that the system might sometimes know that a given mapping is total, but I don't think it could ever know for sure that a given mapping is partial. So I could be wrong, but it seems to me that, in general, the answer to the question ("Does the system know which mappings are partial and which total?") must be *no.*

If the analysis of the previous paragraph is correct, then the next question is: Which assumption is safer?—assume mappings are always partial, or assume they're always total? Let's examine this question.

Suppose the system assumes mappings are always partial. For a given update request, then, the system will have to choose the most appropriate way to respond to that request. In the case at hand, for example, the system will have to choose among the following options:

1. Reject the delete entirely, on the grounds that there isn't enough information to choose any other option.

---

[23] I'm assuming here that an attempt to insert a tuple that already exists has no effect.

[24] I remind you that, in the example under discussion, all the system knows is that SCP is the join of S and P. In the case at hand, therefore, the question becomes: Is the system able to determine unequivocally, from this knowledge alone, that the mapping is partial? To jump ahead of myself for a moment, it seems obvious to me that the answer to this question must be *no.*

2. Delete from just S or just P.

3. Delete from both S and P.

Option 1 seems unsatisfactory, because the update will fail when it could have succeeded (and indeed *should* have succeeded, if the mapping happened to be total). Option 2 raises the question of how the system is to decide which relvar to delete from; not only does there seem to be no good way to answer this question, but (as noted earlier) it raises the unpleasant possibility that the expressions S JOIN P and P JOIN S might have different semantics. What's more, the update will fail in this case (on a **Golden Rule** violation) if the mapping does happen to be total, when again it should have succeeded. Overall, therefore, I think the system should go for Option 3.

But, of course, Option 3 is the only sensible option if the mapping is total (in that case, indeed, it's the only one that's logically correct). I therefore conclude that it's better for the system to adopt the assumption that mappings are always total—with the implication that the view updating rules I gave in references [1] and [3] should be followed in all cases. In other words, I think we should abide by a universal set of rules that do at least always work and do guarantee that mappings are total when they're supposed to be. If those rules do sometimes give rise to consequences that are considered unpalatable for some reason, then there are always certain pragmatic fixes, such as using the system's security subsystem to prohibit certain updates, that can be adopted to avoid those consequences.

Note: Please don't misunderstand me here. I'm not saying we *must* employ those pragmatic fixes in order for the system to work properly. A system that relies for its correct operation on the user, or the DBA, "doing the right thing"—e.g., using the security subsystem appropriately—is obviously not acceptable. So we must always at least permit view updates, even when the mappings aren't total, and we must have a set of rules that work even in that case. That's why I advocate the position I do.

APPENDIX B: AN IMPORTANT LOGICAL DIFFERENCE

Let relational expressions *rx* and *ry* be logically equivalent; i.e., let them be such that, at any given time, the relation denoted by *rx* and the relation denoted by *ry* are one and the same (and I'll continue to use the term *logical equivalence* in this sense throughout the discussion that follows). Let's agree to denote this equivalence thus: $rx \equiv ry$. As is well known, then, any appearance of either *rx* or *ry* in a read-only context—in particular, on the right side of an assignment—can be replaced by an appearance of the other with logical impunity. As I pointed out in reference [1], however, the same is not true, in general, if either of those expressions appears in an update context—in particular, on the left side of an assignment, where it serves as a *pseudovariable reference.*[25] Consider the following example. Suppose for simplicity that (a) relvar S has just one attribute, S#; (b) relvar SP has just two attributes, S# and P#; and (c) those relvars have current values as follows:

---

[25] I assume for the sake of the discussion that pseudovariable references of this kind are supported in **Tutorial D,** though in fact (as noted in Chapter 11) they currently aren't.

S

S#
S1
S2
S5

SP

S#	P#
S1	P1
S1	P2
S1	P3
S2	P2

Now let SSP be a view, defined as the join of S and SP (a one to many join, incidentally):

```
VAR SSP VIRTUAL ( S JOIN SP ) KEY { S# , P# } ;
```

Before we go any further, observe that (to use the terminology of Appendix A) the mapping from relvars S and SP to view SSP is partial, not total, because it's possible for tuples in S to have no counterpart in SSP. Observe further that it follows as a consequence of this first point that the database consisting of S and SP and the database consisting of just SSP aren't information equivalent.

Now consider the effect of the following DELETE on view SSP:

```
DELETE <S2,P2> FROM SSP ;
```

Reference [1] defines the effect of this DELETE by means of the following conceptual algorithm (it also gives what I believe are good arguments for accepting this definition):

```
Temp := SSP ;   /* Temp is a temporary variable */

DELETE <S2,P2> FROM Temp ;   /* deletes just the specified tuple */

SP := ( SP MINUS SSP { S# , P# } ) UNION Temp { S# , P# } ,
S  := ( S MINUS SSP { S# } ) UNION Temp { S# } ;
```

Alternatively, using the terminology and ideas introduced in the present chapter, we could say the applicable compensatory action is as follows:

```
ON DELETE ssp FROM SSP :
   DELETE ssp FROM SP ,
   DELETE ( ( S MATCHING SP ) NOT MATCHING ( SP MINUS ssp ) )
                                                       FROM S ;
```

Of course, we must be sure *The Assignment Principle* (for relvar SSP in particular) and **The Golden Rule** (for relvars S and SP in particular) aren't violated. Assuming they aren't, however (which is certainly the case in the example), we can see that the foregoing definition amounts to saying "Delete tuple(s) from SP as requested, and delete tuple(s) from S that previously had matching tuples in SP but now no longer do so." Given the sample values shown previously, the result looks like this:[26]

[26] By contrast, if the original DELETE specified the tuple <S1,P2> instead of <S2,P2>, then (a) if the compensatory action—i.e., the cascade delete rule—ON DELETE *s* FROM S: DELETE (SP MATCHING *s*) FROM SP is in effect, the effect would be to delete <S1> from S and all tuples except <S2,P2> from SP; otherwise (b) the DELETE would fail.

S

S#
S1
S5

SP

S#	P#
S1	P1
S1	P2
S1	P3

In other words, the tuple <S2,P2> has been deleted from relvar SP, *and the tuple <S2> has also been deleted from relvar S.* So the obvious question is: Why *should* this latter tuple be deleted from relvar S? Given that, thanks to the foreign key constraint from SP to S, the expression S JOIN SP is logically equivalent to just SP, why is relvar S updated at all? Why is updating S JOIN SP not equivalent to updating just SP?

Now, I must confess here that—along with many other people, I'm sure—I've been much vexed by such questions over the years. Indeed, I'm on record, in reference [1] and elsewhere, as making a series of rather dogmatic assertions about such matters, all of them along the following lines: *The semantics of view updating should not depend on the particular syntactic form in which the view definition in question happens to be stated.* And it was only comparatively recently that I began to wonder whether I might not be mistaken in this matter. (To quote Enrico Bombieri: "When things get too complicated, it sometimes make sense to stop and wonder: Have I asked the right question?") Let me elaborate.

Assume again that relational expressions *rx* and *ry* are logically equivalent in the sense previously explained (i.e., $rx \equiv ry$), and let them be the defining expressions for views *VX* and *VY*, respectively:

```
VAR VX VIRTUAL ( rx ) ... ;

VAR VY VIRTUAL ( ry ) ... ;
```

Because $rx \equiv ry$, we can certainly say the following:

- The relation that's the value of *VX* at any given time *t* and the relation that's the value of *VY* at that same time *t* are identical.

- Therefore, the result of evaluating any given query *Q* on *VX* at time *t* and the result of evaluating that same query *Q* on *VY* at that same time *t* will always be identical.

- Moreover, for any given update *UX* on *VX,* there will exist an update *UY* on *VY* such that the effect on *VX* of executing *UX* at time *t* and the effect on *VY* of executing *UY* at that same time *t* will also always be identical.

To repeat, the fact that $rx \equiv ry$ does mean all of the above. But that's *all* it means! As far as I can see, there's no logical reason why it should mean anything more. In particular, there's no logical reason why it should mean that executing some given update *U* on *VX* at time *t* and executing that same update *U* on *VY* at that same time *t* will necessarily have the same effect, either on those views themselves or on the relvars in terms of which those views are defined (i.e., on the relvars mentioned in *rx* and *ry,* respectively). On the contrary, here are some cogent reasons why it shouldn't:

- First of all, there's a logical difference between an expression and a pseudovariable reference—an expression denotes a value, a pseudovariable reference does not. In other words, an expression and a pseudovariable reference have different semantics, even if they're syntactically identical.

- By definition, if two databases aren't information equivalent, there'll be updates on one that have no counterpart on the other. (In the example that introduces this appendix, the database consisting of S and SP and the database consisting of SSP aren't information equivalent; given the specified sample values, then, INSERT <S3> INTO S is an example of an update on the former that has no counterpart on the latter.)

- As we've seen, either of *rx* and *ry* might quite plausibly mention a relvar that's not mentioned in the other. Such was the case—taking *rx* to be SP and *ry* to be S JOIN SP—in the introductory example. As a consequence, it seems on the face of it quite reasonable that updates via the one and updates via the other can have different effects—as indeed they do, in the example, in the case of DELETE <S2,P2> FROM SP vs. DELETE <S2,P2> FROM SSP.

In fact, following on from this last point, updates can have different effects even when neither *rx* nor *ry* mentions a relvar that the other doesn't. By way of example, suppose again that relvar S has just one attribute, S#, and relvar SP has just two attributes, S# and P#. Suppose also that relvar P has just one attribute, P#. Finally, suppose views *VX* and *VY* are defined as follows:[27]

```
VAR VX VIRTUAL ( ( S JOIN SP ) JOIN P ) ... ;

VAR VY VIRTUAL ( ( S JOIN P ) JOIN SP ) ... ;
```

Let's think about this example for a moment. First of all, notice that it differs in kind from the example involving just S and SP, inasmuch as the logical equivalence of the expressions ((S JOIN SP) JOIN P) and ((S JOIN P) JOIN SP) is *absolute*—it doesn't rely on the existence of certain constraints interrelating the relvars. (By contrast, the logical equivalence of the expressions SP and S JOIN SP in the earlier example relied on the fact that there was a foreign key constraint from SP to S.)

Next, however, this example does resemble that earlier example in that the mappings are again partial. That is, each of the three relvars S, SP, and P might contain a tuple with no counterpart in *VX* or no counterpart in *VY* or both. (Note that I don't necessarily assume there's a foreign key constraint from SP to either S or P.) It follows, incidentally, that neither *VX* nor *VY* is information equivalent to the combination of S, SP, and P.

Now let relvars S, SP, and P have values as follows—

S

S#
S1
S2
S5

SP

S#	P#
S1	P1
S1	P2
S2	P1
S2	P2

P

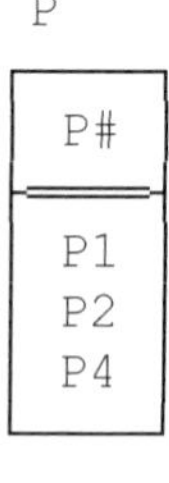

P#
P1
P2
P4

—and consider the effect of deleting the tuple <S1,P1> from each of the two views:

- Deleting <S1,P1> from *VX* causes that same tuple <S1,P1> to be deleted from SP (and nothing more).

- Deleting <S1,P1> from *VY* causes <S1> to be deleted from S, <P1> to be deleted from P, and all tuples except <S2,P2> to be deleted from SP. (I'm assuming here that compensatory actions of the form ON DELETE *s* FROM S: DELETE (SP MATCHING *s*) FROM SP and ON DELETE *p* FROM P: DELETE

[27] Thanks to Hugh Darwen for this example.

(SP MATCHING *p*) FROM SP have both been specified.)

So if you still want to claim, despite the foregoing, that the fact that $rx \equiv ry$ should mean that updating through *rx* and updating through *ry*—apologies for the loose manner of speaking here—always have the same effect, then I think you need to justify your position. In fact, I suspect such claims might be another manifestation of a problem I've had occasion to mention elsewhere (e.g., in Chapter 30 of the present book): viz., a failure to distinguish properly between relation values (relations) and relation variables (relvars).

For clarity, then, from this point forward I'll say that expressions *rx* and *ry* are *read equivalent* if they can safely be interchanged in read-only contexts, and *update equivalent* if they can safely be interchanged in an update context. Of course, if *rx* and *ry* are update equivalent, they're certainly read equivalent, but the converse is not true. *Note:* Read equivalence is essentially what I previously called *logical* equivalence; update equivalence is essentially a very strong form of what I previously called *information* equivalence.

Now I'd like to consider another example, in order to make another point. The example in question is essentially the one I first used in reference [1] to highlight the phenomenon under consideration (i.e., the fact that even if *rx* and *ry* are read equivalent, it doesn't follow that they're update equivalent). Let relvars *A* and *B* have just one attribute each, of type integer, and let their initial values be as follows:

```
A : 0 4 5 7

B : 3 4 6 7 8
```

Also, let the following constraints be in effect (*n* here denotes any integer appearing in either of the two relvars):

```
A : n ⩽ 7

B : n ⩾ 2
```

Note: I talk for simplicity as if the relvars contained integers as such, instead of (as would obviously be more correct) tuples containing such integers. Also, for clarity I show sets of integers as simple lists with adjacent integers separated by a blank, thereby writing, e.g., 0 4 5 7 instead of the more conventional {0,4,5,7}.

Now let *V* be a view defined as follows:

```
VAR V VIRTUAL ( A UNION ( A INTERSECT B ) ) ... ;
```

And now let's execute the following INSERT on *V*:

```
INSERT 1 2 3 5 INTO V ;
```

Applying the rules for updating unions and intersections from reference [1], then, here's what happens (bear in mind throughout that inserting something that's already present has no effect):

- The constraint for *V* is $(n \leqslant 7)$ OR $(n \leqslant 7$ AND $n \geqslant 2)$—which reduces to just $n \leqslant 7$—and the integers 1, 2, 3, and 5 do all satisfy this constraint. (If they didn't, an error—viz., constraint violation—would occur.)

- Since 1, 2, 3, and 5 in fact all satisfy the constraint for *A* (as well as for *V*), they're inserted into *A*.

- 2, 3, and 5 (but not 1) also satisfy the constraint for *A* INTERSECT *B*—viz., $(n \leqslant 7)$ AND $(n \geqslant 2)$—and so they're also inserted into that intersection. Inserting them into that intersection has the effect of inserting all three into both *A* and *B*.

So the final result looks like this:

```
A : 0 1 2 3 4 5 7
B : 2 3 4 5 6 7 8
```

Observe now that, of course, the expression *A* UNION (*A* INTERSECT *B*) is read equivalent to simply *A*.[28] But if we had directed the original INSERT at *A* instead of at *V* = *A* UNION (*A* INTERSECT *B*), we would have obtained this result:

```
A : 0 1 2 3 4 5 7
B : 3 4 6 7 8 /* unchanged */
```

Again, therefore, we see that expressions that are interchangeable in a read-only context aren't necessarily so in an update context. As I explained in reference [1], however, this situation arises in this particular example precisely because it's possible for the very same integer to appear in both *A* and *B*—i.e., the constraints for *A* and *B* "overlap," as it were, meaning the very same integer can satisfy both. And I also showed in reference [1] that this problem (if problem it is) goes away if the constraints don't overlap in this sense.[29] In other words, there's at least one situation—actually, of course, there are many—in which expressions that are read equivalent can be treated as update equivalent also. Some interesting research questions therefore arise. For example:

- Can we characterize precisely those situations in which read equivalent expressions can be treated as update equivalent? (I've shown that view updating semantics can't be independent of syntax 100 percent, but it's surely a desirable goal that it be as independent of syntax as possible.)
- Do those situations depend on the specific expressions in question?
- Do they depend on the specific updates in question?

And probably others.

There's one last point I want to make. Consider the following revised version, also taken from reference [1], of the integers example:

```
A : 0 3   : Constraint : n < 5
B : 6 8 9 : Constraint : n > 5
```

Observe that the constraints here don't overlap (and so the issue I've been discussing in this appendix so far doesn't arise in this example). Now let's define a view:

```
VAR V VIRTUAL ( A UNION B ) ... ;
```

Given the specified sample values, *V* has the value 0 3 6 8 9 (the constraint for *V* is ($n < 5$) OR ($n > 5$)). Now suppose we execute the following update on this view:

---

[28] This example too differs from the earlier one involving S and SP inasmuch as the read equivalence in question (i.e., $A \equiv A$ UNION (*A* INTERSECT *B*)) is absolute.

[29] In reference [1] I also said that enforcing this condition—i.e., that constraints not overlap in this sense—could be regarded as "a strong form of orthogonality." Well, it's certainly true in the example that enforcing that condition will guarantee that relvars *A* and *B* abide by *The Principle of Orthogonal Design* (see, e.g., reference [4] for a discussion of this principle); however, the converse is false—i.e., *A* and *B* might still abide by the principle, even if their constraints overlap. That said, I do suspect *The Principle of Orthogonal Design* might have some role to play in subsequent investigations in this area.

```
INSERT 5 INTO V , UPDATE V WHERE n = 5 : { n := 7 } ;
```

Note that, loosely speaking, the INSERT here is trying to insert a value—viz., 5—that violates the constraint on *V*, but the UPDATE then tries to repair the damage (as it were) by replacing that 5 by 7. So what happens?

Well, for clarity, let's convert the update (which is, of course, a multiple assignment) to pure assignment form:

```
V := V UNION 5 , V := ( V MINUS 5 ) UNION 7 ;
```

Now suppose for a moment that *V* is a base relvar instead of a view. According to the rules for multiple assignment, then (see reference [8]), we would first combine the two individual assignments to *V* into a single assignment, thus:

```
V := WITH ( V := V UNION 5 ) : ( V MINUS 5 ) UNION 7 ;
```

As I hope you can see, the overall effect of this assignment is simply to insert 7 into *V*, as is apparently required. But what happens if *V* is a view and not a base relvar? Well, if we begin by combining the two individual assignments into one, we clearly obtain the same assignment as before:

```
V := WITH ( V := V UNION 5 ) : ( V MINUS 5 ) UNION 7 ;
```

Now we replace the references to view *V* by the corresponding view defining expression:

```
A UNION B := WITH ( V := ( A UNION B ) UNION 5 ) :
                  ( V MINUS 5 ) UNION 7 ;
```

(The remaining references to *V* on the right side here denote not view *V* but a temporary variable of the same name.) Thus, the overall expression on the right denotes the set of integers 0 3 6 7 8 9 (all of which satisfy the pertinent constraint, please observe). Then, by the rules for updating unions, integers from this set that are less than 5 are assigned to *A* and integers from this set that are greater than 5 are assigned to *B*. The net effect is thus to insert 7 into *B* and hence into *V*, as required.

But now suppose by contrast that we start with the original update (i.e., the multiple assignment) and expand the references to *V* before we combine individual assignments. We obtain:

```
A := A UNION 5 , B := B UNION 5 ,
A := ( ( A UNION B ) MINUS 5 ) UNION 7 ,
B := ( ( A UNION B ) MINUS 5 ) UNION 7 ;
```

Next we combine the two assignments to *A* into one, and likewise for *B*:

```
A := WITH ( A := A UNION 5 ) :
          ( ( ( A UNION B ) MINUS 5 ) UNION 7 ,
B := WITH ( A := A UNION 5 ) :
          ( ( ( A UNION B ) MINUS 5 ) UNION 7 ;
```

Clearly, the expressions on the right sides of the two individual assignments are identical, both denoting the set of integers 0 3 6 7 8 9. In other words, we're attempting to assign that entire set of integers to both *A* and *B*—and those assignments will both fail, because in both cases we're trying to violate the pertinent constraint.

I conclude from this example that (as indeed I previously suggested in reference [1]) we need to add another step to the multiple assignment algorithm—see Chapter 1, RM Prescription 21—according to which distinct assignments to the same virtual relvar are combined before Step a. (the syntactic expansion step) is performed.

APPENDIX C: TOWARD PERFECT VIEW UPDATING (?)

As stated in the acknowledgments, David McGoveran reviewed this chapter in draft form and offered numerous helpful comments. For the most part, David agreed with what I was saying; however, he wanted me to add that what I was saying was, in effect, *the best we could do given the state of the art*—by which he meant, the best we could do given the state of current DBMS implementation technology. Meditating on this point made me think it might be worth including some discussion of David's ideas in this connection—hence this appendix (which is, I hasten to say, little more than the briefest of sketches).

Recall first that every relvar has an associated *relvar predicate,* which is, loosely, what the relvar in question means to the user. For example, the predicate for the supplier relvar S is:

> *Supplier S# is under contract, is named SNAME, has status STATUS, and is located in city CITY.*

For brevity, let's refer to this predicate as *pred*(S); more generally, in fact, let's refer to the predicate for any given relvar *R* as *pred*(*R*). Then each tuple in *R* at any given time *t* is supposed to be such that the attribute values from that tuple, if substituted for the parameters in *pred*(*R*), yield a proposition—more precisely, an instantiation of *pred*(*R*)—that we believe to be true at that time *t*. For example, if the tuple <S1,Smith,20,London> appears in relvar S right now, it means we believe the following to be a currently true proposition:

> *Supplier S1 is under contract, is named Smith, has status 20, and is located in city London.*

See, e.g., reference [4] if you want to see the foregoing ideas explained in more detail.

Next, note that in order to use relvar *R* in any meaningful way at all, the user must be aware of and understand that predicate *pred*(*R*). As a consequence, the user of relvar *R* must be informed (by the "owner" or "creator" of that relvar) of the corresponding predicate. Note further that these remarks are true of virtual relvars (views) as well as base ones. For example, the predicate *pred*(NLS) for view NLS ("non London suppliers") from the body of the chapter is:

> *Supplier S# is under contract, is named SNAME, has status STATUS, and is located in city CITY (and CITY is not London).*

Every user of view NLS, for whatever purpose, must be aware of this predicate.

Now, as I've written elsewhere—see, e.g., reference [4]—in an ideal world, the predicate *pred*(*R*) would serve as the criterion for acceptability of updates on relvar *R;* however, this goal is obviously unachievable as stated. In the case of relvar S, for example:

- First, the DBMS can't know what it means for a "supplier" to be "under contract" or to be "located" somewhere; these are matters of *interpretation.* For example, if the supplier number S1 and the city name London happen to appear together in the same tuple, then the user can interpret that fact to mean supplier S1 is located in London, but there's no way the DBMS can do anything analogous.

- Second, even if the DBMS could know what it means for a supplier to be under contract or to be located somewhere, it still couldn't know a priori whether what the user tells it is true! If the user asserts (by means of some update operation) that there's a supplier S6 named Lopez with status 30 and city Madrid, there's no way for the DBMS to know whether that assertion is true; all the DBMS can do is check that the user's assertion doesn't violate any integrity constraints. Assuming it doesn't, the DBMS will then insert the corresponding tuple <S6,Lopez,30,Madrid> into relvar S (in effect, it will then consider that tuple as representing a true proposition from this point forward).

In other words, the pragmatic "criterion for acceptability of updates" in today's DBMSs is not the predicate but the corresponding constraints, which might thus be regarded—with a large dose of rather wishful thinking—as the DBMS's approximation to the predicate.[30] (And this state of affairs explains the emphasis on constraints in the body of the chapter, of course.)

But now suppose we could tell the DBMS the name of the predicate for any given relvar, so that the DBMS would at least know that, e.g., the predicate for relvar S is *pred*(S)—even though, to repeat, it wouldn't "understand" that predicate. Further, suppose we could mention those predicates by name in requests to the DBMS. By way of example, consider the following scenario:

- Imagine we have two relvars, *A* and *B,* with predicates *pred*(*A*) and *pred*(*B*), respectively. To make the example a little more concrete, let *A* be "my friends" and let *B* be "my business contacts," respectively, and suppose *A* and *B* both have just one attribute, viz., NAME. (In other words, *pred*(*A*) is "NAME is the name of one of my friends" and *pred*(*B*) is "NAME is the name of one of my business contacts.")

- Let *C* be a view, defined as the union of *A* and *B*. The predicate for *C* is *pred*(*A*) OR *pred*(*B*) (i.e., *pred*(*C*) is "NAME is the name of one of my friends or one of my business contacts, and possibly both").

- Now consider the following update:

  ```
  INSERT 'Fred' INTO C ;
  ```

  According to the scheme described in references [1] and [3] (and endorsed, implicitly, in the body of the chapter), the effect of this INSERT will be to insert Fred into both of *A* and *B*. Indeed, we have here one of those ambiguous situations that some critics object to so strongly: The effect of the INSERT can be achieved by inserting Fred into *A* or *B* or both, and there's no good reason for choosing any particular one of these options, and so the INSERT should be rejected.

Now, I've argued in Appendix A that such updates should be accepted despite the ambiguity—but (of course) my arguments in that appendix were tacitly assuming "the state of the art" as found in today's implementations. By contrast, if we had a DBMS that behaved as suggested above, then the following would be possible:

- First, we could tell the DBMS that *pred*(*A*) is the predicate for *A* and *pred*(*B*) is the predicate for *B*. We could also tell it that the predicate for *C* is *pred*(*A*) OR *pred*(*B*), though of course it could easily determine this latter fact for itself.

- Second, suppose some user *U* "sees" only view *C* and is unaware of the existence of relvars *A* and *B*. Despite this latter fact, user *U* must nevertheless be aware that the predicate for *C* is of the form *pred*(*A*) OR *pred*(*B*), where *pred*(*A*) is "NAME is the name of one of my friends" and *pred*(*B*) is "NAME is the name of one of my business contacts."

Now suppose user *U* wants to insert Fred into *C*. Then the critical point is this: Even though the DBMS has no way of knowing ahead of time whether Fred is a friend or a business contact or both, *user U does have that knowledge, necessarily*—and user *U* can tell the DBMS which case applies, by explicitly mentioning the appropriate predicate(s) in the update request. For example (to invent some syntax on the fly):

```
INSERT 'Fred' INTO C : pred(A) ;
```

The effect of this INSERT will be to insert Fred into *A* (and hence into *C* as well, as requested) but not into *B*. Another example:

---

[30] Wishful thinking is right! This remark is, unfortunately, more than a little charitable to those DBMSs. The sad truth is, most DBMSs today don't even provide much by way of support for constraints, let alone support for the corresponding predicates as such.

```
INSERT 'Fred' INTO C : pred(A) AND pred(B) ;
```

The effect of this INSERT will be to insert Fred into both *A* and *B* (and hence into *C* as well). Incidentally, note that AND, not OR, is indeed the right connective here.

What about DELETE? Well, the following request—

```
DELETE 'Alice' FROM C : pred(A) ;
```

—will fail if Alice is a business contact but will succeed otherwise.

Whether a scheme like that sketched above can be made to work obviously remains to be seen; certainly the full implications are unclear at this time. But one implication is worth mentioning right away:[31] Taken to its logical conclusion, the scheme implies that database requests become *requests on the database,* rather than requests that are directed at specific relvars—because the DBMS should always be able to work out for itself which relvars are pertinent to any given request. (Observe in passing that these remarks apply to retrieval requests as well as update ones.) In other words, relvar names are best thought of as nothing more than convenient shorthands for the corresponding predicates (after all, it's predicates, not names, that represent semantics). Note finally that this state of affairs is fully consistent with a position articulated in—among several other places—Appendix D of reference [7]:

- From a conceptual point of view, at least, the only variable we're really dealing with is the database itself (the database in its entirety, that is).
- As a consequence of this point, "updating a database relvar" really means updating the database (the relvar acts as a *pseudovariable* in such contexts).

[31] Ideas along the lines described in this paragraph were previously aired—perhaps not as coherently as they might have been—in the paper "A New Database Design Principle," by David McGoveran and myself (first published in 1994 in *Database Programming & Design 7,* No. 7, and reprinted in my book *Relational Database Writings 1991-1994,* Addison-Wesley, 1995).

Part II

LANGUAGE DESIGN

This part of the book consists of eight chapters. Chapter 11 is a self-contained and updated definition of **Tutorial D,** which is a particular **D** we use in the *Manifesto* book (i.e., *Databases, Types, and the Relational Model: The Third Manifesto,* 3rd edition, by C. J. Date and Hugh Darwen, Addison-Wesley, 2006) to illustrate the *Manifesto*'s ideas. Chapters 12-15 discuss four specific database topics in depth—the relational divide operator, foreign keys, "image relations," and *n*-adic operators—and makes a series of language proposals based on those discussions. Chapter 16 examines the question of upgrading **Tutorial D** to what might be called **Industrial D**. Chapter 17 considers the topic of prenex normal form, which could be relevant to the design of a **D** based on relational calculus instead of relational algebra (which is what **Tutorial D** is based on). Finally, Chapter 18 might be considered a little light relief, except that what it describes isn't really funny at all.

Chapter 11

Tutorial D

I never use a big, big D—

—W. S. Gilbert: *HMS Pinafore*

This chapter consists of a heavily edited version of Chapter 5 from the book *Databases, Types, and the Relational Model: The Third Manifesto,* 3rd edition, by C. J. Date and Hugh Darwen, Addison-Wesley, 2006 ("the *Manifesto* book" for short—reference [7] in the list of references near the end of the chapter). Its aim is to provide a reference description for the language **Tutorial D**. **Tutorial D** is computationally complete and includes fully integrated ("native") database functionality, but it's not meant to be industrial strength; rather, it's meant to be a "toy" language, whose principal purpose is to serve as a teaching vehicle. As a consequence, many features that would be needed in an industrial strength language have deliberately been omitted.[1] In particular, I/O support and exception handling are both omitted; so too is all support for type inheritance, though possible extensions to provide this latter support are described in Chapter 21 of the present book [10].

In addition to the foregoing, many minor details, both syntactic and semantic, that would require precise specification in an industrial strength language are also ignored. For example, details of the following are all omitted:

- Language characters, identifiers, scope of names, etc.
- Reserved words (if any), comments,[2] delimiters and separators, etc.
- Operator precedence rules (except for a couple of important special cases)
- "Obvious" syntax rules (e.g., distinct parameters to the same operator must have distinct names)

Despite such omissions, the language is meant to be well designed as far as it goes. Indeed, it must be—for otherwise it wouldn't be a valid **D,** since it would violate RM Prescription 26 (which, as explained in Chapter 1 of the present book, requires every **D** to be constructed according to principles of good language design).

As already noted, **Tutorial D** is computationally complete, implying that entire applications can be written in the language; it isn't just a data sublanguage that relies on some host language to provide the necessary computational capabilities. Also, like most languages currently in widespread use, it's imperative in style—though it's worth mentioning that the "data retrieval" portions of the language, being based as they are on relational algebra, could in fact be regarded as a functional language if considered in isolation. *Note:* In practice we would hope that those portions would be implemented in an interactive form as well as in the form of a programming language per se; in other words, we endorse the *dual mode principle* as described in, e.g., reference [2].

As already indicated, **Tutorial D** is a relational language; in some respects, however, it can be regarded as an object language as well. For one thing, it follows RM Very Strong Suggestion 3 in supporting the concept of single level storage (see Chapter 1 of the present book). More important, it supports what is probably the most fundamental feature of object languages: namely, it allows users to define their own types. And since there's no

[1] At this point the original chapter in reference [7] added that "extending the language to incorporate such features, thereby turning it into what might be called **Industrial D,** could be a worthwhile project." Reference [9] includes some proposals for such extensions.

[2] In examples elsewhere in this book we show comments as text strings bracketed by "/*" and "*/" delimiters.

reliance on a host language, there's no "impedance mismatch" between the types available inside the database and those available outside (i.e., there's no need to map between the arbitrarily complex types used in the database and the probably rather simple types provided by some conventional host language). In other words, we agree with the object community's complaint that there's a serious problem in trying to build an interface between a DBMS that allows user defined types and a programming language that doesn't. For example, if the database contains a value of type POLYGON, then in **Tutorial D** that value can be assigned to a local variable also of type POLYGON—there's no need to break it down into, say, a sequence of number pairs representing the *x* and *y* coordinates of the vertices of the polygon in question. Altogether, then, it seems fair to characterize **Tutorial D** as a true "object/relational" language (inasmuch as that term has any objective meaning, that is!—see the *Manifesto* book for further explanation).

Tutorial D has been designed to support all of the prescriptions and proscriptions (though not all of the very strong suggestions) defined in Chapter 1 of the present book. However, it isn't meant to be minimal in any sense—it includes numerous features that are really just shorthand for certain combinations of others. (This remark applies especially to its relational support.) However, the shorthands in question are all specifically designed to be shorthands;[3] in other words, the redundancies are deliberate, and are included for usability reasons.

The bulk of the rest of the chapter consists of a BNF grammar for **Tutorial D**. The grammar is defined by means of essentially standard BNF notation, except for a couple of simplifying extensions that we now explain. Let *<xyz>* denote an arbitrary syntactic category (i.e., anything that appears, or potentially could appear, on the left side of some production rule). Then:

- The syntactic category *<xyz list>* denotes a sequence of zero or more *<xyz>*s in which adjacent *<xyz>*s are separated by one or more "white space" characters.

- The syntactic category *<xyz commalist>* denotes a sequence of zero or more *<xyz>*s in which adjacent *<xyz>*s are separated by a comma (as well as, optionally, one or more "white space" characters before the comma or after it or both).

Observe in particular that most of the various lists and commalists described in what follows are allowed to be empty. The effect of specifying an empty list or commalist is usually obvious; for example, an *<assignment>* for which the immediately contained commalist of *<assign>*s is empty degenerates to a *<no op>* ("no operation"). Occasionally, however, there's something a little more interesting to be said about such cases (see Appendix B at the end of the chapter).

Finally, a few miscellaneous points:

- All syntactic categories of the form *<... name>* are defined to be *<identifier>*s, barring explicit production rules to the contrary. The category *<identifier>* in turn is terminal and is defined no further here.

- A few of the production rules include an alternative on the right side that consists of an ellipsis "..." followed by plain text. In such cases, the plain text is intended as an informal natural language explanation of the syntactic category being defined (or, more usually, one particular form of that syntactic category).

- Some of the production rules are accompanied by a prose explanation of certain additional syntax rules or the corresponding semantics or both, but only where such explanations seem necessary.

- Braces "{" and "}" in the grammar stand for themselves; i.e., they're symbols in the language being

---

[3] Note the contrast with SQL here. SQL includes many features that are almost but not quite equivalent—"almost but not quite," because the features in question were designed independently of one another. For example, an expression that involves a GROUP BY can usually but not always be replaced by one that doesn't (and, of course, it's that "but not always" that causes the problems).

defined, not (as they usually are) symbols of the metalanguage. To be specific, we use braces to enclose commalists of items when the commalist in question is intended to denote a set of some kind, in which case (a) the order in which the items appear within that commalist is immaterial and (b) if an item appears more than once, it's treated as if it appeared just once. In particular, we use braces to enclose the commalist of argument expressions in certain *n*-adic operator invocations (e.g., JOIN, UNION). *Note:* In such cases, if the operator in question is idempotent,[4] then the argument expression commalist truly does represent a set of arguments, and the foregoing remarks apply 100 percent. If the operator is not idempotent, however, then the argument expression commalist represents a bag of arguments, not a set—in which case the order in which the argument expressions appear is still immaterial, but repetition has significance (e.g., the expression SUM{1,2,2} returns 5, not 3). Of the *n*-adic operators defined in what follows, the following (only) are not idempotent: COUNT, SUM, AVG, XOR, EXACTLY, COMPOSE, and XUNION.

- The grammar reflects the logical difference between expressions and statements. An expression denotes a value; it can be thought of as a rule for computing or determining the value in question. A statement doesn't denote a value; instead, it causes some action to occur, such as assigning a value to some variable or changing the flow of control.

- Following on from the previous point: Expressions in general are of two kinds, open and closed. A closed expression is one that isn't open, and it can appear wherever expressions in general are allowed. By contrast, an open expression is one that can appear only in certain contexts, because it contains certain references (either attribute references or possrep component references) whose meaning depends on the context in question. To be precise, an open expression can appear (a) as the *<bool exp>* following the keyword WHERE in a *<where>*, a *<relation delete>*, or a *<relation update>*; (b) as the *<bool exp>* following the keyword CONSTRAINT in a *<possrep constraint def>*; (c) as the expression denoting the source in a *<possrep component assign>* within a *<scalar update>*; (d) as the expression denoting the source in an *<attribute assign>* within a *<tuple extend>*, an *<extend>*, a *<tuple update>*, or a *<relation update>*; (e) as the *<integer exp>* or *<exp>* within an *<agg op inv>* or a *<summary>*; (f) as a subexpression within any of the foregoing; (g) nowhere else. In all cases, the meaning of the "certain references" (within the open expression in question) is explained under the pertinent production rule(s).

- In line with discussions in Chapter 3 of the present book, we introduce REL and TUP as synonyms for the keywords RELATION and TUPLE, respectively. We also introduce DEE and DUM as abbreviations for TABLE_DEE and TABLE_DUM, respectively. Throughout the language, in other words, the keywords RELATION and REL can be used interchangeably, and the same is true for the keywords TUPLE and TUP, TABLE_DEE and DEE, and TABLE_DUM and DUM. However, these facts aren't explicitly reflected in the grammar that follows.

- The grammar deliberately includes no explicit production rules for the following syntactic categories:

  ```
  <possrep component assign>

  <attribute assign>
  ```

  However, a detailed explanation of the former can be found in the discussion of the production rule for *<scalar update>*, and a detailed explanation of the latter can be found in the discussion of the production

---

[4] The dyadic operator *Op* is idempotent if and only if $x\ Op\ x = x$ for all x. For example, in logic, inclusive OR is idempotent, but exclusive OR (XOR) is not.

rules for *<tuple update>*, *<relation update>*, *<tuple extend>*, *<extend>*, and *<summarize>*.

- Finally, except for certain changes at the detail level, the version of **Tutorial D** defined by this grammar provides essentially the same functionality as that defined in Chapter 5 of the *Manifesto* book [7]. In particular, major changes proposed elsewhere in the present book are excluded. However, the text does include pointers to chapters in the present book where such changes are proposed, where appropriate.

In addition to the changes noted above, minor corrections and cosmetic improvements have been made to almost all of the production rules and prose explanations. Of course, wherever there's a discrepancy between the present chapter and Chapter 5 of the *Manifesto* book, the present chapter should be taken as superseding.

COMMON CONSTRUCTS

```
<type spec>
    ::=   <scalar type spec>
        | <nonscalar type spec>

<scalar type spec>
    ::=   <scalar type name>
        | SAME_TYPE_AS ( <scalar exp> )

<nonscalar type spec>
    ::=   <tuple type spec>
        | <relation type spec>

<tuple type spec>
    ::=   <tuple type name>
        | SAME_TYPE_AS ( <tuple exp> )
        | TUPLE SAME_HEADING_AS ( <nonscalar exp> )

<relation type spec>
    ::=   <relation type name>
        | SAME_TYPE_AS ( <relation exp> )
        | RELATION SAME_HEADING_AS ( <nonscalar exp> )

<user op def>
    ::=   <user update op def>
        | <user read-only op def>

<user update op def>
    ::=   OPERATOR <user op name> ( <parameter def commalist> )
             UPDATES { [ ALL BUT ] <parameter name commalist> } ;
                <statement>
          END OPERATOR
```

The *<parameter def commalist>* is enclosed in parentheses instead of braces, as is the corresponding *<argument exp commalist>* in an invocation of the operator in question (see *<user op inv>*, later), because we follow convention in relying on ordinal position for argument/parameter matching.[5] UPDATES (*<parameter name commalist>*), if specified, identifies parameters that are subject to update; alternatively, UPDATES (ALL BUT *<parameter name commalist>*), if specified, identifies parameters that aren't subject to update. *Note:* The specification ALL BUT has an analogous interpretation in all contexts in which it appears; however, the precise nature of that "analogous interpretation" in other contexts is left as an exercise for the reader.

In practice, it might be desirable to support an external form of *<user update op def>* as well. Syntactically, such a *<user update op def>* would include, not a *<statement>* as above, but rather a reference to an external file that contains the code that implements the operator (possibly written in some different language). It might also be desirable to support a form of *<user update op def>* that includes neither a *<statement>* nor such an external reference; such a *<user update op def>* would define merely what is called a *specification signature* for the operator in question, and the implementation code would then have to be defined elsewhere. Splitting operator definitions into separate pieces in this way is likely to prove particularly useful if type inheritance is supported (see Chapter 21). *Note:* Everything in this paragraph applies to *<user read-only op def>*s as well, mutatis mutandis.

```
<parameter def>
    ::=   <parameter name> <type spec>

<user read-only op def>
    ::=   OPERATOR <user op name> ( <parameter def commalist> )
             RETURNS <type spec> ;
                <statement>
          END OPERATOR
```

The *<user op name>* denotes a scalar, tuple, or relational operator, depending on the *<type spec>* in the RETURNS specification.

```
<user op inv>
    ::=   <user op name> ( <argument exp commalist> )
```

The *i*th entry in the *<argument exp commalist>* corresponds to the *i*th entry in the *<parameter def commalist>* in the *<user op def>* identified by *<user op name>*.

```
<argument exp>
    ::=   <exp>

<exp>
    ::=   <scalar exp>
        | <nonscalar exp>

<scalar exp>
    ::=   <scalar with exp>
        | <scalar nonwith exp>
```

For further details of *<scalar nonwith exp>*s, see the section "Scalar Operations," later.

---

[5] This remark is true of read-only as well as update operators. In particular, it's true of scalar selector operators—i.e., the arguments to a *<scalar selector inv>* (see later) are specified in parentheses, even though the corresponding parameters are specified in braces (see *<possrep def>*). See Appendix A ("A Remark on Syntax") at the end of the chapter.

```
<scalar with exp>
    ::=   WITH ( <name intro commalist> ) : <scalar exp>
```

Let *SWE* be a <*scalar with exp*>, and let *NIC* and *SE* be the <*name intro commalist*> and the <*scalar exp*>, respectively, immediately contained in *SWE*. The individual <*name intro*>s in *NIC* are evaluated in sequence as written. As the next production rule shows, each such <*name intro*> immediately contains an <*introduced name*> and an <*exp*>. Let *NI* be one of those <*name intro*>s, and let the <*introduced name*> and the <*exp*> immediately contained in *NI* be *N* and *X*, respectively. Then *N* denotes the value obtained by evaluating *X*, and it can appear subsequently in *SWE* wherever the expression (*X*)—i.e., *X* in parentheses—would be allowed. *Note:* Everything in this paragraph applies to <*tuple with exp*>s and <*relation with exp*>s as well, mutatis mutandis.

```
<name intro>
    ::=   <introduced name> := <exp>

<nonscalar exp>
    ::=   <tuple exp>
        | <relation exp>

<tuple exp>
    ::=   <tuple with exp>
        | <tuple nonwith exp>
```

For further details of <*tuple nonwith exp*>s, see the section "Tuple Operations," later.

```
<tuple with exp>
    ::=   WITH ( <name intro commalist> ) : <tuple exp>

<relation exp>
    ::=   <relation with exp>
        | <relation nonwith exp>
```

For further details of <*relation nonwith exp*>s, see the section "Relational Operations," later.

```
<relation with exp>
    ::=   WITH ( <name intro commalist> ) : <relation exp>

<user op drop>
    ::=   DROP OPERATOR <user op name>

<selector inv>
    ::=   <scalar selector inv>
        | <nonscalar selector inv>

<nonscalar selector inv>
    ::=   <tuple selector inv>
        | <relation selector inv>

<var ref>
    ::=   <scalar var ref>
        | <nonscalar var ref>

<scalar var ref>
    ::=   <scalar var name>
```

```
<nonscalar var ref>
    ::=   <tuple var ref>
        | <relation var ref>

<tuple var ref>
    ::=   <tuple var name>

<relation var ref>
    ::=   <relation var name>

<attribute ref>
    ::=   <attribute name>

<possrep component ref>
    ::=   <possrep component name>

<assignment>
    ::=   <assign commalist>

<assign>
    ::=   <scalar assign>
        | <nonscalar assign>

<nonscalar assign>
    ::=   <tuple assign>
        | <relation assign>
```

SCALAR DEFINITIONS

```
<scalar type name>
    ::=   <user scalar type name>
        | <built in scalar type name>

<built in scalar type name>
    ::=   INTEGER | RATIONAL | CHARACTER | BOOLEAN
```

As indicated, **Tutorial D** supports the following built in (system defined) scalar types:

- INTEGER (signed integers): synonym INT; literals expressed as an optionally signed decimal integer; usual arithmetic and comparison operators, with usual notation. The (implicit) example value is 0.
- RATIONAL (signed rational numbers): synonym RAT; literals expressed as an optionally signed decimal mantissa (including a decimal point), optionally followed by the letter E and an optionally signed decimal integer exponent (examples: 6., 8.0, 17.5, –4.3E+2); usual arithmetic and comparison operators, with usual notation. The (implicit) example value is 0.0.
- CHARACTER (varying length character strings): synonym CHAR; literals expressed as a sequence, enclosed in single quotes, of zero or more characters; usual string manipulation and comparison operators, with usual notation—"||" (concatenate), SUBSTR (substring), etc. The (implicit) example value is '' (the empty string). By the way, if you're familiar with SQL, don't be misled here; the SQL data type CHAR corresponds to *fixed* length character strings (the varying length analog is called VARCHAR), and an

associated length—default one—must be specified as in, e.g., CHAR(25).[6] **Tutorial D** doesn't support a fixed length character string type.

- BOOLEAN (truth values): synonym BOOL; literals TRUE and FALSE; usual comparison operators ("=" and "≠") and boolean operators (AND, OR, NOT, etc.), with usual notation. The (implicit) example value is FALSE. Note that **Tutorial D**'s support for type BOOLEAN goes beyond that found in many languages in at least three ways:

  1. It includes explicit support for the XOR operator (exclusive OR). The expression *a* XOR *b* (where *a* and *b* are *<bool exp>*s) is semantically equivalent to the expression $a \neq b$.

  2. It supports *n*-adic versions of the operators AND, OR, and XOR. The syntax is:

     ```
     <n-adic bool op name> { <bool exp commalist> }
     ```

     The *<n-adic bool op name>* is AND, OR, or XOR. AND returns TRUE if and only if all specified *<bool exp>*s evaluate to TRUE. OR returns FALSE if and only if all specified *<bool exp>*s evaluate to FALSE. XOR returns TRUE if and only if the number of specified *<bool exp>*s that evaluate to TRUE is odd.

  3. It supports an *n*-adic operator of the form

     ```
     EXACTLY ( <integer exp> , { <bool exp commalist> } )
     ```

     Let the *<integer exp>* evaluate to *n*.[7] Then the overall expression evaluates to TRUE if and only if the number of specified *<bool exp>*s that evaluate to TRUE is *n*.

Type INTEGER is an ordinal type; types RATIONAL and CHARACTER are ordered but not ordinal types. *Note:* In practice we would expect a variety of other system defined scalar types to be supported in addition to the foregoing: DATE, TIME, perhaps BIT (varying length bit strings), and so forth. We omit such types here as irrelevant to our main purpose.

```
<user scalar type def>
    ::=   <user scalar root type def>
```

The syntactic category *<user scalar root type def>* is introduced merely to pave the way for the inheritance support to be described in Chapter 21 (all types are root types—and leaf types too—in the absence of inheritance support).

```
<user scalar root type def>
    ::=   TYPE <user scalar type name>
             [ <ordering> ] <possrep def list>
               INIT ( <literal> )
```

Let *T* be the scalar type being defined. The purpose of the INIT specification is to introduce the example value required for *T* by RM Prescription 1 (and the declared type of the *<literal>* must therefore be *T*). *Note:* Eyebrows might be raised at our choice of keyword here. But RM Prescription 11 requires scalar variables to be

---

[6] It would be more accurate to refer to CHAR and VARCHAR in SQL not as types but as type generators, and the associated length specification (as in, e.g., CHAR(25)) as the argument to an invocation of such a generator.

[7] The detailed syntax of *<integer exp>*s is left unspecified here (as is that of *<literal>* also—see *<user scalar root type def>*, later); however, we note that an *<integer exp>* is of course a numeric expression, and hence a *<scalar exp>* also.

initialized, at the time they're defined, to "either a value specified explicitly as part of the operation that defines [the variable in question] *or some implementation defined value otherwise*" (italics added). In **Tutorial D** in particular, if the variable in question happens to be of a user defined type, we use the applicable example value as the necessary implementation defined value;[8] hence our choice of keyword.

```
<ordering>
    ::=   ORDINAL | ORDERED
```

Let *T* be the scalar type being defined. If *<ordering>* is specified, then:

- Type *T* is an ordered type (i.e., the operator "<" is defined for all pairs of values of the type).
- If and only if ORDINAL is specified, then type *T* is also an ordinal type, in which case certain additional operators must also be defined—*first* and *last* (which return the first and last value, respectively, of type *T* with respect to the applicable ordering), and *next* and *prior* (which, given a particular value of type *T*, return that value's successor and predecessor, respectively, again with respect to the applicable ordering). Further details are beyond the scope of this chapter.

```
<possrep def>
    ::=   POSSREP [ <possrep name> ]
                  { <possrep component def commalist>
                            [ <possrep constraint def> ] }
```

If *<possrep name>* is omitted, a *<possrep name>* equal to the *<user scalar type name>* of the containing *<user scalar root type def>* is assumed by default.

```
<possrep component def>
    ::=   <possrep component name> <type spec>
```

No two distinct *<possrep def>*s within the same *<user scalar type def>* can include a component with the same *<possrep component name>*.

```
<possrep constraint def>
    ::=   CONSTRAINT <bool exp>
```

The *<bool exp>* must not mention any variables, but *<possrep component ref>*s can be used to denote the corresponding components of the applicable possible representation ("possrep") of an arbitrary value of the scalar type in question.

```
<user scalar type drop>
    ::=   DROP TYPE <user scalar type name>

<scalar var def>
    ::=   VAR <scalar var name> <scalar type or init value>

<scalar type or init value>
    ::=   <scalar type spec> | INIT ( <scalar exp> )
        | <scalar type spec> INIT ( <scalar exp> )
```

If *<scalar type spec>* and the INIT specification both appear, the declared type of *<scalar exp>* must be

[8] Indeed, we find it hard to believe for *any* **D** that the necessary implementation defined value would be anything other than the applicable example value.

the type specified by *<scalar type spec>*. If *<scalar type spec>* appears, the declared type of the scalar variable is the specified type; otherwise it's the same as that of *<scalar exp>*. If the INIT specification appears, the scalar variable is initialized to the value of *<scalar exp>*; otherwise it's initialized to the example value of the pertinent type.

TUPLE DEFINITIONS

```
<tuple type name>
    ::=   TUPLE <heading>

<heading>
    ::=   { <attribute commalist> }

<attribute>
    ::=   <attribute name> <type spec>

<tuple var def>
    ::=   VAR <tuple var name> <tuple type or init value>

<tuple type or init value>
    ::=   <tuple type spec> | INIT ( <tuple exp> )
        | <tuple type spec> INIT ( <tuple exp> )
```

If *<tuple type spec>* and the INIT specification both appear, the declared type of *<tuple exp>* must be the type specified by *<tuple type spec>*. If *<tuple type spec>* appears, the declared type of the tuple variable is the specified type; otherwise it's the same as that of *<tuple exp>*. If the INIT specification appears, the tuple variable is initialized to the value of *<tuple exp>*; otherwise it's initialized to the tuple with the default initialization value for each of its attributes, where (a) the default initialization value for a scalar attribute is the example value of the pertinent scalar type; (b) the default initialization value for a tuple valued attribute is the tuple with the default initialization values for each of the attributes of the tuple type in question; and (c) the default initialization value for a relation valued attribute is the empty relation of the pertinent type.

RELATIONAL DEFINITIONS

```
<relation type name>
    ::=   RELATION <heading>

<relation var def>
    ::=   <database relation var def>
        | <application relation var def>

<database relation var def>
    ::=   <real relation var def>
        | <virtual relation var def>
```

A *<database relation var def>* defines a database relvar—i.e., a relvar that's part of the database. In particular, therefore, it causes an entry to be made in the catalog. Note, however, that neither databases nor catalogs are explicitly mentioned anywhere in the syntax of **Tutorial D**.

```
<real relation var def>
    ::=   VAR <relation var name> <real or base>
              <relation type or init value> <key def list>
```

An empty *<key def list>* is equivalent to a *<key def list>* of the form KEY {ALL BUT}.

```
<real or base>
    ::=   REAL | BASE

<relation type or init value>
    ::=   <relation type spec> | INIT ( <relation exp> )
        | <relation type spec> INIT ( <relation exp> )
```

An INIT specification can appear only if either REAL (or BASE) or PRIVATE is specified for the relvar in question (see *<application relation var def>*, later, for an explanation of PRIVATE). If *<relation type spec>* and the INIT specification both appear, the declared type of *<relation exp>* must be the type specified by *<relation type spec>*. If *<relation type spec>* appears, the declared type of the relation variable is the specified type; otherwise it's the same as that of *<relation exp>*. If and only if the relvar is either real or private, then (a) if the INIT specification appears, the relvar is initialized to the value of *<relation exp>*; (b) otherwise it's initialized to the empty relation of the appropriate type.

```
<key def>
    ::=   KEY { [ ALL BUT ] <attribute ref commalist> }
```

Tutorial D uses the unqualified keyword KEY to mean a candidate key specifically. It doesn't explicitly support primary keys as such; in fact, it makes no distinction between primary and alternate keys. *Note:* Elsewhere this book proposes introducing explicit syntax for foreign keys in addition to candidate keys. See references [5] and [9].

```
<virtual relation var def>
    ::=   VAR <relation var name> VIRTUAL
              ( <relation exp> ) <key def list>
```

The *<relation exp>* must mention at least one database relvar and no other variables. An empty *<key def list>* is equivalent to a *<key def list>* that contains exactly one *<key def>* for each key that can be inferred by the system from *<relation exp>*.

```
<application relation var def>
    ::=   VAR <relation var name> <private or public>
              <relation type or init value> <key def list>
```

An empty *<key def list>* is equivalent to a *<key def list>* of the form KEY {ALL BUT}.

```
<private or public>
    ::=   PRIVATE | PUBLIC

<relation var drop>
    ::=   DROP VAR <relation var ref>
```

The *<relation var ref>* must denote a database relvar, not an application one.

```
<constraint def>
    ::=   CONSTRAINT <constraint name> <bool exp>
```

A *<constraint def>* defines a database constraint. The *<bool exp>* must not reference any variables other than database relvars. (**Tutorial D** doesn't support constraints that reference any other kinds of variables, though there's no logical reason why it shouldn't.)

```
<constraint drop>
    ::=   DROP CONSTRAINT <constraint name>
```

SCALAR OPERATIONS

```
<scalar nonwith exp>
    ::=   <scalar var ref>
        | <scalar op inv>
        | ( <scalar exp> )

<scalar op inv>
    ::=   <user op inv>
        | <built in scalar op inv>
```

In the *<user op inv>* case, the operator being invoked must be a read-only operator specifically.

```
<built in scalar op inv>
    ::=   <scalar selector inv>
        | <THE_ op inv>
        | <attribute extractor inv>
        | <agg op inv>
        | ... plus the usual possibilities
```

It's convenient to get "the usual possibilities" out of the way first. By this term, we mean the usual numeric operators ("+", "*", etc.), character string operators ("||", SUBSTR, etc.), and boolean operators, all of which we've already said are built in (system defined) operators in **Tutorial D**. It follows that numeric expressions, character string expressions, and in particular boolean expressions—i.e., *<bool exp>*s—are all *<scalar exp>*s (and we assume the usual syntax in each case). The following are also *<scalar exp>*s:

- Two special forms of *<bool exp>*, IS_EMPTY (*<relation exp>*), which returns TRUE if and only if the relation denoted by *<relation exp>* is empty, and IS_NOT_EMPTY (*<relation exp>*), which returns TRUE if and only if the relation denoted by *<relation exp>* is nonempty.

- CAST expressions of the form CAST_AS_*T* (*<scalar exp>*), where *T* is a scalar type and *<scalar exp>* denotes a scalar value to be converted ("cast") to that type. *Note:* We use syntax of the form CAST_AS_*T* (...), rather than CAST (... AS *T*), because this latter form raises "type TYPE" issues—e.g., what is the type of operand *T*?—that we prefer to avoid.

- IF ... END IF and CASE ... END CASE expressions of the usual form, viz.:

  ```
  IF <bool exp> THEN <scalar exp> [ ELSE <scalar exp> ] END IF

  CASE <when def list> [ ELSE <scalar exp> ] END CASE
  ```

  A *<when def>* in turn takes the form:

  ```
  WHEN <bool exp> THEN <scalar exp>
  ```

  Note: We assume without going into details that tuple and relation analogs of the foregoing scalar IF and CASE expressions are available also.

```
<scalar selector inv>
    ::=   <built in scalar literal>
        | <possrep name> ( <argument exp commalist> )
```

The syntax of *<built in scalar literal>* is explained in the prose following the production rule for *<built in scalar type name>*. In the second format, the *i*th entry in the *<argument exp commalist>* corresponds to the *i*th entry in the *<possrep component def commalist>* in the possrep identified by *<possrep name>*. *Note:* Whether scalar selectors are regarded as system defined or user defined could be a matter of some debate, but the point is unimportant for present purposes. Analogous remarks apply to THE_ operators and attribute extractors also (see the next two production rules).

```
<THE_ op inv>
    ::=    <THE_ op name> ( <scalar exp> )
```

We include this production rule in this section because in practice we expect most *<THE_ op inv>*s to denote scalar values. In fact, however, a *<THE_ op inv>* will be a *<scalar exp>*, a *<tuple exp>*, or a *<relation exp>*, depending on the type of the *<possrep component>* corresponding to *<THE_ op name>*.

```
<attribute extractor inv>
    ::=    <attribute ref> FROM <tuple exp>
```

We include this production rule in this section because in practice we expect most attributes to be scalar. In fact, however, an *<attribute extractor inv>* will be a *<scalar exp>*, a *<tuple exp>*, or a *<relation exp>*, depending on the type of *<attribute ref>*.

```
<agg op inv>
    ::=    <agg op name>
               ( [ <integer exp> , ] <relation exp> [ , <exp> ] )
         | <n-adic count etc>
```

In the first format:

- The *<integer exp>* and following comma must be specified if and only if the *<agg op name>* is EXACTLY. The *<exp>* must be omitted if the *<agg op name>* is COUNT.
- Let the relation denoted by the specified *<relation exp>* be *r*. If the *<agg op name>* is not COUNT, then the *<exp>* can be omitted only if *r* is of degree one, in which case an *<exp>* consisting of an *<attribute ref>* that designates the sole attribute of *r* is specified implicitly. More generally, the *<exp>* is allowed to contain an *<attribute ref>*, *AR* say, wherever a *<selector inv>* would be allowed. During the process of computing the desired aggregation, *<exp>* is effectively evaluated for each tuple of *r* in turn. If the *<attribute name>* of *AR* is that of an attribute of *r*, then (for each such evaluation) *AR* denotes the corresponding attribute value from the corresponding tuple; otherwise the *<agg op inv>* must be contained within some expression in which the meaning of *AR* is defined. In other words, the *<agg op inv>*

  ```
  agg ( rx , x )
  ```

  is equivalent to the following:

  ```
  agg ( EXTEND rx : { Temp := x } , Temp )
  ```

- For SUM, the declared type of the attribute denoted by *<attribute ref>* must be some type for which the operator "+" is defined; for AVG, it must be one for which the operators "+" and "/" are defined; for MAX and MIN, it must be some ordered type; for AND, OR, XOR, and EXACTLY, it must be type BOOLEAN; for UNION, D_UNION, INTERSECT, and XUNION, it must be some relation type.

Note: We include this production rule in this section because in practice we expect most *<agg op inv>*s to denote scalar values. In fact, however, an *<agg op inv>* will be a *<scalar exp>*, a *<tuple exp>*, or a *<relation*

exp> depending on the type of the operator denoted by <*agg op name*>.

```
<agg op name>
     ::=   COUNT | SUM | AVG | MAX | MIN
         | AND | OR | XOR | EXACTLY
         | UNION | D_UNION | INTERSECT | XUNION
```

COUNT returns a result of declared type INTEGER; SUM, AVG, MAX, MIN, UNION, D_UNION, INTERSECT, and XUNION return a result of declared type the same as that of the attribute denoted by the applicable <*attribute ref*>;[9] AND, OR, XOR, and EXACTLY return a result of declared type BOOLEAN. *Note:* **Tutorial D** also includes support for certain conventional operators (as opposed to aggregate operators) that are *n*-adic versions of (a) AND, OR, XOR, and EXACTLY (see the section "Scalar Definitions," earlier) and (b) UNION, D_UNION, INTERSECT, JOIN, TIMES, XUNION, and COMPOSE (see the section "Relational Operations," later).[10] Analogously, it also includes support for *n*-adic versions of COUNT, SUM, AVG, MAX, and MIN (see the production rule immediately following).

```
<n-adic count etc>
     ::=   <agg op name> { <exp commalist> }
```

The <*agg op name*> must be COUNT, SUM, AVG, MAX, or MIN, and the <*exp*>s must all be of the same declared type. For SUM, that type must be one for which the operator "+" is defined; for AVG, it must be one for which the operators "+" and "/" are defined; for MAX and MIN, it must be some ordered type. *Note:* For SUM, MAX, and MIN, the <*agg op name*> can optionally have a suffix of the form _*T,* where *T* is a scalar type name (as in, e.g., SUM_INTEGER or, equivalently, SUM_INT) and every <*exp*> in the <*exp commalist*> is of declared type *T*. Such a suffix must be specified if the <*exp commalist*> is empty.

```
<scalar assign>
     ::=   <scalar target> := <scalar exp>
         | <scalar update>

<scalar target>
     ::=   <scalar var ref>
         | <scalar THE_ pv ref>
```

The abbreviation *pv* stands for *pseudovariable.* The grammar presented in this chapter doesn't say as much explicitly, but the general intent is that a pseudovariable reference should be allowed to appear wherever a variable reference is allowed to appear (speaking a trifle loosely).

```
<scalar THE_ pv ref>
     ::=   <THE_ pv name> ( <scalar target> )
```

The declared type of the <*possrep component*> corresponding to <*THE_ pv name*> must be some scalar type.

---

[9] It might be preferable in practice to define AVG in such a way that, e.g., taking the average of a collection of integers returns a rational number. We do not do so here merely for reasons of simplicity.

[10] It would be possible to define JOIN, TIMES, and COMPOSE aggregate operators also. However, JOIN would always be equivalent to INTERSECT; TIMES would always raise an error, except in the degenerate special case in which the pertinent relations were of degree zero; and COMPOSE would always be equivalent to INTERSECT followed by a projection on no attributes.

```
<scalar update>
    ::=   UPDATE <scalar target> :
              { <possrep component assign commalist> }
```

Let the *<scalar target>, ST* say, be of declared type *T*. Every *<possrep component assign>*, *PCA* say, in the *<possrep component assign commalist>* is syntactically identical to an *<assign>* (i.e., a *<scalar assign>*, a *<tuple assign>*, or a *<relation assign>*, as applicable), except that:

- The target of *PCA* must be a *<possrep component target>*, *PCT* say.
- *PCT* must identify, directly or indirectly,[11] some *Ci* (*i* = 1, 2, ..., *n*), where *C1, C2, ..., Cn* are the components of some possrep *PR* for type *T* (the same possrep *PR* in every case).
- *PCA* is allowed to contain a *<possrep component ref>*, *PCR* say, wherever a *<selector inv>* would be allowed, where *PCR* is some *Ci* (*i* = 1, 2, ..., *n*) and denotes the corresponding possrep component value from *ST*.

Steps a. and b. of the definition given for multiple assignment under RM Prescription 21 (see Chapter 1 of the present book) are applied to the *<possrep component assign commalist>*. The result of that application is a *<possrep component assign commalist>* in which each *<possrep component assign>* is of the form

```
Ci := exp
```

for some *Ci,* and no two distinct *<possrep component assign>*s specify the same target *Ci*. Then the original *<scalar update>* is equivalent to the *<scalar assign>*

```
ST := PR ( X1 , X2 , ... , Xn )
```

(*PR* here is the selector operator corresponding to the possrep with the same name.) The arguments *Xi* are defined as follows:

- If a *<possrep component assign>*, *PCA* say, exists for *Ci,* then let the *<exp>* from *PCA* be *X*. For all *j* (*j* = 1, 2, ..., *n*), replace references in *X* to *Cj* by (THE_*Cj*(*ST*)). The version of *X* that results is *Xi*.
- Otherwise, *Xi* is THE_*Ci*(*ST*).

```
<possrep component target>
    ::=   <possrep component ref>
        | <possrep THE_ pv ref>

<possrep THE_ pv ref>
    ::=   <THE_ pv name> ( <possrep component target> )

<scalar comp>
    ::=   <scalar exp> <scalar comp op> <scalar exp>
```

Scalar comparisons are a special case of the syntactic category *<bool exp>*.

---

[11] The phrase *directly or indirectly* appears several times in this chapter in contexts like this one. In the present context, we can explain it as follows: Again, let *<possrep component assign> PCA* specify *<possrep component target> PCT.* Then *PCA* identifies *Ci* as its target directly if *PCT* is *Ci;* it identifies *Ci* as its target indirectly if *PCT* takes the form of a *<possrep THE_ pv ref> PTR,* where the argument at the innermost level of nesting within *PTR* is *Ci.* The meaning of the phrase *directly or indirectly* in other similar contexts is analogous.

```
<scalar comp op>
    ::=   = | ≠ | < | ≤ | > | ≥
```

The operators "=" and "≠" apply to all scalar types; the operators "<", "≤", ">", and "≥" apply only to ordered types.

TUPLE OPERATIONS

```
<tuple nonwith exp>
    ::=   <tuple var ref>
        | <tuple op inv>
        | ( <tuple exp> )

<tuple op inv>
    ::=   <user op inv>
        | <built in tuple op inv>

<built in tuple op inv>
    ::=   <tuple selector inv>
        | <THE_ op inv>
        | <attribute extractor inv>
        | <tuple extractor inv>
        | <tuple project>
        | <n-adic other built in tuple op inv>
        | <monadic or dyadic other built in tuple op inv>

<tuple selector inv>
    ::=   TUPLE { <tuple component commalist> }

<tuple component>
    ::=   <attribute name> <exp>

<tuple extractor inv>
    ::=   TUPLE FROM <relation exp>
```

The <*relation exp*> must denote a relation of cardinality one.

```
<tuple project>
    ::=   <tuple exp> { [ ALL BUT ] <attribute ref commalist> }
```

The <*tuple exp*> must not be a <*monadic or dyadic other built in tuple op inv*>. *Note:* Although we generally have little to say regarding operator precedence, we find it convenient to assign high precedence to tuple projection in particular. A similar remark applies to relational projection as well (see later).

```
<n-adic other built in tuple op inv>
    ::=   <n-adic tuple union>

<n-adic tuple union>
    ::=   UNION { <tuple exp commalist> }
```

N-adic tuple INTERSECT, COMPOSE, and XUNION operators could also be defined if desired (though *n*-adic tuple COMPOSE and *n*-adic tuple XUNION operators would be logically equivalent).

```
<monadic or dyadic other built in tuple op inv>
    ::=   <monadic other built in tuple op inv>
        | <dyadic other built in tuple op inv>

<monadic other built in tuple op inv>
    ::=   <tuple rename> | <tuple extend>
        | <tuple wrap> | <tuple unwrap>

<tuple rename>
    ::=   <tuple exp> RENAME { <renaming commalist> }
```

The *<tuple exp>* must not be a *<monadic or dyadic other built in tuple op inv>*. The individual *<renaming>*s are effectively executed in parallel.[12]

```
<renaming>
    ::=   <attribute ref> AS <introduced name>
        | PREFIX <character string literal>
              AS <character string literal>
        | SUFFIX <character string literal>
              AS <character string literal>
```

For the syntax of *<character string literal>*, see *<built in scalar type name>*. The *<renaming>* PREFIX *a* AS *b* causes all attributes of the applicable tuple or relation whose name begins with the characters of *a* to be renamed such that their name begins with the characters of *b* instead. The *<renaming>* SUFFIX *a* AS *b* is defined analogously.

```
<tuple extend>
    ::=   EXTEND <tuple exp> : { <attribute assign commalist> }
```

The individual *<attribute assign>*s are effectively executed in parallel. Let *t* be the tuple denoted by the *<tuple exp>*, and let *A1, A2, ..., An* be the attributes of *t*. Every *<attribute assign>*, *AA* say, in the *<attribute assign commalist>* is syntactically identical to an *<assign>* (i.e., a *<scalar assign>*, a *<tuple assign>*, or a *<relation assign>*, as applicable), except that:

- The target of *AA* must be either an *<introduced name> N* or an *<attribute target> AT*.
- If *N* is specified, it must be distinct from every *Ai* (*i* = 1, 2, ..., *n*). If *AT* is specified, then it must identify, directly or indirectly, some *Ai* (*i* = 1, 2, ..., *n*).
- *AA* is allowed to contain an *<attribute ref>*, *AR* say, wherever a *<selector inv>* would be allowed. If the *<attribute name>* of *AR* is that of some *Ai* (*i* = 1, 2, ..., *n*), then *AR* denotes the corresponding attribute value from *t;* otherwise the *<tuple extend>* must be contained within some expression in which the meaning of *AR* is defined.

Steps a. and b. of the definition given for multiple assignment under RM Prescription 21 (see Chapter 1 of the present book) are applied to the *<attribute assign commalist>*. The result of that application is an *<attribute assign commalist>* in which each *<attribute assign>* is of the form

---

[12] RENAME as defined in the *Manifesto* book used parentheses, not braces, and the individual *<renaming>*s were executed in sequence instead of in parallel. Of course, the effect of sequential execution can always be obtained if desired by nesting, as in, e.g., (*t* RENAME {*A* AS *B*}) RENAME {*B* AS *C*}. Similar remarks apply to certain other operators as well—essentially, all of those operators for which the prose explanation in this chapter includes the phrase "effectively executed in parallel."

```
X := exp
```

Here each such *X* is either an *<introduced name>* or some *Ai,* and no two distinct *<attribute assign>*s specify the same target. Now:

- Consider the expression

  ```
  EXTEND t : { X := XX }
  ```

  where *X* is an introduced name. (For simplicity, we consider only the case where there is just one *<attribute assign>*. The considerations involved in dealing with more than one are essentially straightforward.) The value of this expression is a tuple identical to *t* except that it has an additional attribute called *X,* with declared type and value as specified by *XX.*

- Alternatively, consider the expression

  ```
  EXTEND t : { Y := YY }
  ```

  where *Y* is some *Ai.* (Again we consider for simplicity only the case where there is just one *<attribute assign>*.) This expression is equivalent to the following:

  ```
  ( EXTEND t : { X := YY } ) { ALL BUT Y } RENAME { X AS Y }
  ```

  Here *X* is an arbitrary *<introduced name>*, distinct from all existing attribute names in *t*.[13]

```
<attribute target>
    ::=   <attribute ref>
        | <attribute THE_ pv ref>

<attribute THE_ pv ref>
    ::=   <THE_ pv name> ( <attribute target> )

<tuple wrap>
    ::=   <tuple exp> WRAP ( <wrapping> )
```

The *<tuple exp>* must not be a *<monadic or dyadic other built in tuple op inv>*.

```
<wrapping>
    ::=   { [ ALL BUT ] <attribute ref commalist> }
                                         AS <introduced name>

<tuple unwrap>
    ::=   <tuple exp> UNWRAP ( <unwrapping> )
```

The *<tuple exp>* must not be a *<monadic or dyadic other built in tuple op inv>*.

```
<unwrapping>
    ::=   <attribute ref>
```

The declared type of the specified attribute must be some tuple type.

---

[13] Observe that this latter form of *<tuple extend>* replaces *<tuple substitute>* as defined in the *Manifesto* book (and a similar remark applies to *<extend>*, q.v.). *Note*: The keyword EXTEND is perhaps not the best in the circumstances, but it's hard to find a word that catches the overall sense better and yet is equally succinct.

```
<dyadic other built in tuple op inv>
    ::=   <dyadic tuple union> | <dyadic tuple compose>

<dyadic tuple union>
    ::=   <tuple exp> UNION <tuple exp>
```

The *<tuple exp>*s must not be *<monadic or dyadic other built in tuple op inv>*s, except that either or both can be another *<dyadic tuple union>*. *Note:* Dyadic tuple INTERSECT and MINUS operators could also be defined if desired. A dyadic tuple XUNION operator could be defined too, but it would be logically equivalent to *<dyadic tuple compose>* (see the production rule immediately following).

```
<dyadic tuple compose>
    ::=   <tuple exp> COMPOSE <tuple exp>
```

The *<tuple exp>*s must not be *<monadic or dyadic other built in tuple op inv>*s (not even another *<dyadic tuple compose>*).

```
<tuple assign>
    ::=   <tuple target> := <tuple exp>
        | <tuple update>

<tuple target>
    ::=   <tuple var ref>
        | <tuple THE_ pv ref>

<tuple THE_ pv ref>
    ::=   <THE_ pv name> ( <scalar target> )
```

The declared type of the *<possrep component>* corresponding to *<THE_ pv name>* must be some tuple type.

```
<tuple update>
    ::=   UPDATE <tuple target> :
               { <attribute assign commalist> }
```

Let *TT* be the *<tuple target>*, and let *A1, A2, ..., An* be the attributes of *TT*. Every *<attribute assign>*, *AA* say, in the *<attribute assign commalist>* is syntactically identical to an *<assign>*, except that:

- The target of *AA* must be an *<attribute target>*, *AT* say.
- *AT* must identify, directly or indirectly, some *Ai* (*i* = 1, 2, ..., *n*).
- *AA* is allowed to contain an *<attribute ref>*, *AR* say, wherever a *<selector inv>* would be allowed. If the *<attribute name>* of *AR* is that of some *Ai* (*i* = 1, 2, ..., *n*), then *AR* denotes the corresponding attribute value from *TT;* otherwise the *<tuple update>* must be contained within some expression in which the meaning of *AR* is defined.

Steps a. and b. of the definition given for multiple assignment under RM Prescription 21 (see Chapter 1 of the present book) are applied to the *<attribute assign commalist>*. The result of that application is an *<attribute assign commalist>* in which each *<attribute assign>* is of the form

```
Ai := exp
```

for some *Ai,* and no two distinct *<attribute assign>*s specify the same target *Ai*. Now consider the *<tuple update>*

```
UPDATE TT : { X := XX }
```

where *X* is some *Ai*. (For simplicity, we consider only the case where there is just one <*attribute assign*>. The considerations involved in dealing with more than one are essentially straightforward.) This <*tuple update*> is equivalent to the following <*tuple assign*>:

```
TT := EXTEND TT : { X := XX }
```

```
<tuple comp>
    ::=  <tuple exp> <tuple comp op> <tuple exp>
       | <tuple exp> ∈ <relation exp>
       | <tuple exp> ∉ <relation exp>
```

Tuple comparisons are a special case of the syntactic category <*bool exp*>. The symbol "∈" denotes the set membership operator; it can be read as *belongs to* or *is a member of* or just *in* or *is in*. The expression $t \notin r$ is semantically equivalent to the expression NOT ($t \in r$).

```
<tuple comp op>
    ::=  = | ≠
```

RELATIONAL OPERATIONS

Note that definitions of the semantics of many (not all) of the operators described in this section can be found in Appendix A of reference [7].

```
<relation nonwith exp>
    ::=  <relation var ref>
       | <relation op inv>
       | ( <relation exp> )

<relation op inv>
    ::=  <user op inv>
       | <built in relation op inv>

<built in relation op inv>
    ::=  <relation selector inv>
       | <THE_ op inv>
       | <attribute extractor inv>
       | <project>
       | <n-adic other built in relation op inv>
       | <monadic or dyadic other built in relation op inv>

<relation selector inv>
    ::=  RELATION [ <heading> ] { <tuple exp commalist> }
       | TABLE_DEE
       | TABLE_DUM
```

If the keyword RELATION is specified, (a) <*heading*> must be specified if <*tuple exp commalist*> is empty; (b) every <*tuple exp*> in the <*tuple exp commalist*> must have the same heading; (c) that heading must be exactly as defined by <*heading*> if <*heading*> is specified. TABLE_DEE and TABLE_DUM are shorthand for RELATION {} {TUPLE {}} and RELATION {} {}, respectively. *Note:* The proposals of reference [9], q.v., classify TABLE_DEE and TABLE_DUM not as <*relation selector inv*>s but as <*relation const ref*>s ("relation constant references") instead.

```
<project>
    ::=   <relation exp> { [ ALL BUT ] <attribute ref commalist> }
```

The *<relation exp>* must not be a *<monadic or dyadic other built in relation op inv>*. *Note:* As mentioned earlier, although we generally have little to say regarding operator precedence, we find it convenient to assign high precedence to projection in particular.

```
<n-adic other built in relation op inv>
    ::=   <n-adic union> | <n-adic disjoint union>
        | <n-adic intersect> | <n-adic join> | <n-adic times>
        | <n-adic xunion> | <n-adic compose>
```

```
<n-adic union>
    ::=   UNION [ <heading> ] { <relation exp commalist> }
```

Here (a) *<heading>* must be specified if *<relation exp commalist>* is empty; (b) every *<relation exp>* in the *<relation exp commalist>* must have the same heading; (c) that heading must be exactly as defined by *<heading>* if *<heading>* is specified. The same remarks apply to *<n-adic disjoint union>*, *<n-adic intersect>*, and *<n-adic xunion>*, q.v.

```
<n-adic disjoint union>
    ::=   D_UNION [ <heading> ] { <relation exp commalist> }
```

```
<n-adic intersect>
    ::=   INTERSECT [ <heading> ] { <relation exp commalist> }
```

```
<n-adic join>
    ::=   JOIN { <relation exp commalist> }
```

```
<n-adic times>
    ::=   TIMES { <relation exp commalist> }
```

The expression TIMES{*r1,r2,...,rn*} ($n \geqslant 0$) is defined if and only if relations *r1, r2, ..., rn* have no attribute names in common, in which case it's semantically equivalent to JOIN{*r1,r2,...,rn*}.

```
<n-adic xunion>
    ::=   XUNION [ <heading> ] { <relation exp commalist> }
```

Let *r1, r2, ..., rn* ($n \geqslant 0$) be relations all of the same type; then XUNION{*r1,r2,...,rn*} is a relation of that same type with body consisting just of those tuples *t* that appear in exactly *m* of *r1, r2, ..., rn,* where *m* is odd (and possibly different for different tuples *t*). See reference [6] for further explanation.

```
<n-adic compose>
    ::=   COMPOSE { <relation exp commalist> }
```

Let *r1, r2, ..., rn* ($n \geqslant 0$) be relations; then COMPOSE{*r1,r2,...,rn*} is shorthand for the projection on {*X*} of JOIN{*r1,r2,...,rn*}, where {*X*} is all of the attributes of *r1, r2, ..., rn* apart from ones common to at least two of those relations. See reference [6] for further explanation.

```
<monadic or dyadic other built in relation op inv>
    ::=   <monadic other built in relation op inv>
        | <dyadic other built in relation op inv>
```

```
<monadic other built in relation op inv>
    ::=   <rename> | <where> | <extend> | <wrap> | <unwrap>
        | <group> | <ungroup> | <tclose>

<rename>
    ::=   <relation exp> RENAME { <renaming commalist> }
```

The *<relation exp>* must not be a *<monadic or dyadic other built in relation op inv>*. The individual *<renaming>*s are effectively executed in parallel.

```
<where>
    ::=   <relation exp> WHERE <bool exp>
```

The *<relation exp>* must not be a *<monadic or dyadic other built in relation op inv>*. Let *r* be the relation denoted by *<relation exp>*. The *<bool exp>* is allowed to contain an *<attribute ref>*, *AR* say, wherever a *<selector inv>* would be allowed. The *<bool exp>* can be thought of as being evaluated for each tuple of *r* in turn. If the *<attribute name>* of *AR* is that of an attribute of *r*, then (for each such evaluation) *AR* denotes the corresponding attribute value from the corresponding tuple of *r;* otherwise the *<where>* must be contained in some expression in which *AR* is defined. *Note:* The *<where>* operator of **Tutorial D** includes the *restrict* operator of relational algebra as a special case.

```
<extend>
    ::=   EXTEND <relation exp> : { <attribute assign commalist> }
```

The individual *<attribute assign>*s are effectively executed in parallel. Let *r* be the relation denoted by the *<relation exp>*, and let *A1, A2, ..., An* be the attributes of *r*. Every *<attribute assign>*, *AA* say, in the *<attribute assign commalist>* is syntactically identical to an *<assign>* (i.e., a *<scalar assign>*, a *<tuple assign>*, or a *<relation assign>*, as applicable), except that:

- The target of *AA* must be either an *<introduced name> N* or an *<attribute target> AT.*
- If *N* is specified, it must be distinct from every *Ai* (*i* = 1, 2, ..., *n*). If *AT* is specified, then it must identify, directly or indirectly, some *Ai* (*i* = 1, 2, ..., *n*).
- *AA* is allowed to contain an *<attribute ref>*, *AR* say, wherever a *<selector inv>* would be allowed. *AA* can be thought of as being executed for each tuple of *r* in turn. If the *<attribute name>* of *AR* is that of some *Ai* (*i* = 1, 2, ..., *n*), then (for each such application) *AR* denotes the corresponding attribute value from the corresponding tuple of *r;* otherwise the *<extend>* must be contained within some expression in which the meaning of *AR* is defined.

Steps a. and b. of the definition given for multiple assignment under RM Prescription 21 (see Chapter 1 of the present book) are applied to the *<attribute assign commalist>*. The result of that application is an *<attribute assign commalist>* in which each *<attribute assign>* is of the form

```
X := exp
```

Here each such *X* is either an *<introduced name>* or some *Ai,* and no two distinct *<attribute assign>*s specify the same target. Now:

- Consider the expression

  ```
  EXTEND r : { X := XX }
  ```

  where *X* is an introduced name. (For simplicity, we consider only the case where there is just one

<attribute assign>. The considerations involved in dealing with more than one are essentially straightforward.) The value of this expression is a relation with (a) heading the heading of *r* extended with attribute *X* (with declared type as specified by *XX*) and (b) body consisting of all tuples *t* such that *t* is a tuple of *r* extended with a value for attribute *X* that is computed by evaluating the expression *XX* on that tuple of *r*.

- Alternatively, consider the expression

  ```
  EXTEND r : { Y := YY }
  ```

  where *Y* is some *Ai*. (Again we consider for simplicity only the case where there is just one *<attribute assign>*.) This expression is equivalent to the following:

  ```
  ( EXTEND r : { X := YY } ) { ALL BUT Y } RENAME { X AS Y }
  ```

  Here *X* is an arbitrary *<introduced name>*, distinct from all existing attribute names in *r*.

```
<wrap>
    ::=   <relation exp> WRAP ( <wrapping> )
```

The *<relation exp>* must not be a *<monadic or dyadic other built in relation op inv>*.

```
<unwrap>
    ::=   <relation exp> UNWRAP ( <unwrapping> )
```

The *<relation exp>* must not be a *<monadic or dyadic other built in relation op inv>*.

```
<group>
    ::=   <relation exp> GROUP ( <grouping> )
```

The *<relation exp>* must not be a *<monadic or dyadic other built in relation op inv>*.

```
<grouping>
    ::=   { [ ALL BUT ] <attribute ref commalist> }
                                      AS <introduced name>
```

```
<ungroup>
    ::=   <relation exp> UNGROUP ( <ungrouping> )
```

The *<relation exp>* must not be a *<monadic or dyadic other built in relation op inv>*.

```
<ungrouping>
    ::=   <attribute ref>
```

The declared type of the specified attribute must be some relation type.

```
<tclose>
    ::=   TCLOSE ( <relation exp> )
```

The *<relation exp>* must not be a *<monadic or dyadic other built in relation op inv>*. Furthermore, it must denote a relation of degree two, and the declared types of the attributes of that relation must both be the same.

```
<dyadic other built in relation op inv>
    ::=   <dyadic union> | <dyadic disjoint union>
        | <dyadic intersect> | <minus> | <included minus>
        | <dyadic join> | <dyadic times> | <dyadic xunion>
        | <dyadic compose> | <matching> | <not matching>
        | <divide> | <summarize>
```

```
<dyadic union>
    ::=   <relation exp> UNION <relation exp>
```

The <*relation exp*>s must not be <*monadic or dyadic other built in relation op inv*>s, except that either or both can be another <*dyadic union*>.

```
<dyadic disjoint union>
    ::=   <relation exp> D_UNION <relation exp>
```

The <*relation exp*>s must not be <*monadic or dyadic other built in relation op inv*>s, except that either or both can be another <*dyadic disjoint union*>. The operand relations must have no tuples in common.

```
<dyadic intersect>
    ::=   <relation exp> INTERSECT <relation exp>
```

The <*relation exp*>s must not be <*monadic or dyadic other built in relation op inv*>s, except that either or both can be another <*dyadic intersect*>.

```
<minus>
    ::=   <relation exp> MINUS <relation exp>
```

The <*relation exp*>s must not be <*monadic or dyadic other built in relation op inv*>s.

```
<included minus>
    ::=   <relation exp> I_MINUS <relation exp>
```

The <*relation exp*>s must not be <*monadic or dyadic other built in relation op inv*>s. The second operand relation must be included in the first.

```
<dyadic join>
    ::=   <relation exp> JOIN <relation exp>
```

The <*relation exp*>s must not be <*monadic or dyadic other built in relation op inv*>s, except that either or both can be another <*dyadic join*>.

```
<dyadic times>
    ::=   <relation exp> TIMES <relation exp>
```

The <*relation exp*>s must not be <*monadic or dyadic other built in relation op inv*>s, except that either or both can be another <*dyadic times*>.

```
<dyadic xunion>
    ::=   <relation exp> XUNION <relation exp>
```

The dyadic XUNION operator ("exclusive union") is essentially symmetric difference as usually understood. The <*relation exp*>s must not be <*monadic or dyadic other built in relation op inv*>s, except that either or both can be another <*dyadic xunion*>.

```
<dyadic compose>
    ::=   <relation exp> COMPOSE <relation exp>
```

The *<relation exp>*s must not be *<monadic or dyadic other built in relation op inv>*s (not even another *<dyadic compose>*).

```
<matching>
    ::=   <relation exp> MATCHING <relation exp>
```

The *<relation exp>*s must not be *<monadic or dyadic other built in relation op inv>*s. The keyword MATCHING can alternatively be spelled SEMIJOIN.

```
<not matching>
    ::=   <relation exp> NOT MATCHING <relation exp>
```

The *<relation exp>*s must not be *<monadic or dyadic other built in relation op inv>*s. The keywords NOT MATCHING can alternatively be spelled SEMIMINUS.

```
<divide>
    ::=   <relation exp> DIVIDEBY <relation exp> <per>
```

The *<relation exp>*s must not be *<monadic or dyadic other built in relation op inv>*s. *Note:* Elsewhere this book proposes that DIVIDEBY should be dropped. See references [4] and [9].

```
<per>
    ::=   PER ( <relation exp> [ , <relation exp> ] )
```

Reference [1] defines two distinct "divide" operators that it calls the Small Divide and the Great Divide, respectively. In **Tutorial D,** a *<divide>* in which the *<per>* contains just one *<relation exp>* is a Small Divide, a *<divide>* in which it contains two is a Great Divide.

```
<summarize>
    ::=   SUMMARIZE <relation exp> [ <per or by> ] :
                                   { <attribute assign commalist> }
```

The individual *<attribute assign>*s are effectively executed in parallel. Further explanation appears in the prose following the next three production rules. *Note:* Elsewhere this book proposes that SUMMARIZE should be dropped. See references [4] and [9].

```
<per or by>
    ::=   <per>
        | BY { [ ALL BUT ] <attribute ref commalist> }
```

If *<per>* is specified, it must contain exactly one *<relation exp>*. Let *p* be the relation denoted by that *<relation exp>*, let *r* be the relation denoted by the *<relation exp>* immediately following the keyword SUMMARIZE, and let *B1, B2, ..., Bm* and *A1, A2, ..., An* be the attributes of *p* and *r,* respectively. Every *Bi* (*i* = 1, 2, ..., *m*) must be some *Aj* (*j* = 1, 2, ..., *n*). Specifying BY {*Bx,By,...,Bz*} is equivalent to specifying PER (*r*{*Bx,By,...,Bz*}). Omitting *<per or by>* is equivalent to specifying PER (TABLE_DEE).

Every *<attribute assign>*, *AA* say, in the *<attribute assign commalist>* is syntactically identical to an *<assign>* (i.e., a *<scalar assign>*, a *<tuple assign>*, or a *<relation assign>*, as applicable), except that the target must be an *<introduced name>*, distinct from every *Bi* (*i* = 1, 2, ..., *m*), and the source is allowed to contain a *<summary>* wherever a *<selector inv>* would be allowed (see the production rule immediately following). Steps a. and b. of the definition given for multiple assignment under RM Prescription 21 (see Chapter 1 of the present book) are applied to the *<attribute assign commalist>*. The result of that application is an *<attribute assign*

commalist> in which each <*attribute assign*> is of the form

```
X := exp
```

where *X* is an <*introduced name*> that is distinct from every *Bi,* and no two distinct <*attribute assign*>s specify the same target. Now consider the expression

```
SUMMARIZE r PER ( p ) : { X := SUM ( XX ) }
```

(For simplicity, we consider only the case where there is just one <*attribute assign*>, the source consists of just a single <*summary*> in isolation, and the corresponding <*summary spec*> is SUM; the considerations involved in dealing with other cases are tedious but essentially straightforward.) This <*summarize*> is defined to be logically equivalent to the following:

```
EXTEND ( p ) : { X := SUM ( ( ( r ) MATCHING
                 RELATION { TUPLE { B1 B1 , B2 B2 , ... , Bm Bm } } )
                                   { ALL BUT B1 , B2 , ... , Bm } , XX }
```

In other words, the value of the <*summarize*> expression is a relation with (a) heading the heading of *p* extended with attribute *X* (with declared type as specified by *XX*) and (b) body consisting of all tuples *t* such that *t* is a tuple of *p* extended with a value *x* for attribute *X*. That value *x* is computed by evaluating the summary *XX* over all tuples of *r* that have the same value for attributes *B1, B2, ..., Bm* as tuple *t* does.

```
<summary>
    ::=   <summary spec> ( [ <integer exp> , ] [ <exp> ] )
```

Let *r* and *p* be as defined under the production rule for <*per or by*>. Then:

- The <*integer exp*> and following comma must be specified if and only if the <*summary spec*> is EXACTLY or EXACTLYD; the <*exp*> must be specified if and only if the <*summary spec*> is not COUNT. The <*exp*> (if specified) is effectively evaluated for each tuple of *p* in turn. Let *ee* be such an evaluation, and let the corresponding tuple of *p* be *eet*.

- The <*integer exp*> is allowed to contain an <*attribute ref*>, *IAR* say, wherever a <*selector inv*> would be allowed. If the <*attribute name*> of *IAR* is that of some attribute *Bi* (*i* = 1, 2, ..., *m*) of *p,* then (for each evaluation *ee*) *IAR* denotes the corresponding attribute value from tuple *eet;* otherwise the <*summarize*> must be contained within some expression in which the meaning of *AR* is defined.

- The <*exp*> is allowed to contain an <*attribute ref*>, *AR* say, wherever a <*selector inv*> would be allowed. The <*attribute name*> of *AR* can be—and usually is—that of some attribute *Aj* (*j* = 1, 2, ..., *n*) of *r* but must not be that of any attribute *Bi* (*i* = 1, 2, ..., *m*) of *p*. If the <*attribute name*> of *AR* is that of an attribute of *r,* then (for each evaluation *ee*) *AR* denotes the corresponding attribute value from some tuple of *r* that has the same values for *B1, B2, ..., Bm* as tuple *eet* does; otherwise the <*summarize*> must be contained within some expression in which the meaning of *AR* is defined.

- For SUM, SUMD, AVG, and AVGD, the declared type of <*exp*> must be some type for which the operator "+" is defined; for MAX and MIN, it must be some ordered type; for AND, OR, XOR, EXACTLY, and EXACTLYD, it must be type BOOLEAN; for UNION, D_UNION, INTERSECT, and XUNION, it must be some relation type.

```
<summary spec>
    ::=   COUNT | COUNTD | SUM | SUMD | AVG | AVGD | MAX | MIN
        | AND | OR | XOR | EXACTLY | EXACTLYD
        | UNION | D_UNION | INTERSECT | XUNION
```

The suffix "D" ("distinct") in COUNTD, SUMD, AVGD, and EXACTLYD means "eliminate redundant duplicate values before performing the summarization." COUNT and COUNTD return a result of declared type INTEGER; SUM, SUMD, AVG, AVGD, MAX, MIN, UNION, D_UNION, INTERSECT, and XUNION return a result of declared type the same as that of the applicable *<exp>*;[14] AND, OR, XOR, EXACTLY, and EXACTLYD return a result of declared type BOOLEAN.

```
<relation assign>
    ::=   <relation target> := <relation exp>
        | <relation insert>
        | <relation d_insert>
        | <relation delete>
        | <relation i_delete>
        | <relation update>

<relation target>
    ::=   <relation var ref>
        | <relation THE_ pv ref>

<relation THE_ pv ref>
    ::=   <THE_ pv name> ( <scalar target> )
```

The declared type of the *<possrep component>* corresponding to *<THE_ pv name>* must be some relation type. *Note:* Let *rx* be a *<relation exp>* that could appear in the *<virtual relation var def>* that defines some updatable virtual relvar *V* (see references [3] and [8], also Chapter 10 of the present book). Then it would be possible to allow *rx* to serve as a relation pseudovariable also. However, this possibility is not reflected in the grammar defined in this chapter.

```
<relation insert>
    ::=   INSERT <relation target> <relation exp>

<relation d_insert>
    ::=   D_INSERT <relation target> <relation exp>
```

The difference between INSERT and D_INSERT is that, loosely speaking, an attempt to insert a tuple that already exists succeeds with INSERT but fails with D_INSERT. (In other words, INSERT is defined in terms of UNION, while D_INSERT is defined in terms of D_UNION.)

```
<relation delete>
    ::=   DELETE <relation target> <relation exp>
        | DELETE <relation target> [ WHERE <bool exp> ]
```

Let *RT* be a *<relation target>*. Then the *<relation delete>* DELETE *RT* WHERE *bx* is shorthand for the *<relation delete>* DELETE *RT rx,* where the *<relation exp> rx* is a *<where>* of the form *RT* WHERE *bx*.

---

[14] It might be preferable in practice to define the *<summary spec>*s AVG and AVGD in such a way that, e.g., taking the average of a collection of integers returns a rational number. We do not do so here merely for reasons of simplicity.

```
<relation i_delete>
    ::=   I_DELETE <relation target> <relation exp>
```

The relation denoted by the *<relation exp>* must be included in the current value of the *<relation target>*.

```
<relation update>
    ::=   UPDATE <relation target> [ WHERE <bool exp> ] :
                 { <attribute assign commalist> }
```

Let *RT* be the *<relation target>*, and let *A1, A2, ..., An* be the attributes of *RT*. The *<bool exp>* is allowed to contain an *<attribute ref>*, *AR* say, wherever a *<selector inv>* would be allowed. The *<bool exp>* can be thought of as being evaluated for each tuple of *RT* in turn. If the *<attribute name>* of *AR* is that of some *Ai* (*i* = 1, 2, ..., *n*), then (for each such evaluation) *AR* denotes the corresponding attribute value from the corresponding tuple; otherwise the *<relation update>* must be contained within some expression in which the meaning of *AR* is defined. Every *<attribute assign>*, *AA* say, in the *<attribute assign commalist>* is syntactically identical to an *<assign>*, except that:

- The target of *AA* must be an *<attribute target>*, *AT* say.
- *AT* must identify, directly or indirectly, some *Ai* (*i* = 1, 2, ..., *n*).
- *AA* is allowed to contain an *<attribute ref>*, *AR* say, wherever a *<selector inv>* would be allowed. *AA* can be thought of as being applied to each tuple of *r* in turn. If the *<attribute name>* of *AR* is that of some *Ai* (*i* = 1, 2, ..., *n*), then (for each such application) *AR* denotes the corresponding attribute value from the corresponding tuple; otherwise the *<relation update>* must be contained within some expression in which the meaning of *AR* is defined.

Steps a. and b. of the definition given for multiple assignment under RM Prescription 21 (see Chapter 1 of the present book) are applied to the *<attribute assign commalist>*. The result of that application is an *<attribute assign commalist>* in which each *<attribute assign>* is of the form

```
Ai := exp
```

for some *Ai,* and no two distinct *<attribute assign>*s specify the same target *Ai*. Now consider the *<relation update>*

```
UPDATE RT WHERE b : { X := XX }
```

where *X* is some *Ai*. (For simplicity, we consider only the case where there is just one *<attribute assign>*. The considerations involved in dealing with more than one are essentially straightforward.) This *<relation update>* is equivalent to the following *<relation assign>*:

```
RT := ( RT WHERE NOT ( b ) )
        UNION
      ( EXTEND RT WHERE b : { X := XX } )
```

```
<relation comp>
    ::=   <relation exp> <relation comp op> <relation exp>
```

Relation comparisons are a special case of the syntactic category *<bool exp>*.

```
<relation comp op>
    ::=   = | ≠ | ⊆ | ⊇ | ⊂ | ⊃
```

The symbols "⊆" and "⊂" denote "subset of" and "proper subset of," respectively; the symbols "⊇" and

"⊃" denote "superset of" and "proper superset of," respectively.

RELATIONS AND ARRAYS

The Third Manifesto forbids tuple level retrieval from a relation (in other words, it prohibits anything analogous to SQL's FETCH via a cursor). But **Tutorial D** does allow a relation to be mapped to a one-dimensional array (of tuples), so an effect somewhat analogous to such tuple level retrieval can be obtained, if desired, by first performing such a mapping and then iterating over the resulting array.[15] But we deliberately adopt a very conservative approach to this part of the language. A fully orthogonal language would support arrays as "first class citizens"—implying support for a general ARRAY type generator, and arrays of any number of dimensions, and array expressions, and array assignment, and array comparisons, and so on. However, to include such extensive support in **Tutorial D** would complicate the language unduly and might well obscure more important points. For simplicity, therefore, we include only as much array support here as seems absolutely necessary; moreover, most of what we do include is deliberately "special cased." Note in particular that we don't define a syntactic category called *<array type spec>*.

```
<array var def>
    ::=   VAR <array var name> ARRAY <tuple type spec>
```

Let *A* be a **Tutorial D** array variable; then the value of *A* at any given time is a one-dimensional array containing zero or more tuples all of the same type. Let the values of *A* at times *t1* and *t2* be *a1* and *a2*, respectively. Then *a1* and *a2* need not necessarily contain the same number of tuples, and *A*'s upper bound thus varies with time (the lower bound, by contrast, is always zero).[16] Note that the only way *A* can acquire a new value is by means of a *<relation get>* (see below); in practice, of course, additional mechanisms will be desirable, but no such mechanisms are specified here.

```
<relation get>
    ::=   LOAD <array target> FROM <relation exp>
                               ORDER ( <order item commalist> )

<array target>
    ::=   <array var ref>

<array var ref>
    ::=   <array var name>
```

Points arising:

- Tuples from the relation denoted by *<relation exp>* are loaded into the array variable designated by *<array target>* in the order defined by the ORDER specification. If *<order item commalist>* is empty, tuples are loaded in an implementation defined order.
- The headings associated with *<array target>* and *<relation exp>* would normally be the same. But it would be possible, and perhaps desirable, to allow the former to be a proper subset of the latter. Such a feature could allow the sequence in which tuples are loaded into the array variable to be defined in terms of attributes whose values aren't themselves to be retrieved—thereby allowing, e.g., retrieval of employee

---

[15] By contrast, in accordance with RM Proscription 7 (see Chapter 1 of the present book), **Tutorial D** supports nothing comparable to SQL's tuple at a time update operators—i.e., UPDATE or DELETE "WHERE CURRENT OF *cursor*"—at all.

[16] Chapter 7 of the *Manifesto* book includes a coding example in which the lower bound is assumed to be one.

numbers and names in salary order without at the same time actually retrieving those salaries.

- LOAD is really assignment, of a kind (in particular, it has the effect of replacing whatever value the target previously had). However, we deliberately choose not to use assignment syntax for it because it effectively involves an implicit type conversion (i.e., a coercion) between a relation and an array. As a general rule, we prefer not to support coercions at all; in the case at hand, therefore, we prefer to define a new operation (LOAD), with operands that are explicitly defined to be of different types, instead of relying on conventional assignment plus coercion.

```
<order item>
    ::=   <direction> <attribute ref>
```

The attribute identified by *<attribute ref>* must be of some ordered type. A useful extension in practice might be to allow *<scalar exp>* in place of *<attribute ref>* here.

```
<direction>
    ::=   ASC | DESC

<relation set>
    ::=   LOAD <relation target> FROM <array var ref>
```

The array identified by *<array var ref>* must not include any duplicate tuples.

We also need a new kind of *<tuple nonwith exp>* and an *<array cardinality>* operator (a special case of *<integer exp>*):

```
<tuple nonwith exp>
    ::=   ... all previous possibilities, together with:
        | <array var ref> ( <subscript> )
```

We remark that it might be preferable in practice for subscripts to be enclosed in square brackets instead of parentheses. As it is, a *<tuple nonwith exp>* of the form *A(I)* is syntactically indistinguishable from an invocation of an operator called *A* with a single argument *I* of type INTEGER.

```
<subscript>
    ::=   <integer exp>

<array cardinality>
    ::=   COUNT ( <array var ref> )
```

STATEMENTS

```
<statement>
    ::=   <statement body> ;

<statement body>
    ::=   <with statement body>
        | <nonwith statement body>

<with statement body>
    ::=   WITH ( <name intro commalist> ) : <statement body>
```

Let *WSB* be a *<with statement body>*, and let *NIC* and *SB* be the *<name intro commalist>* and the *<statement body>*, respectively, immediately contained in *WSB*. The individual *<name intro>*s in *NIC* are evaluated in sequence as written. By definition, each such *<name intro>* immediately contains an *<introduced*

name> and an <*exp*>. Let *NI* be one of those <*name intro*>s, and let the <*introduced name*> and the <*exp*> immediately contained in *NI* be *N* and *X,* respectively. Then *N* denotes the value obtained by evaluating *X,* and it can appear subsequently in *WSB* wherever the expression (*X*)—i.e., *X* in parentheses—would be allowed.

```
<nonwith statement body>
    ::=   <previously defined statement body commalist>
        | <begin transaction> | <commit> | <rollback>
        | <call> | <return> | <case> | <if> | <do> | <while>
        | <leave> | <no op> | <compound statement body>
```

```
<previously defined statement body>
    ::=   <assignment>
        | <user op def> | <user op drop>
        | <user scalar type def> | <user scalar type drop>
        | <scalar var def> | <tuple var def>
        | <relation var def> | <relation var drop>
        | <constraint def> | <constraint drop>
        | <array var def> | <relation get> | <relation set>
```

```
<begin transaction>
    ::=   BEGIN TRANSACTION
```

BEGIN TRANSACTION can be issued when a transaction is in progress. The effect is to suspend the current transaction and to begin a new ("child") transaction. COMMIT or ROLLBACK terminates the transaction most recently begun, thereby resuming the suspended "parent" transaction, if any. *Note:* An industrial strength **D** might usefully allow BEGIN TRANSACTION to assign a name to the transaction in question and then require COMMIT and ROLLBACK to reference that name explicitly. However, we choose not to specify any such facilities here.

```
<commit>
    ::=   COMMIT
```

```
<rollback>
    ::=   ROLLBACK
```

```
<call>
    ::=   CALL <user op inv>
```

The user defined operator being invoked must be an update operator specifically. Arguments corresponding to parameters that are subject to update must be specified as <*scalar target*>s, <*tuple target*>s, or <*relation target*>s, as applicable.

```
<return>
    ::=   RETURN [ <exp> ]
```

A <*return*> is permitted only within a <*user read-only op def*> or a <*user update op def*>. The <*exp*> is required in the former case and prohibited in the latter. *Note:* A <*user update op def*> need not contain a <*return*> at all, in which case an implicit <*return*> is executed when the END OPERATOR is reached.

```
<case>
    ::=   CASE ; <when spec list> [ ELSE <statement> ]
          END CASE
```

```
<when spec>
    ::=   WHEN <bool exp> THEN <statement>

<if>
    ::=   IF <bool exp> THEN <statement> [ ELSE <statement> ]
          END IF

<do>
    ::=   [ <statement name> : ]
          DO <scalar var ref> := <integer exp> TO <integer exp> ;
             <statement>
          END DO

<while>
    ::=   [ <statement name> : ]
          WHILE <bool exp> ;
             <statement>
          END WHILE

<leave>
    ::=   LEAVE <statement name>
```

A variant of *<leave>* that merely terminates the current iteration of the loop and begins the next might be useful in practice.

```
<no op>
    ::=   ... zero or more "white space" characters

<compound statement body>
    ::=   BEGIN ; <statement list> END
```

One final point to close this section: In other writings we often make use of *end of statement, statement boundary,* and similar expressions to refer to the time when integrity checking is done, among other things. In such contexts, *statement* is to be understood, in **Tutorial D** terms, to mean a *<statement>* that contains no other *<statement>*s nested syntactically inside itself; i.e., it isn't a *<case>*, *<if>*, *<do>*, *<while>*, or compound statement. In other words (loosely): Integrity checking is done at semicolons.

RECENT LANGUAGE CHANGES

As mentioned in the introduction to this chapter, there are a number of differences between **Tutorial D** as defined herein and the version defined in Chapter 5 of the *Manifesto* book. For the benefit of readers who might be familiar with that earlier version, we summarize the main differences here.

- INT, RAT, and BOOL have been introduced as synonyms for INTEGER, RATIONAL, and BOOLEAN, respectively; REL and TUP have been introduced as synonyms for RELATION and TUPLE, respectively; DEE and DUM have been introduced as abbreviations for TABLE_DEE and TABLE_DUM, respectively.

- Scalar types now have an associated example value. Example values for the system defined scalar types INTEGER, RATIONAL, CHARACTER, and BOOLEAN have been defined.

- Those example values are used as a basis for defining the initial value for a scalar or tuple variable that has no such explicitly defined value.

- Scalar types can now be defined to be ORDINAL, ORDERED, or neither. Justification for this revision can be found in the section "Recent *Manifesto* Changes" in Chapter 1.

- Specifying an empty *<key def list>* for a real relvar or an application relvar is now interpreted to mean the entire heading is a key for the pertinent relvar.

- The *<name intro commalist>* in WITH is now enclosed in parentheses—not braces, because the individual *<name intro>* are executed in sequence, not in parallel—and those *<name intro>*s now use assignment-style syntax. WITH is now allowed on statements as well as expressions.

- The second argument to an aggregate operator invocation—or third, in the case of EXACTLY—is now specified as a general *<exp>* instead of just a simple *<attribute ref>*, and a similar change has been made to SUMMARIZE. *Note:* This facility is particularly useful in connection with the aggregate operator AND and what are sometimes called "tuple constraints." A tuple constraint is a constraint that can be checked for a given tuple in isolation (i.e., without having to inspect any other tuples in the pertinent relvar and without having to examine any other relvars). Such constraints take the general form "For all tuples in *rx, x* must be true." Previously, we would typically have had to express such a constraint as "The set of tuples in *rx* for which *rx* is not true must be empty"; but the extended form of the AND aggregate operator lets us express it a little more directly. For example, suppose the familiar suppliers-and-parts database is subject to the constraint that supplier status values must always be positive. Old style:

  ```
  CONSTRAINT ... IS_EMPTY ( S WHERE NOT ( STATUS > 0 ) ) ;
  ```

  New style:

  ```
  CONSTRAINT ... AND ( S , STATUS > 0 ) ;
  ```

- The syntax of *n*-adic aggregate operator invocations has been clarified.

- The *<agg op name>*s and *<summary spec>*s ALL and ANY (previously supported as alternative spellings for AND and OR, respectively) were always somewhat error prone and have been dropped.[17]

- The individual *<renaming>*s in a RENAME invocation are now executed in parallel instead of in sequence, and analogous remarks apply to EXTEND and SUMMARIZE. Braces are now used in all of these operators instead of parentheses.

- The syntax of EXTEND and SUMMARIZE has been revised to use assignment-style syntax.[18] The functionality of the read-only UPDATE or "substitute" operators is now provided by extended forms of the corresponding EXTEND operators (and those "substitute" operators have been dropped).

- The GROUP operator now takes just a single *<grouping>* instead of a *<grouping commalist>*. The reason is that in some cases the order in which individual *<grouping>*s are evaluated in a "multiple grouping" affects the overall result, and we didn't want to have to prescribe a specific evaluation sequence. Similar

---

[17] We are however actively considering FORALL and EXISTS as possible replacements. These keywords work quite well as *<agg op name>*s, less well as *<summary spec>*s. But we're proposing elsewhere (see Chapter 16) that SUMMARIZE be dropped anyway, so this latter objection is perhaps not very significant.

[18] Several writers have criticized this particular revision on the grounds that assignments as such cause "a change in state"—i.e., a change to some variable visible to the user—and EXTEND and SUMMARIZE don't. This observation is clearly correct. But every alternative syntax we've investigated seems to suffer from drawbacks of its own; therefore, given that any such alternative would require rather major surgery on this chapter (surgery for perhaps marginal gain at that), we've decided for the time being to let sleeping dogs lie.

remarks apply to UNGROUP, WRAP, and UNWRAP.

- As previously noted, the commalist of *<assign>*s (of various kinds) in EXTEND and SUMMARIZE, and UPDATE is now enclosed in braces; it is also preceded by a colon. Similar remarks apply to UPDATE (all forms).

- Support for dyadic and *n*-adic cartesian product (TIMES), dyadic and *n*-adic exclusive union (XUNION), *n*-adic COMPOSE, and included minus (I_MINUS) has been added.

- Support for *n*-adic tuple UNION has been added.

- The argument expression in TCLOSE is now enclosed in parentheses.

- Support for D_INSERT and I_DELETE has been added.

- Arrays now always have a lower bound of zero.

- The syntax of *<statement>* has been extended to allow a commalist of any number of *<previously defined statement body>*s preceding the semicolon. Thus, for example, any number of variables, or any number of types, or any number of constraints, can all be defined or destroyed "simultaneously." (Multiple assignment, which was already included in the version of **Tutorial D** defined in the *Manifesto* book, is now just a special case and thus no longer really requires separate production rules of its own.) *Note:* It would be remiss of us not to point out that there's a small unresolved syntax problem in this area, though. One form of *<previously defined statement body>* is a *<user op def>*. But the syntax of a *<user op def>* includes nested semicolons, and those semicolons might be thought to clash with the semicolon that terminates the overall *<statement>*. Possible fixes for this problem include the following:

    1. Do nothing—those semicolons don't actually lead to any syntactic ambiguity, they're just intrusive and awkward.

    2. Require *<user op def>*s to be enclosed in, say, parentheses when they appear in this particular context.

    3. Don't allow *<user op def>*s to appear in this context at all. This fix is probably the least attractive, since it would certainly constitute a violation of orthogonality, and in fact there might be a genuine requirement to be able to define several operators simultaneously (e.g., in cases of mutual recursion).

In addition to the foregoing, many syntactic category names and production rules have been revised (in some cases extensively). However, those revisions in themselves are not intended to induce any changes in the language being defined.

ACKNOWLEDGMENTS

We would like to acknowledge Adrian Hudnott's careful review of an earlier version of this chapter and his several contributions to the final version.

REFERENCES AND BIBLIOGRAPHY

1. Hugh Darwen and C. J. Date: "Into the Great Divide," in C. J. Date and Hugh Darwen, *Relational Database Writings 1989-1991*. Reading, Mass.: Addison-Wesley (1992).

2. C. J. Date: *An Introduction to Database Systems* (8th edition). Boston, Mass.: Addison-Wesley (2004).

3. C. J. Date: "The Logic of View Updating," in *Logic and Databases: The Roots of Relational Theory*. Victoria, B.C.: Trafford Publishing (2007). See *www.trafford.com/07-0690*. See also Chapter 10 of the present book.

4. C. J. Date: "A Brief History of the Relational Divide Operator" (Chapter 12 of the present book).

5. C. J. Date: "Inclusion Dependencies and Foreign Keys" (Chapter 13 of the present book).

6. C. J. Date: "*N*-adic vs. Dyadic Operators: An Investigation" (Chapter 15 of the present book).

7. C. J. Date and Hugh Darwen: *Databases, Types, and the Relational Model: The Third Manifesto* (3rd edition). Boston, Mass.: Addison-Wesley (2006).

8. C. J. Date and Hugh Darwen: "View Updating" (Appendix E of reference [7]).

9. C. J. Date and Hugh Darwen: "Toward an Industrial Strength Dialect of **Tutorial D**" (Chapter 16 of the present book).

10. C. J. Date and Hugh Darwen: "Extending Tutorial D to Support the Inheritance Model" (Chapter 21 of the present book).

APPENDIX A: A REMARK ON SYNTAX

As you might have noticed, the syntax of operator invocations in **Tutorial D** isn't very consistent. To be specific:

- User defined operators use a prefix style, with positional argument/parameter matching.

- System defined operators, by contrast, sometimes use an infix style ("+", "=", MINUS, etc.), sometimes a prefix style (MAX, EXACTLY, *n*-adic JOIN, etc.).

- Some of those system defined operators rely on positional argument/parameter matching ("+", MINUS, AVG, EXACTLY, etc.), while others don't ("=", *n*-adic JOIN, etc.).

- Some but not all of those system defined operators that rely on positional matching use parentheses to enclose their arguments, while those that don't use braces.

- Some operators seem to use a mixture of prefix and infix styles (SUMMARIZE, DIVIDEBY, etc.), or even a wholly private style of their own (project, THE_ operators, CASE, CAST, etc.).

- Finally, it could be argued that reliance on ordinal position for argument/parameter matching violates the spirit, if not the letter, of RM Proscription 1 (which, as explained in Chapter 1 of the present book, prohibits the use of ordinal position to distinguish the attributes of a relation)—especially in the case of scalar selectors, where the sequence of defining parameters (in the corresponding possrep definition) shouldn't matter but does.

Given all of the above, the possibility of adopting a more uniform style seems worth exploring. Now, we deliberately did no such thing earlier in this chapter because we didn't want **Tutorial D** to look even more outlandish than it might do already. Now, however, we can at least offer some thoughts on the subject. The obvious approach would be to do both of the following:

- Permit (if not mandate) a prefix style for everything

- Perform argument/parameter matching on the basis of names instead of position

  In the case of scalar selectors, for example, we might propose

```
CARTESIAN { Y 2.5, X 7.0 }
```

as a possible replacement for

```
CARTESIAN ( 7.0, 2.5 )
```

Note in particular that the parentheses have been replaced by braces; the assumption in the example is that CARTESIAN ("cartesian coordinates") is a possible representation for a user defined scalar type called, perhaps, POINT. In other words, the suggestion is that operator invocations in general should take the form

```
<op name> { <argument spec commalist> }
```

where *<op name>* identifies the operator in question and *<argument spec>* takes the form

```
<parameter name> <argument exp>
```

or even, possibly,

```
<parameter name> := <argument exp>
```

There are some difficulties, however. First, this new prefix style seems clumsier than the old one in the common special case in which the operator takes just one parameter, as with, e.g., SIN, COS, and (usually) COUNT. Second, some common operators (e.g., "+", "=", ":=") have names that do not abide by the usual rules for forming identifiers. Third, system defined operators, at least as currently defined, have no user known parameter names.

Now, we could perhaps fix this last problem by introducing a convention according to which those names are simply defined to be P1, P2, P3, etc., thus making (e.g.) expressions like this one valid:

```
JOIN { P1 r1 , P2 r2 , P3 r3 , ... , P50 r50 }
```

Again, however, the new syntax in this particular case seems clumsier than before, since JOIN is associative and the order in which the arguments are specified makes no difference.

Another difficulty arises in connection with examples like this one:

```
MINUS { P1 r1 , P2 r2 }
```

Here it becomes important to know which parameter is P1 and which P2 (since *r1* MINUS *r2* and *r2* MINUS *r1* aren't equivalent, in general). Some additional apparatus would be required to communicate such information to the user.

APPENDIX B: EMPTY LISTS AND COMMALISTS

For purposes of reference, in this appendix we (a) repeat the production rules for those **Tutorial D** constructs that include either lists or commalists and (b) explain in each case whether the list or commalist in question is allowed to be empty and, if so, what the significance is. *Note:* In some cases, the significance was in fact explained in the body of the chapter, but we repeat it here for convenience.

```
<user update op def>
    ::=   OPERATOR <user op name> ( <parameter def commalist> )
             UPDATES { [ ALL BUT ] <parameter name commalist> } ;
                <statement>
          END OPERATOR
```

If and only if the *<parameter def commalist>* is empty, then the update operator being defined is niladic and must always be invoked with an empty *<argument exp commalist>*. Also, let the UPDATES specification (either form) identify exactly *n* parameters as being subject to update. If the update operator being defined is niladic, then *n* must be zero. If *n* is zero, then the operator being defined is still an update operator, but it isn't allowed to assign to any of its parameters (it might, however, assign to some "global variable").

```
<user read-only op def>
    ::=   OPERATOR <user op name> ( <parameter def commalist> )
             RETURNS <type spec> ;
                <statement>
          END OPERATOR
```

If and only if the *<parameter def commalist>* is empty, then the read-only operator being defined is niladic and must always be invoked with an empty *<argument exp commalist>*.

```
<user op inv>
    ::=   <user op name> ( <argument exp commalist> )
```

If the *<argument exp commalist>* is empty, then the operator being invoked must be niladic and vice versa.

```
<scalar with exp>
    ::=   WITH ( <name intro commalist> ) : <scalar exp>

<tuple with exp>
    ::=   WITH ( <name intro commalist> ) : <tuple exp>

<relation with exp>
    ::=   WITH ( <name intro commalist> ) : <relation exp>
```

For all expressions *x*, the expression WITH () : *x* is logically equivalent to the expression *x* (regardless of whether *x* is a scalar, tuple, or relation expression).

```
<assignment>
    ::=   <assign commalist>
```

An *<assignment>* with an empty *<assign commalist>* is a *<no op>*.

```
<n-adic bool op name> { <bool exp commalist> }
```

AND {} returns TRUE, OR {} and XOR {} both return FALSE.

```
EXACTLY ( <integer exp> , { <bool exp commalist> } )
```

EXACTLY (*n*, {}) returns FALSE unless *n* = 0, in which case it returns TRUE.

```
<user scalar root type def>
    ::=   TYPE <user scalar type name>
             [ <ordering> ] <possrep def list>
               INIT ( <literal> )
```

The *<possrep def list>* is allowed to be empty if and only if type inheritance is supported, in which case, if the *<possrep def list>* is in fact empty, then the scalar root type being invoked must be a dummy type and vice versa. See Chapter 21 for further explanation.

```
<possrep def>
    ::=   POSSREP [ <possrep name> ]
                  { <possrep component def commalist>
                            [ <possrep constraint def> ] }
```

If the *<possrep component def commalist>* is empty, then the scalar root type being defined has at most one value—in fact, exactly one value, since there are no user defined empty scalar types (see RM Prescription 1).

```
<heading>
    ::=   { <attribute commalist> }
```

The (sole) heading with an empty *<attribute commalist>* is the heading of a tuple or relation of degree zero (in particular, it's the heading for TABLE_DEE and TABLE_DUM).

```
<real relation var def>
    ::=   VAR <relation var name> <real or base>
              <relation type or init value> <key def list>
```

To repeat from the body of the chapter: An empty *<key def list>* is equivalent to a *<key def list>* of the form KEY {ALL BUT}.

```
<key def>
    ::=   KEY { [ ALL BUT ] <attribute ref commalist> }
```

The *<key def>* KEY {} implies that the pertinent relvar can never contain more than one tuple. The *<key def>* KEY {ALL BUT} implies that every relation of the pertinent type is a legitimate value for the pertinent relvar (unless prevented by some further constraint, of course).

```
<virtual relation var def>
    ::=   VAR <relation var name> VIRTUAL
              ( <relation exp> ) <key def list>
```

To repeat from the body of the chapter: An empty *<key def list>* is equivalent to a *<key def list>* that contains exactly one *<key def>* for each key that can be inferred by the system from *<relation exp>*.

```
<application relation var def>
    ::=   VAR <relation var name> <private or public>
              <relation type or init value> <key def list>
```

To repeat from the body of the chapter: An empty *<key def list>* is equivalent to a *<key def list>* of the form KEY {ALL BUT}.

```
CASE <when def list> [ ELSE <scalar exp> ] END CASE
```

If ELSE *<scalar exp>* is omitted, the *<when def list>* must not be empty. The expression

```
CASE ELSE x END CASE
```

is equivalent to *x*.

```
<scalar selector inv>
    ::=   <possrep name> ( <argument exp commalist> )
```

An empty *<argument exp commalist>* is allowed (in fact, required) if and only if the *<possrep def>* identified by *<possrep name>* has an empty *<possrep component def commalist>*—in which case the *<scalar selector inv>* returns the sole value of the applicable type.

```
<n-adic count etc>
    ::=   <agg op name> { <exp commalist> }
```

COUNT {} and SUM_*T* {} return zero (of type INTEGER in the case of COUNT and type *T* in the case of SUM); MAX_*T* {} and MIN_*T* {} return the smallest value and the largest value, respectively, of type *T;* AVG {} raises an exception.

```
<scalar update>
    ::=   UPDATE <scalar target> :
               { <possrep component assign commalist> }
```

The *<scalar update>* UPDATE *ST* : {}, where *ST* is a *<scalar target>*, is equivalent to the *<scalar assign>* *ST* := *ST*.

```
<tuple selector inv>
    ::=   TUPLE { <tuple component commalist> }
```

The *<tuple selector inv>* TUPLE {} denotes the 0-tuple.

```
<tuple project>
    ::=   <tuple exp> { [ ALL BUT ] <attribute ref commalist> }
```

The *<tuple project>* *tx* {}, where *tx* is a *<tuple exp>*, returns the 0-tuple. The *<tuple project>* *tx* {ALL BUT} is equivalent to *tx*.

```
<n-adic tuple union>
    ::=   UNION { <tuple exp commalist> }
```

The *<n-adic tuple union>* UNION {} returns the 0-tuple.

```
<tuple rename>
    ::=   <tuple exp> RENAME { <renaming commalist> }
```

The *<tuple rename>* *tx* RENAME {}, where *tx* is a *<tuple exp>*, is equivalent to *tx*.

```
<tuple extend>
    ::=   EXTEND <tuple exp> : { <attribute assign commalist> }
```

The *<tuple extend>* EXTEND *tx* : {}, where *tx* is a *<tuple exp>*, is equivalent to *tx*.

```
<wrapping>
    ::=   { [ ALL BUT ] <attribute ref commalist> }
                                            AS <introduced name>
```

The *<tuple wrap>* *tx* WRAP ({} AS *A*), where *tx* is a *<tuple exp>*, is equivalent to EXTEND *tx* : {*A* := {}}; the *<tuple wrap>* *tx* WRAP ({ALL BUT} AS *A*), where again *tx* is a *<tuple exp>*, is equivalent to EXTEND *tx* : {*A* := {*X*}}, where {*X*} is all of the attributes of *tx*. Analogous remarks apply to the <*wrap*> *rx* WRAP ({} AS *A*) and the <*wrap*> *rx* WRAP ({ALL BUT} AS *A*), where *rx* is a <*relation exp*>.

```
<tuple update>
    ::=   UPDATE <tuple target> :
                   { <attribute assign commalist> }
```

The <*tuple update*> UPDATE *TT* : {}, where *TT* is a <*tuple target*>, is equivalent to the <*tuple assign*> *TT* := *TT*.

```
<relation selector inv>
    ::=   RELATION [ <heading> ] { <tuple exp commalist> }
        | TABLE_DEE
        | TABLE_DUM
```

If an empty <*tuple exp commalist*> is specified, then <*heading*> must be specified, and the <*relation selector inv*> returns the empty relation with the specified heading.

```
<project>
    ::=   <relation exp> { [ ALL BUT ] <attribute ref commalist> }
```

The <*project*> *rx* {}, where *rx* is a <*relation exp*>, returns TABLE_DUM if *rx* is empty and TABLE_DEE otherwise. The <*project*> *rx* {ALL BUT} is equivalent to *rx*.

```
<n-adic union>
    ::=   UNION [ <heading> ] { <relation exp commalist> }
```

If the <*relation exp commalist*> is empty, then <*heading*> must be specified, and the <*n-adic union*> returns the empty relation with the specified heading.

```
<n-adic disjoint union>
    ::=   D_UNION [ <heading> ] { <relation exp commalist> }
```

If the <*relation exp commalist*> is empty, then <*heading*> must be specified, and the <*n-adic disjoint union*> returns the empty relation with the specified heading.

```
<n-adic intersect>
    ::=   INTERSECT [ <heading> ] { <relation exp commalist> }
```

If the <*relation exp commalist*> is empty, then <*heading*> must be specified, and the <*n-adic intersect*> returns the universal relation with the specified heading (i.e., the relation whose body contains every tuple with the specified heading). In practice, the implementation might want to outlaw, or at least flag, any expression that requires such a value to be materialized.

```
<n-adic join>
    ::=   JOIN { <relation exp commalist> }
```

JOIN {} returns TABLE_DEE.

```
<n-adic times>
    ::=   TIMES { <relation exp commalist> }
```

TIMES {} returns TABLE_DEE.

```
<n-adic xunion>
    ::=   XUNION [ <heading> ] { <relation exp commalist> }
```

If the *<relation exp commalist>* is empty, then *<heading>* must be specified, and the *<n-adic xunion>* returns the empty relation with the specified heading.

```
<n-adic compose>
    ::=   COMPOSE { <relation exp commalist> }
```

COMPOSE {} returns TABLE_DEE.

```
<rename>
    ::=   <relation exp> RENAME { <renaming commalist> }
```

The *<rename>* *rx* RENAME {}, where *rx* is a *<relation exp>*, is equivalent to *rx*.

```
<extend>
    ::=   EXTEND <relation exp> : { <attribute assign commalist> }
```

The *<extend>* EXTEND *rx* : {}, where *rx* is a *<relation exp>*, is equivalent to *rx*.

```
<grouping>
    ::=   { [ ALL BUT ] <attribute ref commalist> }
                                       AS <introduced name>
```

The *<group>* *rx* GROUP ({} AS *A*), where *rx* is a *<relation exp>*, is equivalent to EXTEND *rx* : {*A* := TABLE_DEE}; the *<group>* *rx* GROUP ({ALL BUT} AS *A*), where again *rx* is a *<relation exp>*, is equivalent to EXTEND *rx*{} : {*A* := *rx*}.

```
<summarize>
    ::=   SUMMARIZE <relation exp> [ <per or by> ] :
                                   { <attribute assign commalist> }
```

The *<summarize>* SUMMARIZE *rx* PER (*px*) : {}, where *rx* and *px* are *<relation exp>*s, is equivalent to *px*. The *<summarize>* SUMMARIZE *rx* BY {*X*} : {}, where *rx* is a *<relation exp>*, is equivalent to *rx* {*X*}.

```
<per or by>
    ::=   <per>
        | BY { [ ALL BUT ] <attribute ref commalist> }
```

The *<summarize>* SUMMARIZE *rx* BY {} : {...}, where *rx* is a *<relation exp>*, is equivalent to SUMMARIZE *rx* PER (*rx* {}) : {...}. The *<summarize>* SUMMARIZE *rx* BY {ALL BUT} : {...}, where again *rx* is a *<relation exp>*, is equivalent to SUMMARIZE *rx* PER (*rx*) : {...}.

```
<relation update>
    ::=   UPDATE <relation target> [ WHERE <bool exp> ] :
               { <attribute assign commalist> }
```

The *<relation update>* UPDATE *RT* [WHERE *bx*] : {}, where *RT* is a *<relation target>* and *bx* is a *<bool exp>*, is equivalent to the *<relation assign>* *RT* := *RT*.

```
<relation get>
    ::=   LOAD <array target> FROM <relation exp>
                              ORDER ( <order item commalist> )
```

The *<relation get>* LOAD *AT* FROM *rx* ORDER (), where *AT* is an *<array target>* and *rx* is a *<relation exp>*, causes tuples from the relation denoted by *rx* to be loaded into the array variable designated by *AT* in an implementation defined order.

```
<with statement body>
    ::=   WITH ( <name intro commalist> ) : <statement body>
```

The *<with statement body>* WITH () : *S*, where *S* is a *<statement body>*, is logically equivalent to the *<statement body> S*.

```
<nonwith statement body>
    ::=   <previously defined statement body commalist>
        | <begin transaction> | <commit> | <rollback>
        | <call> | <return> | <case> | <if> | <do> | <while>
        | <leave> | <no op> | <compound statement body>
```

The *<nonwith statement body>* consisting of an empty *<previously defined statement body commalist>* is a *<no op>*.

```
<case>
    ::=   CASE ; <when spec list> [ ELSE <statement> ]
          END CASE
```

The statement

```
CASE ; ELSE S ; END CASE ;
```

(where *S* is a *<statement body>*) is equivalent to

```
S ;
```

The statement

```
CASE ; END CASE ;
```

is equivalent to a *<no op>*.

```
<compound statement body>
    ::=   BEGIN ; <statement list> END
```

The compound statement

```
BEGIN ; END ;
```

is equivalent to a *<no op>*.

Chapter 12

A Brief History of the Relational Divide Operator

Where the logic needs dissection
Across the Great Divide

—with apologies to Kate Wolf

The relational divide operator has never been widely understood. To some extent, this state of affairs might be due to the fact that the best known relational (or would-be relational) language, SQL, includes nothing directly analogous—but there are deeper issues involved, as I hope to show. What I plan to do is review the history of the divide operator in some detail, from its introduction by Codd in 1972 all the way up to the present day. Among other things, I'll show that:

- First, the operator suffers from several deficiencies, not the least of which is that it doesn't really solve the problem it was originally intended to address.
- Second, and partly as a consequence of the first point, the definition of the operator has changed several times over the years anyway.

Taken all in all, I believe a careful study of this history will serve to buttress an opinion I've held for a long time: namely, that language design is hard [11].

THE RUNNING EXAMPLE

Most of the examples in this chapter are based on the usual suppliers-and-parts database. A definition of that database, expressed in **Tutorial D** (see the next section), follows immediately; sample values are shown in Fig. 1 overleaf. The comments in italics show the intended interpretations of the three relation variables (relvars) S, P, and SP as suppliers, parts, and shipments, respectively.

```
VAR S BASE RELATION    /* supplier is under contract */
  { S# S# , SNAME NAME , STATUS INTEGER , CITY CHAR }
    KEY { S# } ;

VAR P BASE RELATION    /* part is of interest */
  { P# P# , PNAME NAME , COLOR COLOR , WEIGHT WEIGHT , CITY CHAR }
    KEY { P# } ;

VAR SP BASE RELATION  /* supplier supplies (or ships) part */
  { S# S# , P# P# , QTY QTY }
    KEY { S# , P# } ;
```

S

S#	SNAME	STATUS	CITY
S1	Smith	20	London
S2	Jones	10	Paris
S3	Blake	30	Paris
S4	Clark	20	London
S5	Adams	30	Athens

P

P#	PNAME	COLOR	WEIGHT	CITY
P1	Nut	Red	12.0	London
P2	Bolt	Green	17.0	Paris
P3	Screw	Blue	17.0	Oslo
P4	Screw	Red	14.0	London
P5	Cam	Blue	12.0	Paris
P6	Cog	Red	19.0	London

SP

S#	P#	QTY
S1	P1	300
S1	P2	200
S1	P3	400
S1	P4	200
S1	P5	100
S1	P6	100
S2	P1	300
S2	P2	400
S3	P2	200
S4	P2	200
S4	P4	300
S4	P5	400

Fig. 1: The suppliers-and-parts database—sample values

CODD'S DIVIDE

The first version of the relational divide operator was defined by Codd in reference [2].[1] For reasons I'll get to shortly, I won't give Codd's original definition as such; instead, I'll give one that (a) is simplified or abridged just slightly, compared to that original definition, and (b) captures the intent—most of the intent, at any rate—of that original definition but frames it somewhat differently. You can find Codd's original definition elsewhere in this book, if you're interested (see reference [15]).

- **Definition (Codd's divide, abridged version):** Let relations *r1* and *r2* be such that the heading {*Y*} of *r2* is some subset of the heading of *r1* and the set {*X*} is "the other attributes" of *r1*, as the following diagram suggests:

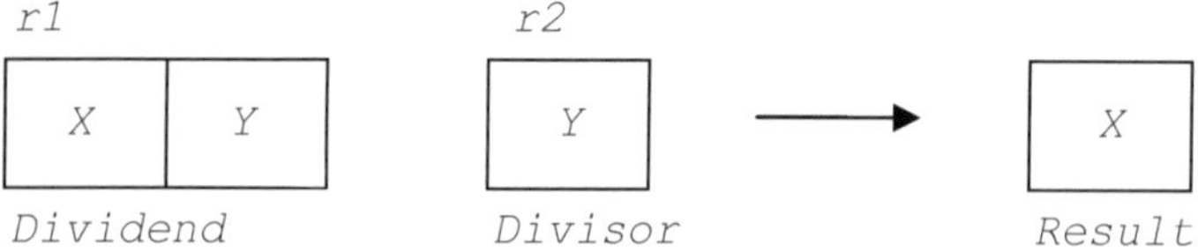

Then the division *r1* DIVIDEBY *r2* (where *r1* is the dividend and *r2* is the divisor) is equivalent to, and thus shorthand for, the following expression:

```
r1 { X } MINUS ( ( r1 { X } JOIN r2 ) MINUS r1 ) { X }
```

---

[1] I remark in passing that most of the standard database textbooks limit their attention to just this first version (if they discuss division at all, that is—some just ignore it entirely).

Note: A couple of points arise immediately that I need to get out of the way before I can get on with the substance of the discussion:

- First, the foregoing "longhand" (expanded) expression, like most other relational expressions in this chapter, is formulated in a language called **Tutorial D,** which is the language used in reference [16] to illustrate the ideas of *The Third Manifesto.* The language is mostly self-explanatory, but it does assume for convenience that projection has the highest precedence of all of the relational operators. *Note:* Projection is expressed in **Tutorial D** by means of braces; e.g., the expression *r1*{*X*} in the expansion above denotes the projection of relation *r1* on the set of attributes {*X*}. Moreover, the expression *r1*{ALL BUT *X*} denotes the projection of relation *r1* on all of its attributes other than {*X*}; in other words, *r1*{ALL BUT *X*} is equivalent to *r1*{*Y*}, where {*X*} and {*Y*} are disjoint and their set theory union is equal to the heading of *r1*.

- The second point is a little tricky: a matter of precision in the use of notation and terminology. I said in the definition that the set {*X*} was a set of attributes. However, I then used that same symbol {*X*} in the **Tutorial D** longhand equivalent:

  ```
  r1 { X } MINUS ( ( r1 { X } JOIN r2 ) MINUS r1 ) { X }
  ```

  But according to **Tutorial D** syntax rules, the symbol {*X*} in this expression is supposed to denote, not a set of attributes as such, but rather a set of attribute *names.* I apologize for this slight sloppiness on my part; more to the point, I hope it won't confuse you, because I intend to indulge in the same kind of sloppiness throughout the rest of the chapter. (In fact, as you might have noticed, I already did the same thing in the previous paragraph.)

Back to the divide operator per se. As the definition given above shows, the operator is clearly not primitive—it can be defined in terms of projection, difference (MINUS, in **Tutorial D**), and join. (This point was recognized by Codd himself in reference [2], and you won't be surprised to learn that a similar remark applies to all of the other divide operators I'll be describing in this chapter.) As a basis for explaining the semantics of the operator, here first is a stepwise version of the expanded form:

```
WITH ( Temp1 := r1 { X } ,
       Temp2 := Temp1 JOIN r2 { Y } ,
       Temp3 := Temp2 MINUS r1 { X , Y } ,
       Temp4 := Temp3 { X } ) :
Temp1 MINUS Temp4
```

For clarity, I've replaced *r2* in the second line by the corresponding identity projection—i.e., the projection of *r2* on all of its attributes, *r2*{*Y*}—and *r1* in the third line likewise by its identity projection *r1*{*X,Y*}. Using an obvious abbreviated notation for tuples, then, the semantics of the foregoing stepwise expansion can be explained (a trifle loosely) as follows:

- By definition, *r1* contains all tuples of the form <*x,y*> such that *x* is related to *y*. (Here and throughout this explanation, I use the phrase "is related to" to refer to the relationship represented by relation *r1* specifically.) Thus, *Temp1* contains all tuples of the form <*x*> such that there exists a *y* that *x* is related to.

- *Temp2* contains all possible tuples of the form <*x,y*> such that *y* appears in *r2* and *x* is related to some *y* (not necessarily the *y* in that same tuple). *Note:* The join here is in fact a cartesian product, since the two operand relations have no attribute names in common.[2] I remark in passing that the notion of two sets of attributes having no attribute names in common crops up several times in this chapter. I remark also that if {*H1*} and {*H2*} are sets of attributes that have no attribute names in common, then a fortiori {*H1*} and {*H2*} have no attributes in common either, since common attributes certainly have the same name. (By definition, an attribute is an ordered pair of the form <*A,T*>, where *A* is an attribute name and *T* is a type name.)

- *Temp3* contains all tuples of the form <*x,y*> that appear in *Temp2* and not in *r1*—in other words, all tuples of the form <*x,y*> such that *x* is related to some *y* but definitely *not* to the *y* in that same tuple.

- *Temp4* contains all tuples of the form <*x*> such that there exists a *y* that *x* is not related to.

- The result contains all tuples of the form <*x*> such that there exists a *y* that *x* is related to and there does not exist a *y* that *x* is not related to. In other words, the result contains *x*'s from *r1* that are related (in *r1*) to all of the *y*'s in *r2*.

  By way of example, consider the expression:

```
SP { S# , P# } DIVIDEBY P { P# }
```

The dividend here is the projection of SP on {S#,P#} and the divisor is the projection of P on {P#}; the heading of the divisor is thus a subset of that of the dividend as required, and the expression overall yields supplier numbers for suppliers mentioned in SP who supply all parts mentioned in P. Given the sample values in Fig. 1, the result is:

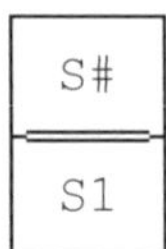

S#
S1

By the way, you might be wondering why the operator is called divide. The answer is that if *r0* and *r2* are relations with no attribute names in common and we form the cartesian product *r1* = *r0* TIMES *r2* (or, equivalently, *r0* JOIN *r2*), and then divide *r1* by *r2,* we get back to *r0;* in other words, product and divide are inverses of each other, in a sense. Well ... they're inverses so long as *r2* isn't empty. If it is, however, then *r1,* and therefore *r1* DIVIDEBY *r2,* are both empty as well, regardless of the value of *r0*. So the justification for the name "divide" is weak at best—but I'll stay with it in this chapter, for historical reasons if nothing else.

Now I can explain why I choose not to quote Codd's original definition verbatim. Actually I have several reasons:

- First, Codd's definition assumed (albeit only "for notational and expository convenience") that attributes were identified by ordinal position, left to right. I prefer a definition that relies on identifying attributes by name.

- Second, Codd's definition relied on a slightly suspect notion called "union compatibility." I prefer a definition that relies on the notion of relation types. (In particular, the operator MINUS is defined, in the version of relational algebra that I support, if and only if its operand relations are of the same relation type. See reference [16] for further details.)

---

[2] The fact that cartesian product (TIMES) is just a special case of join is explained in many places (see, e.g., reference [6]).

- Third, Codd's definition was framed in terms of certain subsidiary concepts that I have no need for in this chapter and would only be distracting for present purposes.

- Fourth, Codd's definition didn't actually require the heading of the divisor to be a subset of that of the dividend; instead, it required only that the heading of the divisor *have a subset* that was a subset of that of the dividend.[3] In the definition I gave, I simplified the requirement—and hence the operator too—mainly for pedagogical reasons. I'll fix the discrepancy in the next section.

  Aside: Honesty compels me to admit that for many years I thought Codd's definition did require the heading of the divisor to be a subset of that of the dividend; I only realized my mistake in working on the present chapter! What's more, I regret to say that the mistake is reflected in many of my earlier writings (in references [8], [9], and [16] in particular). My apologies to Codd for misrepresenting his intentions in this matter, and to anyone else I might have inadvertently misled in this connection. In my own defense, however, let me add that (a) I checked several of the standard database textbooks and found that every one of those that discussed division at all (eight of them, to be precise) made the same mistake, and (b) in any case, I don't believe the mistake is very significant, for reasons that I hope will become apparent as we proceed. *End of aside.*

- Last—this point hardly seems worth mentioning, but I'd like to spell it out anyway—I want all of the definitions in this chapter to be expressed in the same general style, in order to facilitate the task of comparing and contrasting them, and Codd's original style does not readily lend itself to some of the definitions to come (at least, not without a lot of additional groundwork that I prefer not to get into here).

Incidentally, it's interesting to note that Codd apparently failed to notice that his divide operator logically required support for relations of degree zero. (I'll explain in a little while why I say he "apparently failed to notice" this fact.) As I hope you know, there are exactly two such relations: TABLE_DEE (DEE for short), which contains just one tuple—the empty tuple, of course—and TABLE_DUM (DUM for short), which contains no tuples at all (see reference [6]). Here again is Codd's divide (abridged definition): The expression *r1* DIVIDEBY *r2,* where the heading {*Y*} of *r2* is a subset of the heading of *r1* and {*X*} is the other attributes of *r1,* is shorthand for the following:

```
r1 { X } MINUS ( ( r1 { X } JOIN r2 ) MINUS r1 ) { X }
```

Now consider what happens if the heading of *r2* isn't a *proper* subset of that of *r1* (i.e., {*X*} is just {}, the empty set). The expansion becomes:

```
r1 { } MINUS ( ( r1 { } JOIN r2 ) MINUS r1 ) { }
```

It follows that:

- If *r1* is empty (i.e., contains no tuples), *r1*{} is TABLE_DUM, and the overall expression also evaluates to TABLE_DUM.

- Alternatively, if *r1* is nonempty, *r1*{} is TABLE_DEE, *r1*{} JOIN *r2* reduces to just *r2,* and the overall expression evaluates to either TABLE_DEE or TABLE_DUM—TABLE_DEE if every tuple in *r2* also appears in *r1,* TABLE_DUM otherwise.

Either way, of course, the result is of degree zero, and so we see that Codd's divide does logically require support for such relations.

---

[3] Which in fact it always will!—since the empty set is a subset of every set. Codd's definition apparently overlooked this fact.

Note: As a special case of the foregoing, let *r1* = *r2* = *r*, say; then we have *r* DIVIDEBY *r* = TABLE_DUM if *r* is empty, TABLE_DEE otherwise. It's also interesting to ask what happens if the heading of *r2* is the empty set (as noted in a footnote earlier, the empty set is a subset of every set, and so this case too is legitimate). In this case, {*Y*} is (as stated) the empty set, *r2* is either TABLE_DEE or TABLE_DUM, and {*X*} is the entire heading of *r1*. The expansion becomes:

```
r1 MINUS ( ( r1 JOIN r2 ) MINUS r1 )
```

It follows that:

- If *r2* is TABLE_DEE, *r1* JOIN *r2* reduces to just *r1*, the second operand to the outer MINUS is thus empty, and the expression overall degenerates to just *r1*.
- Alternatively, if *r2* is TABLE_DUM, *r1* JOIN *r2* is empty, the second operand to the outer MINUS is thus empty again, and again the expression overall degenerates to just *r1*.

Observe that this result is intuitively reasonable, inasmuch as in both cases, every tuple in *r1* is indeed "related to"—meaning, here, that its projection on no attributes is equal to—every tuple in *r2*.

Another special case: What happens to *r1* DIVIDEBY *r2* if *r2* is empty (i.e., contains no tuples)? As you can easily check for yourself, the division reduces to a simple projection in this case: namely, the projection *r1*{*X*}.

From all of the above, it follows in particular that (a) TABLE_DEE divided by either TABLE_DEE or TABLE_DUM gives TABLE_DEE, and (b) TABLE_DUM divided by either TABLE_DEE or TABLE_DUM gives TABLE_DUM. The following table summarizes these special cases:

dividend	divisor	result
DEE	DEE	DEE
DEE	DUM	DEE
DUM	DEE	DUM
DUM	DUM	DUM

Now I can explain why I said earlier that Codd "apparently failed to notice" that his divide operator logically required support for relations of degree zero. The point is, I'm pretty sure he wrote somewhere—though a precise reference escapes me—that he saw little value in the idea of such relations; certainly he never seemed to acknowledge the fundamental nature of the role played by such relations in the relational algebra. For example, in his book [4], he repeatedly stresses the point that the phrase "*n*-ary relations" includes *n* = 1 as an important special case, and yet he never even mentions the arguably much more important special case *n* = 0. In fact, the only mention of that case I've been able to find in his published writings at all is in a fairly obscure article [5], where he states that "[degree] *n* = 1 is often very useful [and degree] *n* = 0 is occasionally useful." And it seems to me that he wouldn't have (*couldn't* have) been so dismissive of the idea if he had realized that certain of his relational operators—divide in particular, but not just divide—logically required it.

I'll close this section by giving another definition for Codd's divide (though still the abridged version, please note), this one expressed in terms of semidifference—NOT MATCHING, in **Tutorial D**—instead of difference (i.e., MINUS). Here first is a definition of NOT MATCHING, taken from reference [14]:

- **Definition (NOT MATCHING):** The semidifference *r1* NOT MATCHING *r2* between relations *r1* and *r2* (in that order) is equivalent to, and thus shorthand for, the following expression:

  ```
  r1 MINUS ( r1 MATCHING r2 )
  ```

  As you can see, this definition relies on MATCHING, which is **Tutorial D** syntax for the semijoin operator. MATCHING in turn can be defined thus:

- **Definition (MATCHING):** Let relations *r1* and *r2* be such that attributes with the same name are of the same type.[4] Then the semijoin *r1* MATCHING *r2* of *r1* with *r2* (in that order) is equivalent to, and thus shorthand for, the join of *r1* and *r2*, projected back on to the attributes of *r1*.

Examples: The expression S MATCHING SP denotes suppliers who supply at least one part; the expression S NOT MATCHING SP denotes suppliers who supply no parts at all (speaking a trifle loosely in both cases). Given the sample values in Fig. 1, the results are:

```
/* suppliers who supply at least one part */
```

S#	SNAME	STATUS	CITY
S1	Smith	20	London
S2	Jones	10	Paris
S3	Blake	30	Paris
S4	Clark	20	London

```
/* suppliers who supply no parts at all */
```

S#	SNAME	STATUS	CITY
S5	Adams	30	Athens

Now, it's easy to see that NOT MATCHING is a generalization of the familiar MINUS operator. To be specific, let relations *r1* and *r2* be of the same type. Then *r1* NOT MATCHING *r2* is shorthand for *r1* MINUS (*r1* MATCHING *r2*), as usual. In this particular case, however, (a) *r1* MATCHING *r2* degenerates to *r1* JOIN *r2;* (b) *r1* JOIN *r2* in turn degenerates to *r1* INTERSECT *r2;* and (c) *r1* MINUS (*r1* INTERSECT *r2*) degenerates to *r1* MINUS *r2*. No harm is done, therefore, if we revise the definition of Codd's divide (abridged version) to use NOT MATCHING instead of MINUS—a revision that allows us to drop a projection, incidentally—as follows:

```
r1 { X } NOT MATCHING ( ( r1 { X } JOIN r2 ) NOT MATCHING r1 )
```

This revised definition illustrates the general style—*a* NOT MATCHING (*b* NOT MATCHING *c*) for some *a, b,* and *c*—to be used in all of the definitions given later in the body of the chapter (though not in the appendixes).

ISSUES WITH CODD'S DIVIDE

I've already suggested that Codd's divide suffers from problems. In fact, we can identify at least three such problems. However, let me say immediately that the first isn't really a problem with Codd's divide as such, but rather with the simplified form of that operator as I defined it in the previous section. As we've seen, that simplified version requires the heading of the divisor to be a subset of that of the dividend. As a consequence, the operator is somewhat limited in its application; in effect, it can be used only in a certain special case, and arguably

---

[4] Elsewhere this book uses the term *joinable* to refer to such relations. One way to define this concept is as follows: Relations *r1* and *r2* are joinable if and only if the set theory union of their headings is a valid heading.

a somewhat unusual special case at that. Such a state of affairs is very different from what we typically find in mathematics, where operators are usually defined in such a way as to be as general as possible. As a simple analogy, consider the familiar divide operator of conventional arithmetic. That operator allows us to divide any number *a* by any number *b*. But Codd's divide (at least in its simplified form) is like a hypothetical arithmetic divide that would allow us to divide *a* by *b* only if $b < a$; in other words, it suffers from an artificial, and in fact unnecessary, limitation.

> *Aside:* The foregoing analogy does raise another question, though. In arithmetic, there's an exception to the rule that we can divide any number *a* by any number *b*—namely, the case $b = 0$; division by zero is prohibited. So is there any analog of division by zero for Codd's divide, or more generally for any of the various relational divide operators I'll be discussing? That is, is it possible to formulate a relational divide that's correct as far as the compiler is concerned (meaning it satisfies all compile time checks) but nevertheless fails at run time, in a way analogous to the way division by zero fails "at run time" (as it were) in arithmetic? I don't propose to examine this question in detail here; let me just say for the record that (as a careful study of the definitions will show) the answer is *no*. *End of aside.*

Anyway, here's a definition for Codd's divide that does fix the foregoing problem:

- **Definition (Codd's divide, unabridged version):** Let relations *r1* and *r2* be such that attributes with the same name are of the same type, the set {*Y*} is the common attributes of *r1* and *r2*, and the set {*X*} is the other attributes of *r1* (see the following diagram).

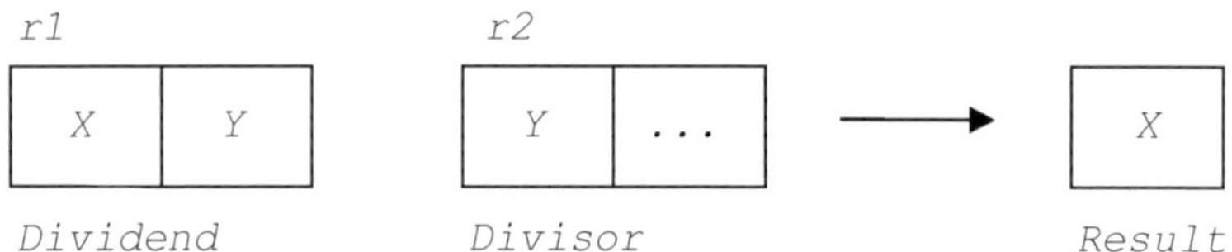

Then the division *r1* DIVIDEBY *r2* (where *r1* is the dividend and *r2* is the divisor) is equivalent to, and thus shorthand for, the following expression:

```
r1 { X } NOT MATCHING
                    ( ( r1 { X } JOIN r2 { Y } ) NOT MATCHING r1 )
```

Note: If the set of attributes {ALL BUT *Y*} of *r2* is empty, *r2*{*Y*} can be replaced by *r2*, and the foregoing definition reduces to the abridged version given earlier.

I turn now to the second issue, which I'll explain in terms of the sample query "Get suppliers who supply all parts." Let the desired set of suppliers be *sallp*. As we saw in the previous section, then, the expression SP{S#,P#} DIVIDEBY P{P#} gives supplier *numbers* (extracted from SP) for suppliers in that set *sallp*. In practice, however, we would probably want entire supplier *tuples* (extracted from S) for suppliers in that set *sallp*, not just the corresponding supplier numbers. In the example, therefore, the divide will need to be either preceded or followed by a join, as in either of the following formulations:

```
( SP { S#, P# } JOIN S ) DIVIDEBY P { P# }

( SP { S#, P# } DIVIDEBY P { P# } ) JOIN S
```

The effect of the join in both cases is to ensure that the result includes the desired SNAME, STATUS, and CITY values as well as the supplier numbers (S# values) as such. In other words, as this example suggests, queries involving a divide often require that divide to be either preceded or followed by a join—the divide by itself is typically not adequate to express the entire query. Of course, this isn't a big deal, but it's annoying nevertheless.

The third and biggest issue with Codd's divide is that it doesn't really solve the problem it was originally meant to solve, anyway. Codd's divide is often characterized, informally, as an algebraic counterpart to the universal quantifier FORALL of predicate logic; indeed, Codd himself characterized it that way in references [2] and [3]. And I said more or less the same thing myself when I said that the expression SP{S#,P#} DIVIDEBY P{P#} returns supplier numbers for suppliers who supply all parts mentioned in P (notice that word *all*). That being said, however, I now observe that discussions of divide in the literature—which, as noted earlier, almost invariably limit themselves to Codd's divide, and the abridged version at that—typically give a simpler interpretation for such expressions, one that could be rendered in the case at hand as just "Get supplier numbers for suppliers who supply all parts" (instead of "Get supplier numbers who supply all parts *mentioned in P*"). But such simpler interpretations are actually oversimplified; indeed, they can be quite misleading, as I'll now demonstrate.

As a basis for that demonstration, let me switch to an example that makes a little more intuitive sense. Consider the query "Get supplier numbers for suppliers who supply all purple parts." The point of this revised example is that, given the sample values in Fig. 1:

a. There are some parts, but there aren't any purple ones (i.e., the set of purple parts is empty), and hence

b. There are no tuples for purple parts in P and no tuples for shipments of purple parts in SP.

I'll begin my analysis of this example by first stating the query a little more precisely, using the universal quantifier FORALL:[5]

```
Get supplier numbers for suppliers s
             where FORALL purple parts pp ( s supplies pp )
```

Now, a user familiar with Codd's divide would probably try to formulate this query as follows:

```
WITH ( PP := P WHERE COLOR = COLOR('Purple') ) :
     SP { S# , P# } DIVIDEBY PP { P# }
```

I'll refer to this formulation as *Expression 1*. Now I appeal to the well known fact that, in logic, the boolean expression

```
FORALL x ( bx )
```

returns TRUE if there aren't any *x*'s, regardless of what form the boolean expression *bx* happens to take.[6] It follows that if there are no purple parts, the expression

```
FORALL purple parts pp ( s supplies pp )
```

returns TRUE no matter which supplier *s* we happen to be talking about (in other words, it returns TRUE for every supplier *s*). So if there are no purple parts, then every supplier supplies all of them!—even suppliers who (like supplier S5 in Fig. 1) supply no parts at all. But Expression 1 can't possibly return supplier numbers for suppliers who supply no parts at all, because such suppliers aren't represented in SP in the first place (they're represented in S, of course, but not in SP). Thus we see that Expression 1 doesn't accurately represent the query "Get supplier numbers for suppliers who supply all purple parts"; rather, it represents the query "Get supplier

---

[5] In case you're not familiar with that quantifier, I should explain that FORALL *x* (*bx*), where *bx* is a boolean expression, is itself a boolean expression, and it evaluates to TRUE if and only if *bx* evaluates to TRUE for all possible values of the variable *x*.

[6] See, e.g., reference [12] if you need to see this aspect of logic explained in detail. In fact I've appealed to it in this chapter already, in passing; to be specific, I said earlier (paraphrasing) that *r1* DIVIDEBY *r2* degenerates to just *r1* if *r2* is TABLE_DUM because, in this case, every tuple in *r1* is related to—i.e., its projection on no attributes is equal to—"every tuple" in *r2*.

numbers for suppliers who *supply at least one part and* supply all purple parts."

As a matter of fact, it should be obvious from the informal explanation of the semantics of (the simplified form of) Codd's divide that I gave in the previous section that the foregoing is the case. The final step in that explanation was as follows:

- The result contains all tuples of the form <*x*> such that there exists a *y* that *x* is related to and there does not exist a *y* that *x* is not related to. In other words, the result contains *x*'s from *r1* that are related (in *r1*) to all of the *y*'s in *r2*.

  Rephrasing these remarks in terms of our example (and simplifying slightly), we get:

- The result contains all tuples of the form <*s#*> such that there exists a part that supplier *s#* supplies and there does not exist a purple part that supplier *s#* does not supply. In other words, the result contains *s#*'s from SP that are related (in SP) to every purple part.

Let me close this section by mentioning that there are at least two alternative formalisms that can be used to tackle the problem that the various divide operators are meant to address (alternatives to the divide formalism as such, I mean—indeed, ones that are preferable in some respects to the divide formalism as such). They're discussed in Appendixes A and B, respectively. See also reference [15], which in some respects can be thought of as a companion to the present chapter.

THE SMALL DIVIDE

The term *Small Divide* was introduced in reference [8] to distinguish the operator in question from another operator it called the Great Divide. At first it used the term to refer to Codd's divide; subsequently, it used it to refer to a revised form of Codd's divide—a revised form that addressed the third, and biggest, of the issues identified in the previous section. And later in this chapter, I'll follow reference [16] in using it to refer to a generalized version of that revised form ... I apologize if you find these denotational shifts confusing, but it's in the nature of the beast (or in the nature of the history of the beast, perhaps I should say).

Actually, it's perfectly reasonable to use the same term to refer to both the revised form of Codd's divide and the generalized version of that revised form, since the generalization truly is a generalization; that is, the second meaning of the term truly is just a special case of the third. But first things first—let's get to some technical substance. We saw in the previous section that what I there called Expression 1 was inadequate to represent the query "Get supplier numbers for suppliers who supply all purple parts," because it missed suppliers who supplied no parts at all, and yet such suppliers ought to be included if there aren't any purple parts. How can we fix this problem? Well, here's a stepwise expansion of Expression 1:

```
WITH ( PP := P WHERE COLOR = COLOR('Purple') ,
       Temp1 := SP { S# } ,
       Temp2 := Temp1 JOIN PP { P# } ,
       Temp3 := Temp2 NOT MATCHING SP { S# , P# } ) :
Temp1 NOT MATCHING Temp3
```

Now suppose we were to replace the reference to SP in the second line by a reference to S instead—a change that (from an intuitive point of view) would mean we're considering suppliers under contract instead of suppliers that supply at least one part:

```
WITH ( PP := P WHERE COLOR = COLOR('Purple') ,
       Temp1 := S { S# } ,
       Temp2 := Temp1 JOIN PP { P# } ,
       Temp3 := Temp2 NOT MATCHING SP { S# , P# } ) :
Temp1 NOT MATCHING Temp3
```

Now we have:

- *Temp1* contains all tuples of the form <*s#*> such that supplier *s#* is under contract.

- *Temp2* contains all tuples of the form <*s#,p#*> such that supplier *s#* is under contract and part *p#* is a purple part (more precisely, a purple part that's "of interest," but for simplicity I'll ignore, for now, the bit about the part being of interest).

- *Temp3* contains all tuples of the form <*s#,p#*> that appear in *Temp2* and not in SP (more precisely, in the projection of SP on {S#,P#})—in other words, all tuples of the form <*s#,p#*> such that supplier *s#* is under contract, part *p#* is purple, and supplier *s#* does not supply part *p#*.

- Hence the result contains all tuples of the form <*s#*> such that supplier *s#* is under contract and there does not exist a purple part that supplier *s#* does not supply.

So the overall expression represents the query "Get supplier numbers for suppliers who *are under contract (i.e., are represented in S) and* supply all purple parts"—in other words, the query we really want—and it does so regardless of whether or not there actually are any purple parts.

The foregoing discussion strongly suggests that it would be desirable to define a revised version of Codd's divide, one that corresponds to the modified stepwise expression discussed in the example; and that's what the Small Divide is all about. Here's the definition:

- **Definition (Small Divide, original version):** Let relations *r1, r2,* and *r3* be such that (a) the headings of *r1* and *r2* are {*X*} and {*Y*}, respectively; (b) the sets {*X*} and {*Y*} have no attribute names in common; and (c) the heading of *r3* is the set theory union of {*X*} and {*Y*} (see the following diagram).

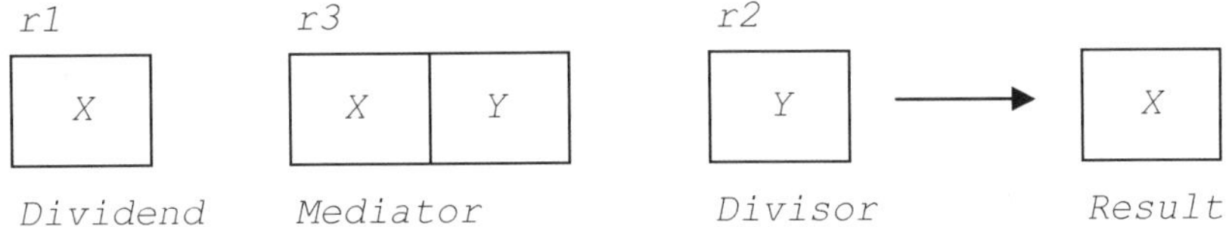

Then the division *r1* DIVIDEBY *r2* PER (*r3*)—where *r1* is the dividend, *r2* is the divisor, and *r3* is the mediator—is equivalent to, and thus shorthand for, the following expression:

```
r1 NOT MATCHING ( ( r1 JOIN r2 ) NOT MATCHING r3 )
```

Informally, this expression yields every tuple <*x*> from *r1* such that *x* is related in *r3* to every *y* such that the tuple <*y*> appears in *r2*. Thus, the query "Get supplier numbers for suppliers who supply all purple parts" can now simply (and correctly) be expressed as:

```
WITH ( PP := P WHERE COLOR = COLOR('Purple') ) :
     S { S# } DIVIDEBY PP { P# } PER SP { S# , P# }
```

So what's happened to the problems with Codd's divide I identified in the previous section? Well, we've certainly solved the third problem—the Small Divide truly is a counterpart to the universal quantifier of predicate logic, in a way that Codd's divide was not (not quite, at any rate). The other two problems remain, however, albeit in revised form: Like Codd's divide, the Small Divide as just defined still typically has to be either preceded or followed by a join; and, again like Codd's divide (at least the abridged version), the Small Divide is still limited in its application, in that it applies only to relations whose headings satisfy a certain rather demanding set of requirements.

Before I can address these issues properly, I need to step back a little and consider another early version of divide, due to Stephen Todd [17], which among other things was an attack on the fact that Codd's divide (at least in its abridged form) was, as I've said, "limited in its application." But before I can do *that,* I need to point out that the Small Divide, while it does obviously solve one big problem, also introduces a small problem of its own: to be specific, a small problem of nomenclature.

As I've already said, Codd's original divide was called divide because it was a kind of inverse of the cartesian product operator: If *r0* and *r2* are relations with no attribute names in common and we form the cartesian product *r1* = *r0* TIMES *r2,* and then divide *r1* by *r2,* we get back to *r0* (except in the case where *r2* is empty). But the Small Divide involves three relations, not two, and no obvious analog of this property holds (or *can* hold); the term "divide" is thus no longer very apt. (Well, as we've seen, it wasn't very apt in the first place, but it's even less so now.) As I said earlier, however, I'll stay with it for historical reasons.

There's one last point I'd like to discuss briefly in closing this section—a question of intuition. I've shown that the Small Divide behaves correctly on queries like "Get supplier numbers for suppliers who supply all purple parts," even when the divisor is empty. But people not trained in formal logic might be forgiven for finding that behavior somewhat counterintuitive. For example, how do you think an only child ought to respond to the question "Are your siblings all boys?" The logically correct answer is, of course, *yes* (though I observe that *yes* is the logically correct answer to the question "Are your siblings all girls?" as well). In practice, however, we would surely expect some more informative response, along the lines of "Well, actually I don't have any siblings." What this thought experiment suggests—at least to me—is that while the relational algebra, or its predicate logic equivalent, is certainly *necessary* as a basis on which to build a user friendly interface to the database, it surely isn't sufficient; some additional mechanism is needed that will enable the system to explain its answers, at least if it's asked to do so.

TODD'S DIVIDE

The big difference between Todd's divide and Codd's—at least as the latter is usually understood—is that Todd's allows any relation to be divided by any relation (just so long as the relations in question satisfy the usual requirement that attributes with the same name are of the same type). I'll begin with an example, or rather two examples. Suppose we're given the following variation on the suppliers-and-parts database (where, as the comments indicate, J stands for *projects*):

```
S  { S# }         /* supplier is under contract */
SP { S#, P# }     /* supplier supplies part     */
P  { P# }         /* part is of interest        */
PJ { P#, J# }     /* part is used in project    */
J  { J# }         /* project is in progress     */
```

Note that, in this version of the database, all nonkey attributes have been discarded from S, SP, and P; in fact, I'll assume for simplicity from this point forward that S, SP, P, PJ, and J contain just the attributes shown above and no others, barring explicit statements to the contrary.

Given this database, then, the expression

```
SP DIVIDEBY PJ
```

gives <*s#,j#*> pairs such that supplier *s#* supplies all parts used in project *j#,* and the expression

```
PJ DIVIDEBY SP
```

gives <*j#,s#*> pairs such that project *j#* uses all parts supplied by supplier *s#*. (At least, these are loose interpretations of the two expressions; however, matters aren't quite as clearcut as these interpretations suggest, as we'll soon see.)

Here now is a definition:

- **Definition (Todd's divide):** Let relations *r1* and *r2* be such that (a) attributes with the same name are of the same type; (b) the set {*Y*} is the common attributes of *r1* and *r2;* and (c) the sets {*X*} and {*Z*} are the other attributes of *r1* and the other attributes of *r2,* respectively (see the following diagram).

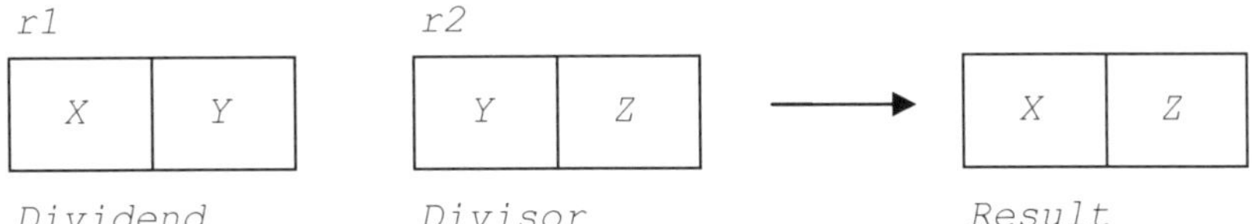

Then the division *r1* DIVIDEBY *r2*—where *r1* is the dividend and *r2* is the divisor—is equivalent to, and thus shorthand for, the following expression:

```
( r1 { X } JOIN r2 { Z } ) NOT MATCHING
          ( ( r1 { X } JOIN r2 ) NOT MATCHING ( r1 JOIN r2 ) )
```

Informally, this expression yields every <*x,z*> pair such that <*x*> appears in *r1*{*X*}, <*z*> appears in *r2*{*Z*}, and *x* is related in *r1* to every *y* that's related in *r2* to *z*.

I don't propose to go into as much detail on Todd's divide as I did for Codd's divide and the Small Divide. Instead, I content myself with the following observations:

- First, Todd's divide clearly solves the "limited application" problem: There are no serious limits on the headings of *r1* and *r2,* and the operator thus does indeed allow us "to divide anything by anything." (The reason I say there are no *serious* limits is because the requirement that attributes with the same name must be of the same type—equivalently, attributes of different types mustn't have the same name—is easily addressed by attribute renaming, if necessary.)

- However, Todd's divide, like Codd's divide and the Small Divide, still often has to be preceded or followed by a join.

- And, more important (and also like Codd's divide, though not the Small Divide), Todd's divide still gets into difficulties over empty relations.

The specifics of this last point are rather more complicated than they were with Codd's divide; for that reason, I choose not to go into details here, but content myself with a couple of simple examples. First, consider again the expression:

```
SP DIVIDEBY PJ
```

I said earlier that this expression represented the query "Get <*s#,j#*> pairs such that supplier *s#* supplies all parts used in project *j#*." However, I did also say this interpretation was loose. A more accurate interpretation is: "Get <*s#,j#*> pairs such that (a) supplier *s#* supplies at least one part, (b) project *j#* uses at least one part, and (c) supplier *s#* supplies all parts used in project *j#*." Observe, therefore, that not only do we have to add a qualification to the dividend, as we did with Codd's divide ("supplier *s#* supplies at least one part"), but we also have to add a similar qualification to the divisor ("project *j#* uses at least one part").

Analogously, the expression

```
PJ DIVIDEBY SP
```

has the following more accurate interpretation: "Get <*j#*,*s#*> pairs such that (a) project *j#* uses at least one part, (b) supplier *s#* supplies at least one part, and (c) project *j#* uses all parts supplied by supplier *s#*."

The foregoing issues are discussed in more detail in reference [8]. Overall, the net of those discussions is that we still have what might be called FORALL-type problems with Todd's divide, just as we did with Codd's. I'll come back to those problems in the next section. First, however, there's a further issue to discuss in connection with Todd's divide. Consider the sets of attributes {*X*}, {*Y*}, and {*Z*} from the definition. In general, any or all of these sets might be empty, of course; in particular, I want to examine the case in which {*Z*} happens to be empty (I'll leave the other cases to you, if you're interested). In this particular case, the definition reduces to the following:

- **Definition (Todd's divide, with {*Z*} empty):** Let relations *r1* and *r2* be such that (a) attributes with the same name are of the same type; (b) the set {*Y*} is the common attributes of *r1* and *r2;* and (c) the set {*X*} is the other attributes of *r1,* and *r2* has no other attributes (see the following diagram).

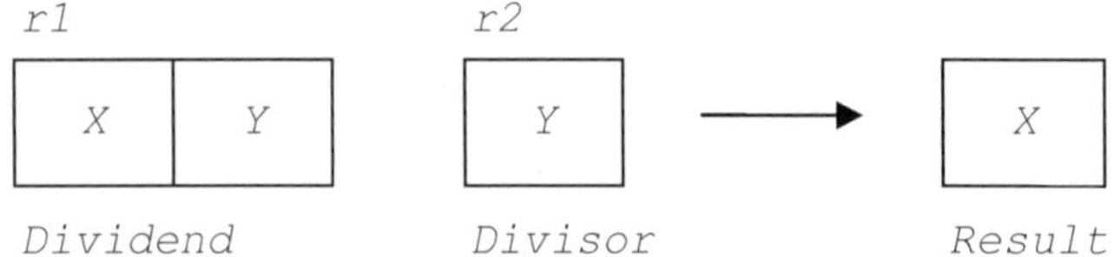

Then the division *r1* DIVIDEBY *r2* is equivalent to, and thus shorthand for, the following expression:

```
( r1 { X } JOIN r2 { } ) NOT MATCHING
             ( ( r1 { X } JOIN r2 ) NOT MATCHING ( r1 JOIN r2 ) )
```

Now, if {*Z*} is empty, *r1* and *r2* conform to the requirements for Codd's divide (in fact, to the requirements for the simplified form of that operator), as well as for Todd's; so the question is, does Todd's divide degenerate to Codd's in this particular case? Well, suppose *r2* happens to be empty (contain no tuples). Then *r2*{} is TABLE_DUM, the first operand to the outer NOT MATCHING in the expansion is thus empty, and the overall expression therefore evaluates to an empty relation also (with heading {*X*}). But as we saw in the section "Codd's Divide," if *r2* is empty, then Codd's divide reduces to *r1*{*X*}, and *r1*{*X*} is not empty, in general—in fact, it's empty only if *r1* itself is empty. It follows that Codd's divide isn't a special case of Todd's (equivalently, Todd's isn't a generalization of Codd's): The two are genuinely different operators. It follows further that we really shouldn't do what I've been doing: namely, use the same syntax for both. (The point isn't very important, however, because I don't believe a real system should support either of these operators, as such, anyway. See the section "Conclusions" for further discussion of this point.)

Exercise for the reader: As we've just seen, if {*Z*} is empty, Todd's divide differs from Codd's in the special case where *r2* is empty. What happens if *r2* does contain at least one tuple?

THE GREAT DIVIDE

The Small Divide was introduced in reference [8] to fix the FORALL-type problems with Codd's divide; analogously, the Great Divide was introduced in that same paper to fix the FORALL-type problems with Todd's divide. And, unfortunately, similar terminological confusions arise ... To be specific, reference [8] first used the term *Great Divide* to refer to Todd's divide as discussed in the previous section; subsequently, however, it used it, at least implicitly, to refer to a revised form of Todd's divide—a revised form that addressed the aforementioned FORALL-type problems. And later in this chapter, I'll follow reference [16] in using it to refer to a generalized version of that revised form. Again I apologize if you find these denotational shifts confusing. At least I should say that it's reasonable to use the same term to refer to both the revised form of Todd's divide and the generalized version of that revised form, since the generalization truly is a generalization; that is, the second meaning of the term truly is just a special case of the third.

Be that as it may, I'll begin by giving a definition of the Great Divide that does at least fix the FORALL-type problems with Todd's divide:

- **Definition (Great Divide, original version):** Let relations *r1, r2, r3,* and *r4* be such that (a) the headings of *r1* and *r2* are {*X*} and {*Z*}, respectively; (b) the sets {*X*} and {*Z*} have no attribute names in common; (c) the headings of *r3* and *r4* are supersets of {*X*} and {*Z*}, respectively; (d) the set {*Y*} is both the other attributes of *r3* and the other attributes of *r4* (see the following diagram).

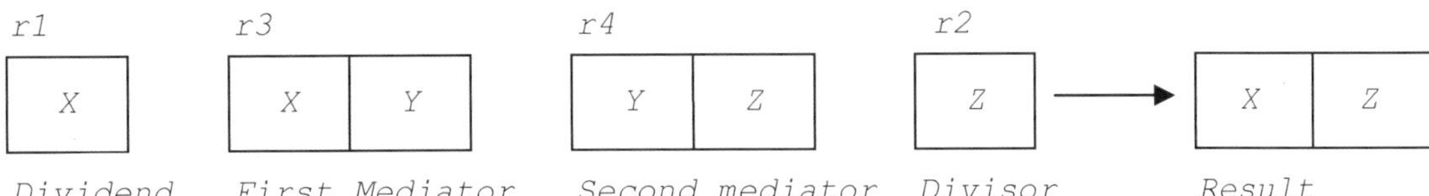

Then the division *r1* DIVIDEBY *r2* PER (*r3,r4*)—where *r1* is the dividend, *r2* is the divisor, and *r3* and *r4* are the mediators—is equivalent to, and thus shorthand for, the following expression:

```
( r1 JOIN r2 ) NOT MATCHING ( ( r1 JOIN r4 ) NOT MATCHING r3 )
```

Informally, this expression yields every *<x,z>* pair such that *<x>* appears in *r1* and *z* appears in *r2* and *x* is related in *r3* to every *y* such that the pair *<y,z>* appears in *r4*. For example, the expression

```
S DIVIDEBY J PER ( SP , PJ )
```

represents the query "Get *<s#,j#>* pairs such that supplier *s#* is under contract, project *j#* is in progress, and supplier *s#* supplies all parts used in project *j#*," as I'll now demonstrate.

As a basis for that demonstration, here first is the stepwise expansion:

```
WITH ( Temp1 := S JOIN PJ ,
       Temp2 := Temp1 NOT MATCHING SP ,
       Temp3 := S JOIN J ) :
Temp3 NOT MATCHING Temp2
```

Taking this expansion one step at a time, we have:

- *Temp1* contains all tuples of the form *<s#,p#,j#>* such that supplier *s#* is under contract and part *p#* is used in project *j#*.

- *Temp2* contains all tuples of the form *<s#,p#,j#>* such that supplier *s#* is under contract, part *p#* is used in project *j#,* and supplier *s#* does not supply part *p#*.

- *Temp3* contains all tuples of the form *<s#,j#>* such that supplier *s#* is under contract and project *j#* is in progress.

- Hence the result contains all tuples of the form *<s#,j#>* such that supplier *s#* is under contract, project *j#* is in progress, and there does not exist a part *p#* that is used in project *j#* but is not supplied by supplier *s#*.

In other words, the expression overall does indeed represent, as advertised, the query "Get *<s#,j#>* pairs such that supplier *s#* is under contract, project *j#* is in progress, and supplier *s#* supplies all parts used in project *j#*." I remind you that, by contrast, the Todd divide

```
SP DIVIDEBY PJ
```

represents the query "Get <*s#,j#*> pairs such that supplier *s# supplies at least one part,* project *j# uses at least one part,* and supplier *s#* supplies all parts used in project *j#*."

GENERALIZING THE SMALL DIVIDE

I said earlier that the Small Divide suffered from two problems: It typically had to be preceded or followed by a join, and it was limited in its application. Todd's divide fixed the second problem (but had problems of its own, which the Great Divide then fixed). It's time to fix the first problem.

Actually, what's needed here was explained, in essence, in reference [8]—basically, all we need do is extend the definition to allow relations *r1, r2,* and *r3* to have headings that are supersets of what were allowed previously, thus:

- **Definition (Small Divide, generalized version):** Let relations *r1, r2,* and *r3* be such that (a) attributes with the same name in *r1* and *r3* are of the same type, and so are attributes with the same name in *r3* and *r2;* (b) the set {*X*} is the common attributes of *r1* and *r3;* (c) the set {*Y*} is the common attributes of *r3* and *r2;* and (d) the sets {*X*} and {*Y*} are disjoint (see the following diagram).

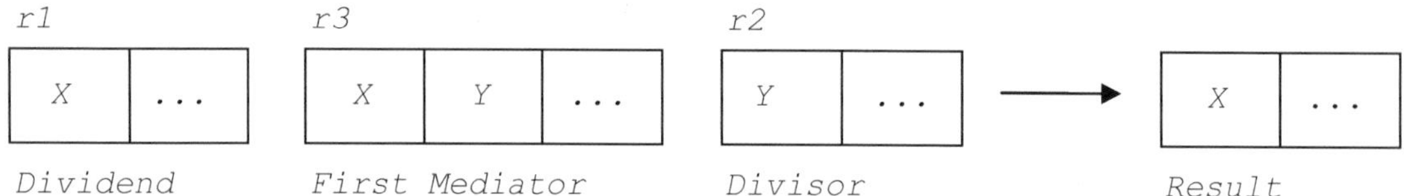

Then the division *r1* DIVIDEBY *r2* PER (*r3*)—where *r1* is the dividend, *r2* is the divisor, and *r3* is the mediator—is equivalent to, and thus shorthand for, the following expression:

```
r1 NOT MATCHING ( ( r1 { X } JOIN r2 { Y } ) NOT MATCHING r3 )
```

By way of example, the expression

```
S DIVIDEBY P PER ( SP )
```

returns, not just supplier numbers, but entire supplier tuples, for suppliers who are under contract and supply every part that's of interest to the enterprise (whatever "the enterprise" might be). Of course, I said earlier that I was assuming until further notice that S# was the sole attribute of S, so "entire supplier tuples" here still basically means just supplier numbers. But if we reinstate the other supplier attributes SNAME, STATUS, and CITY (just for the moment, and just for the sake of this example), then those entire supplier tuples will additionally include supplier names, status values, and city names. What's more, we could also reinstate the other attributes of P and SP without affecting the overall result.

By the way, I hope it's obvious that the Small Divide as just defined is indeed a generalization of the original version. To spell out the details:

- In the original version, the headings of *r1, r2,* and *r3* are {*X*}, {*Y*}, and the set theory union of {*X*} and {*Y*}, respectively, and the sets {*X*} and {*Y*} are disjoint.

- In the generalized version, the headings of *r1* and *r3* both include the set {*X*} (and have no other common attributes), the headings of *r2* and *r3* both include the set {*Y*} (and have no other common attributes), and again the sets {*X*} and {*Y*} are disjoint. These are compatible extensions.

- Here again is the generalized expansion:

  ```
  r1 NOT MATCHING ( ( r1 { X } JOIN r2 { Y } ) NOT MATCHING r3 )
  ```

  But if *r1* and *r2* have headings {*X*} and {*Y*}, respectively, then we can replace *r1*{*X*} and *r2*{*Y*} by *r1* and *r2,* respectively, and the expression then becomes identical to the expansion for the original version of the Small Divide.

GENERALIZING THE GREAT DIVIDE

It should be clear that we can generalize the Great Divide in a manner exactly analogous to that in which we generalized the Small Divide in the previous section. Here's the definition:

- **Definition (Great Divide, generalized version):** Let relations *r1, r2, r3* and *r4* be such that (a) *r1* and *r2* have no attribute names in common; (b) attributes with the same name in *r1* and *r3* are of the same type, and so are attributes with the same name in *r3* and *r4,* and so are attributes with the same name in *r4* and *r2;* (c) the sets {*X*}, {*Y*}, and {*Z*} are the common attributes of *r1* and *r3,* of *r3* and *r4,* and of *r4* and *r2,* respectively; and (d) the sets {*X*} and {*Y*} are disjoint, and so are the sets {*Y*} and {*Z*} (see the following diagram).

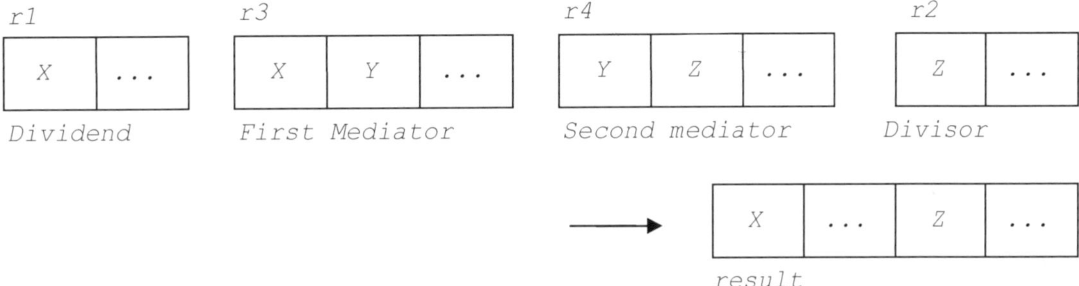

  Then the division *r1* DIVIDEBY *r2* PER (*r3,r4*)—where *r1* is the dividend, *r2* is the divisor, and *r3* and *r4* are the mediators—is equivalent to, and thus shorthand for, the following expression:

  ```
  ( r1 JOIN r2 ) NOT MATCHING
                 ( ( r1 { X } JOIN r4 { Y , Z } ) NOT MATCHING r3 )
  ```

  By way of example, the expression

  ```
  S DIVIDEBY J PER ( SP , PJ )
  ```

returns <*s,j*> pairs where <*s*> is a tuple of S (i.e., *s* represents a supplier under contract), <*j*> is a tuple of J (i.e., *j* represents a project in progress), and supplier *s* supplies all parts used in project *j*. *Note:* I did say earlier that I was assuming until further notice that S tuples contained just a supplier number (*s#,* say) and J tuples just a project number (*j#,* say), so "<*s,j*> pairs where <*s*> is a tuple of S [and] <*j*> is a tuple of J" basically just means <*s#,j#*> pairs. But if we were to reinstate (just for the moment, and just for the sake of the example) the other supplier attributes SNAME, STATUS, and CITY, and likewise introduced various project attributes (e.g., JNAME, BUDGET), then those <*s,j*> pairs would include that additional supplier and project information. I'll leave it as an exercise for the reader to verify this claim.

Incidentally, observe what happens if the operands are switched around, thus:

```
J DIVIDEBY S PER ( PJ , SP )
```

This expression returns <*s,j*> pairs where *s* represents a supplier under contract, *j* represents a project in progress, and project *j* uses all parts supplied by supplier *s*.

Again it should be obvious that we're dealing with a true generalization here—that is, the Great Divide as just defined is indeed a generalization of the original version. I won't bother to spell out the details. However, there's another interesting question we need to consider: Is the Great Divide a generalization of the Small Divide? (You might have noticed that—deliberately, of course—I ducked any discussion of this issue when I first introduced the Great Divide a couple of sections back.)

Well, without getting into too much detail, it should be clear that, in general, given relations *r1, r2,* and *r3,* there's no relation *r4* such that the Small Divide *r1* DIVIDEBY *r2* PER (*r3*) and the Great Divide *r1* DIVIDEBY *r2* PER (*r3,r4*) are equivalent. The reason is as follows: The former expression returns some subset of *r1* and the latter some subset of *r1* JOIN *r2,* and these two results can't possibly be equal unless both of the following conditions are satisfied:

- The heading of *r2* is a subset of that of *r1*.
- Each tuple of *r1* joins to exactly one tuple of *r2*.

In general, of course, neither of these conditions will be satisfied.

However, the Small Divide *r1* DIVIDEBY *r2* PER (*r3*) *is* equivalent to the Great Divide *r1* DIVIDEBY *r4* PER (*r3,r2*)—note the rearrangement of the operands—just so long as *r4* is TABLE_DEE. Thus, for example, the expressions

```
S DIVIDEBY P PER ( SP )
```

and

```
S DIVIDEBY TABLE_DEE PER ( SP , P )
```

are equivalent, as you can easily confirm by checking the expansions. The generalized Great Divide therefore is a generalization of the generalized Small Divide, albeit in a way that might not be immediately obvious. Indeed, I think it's worth stating for the record that the authors of the paper that introduced these operators (reference [8])—viz., Hugh Darwen and myself—didn't explicitly recognize this state of affairs for several years.

DARWEN'S DIVIDE

By now you might be feeling thoroughly confused; in fact, if you aren't, I'm tempted to invoke that well known saying and accuse you of not paying attention. But the end is in sight—well, almost; there's one more divide operator I want to discuss, briefly. In a recent technical note [7], Hugh Darwen has proposed yet another divide operator. Here's the definition:

- **Definition (Darwen's divide):** Let relations *r1, r2, r3* and *r4* be such that attributes with the same name are of the same type. Then the division *r3* PER (*r1*) DIVIDEBY *r4* PER (*r2*)—where *r1* is the dividend, *r2* is the divisor, and *r3* and *r4* are the mediators—is equivalent to, and thus shorthand for, the following expression:

```
( r1 JOIN r2 ) NOT MATCHING ( ( r1 JOIN r4 ) NOT MATCHING r3 )
```

For completeness I also give an "explanatory" diagram (see below). However, that diagram doesn't really explain much, because as you can see the definition imposes no limitations on the headings of the operands, other than the usual requirement that attributes of the same name be of the same type. For the sake of the diagram, however, let the headings of *r1, r2, r3,* and *r4* be {*X1*}, {*X2*}, {*X3*}, and {*X4*}, respectively. Then we have:

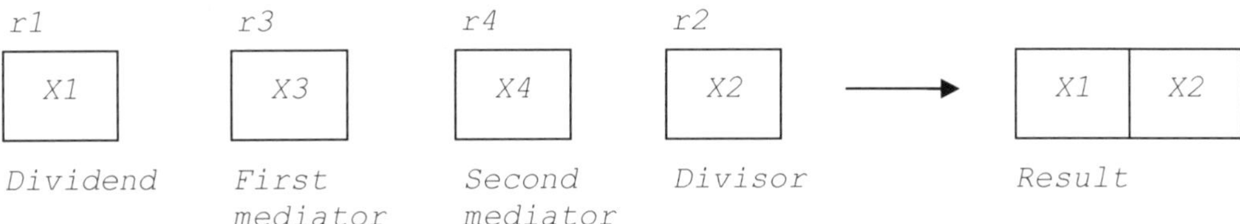

As you can see, the syntax of this operator—*r3* PER (*r1*) DIVIDEBY *r4* PER (*r2*)—differs somewhat from that of all of the divides considered previously in this chapter. However, I want to ignore this point for the moment and focus instead on semantic issues. First let me remind you of the following requirements from the definition of the (generalized) Great Divide:

- Relations *r1* and *r2* must have no attribute names in common.
- The sets {*X*} (the common attributes of *r1* and *r3*) and {*Y*} (the common attributes of *r3* and *r4*) must be disjoint.
- The sets {*Y*} (the common attributes of *r3* and *r4*) and {*Z*} (the common attributes of *r4* and *r2*) must be disjoint.

As I've already pointed out, however, Darwen's divide imposes no such limitations on its operands, and it's thus conceptually simpler than the generalized Great Divide. Moreover, its expansion—

```
( r1 JOIN r2 ) NOT MATCHING ( ( r1 JOIN r4 ) NOT MATCHING r3 )
```

—is also simpler than its generalized Great Divide counterpart:

```
( r1 JOIN r2 ) NOT MATCHING
                        ( ( r1 { X } JOIN r4 { Y } ) NOT MATCHING r3 )
```

It's simpler because it doesn't require those projections on {*X*} and {*Y*}. (It is, however, identical to the expansion for the original Great Divide, but the original Great Divide imposes certain limitations on its operands that Darwen's divide does not.)

Of course, the interesting question is: What exactly is the relationship between Darwen's divide and the Great Divide? (I assume now and for the rest of the chapter that the term *Great Divide* refers to the generalized version of that operator, barring explicit statements to the contrary.) More particularly, does Darwen's divide subsume the Great Divide, in the sense that any given Great Divide can be expressed as a Darwen divide? If so, then we could obviously dispense with the Great Divide in favor of Darwen's divide. Or is the opposite true—i.e., does the Great Divide subsume Darwen's divide? If so, then we could stay with the Great Divide and forget about Darwen's divide. Or is it the case that neither subsumes the other, and that Darwen's divide and the Great Divide are logically distinct operators—in which case we might want to consider supporting both?

Before I go any further, let me spell out for the record what would need to be done in order to investigate these questions properly:

- To show that Darwen's divide subsumes the Great Divide, it would be necessary to show that, given arbitrary relations *r1, r2, r3,* and *r4* satisfying the requirements for a Great Divide, there exist relations *s1, s2, s3,* and *s4* such that the expression *s3* PER (*s1*) DIVIDEBY *s4* PER (*s2*) is logically equivalent to the expression *r1* DIVIDEBY *r2* PER (*r3,r4*).
- To show that the Great Divide subsumes Darwen's divide, it would be necessary to show that, given arbitrary relations *s1, s2, s3,* and *s4* satisfying the requirements for Darwen's divide, there exist relations

r1, r2, r3, and *r4* such that the expression *r1* DIVIDEBY *r2* PER (*r3,r4*) is logically equivalent to the expression *s3* PER (*s1*) DIVIDEBY *s4* PER (*s2*).

I don't propose to explore either of these possibilities further here. Instead, I'd like to inject a small, but I believe pertinent, personal anecdote. In an earlier draft of this chapter, I gave two examples at this point, one purporting to show there exist Darwen divides that can't be expressed as a Great Divide, the other purporting to show the opposite. In his review of that draft, Hugh Darwen claimed that I'd got both examples wrong. However, it turned out that, while he was correct regarding the second example, he was incorrect regarding the first; in other words, I was wrong on one example, and he was wrong on the other![7] This state of affairs seems to both of us to constitute strong empirical evidence in favor of dropping support for divide entirely (i.e., not supporting *any* version of the operator). See the section "Conclusions" for further discussion.

I turn now to a brief discussion of syntax. First of all, it should be clear that the keywords DIVIDEBY and PER play roles in Darwen's divide rather different from the ones they've played in all of the other divides discussed earlier in this chapter. In particular, it seems a little odd (at least to me) that what might be thought of as the primary operands, the dividend and the divisor, are specified in the PER clauses. What makes matters even odder is that those PER clauses are optional, anyway—omitting PER (*r1*) is equivalent to specifying PER *r3* {ALL BUT *X*}, and omitting PER (*r2*) is equivalent to specifying PER *r4* {ALL BUT *X*}, where the set {*X*} is the common attributes of *r3* and *r4*. By way of example, suppose again that S, SP, PJ, and J have just the following attributes:

```
S  { S# }
SP { S# , P# }
PJ { P# , J# }
J  { J# }
```

Then the following expression is a legal Darwen divide:

```
SP DIVIDEBY PJ
```

But SP and PJ are *not* the dividend and divisor here—at least, not in any sense that's close to that in which those terms have been used previously in this chapter. Rather, the dividend is SP{P#}, and the divisor is PJ{P#}. Here's the expansion:

```
SP PER SP { P# } DIVIDEBY PJ PER PJ { P# }
```

And this expression in turn is shorthand for the following:

```
( SP { S# } JOIN PJ { J# } ) NOT MATCHING
             ( ( SP { S# } NOT MATCHING PJ ) NOT MATCHING SP )
```

I'll close this section with Hugh Darwen's own response to the foregoing criticisms of his divide: in particular, to the criticism that the "primary operands"—i.e., the dividend and the divisor—are specified in the PER clauses. Here it is, slightly edited (the italicized remark in brackets is mine):

> In my divide, I regard the dividend as the counterpart to Codd's dividend and the divisor as a generalization of Codd's divisor. I think a mistake was made by the authors of reference [8] [*guess who*] when they put the dividend—and the divisor too, in the case of the Great Divide—into the PER clause.

Well, this argument might be tenable, but I'm not sure I buy it. If you go back to the section of this chapter in which the Small Divide was first discussed, you'll see that it was introduced to address the FORALL-

---

[7] In case you're interested, the original examples and discussion can be found in Appendix D.

type problem with Codd's divide; and it did so (in terms of the example discussed in that section) by replacing SP by S in the stepwise expansion. And SP was certainly the dividend in the Codd divide, so it made (makes?) sense to think of S as the dividend in the Small Divide. But the point is not important; what's important is that, in my opinion (and in Darwen's too, I hasten to add), the whole situation serves only to bolster still further the conclusions of the section immediately following.

CONCLUSIONS

So where does all of this leave us? For what they're worth, here are my own thoughts on the matter:

- This whole subject is amazingly confusing. I've defined seven operators (eight, if we count both forms of Codd's divide) in this chapter, each of which has some claim to being called "divide," and each of which has some unique feature that distinguishes it from all the rest.
- I don't think it's easy to remember the definitions (the semantic definitions, I mean) of all of those operators. And I have to say too that I don't think the name *divide* helps much in this regard—witness the confusions, over what's the dividend and what the divisor, mentioned at the end of the previous section.
- The operators are all defined in terms of other, more primitive ones; in other words, they're all just shorthand for some "longhand" combination of other operators. What's more, the longhand is often not much longer than the shorthand, anyway—not to mention the fact that the longhand is at least arguably easier to understand, relying as it does on operators whose semantics are, or should be, much more familiar and much easier to understand.
- Most of the operators don't do the job they're meant to do, anyway—at least, not very satisfactorily. The principal exceptions here are (a) the generalized Small Divide; (b) the generalized Great Divide (and it's perhaps fortunate that the former is a special case of the latter); and (c) Darwen's divide, possibly.
- As I've just said, the generalized Small Divide is a special case of the generalized Great Divide. It's a rather *special* (not to say awkward) special case, though. Just to remind you, the Small Divide *r1* DIVIDEBY *r2* PER (*r3*) *is* equivalent to the Great Divide *r1* DIVIDEBY TABLE_DEE PER (*r3,r2*). Thus, there could be an argument that explicit support for both operators is desirable. Alternatively, it might be worth trying to come up with a different syntax for the Great Divide that reduces gracefully to a syntax (possibly also different from that described in this chapter) for the generalized Small Divide. But my own feeling is that, frankly, neither of these alternatives is worth the effort.
- *The Third Manifesto* [16] adopts the rather weak position that the Small Divide and the Great Divide must both be supported, but only "directly or indirectly."[8] Any language that supports projection, join, and semidifference (NOT MATCHING) thus satisfies this requirement, because it does at least provide the mandated support indirectly.
- By contrast, **Tutorial D** currently provides explicit support for both operators (i.e., the generalized Small Divide and the generalized Great Divide), as well as—of course—explicit support for projection, join, and semidifference. Partly as a consequence of the investigations reported in the present chapter, however, it is the intention of the designers of **Tutorial D** (viz., Hugh Darwen and myself) to drop explicit support for divide from the next version of that language. (In this connection, I'd like to draw your attention again to

---

[8] As a matter of fact, the sentence advocating this "weak position" has since been dropped from the *Manifesto*, on the grounds that it didn't really add anything. See Chapter 1 of the present book.

reference [15], which proposes among other things a much more user friendly approach to "divide type queries.")

There's one more point I'd like to make, a point not mentioned previously in this chapter. The title of the paper [2] in which Codd originally introduced the divide operator was "Relational Completeness of Data Base Sublanguages." In that paper, Codd did the following:

- He defined a relational algebra (similar but not identical to the version of the algebra embraced in reference [16]), consisting of the operators cartesian product, union, intersect, difference, restrict, project, theta join, and divide.

- He defined a relational calculus (essentially an applied form of predicate logic, tailored to operating on relations). Appendix B of the present chapter gives some idea of what that calculus looks like.

- He defined the notion of relational completeness. Relational completeness is a measure of the expressive power of a language; essentially, a language is relationally complete if and only if it's at least as powerful as the relational calculus, meaning that any relation definable by some relational calculus expression is also definable by some expression of the language in question.

- In particular, he showed that the relational algebra defined in the paper is relationally complete. He did this by providing an algorithm—"Codd's reduction algorithm"—for translating an arbitrary calculus expression into a semantically equivalent algebraic expression (and thereby, incidentally, providing a basis for implementing the calculus).

An informal description of Codd's reduction algorithm can be found in reference [9]. For our purposes, the crucial point about that algorithm is that it explicitly treats divide as an algebraic counterpart to the universal quantifier FORALL; that is, it translates occurrences of FORALL in the source (calculus) expression to occurrences of divide in the target (algebraic) expression. It seems likely, therefore, that Codd's reason for introducing divide in the first place was precisely so that he could use it in his reduction algorithm, in order to facilitate the proof of completeness. Certainly he used it for that purpose. But, of course, it doesn't follow that exposing the divide operator, as such, to the user is a good idea[9]—and, after meditating on the question for many years, I've come to the conclusion that it isn't.

This marks the end of the body of the chapter. But I strongly recommend that you take a look at Appendixes A and B, which describe two quite different approaches to "the divide problem," and then make up your own mind. Darwen and I are still open to arguments in favor of explicit divide support—just so long as those arguments are cogent ones.

ACKNOWLEDGMENTS

I'd like to thank Hugh Darwen for his extremely careful review of an earlier draft of this chapter and much helpful discussion.

---

[9] I remark in passing that in any case it's possible, and perhaps preferable, to show the algebra is complete without using divide at all. See, e.g., reference [18].

REFERENCES AND BIBLIOGRAPHY

1. E. F. Codd: "Derivability, Redundancy, and Consistency of Relations Stored in Large Data Banks," IBM Research Report RJ599 (August 19th, 1969).

2. E. F. Codd: "Relational Completeness of Data Base Sublanguages," in R. Rustin (ed.), *Data Base Systems*, Courant Computer Science Symposia Series 6. Englewood Cliffs, N.J.: Prentice-Hall (1972).

3. E. F. Codd: "Extending the Database Relational Model to Capture More Meaning," *ACM TODS 4,* No. 4 (December 1979).

4. E. F. Codd: *The Relational Model for Database Management Version 2.* Reading, Mass.: Addison-Wesley (1990).

5. E. F. Codd: *The 25th Anniversary of the Creation of the Relational Model for Database Management* (published by the consulting company Codd & Date Inc. in 1994). *Note:* That company no longer exists, so this reference might be hard to track down.

6. Hugh Darwen: "The Nullologist in Relationland," in C. J. Date and Hugh Darwen, *Relational Database Writings 1989-1991.* Reading, Mass.: Addison-Wesley (1992).

7. Hugh Darwen: Private communication (March 2007).

8. Hugh Darwen and C. J. Date: "Into the Great Divide," in C. J. Date and Hugh Darwen, *Relational Database Writings 1989-1991.* Reading, Mass.: Addison-Wesley (1992).

9. C. J. Date: *An Introduction to Database Systems* (8th edition). Boston, Mass.: Addison-Wesley (2004).

10. C. J. Date: "Notes Toward a Reconstituted Definition of the Relational Model Version 1 (RM/V1)," in C. J. Date and Hugh Darwen, *Relational Database Writings 1989-1991.* Reading, Mass.: Addison-Wesley (1992).

11. C. J. Date: Review of February 5th, 1995, draft of "Data Cube: A Relational Aggregation Operator Generalizing GROUP BY, Cross Tab, and Subtotals," by Jim Gray, Adam Bosworth, Andrew Layman, and Hamid Pirahesh. Privately published (February 23rd, 1995).

12. C. J. Date: "The Building Blocks of Logic," in *Databases and Logic: The Roots of Relational Theory.* Victoria, B.C.: Trafford Publishing (2007). See *www.trafford.com/07-0690.*

13. C. J. Date: "Why Is It Called Relational Algebra?", in *Databases and Logic: The Roots of Relational Theory.* Victoria, B.C.: Trafford Publishing (2007). See *www.trafford.com/07-0690.*

14. C. J. Date: "Semijoin and Semidifference," in *Databases and Logic: The Roots of Relational Theory.* Victoria, B.C.: Trafford Publishing (2007). See *www.trafford.com/07-0690.*

15. C. J. Date: "Image Relations" (Chapter 14 of the present book).

16. C. J. Date and Hugh Darwen: *Databases, Types, and the Relational Model: The Third Manifesto* (3rd edition). Boston, Mass.: Addison-Wesley (2006).

17. Stephen Todd: Private communication (1988).

18. Günter von Bültzingsloewen: "Translating and Optimizing SQL Queries Having Aggregates," Proc. 13th Int. Conf. on Very Large Data Bases, Brighton, U.K. (September 1987).

APPENDIX A: RELATIONAL COMPARISONS

As I've explained elsewhere [13], the algebra of sets is usually thought of as including a partial ordering operator called *set inclusion,* denoted by the symbol "⊆". Here's the definition: The expression *s1* ⊆ *s2,* where *s1* and *s2* are sets, evaluates to TRUE if and only if every element of *s1* is also an element of *s2* (i.e., if and only if *s1* is a subset of *s2*). So if, as seems not unlikely, Codd meant to pattern his algebra of relations after the algebra of sets, it would have been reasonable to define an analogous relational inclusion operator. More generally, it would have been appropriate, and indeed useful, to define a full array of relational comparison operators: equality, inclusion, proper inclusion, and so on.

Sadly, of course, Codd never did define any such operators as part of his original relational model.[10] (Actually this omission is a trifle odd, inasmuch as several of Codd's relational writings—including his very first paper on the relational model [1]—certainly required the ability to compare two relations for equality if nothing else. What's more, the definitions he gave for divide in references [2], [3], and [4] all explicitly invoke the notion of relational inclusion!) However, a proposal to extend the original model to include such operators was made by myself in reference [10], and *The Third Manifesto* requires them, and of course **Tutorial D** supports them [16].

Given the availability of such operators, the query "Get suppliers who are under contract and supply all parts" (for example) can easily be formulated:

```
S WHERE P { P# } ⊆
      ( SP MATCHING RELATION { TUPLE { S# S# } } ) { P# }
```

Explanation: For a given tuple *s,* say, in S, the expression (actually a relation selector invocation [16])

```
RELATION { TUPLE { S# S# } }
```

evaluates to a relation with one attribute, S#, and one tuple, and that tuple contains just the S# value from *s*. (The first S# in the expression TUPLE{S# S#} here is an attribute name; the second denotes the value of the attribute of that name in *s*.) Thus, the expression

```
SP MATCHING RELATION { TUPLE { S# S# } }
```

evaluates to that restriction of SP containing just the SP tuples that match the S tuple *s,* and the expression

```
( SP MATCHING RELATION { TUPLE { S# S# } } ) { P# }
```

evaluates to a relation *ps,* say, with one attribute, P#, giving part numbers for all parts supplied by the supplier corresponding to tuple *s*. (Note in particular that if that supplier supplies no parts, then relation *ps* will contain no tuples.) For that supplier, therefore, the overall restriction (S WHERE ...) tests the corresponding relation *ps* to see whether the relation that's the projection of P on {P#} is included in it. Clearly, that test will give TRUE if and only if the supplier corresponding to tuple *s* does in fact supply all parts mentioned in P.

Note: Given the semantics of the situation—more precisely, given the fact that {P#} is a foreign key in SP, referencing the key {P#} in P[11]—we could in fact replace the relation inclusion operator in the foregoing example by the relation equality operator, thus:

```
S WHERE P { P# } =
      ( SP MATCHING RELATION { TUPLE { S# S# } } ) { P# }
```

---

[10] He did subsequently call for one such operator to be added to what he called Version 2 of the model—see reference [4]—but he didn't discuss it in detail or even define it. (The pertinent text, on page 365 of that reference, reads in its entirety thus: "[The relational language] also includes set comparators such as SET INCLUSION.")

[11] Though I didn't actually declare it as such at the beginning of the chapter.

In like manner, the query "Get suppliers who are under contract and supply all purple parts" can be expressed thus:

```
WITH ( PP := P WHERE COLOR = COLOR('Purple') ) :
     S WHERE PP { P# } ⊆
        ( SP MATCHING RELATION { TUPLE { S# S# } } ) { P# }
```

On the basis of examples like the foregoing, it's tempting to suggest that there would never have been any need for an explicit divide operator at all if relational comparisons had been part of the relational model from the very beginning. What's more, if this approach had been adopted, the difficulties discussed in the body of this chapter, over empty sets in particular, might never have occurred.

Be that as it may, here's a definition of the (generalized) Small Divide in terms of relational comparisons:

- **Definition (Small Divide, generalized version, using relational comparisons):** Let relations *r1, r2,* and *r3* be such that (a) attributes with the same name in *r1* and *r3* are of the same type, and so are attributes with the same name in *r3* and *r2;* (b) the set {*X*} is the common attributes of *r1* and *r3;* (c) the set {*Y*} is the common attributes of *r3* and *r2;* and (d) the sets {*X*} and {*Y*} are disjoint. Assume for simplicity that the set {*X*} is of cardinality one (extending the definition to cater for cardinality greater than one is tedious but straightforward). Then the division *r1* DIVIDEBY *r2* PER (*r3*)—where *r1* is the dividend, *r2* is the divisor, and *r3* is the mediator—is equivalent to, and thus shorthand for, the following expression:

```
r1 WHERE r2 { Y } ⊆
       ( r3 MATCHING RELATION { TUPLE { X X } } ) { Y }
```

As you would surely expect, the generalized Great Divide can be defined analogously:

- **Definition (Great Divide, generalized version, using relational comparisons):** Let relations *r1, r2, r3* and *r4* be such that (a) *r1* and *r2* have no attribute names in common; (b) attributes with the same name in *r1* and *r3* are of the same type, and so are attributes with the same name in *r3* and *r4,* and so are attributes with the same name in *r4* and *r2;* (c) the sets {*X*}, {*Y*}, and {*Z*} are the common attributes of *r1* and *r3,* of *r3* and *r4,* and of *r4* and *r2,* respectively; and (d) the sets {*X*} and {*Y*} are disjoint, and so are the sets {*Y*} and {*Z*}. Assume for simplicity that the sets {*X*} and {*Z*} are both of cardinality one (extending the definition to cater for cardinalities greater than one is tedious but straightforward). Then the division *r1* DIVIDEBY *r2* PER (*r3,r4*)—where *r1* is the dividend, *r2* is the divisor, and *r3* and *r4* are the mediators—is equivalent to, and thus shorthand for, the following expression:

```
( r1 JOIN r2 ) WHERE
           ( ( r4 MATCHING RELATION { TUPLE { Z Z } } ) { Y }
        ⊆  ( ( r3 MATCHING RELATION { TUPLE { X X } } ) { Y }
```

The examples given earlier in this appendix were both "small divides." Here by contrast is a "great divide" example. Given S, SP, PJ, and J as follows—

```
S  { S# }         /* supplier is under contract */
SP { S# , P# }    /* supplier supplies part     */
PJ { P# , J# }    /* part is used in project    */
J  { J# }         /* project is in progress     */
```

—the following expression represents the query "Get <*s#,j#*> pairs such that supplier *s#* is under contract, project *j#* is in progress, and supplier *s#* supplies all parts used in project *j#,*" or in other words the Great Divide S DIVIDEBY J PER (SP,PJ):

```
( S JOIN J ) WHERE
            ( PJ MATCHING RELATION { TUPLE { J# J# } } { P# }
        ⊆   ( SP MATCHING RELATION { TUPLE { S# S# } } { P# }
```

Note: I should add that, based on the ideas discussed in this appendix, I've elsewhere proposed a new relational operator called *imaging* whose use greatly simplifies the formulation of "divide type queries" (among other things). As noted in the body of this chapter, you can find the specifics of this proposal in reference [15].

APPENDIX B: PREDICATE LOGIC

It won't come as a surprise to learn that the various divide operators can all be defined straightforwardly in terms of the quantifiers of predicate logic; indeed, the various references to FORALL in the body of the chapter effectively suggested as much. For the record, I'll give definitions in such terms of the generalized Small Divide and generalized Great Divide. Note that, like the ones in Appendix A, these definitions avoid many of the difficulties discussed in the body of the chapter (the difficulties over empty sets in particular).

- **Definition (Small Divide, generalized version, using predicate logic):** Let relations *r1, r2,* and *r3* be such that (a) attributes with the same name in *r1* and *r3* are of the same type, and so are attributes with the same name in *r3* and *r2;* (b) the set {*X*} is the common attributes of *r1* and *r3;* (c) the set {*Y*} is the common attributes of *r3* and *r2;* and (d) the sets {*X*} and {*Y*} are disjoint. Assume for simplicity that the sets {*X*} and {*Y*} are each of cardinality one (extending the definition to cater for cardinalities greater than one is tedious but straightforward). Then the division *r1* DIVIDEBY *r2* PER (*r3*)—where *r1* is the dividend, *r2* is the divisor, and *r3* is the mediator—yields a relation defined as follows:

```
{ t1 ∈ r1 : FORALL t2 ∈ r2 EXISTS t3 ∈ r3
                                  ( t1.X = t3.X AND t3.Y = t2.Y ) }
```

By way of example, here's a predicate logic formulation of the query "Get suppliers who are under contract and supply all parts":

```
{ s ∈ S : FORALL p ∈ P EXISTS sp ∈ SP
                             ( s.S# = sp.S# AND sp.P# = p.P# ) }
```

What about the query "Get suppliers who are under contract and supply all purple parts"? Here the divisor is a certain restriction of P: namely, the restriction to just those tuples for parts that are purple. But there's no need to define that restriction "ahead of time," as it were, before formulating the desired division as a predicate logic expression—instead, we can effectively incorporate the necessary definition "inline" within that expression, as follows:

```
{ s ∈ S : FORALL p ∈ P
    ( IF p.COLOR = COLOR('Purple') THEN EXISTS sp ∈ SP
                                  ( s.S# = sp.S# AND sp.P# = p.P# ) }
```

In stilted English: "Get suppliers *s* such that for all parts *p,* if *p* is purple, then there exists a shipment *sp* linking that supplier *s* to that part *p.*" The subexpression IF ... THEN ... here is a logical implication; the logical implication IF *p* THEN *q* is defined to be logically equivalent to (NOT *p*) OR *q,* and thus returns TRUE if and only if *p* is false or *q* is true.

- **Definition (Great Divide, generalized version, using predicate logic):** Let relations *r1, r2, r3* and *r4* be such that (a) *r1* and *r2* have no attribute names in common; (b) attributes with the same name in *r1* and *r3* are of the same type, and so are attributes with the same name in *r3* and *r4,* and so are attributes with the same name in *r4* and *r2;* (c) the sets {*X*}, {*Y*}, and {*Z*} are the common attributes of *r1* and *r3,* of *r3* and *r4*, and of *r4* and *r2*, respectively; and (d) the sets {*X*} and {*Y*} are disjoint, and so are the sets {*Y*} and {*Z*}. Assume for simplicity that the sets {*X*}, {*Y*}, and {*Z*} are each of cardinality one (extending the definition to cater for cardinalities greater than one is tedious but straightforward). Then the division *r1* DIVIDEBY *r2* PER (*r3,r4*)—where *r1* is the dividend, *r2* is the divisor, and *r3* and *r4* are the mediators—yields a relation defined as follows:

```
{ t1 ∈ r1 , t2 ∈ r2 : FORALL t4 ∈ r4 EXISTS t3 ∈ r3
              ( t1.X = t3.X AND t3.Y = t4.Y AND t4.Z = t2.Z ) }
```

Example: Here's a predicate logic formulation of the query "Get <*s#,j#*> pairs such that supplier *s#* is under contract, project *j#* is in progress, and supplier *s#* supplies all parts used in project *j#*":

```
{ s ∈ S , j ∈ J : FORALL pj ∈ PJ EXISTS sp ∈ SP
              ( s.S# = sp.S# AND sp.P# = pj.P# AND pj.J# = j.J# ) }
```

APPENDIX C: A REMARK ON SQL

You might have noticed that throughout this chapter so far, I've given neither definitions nor examples in terms of SQL. Now I can explain why not.

- *(With reference to the body of the chapter:)* SQL doesn't directly support either MATCHING or NOT MATCHING. As a result, relational algebra expressions involving either MATCHING or NOT MATCHING are quite awkward to translate into SQL.
- *(With reference to Appendix A:)* SQL doesn't support relational comparisons at all. As a result, relational algebra expressions involving such comparisons can't be directly translated into SQL at all.
- *(With reference to Appendix B:)* SQL doesn't directly support FORALL. As a result, logical expressions involving FORALL are very awkward to translate into SQL.

For the record, however, I'll give just one example in SQL—the query "Get suppliers who are under contract and supply all purple parts":

```
SELECT DISTINCT s.*
FROM   S AS s
WHERE  NOT EXISTS
     ( SELECT DISTINCT p.*
       FROM   P AS p
       WHERE  p.COLOR = COLOR('Purple')
       AND    NOT EXISTS
            ( SELECT DISTINCT sp.*
              FROM   SP AS sp
              WHERE  s.S# = sp.S#
              AND    sp.P# = p.P# ) )
```

In stilted English: "Get suppliers *s* such that there does not exist a purple part *p* such that there does not exist a shipment *sp* linking that supplier *s* to that part *p*." By way of comparison, here repeated from Appendix B is a predicate logic version of this query:

```
{ s ∈ S : FORALL p ∈ P
    ( IF p.COLOR = COLOR('Purple') THEN EXISTS sp ∈ SP
                                        ( s.S# = sp.S# AND sp.P# = p.P# ) }
```

Observe in passing, therefore, that this example also illustrates the point that SQL doesn't directly support logical implication, either.

Exercise for the reader: Give an SQL formulation of the query "Get *<s#,j#>* pairs such that supplier *s#* is under contract, project *j#* is in progress, and supplier *s#* supplies all parts used in project *j#*."

APPENDIX D: WE CAN ALL MAKE MISTAKES

As noted in the section "Darwen's Divide," in an earlier draft of this chapter I gave two examples, one purporting to show there exist Darwen divides that can't be expressed as a Great Divide, the other purporting to show the opposite. However, I also indicated that I'd made some mistakes in my analysis of those examples, and hence that the conclusions I'd drawn were not to be trusted—which is why I dropped the examples and associated discussion from the body of the chapter, of course. At the same time, it seemed to me that it could be worth retaining my original text as a kind of "case study" appendix ... You might be interested in trying to analyze the examples for yourself and confirming that my original conclusions were erroneous. (*Were* they erroneous?)

I've edited what follows for reasons of flow and so forth, but I haven't changed the sense. *Note:* To take any portion of what follows out of context could be misleading in the extreme!—and I categorically refuse to accept responsibility if anybody does so.

———♦♦♦♦♦———

My first example is meant to show that there exist Darwen divides that can't be expressed as a Great Divide. Suppose S, SP, PJ, and J have attributes as follows (and no others):

```
S  { S# , CITY }     /* r1 */
SP { S# , P# }       /* r3 */
PJ { P# , J# }       /* r4 */
J  { J# , CITY }     /* r2 */
```

The comments indicate which relations play which roles with respect to the various divide definitions. Now, the crucial point regarding this example is that S and J (in other words, *r1* and *r2*) have a common attribute, CITY; as a consequence, they can't be the dividend and divisor, respectively, for a Great Divide. By contrast, the following Darwen divide is legitimate:

```
SP PER ( S ) DIVIDEBY PJ PER ( J )
```

It represents the following query:

> Get *<s#,c,j#>* triples such that *<s#,c>* is a tuple of S and *<j#,c>* is a tuple of J (implying that supplier *s#* is under contract, project *j#* is in progress, and supplier *s#* and project *j#* are both located in city *c*), and supplier *s#* supplies all parts used in project *j#*.

As previously indicated, I think this is a query that can't be formulated as a Great Divide.

My second example is meant to show that there exist Great Divides that can't be expressed as a Darwen divide. Let S, SP, PJ, and J have attributes as follows and no others (the crucial point here is that S and PJ—i.e., *r1* and *r4*—have a common attribute, a possibility not prohibited by the Great Divide definition):

```
S  { S# , CITY }          /* r1 */
SP { S# , P# }            /* r3 */
PJ { P# , J#, CITY }      /* r4 */
J  { J# }                 /* r2 */
```

Now the following expressions (a Great Divide and a Darwen divide, respectively) are both legal:

```
S DIVIDEBY J PER ( SP , PJ )

SP PER ( S ) DIVIDEBY PJ PER ( J )
```

However, the two expressions aren't equivalent. For example, suppose the relation values are as follows:

S (*r1*)

S#	CITY
S1	London

SP (*r3*)

S#	P#
S2	P2

PJ (*r4*)

P#	J#	CITY
P1	J1	Athens

J (*r2*)

J#
J1

Then the Great Divide returns an empty relation, while the Darwen divide returns a relation containing one tuple, viz., <S1,London,J1>. This relation is the result of the query:

> Get <*s#,c,j#*> triples such that <*s#,c*> is a tuple of S (implying that supplier *s#* is under contract and is located in city *c*), <*j#*> is a tuple of J (implying that project *j#* is in progress), and supplier *s#* supplies all parts used by project *j#* in city *c*.

By contrast, the Great Divide expression represents the query:

> Get <*s#,c,j#*> triples such that <*s#,c*> is a tuple of S (implying that supplier *s#* is under contract and is located in city *c*), <*j#*> is a tuple of J (implying that project *j#* is in progress), and supplier *s#* supplies all parts used by project *j#* (in city *c* or in any other city).

As previously indicated, I think this is a query that can't be formulated as a Darwen divide. So it seems to me, though I could be wrong, that Darwen's divide and the Great Divide are logically distinct operators (i.e., neither is a special case of the other). But—lacking the courage of my convictions here—let me spell out for the record what would have to be done in order to show that I *am* wrong in this regard [*here follows text repeated from the body of the chapter*]:

- To show that Darwen's divide subsumes the Great Divide, it would be necessary to show that, given arbitrary relations *r1, r2, r3,* and *r4* satisfying the requirements for a Great Divide, there exist relations *s1, s2, s3,* and *s4* such that the expression *s3* PER (*s1*) DIVIDEBY *s4* PER (*s2*) is logically equivalent to the expression *r1* DIVIDEBY *r2* PER (*r3,r4*).

- To show that the Great Divide subsumes Darwen's divide, it would be necessary to show that, given arbitrary relations *s1, s2, s3,* and *s4* satisfying the requirements for Darwen's divide, there exist relations *r1, r2, r3,* and *r4* such that the expression *r1* DIVIDEBY *r2* PER (*r3,r4*) is logically equivalent to the expression *s3* PER (*s1*) DIVIDEBY *s4* PER (*s2*).

Chapter 13

Inclusion Dependencies and Foreign Keys

This article may contain URLs that were valid when originally published, but now link to sites or pages that no longer exist. To maintain the flow of the article, we've left these URLs in the text, but deleted the links.
—from "Why We Need XML Server Technology" (*www.software.ag,* August 1999)

Include me out.
—Samuel Goldfish

The term, though possibly not the concept, *inclusion dependency* (IND for short) seems to have originated in a paper by Fagin [31]. Simplifying slightly—the simplification has to do with an occasional need to rename attributes and is discussed under Example 4, later—an inclusion dependency is an integrity constraint to the effect that, at all times, some specified projection of some relvar *R2* is required to be included in, or in other words to be a subset of, some specified projection of some relvar *R1* (*R1* and *R2* not necessarily distinct):

```
R2 { X } ⊆ R1 { X }
```

Note: Throughout this chapter I use the symbol "⊆" to represent the operator *is included in* (also known, in the relational context specifically, as *relational inclusion*). I also use the terms *source relvar* and *target relvar* (source and target for short) to refer to relvars *R2* and *R1,* respectively

By way of example, consider the well known suppliers-and-parts database, with its relvars S, P, and SP representing suppliers, parts, and shipments, respectively:

```
VAR S BASE RELATION     /* supplier is under contract */
  { S# S# , SNAME NAME , STATUS INTEGER , CITY CHAR }
    KEY { S# } ;

VAR P BASE RELATION     /* part is of interest */
  { P# P# , PNAME NAME , COLOR COLOR , WEIGHT WEIGHT ,
    CITY CHAR }
    KEY { P# } ;

VAR SP BASE RELATION    /* supplier supplies (or ships) part */
  { S# S# , P# P# , QTY QTY }
    KEY { S# , P# } ;
```

Suppose this database is subject to the constraint that no part can be stored in a city unless there's at least one supplier in that city. Then that constraint—let's call it IND1—is in fact an inclusion dependency, and it can be specified as follows:

```
CONSTRAINT IND1 P { CITY } ⊆ S { CITY } ;
/* every part city must be a supplier city as well */
```

Note: Examples in this chapter are formulated in **Tutorial D,** which is the language used in reference [28] to illustrate the ideas of *The Third Manifesto*. The language is mostly self-explanatory, but there are a couple of points to do with the relational projection operator in particular that I need to call out explicitly:

- Projection is expressed in **Tutorial D** by means of braces; thus, for example, the expression P{CITY} denotes the projection of the relation that's the current value of relvar P on the set of attributes {CITY}—a set that contains just one attribute, as it happens. *Note:* For user convenience, **Tutorial D** also allows the projection *r*{*X*} to be expressed in the form *r*{ALL BUT *Y*}, where {*X*} and {*Y*} are disjoint and their set theory union is equal to the heading of relation *r*.

- Projection has the highest precedence in **Tutorial D** of all of the familiar relational operators; thus, for example, the expression S JOIN P{P#} means S JOIN (P{P#}), not (S JOIN P){P#}.

Now, in the version of relational algebra supported by *The Third Manifesto*—and therefore by **Tutorial D** also—(a) the comparands in a relational comparison like the one shown in constraint IND1 are required to be of the same type, and (b) two relations are considered to be of the same type if and only if they have the same heading. That's why, in the inclusion dependency definition given above, relvars *R2* and *R1* were both projected on the same set of attributes {*X*}; it's also why, in the example constraint IND1, relvars P and S were both projected on the same set of attributes {CITY}. So the obvious question is: What happens if the pertinent projections involve differently named attributes? The answer, of course, is that we have to do some attribute renaming in such a case. As I've already said, I'll consider this issue in detail later, under Example 4.

Another question that arises in connection with inclusion dependencies as defined above is this: Are *R1* and *R2* required to be base relvars specifically? Or even relvars, as such, at all? In fact these questions aren't addressed in reference [31]; however, I believe there's a strong implication in that reference that the answer to both is *yes,* and in the present chapter I'll assume as much until further notice.

One last introductory point: The purpose of this chapter is, in essence, to offer a series of language proposals for IND and foreign key support. However, those proposals are to some extent only proposals, and of course I'm open to cogent arguments in favor of alternatives. In other words, the chapter isn't necessarily meant to be definitive.

FOREIGN KEYS

Foreign key constraints are a special case of INDs in general. To be specific, they're the special case in which the set of attributes on which the target relvar *R1* is to be projected constitutes a key for that relvar.[1] For example, the following IND is satisfied by the suppliers-and-parts database:

```
SP { S# } ⊆ S { S# }
```

And since {S#} is a key for relvar S, this IND is in fact a foreign key constraint (and the set of attributes {S#} of relvar SP is a foreign key, referencing the key {S#} of relvar S).

Of course, the following IND (also satisfied by the suppliers-and-parts database) is a foreign key constraint as well:

```
SP { P# } ⊆ P { P# }
```

So the set of attributes {P#} of relvar SP is also a foreign key, referencing the key {P#} of relvar P.

Now, the foreign key concept was invented before INDs in general were defined (see Appendix A)—

---

[1] Throughout this chapter I follow *The Third Manifesto* in using the unqualified term *key* to mean a candidate key specifically, unless the context demands otherwise. I remark in passing that the key in question is often required to be (even more specifically) the *primary* key for the target relvar; for reasons explained in reference [15], however, I reject this stronger requirement, and *The Third Manifesto* doesn't support it. Nor does SQL, incidentally [32].

indeed, I dare say it's more familiar to you than INDs in general are—and a great deal of special terminology has grown up around it. For the record, I give here definitions for some of the terms most commonly encountered in practice. I'll begin with a definition of the term *foreign key* itself. *Note:* The definition mentions the occasional need to do some attribute renaming, but you can ignore that issue until further notice. Also, since foreign key constraints are INDs and I've already said I'm assuming until further notice that INDs apply to relvars specifically, the definition assumes that foreign key constraints too apply to relvars specifically—but this assumption too will be revisited later in the chapter.

- **Definition (foreign key):** Let *R1* and *R2* be relvars, not necessarily distinct, and let *K* be a key for *R1*. Let *FK* be a subset of the heading of *R2* such that there exists a possibly empty sequence of attribute renamings on *R1* that maps *K* into *K'* (say), where *K'* and *FK* contain exactly the same attributes. Further, let *R2* and *R1* be subject to the constraint that, at all times, every tuple *t2* in *R2* has an *FK* value that's the *K'* value for some (necessarily unique) tuple *t1* in *R1* at the time in question. Then *FK* is a **foreign key,** the associated constraint is a **referential constraint** (also known as a **foreign key constraint**), and *R2* and *R1* are the **referencing relvar** and the corresponding **referenced relvar,** respectively, for that constraint. Also, *K* (not *K'*) is referred to, sometimes, as the **referenced key** or **target key**. *Note:* The referencing and referenced terminology carries over to tuples in the obvious way; that is, tuples *t2* and *t1* from the foregoing discussion are a **referencing tuple** and the corresponding **referenced tuple,** respectively.

  Aside: The foregoing definition, like all definitions in this chapter, is stated relationally and doesn't necessarily accord with the way things are in SQL. In particular (as the definition states), in the relational model an attribute of a given foreign key and the corresponding attribute of the corresponding target key are matched up by virtue of being the very same attribute. In SQL, by contrast, such matching is performed on the basis of ordinal position—the "first" attribute (or column, rather) of the foreign key matches the "first" attribute (or column) of the target key, the "second" matches the "second," and so on—where "first," "second," etc., refer to the order in which those columns are mentioned in the applicable FOREIGN KEY specification. In other words, an SQL FOREIGN KEY specification looks like this:

  ```
  FOREIGN KEY ( B1 , B2 , ... , Bn ) REFERENCES T ( A1 , A2 , ... , An )
  ```

  Given this specification, column *Bi* is matched up with column *Ai* ($1 \leqslant i \leqslant n$); those columns must be of the same type, but they don't have to have the same name. Also, of course, *A1, A2, ..., An* must be named in some UNIQUE or PRIMARY KEY specification for the target table *T,* though they needn't appear in that specification in the same sequence as they do in the FOREIGN KEY specification. (Optionally, they and the parentheses surrounding them can be omitted entirely from the FOREIGN KEY specification—but then they must appear in a PRIMARY KEY specification, not a UNIQUE specification, for table *T,* and of course they must also appear in that specification in the appropriate sequence.) *End of aside.*

- **Definition (source relvar):** For the general meaning, see the definition of inclusion dependency in the opening section. In the foreign key context in particular, the term becomes a synonym for referencing relvar.

- **Definition (target relvar):** For the general meaning, see the definition of inclusion dependency in the opening section. In the foreign key context in particular, the term becomes a synonym for referenced relvar.

- **Definition (source tuple):** Synonym for referencing tuple.

- **Definition (target tuple):** Synonym for referenced tuple.

- **Definition (child):** Deprecated, because inappropriate, term sometimes used in SQL contexts to mean a referencing relvar (or the SQL analog of such a relvar, rather).

- **Definition (parent):** Deprecated, because inappropriate, term sometimes used in SQL contexts to mean a referenced relvar (or the SQL analog of such a relvar, rather).

- **Definition (referential integrity):** Loosely, the rule that no referencing tuple is allowed to exist if the corresponding referenced tuple doesn't exist. More precisely, let *FK* be some foreign key in some referencing relvar *R2;* let *K* be the corresponding target key in the corresponding referenced relvar *R1;* and let *K′* be derived from *K* as explained under the definition of foreign key. Then the **referential integrity rule** requires there never to be a time at which there exists an *FK* value in *R2* that isn't the *K′* value for some (necessarily unique) tuple in *R1*.

  For completeness, let me also give a definition for the term *candidate key:*

- **Definition (candidate key):** Let *K* be a subset of the heading of relvar *R;* then *K* is a **candidate key**—**key** for short—for *R* if and only if (a) no possible value for *R* contains two distinct tuples with the same value for *K* (the uniqueness property), while (b) the same can't be said for any proper subset of *K* (the irreducibility property).

Syntax

Foreign keys are usually regarded as an integral part of the relational model (see Appendix A). In *The Third Manifesto,* however [28], we—i.e., Hugh Darwen and I, the authors of that *Manifesto*—don't insist that foreign keys as such be explicitly supported; we insist only that the system support a language that allows constraints of arbitrary complexity to be defined, and foreign key constraints in particular can then be defined using that general purpose language. And one reason we don't insist on such explicit support is that foreign key constraints are self-evidently not fundamental—unlike, e.g., the notion of integrity constraints in general, or candidate key constraints in particular.[2]

Given the foregoing, it won't surprise you to learn that **Tutorial D** doesn't include explicit foreign key support either. And yet ... in other writings and live presentations, I've often found it necessary to use a hypothetical dialect of **Tutorial D** that does include such support—partly because foreign keys are indeed part of the relational model as usually understood and therefore often need to be discussed, and partly because there's no question that foreign keys are very important in practice. What's more, although it's true that the *Manifesto* doesn't insist that foreign keys be explicitly supported, it does at least "very strongly suggest" such support. To be specific, RM Very Strong Suggestion 2 [28] reads as follows:

> **D** should include some declarative shorthand for expressing **referential constraints** (also known as **foreign key** constraints).

So one aim of the present chapter is to suggest some possible extensions to **Tutorial D** that do provide explicit foreign key support after all.[3]

As a first step toward such extensions, consider the following extended definition for relvar SP, which illustrates some obvious syntax for specifying the foreign keys that apply to that particular relvar:

---

[2] Actually candidate key constraints aren't fundamental either (or an argument could be made to that effect, at any rate), but in this case the practical benefits of providing explicit support are overwhelming.

[3] As noted in Chapter 1 of this book, we've dropped the foregoing "very strong suggestion" from the most recent version of the *Manifesto.* But the fact that we've dropped the suggestion shouldn't be taken to mean we're opposed to support for foreign keys as such; rather, we're opposed to the form such support usually takes. Indeed, part of the point of the present chapter is precisely to indicate what we think such support ought to look like.

```
VAR SP BASE RELATION
  { S# S# , P# P# , QTY QTY }
    KEY { S# , P# }
    FOREIGN KEY { S# } REFERENCES S
    FOREIGN KEY { P# } REFERENCES P ;
```

Now let me concentrate on the specification—which I'll refer to henceforth as a *<foreign key def>*—FOREIGN KEY {S#} REFERENCES S. (For simplicity, I'll ignore the fact that relvar SP has another foreign key, {P#}, almost entirely throughout the remainder of this chapter.) The semantics of that specification are intuitively obvious, but for the record let me spell them out here:

- The source relvar with respect to this particular *<foreign key def>* is relvar SP, because the *<foreign key def>* is contained within the definition of that relvar.
- The set of attributes {S#} of that source relvar constitutes a foreign key for that relvar, because that set of attributes is the one specified following the keywords FOREIGN KEY in the *<foreign key def>*.
- The target relvar with respect to that *<foreign key def>* is relvar S, because that relvar is the one specified following the keyword REFERENCES in that *<foreign key def>*.
- The target relvar S is required to have an attribute called S# such that {S#} is defined, via an appropriate KEY specification, to be a key for that relvar.
- Attribute S# of S is required to be of the same type as attribute S# of SP (formally, in fact, they're required to be the very same attribute).
- Relvars SP and S are required to satisfy the following IND:

  ```
  SP { S# } ⊆ S { S# }
  ```

  So far, then, we can say that a *<foreign key def>* looks like this:

  ```
  <foreign key def>
       ::=   FOREIGN KEY { <attribute ref commalist> }
                  REFERENCES <relation var ref>
  ```

The syntax has to permit a commalist of *<attribute ref>*s, of course, in order to cater for foreign keys consisting of two or more attributes. Every *<attribute ref>* in that *<attribute ref commalist>* must identify an attribute of the relvar in whose definition the *<foreign key def>* appears; moreover, the same set of *<attribute ref>*s must together identify a key of the relvar identified by the specified *<relation var ref>*. *Note:* For convenience, we ought to support an ALL BUT form too, and so the syntax becomes:

```
<foreign key def>
     ::=   FOREIGN KEY { [ ALL BUT ] <attribute ref commalist> }
                REFERENCES <relation var ref>
```

We ought really to allow the *<foreign key def>* to be named, too, so that error messages arising from attempts to violate the constraint can be specific as to just which constraint it is that's been violated. For simplicity, however, I'll ignore this detail for the remainder of the chapter.

Superkeys

I've said, in effect, that a *<foreign key def>* of the form FOREIGN KEY {*K*} REFERENCES *R* requires the definition of relvar *R* to include a key definition of the form KEY {*K*}. Note, however, that while the system will certainly enforce the uniqueness property implied by such a definition, it can't in general enforce the corresponding irreducibility property as well. With respect to relvar S, for example, we know—because we know what the relvar means—that the combination {S#,CITY} doesn't have the irreducibility property (though of course it does have the uniqueness property). To repeat, we know that—but the system doesn't. So if we were to specify {S#,CITY} instead of {S#} as a key for relvar S, the system wouldn't—*couldn't*—enforce the constraint that supplier numbers as such, as opposed to supplier-number/city combinations, were unique. More generally, when we specify KEY {*K*} as part of the definition of relvar *R*, the system can and will guarantee that {*K*} is a *superkey,* but not necessarily a key as such, for *R*. Here's the definition:

- **Definition (superkey):** Let *K* be a subset of the heading of relvar *R;* then *K* is a **superkey** for *R* if and only if no possible value for *R* contains two distinct tuples with the same value for *K*. In other words (speaking a trifle loosely), a superkey is a superset of a key—it has the uniqueness property but not necessarily the irreducibility property. Every key is a superkey, but most superkeys aren't keys. *Note:* A superkey that isn't a key is sometimes called a *proper* superkey.

To repeat, if we were to specify KEY {S#,CITY} instead of KEY {S#} in the definition of relvar S, the system wouldn't be able to enforce the constraint that supplier numbers are unique. However, if we were to specify both KEY {S#} and KEY {S#,CITY}, then the system should at least be able to recognize that {S#} is a proper subset of {S#,CITY} and so reject the latter specification. Whether it will actually do so is another matter, of course.[4]

Advantages of Special Syntax

Why might it be desirable to invent special syntax for foreign key constraints, given that (as noted earlier) we're certainly guaranteed a means for expressing constraints in general—i.e., constraints of arbitrary complexity? There are several possible answers to this question; here are some of them.

1. Special syntax effectively raises the level of abstraction, and hence the level of discourse, by giving an explicit name to, and thereby allowing us to talk explicitly in terms of, certain "bundles" of concepts that fit naturally together and often need to be discussed in the same breath, as it were. *Note:* To me, this first advantage is the most important one. It accords well with what I've referred to elsewhere—see reference [17]—as *The Naming Principle,* which simply says that *Everything we need to talk about should have a name* (including that principle itself, of course!).

2. Special syntax can be more user friendly; in particular, it can act as shorthand for what might otherwise require a comparatively longwinded formulation.[5] (Actually this point might be a little debatable in the case of foreign keys in particular. For example, the specification

   ```
   FOREIGN KEY { S# } REFERENCES S
   ```

   can hardly be said to be "shorthand" for the specification

   ```
   SP { S# } ⊆ S { S# }
   ```

---

[4] It won't in SQL, because the SQL standard does permit "keys" to be declared that the user *and the system* both know to be proper superkeys. The justification for this hack—for hack it certainly is—is that it allows SQL's FOREIGN KEY syntax to be used to express certain inclusion dependencies that aren't foreign key constraints as such (at least as that concept is defined in SQL). Without getting into details, let me just say that such a hack will never be necessary if the proposals of this chapter are implemented.

[5] As Jonathan Leffler points out (in a private communication), the shorthand means among other things that users don't have to devote time and effort to checking whether the constraint they've laboriously typed out in longhand is really the one they meant; in particular, they don't have to check that it doesn't have a subtle typo in it that converts it into something completely different.

—except inasmuch as the former implies that {S#} must have been defined as a key for relvar S while the latter doesn't. On the other hand, the explicit IND syntax does require the pertinent attribute names to be written out twice, a consideration that could have the effect of making the FOREIGN KEY analog truly a shorthand after all, in some cases.)

3. Special syntax can make it easier for the system to recognize the special case and give it special treatment (by which I mean it can implement it more efficiently). Let me immediately add that I regard this particular advantage merely as a kind of bonus; I'm very much opposed to the idea of adding features to the user language, or to the model, if the sole, or even just the primary, motivation for them is performance.[6]

All of that being said, in practice it's clearly a judgment call as to which particular special cases merit special syntactic treatment. Codd obviously felt that foreign keys did (see Appendix A). By contrast, Darwen and I felt otherwise, at least so far as reference [28] was concerned. Part of the point of this chapter, therefore, is to see whether the foreign key notion can be sufficiently extended—in other words, be made sufficiently useful—as to merit such special casing after all. Thus, the bulk of the remainder of the chapter consists in effect of a series of arguments in favor of extending the foreign key notion in various ways, with the ultimate goal of pinning down exactly what that notion might reasonably, and usefully, be expected to encompass.

EXAMPLE 1: A ONE TO ONE RELATIONSHIP

I now embark on a series of detailed examples, each of which is intended to introduce one new point. My first is taken from reference [12]; it concerns two "entity types," invoices and shipments, with a one to one relationship between them (by which I mean that each shipment has exactly one invoice and each invoice has exactly one shipment).[7] The obvious first attempt at a database design looks like this (INV# = invoice number, SHIP# = shipment number):

```
VAR INVOICE BASE RELATION
  { INV# ... , SHIP# ... , INV_DETAILS ... }
    KEY { INV# }
    KEY { SHIP# }
    FOREIGN KEY { SHIP# } REFERENCES SHIPMENT ;

VAR SHIPMENT BASE RELATION
  { SHIP# ... , INV# ... , SHIP_DETAILS ... }
    KEY { SHIP# }
    KEY { INV# }
    FOREIGN KEY { INV# } REFERENCES INVOICE ;
```

Well ... perhaps the design isn't so obvious, after all. It clearly involves some redundancy (a point I'll come back to later); in particular, it's not at all obvious why we should have to deal with both invoice numbers and shipment numbers when the two are clearly in lock step, as it were. Suffice it to say, therefore, that the example is based on a real application, and the company in question really did use both invoice numbers to

---

[6] Hugh Darwen has asked me to add that he agrees strongly with this sentiment.

[7] I apologize for my use of the term "entity type" here, which, because it's so vague, is a term I usually try to avoid; at least I'm not relying on it in any formal sense. By contrast, I *am* relying on the term *one to one relationship* in a formal sense. Here's the definition: A one to one relationship is a correspondence between two sets *s1* and *s2* (not necessarily distinct) such that each element of *s1* corresponds to exactly one element of *s2* and each element of *s2* corresponds to exactly one element of *s1*.

identify invoices and shipment numbers to identify shipments, and the database really was designed in essentially the manner shown.

Observe, then, that (a) each relvar has two keys; (b) each relvar has a foreign key referencing the other; (c) each foreign key is in fact also a key for the relvar that contains it. *Note:* Because of point (b), the example involves a *referential cycle*. Here are the pertinent definitions:

- **Definition (referential cycle):** A referential path from some relvar to itself.

- **Definition (referential path):** Let relvars *Rz, Ry, Rx, ..., Rb, Ra* be such that there exists a referential constraint from *Rz* to *Ry*, a referential constraint from *Ry* to *Rx*, ..., and a referential constraint from *Rb* to *Ra*. Then the chain of such constraints from *Rz* to *Ra* constitutes a **referential path** from *Rz* to *Ra* (and the number of constraints in the chain is the **length** of that path).

Incidentally, you might be wondering how we can ever "get started," as it were, with a database that involves a referential cycle; in the case of invoices and shipments, for example, it looks as if we can't insert an invoice until we've inserted the corresponding shipment, and we can't insert a shipment until we've inserted the corresponding invoice. *The Third Manifesto* solves this problem by means of a *multiple assignment* operation [30], which (among other things) allows tuples to be inserted into both relvars simultaneously. See references [28] and [30] for further explanation.[8]

However, the main point about the example is precisely its one to one nature. To be specific, while the database clearly does satisfy the INDs implied by the two *<foreign key def>*s—

```
INVOICE { SHIP# } ⊆ SHIPMENT { SHIP# }

SHIPMENT { INV# } ⊆ INVOICE { INV# }
```

—it clearly satisfies the following INDs as well, because of that one to one relationship:

```
INVOICE { INV# } ⊆ SHIPMENT { INV# }

SHIPMENT { SHIP# } ⊆ INVOICE { SHIP# }
```

On the face of it, therefore, it looks as if we need two more *<foreign key def>*s, and so the relvar definitions now look like this:

```
VAR INVOICE BASE RELATION
  { INV# ... , SHIP# ... , INV_DETAILS ... }
    KEY { INV# }
    KEY { SHIP# }
    FOREIGN KEY { SHIP# } REFERENCES SHIPMENT
    FOREIGN KEY { INV# } REFERENCES SHIPMENT ;
```

[8] Something akin to multiple assignment—probably the ability to bundle up several relvar definitions into a single statement—will also be needed in order to permit the cycle to be defined in the first place. I remark in passing that multiple assignments are involved implicitly in a variety of other operations: for example, updating a join view, or updating a relvar in such a way as to cause some compensatory action to be performed (see Example 10, later).

```
VAR SHIPMENT BASE RELATION
  { SHIP# ... , INV# ... , SHIP_DETAILS ... }
    KEY { SHIP# }
    KEY { INV# }
    FOREIGN KEY { INV# } REFERENCES INVOICE
    FOREIGN KEY { SHIP# } REFERENCES INVOICE ;
```

In fact, of course, the database really satisfies two constraints (actually two *relational equalities*) that look like this:

```
INVOICE { SHIP# } = SHIPMENT { SHIP# }

SHIPMENT { INV# } = INVOICE { INV# }
```

These constraints aren't just INDs, because of those "=" symbols; instead, let's agree to call them *equality dependencies* (EQDs for short). Here's a loose definition: An equality dependency is a special case of an inclusion dependency—to be specific, an inclusion dependency in which the "⊆" symbol is replaced by an equality ("=") symbol, thus:

```
R2 { X } = R1 { X }
```

Note: The equality dependency $R2\{X\} = R1\{X\}$ clearly holds if and only if the INDs $R2\{X\} \subseteq R1\{X\}$ and $R1\{X\} \subseteq R2\{X\}$ both hold.

Now, we might consider extending the syntax of a *<foreign key def>* to make it explicit when the implied dependency is in fact an EQD instead of just an IND—perhaps by means of an AND VICE VERSA specification, as here:

```
<foreign key def>
    ::=   FOREIGN KEY { [ ALL BUT ] <attribute ref commalist> }
              REFERENCES <relation var ref> AND VICE VERSA
```

The trouble with any such extension, however, is that symmetry would dictate that it be specified for each of the foreign keys involved:

```
VAR INVOICE BASE RELATION ...
    FOREIGN KEY { SHIP# } REFERENCES SHIPMENT AND VICE VERSA
    FOREIGN KEY { INV# } REFERENCES SHIPMENT AND VICE VERSA ;

VAR SHIPMENT BASE RELATION ...
    FOREIGN KEY { INV# } REFERENCES INVOICE AND VICE VERSA
    FOREIGN KEY { SHIP# } REFERENCES INVOICE AND VICE VERSA ;
```

Matters are getting worse, not better! The fact is, the syntax of *<foreign key def>*s as discussed previously works, more or less, precisely because the implied constraint is usually an IND as such; it's the asymmetry inherent in INDs in general—i.e., their intrinsic many to one nature—that makes it intuitively reasonable to attach the *<foreign key def>* to just one of the relvars involved (namely, the source relvar). But when that implied constraint is an EQD instead, the asymmetry goes away, and there's no longer any good reason to attach the *<foreign key def>* to one of the relvars and not the other. (And attaching it to both is obviously redundant.)

For such reasons, I don't offer AND VICE VERSA as a serious syntax proposal. Indeed, I see no reasonable alternative to simply stating the EQDs explicitly—in which case, of course, the *<foreign key def>*s become 100 percent redundant (since they're implied by those EQDs) and can be dropped, and the database design becomes:

```
VAR INVOICE BASE RELATION
  { INV# ... , SHIP# ... , INV_DETAILS ... }
    KEY { INV# }
    KEY { SHIP# } ;

VAR SHIPMENT BASE RELATION
  { SHIP# ... , INV# ... , SHIP_DETAILS ... }
    KEY { SHIP# }
    KEY { INV# } ;

CONSTRAINT EQD1A INVOICE { SHIP# } = SHIPMENT { SHIP# } ;

CONSTRAINT EQD1B SHIPMENT { INV# } = INVOICE { INV# } ;
```

I haven't finished with this example—I'll come back to it in the section immediately following.

EXAMPLE 2: MORE ON ONE TO ONE RELATIONSHIPS

Perhaps you've already realized that there's still a problem with the invoices-and-shipments design, even with its explicit EQDs and no <*foreign key def*>s. To be specific, the database is clearly required to satisfy the constraint that if relvar INVOICE shows invoice *i* as corresponding to shipment *s*, then relvar SHIPMENT must show shipment *s* as corresponding to invoice *i* (and vice versa); but the foregoing design does not capture or enforce this constraint. For example, the configuration of values shown below is permitted by that design and yet violates the constraint:

INVOICE

INV#	SHIP#	...
i1	*s1*	...
i2	*s2*	...

SHIPMENT

SHIP#	INV#	...
s1	*i2*	...
s2	*i1*	...

It might appear, therefore, that the pertinent constraint needs to be separately stated and separately enforced (where by "separately" I mean over and above the explicit KEY specifications and explicit EQDs). The constraint in question is in fact another EQD:

```
CONSTRAINT EQD2A
    INVOICE { INV# , SHIP# } = SHIPMENT { INV# , SHIP# } ;
```

Observe, however, that enforcing this constraint has the effect of enforcing constraints EQD1A and EQD1B automatically!—which means there's now no need to state those constraints explicitly, and they can be dropped.

Note: In practice, faced with a situation like the one just discussed, users sometimes "cheat" by (a) declaring the sole key for each of the relvars to be the combination {INV#,SHIP#} and then (b) declaring that combination additionally to be a foreign key in each of the relvars that references the other. Now, it's true that this subterfuge will have the effect of enforcing constraint EQD2A. However, it will also have the effect of *not* enforcing uniqueness for any of the true keys! Moreover, suppose the user attempts to overcome this latter objection by additionally defining {INV#} and {SHIP#} to be keys for both relvars. Then the system should reject the attempt to define the combination {INV#,SHIP#} as a key as well, since it manifestly violates the irreducibility requirement. As noted earlier, whether the system will indeed reject that attempt is another matter, however. In fact, in the case of SQL in particular, an implementation that did reject the attempt would actually be "nonconforming"—that is, it would actually be in violation of the standard (believe it or not). See reference [32].

By the way, another criticism that might be leveled at the invoices-and-shipments design is that it's redundant, in the sense that (as we've seen) every {INV#,SHIP#} combination appearing in either of the two relvars necessarily also appears in the other. I don't want to get into a detailed discussion of that issue here, however, since it's somewhat tangential to the main aim of the chapter; suffice it to say that at least that redundancy won't cause any "update anomalies" (as they're usually called), just so long as constraint EQD2A is enforced. See reference [23].

EXAMPLE 3: A SIXTH NORMAL FORM DESIGN

For my next example, I return to suppliers and parts. Suppose we decide to represent suppliers, not by a single relvar S as before, but rather by a set of relvars in *sixth normal form,* 6NF. Here's a definition of 6NF, taken from reference [21]:

- **Definition (sixth normal form):** Relvar *R* is in **sixth normal form,** 6NF, if and only if it can't be nonloss decomposed at all (other than into the identity projection of *R*). Equivalently, relvar *R* is in 6NF if and only if it's in 5NF, is of degree *n,* and has no key of degree less than *n*–1.

And here's the 6NF design:

```
VAR SN BASE RELATION { S# S# , SNAME NAME } KEY { S# } ;

VAR ST BASE RELATION { S# S# , STATUS INTEGER } KEY { S# } ;

VAR SC BASE RELATION { S# S# , CITY CHAR } KEY { S# } ;
```

Let's assume that if a given supplier is represented in any of these relvars, then that supplier is in fact represented in all of them—implying that we have an EQD between relvars SN and ST, and another between relvars ST and SC, and another between relvars SC and SN:[9]

```
CONSTRAINT EQD3A SN { S# } = ST { S# } ;

CONSTRAINT EQD3B ST { S# } = SC { S# } ;

CONSTRAINT EQD3C SC { S# } = SN { S# } ;
```

This example thus has certain points in common with the invoices-and-shipments example. It differs from that example in at least one respect, however. To be specific, it's likely in practice that, in addition to the three binary relvars shown, we would have another (unary) relvar whose purpose is simply to record the supplier numbers for all suppliers currently represented in the database.[10] Let's call that unary relvar S:

```
VAR S BASE RELATION { S# S# } KEY { S# } ;
```

Now there are three more EQDs:

```
CONSTRAINT EQD3D SN { S# } = S { S# } ;

CONSTRAINT EQD3E ST { S# } = S { S# } ;

CONSTRAINT EQD3F SC { S# } = S { S# } ;
```

---

[9] Note, however, that enforcing any two of these EQDs is sufficient to enforce the third. What does this fact suggest regarding explicit statement of those constraints?

[10] See, e.g., the "RM/T" design discipline recommended by Codd in reference [4] and discussed further by myself in reference [23].

Note, however, that now there's no need to state constraints EQD3A, EQD3B, and EQD3C explicitly, because enforcing constraints EQD3D, EQD3E, and EQD3F will enforce constraints EQD3A, EQD3B, and EQD3C a fortiori. What's more, there's something intuitively appealing in regarding relvar S as a kind of "master" relvar and relvars SN, ST, and SC as somehow subordinate to that "master" (which is what constraints EQD3D, EQD3E, and EQD3F together suggest).

Incidentally, another strong argument in favor of including that master relvar S has to do with the shipments relvar SP (which in fact is already in 6NF): Given that master relvar, we can retain the conventional *<foreign key def>* from SP to S (viz., FOREIGN KEY {S#} REFERENCES S). Without it, the situation is much messier (for further discussion, see Example 9).

Furthermore, suppose that (as is not unlikely) it's not the case after all that if a given supplier is represented in any of relvars SN, ST, and SC, then that supplier is represented in all of them; more precisely, suppose it's the case only that no supplier can be represented in any of relvars SN, ST, and SC without also being represented in relvar S. Then none of the foregoing EQDs will apply any more; instead, we'll be back to a situation involving nothing more than conventional foreign keys, and conventional foreign key syntax—i.e., *<foreign key def>*s as so far defined—will suffice. The design will now look like this:

```
VAR S BASE RELATION { S# S# } KEY { S# } ;

VAR SN BASE RELATION { S# S# , SNAME NAME } KEY { S# }
    FOREIGN KEY { S# } REFERENCES S ;

VAR ST BASE RELATION { S# S# , STATUS INTEGER } KEY { S# }
    FOREIGN KEY { S# } REFERENCES S ;

VAR SC BASE RELATION { S# S# , CITY CHAR } KEY { S# }
    FOREIGN KEY { S# } REFERENCES S ;
```

Note that this design allows us to represent a supplier with no known name or no known status or no known city without having to resort to nulls, three-valued logic, or other such suspect methods of dealing with "missing information" (see, e.g., references [25] and [33]). Indeed, this fact in itself is a strong argument in favor of such a design.

EXAMPLE 4: SIMPLE RENAMING

As promised earlier, I now take up the issue of attribute renaming. Let's go back to the original suppliers-and-parts database as defined in the opening section, where relvars S and P are in fifth normal form (5NF) but not sixth. For the sake of the example, however, suppose the supplier number attribute in relvar S is named SNO, say, instead of S#. Now, in **Tutorial D,** an expression of the form

```
SP { S# } ⊆ S { SNO }     /* warning: illegal! */
```

is illegal—it fails on a type error, because (as explained earlier) the relational algebra of reference [28] defines relations with different headings to be of different types. In this example, therefore, some attribute renaming is required in order to make the comparison legal.

Now, in principle we could do that renaming either on the source side or on the target side. Renaming on the source side gives:

```
( SP RENAME { S# AS SNO } ) { SNO } ⊆ S { SNO }
```

By contrast, renaming on the target side gives:

```
S { S# } ⊆ ( S RENAME { SNO AS S# } ) { S# }
```

Both of these comparisons are legal. Corresponding *<foreign key def>*s might look like this:

```
FOREIGN KEY { RENAME { S# AS SNO } } REFERENCES S

FOREIGN KEY { S# } REFERENCES S RENAME { SNO AS S# }
```

Syntactically speaking, therefore, it might seem as if we could go either way, as it were (i.e., we could do the renaming on either side). However, there are reasons—possibly not overwhelming ones, but reasons nevertheless—to prefer the option of renaming on the target side:[11]

- Renaming on the source side requires us to introduce a new syntactic construct—to be specific, a new kind of *<attribute ref>*, of the form RENAME {*<attribute ref>* AS *<introduced name>*}. The question then arises as to whether such *<attribute ref>*s should be allowed in other contexts (and if so, what they might mean).

- Renaming on the source side also means that what we surely think of intuitively as the foreign key as such—{S#} in SP, in the example—is not what actually appears following the keywords FOREIGN KEY in the definition.

By contrast, renaming on the target side avoids these two problems. So we've arrived at the point where a *<foreign key def>* looks like this:

```
<foreign key def>
    ::=   FOREIGN KEY { [ ALL BUT ] <attribute ref commalist> }
              REFERENCES <relation var ref>
                 [ RENAME { <renaming commalist> } ]
```

A *<renaming>* in turn looks like this:

```
<renaming>
    ::=   <attribute ref> AS <introduced name>
```

Now, you might be thinking that renaming on the target side as just proposed simply means we have to introduce a new syntactic construct on the target side instead of the source side. But it doesn't; the syntactic construct

```
<relation var ref> RENAME { <renaming commalist> }
```

is just a special case of a syntactic construct that already exists in **Tutorial D**. To be specific, it's a special case of a *<rename>*, whose more general form is as follows:

```
<relation exp> RENAME { <renaming commalist> }
```

And a *<rename>* in turn is itself just a special case of a *<relation exp>*. So now we've reached the point where the target in a *<foreign key def>* might be specified by means of a certain special case, at least, of a general *<relation exp>*.

Observe now that if we agree to interpret the syntactic construct *<relation var ref>* RENAME {*<renaming commalist>*}, when it's used to specify the target in a *<foreign key def>*, as a *<relation exp>*, then

---

[11] And I now therefore explicitly disavow the syntax tentatively proposed in references [18] and [28], which effectively involved renaming on the source side. In fact, as you might have noticed, the foreign key definition I gave earlier in the chapter reflects this decision to do the renaming on the target side—though of course it would be perfectly possible to define the concept one way and still go the other way in concrete syntax.

we've tacitly also agreed that a foreign key target doesn't necessarily have to be a base relvar! After all, we could certainly define S RENAME {SNO AS S#} as a *virtual relvar* (i.e., a view), like this:

```
VAR SV VIRTUAL
  ( S RENAME { SNO AS S# } )
    KEY { S# } ;
```

And now we could define {S#} as a foreign key from relvar SP to that relvar SV:

```
VAR SP BASE RELATION
  { S# S# , P# P# , QTY QTY }
    KEY { S# , P# }
    FOREIGN KEY { S# } REFERENCES SV ;
```

So now we have the idea that the target for a given foreign key might be a view—or, more generally, something that could be a view if we chose to define it as such.[12] I'll explore this possibility in more detail later (see Example 6). First, however, I want to say a little more (in the next section) about attribute renaming as such; and before I can do that, I need to take care of a small piece of unfinished business by giving for the record a more precise definition for the term *inclusion dependency*.

- **Definition (inclusion dependency):** Let *R1* and *R2* be relvars, not necessarily distinct. Let *X1* and *X2* be a subset of the heading of *R1* and a subset of the heading of *R2*, respectively, such that there exists a possibly empty sequence of attribute renamings on *R1* that maps *X1* into *X1'* (say), where *X1'* and *X2* contain exactly the same attributes. Further, let *R2* and *R1* be subject to the constraint that, at all times, every tuple *t2* in *R2* has an *X2* value that's the *X1'* value for at least one tuple *t1* in *R1* at the time in question. Then that constraint is an **inclusion dependency** (IND for short), and *R2* and *R1* are the **source relvar** and corresponding **target relvar,** respectively, for that IND.

Note, however, that the foregoing definition still doesn't take into account the possibility that the target—and perhaps the source as well?—might be specified by something more general than a simple <*relation var ref*>.

EXAMPLE 5: MORE ON RENAMING

Consider the following relvar definition:

```
VAR EMP BASE RELATION      /* employees */
  { EMP# EMP# , MGR# EMP# , EMP_DETAILS ... }
    KEY { EMP# }
    FOREIGN KEY { MGR# } REFERENCES
            EMP { EMP# } RENAME { EMP# AS MGR# } ;
```

Attribute MGR# here denotes the employee number of the manager of the employee identified by EMP#; for example, the EMP tuple for employee E2 might contain a MGR# value of E1, which constitutes a reference to the EMP tuple for employee E1. Note, therefore, that (as in Example 1) we have a referential cycle on our hands: a cycle of length one, as it happens. *Note:* A relvar that's involved in a referential cycle of length one is sometimes called a *self-referencing* relvar. Here's the definition:

- **Definition (self-referencing relvar):** A relvar *R* with a foreign key corresponding to some target key in *R*

[12] The more fundamental implication is that the target for an arbitrary IND might be a view, or something that could be a view if we were to define it as such.

itself (thereby giving rise to a referential cycle of length one).

Be that as it may, observe now that the *<foreign key def>* in this example involves renaming on the target side once again. More specifically, the target is specified by means of an expression that is, again, more complicated than a simple *<relation var ref>*:

```
EMP { EMP# } RENAME { EMP# AS MGR# }
```

But this expression doesn't just involve a RENAME as in Example 4—it involves a projection (of EMP on {EMP#}) as well. And in fact it must. For suppose we tried to write the *<foreign key def>* as follows, without that projection:

```
FOREIGN KEY { MGR# } REFERENCES EMP RENAME { EMP# AS MGR# }
```

Then the RENAME would fail—more precisely, the expression EMP RENAME {EMP# AS MGR#} would fail—because relvar EMP already has an attribute called MGR#. By contrast, the projection of EMP on {EMP#} doesn't.

Here for the record is the relational comparison (to be more specific, the IND) that's implied by the *<foreign key def>* in the example:

```
EMP { MGR# } ⊆ ( EMP { EMP# } RENAME { EMP# AS MGR# } ) { MGR# }
```

Again, therefore, the example illustrates the point that a foreign key target doesn't necessarily have to be a base relvar. In particular, we could define a view like this:

```
VAR EMPV VIRTUAL
  ( EMP { EMP# } RENAME { EMP# AS MGR# } )
    KEY { MGR# } ;
```

And now we could define {MGR#} to be a foreign key from the base relvar EMP to the virtual relvar EMPV:

```
VAR EMP BASE RELATION
  { EMP# EMP# , MGR# EMP# , EMP_DETAILS ... }
    KEY { EMP# }
    FOREIGN KEY { MGR# } REFERENCES EMPV ;
```

But this example raises another point. (Actually, Example 4 raised the same point, but I deliberately ducked the issue when I discussed that example in the previous section.) In the *<foreign key def>* FOREIGN KEY {*K*} REFERENCES *R*, the target *R* is supposed to have a key of the same type—involving, therefore, the same attribute name(s)—as {*K*}; thus, in the example under discussion, the target is supposed to have {MGR#} as a key.

Now, in the version of the example that specified the target relvar as view EMPV, I explicitly defined {MGR#} to be a key for that view,[13] and so the *<foreign key def>* FOREIGN KEY {MGR#} REFERENCES EMPV clearly satisfied the foregoing requirement. But what about the original version of the example? Here again is the *<foreign key def>* from that version:

---

[13] I did this in order to avoid complicating the example unnecessarily. However, **Tutorial D** doesn't actually require explicit KEY specifications on views; if they're omitted, then the system is supposed to work out for itself what keys the view in question might possess. As for SQL, explicit KEY specifications—or their analog, rather—on views aren't even permitted.

```
FOREIGN KEY { MGR# } REFERENCES
        EMP { EMP# } RENAME { EMP# AS MGR# }
```

The question here is: Does the system know in this case that a specification of the form KEY {MGR#} applies to the target? Well, first let me remind you that specifying KEY {*K*} as part of the definition of relvar *R* means only that {*K*} is a superkey, and not necessarily a key as such, for relvar *R*. In the case at hand, then, the system does at least know that {EMP#} is a superkey for EMP, thanks to the specification KEY {EMP#} in the definition of that relvar. From this fact, it follows that {EMP#} is certainly a superkey for the projection of EMP on {EMP#}. And from *this* fact, it follows that {MGR#} is at least a superkey for the result of the renaming. Thus, the system should certainly be able to infer that {MGR#} is a superkey for the foreign key target in this particular example—and so the situation is logically equivalent to that in which the foreign key target is specified as view EMPV and the definition of that view includes the explicit specification KEY {MGR#}. In other words, in this example at least, the requirement under discussion is again clearly satisfied. (And I hope it's obvious that it was satisfied in Example 4 also.)

EXAMPLE 6: GENERALIZING THE TARGET

I now return to the original supplier-and-parts database as defined in the opening section. Suppose that database is subject to the following constraint: *At this time there's a trade embargo in effect, such that no supplier in Athens is allowed to supply any parts.* Formally, then, we have:

```
SP { S# } ⊆ ( S WHERE CITY ≠ 'Athens' ) { S# }
```

This constraint is clearly another example of an inclusion dependency (by which I mean the generalized form of such a dependency, in which the target is not necessarily a base relvar). However, it's not a foreign key constraint—at least, not as foreign key constraints are conventionally understood. But it does look awfully like one! Now, we've already seen cases in which the target for a *<foreign key def>* has to be specified by means of a *<relation exp>* that's more general than a simple *<relation var ref>*. So why not go the whole hog, as it were, and extend the syntax of *<foreign key def>*s to allow the target to be specified by a *<relation exp>* of arbitrary complexity, like this?—

```
<foreign key def>
    ::=   FOREIGN KEY { [ ALL BUT ] <attribute ref commalist> }
              REFERENCES <relation exp>
```

The example at hand could then be expressed as follows:

```
VAR SP BASE RELATION
  { S# S# , P# P# , QTY QTY }
    KEY { S# , P# }
    FOREIGN KEY { S# } REFERENCES ( S WHERE CITY ≠ 'Athens' ) ;
```

(The parentheses surrounding the expression S WHERE CITY ≠ 'Athens' are legal, because one form of *<relation exp>* in **Tutorial D** consists of a *<relation exp>* enclosed in parentheses. I include them for clarity.)

Note, moreover, that if this solution isn't available to us, then we'll have to write something like this:

```
VAR SP BASE RELATION
  { S# S# , P# P# , QTY QTY }
    KEY { S# , P# }
    FOREIGN KEY { S# } REFERENCES S ;
```

```
CONSTRAINT ...
    IS_EMPTY ( ( SP JOIN ( S WHERE CITY = 'Athens' ) ) ) ;
```

But if we have to write a separate constraint definition anyway, why not just write one that takes care of the foreign key constraint as well, like this?—

```
CONSTRAINT ...
    SP { S# } ⊆ ( S WHERE CITY ≠ 'Athens' ) { S# } ;
```

Then there wouldn't be any need for the <*foreign key def*> as such (i.e., FOREIGN KEY {S#} REFERENCES S) at all! So what exactly does the conventional FOREIGN KEY syntax buy us, in this particular example?

On the other hand, suppose we did in fact extend the syntax of <*foreign key def*>s to allow specifications like the one under discussion:

```
FOREIGN KEY { S# } REFERENCES ( S WHERE CITY ≠ 'Athens' )
```

Once again, then, we'd be faced with a key inference problem: to be specific, the problem of ensuring that, in the case of this particular example, if (a) the expression S WHERE CITY ≠ 'Athens' were used to define a view, say *V*, then (b) *V* would be subject to the constraint KEY {S#}. But in this particular case the inference is again straightforward, because the system certainly knows that {S#} is a superkey for S, and from this fact it follows immediately that {S#} is also a superkey for any restriction of S (which is what S WHERE CITY ≠ 'Athens' is, of course).

More generally, if we want to permit <*relation exp*>s of arbitrary complexity to be used to specify foreign key targets, then we need to be sure that the key inference problem can be solved for any such <*relation exp*>. But that problem *has* been solved, at least to a large extent. To be specific, Hugh Darwen has given solutions in reference [8] for <*relation exp*>s involving any of the following relational operations: rename, project, restrict, join, product, intersect, union, difference, extend, and summarize.[14]

EXAMPLE 7: MORE ON GENERALIZING THE TARGET

I'd like to show another example, briefly, to illustrate the usefulness of being able to specify the target of a foreign key constraint by means of an arbitrarily complex <*relation exp*>. Suppose the suppliers-and-parts database (original version, as defined in the opening section) is subject to the following constraint: *If supplier s supplies part p, then supplier s and part p must be in the same city.* This constraint is easily expressed by means of an appropriate <*foreign key def*> for relvar SP, thus:

```
VAR SP BASE RELATION
  { S# S# , P# P# , QTY QTY }
    KEY { S# , P# }
    FOREIGN KEY { S# , P# } REFERENCES ( S JOIN P ) ;
```

Observe that (a) the expression S JOIN P denotes the join of suppliers and parts on {CITY} (since CITY is the sole attribute common to relvars S and P), and (b) the combination {S#,P#} is clearly a key for that join.

---

[14] Darwen also reports that an attempt has been made to incorporate those solutions into the SQL standard [32].

EXAMPLE 8: GENERALIZING THE SOURCE

Again I refer to the original supplier-and-parts database as defined in the opening section. Suppose that database is subject to the following constraint: *Only suppliers in London can supply parts in a quantity greater than 200.* Formally:

```
( SP WHERE QTY > 200 ) { S# } ⊆
                             ( S WHERE CITY = 'London' ) { S# }
```

Now, we've already agreed that we can allow the target of a *<foreign key def>* (or, more generally, an IND) to be specified by means of an arbitrarily complex *<relation exp>*—so the obvious question is: Can't we do the same with the source?

Well, note first that, as the formal statement of the constraint under discussion suggests, we've effectively already done this in connection with inclusion dependencies in general; that is, we've already allowed the source in an IND to be specified by means of an arbitrarily complex relational expression.[15] Turning to *<foreign key def>*s in particular, here's a formulation that looks as if it might work:

```
VAR SP BASE RELATION
  { S# S# , P# P# , QTY QTY }
    KEY { S# , P# }
    WHEN QTY > 200 THEN FOREIGN KEY { S# } REFERENCES
                             ( S WHERE CITY = 'London' ) ;
```

Of course, we would still need to say that every supplier number in relvar SP also appears in relvar S, even if the quantity is 200 or less. A conventional *<foreign key def>* of the form FOREIGN KEY {S#} REFERENCES S would suffice. But we might want to be a little more sophisticated:

```
VAR SP BASE RELATION
  { S# S# , P# P# , QTY QTY }
    KEY { S# , P# }
    WHEN QTY > 200 THEN FOREIGN KEY { S# } REFERENCES
                             ( S WHERE CITY = 'London' )
    WHEN QTY ≤ 200 THEN FOREIGN KEY { S# } REFERENCES S ;
```

Or even:

```
VAR SP BASE RELATION
  { S# S# , P# P# , QTY QTY }
    KEY { S# , P# }
    CASE
       WHEN QTY > 200 THEN FOREIGN KEY { S# } REFERENCES
                                ( S WHERE CITY = 'London' )
       WHEN QTY ≤ 200 WHEN FOREIGN KEY { S# } REFERENCES S
    END CASE ;
```

---

[15] It's worth noting in passing that this fact implies that all possible database constraints can be expressed as INDs! By definition, any constraint implies that some *<relation exp>*—namely, one that denotes the set of tuples that cause the constraint in question to be violated—must always evaluate to an empty relation. Thus, the constraint is conceptually of the form IS_EMPTY(*rx*) for some *<relation exp> rx*. But IS_EMPTY(*rx*) is logically equivalent to an expression of the form *rx*{} ⊆ TABLE_DUM—in other words, to a certain generalized IND (more precisely, to an EQD of the form *rx*{} = TABLE_DUM). See reference [9] for further explanation.

Here's the same example formulated in terms of explicit views:

```
VAR SPV VIRTUAL ( SP WHERE QTY > 200 ) KEY { S# , P# }
    FOREIGN KEY { S# } REFERENCES ( S WHERE CITY = 'London' ) ;

VAR SPW VIRTUAL ( SP WHERE QTY ≤ 200 ) KEY { S# , P# }
    FOREIGN KEY { S# } REFERENCES S ;
```

In other words, it should be possible to specify a view as the source, as well as the target, for a *<foreign key def>*; indeed, *The Principle of Interchangeability* (of base relvars and views) effectively demands as much [18]. For the record, here's a definition of that principle:

- **Definition (*The Principle of Interchangeability*):** There should be no arbitrary and unnecessary distinctions between base and virtual relvars; i.e., virtual relvars should "look and feel" just like base ones so far as users are concerned.

However, I don't think I want to offer the foregoing syntax, using WHEN, as a serious proposal (except possibly as a basis for a well defined shorthand), because it isn't sufficiently general. Consider the following constraint: *If supplier s and part p are in the same city, then supplier s must supply part p.* (This constraint is the inverse of the one discussed under Example 7, in a sense.) Formally:

```
( S JOIN P ) { S# , P# } ⊆ SP { S# , P# }
```

Now, we might consider representing this IND by means of a *<foreign key def>* for which an appropriate view serves as the source, like this:

```
VAR SPZ VIRTUAL ( S JOIN P ) KEY { S# , P# }
    FOREIGN KEY { S# , P# } REFERENCES SP ;
```

But we surely don't want to have to go through the effort and overhead of defining a view if the sole purpose of that view is merely to serve as the source for some *<foreign key def>*. Instead, why not allow *<foreign key def>*s to be attached directly (within a constraint definition) to an arbitrary *<relation exp>*?[16] Then we could formulate the example at hand as follows:

```
CONSTRAINT ...
    ( S JOIN P ) FOREIGN KEY { S# , P# } REFERENCES SP ;
```

Now, this particular example is slightly longer than its IND equivalent—which, to remind you, looks like this:

```
CONSTRAINT ...
    ( S JOIN P ) { S# , P# } ⊆ SP { S# , P# } ;
```

But note that this latter syntax requires the pertinent attribute names to be written out twice, which the FOREIGN KEY analog doesn't. Thus, the FOREIGN KEY equivalent might truly be a shorthand in more complicated cases. I conclude that (a) as we know, *<foreign key def>*s are certainly a useful shorthand in

---

[16] I'm already on record—see, e.g., references [14] and [24]—as proposing that we should be able to attach conventional KEY specifications to *<relation exp>*s within constraint definitions. By way of example, suppose the following constraint is in effect: *If suppliers Sx and Sy (x ≠ y) supply the same part, then they must be in different cities.* One way of formulating this constraint is as follows: CONSTRAINT ... (S JOIN SP) KEY {P#,CITY}. (Of course, the key constraint KEY {S#,P#} also applies to S JOIN SP.) So what I'm suggesting here, regarding FOREIGN KEY specifications, is an obvious extension of that earlier proposal. But I should add that neither proposal has been checked for syntactic soundness.

connection with explicit relvar definitions (where the relvars in question can be either base relvars or views), and (b) they can also be useful on occasion in connection with arbitrary *<relation exp>*s.

EXAMPLE 9: MORE THAN ONE TARGET

In reference [10], I proposed an extension to the basic foreign key concept according to which *<foreign key def>*s would look something like this:

```
<foreign key def>
    ::=   FOREIGN KEY { [ ALL BUT ] <attribute ref commalist> }
              REFERENCES
                 [ <quantifier> ] { <relation exp commalist> }
```

The *<quantifier>* is EXACTLY ONE OF, AT LEAST ONE OF, or ALL OF; it can be omitted, along with the braces enclosing the *<relation exp commalist>*, if and only if that commalist contains exactly one *<relation exp>*. *Note:* I assume for the purposes of the present discussion that the various *<quantifier>*s all have the intuitively obvious semantics.

In a later paper [11], however, I backed down from the foregoing proposals somewhat. But I think it's worth taking a closer look at them here, if only in the interest of completeness (of some kind).

EXACTLY ONE OF

EXACTLY ONE OF is arguably the most useful of the three cases. By way of a motivating example, suppose the database contains a relvar representing an audit trail for a certain bank, and suppose that relvar contains a tuple for every commercial transaction carried out by that bank over a certain period of time. Suppose also that each such transaction is exactly one of the following: a deposit, a withdrawal, or a request for balance information. Then we could certainly imagine a situation in which each tuple in the audit trail relvar has to reference exactly one of the following: a tuple in the deposits relvar, a tuple in the withdrawals relvar, or a tuple in the balance requests relvar.

For a more concrete example, I turn to suppliers and parts once again. Suppose the original suppliers relvar S is replaced by a set of relvars, one for each supplier city, thus:

```
VAR AS BASE RELATION      /* Athens suppliers */
  { S# S# , SNAME NAME , STATUS INTEGER }
    KEY { S# } ;

VAR LS BASE RELATION      /* London suppliers */
  { S# S# , SNAME NAME , STATUS INTEGER }
    KEY { S# } ;

VAR PS BASE RELATION      /* Paris suppliers  */
  { S# S# , SNAME NAME , STATUS INTEGER }
    KEY { S# } ;
```

(For simplicity, I assume there are just three possible supplier cities.) In relvar SP, then, we might have a *<foreign key def>* involving EXACTLY ONE OF:

```
VAR SP BASE RELATION
  { S# S# , P# P# , QTY QTY }
    KEY { S# , P# }
    FOREIGN KEY { S# } REFERENCES EXACTLY ONE OF { AS , LS , PS } ;
```

However, I now observe that this EXACTLY ONE OF syntax is logically redundant. To see why, note first that (in terms of the example under discussion) we'll need a constraint to ensure that no supplier number appears at any given time in more than one of AS, LS, and PS:

```
CONSTRAINT S#_GLOBALLY_UNIQUE IS_EMPTY
  ( UNION { AS { S# } INTERSECT LS { S# } ,
            LS { S# } INTERSECT PS { S# } ,
            PS { S# } INTERSECT AS { S# } } ) ;
```

Explanation: The union of these three intersections will be empty if and only if each of those individual intersections is itself empty. If each individual intersection is empty, then no supplier number is common to any two of AS, LS, and PS; hence, no supplier number is common to all three, a fortiori.[17]

Clearly, then, if constraint S#_GLOBALLY_UNIQUE is enforced (as it should be), the *<foreign key def>* can be stated more simply as:

```
FOREIGN KEY { S# } REFERENCES UNION { AS , LS , PS }
```

Or even:[18]

```
FOREIGN KEY { S# } REFERENCES D_UNION { AS , LS , PS }
```

For such reasons, I don't offer EXACTLY ONE OF as a serious syntax proposal at this time.

AT LEAST ONE OF

It's hard to come up with an intuitively reasonable example to justify support for AT LEAST ONE OF—but in any case there's no need to, because (like EXACTLY ONE OF) it's clearly logically redundant. To be specific, the *<foreign key def>*—

```
FOREIGN KEY { FK }
        REFERENCES AT LEAST ONE OF { R1 , R2 , ... , Rn }
```

—is clearly equivalent to this one (at least, it is so long as *R1, R2, ..., Rn* are all of the same type; otherwise some projections and/or renamings will be required, as in Examples 4 and 5):

```
FOREIGN KEY { FK } REFERENCES UNION { R1 , R2 , ... , Rn }
```

So I don't offer AT LEAST ONE OF as a serious syntax proposal at this time, either.

ALL OF

Finally, consider the *<foreign key def>*

```
FOREIGN KEY { FK } REFERENCES ALL OF { R1 , R2 , ... , Rn }
```

I note in passing that such a *<foreign key def>* might appear as part of the definition of relvar SP if—as in Example 3 earlier—suppliers are represented by the three 6NF relvars SN, ST, and SC (only, i.e., without the master relvar S). Be that as it may, every pair of targets in *R1, R2, ..., Rn* clearly has to satisfy a certain equality dependency (EQD), and we need a constraint to ensure that this is so:[19]

---

[17] I note in passing that support for an operator of the form DISJOINT {*<relation exp commalist>*}, defined to return TRUE if and only if no two of its argument relations have a tuple in common, might be a useful thing to have in practice.

[18] But see Chapter 10 of the present book regarding the possible undesirability of using D_UNION in constraints. *Note:* The keyword D_UNION denotes the *disjoint union* operator. For further explanation, see, e.g., reference [28].

[19] Again a shorthand might be useful—perhaps an operator of the form IDENTICAL {*<relation exp commalist>*}, defined to return TRUE if and only if its argument relations are all equal.

```
CONSTRAINT ...
    UNION     { R1 { FK } , R2 { FK } , ... , Rn { FK } } =
    INTERSECT { R1 { FK } , R2 { FK } , ... , Rn { FK } } ;
```

(The union and the intersection of a given collection of sets will be equal if and only if all of the sets in the collection are in fact the same set.) And if this constraint is enforced, the *<foreign key def>* can be stated more simply as, e.g.:[20]

```
FOREIGN KEY { FK } REFERENCES R1
```

So I don't offer ALL OF as a serious syntax proposal at this time, either. The net of the discussions in these three subsections is thus that I don't believe it's necessary to extend the syntax of *<foreign key def>*s to allow more than one target, just so long as other recommendations in this chapter are implemented—in particular, the recommendation that it should be possible to specify the target by means of an arbitrarily complex *<relation exp>*.

EXAMPLE 10: COMPENSATORY ACTIONS

For my final example I return once again to the original suppliers-and-parts database from the opening section, and in particular to the *<foreign key def>* relating shipments to suppliers:

```
FOREIGN KEY { S# } REFERENCES S
```

Here is an exhaustive list of the updates that could cause this constraint to be violated. *Note:* For reasons explained in detail in reference [20] and elsewhere, all of the following characterizations are loose in the extreme; however, they're accurate enough for present purposes.

1. Inserting an SP tuple, if the S# value doesn't currently appear in relvar S
2. Changing the S# value in an SP tuple, if the new S# value doesn't currently appear in relvar S
3. Deleting an S tuple, if the S# value currently appears in relvar SP
4. Changing the S# value in an S tuple, if the old S# value currently appears in relvar SP
5. Any relational assignment that's logically equivalent to one of the preceding cases

Now, so far in this chapter I've tacitly assumed that—as with constraints in general—any update that, if accepted, would cause some foreign key constraint to be violated is simply rejected. For example, consider the following **Tutorial D** DELETE statement:

```
DELETE S WHERE S# = S#('S1') ;
```

If this DELETE means exactly what it says (i.e., if it means *Delete the tuple for supplier S1 from relvar S,* no more and no less), and if relvar SP does contain at least one tuple for supplier S1, then the DELETE will fail. But sometimes we can do better than that—and that's what *foreign key rules* are all about. The basic idea is that sometimes it might be possible for the system to perform an appropriate *compensatory action* that will guarantee that the overall result does still satisfy the foreign key constraint. In the example, the obvious compensatory action is for the system to "cascade" the DELETE to delete the SP tuples for supplier S1 as well. We can achieve this effect by extending the *<foreign key def>* as follows:

---

[20] Though I admit that the arbitrariness of the choice as to which of *R1, R2, ..., Rn* is to play the role of the target is a little bothersome.

```
FOREIGN KEY { S# } REFERENCES S ON DELETE CASCADE
```

The specification ON DELETE CASCADE defines a *DELETE rule* for this particular foreign key, and the specification CASCADE is the corresponding compensatory action.

Foreign key rules were first proposed by myself in reference [10]. The discussion that follows is based on ideas from that reference, therefore, but it differs considerably at the detail level.[21] First let me give some definitions:

- **Definition (foreign key rule):** A rule specifying the action to be taken by the system—typically but not necessarily a compensatory action—to ensure that updates affecting the foreign key in question don't violate the associated foreign key constraint.

- **Definition (DELETE rule):** A foreign key rule that specifies the action to be taken by the system if some tuple *t2* exists that contains a foreign key value referencing some tuple *t1* and—speaking rather loosely—tuple *t1* is deleted.

- **Definition (UPDATE rule):** A foreign key rule that specifies the action to be taken by the system if some tuple *t2* exists that contains a foreign key value referencing some tuple *t1* and—speaking very loosely—the corresponding target key in tuple *t1* is updated.

- **Definition (referential action):** The action specification portion of a foreign key rule (e.g., CASCADE, in a DELETE rule); also used to mean the corresponding action itself.

- **Definition (compensatory action):** An update performed automatically by the system in addition to some requested update, with the aim of avoiding some integrity violation that might otherwise occur. Cascading a delete operation is a typical example. Such actions should be specified declaratively, and users should be aware of them; that is, users should know when their update requests are shorthand for some more extensive set of actions, for otherwise they might perceive an apparent violation of *The Assignment Principle* (see later).

Several points arise from the foregoing definitions. First, note that compensatory actions in general are not actually prescribed by the relational model—but neither are they proscribed. In other words, while the relational model is certainly the foundation of the database field, it's *only* the foundation, and there's no reason why additional features shouldn't be built on top of, or alongside, that foundation—just so long as those additions don't violate the prescriptions of the model, of course (and are in the spirit of the model and can be shown to be useful, I suppose I should add).

Second, observe that I distinguish between compensatory and referential actions. A referential action is what the system has to do when an update is attempted that might violate some referential constraint. A compensatory action is what the system has to do when an update is attempted that otherwise definitely would violate some constraint (not necessarily a referential constraint). Thus, some referential actions are compensatory actions and some compensatory actions are referential actions, but the concepts are distinct.

Third, note that I propose a foreign key DELETE rule and a foreign key UPDATE rule but no foreign key INSERT rule. The rationale here—with reference to suppliers and shipments specifically—is that shipments are subordinate to suppliers, in a sense (certainly they're "existence dependent" on them). And an INSERT rule, if such a thing were defined, would presumably mean that the insertion of a shipment could cause some kind of compensatory action to be performed on suppliers—an intuitively unreasonable "tail wags the dog" situation, it seems to me. For analogous reasons, there's no UPDATE rule that applies to UPDATEs on relvar SP, though

---

[21] Mostly because I no longer believe in nulls, and therefore now reject some of the options proposed in the original paper.

there is one that applies to UPDATEs on relvar S. *Note:* This paragraph should not be construed as saying that such INSERT and UPDATE rules could never make sense—it's just that they don't make sense in the context of suppliers and shipments specifically, and no such rules are proposed in this chapter.

Fourth, the only referential actions that I believe (at the time of writing) make sense are CASCADE and NO CASCADE:[22]

- CASCADE is a compensatory action, and I've already explained its effect, informally, in the context of a DELETE rule. In the context of an UPDATE rule, its effect is as follows (I'll explain it in terms of suppliers and shipments, for definiteness): If the S# value in an S tuple is changed, then that same change is cascaded to all corresponding SP tuples.

- NO CASCADE (which is the default) is a referential action but not a compensatory action, and it means what it says: *Don't do any cascading*. Thus, in terms of suppliers and shipments, ON DELETE NO CASCADE means that deleting an S tuple (or attempting to, rather) will fail if there are any corresponding SP tuples; ON UPDATE NO CASCADE means that changing the S# value in an S tuple (or attempting to, rather) will fail if there are any corresponding SP tuples.

So I'm extending the syntax of *<foreign key def>*s once again:

```
<foreign key def>
    ::=   FOREIGN KEY { [ ALL BUT ] <attribute ref commalist> }
              REFERENCES <relation exp>
            [ ON DELETE [ NO ] CASCADE ]
            [ ON UPDATE [ NO ] CASCADE ]
```

Fifth, note that the definition of compensatory actions explicitly requires that such actions be made visible to users, for otherwise those users might perceive an apparent violation of *The Assignment Principle*. Here's a definition of that principle:

- **Definition (*The Assignment Principle*):** After assignment of value *v* to variable *V*, the comparison *v* = *V* is required to evaluate to TRUE.

Clearly, this principle—which is, in effect, nothing but a definition of the semantics of assignment—could be violated if the system is allowed to update some variable (meaning, more specifically, some variable that's visible to the user) without the user being aware of that fact. Thus, for example, if ON DELETE CASCADE is specified in connection with the foreign key from relvar SP to relvar S, then the user must be aware that the statement

```
DELETE S WHERE S# = S#('S1') ;
```

is really shorthand for the following multiple assignment:[23]

```
DELETE S  WHERE S# = S#('S1') ,
DELETE SP WHERE S# = S#('S1') ;
```

---

[22] I reject SQL's SET NULL for obvious reasons. I also reject SET DEFAULT, because any such support would clearly have to be part of some kind of comprehensive scheme for default values and **Tutorial D** includes no such scheme at this time. As for RESTRICT and NO ACTION, I believe these are both equivalent to NO CASCADE if updates are treated—as they should be—as proper set level operators, not tuple level operators (see the discussion of this question in the section "Some Implementation Issues," later).

[23] Note that this "multiple DELETE" is indeed a multiple assignment, logically speaking; to be specific, it's one that assigns something to relvar S and something to relvar P.

For otherwise the variable that's the entire database will be perceived, in general, as having changed its overall value in a way that's not consistent with the idea that a single tuple (only) has been removed fom a single relvar (only). *Note:* For an extended discussion of this idea—the idea, that is, that compensatory updates must be exposed to the user—see reference [26]. Also, for a discussion of the idea that the entire database is a variable, see reference [28].

Sixth, as the foregoing example indicates, if some update does cause some compensatory action to be performed, then the original update and the compensatory action together must be regarded as semantically atomic (all or nothing); in other words, they must definitely be regarded as part of the same overall multiple assignment.

Seventh, I haven't lost sight of the fact that *<foreign key def>*s, and therefore compensatory actions, can be specified for views as well as base relvars (and possibly even for arbitrary *<relation exps>*s as well, within a general constraint definition). Thus, compensatory actions in general imply the need to support at least some kinds of view updating. See references [19] and [26] for further discussion.

Eighth, I observe that if foreign key constraints are *not* specified by means of special case syntax—i.e., by *<foreign key def>*s, to use the terminology of the present chapter—but instead by means of expressions in some general purpose constraint language, then it might not be possible, in the case of those constraints in particular, to specify foreign key rules declaratively. The implications of this point are unclear at this time.

Finally, the question arises: If some specific update would require some compensatory action to be performed if it were expressed as an explicit DELETE or UPDATE, what should happen if that update is expressed by some means of some general relational assignment instead? This is another issue that I believe requires more study at this time.

SOME IMPLEMENTATION ISSUES

Although this chapter is deliberately not much concerned with matters of implementation, I do want to make a couple of remarks in connection with the implementation of DELETE rules in particular. The first concerns certain implementation restrictions to be found in certain SQL products today. For example, IBM's DB2 has (or used to have) a restriction in connection with self-referencing relvars to the effect that the DELETE rule must specify CASCADE. Part of the justification for this state of affairs is as follows. Consider the following self-referencing relvar (repeated from Example 5):

```
VAR EMP BASE RELATION
  { EMP# EMP# , MGR# EMP# , EMP_DETAILS ... }
    KEY { EMP# }
    FOREIGN KEY { MGR# } REFERENCES
            EMP { EMP# } RENAME { EMP# AS MGR# } ;
```

Here's a sample value for this relvar:

EMP

EMP#	MGR#	...	
E1	E1	...	(tuple 1)
E2	E1	...	(tuple 2)

Observe now that the DELETE rule for the foreign key in this example is, by default, ON DELETE NO CASCADE. So consider the following DELETE statement:

```
DELETE EMP WHERE EMP# > EMP#('E0') ;
```

(I assume for the sake of the example that the comparison operator ">" makes sense for values of type EMP#.) Now suppose the system tries to delete tuple 2 first and then tuple 1, checking the foreign key constraint for each tuple in turn as it goes; then the DELETE overall will succeed. But if it tries to delete tuple 1 first, then after that tuple has been deleted tuple 2 will contain a reference to a tuple that no longer exists, and the DELETE overall will fail. So the argument goes like this: In order to guarantee a predictable result no matter which tuple is deleted first, the DELETE rule *must* specify CASCADE. (I leave it as an exercise for the reader to determine exactly why CASCADE does provide such a guarantee in this situation.)

However, I regard the foregoing argument as logically flawed.[24] The flaw consists in checking (or attempting to check) the foreign key constraint one tuple at a time. Operations in the relational model are set at a time, not tuple at a time—which means, in the case of update operations in particular, that they update entire relvars en bloc, not piecemeal (i.e., not one tuple at a time). And one consequence of this fact is that compensatory actions and database constraint checking mustn't be done until all of the updating has been done; to say it again, a set level update mustn't be treated as a sequence of individual tuple level updates. Thus, the conceptual algorithm for implementing the DELETE statement under discussion, with the DELETE rule specifying NO CASCADE, is as follows:

```
unmark all tuples in EMP ;

do for each tuple t in EMP in some sequence ;
   if EMP# FROM t > EMP#('E0')
      then mark t for deletion ;
end do ;

do for each unmarked tuple t in EMP in some sequence ;
   if MGR# FROM t = EMP# FROM some marked tuple in EMP
      then quit /* DELETE fails */ ;
end do ;

do for each marked tuple t in EMP in some sequence ;
   remove t from EMP ;
end do /* DELETE succeeds */ ;
```

Of course, it goes without saying that the foregoing algorithm can and should be improved in numerous ways in practice; however, such matters are beyond the scope of this chapter.

The other implementation issue I want to discuss briefly is as follows.[25] It's well known—or frequently claimed, at any rate—that certain combinations of (a) referential structures (by which I mean sets of relvars that are interrelated via foreign key constraints), (b) specific foreign key rules, and (c) specific data values in the database, can together lead to conflicts. Consider, for example, the situation shown symbolically opposite (this example is taken from reference [11]):

---

[24] The positions I advocate in the present section are somewhat at odds with those I advocated when I first discussed such examples in reference [11]. If this change on my part causes confusion, I apologize.

[25] Actually I think it's the same issue, though some might dispute this claim.

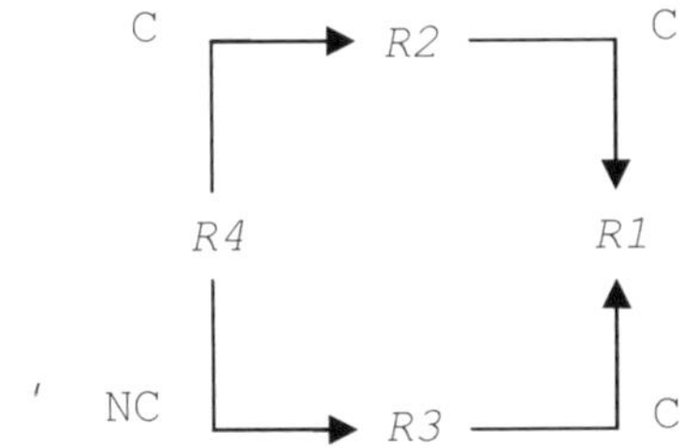

In this example, relvar *R4* has foreign key constraints (shown as arrows) to both relvars *R2* and *R3,* each of which in turn has a foreign key constraint to relvar *R1*. Thus, there are two referential paths from *R4* to *R1*. I'll refer to the path via *R2* as the upper path and the path via *R3* as the lower path.

Now let me focus on the DELETE rules, which I take to be as indicated in the diagram (C = CASCADE, NC = NO CASCADE). Suppose for simplicity that each relvar has just one attribute, *A,* and {*A*} is the sole key for each relvar and also the foreign key in relvars *R2, R3,* and *R4* (actually, both foreign keys, in the case of *R4*); suppose also that each relvar contains just one tuple, containing the same value in every case; and suppose finally that we try to delete the single tuple from relvar *R1*. What happens?

- If the system applies the DELETE rules in the upper path first, the single tuple in *R4* (and the single tuple in *R2*) will be deleted, because the rules both specify CASCADE. When the system then applies the DELETE rule in the lower path, an attempt will be made to delete the single tuple from *R3;* this attempt will succeed, because there is now no tuple in *R4* to cause that attempt to fail. The net effect is that all four tuples will be deleted.

- On the other hand, if the system applies the DELETE rules in the lower path first, the net effect is that the database will remain unchanged—because the tuple in *R4* will cause the attempt to delete the tuple from *T3* to fail (because the DELETE rule on the path from *R4* to *R3* specifies NO CASCADE), and the overall operation will therefore fail as well.

In other words, the overall result is unpredictable—and if so, then it's to be hoped that the implementation will detect and reject the conflicting definitions in the first place, so that such a situation cannot arise.

But is the foregoing argument valid? Again it looks to me as if there's tuple at a time thinking going on here. It seems to me, rather, that the system should go through essentially the same algorithm as described in connection with the previous example:

- First, it should unmark all tuples.

- Next, it should mark tuples that are to be deleted (note that the procedure for this step will be invoked recursively, because of the CASCADE specifications). Following the upper path causes the tuples in *R1, R2,* and *R4* to be marked; following the lower path causes the tuples in *R1* and *R3* to be marked. No matter which path is followed first, therefore, the net effect is that all four tuples are marked.

- Next, it should check to see that no unmarked tuple includes a reference to any marked tuple. In the example, this check succeeds.

- Finally, it should actually delete all marked tuples. In the example, this step has the effect of deleting the tuples from all four of *R1, R2, R3,* and *R4*.

Incidentally, I deliberately chose to illustrate the foregoing issue by means of a slightly complicated example, but a simpler one might have sufficed. To be specific, suppose relvar *R2* has two foreign keys, both referencing relvar *R1,* but the DELETE rules specify CASCADE for one of them and NO CASCADE for the other. Clearly there's just as much potential for conflict here as in the previous example (?). But that combination of rules might be exactly what's wanted! For example, consider the well known "bill of materials" application, in which relvar PP shows which parts ("major" parts) contain which parts ("minor" parts) as components:

```
VAR P BASE RELATION { P# P# , ... } KEY { P# } ;

VAR PP BASE RELATION { MAJOR_P# P# , MINOR_P# P# , ... }
    KEY { MAJOR_P# , MINOR_P# }
    FOREIGN KEY { MAJOR_P# } REFERENCES
                P RENAME { P# AS MAJOR_P# } ON DELETE CASCADE
    FOREIGN KEY { MINOR_P# } REFERENCES
                P RENAME { P# AS MINOR_P# } ON DELETE NO CASCADE;
```

It seems perfectly reasonable to me to say that deleting a part does cascade to those tuples where the pertinent part number appears as a MAJOR_P# value (meaning the part in question contains other parts as components), but not to those tuples where the same part number appears as a MINOR_P# value (meaning the part in question is a component of other parts).

Be that as it may, some critics have used examples like the ones discussed above as a basis for arguing that the notion of foreign key rules as such (or compensatory actions, at least) is problematic, possibly logically flawed. Myself, I don't find such arguments convincing. The rules and compensatory actions specified in any given situation are surely supposed to reflect policies in operation in whatever the enterprise is that the database is intended to serve. Thus, it seems to me that if some combination of definitions leads to unpredictability,[26] then those definitions must be logically incorrect—i.e., they can't properly reflect the situation existing in the real world. (Unless the "real world" is logically incorrect too, I suppose I should add; but then I would argue that having the policies stated declaratively instead of procedurally can only improve the chances of the enterprise detecting the error and coming up with a remedy.)

CONCLUDING REMARKS

This chapter grew in the writing. My original motivation for embarking on it was a nagging concern over the attribute renaming issue (see Examples 4 and 5); I'd been worrying about that issue off and on for quite a long time, and I wanted to get it pinned down once and for all. However, the more I thought about the subject in general, the more I found I wanted to say. And now I have a somewhat embarrassing confession to make ... As I concocted the various examples and as I worked through the various supporting arguments, I began to get an extreme sense of *déjà vu*. Eventually I recalled that several years ago, Hugh Darwen had proposed an article on the same general subject for inclusion in one of our earlier "Writings" books [27]; however, I rejected his article because I disagreed at that time with many of the things he had to say. So I searched through my archives and found Hugh's original draft [7]—and discovered to my chagrin that Hugh had raised many of the same issues (though not all), and come to many of the same conclusions (though again not all), as I have in the present chapter. So I guess I owe Hugh a huge apology, and I hope he'll take it in good part.[27]

Anyway, let me summarize what I've proposed in this chapter:

---

[26] Or to a situation in which CASCADE "trumps" NO CASCADE (as it were), as in the earlier example.

[27] Which of course he does. In passing, let me acknowledge Hugh's meticulous review of earlier drafts of this chapter, too.

- A relational database language like **Tutorial D** should allow *<foreign key def>*s of the following form to be specified as part of a base or virtual relvar definition:

  ```
  <foreign key def>
      ::=   FOREIGN KEY { [ ALL BUT ] <attribute ref commalist> }
                REFERENCES <relation exp>
              [ ON DELETE [ NO ] CASCADE ]
              [ ON UPDATE [ NO ] CASCADE ]
  ```

  Note: Suppose the specified *<relation exp>* is used as the view defining expression for some view *V*. Then the specified *<attribute ref commalist>* must constitute a superkey for *V*.

- A relational database language should also allow *<foreign key def>*s on arbitrary *<relation exp>*s (within constraint definitions)—though what should be done about any associated foreign key rules in such a case is still open to discussion.

- A relational database language should support the relational inclusion operator, "⊆". *Note:* Actually I proposed such support in an earlier paper [13], and **Tutorial D** does already support it; I mention it again here simply because of its particular relevance to the topic of this chapter. Specifically, of course, it's required for the formulation of inclusion dependencies (and hence, in effect, for the formulation of integrity constraints of arbitrary complexity).

- A relational database language must also support the relational equality operator, "=". *Note:* In fact, *The Third Manifesto* [28] requires the equality operator to be supported for every type, anyway, and of course **Tutorial D** does so; I mention relational equality in particular here only because of its relevance to the specification of what in the body of the chapter I called equality dependencies.

- I do *not* propose support—in the foreign key context, at any rate—for the *<quantifier>*s EXACTLY ONE OF, AT LEAST ONE OF, and ALL OF, because they're logically unnecessary if the system allows (as I believe it should) foreign key target specifications to be *<relation exp>*s of arbitrary complexity.

———◆◆◆◆◆———

One last point. Recall constraint IND1 from the beginning of this chapter:

```
CONSTRAINT IND1 P { CITY } ⊆ S { CITY } ;
/* every part city must be a supplier city as well */
```

Clearly, this IND isn't a foreign key constraint as conventionally understood. But it can be expressed as one! Since the target of a *<foreign key def>* can be specified as a *<relation exp>* of arbitrary complexity, we can certainly write the following as part of the definition of the parts relvar P:

```
FOREIGN KEY { CITY } REFERENCES S { CITY }
```

Since {CITY} certainly constitutes a superkey (in fact, a key) for the projection of S on {CITY}, this specification is indeed legitimate as a foreign key constraint. And, of course, analogous remarks apply to INDs of arbitrary complexity. Thus, the proposals of this chapter allow not just conventional foreign key constraints, but INDs of arbitrary complexity, to be expressed by means of special case syntax: specifically, FOREIGN KEY syntax.

REFERENCES AND BIBLIOGRAPHY

1. E. F. Codd: "Derivability, Redundancy, and Consistency of Relations Stored in Large Data Banks," IBM Research Report RJ599 (August 19th, 1969).

2. E. F. Codd: "A Relational Model of Data for Large Shared Data Banks," *Communications of the ACM 13,* No. 6 (June 1970).

3. E. F. Codd: "Further Normalization of the Data Base Relational Model," in Randall J. Rustin (ed.), *Data Base Systems: Courant Computer Science Symposia Series 6.* Englewood Cliffs, N.J.: Prentice-Hall (1972).

4. E. F. Codd: "Extending the Database Relational Model to Capture More Meaning," *ACM Transactions on Database Systems 4,* No. 4 (December 1979).

5. E. F. Codd: "Domains, Keys, and Referential Integrity in Relational Databases," *InfoDB 3,* No. 1 (Spring 1988).

6. E. F. Codd: *The Relational Model for Database Management Version 2.* Reading, Mass.: Addison-Wesley (1990).

7. Hugh Darwen: "Some Doubts Concerning Foreign Keys" (private communication, 1991).

8. Hugh Darwen: "The Role of Functional Dependence in Query Decomposition," in reference [27].

9. Hugh Darwen: "The Nullologist in Relationland," in reference [27].

10. C. J. Date: "Referential Integrity," Proc. 7th International Conference on Very Large Data Bases, Cannes, France (September 1981); revised version in *Relational Database: Selected Writings.* Reading, Mass.: Addison-Wesley (1986).

11. C. J. Date: "Referential Integrity and Foreign Keys—Part I: Basic Concepts; Part II: Further Considerations," in *Relational Database Writings 1985-1989.* Reading, Mass.: Addison-Wesley (1990).

12. C. J. Date: "A Note on One to One Relationships," in *Relational Database Writings 1985-1989.* Reading, Mass.: Addison-Wesley (1990).

13. C. J. Date: "Notes Toward a Reconstituted Definition of the Relational Model Version 1 (RM/V1)," in reference [27].

14. C. J. Date: "A Normalization Problem," in *Relational Database Writings 1991-1994.* Reading, Mass.: Addison-Wesley (1995).

15. C. J. Date: "The Primacy of Primary Keys: An Investigation," in *Relational Database Writings 1991-1994.* Reading, Mass.: Addison-Wesley (1995).

16. C. J. Date: "A Network System: IDMS," in *Relational Database Writings 1991-1994.* Reading, Mass.: Addison-Wesley (1995).

17. C. J. Date: "Database Graffiti," in C. J. Date, Hugh Darwen, and David McGoveran, *Relational Database Writings 1994-1997.* Reading, Mass.: Addison-Wesley (1998).

18. C. J. Date: *An Introduction to Database Systems* (8th edition). Boston, Mass.: Addison-Wesley (2004).

19. C. J. Date and Hugh Darwen: "View Updating," in reference [28].

20. C. J. Date: *Database in Depth: Relational Theory for Practitioners.* Sebastopol, Calif.: O'Reilly Media, Inc. (2005). *Note:* This book has since been superseded by the book *SQL and Relational Theory: How to Write Accurate SQL Code.* Sebastopol, Calif.: O'Reilly Media, Inc. (2009).

21. C. J. Date: *The Relational Database Dictionary, Extended Edition.* Berkeley, Calif.: Apress (2008).

22. C. J. Date: "On the Logical Differences Between Types, Values, and Variables," in *Date on Database: Writings 2000-2006.* Berkeley, Calif.: Apress (2006).

23. C. J. Date: "Data Redundancy and Database Design," in *Date on Database: Writings 2000-2006.* Berkeley, Calif.: Apress (2006).

24. C. J. Date: "Data Redundancy and Database Design: Further Thoughts Number One," in *Date on Database: Writings 2000-2006.* Berkeley, Calif.: Apress (2006).

25. C. J. Date: "The Closed World Assumption," in *Logic and Databases: The Roots of Relational Theory.* Victoria, B.C.: Trafford Publishing (2007). See *www.trafford.com/07-0690.*

26. C. J. Date: "The Logic of View Updating," in *Logic and Databases: The Roots of Relational Theory.* Victoria, B.C.: Trafford Publishing (2007). See *www.trafford.com/07-0690.* See also Chapter 10 in the present book.

27. C. J. Date and Hugh Darwen, *Relational Database Writings 1989-1991.* Reading, Mass.: Addison-Wesley (1992).

28. C. J. Date and Hugh Darwen: *Databases, Types, and the Relational Model: The Third Manifesto* (3rd edition). Boston, Mass.: Addison-Wesley (2006).

29. C. J. Date and Hugh Darwen: "A Closer Look at Specialization by Constraint," in reference [28].

30. C. J. Date and Hugh Darwen: "Multiple Assignment," in *Date on Database: Writings 2000-2006.* Berkeley, Calif.: Apress (2006).

31. Ronald Fagin: "A Normal Form for Relational Databases that Is Based on Domains and Keys," *ACM TODS 6,* No. 3 (September 1981).

32. International Organization for Standardization (ISO): *Database Language SQL,* Document ISO/IEC 9075:2008 (2008).

33. David McGoveran: "Nothing from Nothing" (in four parts), in C. J. Date, Hugh Darwen, and David McGoveran, *Relational Database Writings 1994-1997.* Reading, Mass.: Addison-Wesley (1998).

APPENDIX A: A LITTLE HISTORY

The term and the concept *foreign key* are both due to Codd, but the definitions have changed considerably over the years (as can be seen even in Codd's own writings), and so too has the terminology to some extent. By way of historical review, in this appendix I present a series of extracts—most of them edited slightly, but never in such a way as to change the original meaning[28]—from Codd's writings on the subject, with commentary by myself (all of it with the benefit of considerable hindsight, I hasten to add). Of course, it goes without saying that when that commentary is critical of something that Codd wrote, my criticisms are not meant to be ad hominem. However, it would be remiss of me—indeed, it would undermine a large part of the point of this chapter—to overlook shortcomings when they exist, and I won't. (Perhaps I should say again that I too have changed my opinions in this area, somewhat, over time.)

Codd's 1969 Definitions

Here's an extract from Codd's very first (1969) paper on the relational model [1]:

> The set of entities of a given entity type can be viewed as a relation, and we shall call such a relation an *entity type relation* ... Normally, one attribute (or combination of attributes) of a given entity type has values which uniquely identify each entity. Such an attribute (or combination) is called a *key* ... A key is *nonredundant* if it is either a simple attribute (not a combination) or a combination such that none of the participating attributes is superfluous in uniquely identifying each entity ... The remaining relations ... are between entity types, and are, therefore, called *inter-entity*

---

[28] Except that I've deleted all mention of "missing information" and nulls. Codd believed that foreign keys should be allowed to accept nulls; I don't. (I used to, but I changed my mind on the matter many years ago. As indicated in an earlier footnote, in fact, I now reject the whole notion of nulls as usually understood.)

relations. An essential property of every inter-entity relation is that its domains include at least two keys which either refer to distinct entity types or refer to a common entity type serving distinct roles.

Comments: It's clearly possible (as I've said, with hindsight) to criticize this extract on many grounds. For example:

- Although it does at least mention the foreign key concept, tacitly (the final sentence talks about "keys" that "refer to entity types"), it doesn't give a name for that concept. As I've had occasion to remark elsewhere—again, see the discussion of *The Naming Principle* in reference [17]—it's very hard to talk about concepts that have no names.

- The talk of "entities" is unfortunate, in my opinion; it represents an unpleasant and unnecessary mixing of formal and informal concepts. (Relational concepts are formal; "entity"-related concepts aren't.) Indeed, when he revised reference [1] and republished it the following year [2], Codd dropped such talk.

- It's really relvars, not relations, that have keys and sometimes foreign keys.[29] Of course, the term *relvar* wasn't introduced until 1998 (in the first edition of reference [28])—but the concept certainly existed, in the form of "time-varying relations," even in Codd's very first paper (i.e., the paper under discussion). This confusion between relations and relvars is one that I believe could and should have been avoided but, sadly, continues to this day. *Note:* In the remainder of this appendix, I'll keep to the term *relation* when quoting from original sources, but I'll use the term *relvar* everywhere else (when *relvar* is the mot juste, of course).

- The qualifier "Normally" in the second sentence is a little puzzling!—suggesting, as it does, that there might be situations in which no such unique identifier exists. Now, Codd might have injected that qualifier because of the fuzzy context of entities ... but in fact he retains it in reference [2], where he's definitely talking in terms of relations (or relvars, rather), not entities.

- Keys aren't really attributes (or combinations of attributes) but sets: subsets of the pertinent heading, to be precise. Confusion over this simple point has led to a great deal of further confusion over the years. However, I'm glad to see that Codd does at least say that keys consist of attributes, not domains. On the other hand, he doesn't actually define the term *attribute,* and in fact this sentence seems to be the only place in the paper where it's used!—indeed, he later switches, in the very same paper, to saying that keys consist of domains, not attributes. As I'm sure you know, this muddle over attributes vs. domains has also caused a great deal of confusion over the years.

- The talk of "nonredundant" keys implicitly suggests the possibility of *redundant* keys—i.e., "keys" that aren't keys at all, as we now understand the concept, but proper superkeys. What's more, a "key" could contain just one "simple attribute" and still be redundant in the foregoing sense; in particular, any such "key" will certainly be redundant in that sense if the relvar it applies to is constrained never to contain more than one tuple. *Note:* My preferred term for "nonredundant" in the foregoing sense is *irreducible,* and that's the term I used in the body of the chapter. Elsewhere, Codd uses the term *minimal* for this same concept—see, e.g., reference [5]—but I reject that term as not very apt.

- Of course it isn't necessary for a relvar with foreign keys to have at least two such! (It's necessary if the

[29] Key and foreign key specifications represent constraints, and constraints (by definition) constrain variables. However, it does sometimes make sense to say of a given relation *r*—i.e., of a given relation value—that it either does or does not *satisfy* some key or foreign key constraint. And if relation *r* does satisfy some such constraint, we might even say that *r* "has" the key or foreign key in question; but it must be understood that all such talk is fairly loose.

relvar does indeed represent a relationship between two or more other relvars, which is the case that Codd is considering here, but it obviously isn't necessary in all cases. For example, consider what would happen if we removed the parts relvar P and the shipments attribute P# from the suppliers-and-parts database.)

- One good thing about the extract is that it does *not* require a given foreign key to reference a primary key specifically. As should be clear from the body of the chapter, this is a point I do agree with (though I should add that it's another point I've changed my mind on myself, over the years; I used to believe in primary keys rather more than I do now).

- Finally, the extract doesn't say as much explicitly, but it's clear from the context that all of the relations (or relvars) under consideration are supposed to be base relations (or relvars) specifically; i.e., the possibility that other relations (or relvars) might have keys or foreign keys is never addressed. It's also clear that, for any particular foreign key, there's supposed to be exactly one referenced relvar. I'll have more to say on this latter point at the very end of this appendix.

Codd's 1970 Definitions

A revised version of reference [1] was published the following year (1970) in *Communications of the ACM* [2]. (This revised version is usually credited with being the seminal paper in the whole relational field, though that characterization is a little unfair to its 1969 predecessor.) The following extract is the counterpart in that 1970 paper to the text already quoted from its 1969 predecessor:[30]

> Normally, one domain (or combination of domains) of a given relation has values which uniquely identify each element (*n*-tuple) of that relation. Such a domain (or combination) is called a *primary key* ... A primary key is *nonredundant* if it is either a simple domain (not a combination) or a combination such that none of the participating simple domains is superfluous in uniquely identifying each element. A relation may possess more than one nonredundant primary key ... Whenever a relation has two or more nonredundant primary keys, one of them is arbitrarily selected and called *the* primary key of that relation ... We shall call a domain (or domain combination) of relation *R* a *foreign key* if it is not the primary key of *R* but its elements are values of the primary key of some relation *S* (the possibility that *S* and *R* are identical is not excluded).

Comments: Again it's possible to criticize this text, with hindsight, in a variety of ways:[31]

- The talk of "entities" has gone (good) ... but now the qualifier "Normally" suggests that there might be *relations* (or relvars, rather) for which no unique identifier exists (?).

- The talk of "attributes" has been replaced by talk of "domains" (bad).

- "Keys" have become *primary* keys; such keys can be "redundant," but we're supposed to choose, arbitrarily, exactly one nonredundant primary key as *the* primary key for the relvar in question (and for the rest of this appendix I'll use the term *primary key* in this latter, and more demanding, sense, barring explicit statements to the contrary).

- The term *foreign key* is now explicitly introduced. More important, a given foreign key is now required to

---

[30] A definition virtually identical to the final sentence in this extract (except that it talked in terms of attributes instead of domains) was included in the second (1977) edition of my book *An Introduction to Database Systems* [18]. The first (1975) edition, I regret to say, did not mention the term *foreign key* at all—though, like reference [1], it did at least discuss the concept.

[31] Of course, I won't repeat criticisms I've already made in connection with the 1969 paper. More generally, in fact, I won't raise criticisms in this appendix of any of Codd's definitions if I've effectively made those same criticisms in connection with some earlier definition, unless there's some specific point I want to make.

reference a primary key specifically—but I've already stated my opinion on this issue.

- The requirement that a foreign key not be the primary key of its containing relvar is strange, and in fact both undesirable and unnecessary.

One last point on the foregoing extract: To say it one more time, keys and foreign keys aren't really attributes (or combinations of attributes) but sets—subsets of the pertinent heading, to be precise. And it follows that key and foreign key values aren't attribute values, either, but tuples. Codd almost but not quite acknowledges these facts in reference [2]; or, rather, the extract quoted does at least use the term *element* in such a way as to be capable of supporting such an interpretation. First, that extract talks about "elements" of a relation, which it says are *n*-tuples (or just tuples for short). Then it talks about "elements" of foreign keys, which it says are values of the corresponding primary key.[32] So the question is: Is the term *elements* being used here in two different senses, or are those senses really one and the same? Well, let *FK* be a foreign key for a referencing relvar *R2* and let *PK* be the primary key for the corresponding referenced relvar *R1*. Further, let *R2FK* be the projection of *R2* on the attributes of *FK* and let *R1PK* be the projection of *R1* on the attributes of *PK*. Then we might say that "elements" of *FK* are tuples in *R2FK* and "elements" of *PK* are tuples in *R1PK*—in which case we can agree that (a) *FK* is a subset of the heading of *R2,* (b) *PK* is a subset of the heading of *R1,* (c) *FK* and *PK* values are tuples, and (d) the foreign key constraint is logically equivalent to a constraint (actually an IND) that says that *R2FK* is included in *R1PK:*

```
R2 { fk } ⊆ R1 { pk }
```

(where *{fk}* is the attributes of *FK* and *{pk}* is the attributes of *PK*).[33]

Codd's 1979 Definitions

In 1979 Codd published a paper [4] whose primary purpose was to define a set of extensions to the original relational model, to yield what he called the extended model RM/T. Before describing those proposed extensions, however, he first gave a summary of the original model as he saw it at the time, and the following edited extract is taken from that summary:

> With each relation is associated a set of candidate keys. *K* is a *candidate key* of relation *R* if it is a collection of attributes of *R* with the following time-independent properties.
>
> 1. No two rows of *R* have the same *K*-component.
> 2. If any attribute is dropped from *K,* the uniqueness property (1) is lost.
>
> For each base relation one candidate key is selected as the *primary key*. For a given database, those domains upon which the simple (i.e., single attribute) primary keys are defined are called the *primary domains* of that database ... All insertions into, updates of, and deletions from base relations are constrained by the following [rule] ... (Referential integrity): Suppose an attribute *A* of a compound (i.e., multiattribute) primary key of a relation *R* is defined on a primary domain *D*. Then, at all times, for each value *v* of *A* in *R* there must exist a base relation (say *S*) with a simple primary key (say *B*) such that *v* occurs as a value of *B* in *S*.

Comments:

- The talk of "domains" has been replaced by talk of "attributes" (good).

---

[32] For simplicity, I assume throughout this paragraph (as indeed Codd does also in reference [2], despite definitions in his own later writings) that a given referencing relvar has precisely one corresponding referenced relvar. Under this assumption, it's legitimate to talk about "the" corresponding primary key.

[33] Of course, the formalism used in the body of the chapter would require those two sets of attributes to be identical.

- The talk of "tuples" has been replaced by talk of "rows." Personally, I don't feel this is an improvement, for reasons discussed in reference [20].
- Relvars are now required to have at least one candidate key, instead of at least one primary key; the term *primary key* is now reserved for that particular candidate key that has been chosen, somehow, as being "more equal than the others." Distinguishing between candidate keys in general and primary keys in particular is clearly an improvement (at least in clarity, if not in substance). *Note:* The term *candidate key* was originally introduced in reference [3].
- Keys of all kinds are now explicitly required to be irreducible.
- The term *foreign key* has disappeared!—though the concept survives, of course, at least implicitly, as part of the referential integrity rule. (Incidentally, I believe the paper under discussion was the first of Codd's writings to mention this latter term.)
- The referential integrity rule should, but in fact does not, require attribute *B* to be defined on domain *D*.
- Note, however, that the referential integrity rule explicitly requires foreign keys to be components of composite primary keys. No justification for this unnecessary and undesirable restriction is given.
- Note too that the referential integrity rule also requires foreign keys to consist of exactly one attribute—no more, no less. No justification for this unnecessary and undesirable restriction is given.
- The concept of *primary domain* is new, as well as being both unnecessary and undesirable. Even if we accept the concept, in fact, it's easy to see—see. e.g., reference [11]—that attributes defined on such domains aren't necessarily foreign keys, and foreign keys aren't necessarily defined on such domains.
- Note finally that the referential integrity rule no longer requires a given foreign key to have just one corresponding referenced relvar. Again, I'll comment on this issue at the very end of this appendix.

Codd's 1988 Definitions

In 1988 Codd published a paper [5] that he intended, I believe, to serve as a definitive statement on foreign keys and related matters. The following edited extract is taken from that paper:

> A *foreign key* is a single column or combination of columns of a relation *S*, whose domain *D* is that of a primary key in the database, and each of whose ... values is required at all times ... to equal the value of some primary key (with domain *D*) of at least one relation *R*, where relations *R* and *S* are not *required* to be distinct (but are *permitted* to be distinct, and this is the usual case) ... A foreign key may have *N* corresponding primary keys (where *N* is any integer greater than or equal to 1, and $N = 1$ is the usual case). When $N > 1$, ... any selected foreign key value *may happen to equal* any number of values of the corresponding *N* primary keys, but is *required to equal* at least one of them ... A foreign key within relation *R* is not necessarily a component of the primary key of relation *R*.

Comments:

- The talk of "attributes" has been replaced by talk of "columns." Personally, I don't feel this is an improvement, for reasons discussed in reference [20].
- The wording is not always as accurate as it might be. For example: "Each [foreign key value] is required ... to equal the value of some primary key." Surely, "the value of some primary key" here should be "some value of the primary key"?
- At least it's good to see that foreign keys now (a) are allowed to be composite and (b) don't have to be components of the pertinent primary key.

- But overall the most interesting thing about this extract is the emphasis it lays on the possibility that *N*—i.e., the number of primary keys corresponding to a given foreign key—might be greater than one. More specifically, the wording "*may happen to equal* any number of values of the corresponding *N* primary keys, but is *required to equal* at least one of them" shows clearly that Codd is talking about the case that I referred to in the body of the chapter as AT LEAST ONE OF, which is, of the three cases I discussed, the one that seems to be hardest to justify intuitively! Once again, see my further remarks on this topic at the end of the appendix.

Codd's 1990 Definitions

In 1990 Codd published his book [6] on what he called the Relational Model Version 2 (RM/V2). Here's what that book has to say regarding foreign keys:

> The value of the primary key in each row of the pertinent R-table identifies the particular object represented by that row uniquely within the type of objects that are represented by that relation. Everywhere else in the database that there is a need to refer to that particular object, the *same* identifying value drawn from the *same* domain is used. Any column containing those values is called a *foreign key* ... *Referential integrity* is defined as follows: Let *D* be a domain from which one or more primary keys draw their values. Let *K* be a foreign key, which draws its values from domain *D*. Every ... value which occurs in *K* must also exist in the database as the value of the primary key on domain *D* of some base relation.

Comments:

- "R-table" is a new term. However, it means, precisely, a relation or relvar (depending on context) in the relational model sense; the "R-" prefix is intended to stress the point that certain properties commonly associated with tables in general (e.g., top to bottom row ordering, left to right column ordering) do *not* apply to R-tables.

- "Everywhere ... there is a need to refer to that particular object, the *same* identifying value drawn from the *same* domain is used." I find this requirement too strong; it might often be good practice, but I can certainly imagine situations where the very same "object" is referenced by, say, employee number in some situations and social security number in others.

- "Any column containing those values is called a *foreign key*": What about foreign keys involving two or more "columns"?

- I continue to reject the notion of primary domains (which survive in concept in the extract quoted, even though the term doesn't).

Finally, Codd says that every foreign key value "must also exist in the database as the value of the primary key ... of *some* base relation" (my italics). Again, therefore, Codd is at least allowing, and in fact tacitly requiring, support for the idea that a given foreign key might have two or more corresponding target relvars. As I've said several times, I don't fully support this idea. In part, I don't support it because if the system allows (as I believe it should) foreign key targets to be defined by means of <*relation exp*>s of arbitrary complexity, then support for more than one target relvar as such is logically redundant. More specifically, even if I were persuaded to support the EXACTLY ONE OF and ALL OF cases, I don't think I would support the AT LEAST ONE OF case (which as noted earlier in this appendix seems to be just the case that Codd requires), because I don't think it's useful. And it's interesting to note in this connection that Codd himself explicitly insists on there always being just one target relvar (a base relvar at that) in his extended model RM/T [4]—implying, incidentally, that a conventional relational database not designed in accordance with the single target relvar discipline might be difficult to upgrade to conform to that extended model.

APPENDIX B: FOREIGN KEYS vs. POINTERS

Critics of the relational model have been known to suggest that foreign keys are nothing more than pointers in disguise (pointers, of course, being prohibited in the relational model). The following list of differences between the two concepts shows why that suggestion is incorrect.

- Pointers in general require special referencing and dereferencing operators [22]; foreign keys don't.
- In the database context in particular, pointers typically require their own special retrieval and update operators—e.g., FIND FIRST, FIND NEXT, FIND OWNER, FIND CURRENT, CONNECT, DISCONNECT, and RECONNECT (these examples are taken from CODASYL [16]). Foreign keys don't.
- Pointers *point:* They have directionality, and they have a single, specific target. Foreign key values, by contrast, are regular data values, and they're thus, like all data values in a relational database, what might be called "multiway associative." For example, the part number P4, acting as a foreign key value, is simultaneously linked—speaking purely logically—not just to the pertinent part tuple but to all shipment tuples, and indeed all tuples anywhere (in the database or otherwise), that happen to include that same data value.
- Pointers are addresses; foreign keys aren't. Since variables have addresses and values don't (again, see reference [22]), it follows that pointers, by definition, point to variables, not values. By contrast, foreign keys "point to" tuples, which are values, not variables (excuse my sloppy phrasing here). *Note:* I don't mean to suggest that a given foreign key value "points to" the same tuple all the time; obviously, it can, and typically does, "point to" different tuples at different times.
- Foreign keys have a real world interpretation—i.e., they can be understood "outside the system"—while pointers certainly don't and can't. For example, consider the difference between the foreign key value P#('P4'), which does have meaning outside the system, vs. the address of the storage location containing the stored representation of that part, which doesn't.
- Foreign keys can be composite; pointers can't.
- As we've seen, foreign key constraints are a special case of inclusion dependencies—and even if it's argued that a foreign key is "something like" a pointer, INDs in general certainly aren't.
- Reference [29] shows that pointers—at least if "typed"—and a good model of type inheritance are logically incompatible; it also shows that the same criticism doesn't apply to foreign keys.
- Pointers are subject to the phenomenon known as "dangling references"; foreign keys aren't.
- Foreign keys are logical; pointers are physical. More precisely: Foreign keys are defined at the relational (logical) level, pointers are defined at the storage (physical) level. The idea that "foreign keys are just pointers" thus stems from a basic confusion over levels of abstraction; foreign keys are a higher level concept than pointers. *Note:* It's true that pointers might be used to implement foreign keys, but in practice they almost never are, at least in today's mainstream SQL products. In any case, they're certainly not the only possible implementation.
- Following on from the previous point, pointers almost certainly have physical performance connotations;

foreign keys don't.[34]

- Pointers might have to change their value if the object they refer to moves to another location. No such criticism applies to foreign keys (in fact, of course, the relational model deliberately includes no notion of "location" in this sense, anyway).
- Pointers tend to be implementation dependent: Their properties and behavior depend to some extent on the underlying hardware and/or operating system and/or DBMS. In particular, they're likely to be machine local; for example, in a distributed system, a pointer probably won't be able to point from one machine to another. Foreign keys aren't implementation dependent in any such sense at all.
- Adding new foreign keys and adding new pointers to an existing database are very different operations—the first might be quite trivial, while the second might require a physical reorganization. Similar remarks apply to dropping foreign keys vs. dropping pointers.

---

[34] Even if they involve some levels of indirection (which they might), they'll still have such connotations—because if they don't, there's no reason to have them! *Note:* Here's as good a place as any to observe that I do regard *object IDs,* unlike foreign keys, as "pointers in disguise" (at least to a first approximation), and so my implicit criticisms in this appendix of pointers in general apply to object IDs in particular.

Chapter 14

Image Relations

What do you mean by "relational image"?
Do you mean "her-age," or do you mean "him-age"?
I hope you don't mean just some general scrimmage.

—Anon.: *Where Bugs Go*

I propose a new relational operator called *imaging* and an associated construct called an *image relation*. Like many other relational operators (including most of those commonly encountered in practice), the imaging operator is, in the final analysis, just shorthand for a certain combination of previously defined operators; like those other shorthands, however, it has the effect of simplifying the formulation of certain expressions and (perhaps more important) thereby raising the level of abstraction somewhat.

By way of a motivating example, consider the usual suppliers-and-parts database, with definition as follows:[1]

```
VAR S BASE RELATION   /* supplier is under contract */
  { S# S# , SNAME NAME , STATUS INTEGER , CITY CHAR }
    KEY { S# } ;

VAR P BASE RELATION   /* part is of interest */
  { P# P# , PNAME NAME , COLOR COLOR , WEIGHT WEIGHT , CITY CHAR }
    KEY { P# } ;

VAR SP BASE RELATION  /* supplier supplies (or ships) part */
  { S# S# , P# P# , QTY INTEGER }
    KEY { S# , P# }
    FOREIGN KEY { S# } REFERENCES S
    FOREIGN KEY { P# } REFERENCES P ;
```

The comments in italics show the intended interpretations of relvars S, P, and SP as suppliers, parts, and shipments, respectively. Sample values are shown in Fig. 1 overleaf. *Note:* The relvar definitions are expressed in a language called **Tutorial D** (more precisely, a dialect of **Tutorial D** that includes explicit foreign key support), which is the language used in reference [12] to illustrate the ideas of *The Third Manifesto*. The language is mostly self-explanatory, but it does assume for convenience that projection has the highest precedence of all of the conventional relational operators. (Projection is expressed in **Tutorial D** by means of braces; e.g., the expression *r*{*X*} denotes the projection of relation *r* on the set of attributes {*X*}. Also, the expression *r*{ALL BUT *X*} denotes the projection of relation *r* on all of its attributes other than {*X*}; in other words, *r*{ALL BUT *X*} is equivalent to *r*{*Y*}, where {*X*} and {*Y*} are disjoint and their set theory union is equal to the heading of *r*.)

[1] The definition differs from the one I usually use in that attribute QTY is defined to be of type INTEGER instead of type QTY. I make this change purely in order to simplify some of the examples later in the chapter.

S

S#	SNAME	STATUS	CITY
S1	Smith	20	London
S2	Jones	10	Paris
S3	Blake	30	Paris
S4	Clark	20	London
S5	Adams	30	Athens

P

P#	PNAME	COLOR	WEIGHT	CITY
P1	Nut	Red	12.0	London
P2	Bolt	Green	17.0	Paris
P3	Screw	Blue	17.0	Oslo
P4	Screw	Red	14.0	London
P5	Cam	Blue	12.0	Paris
P6	Cog	Red	19.0	London

SP

S#	P#	QTY
S1	P1	300
S1	P2	200
S1	P3	400
S1	P4	200
S1	P5	100
S1	P6	100
S2	P1	300
S2	P2	400
S3	P2	200
S4	P2	200
S4	P4	300
S4	P5	400

Fig. 1: The suppliers-and-parts database—sample values

Now consider the query "Get supplier details for suppliers who supply all parts." Here's one possible formulation of that query, using NOT MATCHING (in case you're not familiar with it, the NOT MATCHING operator is defined in the next section):

```
S NOT MATCHING ( ( S JOIN P { P# } ) NOT MATCHING SP )
```

Though accurate, this formulation is a little hard to understand, relying as it does on what is in effect a double negation. Perhaps I should note before going any further that double negation is also involved in the most straightforward SQL version of the query:[2]

```
SELECT S.S# , S.SNAME , S.STATUS , S.CITY
FROM   S
WHERE  NOT EXISTS
     ( SELECT P.*
       FROM   P
       WHERE  NOT EXISTS
            ( SELECT SP.*
              FROM   SP
              WHERE  S.S# = SP.S#
              AND    SP.P# = P.P# ) )
```

Here by contrast is a slightly more succinct **Tutorial D** formulation that does at least avoid that explicit

---

[2] Throughout this chapter, all references to "SQL" should be understood to mean the standard dialect of that language [14]—with the tiny exception that I frequently use the character "#" in what the standard calls "regular identifiers," a state of affairs the standard doesn't actually permit.

double negation:[3]

```
S DIVIDEBY P { P# } PER SP { S# , P# }
```

This latter formulation makes use of a relational operator called the Small Divide (more precisely, it uses the original version of that operator; a generalized version can be defined, but there's no need to bring that complication into the present discussion). As reference [10] demonstrates, however, all of the so called "relational divide" operators—the original Small Divide is just one of several such—suffer from a number of problems and are probably best avoided. Under the proposals of the present chapter, the query could be expressed more simply thus:

```
S WHERE ( !!SP ) { P# } = P { P# }
```

Explanation: For a given supplier, *s* say, the expression (!!SP){P#} denotes the set of part numbers from SP for parts supplied by *s*. The expression overall thus denotes those suppliers for whom that corresponding set of part numbers is equal to the set of all part numbers from P (denoted by the expression P{P#})—in other words, suppliers who supply all parts, loosely speaking. The expression !!SP is an invocation of the imaging operator; in other words, it's an *image relation reference*. *Note:* In mathematics, the expression "*n*!" (*n* factorial) is often pronounced "*n* bang." Following this precedent, I propose that the symbol "!!" be pronounced "bang bang" or "double bang."

There's one other preliminary I need to get out of the way before I can proceed: a small matter of precision in the use of notation and terminology. The foregoing example involved a couple of projection operations. Now, I said earlier that the **Tutorial D** expression *r*{*X*} denoted the projection of relation *r* on the set of attributes {*X*}. But according to **Tutorial D** syntax rules, the symbol {*X*} in this expression is supposed to denote, not a set of attributes as such, but rather a set of attribute *names*. I apologize for this slight sloppiness on my part; more to the point, I hope it won't confuse you, because I intend to indulge in the same kind of sloppiness (i.e., using symbols such as {*X*} to mean sometimes a set of attribute names and sometimes a set of attributes per se) throughout the remainder of this chapter.

DEFINITIONS

In mathematics, an *equivalence class* is a subset *T* of some given set *S* such that the elements of *T* are (a) all equivalent to one another (under some stated definition of equivalence) and (b) not equivalent to any other element of *S* (under that same definition of equivalence). Here are a couple of examples:

- Let *H* be the set of "headwords" in entries in some natural language dictionary. Define two such headwords to be equivalent if and only if they begin with same letter. Then the set of all headwords in *H* beginning with the letter *a* is an equivalence class under this definition of equivalence; so too is the set of all headwords in *H* beginning with the letter *b*, and the set of all headwords in *H* beginning with the letter *c*, and so on.

- Let *B* be the body of the relation that's the current value of relvar SP. Define two tuples of *B* to be equivalent if and only if they contain the same S# value. Then the set of all tuples in *B* for supplier number S1 is an equivalence class under this definition of equivalence; so too is the set of all tuples in *B* for supplier S2, and the set of all tuples in *B* for supplier S3, and so on.

---

[3] In case you might be thinking double negation surely isn't all that bad, I invite you to construe the following (from *The Turn of The Screw*, by Henry James): "This was not so good a thing, I admit, as not to leave me to judge that what, essentially, made nothing else much signify was simply my charming work."

As these examples demonstrate, given the set *S* and an appropriate definition of equivalence:

- The corresponding equivalence classes *T* are pairwise disjoint.
- Together, they partition the set *S*.

A note on terminology: Mathematicians typically use the term *partition* (of a given set *S*) to mean the corresponding set of disjoint subsets *T* of *S* considered collectively. My preference is to refer to that set of subsets as a *partitioning,* and to use the term *partition* to mean an individual subset (or equivalence class) from that partitioning. And when the partitioning is applied to a relation (*r,* say), then I use the term *partition* with an even more specific meaning—I use it to mean, specifically, a relation: namely, a relation whose heading is identical to that of *r* and whose body is some subset of that of *r*. (A partition of relation *r* is thus in fact a certain *restriction* of relation *r*.)

The relevance of the foregoing concepts to various relational operations, such as grouping and summarization, should be obvious. Indeed, we already have operators whose effect can best be explained in terms of partitioning a relation, including in particular the GROUP and SUMMARIZE operators of **Tutorial D** and the GROUP BY operator of SQL. However, these operators all produce a result that effectively consists of, or is derived from, the set of *all* of the pertinent partitions. By contrast, it occurred to me that there are situations in which we need to treat those partitions one at a time, as it were. We've already seen one example of such a situation: In the query in the previous section, we effectively needed to treat (in the WHERE clause, for each individual supplier in turn) just those shipments that corresponded to the supplier currently under consideration. And it turns out that such situations are ubiquitous; that is, the need to be able to refer to just one partition (out of the set of all such) crops up in relational expressions in general—in queries in particular—in all kinds of contexts.

My idea, then, was to come up with a shorthand notation that could be used to represent, succinctly, that partition of some relation *ry* that corresponded in some specific manner to some specific tuple of some relation *rx*.[4] Now, since it would certainly denote a relation, any such shorthand would constitute a new kind of relational expression, by definition. However, such a shorthand could clearly appear, not in all possible contexts in which relational expressions in general can appear, but only in certain specific contexts: namely, those in which the pertinent tuple of relation *rx* is well defined.

> *Aside:* Any such shorthand might thus be criticized on the grounds that it violates orthogonality. But there are precedents for such a state of affairs. For example, what **Tutorial D** calls a <*summary*>—an example is the expression SUM(QTY)—can appear only in the context of a SUMMARIZE invocation: It can't appear in any other context, and in fact it wouldn't have any meaning in any other context. *End of aside.*

The notation I decided on was as follows. Let *rx* and *ry* be relational expressions, and let the relations denoted by those expressions be joinable—by which I mean the set theory union of their headings is a valid relational heading: equivalently, attributes with the same name are of the same type ("common attributes"). Let those common attributes be *A1, A2, ..., An* ($n \geqslant 0$). Then the expression !!*ry*—in those contexts in which it's allowed to appear, which are of course always ones in which the pertinent tuple of the relation denoted by *rx* is well defined as required (see later)—is defined to be shorthand for the following expression:

```
( ( ry ) MATCHING
         RELATION { TUPLE { A1 A1 , A2 A2 , ... , An An } } )
                                 { ALL BUT A1 , A2 , ... , An }
```

[4] As will soon be clear, what I'm actually going to propose is, more precisely and more usefully, a notation for representing a certain *projection* of such a partition: namely, the projection that removes attributes that are common to *rx* and *ry*.

Explanation: As you can see, this expansion makes use of the MATCHING operator, so let me digress for a moment to give a definition for that operator:

- **Definition (MATCHING, also known as semijoin):** Let relations *r1* and *r2* be joinable. Then the semijoin *r1* MATCHING *r2* of *r1* with *r2* (in that order) is equivalent to, and thus shorthand for, the join of *r1* and *r2,* projected back on to the attributes of *r1*.

For example, the expression S MATCHING SP denotes suppliers who supply at least one part. Given the sample values in Fig. 1, the result is:

```
/* suppliers who supply at least one part */
```

S#	SNAME	STATUS	CITY
S1	Smith	20	London
S2	Jones	10	Paris
S3	Blake	30	Paris
S4	Clark	20	London

And here's a definition for NOT MATCHING:

- **Definition (NOT MATCHING, also known as semidifference):** The semidifference *r1* NOT MATCHING *r2* between relations *r1* and *r2* (in that order) is equivalent to, and thus shorthand for, the following expression:

```
r1 MINUS ( r1 MATCHING r2 )
```

For example, the expression S NOT MATCHING SP denotes suppliers who supply no parts at all. Given the sample values in Fig. 1, the result is:

```
/* suppliers who supply no parts at all */
```

S#	SNAME	STATUS	CITY
S5	Adams	30	Athens

Now to get back to !!*ry* per se: Let the context in which that expression appears be such that the pertinent tuple of relation *rx* is *tx*. Then the (sub)expression

```
TUPLE { A1 A1 , A2 A2 , ... , An An }
```

—which is an example of what reference [12] calls a *tuple selector invocation*—denotes a tuple whose *A1* value is equal to the *A1* value from *tx,* whose *A2* value is equal to the *A2* value from *tx,* ..., and whose *An* value is equal to the *An* value from *tx*. (In that tuple selector invocation, and in the context under consideration, the pair *Ai Ai* (*i* = 1, 2, ..., *n*) is interpreted as follows: The first *Ai* is an attribute name; the second denotes the value of the attribute of that name in tuple *tx*.) In other words, the expression TUPLE {...} denotes the projection of tuple *tx* over attributes {*A1,A2,...,An*}. *Note:* I'm following reference [12] here in taking projection to be an operator that can be applied to individual tuples as well as to relations.

Next, the expression

```
RELATION { TUPLE { A1 A1 , A2 A2 , ... , An An } }
```

—which is an example of what reference [12] calls a *relation selector invocation*—denotes a relation whose heading is {*A1,A2,...,An*} and whose body contains just one tuple: namely, the projection of tuple *tx* over {*A1,A2,...,An*}. Hence, the expression

```
( ry ) MATCHING RELATION { TUPLE { A1 A1 , A2 A2 , ... , An An } }
```

denotes a restriction (or partition) of *ry:* namely, that restriction or partition whose body contains all and only those tuples *ty* of *ry* that have the same values for attributes *A1, A2, ..., An* as tuple *tx* does (equivalently, it's that restriction or partition whose body contains all and only those tuples *ty* of *ry* whose projection over {*A1,A2,...,An*} is the same as that of tuple *tx* over those same attributes).

Finally, the expression overall—i.e., the complete expansion of the image relation reference !!*ry*—denotes a projection of the foregoing partition of *ry:* namely, the projection of that partition over all attributes except {*A1,A2,...,An*}. Note that, by definition, the specified partition of *ry* is such that every tuple has the same value for {*A1,A2,...,An*}, and further that that value is known, in the sense that it's precisely the {*A1,A2,...,An*} value from tuple *tx*. Projecting those attributes away in the final result thus (a) doesn't lose any information and (b) doesn't affect the cardinality of that final result.

One last point: Suppose relations *rx* and *ry* are not just joinable but in fact are of the same type (meaning they have exactly the same set of attributes each). Let *tx* be a tuple in *rx*. For that tuple *tx,* then, !!*ry* evaluates to either TABLE_DEE or TABLE_DUM:[5] TABLE_DEE if *tx* also appears in *ry,* and TABLE_DUM otherwise. In particular, if *rx* and *ry* are not just of the same type but in fact are the very same relation, then !!*ry* evaluates to TABLE_DEE for every tuple in that relation.

TERMINOLOGY AND NOTATION

Consider once again the example from the opening section:

```
S WHERE ( !!SP ) { P# } = P { P# }
```

With reference to the definitions in the previous section, the roles of *rx* and *ry* are being played here by the relations that are the current values of relvars S and SP, respectively. Let *s* be the relation that's the current value of relvar S; let *t* be some tuple in *s;* and let *s#* be the S# value in *t*. For that tuple *t,* then, the expression !!SP can be thought of as being equivalent to the following:

```
( SP WHERE S# = s# ) { ALL BUT S# }
```

Since SP has heading {S#,P#,QTY}, this expression in turn is equivalent to the following:

```
( SP WHERE S# = s# ) { P# , QTY }
```

Now let *sp* be the relation that's the current value of relvar SP. Then *sp* can be regarded as a function (in the mathematical sense of that term) that maps S# values such as *s#* to relations *pq,* where each such relation *pq* has heading {P#,QTY} and body a set of tuples of the form <*p#,qty*>. (Please note that I'll be using this shorthand notation for tuples—which I hope and assume is self-explanatory—at several points in this chapter, in the interest of simplicity.) In terms of the sample values in Fig. 1, for example, that function maps the supplier number S2 to a relation containing just the tuples <P1,300> and <P2,400>. Using the normal terminology associated with functions, therefore, we can say that the relation containing just the tuples <P1,300> and <P2,400> is the *image* of supplier number S2 under that function (see Fig. 2 opposite). Hence the term *image relation,* and the term *imaging* for the corresponding operator.

---

[5] TABLE_DEE is the unique relation with no attributes and just one tuple (the empty tuple, of course); TABLE_DUM is the unique relation with no attributes and no tuples at all. See reference [6] for further discussion.

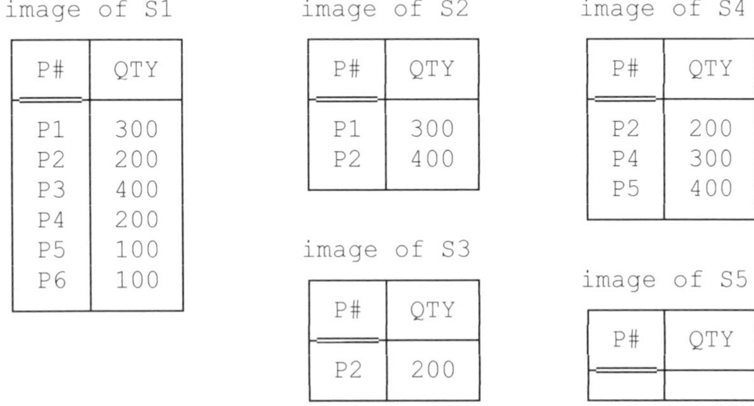
image of S1

P#	QTY
P1	300
P2	200
P3	400
P4	200
P5	100
P6	100

image of S2

P#	QTY
P1	300
P2	400

image of S3

P#	QTY
P2	200

image of S4

P#	QTY
P2	200
P4	300
P5	400

image of S5

P#	QTY

Fig. 2: Images in SP of the five supplier numbers in S from Fig. 1

So much for terminology; I turn now to notation, and in particular to my choice of the symbol "!!" to denote the imaging operator. The choice was arbitrary, of course, and naturally I'm open to alternative suggestions. In fact, however, I rather like the symbol "!!", for the following reasons among others:

1. It happens to be a single character in the character set most readily available to me.

2. It's not currently used for anything else in **Tutorial D** (nor in any other language I'm aware of, either).

3. I actually prefer the use of a special symbol like "!!" instead of a more conventional keyword, because it tends to reinforce the idea that the imaging operator is slightly special (*unconventional* might be a better word). In fact, I even toyed for a while with the idea of calling the imaging operator a pseudo operator; I dropped the idea because the term *pseudo* does tend to have certain negative connotations.

4. I also like the fact that the expressions *r* and !!*r* have very similar, yet strikingly distinct, syntax. See Example 14 later in this chapter.

Note: One correspondent suggested using the keyword MATCH in place of the symbol. Well, it's certainly true that imaging is closely related to the semijoin operator MATCHING (indeed, it's defined in terms of it, as we've seen). However, I don't much care for the suggestion because, e.g., S MATCHING SP denotes a restriction of S, whereas MATCH(SP), if it were supported, would have to denote a restriction of SP (or a projection of a restriction of SP, rather); in other words, the two kinds of matching would go in opposite directions, as it were. What's more, S MATCHING SP refers to tuples of S that match *at least one* tuple of SP (loosely speaking), whereas MATCH(SP), if it were supported, would have to refer to tuples of SP that match *precisely one* tuple of S—namely, the tuple of S currently under consideration.

One further point: Again, consider the example

```
S WHERE ( !!SP ) { P# } = P { P# }
```

In practice, we might want to define "!!" to have higher precedence than projection, so that we could drop the parentheses in this example, thus:

```
S WHERE !!SP { P# } = P { P# }
```

In other words, the expression !!SP{P#} would be interpreted as (!!SP){P#} and not as !!(SP{P#}). In what follows, however, I won't make any such assumptions regarding precedence; instead, I'll use parentheses (as in the example), as needed, for clarity.

IMAGE RELATIONS AND WHERE CLAUSES

Much of the rest of this chapter consists of a series of detailed examples illustrating the utility of the proposed shorthand. First of all, as the example from the opening section suggests, one obvious context in which image relations make sense is WHERE clauses. In **Tutorial D,** a WHERE clause can appear in a *<where>* (which is a special kind of *<relation exp>*), in a *<relation delete>*, and in a *<relation update>*. This section gives examples of all of these cases. I'll number the examples for purposes of subsequent reference.

Example 1: Get suppliers for whom the total shipment quantity, taken over all shipments for the supplier in question, is less than 1000.

```
S WHERE SUM ( !!SP , QTY ) < 1000
```

For any given supplier, the expression SUM(...) here denotes, precisely, the total shipment quantity for the supplier in question. An equivalent formulation without the image relation is:

```
S WHERE
  SUM ( SP MATCHING RELATION { TUPLE { S# S# } } , QTY ) < 1000
```

Another is:

```
WITH ( Temp := SP RENAME { S# AS X } ) :
   S WHERE SUM ( Temp WHERE X = S# , QTY ) < 1000
```

Here for interest is an SQL "analog"—"analog" in quotes because actually there's a trap in this example; the SQL expression shown is not quite equivalent to the **Tutorial D** expressions shown previously (why not?):[6]

```
SELECT S.S# , S.SNAME , S.STATUS , S.CITY
FROM   S , SP
WHERE  S.S# = SP.S#
GROUP  BY S.S# , S.SNAME , S.STATUS , S.CITY
HAVING SUM ( SP.QTY ) < 1000
```

Example 2: Get suppliers with fewer than three shipments.

```
S WHERE COUNT ( !!SP ) < 3
```

SQL analog (or is there a trap here too?):

```
SELECT S.S# , S.SNAME , S.STATUS , S.CITY
FROM   S
WHERE  ( SELECT COUNT (*)
         FROM   SP
         WHERE  SP.S# = S.S# ) < 3
```

Example 3: Get suppliers for whom the minimum shipment quantity is less than half the maximum shipment quantity (taken over all shipments for the supplier in question in both cases).

```
S WHERE MIN ( !!SP , QTY ) < 0.5 * MAX ( !!SP , QTY )
```

SQL analog (or is it?):

---

[6] Correct SQL analogs, where they exist, of numbered examples are given in Appendix B.

```
SELECT S.S# , S.SNAME , S.STATUS , S.CITY
FROM   S
WHERE  ( SELECT MIN ( SP.QTY )
         FROM   SP
         WHERE  SP.S# = S.S# ) <
 0.5 * ( SELECT MAX ( SP.QTY )
         FROM   SP
         WHERE  SP.S# = S.S# )
```

In the remaining examples, I won't bother to show SQL formulations or alternative **Tutorial D** formulations unless there's some specific point I want to make.

Example 4: Get suppliers who supply all parts (same as opening example).

```
S WHERE ( ‼SP ) { P# } = P { P# }
```

I repeat this example because (as previously noted) it can alternatively be expressed in terms of DIVIDEBY:

```
S DIVIDEBY P { P# } PER SP { S# , P# }
```

DIVIDEBY here denotes what I previously referred to as "the original version of the Small Divide." Here's a definition of that operator, taken from reference [10]:

- **Definition (Small Divide, original version):** Let relations *r1, r2,* and *r3* be such that (a) the headings of *r1* and *r2* are {*X*} and {*Y*}, respectively; (b) the sets {*X*} and {*Y*} have no attribute names in common; and (c) the heading of *r3* is the set theory union of {*X*} and {*Y*} (see the following diagram).

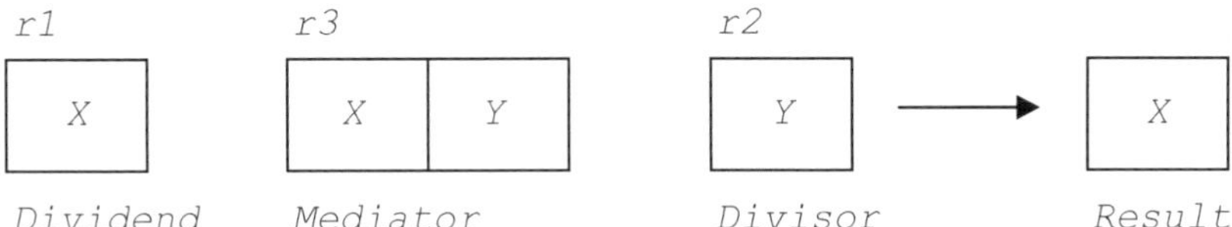

Then the division *r1* DIVIDEBY *r2* PER (*r3*)—where *r1* is the dividend, *r2* is the divisor, and *r3* is the mediator—is equivalent to, and thus shorthand for, the following expression:

```
r1 NOT MATCHING ( ( r1 JOIN r2 ) NOT MATCHING r3 )
```

The point I want to make now is that we could actually, and potentially much more clearly, define this operator in terms of image relations, thus: The division *r1* DIVIDEBY *r2* PER (*r3*) is equivalent to, and thus shorthand for, the following expression:

```
r1 WHERE r2 ⊆ ‼r3
```

Analogous remarks apply to all of the other forms of divide discussed in reference [10]. *Note:* The symbol "⊆" here denotes relation inclusion; the expression *ra* ⊆ *rb* returns TRUE if and only if every tuple appearing in relation *ra* also appears in relation *rb*. Relations *ra* and *rb* must be of the same type. *Exercise for the reader:* Applying the foregoing definition to Example 4, we obtain the following formulation of the query:

```
S WHERE P { P# } ⊆ ( ‼SP ) { P# }
```

How do you account for the discrepancies between this formulation and the one I showed immediately following the original (natural language) statement of the query?

Example 5: Suppose we're given a revised version of the suppliers-and-parts database (one that's simultaneously both extended and simplified, compared to the original version) that looks like this:

```
S    { S# }
SP   { S# , P# }
PJ   { P# , J# }
J    { J# }
```

Relvar J here represents *projects* (J# stands for project number), and relvar PJ indicates which parts are used in which projects. Now consider the query "Get all <*s#,j#*> pairs such that *s#* is an S# value currently appearing in relvar S, *j#* is a J# value currently appearing in relvar J, and supplier *s#* supplies all parts used in project *j#*." This query is one that's often used to illustrate more complicated forms of divide (see, e.g., reference [10]). But a formulation using image relations is almost trivial:

```
( S JOIN J ) WHERE ‼PJ ⊆ ‼SP
```

Exercise for the reader: How would you formulate this query in SQL?

Example 6: With the same database as in Example 5, consider the expression:

```
( S JOIN J ) WHERE ‼SP ⊆ ‼PJ
```

This expression represents the query "Get all <*s#,j#*> pairs such that *s#* is an S# value currently appearing in relvar S, *j#* is a J# value currently appearing in relvar J, and project *j#* uses all parts supplied by supplier *s#*." Note the logical difference between this query and the query discussed under Example 5. *Exercise for the reader:* How would you formulate *this* query in SQL? How easy is it to produce such a formulation from your answer to the exercise under Example 5?

Example 7: Reverting to the original suppliers-and-parts database, find shipments such that at least two other shipments involve the same quantity.

```
SP WHERE COUNT ( ‼(SP RENAME { S# AS SX , P# AS PX }) ) > 2
```

This example is very contrived, of course, but the point is to illustrate the occasional need for some attribute renaming in connection with image relation references. (The renaming is needed in the example in order to ensure that the image relation we want, in connection with a given shipment tuple, is defined in terms of attribute QTY only. The introduced names SX and PX are arbitrary.)

Example 8: Delete shipments by suppliers in London.

```
DELETE SP WHERE IS_NOT_EMPTY ( ‼(S WHERE CITY = 'London') ) ;
```

For a given shipment, the specified image relation ‼(S WHERE ...) either is empty, if the corresponding supplier isn't in London, or contains exactly one tuple otherwise. (This example is the first we've seen in which the argument to the imaging operator invocation is not just a simple relvar reference but is, rather, a more general relational expression.) SQL analog:

```
DELETE
FROM   SP
WHERE  SP.S# IN ( SELECT S.S#
                  FROM   S
                  WHERE  S.CITY = 'London' ) ;
```

Example 9: Delete suppliers for whom the total shipment quantity, taken over all shipments for the supplier in question, is less than 1000.

```
DELETE S WHERE SUM ( ‼SP , QTY ) < 1000 ;
```

Note: Given that there's a foreign key constraint from SP to S, the foregoing DELETE is almost certain to fail on a referential integrity violation (unless ... what, exactly?). The following *multiple* DELETE, by contrast, doesn't suffer from the same drawback:

```
DELETE S  WHERE SUM ( ‼SP , QTY ) < 1000 ,
DELETE SP WHERE SUM ( ‼Temp , QTX ) < 1000 ;
```

The name *Temp* here stands for an expression of the following form:

```
SP RENAME { P# AS PX , QTY AS QTX }
```

The introduced name PX is arbitrary (so is the introduced name QTX, of course, except that whatever name is used must then be referenced in the corresponding SUM invocation). For further explanation—in particular, for an explanation of the fact that the two individual DELETEs do indeed have exactly the desired effect, any possible appearance to the contrary notwithstanding—see reference [13].

Example 10: Update suppliers for whom the total shipment quantity, taken over all shipments for the supplier in question, is less than 1000, reducing their status to half its previous value.

```
UPDATE S WHERE SUM ( ‼SP , QTY ) < 1000 :
                 { STATUS := 0.5 * STATUS } ;
```

IMAGE RELATIONS AND EXTEND

Another obvious context in which image relations make sense is EXTEND; in fact, they're arguably even more useful in this context than they are in WHERE clauses. Some examples follow.

Example 11: For each supplier, find supplier details and total shipment quantity, taken over all shipments for the supplier in question.

```
EXTEND S : { TOTQ := SUM ( ‼SP , QTY ) }
```

Given the sample values in Fig. 1, the result is:

/ suppliers and total shipment quantities */*

S#	SNAME	STATUS	CITY	TOTQ
S1	Smith	20	London	1300
S2	Jones	10	Paris	700
S3	Blake	30	Paris	200
S4	Clark	20	London	900
S5	Adams	30	Athens	0

A conventional **Tutorial D** formulation of this query (i.e., not using image relations) would look like this:

```
S JOIN ( SUMMARIZE SP PER ( S { S# } ) : { TOTQ := SUM ( QTY ) } )
```

Note: SUMMARIZE in **Tutorial D** requires the heading of the PER relation to be a subset of that of the relation to be summarized; that's why the join is needed. If the query had asked just for supplier *numbers* and corresponding total shipment quantities, the SUMMARIZE portion of the expression by itself would have sufficed:

```
SUMMARIZE SP PER ( S { S# } ) : { TOTQ := SUM ( QTY ) }
```

Here's the corresponding EXTEND formulation, using an image relation:

```
EXTEND S { S# } : { TOTQ := SUM ( !!SP , QTY ) }
```

Either way, however (i.e., no matter which version of the query we're talking about), the EXTEND formulation is more succinct than the corresponding SUMMARIZE formulation. In fact, there would no need to support SUMMARIZE at all as currently understood if image relations in EXTEND were supported. What's more, the EXTEND formulation actually enjoys another advantage over its SUMMARIZE counterpart—a more important one than mere succinctness, or so it seems to me—which I'll get to in the section titled "Conclusions." *Exercise for the reader:* How would you formulate the foregoing query (either version) in SQL?

Let me return for a moment to Example 1: "Get suppliers for whom the total shipment quantity, taken over all shipments for the supplier in question, is less than 1000)." Here's the formulation I gave earlier:

```
S WHERE SUM ( !!SP , QTY ) < 1000
```

I can now explain that this formulation is in fact equivalent to—and can be regarded as shorthand for—something like the following:

```
( ( EXTEND S : { TOTQ := SUM ( !!SP , QTY ) } )
                        WHERE TOTQ < 1000 ) { ALL BUT TOTQ }
```

As a matter of fact, all forms of <*where*> in **Tutorial D** can be explained in similar fashion—in terms of EXTEND, I mean, not necessarily in terms of image relations as such—other than the (arguably) simplest possible form in which the operands in the WHERE clause are simple references to attributes of the relation identified by the relational expression preceding that WHERE clause. *Note:* That "simplest possible form" corresponds to the pure *restrict* operator of relational algebra.

Example 12: For each supplier, find supplier details and total, maximum, and minimum shipment quantity, taken over all shipments for the supplier in question.

```
EXTEND S : { TOTQ := SUM ( !!SP , QTY ) ,
             MAXQ := MAX ( !!SP , QTY ) ,
             MINQ := MIN ( !!SP , QTY ) }
```

This example illustrates what might be regarded as a small weakness in what I'm proposing: namely, the need for a certain amount of repetition in complex examples (in the case at hand, it's the image relation reference !!SP that's repeated). My own feeling is that it's worth living with such repetition, in what in practice might be rather unusual situations anyway, to obtain what seem to me significant improvements in clarity and explicitness. Let me immediately admit that the SQL analog (well, rough analog; once again, the equivalence is not exact) doesn't suffer from quite the same drawback:

```
SELECT S.S# , S.SNAME , S.STATUS , S.CITY ,
       SUM ( SP.QTY ) AS TOTQ ,
       MAX ( SP.QTY ) AS MAXQ ,
       MIN ( SP.QTY ) AS MINQ
FROM   S , SP
WHERE  S.S# = SP.S#
GROUP  BY S.S# , S.SNAME , S.STATUS , S.CITY
```

In SQL, therefore, as opposed to what I'm proposing, it might be easier for the optimizer to determine that TOTQ, MAXQ, and MINQ can all be computed in the same pass over (the stored version of) relvar SP. On the other hand, it's well known that defining the semantics of an expression like SUM(SP.QTY) in SQL is a nontrivial exercise anyway—a state of affairs that can cause serious problems for implementers, teachers, learners, and documentation writers (not to mention users!), as well as for language definers per se. I regard it as an interesting question, therefore, to determine how much of a challenge it would be for the optimizer to factor out the repetitions (as it were) in what I'm proposing.[7]

Let me also point out that there are cases in which the repetition is surely unavoidable, anyway, at least in a straightforward representation of the query; Example 3 is a case in point, where the SQL and **Tutorial D** formulations both involved some repetition. Now, the SQL version of that example might have been reformulated to avoid that repetition, perhaps as follows (note the need to introduce a name for the result of the nested subquery):[8]

```
SELECT Temp.*
FROM ( SELECT S.S# , S.SNAME , S.STATUS , S.CITY ,
              MIN ( SP.QTY ) AS MINQ ,
              MAX ( SP.QTY ) AS MAXQ
       FROM   S , SP
       WHERE  S.S# = SP.S#
       GROUP  BY S.S# , S.SNAME , S.STATUS , S.CITY ) AS Temp
WHERE  MINQ < 0.5 * MAXQ
```

But is this a formulation that the typical SQL user is likely to come up with? And even if it is, isn't it likely to be so because the user is motivated by performance considerations and, in effect, feels it necessary to do part of the optimizer's job? If so, is this a desirable state of affairs, or is it a weakness on the part of SQL? And in any case, is the formulation even correct? (No, it isn't. Did you spot the error?)

Example 13: Suppose we're given a revised version of the suppliers-and-parts database that looks like this:

```
S    { S# }
SP   { S# , P# }
SJ   { S# , J# }
J    { J# }
```

As in Examples 5 and 6, relvar J here represents projects (J# stands for project number); relvar SJ indicates which suppliers supply which projects. Now consider the query "For each supplier, find supplier details, the number of parts supplied by that supplier, and the number of projects supplied by that supplier."

```
EXTEND S : { NP := COUNT ( !!SP ) , NJ := COUNT ( !!SJ ) }
```

The SUMMARIZE analog is quite cumbersome:

```
S JOIN
( SUMMARIZE SP PER ( S { S# } ) : { NP := COUNT ( ) } )
  JOIN
( SUMMARIZE SJ PER ( S { S# } ) : { NJ := COUNT ( ) } )
```

---

[7] Of course, I'm assuming, in terms of the example, that it's important for the optimizer to be able to determine that TOTQ, MAXQ, and MINQ can all be computed in the same pass over the stored version of relvar SP—but whether that assumption is always valid is something that might be worth examining in itself. However, this is not the place to conduct such an examination.

[8] I remark in passing that the introduced name is required according to the standard even if it's never explicitly referenced!—e.g., in the case at hand, if the outer SELECT clause takes the form SELECT * (which it could) instead of the form shown.

The same goes for the SQL counterpart:

```
SELECT S.S# , S.SNAME , S.STATUS , S.CITY ,
     ( SELECT COUNT(*)
       FROM   SP
       WHERE  SP.S# = S.S# ) AS NP ,
     ( SELECT COUNT(*)
       FROM   SJ
       WHERE  SJ.S# = S.S# ) AS NJ
FROM   S
```

Example 14: For each supplier, find supplier details, total shipment quantity taken over all shipments for the supplier in question, and total shipment quantity taken over all shipments for all suppliers.

```
EXTEND S : { TOTQ  := SUM ( !!SP , QTY ) ,
             GTOTQ := SUM (   SP , QTY ) }
```

Result:

S#	TOTQ	GTOTQ
S1	1300	3100
S2	700	3100
S3	200	3100
S4	900	3100
S5	0	3100

Example 15: For each city *c*, get *c* and the total and average shipment quantities for all shipments for which the supplier city and part city are both *c*.

```
WITH ( Temp := S JOIN SP JOIN P ) :
EXTEND Temp { CITY } : { TOTQ := SUM ( !!Temp , QTY ) ,
                         AVGQ := AVG ( !!Temp , QTY ) }
```

The point of this rather contrived example is to illustrate the usefulness of WITH in avoiding the need to write out some possibly lengthy subexpression several times.

Example 16: Consider the following expression:

```
SP GROUP ( { P# , QTY } AS PQ )
```

Given the sample data from Fig. 1, this expression yields the following result:

<table>
<tr><th>S#</th><th>PQ</th></tr>
<tr><td>S1</td><td><table><tr><th>P#</th><th>QTY</th></tr><tr><td>P1</td><td>300</td></tr><tr><td>P2</td><td>200</td></tr><tr><td>P3</td><td>400</td></tr><tr><td>P4</td><td>200</td></tr><tr><td>P5</td><td>100</td></tr><tr><td>P6</td><td>100</td></tr></table></td></tr>
<tr><td>S2</td><td><table><tr><th>P#</th><th>QTY</th></tr><tr><td>P1</td><td>300</td></tr><tr><td>P2</td><td>400</td></tr></table></td></tr>
</table>

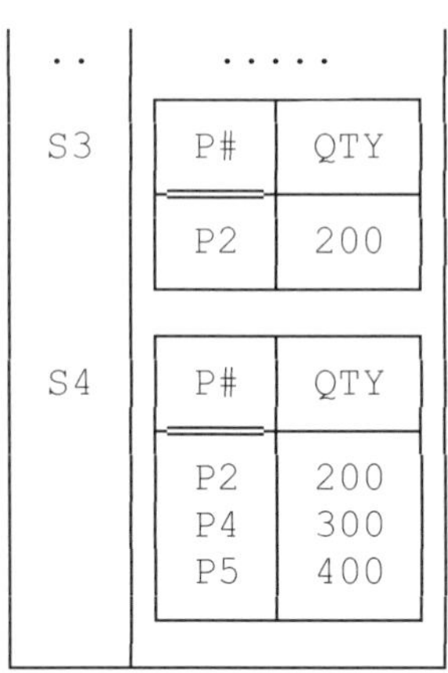

<table>
<tr><td>..</td><td>.....</td></tr>
<tr><td>S3</td><td><table><tr><th>P#</th><th>QTY</th></tr><tr><td>P2</td><td>200</td></tr></table></td></tr>
<tr><td>S4</td><td><table><tr><th>P#</th><th>QTY</th></tr><tr><td>P2</td><td>200</td></tr><tr><td>P4</td><td>300</td></tr><tr><td>P5</td><td>400</td></tr></table></td></tr>
</table>

In other words—speaking very loosely indeed—the effect of the GROUP operator is to convert a relation that has no relation valued attributes into one that has exactly one such attribute. But observe now that the very same effect can be achieved by means of the following expression:

```
EXTEND SP { S# } : { PQ := ‼SP }
```

Now, I'm not saying we should get rid of our useful GROUP operator. Quite apart from anything else, a language that had an explicit UNGROUP operator (as **Tutorial D** does) but no explicit GROUP operator could certainly be criticized on ergonomic grounds, if nothing else. But it's at least interesting, and potentially helpful from a pedagogic point of view, to note that the semantics of GROUP can so easily be explained in terms of EXTEND and image relation references.

Example 17: What are the semantics of the following expression?

```
S WHERE ( ‼(‼SP) ) { P# } = P { P# }
```

Answer: As we already know from the section "Terminology and Notation," for a given supplier number, *s#* say, the expression ‼SP here denotes a relation with heading {P#,QTY} and body consisting of those <*p#,qty*> pairs that correspond in SP to that supplier number *s#*. Call that relation *ir* (for image relation). By definition, then, for that supplier number *s#,* the expression ‼(‼SP) is shorthand for the following:

```
( ( ir ) MATCHING RELATION { TUPLE { } } ) { ALL BUT }
```

This expression in turn is equivalent to the following:

```
( ( ir ) MATCHING TABLE_DEE ) { P# , QTY }
```

And *this* expression reduces to just *ir*. Thus, "‼" is *idempotent* (i.e., ‼(‼*r*) is equivalent to ‼*r* for all *r*), and the overall expression

```
S WHERE ( ‼(‼SP) ) { P# } = P { P# }
```

is equivalent to this one:

```
S WHERE ( !!SP ) { P# } = P { P# }
```

Example 18: What's the logical difference between the following two expressions?

```
EXTEND TABLE_DEE : { NSP := COUNT (   SP ) }

EXTEND TABLE_DEE : { NSP := COUNT ( !!SP ) }
```

Answer: The two expressions are logically equivalent; both return a relation with heading {NSP} and body consisting of just one tuple, containing a count of the number of tuples currently appearing in relvar SP. In fact, both are equivalent to the following simpler expression:

```
RELATION { TUPLE { NSP COUNT ( SP ) } }
```

IMAGE RELATIONS AND CONSTRAINTS

In **Tutorial D,** integrity constraints (constraints for short) can be defined by means of a standalone CONSTRAINT statement, with syntax as follows:

```
CONSTRAINT <constraint name> <bool exp> ;
```

For example:

```
CONSTRAINT IC49 IS_EMPTY
              ( ( S JOIN SP ) WHERE STATUS < 20 AND QTY > 500 ) ;
```

This statement represents the constraint "No supplier with status less than 20 can supply any part in a quantity greater than 500." The name IC49 is just for illustration.

The SQL analog of **Tutorial D**'s CONSTRAINT statement is CREATE ASSERTION.[9] Here's the same example in SQL:

```
CREATE ASSERTION IC49 CHECK
     ( NOT EXISTS ( SELECT S.*
                    FROM   S
                    WHERE  S.STATUS < 20
                    AND    EXISTS ( SELECT SP.*
                                    FROM   SP
                                    WHERE  S.S# = SP.S#
                                    AND    SP.QTY > 500 ) ) ) ;
```

Unlike **Tutorial D,** however, SQL also supports an alternative style—in effect, a kind of shorthand—according to which a constraint can be explicitly attached "inline," as it were, to a specific base relvar (or base table, in SQL terms). For example:

[9] Supported, sadly enough, by few if any of the current mainstream SQL products.

```
CREATE TABLE S
   ( S# ... , SNAME ... , STATUS ... , CITY ... ,
     UNIQUE ( S# ) ,
     CONSTRAINT IC49 CHECK ( S.STATUS > 19 OR NOT EXISTS
                           ( SELECT SP.*
                             FROM   SP
                             WHERE  S.S# = SP.S#
                             AND    SP.QTY > 500 ) ) ) ;
```

As you can see, the advantage of the inline style is that the constraint as such is specified a little more succinctly. And the reason for that comparative succinctness is this: In the inline style, the constraint is understood to apply to each and every tuple of the pertinent relvar; thus, there's no need to spell that fact out explicitly within the constraint definition itself.

At the time of writing, **Tutorial D** includes nothing analogous to inline constraints.[10] But it could—and if it did, the image relation concept could be very helpful. For example, the constraint "No supplier with status less than 20 can supply any part in a quantity greater than 500" might be specified as part of the definition of relvar S, like this:

```
VAR S BASE RELATION
  { S# S# , SNAME NAME , STATUS INTEGER , CITY CHAR }
    KEY { S# }
    CONSTRAINT IC49 STATUS > 19 OR
                    IS_EMPTY ( ‼(SP WHERE QTY > 500) ) ;
```

Here's another example:

```
VAR SP BASE RELATION { S# S# , P# P# , QTY INTEGER }
    KEY { S# , P# }
    CONSTRAINT SFK IS_NOT_EMPTY ( ‼S )
    CONSTRAINT PFK IS_NOT_EMPTY ( ‼P ) ;
```

It should be clear that, given that {S#} is a key for S and {P#} is a key for P, constraints SFK and PFK here are essentially just the conventional foreign key constraints from SP to S and P, respectively.

All of that being said, I should point out that there's a trap for the unwary in this area (which is one reason why **Tutorial D** differs from SQL, currently, in not supporting such inline constraint definitions). Suppose the SQL definition for base table *BT* includes the following constraint definition:

```
CONSTRAINT icx CHECK ( bx )
```

Then this constraint definition is defined to be semantically equivalent to the following:

```
CREATE ASSERTION icx CHECK
 ( NOT EXISTS ( SELECT BT.* FROM BT WHERE NOT ( bx ) ) ) ;
```

And this latter constraint is always satisfied if *BT* happens to be empty, no matter what form *bx* might take—even if takes the form, say, "*BT* must not be empty" (i.e., COUNT(*BT*) > 0) ... or even the form "1 = 0," come to that.

Back to image relations per se. As a matter of fact, there could still be a use for image relations in constraint definitions even if the inline style is not adopted. For example, here's a standalone definition of the foreign key constraint from SP to S:

---

[10] Except for KEY (and, in the dialect used in this chapter, FOREIGN KEY) constraints, which are a special case.

```
CONSTRAINT SFK IS_EMPTY ( SP WHERE IS_EMPTY ( !!S ) ) ;
```

It's interesting to note, incidentally, that this constraint can very easily be extended to represent the foreign key constraint from SP to P as well:

```
CONSTRAINT ...
   IS_EMPTY ( SP WHERE IS_EMPTY ( !!S ) OR IS_EMPTY ( !!P ) ) ;
```

In the interest of accuracy, I should add that constraint SFK above is really an *inclusion dependency* [1]. Foreign key constraints are a special case; to be specific, a foreign key constraint is an inclusion dependency in which what might be called the "target attribute set" is a key for the pertinent relvar. (The sole target attribute in the example is attribute S#, and of course the set of attributes that is {S#} is indeed a key for S.) See reference [11] for further discussion.

DETAILED SPECIFICATIONS

Note: This section is included for completeness; it can be skipped without much loss. It relies on—in fact, it quotes fairly heavily from—the grammar of **Tutorial D** as given in reference [12], though the quotes are deliberately simplified and edited somewhat here.

Let *ry* be a relational expression; then !!*ry* is also a relational expression, and it denotes a certain *image relation.* An image relation is the "image" within some given relation of some given tuple; it consists of a certain projection of a certain restriction of that given relation, where (a) the given relation is the relation denoted by *ry,* and (b) the restriction and projection in question are defined by the given tuple in a manner to be explained below. The expression !!*ry,* which constitutes an *image relation reference,* represents an invocation of the *imaging operator,* and the symbol "!!" (which can be pronounced either "bang bang" or "double bang") denotes that operator.

Since the semantics of the expression !!*ry* are defined in terms of some given tuple, it follows that the expression can appear only in contexts in which that given tuple is well defined.[11] Two such contexts, WHERE clauses and EXTEND invocations, are explained below; as noted in the previous section, however, it might be desirable to include "inline constraint definitions" as another such context also.[12]

——— ♦♦♦♦♦ ———

WHERE clauses (I): The expression !!*<relation exp>* is an *<image relation ref>*. Such an expression can appear within the *<bool exp>* immediately following the keyword WHERE in a *<where>*, a *<relation delete>*, or a *<relation update>*, wherever a *<relation exp>* is currently permitted. I consider each case in turn (and I apologize up front for the repetition involved, which arises out of an attempt to make the definitions more self-contained). First *<where>*:

```
<where>
    ::=    <relation exp> WHERE <bool exp>
```

Let *rx* be the relation denoted by *<relation exp>*. Then:

- The *<bool exp>* is allowed to contain an *<attribute ref>*, *AR* say, wherever a literal would be allowed.

---

[11] Technically speaking, the expression !!*ry* is an example of an *open expression* (see Chapter 11).

[12] Another possible context, not discussed in detail here, is the expression whose values are to be aggregated in an aggregate operator invocation (so long as the expression in question is one that's required to be relation valued, as in, e.g., the aggregate operator invocation UNION (S, !!SP)).

The <*bool exp*> can be thought of as being evaluated for each tuple of *rx* in turn. If the <*attribute name*> of *AR* is that of an attribute of *rx*, then for each such evaluation *AR* denotes the corresponding attribute value from the corresponding tuple; otherwise the <*where*> must be contained in some expression in which the meaning of *AR* is defined.

- Let the <*image relation ref*> !!<*relation exp*> directly appear in the <*bool exp*> (where *directly appear* means the <*image relation ref*> appears within the <*bool exp*> as such and not within some <*where*> or <*extend*> within that <*bool exp*>). Let *ry* be the relation denoted by the <*relation exp*> immediately following the "!!" symbol within that <*image relation ref*>. Relations *rx* and *ry* must be joinable. Let their common attributes be *A1, A2, ..., An* ($n \geqslant 0$). In this context, then, the specified <*image relation ref*> is defined to be equivalent to the expression

```
( ( ry ) MATCHING
     RELATION { TUPLE { A1 A1 , A2 A2 , ... , An An } } )
                              { ALL BUT A1 , A2 , ... , An }
```

♦♦♦♦♦

WHERE clauses (II): Next I consider DELETE operations:

```
<relation delete>
    ::=   DELETE <relvar ref> [ WHERE <bool exp> ]
```

Let *Rx* be the relvar denoted by <*relvar ref*>, and let *rx* be the current value of *Rx*. Then:

- The <*bool exp*> is allowed to contain an <*attribute ref*>, *AR* say, wherever a literal would be allowed. The <*bool exp*> can be thought of as being evaluated for each tuple of *rx* in turn. If the <*attribute name*> of *AR* is that of an attribute of *rx*, then for each such evaluation *AR* denotes the corresponding attribute value from the corresponding tuple; otherwise the <*where*> must be contained in some expression in which the meaning of *AR* is defined.

- Let the <*image relation ref*> !!<*relation exp*> directly appear in the <*bool exp*> (where *directly appear* means the <*image relation ref*> appears within the <*bool exp*> as such and not within some <*where*> or <*extend*> within that <*bool exp*>). Let *ry* be the relation denoted by the <*relation exp*> immediately following the "!!" symbol within that <*image relation ref*>. Relations *rx* and *ry* must be joinable. Let their common attributes be *A1, A2, ..., An* ($n \geqslant 0$). In this context, then, the specified <*image relation ref*> is defined to be equivalent to the expression

```
( ( ry ) MATCHING
     RELATION { TUPLE { A1 A1 , A2 A2 , ... , An An } } )
                              { ALL BUT A1 , A2 , ... , An }
```

♦♦♦♦♦

WHERE clauses (III): Next, UPDATE operations:

```
<relation update>
    ::=   UPDATE <relvar ref> [ WHERE <bool exp> ] :
                        { <attribute assign commalist> }
```

Let *Rx* be the relvar denoted by <*relvar ref*>, and let *rx* be the current value of *Rx*. Then:

- The <*bool exp*> is allowed to contain an <*attribute ref*>, *AR* say, wherever a literal would be allowed. The <*bool exp*> can be thought of as being evaluated for each tuple of *rx* in turn. If the <*attribute name*>

of *AR* is that of an attribute of *rx,* then for each such evaluation *AR* denotes the corresponding attribute value from the corresponding tuple; otherwise the *<where>* must be contained in some expression in which the meaning of *AR* is defined.

- Every *<attribute assign>*, *AA* say, in the *<attribute assign commalist>* is syntactically identical to an *<assign>*, except that (a) the target of *AA* must identify, directly or indirectly, some attribute of *Rx,* and (b) *AA* is allowed to contain an *<attribute ref>*, *AR* say, wherever a literal would be allowed. *AA* can be thought of as being applied to each tuple of *rx* in turn. If the *<attribute name>* of *AR* is that of an attribute of *rx,* then for each such application *AR* denotes the corresponding attribute value from the corresponding tuple; otherwise the *<relation update>* must be contained in some expression in which the meaning of *AR* is defined.

- Let the *<image relation ref>* !!*<relation exp>* directly appear in the *<bool exp>* (where *directly appear* means the *<image relation ref>* appears within the *<bool exp>* as such and not within some *<where>* or *<extend>* within that *<bool exp>*). Let *ry* be the relation denoted by the *<relation exp>* immediately following the "!!" symbol within that *<image relation ref>*. Relations *rx* and *ry* must be joinable. Let their common attributes be *A1, A2, ..., An* ($n \geqslant 0$). In this context, then, the specified *<image relation ref>* is defined to be equivalent to the expression

```
( ( ry ) MATCHING
        RELATION { TUPLE { A1 A1 , A2 A2 , ... , An An } } )
                                { ALL BUT A1 , A2 , ... , An }
```

———♦♦♦♦♦———

EXTEND invocations: The expression !!*<relation exp>* is an *<image relation ref>*. Such an expression can appear within an *<attribute assign>* within an *<extend>*, wherever a *<relation exp>* is currently permitted.[13]

```
<extend>
    ::=   EXTEND <relation exp> : { <attribute assign commalist> }
```

Let *rx* be the relation denoted by *<relation exp>*. Then:

- An *<attribute assign>* directly contained in the *<attribute assign commalist>* (where directly contained means the *<attribute assign>* appears within the *<attribute assign commalist>* as such and not within some *<attribute assign>* within that *<attribute assign commalist>*) is allowed to include an *<attribute ref>*, *AR* say, wherever a literal would be allowed. The *<attribute assign>* can be thought of as being executed for each tuple of *rx* in turn. If the *<attribute name>* of *AR* is that of an attribute of *rx*, then for each such evaluation *AR* denotes the corresponding attribute value from the corresponding tuple; otherwise the *<extend>* must be contained in some expression in which the meaning of *AR* is defined.

- Let the *<image relation ref>* !!*<relation exp>* directly appear in some *<attribute assign>* directly contained in the *<attribute assign commalist>* (where directly appear means the *<image relation ref>* appears within the *<attribute assign>* as such and not within some *<where>* or *<extend>* within that *<attribute assign>*). Let *ry* be the relation denoted by the *<relation exp>* immediately following the "!!" symbol within that *<image relation ref>*. Relations *rx* and *ry* must be joinable. Let their common attributes be *A1, A2, ..., An* ($n \geqslant 0$). In this context, then, the expression !!*ry* is defined to be equivalent to

[13] It follows (without going into a lot of detail) that *<image relation ref>*s are also permitted within the expression on the right side of an *<attribute assign>* within a *<relation update>* invocation, since such invocations are defined in terms of EXTEND.

the expression

```
( ( ry ) MATCHING
       RELATION { TUPLE { A1 A1 , A2 A2 , ... , An An } } )
                                { ALL BUT A1 , A2 , ... , An }
```

———♦♦♦♦♦———

A final observation to close this section: As you can see, the foregoing detailed specifications all define the <*image relation ref*> !!*ry* in terms of a relation selector invocation of the form

```
RELATION { TUPLE { A1 A1 , A2 A2 , ... , An An } }
```

In each of those detailed specifications, that relation selector invocation denotes the relation with heading the same as that of a certain relation *rx* and body consisting just of what might be called, loosely, "the current tuple" of that relation *rx*. Several correspondents have suggested introducing an additional shorthand—say "$"—to represent such a relation selector invocation; that shorthand would be allowed to appear in WHERE clauses and EXTEND invocations, just like the "!!" shorthand. (Indeed, some have proposed introducing a shorthand to represent "the current tuple" as such.) Now, that "$" suggestion does have the effect of making the formulation of Example 7 (q.v.) a little simpler, inasmuch as it avoids the need to do any attribute renaming:

```
SP WHERE COUNT ( SP MATCHING $ { QTY } ) > 2
```

It doesn't seem to help much with any of the other examples, however. More study is required.

CONCLUSIONS

I think it's clear from everything I've said to this point that support for image relations is highly desirable. I've already indicated some of the benefits, but here I'd like to pull together all of the advantages discussed so far for purposes of subsequent reference.

First of all, then, image relations mean we can get rid of the relational divide operator entirely. I see this fact as an advantage for several reasons:

- There are at least eight distinct "divide" operators (they're explained in detail in reference [10]). Teaching, learning, and remembering the differences among them is quite difficult—not to mention the difficulty of choosing the right one to use in any given situation.

- As reference [10] also demonstrates, most if not all of those eight operators don't really do the job they were meant to do, anyway. And even when they do, they often don't do the *whole* job—by which I mean that real queries often require the divide invocation to be embedded within some larger expression in order to represent the query overall.

- All eight of those operators can be defined in terms of other (and simpler) operators, anyway—and invocations of the various divide operators are often longer, syntactically speaking, than the expressions they're meant to be shorthand for!

- Dropping the divide operator can be regarded as a genuine simplification, and genuine simplifications are always a good thing.

Second, image relations mean we can get rid of the relational SUMMARIZE operator as well. Again I have several reasons for seeing this state of affairs as an advantage. The big point is that it implies that we can also drop what **Tutorial D** calls "summaries" (this is the "more important advantage" I was referring to under Example 11). As noted earlier in this chapter, a <*summary*> is a construct that can appear only within the context of a SUMMARIZE invocation; SUM(QTY) is an example. Of course, I don't mean to suggest that some construct is bad just because it can appear only in certain limited contexts (after all, what I'm proposing in this chapter, image relations, can also appear only in certain limited contexts). But summaries in particular suffer from the problem that they "look and feel" very much like another important linguistic construct: namely, aggregate operator invocations. As a result, it's all too easy to confuse the two concepts (I can attest to this fact from a great deal of personal experience). This state of affairs in turn has negative implications for teaching, learning, remembering, and using both concepts.

In fact ... to pursue the point a moment longer, we can observe exactly the confusion I'm referring to in the very design of the language SQL. Let me elaborate. For definiteness, I'll focus on the case of SUM explicitly. First let me explain how SUM works in **Tutorial D:**

- A SUM invocation in **Tutorial D** is a scalar expression (i.e., it's an expression—formally, an *<agg op inv>*—that denotes a scalar value). Thus, for example, the following assignment statement—

  ```
  TOTQ := SUM ( SP , QTY ) ;
  ```

  —has the effect of assigning the grand total of all shipment quantities (i.e., 3100, given the sample values in Fig. 1) to the variable TOTQ.

- In contrast to the foregoing, a SUMMARIZE invocation is a relational expression (i.e., it's an expression that denotes a relation, not a scalar value). Given the sample values in Fig. 1, for example, the following expression—

  ```
  SUMMARIZE SP PER ( S { S# } ) : { TOTQ := SUM ( QTY ) }
  ```

  —produces the following result:

  ```
  /* supplier numbers and total shipment quantities */
  ```

S#	TOTQ
S1	1300
S2	700
S3	200
S4	900
S5	0

- Note very carefully from the two foregoing examples that (a) the *<agg op inv>* SUM(SP,QTY) includes a specification of the relation to be "aggregated," but (b) the analogous *<summary>* SUM(QTY) *doesn't* include a specification of the relation to be "summarized." Thus, the syntax of the two constructs is certainly distinct (though at the same time confusingly similar)—and the same might be said for the semantics, though perhaps with less justification.

- Turning now to SQL: SQL doesn't really have a notion of aggregate operators, as such, at all; in effect, it treats an aggregate operator invocation as just a special case of a summarization, implying among other things that the two constructs have to have the same syntax. Here are the same two examples in SQL (shown side by side for ease of comparison; I ignore the question of assigning the result of the "aggregation" to the variable TOTQ, since details of that assignment per se aren't what I want to focus on here):

```
SELECT SUM ( QTY )       |   SELECT S# , SUM ( QTY )
FROM   SP                |   FROM   SP
                         |   GROUP  BY S#
```

Here are some of the problems arising from the SQL approach:

- The expression on the left must not include an S# specification in the SELECT clause, whereas the expression on the right must include such a specification (at least, if the expression overall is to represent a sensible query). So the rules governing the formulation, and hence syntax and semantics, of the SELECT clause are dependent upon the presence or absence of other clauses (the GROUP BY clause in particular) within the overall expression.

- At the same time, the expression on the right doesn't *have* to include an S# specification; so another criticism of the SQL approach is that it permits the formulation of queries that aren't very sensible, and users have to be educated regarding this fact and have to make choices accordingly. *Note:* I'm not claiming it's impossible to formulate queries in **Tutorial D** that aren't very sensible. What I am claiming, however, is that, in SQL, the user has to make an explicit decision in order for the query expression to be sensible; in **Tutorial D,** the user has to make an explicit decision in order for the query expression *not* to be sensible. The latter state of affairs is surely to be preferred.

- The true argument to the "aggregate operator invocation" in the expression on the left isn't really just QTY, although the syntax makes it look as if it is; instead, it's really QTY FROM SP, and a more orthodox approach to the syntax of function invocation would move the closing parenthesis to after the full argument specification (after the FROM clause, in the example). One consequence of SQL's unorthodox approach is that aggregate operator invocations can't be nested! For example, an expression such as SELECT AVG(SUM(QTY)) FROM SP is illegal (at least in the standard; I believe—though I could be wrong—that there's at least one commercial product in which it's legal, though I have no idea what it might mean).

Anyway, to get back to image relations: As I've said, image relations allow us to dispense with SUMMARIZE, and hence with summaries, entirely.[14] In place of SUMMARIZE, we can now use EXTEND; in place of summaries, we can now use proper aggregate operator invocations (which, unlike summaries, explicitly mention the relation to be aggregated as one of their arguments). Hence, the confusion over aggregate operators vs. summaries goes away too.

There are several further advantages that accrue from eliminating SUMMARIZE that I think are also worth mentioning:

- Summaries in **Tutorial D** have (or had) names, called *<summary spec>*s. Unfortunately, the list of available *<summary spec>*s included, not only obvious ones like SUM and AVG, but also some rather unobvious ones like SUMD and AVGD—where the suffix "D" ("distinct") meant "Eliminate redundant duplicate values before performing the summarization." This scheme was, to be frank, a fairly grotesque piece of adhoc'ery (if that's a word), and I'm glad to be able to get rid of it. For the record, however, let me at least give an example of SUM vs. SUMD:

```
SUMMARIZE SP PER ( S { S# } ) : { TOTQ  := SUM  ( QTY ) }

SUMMARIZE SP PER ( S { S# } ) : { TOTQD := SUMD ( QTY ) }
```

---

[14] Of course we could also retain those constructs, redundantly, if desired.

Here are EXTEND analogs:

```
EXTEND S : { TOTQ  := SUM ( !!SP , QTY ) }

EXTEND S : { TOTQD := SUM ( ( !!SP ) { QTY } ) }
```

Given the sample values in Fig. 1, the results look like this:

S#	TOTQ
S1	1300
S2	700
S3	200
S4	900
S5	0

S#	TOTQD
S1	1000
S2	700
S3	200
S4	900
S5	0

(The only difference is in the quantity for supplier S1, as it happens.)

- SUMMARIZE in **Tutorial D** actually existed in two distinct forms, a PER form and a BY form: another complication that now goes away.

- In fact the PER or BY specification was optional, and a rule was needed to specify the default if neither was specified. That complication goes away too.

- COUNT now always has an explicit argument; i.e., COUNT() is no longer valid syntax, in any context. Of course, COUNT as an <*agg op inv*> always did have an argument, but COUNT as a <*summary*> didn't (see Example 13).[15] This situation also caused confusion but now goes away.

- SUMMARIZE suffers from the at least psychological disadvantage that what might be called the primary operand—i.e., the one that drives the operation, as it were—is the PER relation, not the SUMMARIZE relation (by which I mean the relation identified by the expression in the PER specification, not the one identified by the expression immediately following the keyword SUMMARIZE). No such criticism applies to EXTEND.

- Finally, SUMMARIZE invocations are often longer, syntactically speaking, than the expressions they're now "shorthand" for.

In addition to all of the above, this chapter has shown that image relations can simplify the formulation of certain constraints. There might be other uses too. As I said near the beginning of the chapter, I believe such simplifications, taken together, have the overall effect of raising the level of abstraction, and hence raising the level of discourse somewhat also.

One last point: As Darwen points out in reference [5], there are many advantages to being able to write, e.g., S JOIN SP, instead of effectively having to spell out the algorithm for computing that join (form a cartesian product, then restrict that product, then take a projection of that restriction), as in conventional SQL:

---

[15] Cf. COUNT(<*column ref*>) vs. COUNT(*) in SQL.

```
SELECT S# , SNAME , STATUS , CITY , P# , QTY
FROM   S , SP
WHERE  S.S# = SP.S#
```

I don't want to repeat all of those advantages here; I just want to observe that they all apply, mutatis mutandis, to the ability to write, e.g., !!SP, instead of effectively having to write out the algorithm for computing that image relation:

```
( ( SP ) MATCHING RELATION { TUPLE { S# S# } } ) { P# , QTY }
```

ACKNOWLEDGMENTS

I'd like to thank Jonathan Gennick and Jim Melton for assistance with certain technical questions regarding the SQL standard, and Hugh Darwen for his meticulous review of several earlier drafts of this chapter.

REFERENCES AND BIBLIOGRAPHY

1. Marco A. Casanova, Ronald Fagin, and Christos H. Papadimitriou: "Inclusion Dependencies and their Interaction with Functional Dependencies," Proc. 1st ACM SIGACT-SIGMOD Symposium on Principles of Database Systems, Los Angeles, Calif. (March 1982).

2. E. F. Codd: "A Data Base Sublanguage Founded on the Relational Calculus," Proc. 1971 ACM SIGFIDET Workshop on Data Description, Access and Control, San Diego, Calif. (November 1971).

3. E. F. Codd: "Relational Completeness of Data Base Sublanguages," in Randall J. Rustin (ed.), *Data Base Systems: Courant Computer Science Symposia Series 6*. Englewood Cliffs, N.J.: Prentice-Hall (1972).

4. E. F. Codd: *The Relational Model for Database Management Version 2*. Reading, Mass.: Addison-Wesley (1990).

5. Hugh Darwen (writing as Andrew Warden): "In Praise of Marriage," in C. J. Date, *Relational Database Writings 1985-1989*. Reading, Mass.: Addison-Wesley (1990).

6. Hugh Darwen: "The Nullologist in Relationland," in C. J. Date and Hugh Darwen, *Relational Database Writings 1989-1991*. Reading, Mass.: Addison-Wesley (1992).

7. C. J. Date: *An Introduction to Database Systems* (6th edition). Reading, Mass.: Addison-Wesley (1995).

8. C. J. Date: "We Don't Need Composite Columns," in *Relational Database Writings 1994-1997*. Reading, Mass.: Addison-Wesley (1998).

9. C. J. Date: *The Database Relational Model: A Retrospective Review and Analysis.* Reading, Mass.: Addison-Wesley (2001).

10. C. J. Date: "A Brief History of the Relational Divide Operator" (Chapter 12 of the present book).

11. C. J. Date: "Inclusion Dependencies and Foreign Keys" (Chapter 13 of the present book).

12. C. J. Date and Hugh Darwen: *Databases, Types, and the Relational Model: The Third Manifesto* (3rd edition). Boston, Mass.: Addison-Wesley (2006).

13. C. J. Date and Hugh Darwen: "Multiple Assignment," in C. J. Date, *Date on Database: Writings 2000-2006.* Berkeley, Calif.: Apress (2006).

14. International Organization for Standardization (ISO): *Database Language SQL,* Document ISO/IEC 9075:2008 (2008).

APPENDIX A: A LITTLE HISTORY

The image relation idea isn't entirely new; Codd touched on it in a couple of early papers in 1971 and 1972, respectively, and I proposed explicit support for it myself, independently, in 1995 in the 6th edition of my book *An Introduction to Database Systems* [7]. None of those early publications took the idea very far, but I'd like to take a quick look at what they did say, if only to forestall any complaints that I might be making unwarranted claims of originality now. *Note:* I should say up front, however, that neither Codd nor I followed up on the idea in any subsequent writings, until now.

——— ♦♦♦♦♦ ———

The following extended quote is taken from Codd's 1971 paper on Data Sublanguage ALPHA [2], a hypothetical language based on the tuple relational calculus. ALPHA as such was never implemented, but its ideas were influential on the design of several languages that were, including QUEL and (to some extent) SQL. I'll present the quote verbatim, then offer some comments on it.

> Consider the SUPPLY relation. The set of supplier numbers associated under this relation with a given part number is an example of what may be called an *image set*. The function COUNT applied to this set would yield the number of suppliers who supply this particular part.
>
> So common is this kind of construction and so often can the actual generation of the image set be avoided that we introduce composite functions called I-functions. For example, ICOUNT applied to a SUPPLY tuple, the P# attribute, and the S# attribute yields the count of suppliers who supply the part identified by the P# component of that SUPPLY tuple. ITOTAL applied to a SUPPLY tuple and the attributes P#, QUANTITY yields the total quantity being supplied of the part identified by the P# component of that SUPPLY tuple. IMAX, IMIN, IAVERAGE correspond in an analogous way to MAX, MIN, AVERAGE.
>
> ** For each part number being supplied to a project, find as a triple the part number, the project number, and the total quantity of that part being supplied to that project.
>
> ```
> RANGE SUPPLY Z
>
> GET W ( Z.P# , Z.J# , ITOTAL ( Z , ( P# , J# ) , QUANTITY ) )
> ```
>
> Note that, in this query, image sets of QUANTITY values are conceptually formed for each distinct pair of values (Z.P#,Z.J#). The first argument of the function ITOTAL is Z, the second is the compound attribute (P#,J#), and the third is quantity.
>
> ...
>
> ** Find the part number of parts supplied to more than two projects.
>
> ```
> RANGE SUPPLY Z
>
> GET W Z.P# :  ICOUNT ( Z , P# , J# ) > 2
> ```
>
> Image functions can, of course, appear in both the target list and the qualification.

Comments:

- "Consider the SUPPLY relation": Codd uses the term *relation* here for what we would now call a relvar. Relvar SUPPLY has attributes S# (supplier number), P# (part number), J# (project number), SHIPDATE, and QUANTITY.

- "The set of supplier numbers associated under this relation with a given part number is an example of what may be called an *image set*": When I first read this sentence, I assumed that no real significance attached to the fact that Codd was using the term *image set* rather than the term *image relation*. On further reading in reference [2] and other writings by Codd, however (reference [4] in particular), I came to the conclusion that Codd really did mean sets and not relations. For example, in reference [4], he says (in connection with conventional aggregate functions such as SUM):[16] "Note that an aggregate function ... transforms many scalar values into a single scalar value. The usual *source* of the many scalar values is a ... column" (my italics). This quote seems to be saying that the argument to such a function isn't a column (or attribute) per se, but, rather, the set or bag of values contained in such a column (or attribute). Personally, I would prefer the argument in question to be a relation: specifically, the relation that's the projection of the relation in question over the attribute in question.

- "So ... often can the actual generation of the image set be avoided that we introduce composite functions called I-functions" (referred to elsewhere in reference [2] as *image functions*): I find this remark a little strange. It tends to suggest that Codd's introduction of image functions was motivated by performance considerations, instead of issues of usability and the like. (Also, I don't know what the qualifier *composite* means in this context.) For my part I see the advantage of image relations (or "image sets") as, primarily, a usability advantage; if they lead to better performance as well, then that's a bonus, but I certainly don't want performance considerations to be the primary concern or driving force behind the idea.

- "For example, ... ITOTAL applied to a SUPPLY tuple and the attributes P#, QUANTITY yields the total quantity being supplied of the part identified by the P# component of that SUPPLY tuple": Here I think Codd's focus on sets as opposed to relations might have led him astray, slightly. Clearly, a given QUANTITY value might appear any number of times within the set of SUPPLY tuples for a given part number; for example, supplier S1 might supply part P1 to both project J1 and project J2 in a quantity of 100. Thus, what's needed is a form of aggregation that doesn't eliminate duplicates. Of course, a form of aggregation that does eliminate duplicates is needed too! Reference [4] has this to say on the issue: "When an aggregate function is applied to a column that happens to contain duplicate values, all occurrences of those values participate in the action." Obviously this behavior is inadequate; to repeat, both forms of aggregation are clearly necessary.[17]

- Here again is the first of Codd's two examples:

```
RANGE SUPPLY Z

GET W ( Z.P# , Z.J# , ITOTAL ( Z , ( P# , J# ) , QUANTITY ) )
```

  Explanation: The RANGE statement defines Z to be a range variable that ranges over the relation that's the current value of the SUPPLY relvar. The W in the GET statement identifies a "workspace" into which the relation denoted by the parenthesized expression "(Z.P#, ...)" is to be retrieved. Here for interest is an analog of that expression in terms of the proposals of the body of this chapter:

```
EXTEND SUPPLY { P# , J# } : { QPJ := SUM ( !!SUPPLY , QTY ) }
```

  This formulation differs from Codd's in that (a) it's based on relational algebra, not relational calculus; (b) it handles duplicates properly; and (c) it gives a name, QPJ, to the "sum" attribute of the result relation. (I also think the syntax is better from a human factors point of view, but let that pass.)

---

[16] Like many other writers, Codd uses the term *aggregate function* for what I prefer to call an aggregate operator.

[17] In **Tutorial D** terms, and using relvar SP from the body of the chapter, the distinction shows up in the logical difference between (e.g.) the invocation SUM(SP,QTY) and the invocation SUM(SP{QTY},QTY). *Note:* As explained in the section "A Note on Aggregate Operators" in the body of the chapter, the second of these expressions can be abbreviated to just SUM(SP{QTY}).

One last point on reference [2]: In a private communication to Codd dated February 19th, 1972, I pointed out—and in his response Codd agreed—that, given range variable Z as previously defined, the following ALPHA queries were identical in their effect:

```
GET W ( ICOUNT ( Z , S# , P# ) ) : ( Z.S# = 4 )

GET W (  COUNT ( Z , S# , P# ) ) : ( Z.S# = 4 )
```

For this reason and all of the others indicated above, as well as ones I choose not to go into here, I felt motivated some years later to criticize the image functions idea, as follows (from an essay on ALPHA in reference [9]):

> ... ALPHA does not directly permit aggregate functions to appear in the qualification; instead, it makes use of a shorthand version called image functions (which can also be used in the target commalist). I'll skip the details here, since frankly I don't think image functions were one of ALPHA's better ideas. Indeed, they might well have been the source of the strange syntax used in ... SQL for aggregate function invocations, and hence for the complexities caused in [that language] by that unorthodox syntax.

With hindsight, I think these remarks were a little unfair; I now think "image functions"—or image relations, rather—were a pretty good idea! But it's true to say that Codd's version of that idea suffered from several problems, and as far as I know he never developed it any further.

As I've just said, so far as I know Codd never developed his image functions idea any further. However, he did make one further reference to image *sets,* as such, in his 1972 paper on relational completeness [3]: namely, in his definition of the divide operator. *Note:* Although the final versions of references [2] and [3] were published in 1971 and 1972, respectively, the original IBM Research Report versions were published only a month apart (July and August, 1971). Thus, it seems likely that Codd was working on both at the same time.

> *Division* — Suppose *T* is a binary relation. The *image set* of *x* under *T* is defined by
>
> $$g_T(x) = \{y: (x,y) \in T\}.$$
>
> Consider the question of dividing a relation *R* of degree *m* by a relation *S* of degree *n*. Let *A* be a domain identifying list (without repetitions) for *R,* and let *A′* denote the domain identifying list that is complementary to *A* and in ascending order. For example, if the degree *m* of *R* were 5 and *A* = (2,5), then *A′* = (1,3,4). We treat the dividend *R* as if it were a binary relation with the (possibly compound) domains *A′, A* in that order. Accordingly, given any tuple $r \in R$, we can speak of the image set $g_R(r[A'])$, and we note that this is a subset of *R*[*A*] ... Providing *R*[*A*] and *S*[*B*] are union compatible, the division of *R* on *A* by *S* on *B* is defined by
>
> $$R[A \div B]S = \{r[A']: r \in R \text{ AND } S[B] \subseteq g_R(r[A'])\}.$$

Comments (most of which are concerned merely with explicating Codd's definition of division, not with image sets as such):

- First of all, it's interesting to see that Codd uses the notion of an image set as a basis for defining his divide operator; indeed, he introduces the notion in reference [3] purely for that purpose, and makes no mention of it anywhere else in the paper. I did mention more or less the same point myself in the body of the present chapter—the point, that is, that divide can be defined in terms of image relations—but of course I took the idea further; in particular, I suggested that we should actually use image relations, and not the divide operator, in formulating the kinds of queries that divide was originally intended for.

- Codd assumes throughout reference [3], for "notational and expository convenience," that attributes—actually he uses the term *domains*—are ordered left to right, and hence identified by ordinal position instead of by name (though he does also explicitly recognize that names are better in practice). This assumption (in my opinion, a most unfortunate one) is reflected throughout his divide definition in particular.

- As for "compound" domains (or attributes), I have problems with that notion as well—see reference [8]—and much prefer my own definition of divide, which relies on no such notion (it talks in terms of *sets of attributes* instead).

- Reference [3] uses brackets, not braces, to denote projection; thus, e.g., *R*[*A*] denotes what in **Tutorial D** would be written *R*{*A*}. Also, for typographical reasons, I've had to make some tiny changes to the symbols used in Codd's original text.

- "Providing *R*[*A*] and *S*[*B*] are union compatible": Reference [12] rejects the rather weak notion of "union compatibility" in favor of the much stronger notion of *same relation type*. That notion would require the projections of *R* on *A* and *S* on *B* to be, not just "union compatible," but actually of the same type; and that requirement in turn would require *A* and *B*, considered as sets of attributes, to be identical (i.e., to be the very same set of attributes).

——— ♦♦♦♦♦ ———

Finally I turn to reference [7]. *Note:* I've made some very minor changes in what follows in order to bring the syntax more into line with **Tutorial D,** and I've omitted some irrelevant material, but otherwise the text is as I originally wrote it.

[Consider the following example:]

```
EXTEND S : { NP := COUNT ( ( SP RENAME { S# AS X } ) WHERE X = S# ) }
```

Subexpressions [within EXTEND] such as the one shown in the example—

```
( ( SP RENAME { S# AS X } ) WHERE X = S#
```

(i.e., expressions that involve an attribute renaming, followed by an equality comparison that compares that renamed attribute with an attribute of the relation to be "extended" that has the same name as the renamed attribute before the renaming)—are needed sufficiently often in practice that it seems worthwhile to introduce an appropriate shorthand. Let us therefore agree to define

```
( MATCHING expression )
```

(where *expression* is an arbitrary relational expression) to be an expression that is permitted as an argument to an aggregate function reference within an EXTEND, with interpretation as follows. First, let the EXTEND be

```
EXTEND R1 : { ... := agg-op ( MATCHING R2 ) }
```

Let the set of attributes common to *R1* and *R2* be *Y*. Then the appearance of the subexpression "(MATCHING *R2*)" is defined to be shorthand for the expression

```
( ( R2 RENAME { Y AS X } ) WHERE X = Y )
```

for some appropriate (but essentially arbitrary) name *X*. With this simplification, the overall expression for the original query becomes

```
EXTEND S : { NP := COUNT ( MATCHING SP ) }
```

[Now consider the following example:]

```
S WHERE ( ( SP RENAME { S# AS X } ) WHERE X = S# ) { P# } = P { P# }
```

Of course, we can make use of the same MATCHING shorthand introduced in the section on EXTEND, thereby simplifying the overall expression to just

```
S WHERE ( MATCHING SP ) { P# } = P { P# }
```

Comments: It's pretty clear that I was thinking along very much the same lines in 1995 as I am now; I even used some of the same examples! Note that I was explicitly proposing to use image relations (though I didn't use that term) in both WHERE clauses and EXTEND invocations, and in particular in aggregate operator invocations, all more or less as in the present chapter. Of course, I used the keyword MATCHING instead of the "!!" notation (that keyword was available because it wasn't being used for its present purpose in **Tutorial D** at the time); as noted in the body of the chapter, however, I now prefer the "!!" notation, because I think it helps to stress the fact that the operator in question is slightly special, in a sense. A couple of more detailed observations:

- In the body of the present chapter, I defined !!*ry* to be equivalent to the following:

  ```
  ( ( ry ) MATCHING
           RELATION { TUPLE { A1 A1 , A2 A2 , ... , An An } } )
                                  { ALL BUT A1 , A2 , ... , An }
  ```

  By contrast, "MATCHING *ry*" (where by MATCHING I mean the operator "defined" in reference [7]) would not have performed that final projection to remove the attributes *A1, A2, ..., An.*

- The "definition" in reference [7] involves a renaming of *Y* as *X* and a subsequent comparison of the form *X* = *Y*. But *Y* is supposed to be a *set* of attributes, and those renaming and comparison operations aren't valid, strictly speaking.

More to the point, I didn't really explain the idea overall in sufficient detail; but then I don't think reference [7] would have been the appropriate forum for such detail, in any case. Anyway, I liked the idea then, and I like it even more now, and at this distance I can't think why I didn't pursue it further at the time—nor why I dropped it from subsequent editions of the book.

APPENDIX B: EXAMPLES 1-15 IN SQL

For interest, I repeat in this appendix Examples 1-15 from the body of the chapter and show what I believe to be an accurate SQL formulation in each case. For purposes of comparison I also repeat the **Tutorial D** formulations from the body of the chapter (where by **Tutorial D** I mean a version of that language that has been extended to include support for image relations as proposed in this chapter). *Note:* For simplicity, I assume throughout what follows that the SQL versions of the databases don't contain any nulls.

Example 1: Get suppliers for whom the total shipment quantity, taken over all shipments for the supplier in question, is less than 1000.

```
SELECT S.S# , S.SNAME , S.STATUS , S.CITY
FROM   S
WHERE  ( SELECT COALESCE ( SUM ( SP.QTY ) , 0 )
         FROM   SP
         WHERE  SP.S# = S.S# ) < 1000
```

As the body of the chapter tends to suggest, however, most SQL users would probably attempt to formulate queries like this one in terms of GROUP BY and HAVING. Here for interest, then, is such a formulation:

```
SELECT S# , S.SNAME , S.STATUS , S.CITY
FROM   S NATURAL LEFT OUTER JOIN SP
GROUP  BY S# , S.SNAME , S.STATUS , S.CITY
HAVING COALESCE ( SUM ( SP.QTY ) , 0 ) < 1000
```

I remark in passing that neither S.* nor S.S# would be correct in the SELECT clause here—in fact, they'd be incorrect for two different reasons! I leave the details as an exercise for the reader.

Tutorial D:

```
S WHERE SUM ( ‼SP , QTY ) < 1000
```

Example 2: Get suppliers with fewer than three shipments.

```
SELECT S.S# , S.SNAME , S.STATUS , S.CITY
FROM   S
WHERE  ( SELECT COUNT (*)
         FROM   SP
         WHERE  SP.S# = S.S# ) < 3
```

(This one was correct in the body of the chapter.) **Tutorial D:**

```
S WHERE COUNT ( ‼SP ) < 3
```

Example 3: Get suppliers for whom the minimum shipment quantity is less than half the maximum shipment quantity (taken over all shipments for the supplier in question in both cases).

```
SELECT S# , S.SNAME , S.STATUS , S.CITY
FROM   S NATURAL LEFT OUTER JOIN SP
GROUP  BY S# , S.SNAME , S.STATUS , S.CITY
HAVING ( MIN ( SP.QTY ) < 0.5 * MAX ( SP.QTY ) ) IS NOT FALSE
```

Tutorial D:

```
S WHERE MIN ( ‼SP , QTY ) < 0.5 * MAX ( ‼SP , QTY )
```

Example 4: Get suppliers who supply all parts.

```
SELECT S.S# , S.SNAME , S.STATUS , S.CITY
FROM   S
WHERE  NOT EXISTS
     ( SELECT P.*
       FROM   P
       WHERE  NOT EXISTS
            ( SELECT SP.*
              FROM   SP
              WHERE  S.S# = SP.S#
              AND    SP.P# = P.P# ) )
```

Tutorial D:

```
S WHERE ( ‼SP ) { P# } = P { P# }
```

Example 5: Given the following revised version of the suppliers-and-parts database—

```
S    { S# }
SP   { S# , P# }
PJ   { P# , J# }
J    { J# }
```

—(where relvar J represents projects and relvar PJ indicates which parts are used in which projects), find all <*s#,j#*> pairs such that *s#* is an S# value currently appearing in relvar S, *j#* is a J# value currently appearing in relvar J, and supplier *s#* supplies all parts used in project *j#*.

```
SELECT S.S# , J.J#
FROM   S , J
WHERE  NOT EXISTS
     ( SELECT PJ.*
       FROM   PJ
       WHERE  NOT EXISTS
            ( SELECT SP.*
              FROM   SP
              WHERE  S.S# = SP.S#
              AND    SP.P# = PJ.P#
              AND    PJ.J# = J.J# ) )
```

Tutorial D:

```
( S JOIN J ) WHERE ‼PJ ⊆ ‼SP
```

Example 6: With the same database as in Example 5, find all <*s#,j#*> pairs such that *s#* is an S# value currently appearing in relvar S, *j#* is a J# value currently appearing in relvar J, and project *j#* uses all parts supplied by supplier *s#*.

```
SELECT S.S# , J.J#
FROM   S , J
WHERE  NOT EXISTS
     ( SELECT SP.*
       FROM   SP
       WHERE  NOT EXISTS
            ( SELECT PJ.*
              FROM   PJ
              WHERE  S.S# = SP.S#
              AND    SP.P# = PJ.P#
              AND    PJ.J# = J.J# ) )
```

Tutorial D:

```
( S JOIN J ) WHERE ‼SP ⊆ ‼PJ
```

Example 7: Reverting to the original suppliers-and-parts database, find shipments such that at least two other shipments involve the same quantity.

```
SELECT Temp.S# , Temp.P# , Temp.QTY
FROM   SP AS Temp
WHERE  ( SELECT COUNT(*)
         FROM   SP
         WHERE  SP.QTY = Temp.QTY ) > 2
```

Tutorial D:

```
SP WHERE COUNT ( ‼( SP RENAME { S# AS SX , P# AS PX } ) ) > 2
```

Example 8: Delete shipments by suppliers in London.

```
DELETE
FROM   SP
WHERE  SP.S# IN ( SELECT S.S#
                  FROM   S
                  WHERE  S.CITY = 'London' ) ;
```

Tutorial D:

```
DELETE SP WHERE IS_NOT_EMPTY ( ‼(S WHERE CITY = 'London') ) ;
```

Example 9: Delete suppliers for whom the total shipment quantity, taken over all shipments for the supplier in question, is less than 1000.

```
START TRANSACTION READ WRITE SERIALIZABLE DIAGNOSTICS SIZE 5000 ;

DELETE
FROM   SP
WHERE  SP.S# IN
     ( SELECT S#
       FROM   S NATURAL LEFT OUTER JOIN SP
       GROUP  BY S#
       HAVING COALESCE ( SUM ( SP.QTY ) , 0 ) < 1000 ) ;

DELETE
FROM   S
WHERE  S.S# IN
     ( SELECT S#
       FROM   S NATURAL LEFT OUTER JOIN SP
       GROUP  BY S#
       HAVING COALESCE ( SUM ( SP.QTY ) , 0 ) < 1000 ) ;

COMMIT ;
```

Tutorial D:

```
DELETE S  WHERE SUM ( ‼SP , QTY ) < 1000 ,
DELETE SP WHERE SUM
     ( ‼(SP RENAME { P# AS PX , QTY AS QTX }) , QTX ) < 1000 ;
```

Example 10: Update suppliers for whom the total shipment quantity, taken over all shipments for the supplier in question, is less than 1000, reducing their status to half its previous value.

```
UPDATE S
SET    STATUS = 0.5 * STATUS
WHERE  ( SELECT COALESCE ( SUM ( SP.QTY ) , 0 )
         FROM   SP
         WHERE  SP.S# = S.S# ) < 1000 ;
```

Tutorial D:

```
UPDATE S WHERE SUM ( !!SP , QTY ) < 1000 :
                  { STATUS := 0.5 * STATUS } ;
```

Example 11: For each supplier, find supplier details and total shipment quantity, taken over all shipments for the supplier in question.

```
SELECT S.S# , S.SNAME , S.STATUS , S.CITY ,
     ( SELECT COALESCE ( SUM ( SP.QTY ) , 0 )
       FROM   SP
       WHERE  SP.S# = S.S# ) AS TOTQ
FROM   S
```

Tutorial D:

```
EXTEND S : { TOTQ := SUM ( !!SP , QTY ) }
```

Example 12: For each supplier, find supplier details and total, maximum, and minimum shipment quantity, taken over all shipments for the supplier in question.

```
SELECT S.S# , S.SNAME , S.STATUS , S.CITY ,
       COALESCE ( SUM ( SP.QTY ) , 0 ) AS TOTQ ,
       COALESCE ( MAX ( SP.QTY ) , -99999 ) AS MAXQ ,
       COALESCE ( MIN ( SP.QTY ) , +99999 ) AS MINQ
FROM   S NATURAL LEFT OUTER JOIN SP
GROUP  BY S.S# , S.SNAME , S.STATUS , S.CITY
```

Note: I've made an assumption here for the sake of the example that the maximum and minimum possible quantities are +99999 and –99999, respectively. (Reference [12] requires MAX and MIN to return the lowest and highest values, respectively, of the pertinent type if their argument is empty.)

Tutorial D:

```
EXTEND S : ( TOTQ := SUM ( !!SP , QTY ) ,
             MAXQ := MAX ( !!SP , QTY ) ,
             MINQ := MIN ( !!SP , QTY ) }
```

Example 13: Given the following revised version of the suppliers-and-parts database—

```
S    { S# }
SP   { S# , P# }
SJ   { S# , J# }
J    { J# }
```

—(where relvar J represents projects and relvar SJ indicates which suppliers supply which projects), find, for each supplier, full supplier details, the number of parts supplied by that supplier, and the number of projects supplied by that supplier.

```
SELECT S.S# , S.SNAME , S.STATUS , S.CITY,
     ( SELECT COUNT(*)
       FROM   SP
       WHERE  SP.S# = S.S# ) AS NP ,
     ( SELECT COUNT(*)
       FROM   SJ
       WHERE  SJ.S# = S.S# ) AS NJ
FROM   S
```

(This one was correct in the body of the chapter.) **Tutorial D:**

```
EXTEND S : { NP := COUNT ( ‼SP ) , NJ := COUNT ( ‼SJ ) }
```

Example 14: For each supplier, find supplier details, total shipment quantity taken over all shipments for the supplier in question, and total shipment quantity taken over all shipments for all suppliers.

```
SELECT S.S# , S.SNAME , S.STATUS , S.CITY ,
     ( SELECT COALESCE ( SUM ( SP.QTY ) , 0 )
       FROM   SP
       WHERE  SP.S# = S.S# ) AS TOTQ ,
     ( SELECT COALESCE ( SUM ( SP.QTY ) , 0 )
       FROM   SP ) AS GTOTQ
FROM   S
```

Tutorial D:

```
EXTEND S : { TOTQ  := SUM ( ‼SP , QTY ) ,
             GTOTQ := SUM (  SP , QTY ) }
```

Example 15: For each city *c*, get *c* and the total and average shipment quantities for all shipments for which the supplier city and part city are both *c*.

```
SELECT CITY , SUM ( SP.QTY ) AS TOTQ , AVG ( SP.QTY ) AS AVGQ
FROM   S NATURAL JOIN SP NATURAL JOIN P
GROUP  BY CITY
```

Tutorial D:

```
WITH ( Temp := S JOIN SP JOIN P ) :
EXTEND Temp { CITY } : { TOTQ := SUM ( ‼Temp , QTY ) ,
                         AVGQ := AVG ( ‼Temp , QTY ) }
```

Chapter 15

N-adic vs. Dyadic Operators: An Investigation

All generalizations are dangerous
(often quoted in the form *All generalizations are false).*

—Alexandre Dumas *fils*

Let *Op* be a dyadic operator. In many cases, it turns out to be both easy and desirable to define an *n*-adic version of such an operator—i.e., an extended version of *Op* that takes *n* operands, where *n* is an arbitrary nonnegative integer, instead of being limited to the case $n = 2$. By way of example, consider the logical connective AND, which is conventionally defined to be a dyadic operator, returning TRUE if and only if both of its operands have truth value TRUE. We can define an *n*-adic version of AND as follows. Let the operands be *p1, p2, ..., pn* ($n \geqslant 0$). Then:

- If $n = 0$, the result is TRUE.
- If $n = 1$, the result is the truth value of *p1*.
- If $n > 1$, the result is TRUE if and only if *p1, p2, ..., pn* all have truth value TRUE.

Of course, given that, in logic, universally quantifying over an empty set always yields TRUE, we can combine the foregoing three statements into one:

- AND returns TRUE if and only if all of its operands have truth value TRUE.

In other words, using the expression AND{*p1,p2,...,pn*} to represent the *n*-adic version, we can say that expression is shorthand for:

```
TRUE AND p1 AND p2 AND ... AND pn
```

Observe that this definition agrees with the conventional definition of AND for the special case $n = 2$; in other words, *n*-adic AND degenerates to dyadic AND in this case (as is of course desirable).

In like manner, we can define the expression OR{*p1,p2,...,pn*} to be shorthand for:

```
FALSE OR p1 OR p2 OR ... OR pn
```

In other words, OR returns FALSE if and only if all of its operands have truth value FALSE. And, of course, *n*-adic OR degenerates to dyadic OR when $n = 2$, as is again desirable.

> *Aside:* Let *p*(*x*) be a predicate with sole parameter *x*. If *p1, p2, ..., pn* are all of the possible instantiations of *p,* then (as you might have realized) AND{*p1,p2,...,pn*} and OR{*p1,p2,...,pn*} are logically equivalent to, and in effect formal definitions of, the quantified expressions FORALL *x* (*p*(*x*)) and EXISTS *x* (*p*(*x*)), respectively. *End of aside.*

By way of further examples, we might define *n*-adic versions of the set theory operators INTERSECT and UNION (both of which are conventionally defined to be dyadic, of course). Here for the record are such definitions. Let *s1, s2, ..., sn* be sets. Then:

- The intersection of *s1, s2, ..., sn* is the set of elements *x* such that *x* appears in all of *s1, s2, ..., sn.*

- The union of $s1, s2, \ldots, sn$ is the set of elements x such that x appears in at least one of $s1, s2, \ldots, sn$.

Note: If $n = 0$, INTERSECT returns the universal set, UNION returns the empty set.

Likewise, in relational algebra, we can and do define *n*-adic versions of JOIN and UNION (and hence of INTERSECT, TIMES, and D_UNION as well, since INTERSECT and TIMES are both special cases of JOIN and D_UNION is a special case of UNION). Here are the definitions (they're a little more complicated than their set theory counterparts because a relation in the relational model isn't just a simple set but has some internal structure):

- (*Dyadic JOIN*) Let relations *r1* and *r2* be such that attributes with the same name are of the same type. Then the expression *r1* JOIN *r2* denotes a relation with heading the set theory union of the headings of *r1* and *r2* and with body the set of all tuples *t* such that *t* is the set theory union of a tuple from *r1* and a tuple from *r2*.

- (*N-adic JOIN*) Let relations $r1, r2, \ldots, rn$ ($n \geqslant 0$) be such that attributes with the same name are of the same type. Then the expression JOIN{*r1*,*r2*,...,*rn*} denotes a relation with heading the set theory union of the headings of $r1, r2, \ldots, rn$ and with body the set of all tuples *t* such that *t* is the set theory union of a tuple from *r1*, a tuple from *r2*, ..., and a tuple from *rn*.[1] Equivalently, we can say that JOIN{*r1*,*r2*,...,*rn*} is defined as follows: If $n = 0$, the result is TABLE_DEE; if $n = 1$, the result is *r1;* otherwise, choose any two distinct relations from the set $r1, r2, \ldots, rn$ and replace them by their dyadic join, and repeat this process until the set consists of just one relation, which is the overall result.

- (*Dyadic UNION*) Let relations *r1* and *r2* be of the same type *T*. Then the expression *r1* UNION *r2* denotes a relation of type *T* with body the set of all tuples *t* such that *t* appears in either or both of *r1* and *r2*.

- (*N-adic UNION*) Let relations $r1, r2, \ldots, rn$ ($n \geqslant 0$) all be of the same type *T*. Then the expression UNION{*r1*,*r2*,...,*rn*} denotes a relation of type *T* with body the set of all tuples *t* such that *t* appears in at least one of $r1, r2, \ldots, rn$. *Note:* If $n = 0$, (a) some syntactic mechanism, not shown here, is needed to specify the pertinent type *T* and (b) the result is the empty relation of that type.[2]

To close this introductory section, I observe that we could also, if we liked, define *n*-adic versions of the familiar arithmetic operators "+" and "*". In fact, the aggregate operator SUM is essentially just *n*-adic "+" (though not in SQL), and a similar remark applies to most of the other well known aggregate operators.

COMMUTATIVITY AND ASSOCIATIVITY

Until recently I had always assumed, without investigating the matter too deeply, that in order for it to be possible to define an *n*-adic version of some dyadic operator *Op,* it was necessary that *Op* be both commutative and associative. Indeed, I actually stated as much in the first printing of *The Relational Database Dictionary, Extended Edition* (Apress, 2009). Just to review, dyadic operator *Op* is commutative if and only if

```
x Op y = y Op x
```

for all *x* and *y,* and associative if and only if

---

[1] Observe that this definition appeals (twice) to the definition of *n*-adic UNION for sets.

[2] If *T* is of degree zero, the result is TABLE_DUM. We are currently exploring the implications of making this result the default if no type *T* is specified explicitly.

```
x Op ( y Op z ) = ( x Op y ) Op z
```

for all *x, y,* and *z*. Note that all of the operators discussed so far in this chapter—logical AND and OR, set theory INTERSECT and UNION, relational JOIN and UNION, and arithmetic "+" and "*"—are indeed both commutative and associative by these definitions, and of course we were able to define *n*-adic versions of all of them.

Aside: Perhaps it would be helpful to give some examples of operators that aren't commutative or aren't associative or both:

- *Neither commutative nor associative:* All of the following are dyadic operators that are neither commutative nor associative: the logical operator IMPLIES, which returns FALSE if and only if its first and second operands have truth values FALSE and TRUE, respectively; the set theory operator MINUS, which returns the set of elements *x* such that *x* appears in its first operand and not its second; its relational counterpart (also called MINUS), to which an analogous remark applies; and the arithmetic operators "–" and "/".

- *Associative but not commutative:* A familiar example of an operator that's associative but not commutative is string concatenation ("||"). Another example is the conventionally unnamed dyadic logical operator that simply returns the truth value of its first operand.

- *Commutative but not associative:* One familiar example of an operator that's commutative but not associative is the arithmetic mean operator, AVG. Two further (and important) examples are the dyadic logical operators NAND and NOR. Here are the definitions: NAND returns FALSE if and only if both of its operands have truth value TRUE; NOR returns TRUE if and only if both of its operands have truth value FALSE. Each of these definitions is symmetric with respect to its operands, and the operators are thus clearly both commutative. However, they're not associative. For example, the expressions

  ```
  ( TRUE NAND FALSE ) NAND FALSE
  ```

  and

  ```
  TRUE NAND ( FALSE NAND FALSE )
  ```

  return TRUE and FALSE, respectively, and are thus not equivalent.

End of aside.

To return to the main thread of the discussion: If dyadic operator *Op* is both commutative and associative, then we can clearly generalize it and define an *n*-adic version. I'll use the expression *Op{x1,x2,...xn}* to represent that version—and I'll assume for the moment that *n* is greater than one—and I'll define that expression to be shorthand for the following repeated invocation of the dyadic version:

```
xi Op ( xj Op ( ... Op xk ) )
```

(where *i, j, ... k* is some permutation of 1, 2, ..., *n*).

Why is this definition valid? The answer is that the commutativity and associativity of *Op* together guarantee that the latter expression is well defined and has a unique value, independent of the particular permutation of 1, 2, ..., *n* involved. Indeed, the fact that *Op* is associative means we can drop the parentheses without ambiguity:

```
xi Op xj Op ... Op xk
```

And the fact that *Op* is commutative means we can take the permutation to be the *identity* permutation (i.e., $i = 1$, $j = 2$, ..., $k = n$) without loss of generality. The defining expression can thus be simplified to:

```
x1 Op x2 Op ... Op xn
```

Thus, the value of the expression *Op*{*x1*,*x2*,...,*xn*} is independent of the order in which the operands *x1, x2, ..., xn* are specified. What's more, the definition clearly has the property that the *n*-adic version of *Op* degenerates to the dyadic version in the special case where $n = 2$.

So much for the case $n > 1$. What happens if $n = 1$ or $n = 0$? Well, the case $n = 1$ is easy: We simply define *Op*{*x*} to return the value of *x*. But the case $n = 0$ is a little more tricky. Fundamentally, it makes sense to assign a meaning to the expression *Op*{} only if the dyadic version of *Op* has an associated *identity value.* Here's a definition of this latter concept:

- If *Op* is a commutative dyadic operator, and if there exists a value *i* such that *i Op x* and *x Op i* are both equal to *x* for all *x,* then *i* is the identity value with respect to *Op. Note:* Identity values are also known as *identity elements; identities; neutral elements; unit elements;* or just *units.* Note too that it isn't necessary for *Op* to be associative in order for it to have a corresponding identity value. (Relational COMPOSE is a case in point. See the next section.)

Here are some examples:

- The identity values for AND and OR are TRUE and FALSE, respectively.
- The identity values for INTERSECT and UNION are the universal set and the empty set, respectively.
- The identity values for JOIN and (relational) UNION are TABLE_DEE and the empty relation of the pertinent type, respectively.
- The identity values for "+" and "*" are 0 and 1, respectively.

And as these examples should be sufficient to suggest, we define the expression *Op*{} to have a meaning in general if and only if a corresponding identity value is defined, in which case the meaning is precisely that identity value.

THE COMPOSE OPERATOR

It was consideration of the relational operator COMPOSE that originally spurred me to write this chapter. Since that operator might be novel to some readers, I'll begin with a definition, at least of the dyadic version (and I'll take the name "COMPOSE" to refer to that dyadic version until further notice):[3]

- (*Dyadic COMPOSE*) Let *r1* and *r2* be relations; then *r1* COMPOSE *r2* is shorthand for the projection on {*X*} of *r1* JOIN *r2,* where {*X*} is all of the attributes of *r1* and *r2* apart from common ones. *Note:* COMPOSE is defined in terms of JOIN, as you can see; hence, attributes with the same name in relations *r1* and *r2* are required to be of the same type, and those attributes are precisely the common ones referred to in the definition. Note too that if the set of common attributes is empty, then *r1* COMPOSE *r2*

---

[3] The name "COMPOSE" is meant to be suggestive of the fact that relational composition is a natural generalization of functional composition. In case you're not familiar with this latter notion, the composition of two functions *f*(...) and *g*(...), in that order, is the function *f*(*g*(...)). It's interesting to note that Codd included such an operator in his earliest papers on the relational model, but subsequently discarded it for some reason. (Of course, it's true that it's just shorthand for something that can easily be expressed otherwise, as the definition makes clear.)

degenerates to *r1* TIMES *r2*.

By way of example, let relations SS and SC be as follows:

SS

S#	STATUS
S1	20

SC

S#	CITY
S1	London
S2	Paris

Then, assuming attributes with the same name are of the same type (an assumption I'll make throughout this chapter for simplicity), the expression

```
SS COMPOSE SC
```

yields this result:

STATUS	CITY
20	London

Now, COMPOSE is clearly commutative, since its definition is symmetric in *r1* and *r2;* what's more, it's easy to see that it has a corresponding identity value, viz., TABLE_DEE. However, it isn't associative. In order to illustrate this fact, let relations SS, SC, and SP be as shown below (SS and SC are the same as before). Then:

SS

S#	STATUS
S1	20

SC

S#	CITY
S1	London
S2	Paris

SP

S#	P#
S1	P1
S2	P2

- The expression

  ```
  ( SS COMPOSE SC ) COMPOSE SP
  ```

  yields this result:

STATUS	CITY	S#	P#
20	London	S1	P1
20	London	S2	P2

- By contrast, the expression

  ```
  SS COMPOSE ( SC COMPOSE SP )
  ```

  yields this result:

STATUS	CITY	S#	P#
20	London	S1	P1
20	Paris	S1	P2

So COMPOSE isn't associative. *But we can still define an n-adic version of it*—a version, that is, for arbitrary $n \geqslant 0$ that possesses both of the following desirable properties:

- The value of the expression COMPOSE{*r1,r2,...,rn*} is independent of the order in which the operand relations *r1, r2, ..., rn* are specified.

- The expression COMPOSE{*r1,r2*} is logically equivalent to the expression *r1* COMPOSE *r2*. In other words, the *n*-adic version degenerates to the dyadic version in the special case where $n = 2$.

Here's the definition:

- (*N-adic COMPOSE*) Let *r1, r2, ..., rn* ($n \geqslant 0$) be relations; then COMPOSE{*r1,r2,...,rn*} is shorthand for the projection on {*X*} of JOIN{*r1,r2,...,rn*}, where {*X*} is all of the attributes of *r1, r2, ..., rn* apart from ones common to at least two of those relations. Note in particular that COMPOSE{*r*} returns *r* and COMPOSE{} returns TABLE_DEE.

  For example, if relations SS, SC, and SP are as shown above, then the expression

  ```
  COMPOSE { SS , SC , SP }
  ```

  yields this result:

STATUS	CITY	P#
20	London	P1

It follows from this example that (to spell the point out) although *n*-adic COMPOSE does possess the two desirable properties identified above, and although it's commutative[4] and does have an associated identity value, the following expressions are not in general equivalent:

```
COMPOSE { r1 , COMPOSE { r2 , ... , rm , rn } }

COMPOSE { COMPOSE { r1 , r2 , ... , rm } , rn }

COMPOSE { r1 , r2 , ... , rm , rn }
```

(where $n > 2$ and $m = n - 1$).[5] In other words, *n*-adic COMPOSE as defined above is not just shorthand for repeated dyadic COMPOSE; it truly is a distinct operator. (Contrast the situation with, e.g., *n*-adic JOIN, which *is* shorthand for repeated dyadic JOIN.)

---

[4] I'm speaking loosely here. Commutativity is a property that applies to dyadic operators specifically. What I mean when I say an *n*-adic operator is commutative is merely that the order in which the operands are specified is immaterial.

[5] The expressions would be equivalent if COMPOSE were associative, but of course it isn't. In other words, associativity is sufficient but not necessary for "the two desirable properties" to hold; but it's necessary if we want expressions such as those shown to be equivalent as well.

LOGICAL OPERATORS (I)

Given that *n*-adic COMPOSE as defined in the previous section fails to preserve the equivalence of expressions such as COMPOSE{*r1*,COMPOSE{*r2*,*r3*}} and COMPOSE{COMPOSE{*r1*,*r2*},*r3*}}, it might be felt better not to support it.[6] Before we reject it out of hand, however, I'd like to draw your attention to the fact that at least there's some precedent for this state of affairs. To be specific, I want to consider the logical connectives EQ (equivalence) and XOR (exclusive OR). These operators are of course well known, at least in their dyadic versions, but let me give definitions for the record anyway:

- (*Dyadic equivalence*) EQ returns TRUE if and only if both of its operands have the same truth value.
- (*Dyadic exclusive OR*) XOR returns FALSE if and only if both of its operands have the same truth value.

It's immediate from these definitions that (a) EQ and XOR are, respectively, the equality operator "=" and the inequality operator "≠" for truth values (equivalently, for values of type BOOLEAN), and hence that (b) EQ returns TRUE just when XOR returns FALSE, and FALSE just when XOR returns TRUE.

Now let me focus on EQ for definiteness (I'll come back to XOR in the next section but one). EQ is obviously commutative. Also, there's an obvious identity value, viz., TRUE (the expression *x* EQ TRUE returns *x* for all truth values *x*). What's more, the operator is certainly associative, as can easily be seen by checking the truth tables, and so we can define an *n*-adic version: The expression EQ{*p1*,*p2*,...,*pn*} is shorthand for, and thus logically equivalent (!) to, the expression

```
TRUE EQ p1 EQ p2 EQ ... EQ pn
```

However, I now observe that *n*-adic EQ as just defined has the arguably counterintuitive property that, e.g., the expression

```
EQ { FALSE , TRUE , FALSE }
```

evaluates to TRUE. Surely we wouldn't want to say, in ordinary parlance, that FALSE, TRUE, and FALSE are all equivalent; yet the foregoing expression seems to be saying exactly that. Indeed, the following definition—taken from *The McGraw-Hill Dictionary of Mathematics* (McGraw-Hill, 1994)—seems to accord better with our intuition in this respect:

- [Equivalence is a] logic operator having the property that if P, Q, R, etc., are statements, then the equivalence of P, Q, R, etc., is true if and only if all statements are true or all statements are false.

Note, however, that this definition explicitly defines equivalence to be an *n*-adic operator; it agrees with the definition I gave earlier for $n = 2$ but not for, e.g., $n = 3$. So *n*-adic equivalence as I defined it previously and *n*-adic equivalence as defined by McGraw-Hill are two distinct operators. For clarity, I'll use "MEQ" for the McGraw-Hill operator, retaining "EQ" for equivalence as previously defined; then we can say that, e.g., EQ{*p1*,*p2*,*p3*} and MEQ{*p1*,*p2*,*p3*} are not equivalent.[7]

I now observe that MEQ isn't very precisely defined; in particular, the definition doesn't adequately address the cases $n = 1$ and $n = 0$. However, for $n = 1$, it seems reasonable to say the result is just TRUE (since

---

[6] It's not my purpose here to argue in favor of either side of this issue; I'm merely trying to get some of the relevant facts down in writing, in order to assist with possible debates on the matter.

[7] Given that we now have two distinct meanings for the term *logical equivalence*, it becomes necessary in general to be very careful over natural language claims to the effect that various items are "equivalent." In this chapter, however, all such claims concern the relationship between exactly two items; and since the meanings coincide in this particular case, the problem goes away.

it's certainly true that "all statements are true or all statements are false" in this case).[8] And for $n = 0$, given that TRUE is the identity value for equivalence as usually understood, it seems reasonable to say the result is again just TRUE.

I observe also that we have another slightly counterintuitive situation on our hands: Whereas it is the case that, e.g., EQ{*p1,p2,p3*} is logically equivalent to EQ{*p1*,EQ{*p2,p3*}}, it is *not* the case that MEQ{*p1,p2,p3*} is logically equivalent to MEQ{*p1*,MEQ{*p2,p3*}}—despite the fact that dyadic MEQ, being identical to dyadic EQ, is associative. In other words, *n*-adic MEQ is not just shorthand for repeated dyadic MEQ; it truly is a distinct operator.

Let's get back to EQ as previously defined (where EQ{*p1,p2,...,pn*} is shorthand for TRUE EQ *p1* EQ *p2* EQ ... EQ *pn*). Another question that arises is this: Given that EQ{*p1,p2,...,pn*} doesn't mean that *p1, p2, ..., pn* all have the same truth value, is there nevertheless some pleasing intuitive interpretation of what it does mean? The answer is *yes* (sort of). To be specific, we can define *n*-adic EQ thus:

- EQ returns TRUE if and only if the number of its operands that have truth value FALSE is even. (Note, therefore, that the result doesn't depend at all on those operands that have truth value TRUE, and it doesn't even depend on how many such operands there are. In fact, all of those operands can simply be ignored.)

In other words, the expression EQ{*p1,p2,...,pn*} is defined thus (of course, the following definition is 100 percent redundant; I include it purely for clarity):

- If $n = 0$, the result is TRUE (0 is an even number).
- If $n = 1$, the result is the truth value of *p1*.
- If $n = 2$, the result is TRUE if and only if neither *p1* nor *p2* has truth value FALSE or both do (as with conventional dyadic EQ).
- If $n > 2$, the result is TRUE if and only if exactly *m* of *p1, p2, ..., pn* have truth value FALSE, where *m* is even.

Here are some examples:

- `EQ { }                                : TRUE`
- `EQ { TRUE }                           : TRUE`
- `EQ { FALSE }                          : FALSE`
- `EQ { FALSE , FALSE }                  : TRUE`
- `EQ { TRUE , TRUE , TRUE }             : TRUE`
- `EQ { FALSE , FALSE , FALSE }          : FALSE`
- `EQ { TRUE , TRUE , FALSE }            : FALSE`
- `EQ { TRUE , FALSE , FALSE }           : TRUE`

---

[8] On the other hand, this definition does mean, for what it's worth, that MEQ{FALSE} returns TRUE while EQ{FALSE} returns FALSE.

A REMARK ON SYNTAX

Consider again this example from the previous section:

```
EQ { FALSE , TRUE , FALSE }
```

Now, you might have noticed something a little strange in the syntax here. Normally, we use braces to enclose commalists of items when the commalist in question is intended to denote a set of some kind, in which case (a) the order in which the items appear within that commalist is immaterial and (b) if an item appears more than once, it's treated as if it appeared just once. In particular, as we've seen, we use braces to enclose the commalist of argument expressions in certain *n*-adic operator invocations. Now, if the operator in question is idempotent,[9] then the argument expression commalist truly does represent a set of arguments, and the foregoing remarks apply. If the operator is not idempotent, however, then the argument expression commalist represents a *bag* of arguments, not a set—in which case the order in which the argument expressions appear is still immaterial, but repetition has significance. Thus, for example, EQ isn't idempotent, and so (e.g.) the expressions EQ{FALSE,TRUE,FALSE} and EQ{FALSE,TRUE} aren't equivalent (the first returns TRUE, the second returns FALSE). For another example, the expressions COMPOSE{*r*} and COMPOSE {*r*,*r*} aren't equivalent either (the first returns *r*, the second returns either TABLE_DEE or TABLE_DUM).

LOGICAL OPERATORS (II)

I turn now to the logical connective XOR (exclusive OR). Like EQ, XOR is obviously commutative. The identity value is FALSE (the expression *x* XOR FALSE returns *x* for all truth values *x*). And the operator is associative, as can be seen by checking the truth tables, and so we can define an *n*-adic version: The expression XOR{*p1*,*p2*,...,*pn*} is shorthand for, and thus logically equivalent to, the expression

```
FALSE XOR p1 XOR p2 XOR ... XOR pn
```

However, I now observe that *n*-adic XOR as just defined has the arguably counterintuitive property that, e.g., the expression

```
XOR { FALSE , TRUE , FALSE }
```

evaluates to TRUE. Surely we wouldn't want to say, in ordinary parlance, that FALSE, TRUE, and FALSE are all different; yet the foregoing expression seems to be saying exactly that (or something like that, at any rate).

Now, we've seen that EQ and XOR are inverse operators, in a sense. Interestingly, however, the McGraw-Hill dictionary referenced earlier, although it does (as we've seen) define equivalence as an *n*-adic operator, makes no attempt to define an *n*-adic version of exclusive OR; rather, it explicitly defines it to be dyadic. For the record, here is that definition:

- [Exclusive OR is a] logic operator having the property that if P is a statement and Q is a statement, then P exclusive or Q is true if either but not both statements are true, false if both are true or both are false.

But we might reasonably attempt to come up with an *n*-adic definition along the lines of the *n*-adic definition of MEQ from the previous section but one. In keeping with the McGraw-Hill style, we might try:

- Exclusive OR is a logic operator having the property that if P, Q, R, etc., are statements, then the exclusive OR of P, Q, R, etc., is true if and only if some of the statements are true and some of the statements are

---

[9] The dyadic operator *Op* is idempotent if and only if *x Op x* = *x* for all *x*. I'll leave it as an exercise to determine which of the operators already discussed in this chapter are idempotent and which not.

false. (In other words, at least one of the statements is true and at least one of the statements is false.)

This definition agrees with the definition I gave earlier for *n*-adic XOR for $n = 2$ but not for, e.g., $n = 3$. I'll refer to this new operator as "MXOR," retaining "XOR" for exclusive OR as previously defined; so now we can say that, e.g., XOR{*p1,p2,p3*} and MXOR{*p1,p2,p3*} are not equivalent.

Of course, the foregoing definition, like the one given earlier for MEQ, isn't very precise; in particular, it doesn't adequately address the cases $n = 1$ and $n = 0$. However, for $n = 1$, it seems reasonable to say the result is just FALSE (since it's certainly false that "some of the statements are true and some of the statements are false" in this case).[10] And for $n = 0$, given that FALSE is the identity value for exclusive OR as usually understood, it seems reasonable to say the result is again just FALSE.

And now we have a slightly counterintuitive situation on our hands once again: Whereas it is the case that, e.g., XOR{*p1,p2,p3*} is logically equivalent to XOR{*p1*,XOR{*p2,p3*}}, it is not the case that MXOR{*p1,p2,p3*} is logically equivalent to MXOR{*p1*,MXOR{*p2,p3*}}—despite the fact that dyadic MXOR, being identical to dyadic XOR, is associative. In other words, *n*-adic MXOR is not just shorthand for repeated dyadic MXOR but is truly a distinct operator.

Let's get back to XOR as previously defined (where XOR{*p1,p2,...,pn*} is shorthand for FALSE XOR *p1* XOR *p2* XOR ... XOR *pn*). Another question that arises is this: Given that XOR{*p1,p2,...,pn*} doesn't mean that *p1, p2, ..., pn* all have different truth values—apologies for the loose manner of speaking here—is there nevertheless some pleasing intuitive interpretation of what it does mean? As with EQ, the answer is *yes* (sort of). To be specific, we can define *n*-adic XOR thus:

- XOR returns TRUE if and only if the number of its operands that have truth value TRUE is odd. (So the result doesn't depend at all on those operands that have truth value FALSE, and it doesn't even depend on how many such operands there are. In fact, all of those operands can simply be ignored.)

In other words, the expression XOR{*p1,p2,...,pn*} is defined as follows (again I realize this definition is 100 percent redundant, but I include it for clarity):

- If $n = 0$, the result is FALSE.
- If $n = 1$, the result is the truth value of *p1*.
- If $n = 2$, the result is TRUE if and only if one of *p1* and *p2* has truth value TRUE and the other has truth value FALSE (as with conventional dyadic XOR).
- If $n > 2$, the result is TRUE if and only if exactly *m* of *p1, p2, ..., pn* have truth value TRUE, where *m* is odd.

Here are some examples:

- `XOR { }` : `FALSE`
- `XOR { TRUE }` : `TRUE`
- `XOR { FALSE }` : `FALSE`
- `XOR { FALSE , FALSE }` : `FALSE`
- `XOR { TRUE , TRUE , TRUE }` : `TRUE`

---

[10] On the other hand, this definition does mean, for what it's worth, that MXOR{TRUE} returns FALSE while XOR{TRUE} returns TRUE.

- `XOR { FALSE , FALSE , FALSE } : FALSE`
- `XOR { TRUE , TRUE , FALSE }   : FALSE`
- `XOR { TRUE , FALSE , FALSE }  : TRUE`

But there's yet another fly in the ointment here (perhaps you've spotted it already). Consider the expressions EQ{*p1,p2,...,pn*} and XOR{*p1,p2,...,pn*}. Let the value *n* (the total number of operands in each case) be equal to $i+j$, say, where *i* is even and *j* is odd (so *n* too is odd). Then it's possible for *i* of those operands to have truth value FALSE and *j* of them to have truth value TRUE, and hence for the expressions EQ{*p1,p2,...,pn*} and XOR{*p1,p2,...,pn*} both to return TRUE. (As a trivial example, EQ{TRUE} and XOR{TRUE} both return TRUE. More generally, EQ(*p*) and XOR(*p*) always return the same value.) As a consequence, although we can say (as indeed I did say, earlier) that dyadic EQ and XOR are inverses of one another—EQ returns TRUE just when XOR returns FALSE—we can't say the same for *n*-adic EQ and XOR, in general. Or, to be more precise about the matter: The operators *n*-adic EQ and *n*-adic XOR are inverses of each other when *n* is even, but are equivalent when *n* is odd.

Perhaps I should add that, by contrast, the operators MEQ and MXOR are inverses of each other in all cases.

EXCLUSIVE UNION

Discussion of exclusive OR brings me to its set theory counterpart, the operator *exclusive union* (more usually known as *symmetric difference*), which I'll denote by XUNION. Like XOR, XUNION is conventionally defined to be a dyadic operator. For the record, here is that definition:

- Let *s1* and *s2* be sets. Then the exclusive union of those two sets is the set of elements *x* such that *x* appears in *s1* or *s2* but not both.

Now, this operator is clearly commutative, since its definition is symmetric in *s1* and *s2;* what's more, it's easy to see that it has a corresponding identity value., viz., the empty set. It's not idempotent; however, it is associative (as should indeed be expected, since XOR is associative). Here's the proof:

```
      x ∈ s1 XUNION ( s2 XUNION s3 )
iff   x ∈ s1 XOR x ∈ ( s2 XUNION s3 )
iff   x ∈ s1 XOR ( x ∈ s2 XOR x ∈ s3 )
iff   ( x ∈ s1 XOR x ∈ s2 ) XOR x ∈ s3     —because XOR is associative
iff   ( x ∈ s1 XUNION s2 ) XOR x ∈ s3
iff   x ∈ ( s1 XUNION s2 ) XUNION s3
```

So what about an *n*-adic version? Well, the situation is (of course) precisely analogous to the situation with XOR; that is, we can define an *n*-adic version in two logically distinct ways. To be precise, we can define it *either* as shorthand for repeated application of the dyadic version *or* as an explicit function of *n*. Let's agree, at least for the moment, to use XUNION for the repeated dyadic version and MXUNION for the other version. Then the definitions look like this. Let *s1, s2, ..., sn* ($n \geqslant 0$) be sets. Then:

- (*XUNION*) XUNION{*s1,s2,...,sn*} is the set of elements *x* such that *x* appears in exactly *m* of *s1, s2, ..., sn,* where *m* is odd (and possibly different for different elements *x*).
- (*MXUNION*) MXUNION{*s1,s2,...,sn*} is the set of elements *x* such that *x* appears in at least one but not all of *s1, s2, ..., sn*.

These definitions coincide for $n = 2$, of course. They also coincide for $n = 0$ (in which case the result is the empty set), but not for the case $n = 1$ (in which case the result is the empty set for MXUNION but *s1* for XUNION).

Finally, here for the record are relational analogs of the foregoing definitions:

- *(Dyadic XUNION)*[11] Let relations *r1* and *r2* be of the same type *T*. Then the expression *r1* XUNION *r2* denotes a relation of type *T* with body the set of all tuples *t* such that *t* appears in one but not both of *r1* and *r2*.

- *(N-adic XUNION)* Let relations *r1, r2, ..., rn* ($n \geqslant 0$) all be of the same type *T*. Then the expression XUNION{*r1,r2,...,rn*} denotes a relation of type *T* with body the set of all tuples *t* such that *t* appears in exactly *m* of *r1, r2, ..., rn,* where *m* is odd (and possibly different for different tuples *t*). *Note:* If $n = 0$, (a) some syntactic mechanism, not shown here, is needed to specify the pertinent type *T* and (b) the result is the empty relation of that type.

- *(N-adic MXUNION)* Let relations *r1, r2, ..., rn* ($n \geqslant 0$) all be of the same type *T*. Then the expression XUNION{*r1,r2,...,rn*} denotes a relation of type *T* with body the set of all tuples *t* such that *t* appears in at least one but not all of *r1, r2, ..., rn*. *Note:* If $n = 0$, (a) some syntactic mechanism, not shown here, is needed to specify the pertinent type *T* and (b) the result is the empty relation of that type.

CONCLUDING REMARKS

So where do we go from here? In **Tutorial D,** as you can see from Chapter 11, we do support *n*-adic AND, OR, UNION, D_UNION, JOIN, INTERSECT, and TIMES—but these operators are comparatively noncontroversial. With respect to the more controversial ones, we've plumped for supporting *n*-adic COMPOSE, XOR (not MXOR), and XUNION (not MXUNION); but these decisions are perhaps subject to change. After all, as you'll have gathered by now, the matters discussed in this chapter are surprisingly subtle, and more than a little confusing. Perhaps that's why logic texts (so far as I know) concentrate on dyadic connectives only—or monadic and dyadic connectives only, rather—and have little or nothing to say about possible triadic, tetradic, etc., connectives. I don't know. I'm not a logician.

---

[11] Dyadic MXUNION is the same operator, of course.

Chapter 16

Toward an Industrial Strength Dialect of Tutorial D

This [is] known as the Industrial Revelation.
—W. C. Sellar and R. J. Yeatman: *1066 and All That*

Reference [6] includes a fairly formal, though certainly not rigorous, definition of a database programming language called **Tutorial D**. Here's a lightly edited quote from that reference:

> **Tutorial D** is a computationally complete programming language with fully integrated database functionality. It is deliberately not meant to be industrial strength; rather, it is a "toy" language, whose principal purpose is to serve as a teaching vehicle ... Many features that would be required in an industrial strength language are intentionally omitted.

The first published definition of **Tutorial D** appeared in 1998, in reference [4]. Since that time, the language has received extensive use, both in technical writings and in live classes, as a basis for teaching and exploring database concepts in general and type theory concepts in particular. Experience with the language has also been gained from the use of certain prototype implementations, especially *Rel* [8]. Partly as a result of this history, the language has evolved over the years (a number of differences can be observed between the versions defined in references [4], [5], [6], and [7]). The purpose of the present chapter is to propose a series of further changes—more precisely, to propose a series of changes that we believe can serve to move the language a little closer to what might be called **Industrial D**. Note, however, that those proposals, though stated in what follows as matters of fact, are indeed only proposals; more discussion is needed (probably) before they can be cast in concrete, as it were.

Note: The syntax rules shown in what follows are based for the most part not on those given in reference [6] but on the revised version of those rules to be found in reference [7]. Some of the rules are repeated from this latter reference unchanged in order to make the present chapter a little more self-contained. You can assume that anything included in **Tutorial D** as defined in reference [7] that's not revised here is meant to be incorporated into **Industrial D** unchanged. Note too that (like **Tutorial D** as defined in reference [7]) **Industrial D** as described herein includes no support for type inheritance. Possible extensions to provide such support are described in Chapter 21 of this book.

BUILT IN SCALAR DATA TYPES

INT, RAT, and BOOL are introduced as system defined synonyms for the built in scalar data type names INTEGER, RATIONAL, and BOOLEAN, respectively. *Note:* These synonyms are already included in the dialect of **Tutorial D** defined in reference [7].

NAMED CONSTANTS

The ability to define named constants is introduced. *Note:* We treat the terms *constant* and *value* as synonymous. Thus, there's a logical difference between a constant and a literal; a literal isn't a constant but, rather, a symbol—sometimes referred to as a "self defining" symbol—that denotes a constant (or value). There's also a logical difference between a constant and a *named* constant; a constant is a value, but a named constant is a holder for such a value (in other words, it's like a variable, except that its value can't be changed). That said, however, for the remainder of this discussion we take the term *constant* to mean a named constant specifically. For syntactic purposes, it's convenient to distinguish scalar, tuple, and relation constants. Here's the syntax for a defining a scalar constant:[1]

```
<scalar const def>
    ::=   CONST <scalar const name> INIT ( <scalar const exp> )
```

The declared type and value of the scalar constant are the declared type and value, respectively, of the specified *<scalar const exp>*.

```
<scalar const exp>
    ::=   <scalar exp>
```

The *<scalar exp>* must not include any variable references, at any level of nesting. (In practice, we would usually expect it to be a literal.)

Tuple and relation constants are defined analogously:

```
<tuple const def>
    ::=   CONST <tuple const name> INIT ( <tuple const exp> )
```

The declared type and value of the tuple constant are the declared type and value, respectively, of the specified *<tuple const exp>*.

```
<tuple const exp>
    ::=   <tuple exp>
```

The *<tuple exp>* must not include any variable references, at any level of nesting. (In practice, we would usually expect it to be a literal.)

```
<relation const def>
    ::=   CONST <relation const name> INIT ( <relation const exp> )
```

The declared type and value of the relation constant are the declared type and value, respectively, of the specified *<relation const exp>*.

```
<relation const exp>
    ::=   <relation exp>
```

The *<relation exp>* must not include any variable references, at any level of nesting. (In practice, we would usually expect it to be a literal.)

Here's an example of a relation constant definition:

```
CONST STATES_OF_THE_USA INIT
    ( RELATION { TUPLE { STATE NAME('Alabama') } ,
                 TUPLE { STATE NAME('Alaska' ) } ,
                              ..............
                 TUPLE { STATE NAME('Wyoming') } } ) ;
```

Note: TABLE_DEE and TABLE_DUM are built in relation constants. (They were referred to in reference [7] as relation selector invocations, not constants, but that was because constants as such weren't

---

[1] Observe that we use the keyword INIT for the specification that defines the value of the scalar constant (and likewise for tuple and relation constants, q.v.). Some have questioned the appropriateness of that keyword, since the value in question is obviously more than just the "initial" value of the constant in question. We don't feel strongly about the issue, but as a general rule we'd rather not introduce a new keyword when there's already one available that seems to do the job adequately.

formally defined in that reference.)

For completeness, we also need to add the following:

```
<const ref>
    ::=   <scalar const ref>
        | <nonscalar const ref>

<scalar const ref>
    ::=   <scalar const name>
```

A *<scalar const ref>* is a new form of *<scalar op inv>* (see later).

```
<nonscalar const ref>
    ::=   <tuple const ref>
        | <relation const ref>

<tuple const ref>
    ::=   <tuple const name>
```

A *<tuple const ref>* is a new form of *<tuple op inv>* (see later).

```
<relation const ref>
    ::=   <relation const name> | TABLE_DEE | TABLE_DUM
```

A *<relation const ref>* is a new form of *<relation op inv>* (see later). *Note:* As indicated previously, the names TABLE_DEE and TABLE_DUM can be regarded as built in *<relation const name>*s.

KEYS

The syntax of *<key def>*s is extended to include an optional constraint name:

```
<key def>
    ::=   [ CONSTRAINT <constraint name> ]
            KEY { [ ALL BUT ] <attribute ref commalist> }
```

Details of what it means to omit CONSTRAINT *<constraint name>* remain to be decided, though several obvious possibilities suggest themselves.

In addition, the syntax of *<constraint def>*s is extended to allow a shorthand form involving explicit *<key def>*s or *<foreign key def>*s or both, thus:

```
<constraint def>
    ::=   <bool constraint def>
        | <key or foreign key constraint def>

<bool constraint def>
    ::=   CONSTRAINT <constraint name> <bool exp>

<key or foreign key constraint def>
    ::=   CONSTRAINT <constraint name> <relation exp>
                     <key or foreign key def list>
```

The *<key or foreign key def list>* must not be empty.

```
<key or foreign key def>
    ::=   <key def> | <foreign key def>
```

The semantics of a *<key or foreign key constraint def>* can be explained thus: If that *<relation exp>* were used as the defining expression in the *<virtual relation var def>* for virtual relvar *V* (say), then *V* would be subject to the key and foreign key constraints specified by that *<key or foreign key def list>*. *Note:* For further details of *<foreign key def>*s, see the section immediately following.

FOREIGN KEYS

Following reference [2], the ability to define explicit foreign key constraints is introduced. Here's the syntax:

```
<foreign key def>
    ::=   [ CONSTRAINT <constraint name> ]
            FOREIGN KEY { [ ALL BUT ] <attribute ref commalist> }
                        REFERENCES <relation exp>
```

A *<foreign key def>* can appear wherever a *<key def>* can appear (within a *<constraint spec>* in particular, as noted in the previous section). For complete details of the semantics of *<foreign key def>*s, see reference [2]; here we content ourselves with the following observations.

- No "referential actions" are proposed at this time (apart from NO CASCADE, and even that one can be specified only implicitly).
- The proposed syntax permits the definition, not just of foreign key constraints as traditionally understood, but in fact of inclusion dependencies of arbitrary complexity (a foreign key constraint as traditionally understood is, of course, just a special case of an inclusion dependency). Again, for further explanation see reference [2].
- In reference [7], we proposed that the syntax of statements in general should be extended to allow (e.g.) any number of variables, or any number of types, or any number of constraints, all to be defined or destroyed "simultaneously." Even if **Industrial D** fails to support this idea in its full generality, it will probably at least require the ability to bundle up several relvar definitions into a single statement, in order to support the definition of referential cycles—where a referential cycle consists of a sequence of relvars *R1, R2, ..., Rn* ($n > 0$) such that there's a foreign key constraint from each relvar in the sequence to the next and a foreign key constraint from the last one in the sequence back to the first.
- Note finally that we propose explicit foreign key support even though, as reference [2] shows, foreign keys as conventionally understood are both (a) limited in their applicability and (b) redundant. (Actually, foreign key support as we propose it here is *not* limited in that same sense; however, it is redundant. But then so is key support, come to that.) Be that as it may, the fact is that foreign keys as a concept are firmly embedded in the community psyche, as it were, and to reject them at this stage would simply be foolish.

RELATIONAL READ-ONLY OPERATORS

It's convenient to include here, edited from reference [7], the entire set of production rules for relational expressions. Significant changes are noted at appropriate points.

```
<relation exp>
    ::=   <relation with exp> | <relation nonwith exp>

<relation with exp>
    ::=   WITH ( <name intro commalist> ) : <relation exp>
```

```
<name intro>
    ::=   <introduced name> := <exp>

<relation nonwith exp>
    ::=   <relation op inv> | ( <relation exp> )

<relation op inv>
    ::=   <relation const ref>
        | <relation var ref>
        | <other relation op inv>
```

This production rule is changed to reflect (a) the fact that named constants have been introduced and (b) the fact that constant references and variable references are both explicitly regarded as (read-only) operator invocations. *Note:* Analogous changes are required to *<scalar op inv>* and *<tuple op inv>* as well but are omitted here.

```
<relation const ref>
    ::=   <relation const name> | TABLE_DEE | TABLE_DUM
```

We include this production rule here for completeness, even though it merely repeats one from the section "Named Constants."

```
<relation var ref>
    ::=   <relation var name>

<other relation op inv>
    ::=   <user op inv> | <built in relation op inv>
```

The declared type of the operator invoked by *<user op inv>* must be some relation type.

```
<built in relation op inv>
    ::=   <relation selector inv>
        | <THE_ op inv>
        | <attribute extractor inv>
        | <other built in relation op inv>

<relation selector inv>
    ::=   RELATION [ <heading> ] { <tuple exp commalist> }

<THE_ op inv>
    ::=   <THE_ op name> ( <scalar exp> )
```

We include this production rule here for completeness, even though we expect most *<THE_ op inv>*s in practice to denote scalar values. An analogous remark also applies to the production rule for *<attribute extractor inv>*, which follows immediately.

```
<attribute extractor inv>
    ::=   ATTR_FROM ( <tuple exp> , <attribute ref> )
```

In reference [7], an *<attribute extractor inv>* took the form *<attribute ref>* FROM *<tuple ref>*. Here, by contrast, we propose that all relational read-only operators be expressed in a functional or prefix style;[2] hence the

---

[2] Presumably it would be possible to retain support for the **Tutorial D** style as well, if sufficient cause were shown.

revised syntax for <*attribute op inv*>, and analogous revisions to all of the following: <*rename*>, <*restrict*> (i.e., <*where*>, in reference [7]), <*project*>, <*extend*>, <*wrap*>, <*unwrap*>, <*group*>, <*ungroup*>, <*tclose*>, <*rank*>, <*minus*>, <*matching*>, and <*not matching*> (as will be seen). *Note:* We recognize that this approach is subject to the "LISP syndrome" criticism,[3] but we believe the advantages of a consistent style outweigh the disadvantages in an industrial strength language. Also, the prefix approach means that monadic, dyadic, and *n*-adic operators can all use the same general style. It also means we have no need to specify any precedence rules for the operators under discussion.[4]

```
<other built in relation op inv>
    ::=   <monadic other built in relation op inv>
        | <dyadic other built in relation op inv>
        | <n-adic other built in relation op inv>
```

The set of "other built in relation operators" (a) no longer includes DIVIDEBY and SUMMARIZE (see the section "Image Relations," later) but (b) does now include RANK and TIMES, q.v. *Note:* In fact, TIMES is already included in **Tutorial D** as defined in reference [7].

```
<monadic other built in relation op inv>
    ::=   <rename> | <restrict> | <project> | <extend>
        | <wrap> | <unwrap> | <group> | <ungroup>
        | <tclose> | <rank>

<rename>
    ::=   RENAME ( <relation exp> , { <renaming commalist> } )

<renaming>
    ::=   <attribute ref> AS <introduced name>
        | PREFIX <character string literal>
                 AS <character string literal>
        | SUFFIX <character string literal>
                 AS <character string literal>

<restrict>
    ::=   RESTRICT ( <relation exp> , <bool exp> )
```

RESTRICT might not be the best keyword here, since the <*bool exp*> isn't limited to being a restriction condition as formally defined.[5] Other possibilities include WHERE (but WHERE isn't a verb); SELECT (but SELECT is usually used in relational contexts as a synonym for RESTRICT and thus suffers from exactly the same drawbacks, and there's the conflict with SELECT in SQL to worry about too, and in any case we're already using the term *selector* with a very different meaning); FIND; LOCATE; and probably others besides.

```
<project>
    ::=   PROJECT ( <relation exp> ,
                 { [ ALL BUT ] <attribute ref commalist> } )
```

---

[3] LISP = Lots of Irritating Single Parentheses.

[4] This isn't to say we do have such a need with the **Tutorial D** style.

[5] Formally, a restriction condition is a boolean expression in which all attribute references identify attributes of the same relation and there aren't any relvar references.

In reference [7], a *<project>* took the form *<relation exp>* {*<attribute ref commalist>*} or *<relation exp>* {ALL BUT *<attribute ref commalist>*}, and the operator was defined to have the highest precedence of all of the relational read-only operators. Even with that precedence rule, however, we found that not having a keyword led to certain potential ambiguities and other syntactic difficulties; with hindsight, in fact, we recognize that not having a keyword was always a mistake (even though we could claim merely to be following the style Codd used in reference [1]).

```
<extend>
    ::=   EXTEND ( <relation exp> ,
                 { <attribute assign commalist> } )

<wrap>
    ::=   WRAP ( <relation exp> , ( <wrapping> ) )
```

The inner parentheses here might not be necessary in practice; we include them partly in case it might ever be decided to extend *<wrap>* to allow a *<wrapping commalist>*, in which case we would want it to be clear that the individual *<wrapping>*s were to be exceuted in sequence as written, not in parallel. Analogous remarks apply to *<unwrap>*, *<group>*, and *<ungroup>* (see below).

```
<wrapping>
    ::=   { [ ALL BUT ] <attribute ref commalist> }
                                    AS <introduced name>

<unwrap>
    ::=   UNWRAP ( <relation exp> , ( <unwrapping> ) )

<unwrapping>
    ::=   <attribute ref>

<group>
    ::=   GROUP ( <relation exp> , ( <grouping> ) )

<grouping>
    ::=   { [ ALL BUT ] <attribute ref commalist> }
                                    AS <introduced name>

<ungroup>
    ::=   UNGROUP ( <relation exp> , ( <ungrouping> ) )

<ungrouping>
    ::=   <attribute ref>

<tclose>
    ::=   TCLOSE ( <relation exp> )

<rank>
    ::=   RANK ( <relation exp> ,
                 ( <order item commalist> ) AS <attribute name> )
```

RANK is discussed in reference [6]—see Chapter 10, RM Very Strong Suggestion 5 (quota queries).

```
<dyadic other built in relation op inv>
    ::=   <minus> | <included minus> | <matching> | <not matching>
```

```
<minus>
    ::=   MINUS ( <relation exp> , <relation exp> )

<included minus>
    ::=   I_MINUS ( <relation exp> , <relation exp> )

<matching>
    ::=   MATCHING ( <relation exp> , <relation exp> )
```

We propose that the keyword SEMIJOIN be dropped.

```
<not matching>
    ::=   NOT_MATCHING ( <relation exp> , <relation exp> )
```

We propose that the keyword SEMIMINUS be dropped.

```
<n-adic other built in relation op inv>
    ::=   <union> | <disjoint union> | <intersect> | <join>
        | <times> | <xunion> | <compose>
```

Dyadic versions of these operators no longer have their own special case (infix) syntax.

```
<union>
    ::=   UNION [ <heading> ] { <relation exp commalist> }

<disjoint union>
    ::=   D_UNION [ <heading> ] { <relation exp commalist> }

<intersect>
    ::=   INTERSECT [ <heading> ] { <relation exp commalist> }

<join>
    ::=   JOIN { <relation exp commalist> }

<times>
    ::=   TIMES { <relation exp commalist> }

<xunion>
    ::=   XUNION { <relation exp commalist> }

<compose>
    ::=   COMPOSE { <relation exp commalist> }
```

IMAGE RELATIONS

Following reference [3], image relations are introduced. Here's a definition:

- Let relations *r1* and *r2* be joinable (i.e., such that attributes with the same name are of the same type); let *t1* be a tuple of *r1;* let *t2* be a tuple of *r2* that has the same values for those common attributes as tuple *t1* does; let relation *r3* be that restriction of *r2* that contains all and only such tuples *t2;* and let relation *r4* be the projection of *r3* that removes those common attributes. Then *r4* is the image relation (with respect to *r2*) corresponding to *t1*.

  Here's an example that makes use of image relations:

  ```
  RESTRICT ( S , ( !!(SP) ) { P# } = P { P# } )
  ```

This example is based on the familiar suppliers-and-parts database. *Explanation:*

- First of all, the roles of *r1* and *r2* from the definition are being played by the relations that are the current values of relvar S and relvar SP, respectively.

- Next, we can imagine the boolean expression that denotes the second RESTRICT argument being evaluated for each tuple *t1* in *r1* (i.e., each tuple in relvar S) in turn.

- Consider one such tuple, say that for supplier S*x*. For that tuple, then, the expression !!(SP) (where the symbol "!!" is pronounced "bang bang" or "double bang") denotes the corresponding image relation *r4* within *r2;* in other words, it denotes the set of part-number/quantity pairs within SP for parts supplied by that supplier S*x*. (Formally, the expression !!(SP) is an *image relation reference.*)

- The expression (!!(SP)){P#}—i.e., the projection of the image relation on {P#}—thus denotes the set of part numbers for parts supplied by supplier S*x*.

- The expression overall (i.e., RESTRICT(...)) thus denotes suppliers from relvar S for whom that set of part numbers is equal to the set of all part numbers in the projection of relvar P on {P#}. In other words, it represents the query "Get suppliers who supply all parts" (speaking a little loosely).

Reference [3] shows that any expression involving either DIVIDEBY or SUMMARIZE is logically equivalent to another expression—usually more succinct, and usually easier to understand—involving image relations instead. The DIVIDEBY and SUMMARIZE operators, as such, can therefore be dropped. *Note:* Detailed arguments in favor of dropping these operators can be found in reference [3] and aren't worth repeating here.

Here now is a more formal definition. Let *ry* be a relational expression; then the *<image relation ref>* !!(*ry*) is also a relational expression, and it denotes a certain image relation.[6] However, it can appear only in the following contexts:[7]

- The *<bool exp>* within a *<restrict>*

- The *<bool exp>* within the RESTRICT form of a *<restricted target>* (see the section "Relational Update Operators," later)

- An *<attribute assign>* within an *<extend>*

Consider the *<restrict>* RESTRICT (*rx,bx*). Let *r* be the relation denoted by *rx,* and let the *<image relation ref>* !!(*ry*) directly appear in *bx* (where *directly appear* means that !!(*ry*) appears within *bx* as such and not within some *<restrict>* or *<extend>* contained within *bx*). Let *r'* be the relation denoted by *ry; r* and *r'* must be joinable. Let their common attributes be *A1, A2, ..., An* ($n \geqslant 0$). Then the *<image relation ref>* !!(*ry*) is defined to be equivalent to the expression

---

[6] Technically speaking, the expression !!(*ry*) is an example of an *open expression* (see Chapter 11). *Note:* In simple cases—in particular, if *ry* consists of a simple *<relation var ref>*—the parentheses surrounding *ry* shouldn't be necessary.

[7] Another possible context, not discussed in detail here, is the expression whose values are to be aggregated in an aggregate operator invocation (so long as the expression in question is one that's required to be relation valued, as in, e.g., the aggregate operator invocation UNION (S, !!SP)).

```
PROJECT
 ( MATCHING
   ( r' , RELATION { TUPLE { A1 A1 , A2 A2 , ... , An An } } ) ,
                                  { ALL BUT A1 , A2 , ... , An } )
```

Next, consider the *<relation delete>* DELETE RESTRICT (*R,bx*) and the *<relation update>* UPDATE RESTRICT (*R,bx*) {...}—again, see the section "Relational Update Operators"—and let *r* be the relation denoted by *R*. The remaining definitions in the previous paragraph then apply unchanged.

Finally, consider the *<extend>* EXTEND (*rx,*{*A* := *x*}). Let *r* be the relation denoted by *rx,* and let the *<image relation ref>* !!(*ry*) directly appear in *x* (where *directly appear* means that !!(*ry*) appears within *x* as such and not within some *<restrict>* or *<extend>* within *x*). Again, then, the remaining definitions in the previous paragraph but one apply unchanged. *Note:* It follows (without going into a lot of detail) that *<image relation ref>*s are also permitted within the expression on the right side of an *<attribute assign>* within a *<relation update>*, since *<relation update>* is defined in terms of EXTEND.

RELATIONAL UPDATE OPERATORS

It's convenient to include here, edited from reference [7], the entire set of production rules for *<relation assign>*s. Significant changes are noted at appropriate points (actually there's only one).

```
<relation assign>
    ::=   <relation target> := <relation exp>
        | <relation insert>
        | <relation d_insert>
        | <relation delete>
        | <relation i_delete>
        | <relation update>

<relation target>
    ::=   <relation var ref>
        | <relation THE_ pv ref>

<relation THE_ pv ref>
    ::=   <THE_ pv name> ( <scalar target> )

<relation insert>
    ::=   INSERT <relation target> <relation exp>

<relation d_insert>
    ::=   D_INSERT <relation target> <relation exp>

<relation delete>
    ::=   DELETE <relation target> <relation exp>
        | DELETE <restricted target>
```

The syntax of the second format of *<relation delete>* in reference [7] was DELETE *<relation target>* [WHERE *<bool exp>*]; the proposed change is for consistency with the proposed change to *<restrict>*. *Note:* Analogous remarks apply to *<relation update>*, q.v.

```
<restricted target>
    ::=   <relation target>
        | RESTRICT ( <relation target> , <bool exp> )
```

```
<relation i_delete>
    ::=   I_DELETE <relation target> <relation exp>

<relation update>
    ::=   UPDATE <restricted target> :
               { <attribute assign commalist> }
```

OTHER CHANGES

Several of the proposed changes to the syntax of relational operators imply (for consistency, at least) analogous changes to the syntax of tuple operators also. We omit the details here, except for the case of <*tuple extractor inv*>s, which is revised as follows:

```
<tuple extractor inv>
    ::=   TUPLE_FROM ( <relation exp> )
```

We also propose two new boolean operators, DISJOINT and IDENTICAL:

- The boolean expression DISJOINT {<*relation exp commalist*>} returns TRUE if and only if no two of the relations represented by the <*relation exp*>s in the <*relation exp commalist*> have any tuples in common.
- The boolean expression IDENTICAL {<*exp commalist*>} returns TRUE if and only if no two of the values represented by the <*exp*>s in the <*exp commalist*> are all equal. We remark that this operator might be thought of as an *n*-adic version of "=".

FURTHER POSSIBILITIES

In this section we simply list a few additional potential changes or extensions that might be—in some cases, certainly are—worthy of further consideration.

- *Overloading:* **Tutorial D** currently uses the same syntax for most tuple operators as it does for their relational counterparts. It might be better to introduce a systematic new nomenclature for those tuple operators (e.g., T_UNION instead of UNION).
- *Transition constraints: The Third Manifesto* currently includes the following as RM Very Strong Suggestion 4:

  > **D** should support **transition constraints**—i.e., constraints on the transitions that a given database can make from one value to another.

  Some might feel it high time that this suggestion be acted on, in **Industrial D** if not **Tutorial D**.
- *Possrep component name uniqueness:* It's a slight weakness of **Tutorial D** in its present form that (to quote from reference [7]) "no two distinct <*possrep def*>s within the same <*user scalar type def*> can include a component with the same <*possrep component name*>." It might be desirable to try and find a way to work around this restriction.
- *Authorization:* An industrial strength database language clearly needs an appropriate set of authorization features.
- *Exception handling:* Finally, an industrial strength language also clearly needs an appropriate set of exception handling features.

REFERENCES AND BIBLIOGRAPHY

1. E. F. Codd: "Relational Completeness of Data Base Sublanguages," *Data Base Systems: Courant Computer Science Symposia Series 6*. Englewood Cliffs, N.J.: Prentice-Hall (1972).

2. C. J. Date: "Inclusion Dependencies and Foreign Keys" (Chapter 13 of the present book).

3. C. J. Date: "Image Relations" (Chapter 14 of the present book).

4. C. J. Date and Hugh Darwen: *Foundation for Object/Relational Databases: The Third Manifesto* (1st edition). Reading, Mass.: Addison-Wesley (1998).

5. C. J. Date and Hugh Darwen: *Foundation for Future Database Systems: The Third Manifesto* (2nd edition). Reading, Mass.: Addison-Wesley (2000).

6. C. J. Date and Hugh Darwen: *Databases, Types, and the Relational Model: The Third Manifesto* (3rd edition). Boston, Mass.: Addison-Wesley (2006).

7. C. J. Date and Hugh Darwen: "**Tutorial D**" (Chapter 11 of the present book).

8. Dave Voorhis: *Rel*. *http://dbappbuilder.sourceforge.net/rel.html*.

Chapter 17

A Remark on Prenex Normal Form

Logic, n. The art of thinking and reasoning in strict accordance with the limitations and incapacities of the human misunderstanding

—Ambrose Bierce: *The Devil's Dictionary*

I wrote this chapter for my own benefit as much as anyone's. What I wanted to do was try and get clear in my own mind an issue in logic that I'd been worrying about, a trifle vaguely perhaps, for quite some time. The issue in question is explained in the chapter, of course; before I get to that explanation, however, I must make it clear—though I fear it'll soon become obvious enough—that I'm not a logician myself. One consequence of this fact is that my use of certain terms might not always accord with the way the logicians use them, though I believe it does accord with the way they're used in the database world. At any rate, I've tried to define what I mean by terms whenever I think some problem of interpretation might otherwise occur—but it's only fair to warn you up front to be on your guard, especially if you're a logician rather than a database person. *Caveat lector.*

Note: The reason this chapter is included in this part of the book is as follows. **Tutorial D** (which is, of course, only one possible **D**) is based on relational algebra; but a **D** based on relational calculus might be more to some people's taste, and the observations in this chapter could be relevant to the design of such a **D**.

BACKGROUND

One of Codd's foundational papers on the relational model (first published in 1971) was titled "Relational Completeness of Data Base Sublanguages" [1]. In that paper, Codd did three things:

1. He defined a relational calculus (sometimes known more specifically as the tuple calculus, because its variables range over relations—which is to say, over certain specified sets of tuples—and thus denote tuples in those relations).

2. He defined a relational algebra, consisting of the following operations: extended cartesian product, union, intersection, difference, θ-restriction, projection, natural join (also θ-join), and division.

3. He defined a notion he called *relational completeness*—briefly, a language is relationally complete if and only if it's as expressive as the tuple calculus—and he proved his algebra was complete in this sense. *Note:* Relational completeness mustn't be confused with completeness in any other sense, of course (e.g., computational completeness).

With regard to the last of these points in particular, Codd proved the completeness of his algebra by giving an algorithm—"Codd's reduction algorithm"—for translating an arbitrary tuple calculus expression into a logically equivalent algebraic expression (the completeness of the algebra being, of course, a logical consequence of the existence of such an algorithm).

Now, I mention these matters mostly just by way of preamble. What I want to focus on in this chapter is the very first step in Codd's reduction algorithm, which reads as follows:

> Convert *V* to prenex normal form (if it is not already in this form).

V here refers to what can be thought of, at least for present purposes, as "the predicate in the WHERE clause." For example, consider the following tuple calculus query against the usual suppliers-and-parts database ("Get suppliers who supply at least one red part"):[1]

```
SX  RANGES OVER { S }  ;
SPX RANGES OVER { SP } ;
PX  RANGES OVER { P }  ;

SX WHERE EXISTS PX ( PX.COLOR = 'Red' AND
                     EXISTS SPX ( SPX.S# = SX.S# AND
                                  SPX.P# = PX.P# ) )
```

In this example, the predicate *V* consists of the entire expression "EXISTS PX (...)" following the keyword WHERE. *Note:* I'll assume these same *range variables*—SX, SPX, and PX—throughout my examples in this chapter. Moreover, I won't bother to repeat their definitions in subsequent examples, letting the foregoing definitions do duty for all.

PRENEX NORMAL FORM

Loosely, a predicate is in prenex normal form if and only if the quantifiers all appear at the beginning; more precisely, it's in prenex normal form (hereinafter abbreviated PNF) if and only if (a) it's quantifier free or (b) it's of the form EXISTS *x* (*p*) or FORALL *x* (*p*), where *p* is in PNF in turn. Thus, a PNF predicate takes the form

```
Q1 x1 ( Q2 x2 ( ... ( Qn xn ( q ) ) ... ) )
```

where (a) $n \geqslant 0$, (b) each of *Q1, Q2, ..., Qn* is either EXISTS or FORALL and (c) the predicate *q*—which is sometimes called the *matrix*—is quantifier free. Note in particular that *q* is within the scope, as it were, of each of *Q1, Q2, ..., Qn*. Thus, the predicate *V* in the example in the previous section isn't in PNF—but it's logically equivalent to the following one, which is:

```
EXISTS PX ( EXISTS SPX ( PX.COLOR = 'Red' AND
                         SPX.S# = SX.S# AND
                         SPX.P# = PX.P# ) )
```

Note: One small advantage of PNF is that it lets us drop some unnecessary parentheses. For example, the foregoing example can be unambiguously abbreviated to:

```
EXISTS PX EXISTS SPX ( PX.COLOR = 'Red' AND
                       SPX.S# = SX.S# AND
                       SPX.P# = PX.P# )
```

More generally, the PNF predicate

```
Q1 x1 ( Q2 x2 ( ... ( Qn xn ( q ( x1 , x2 , ... , xn ) ) ) ... ) )
```

(where *q*(*x1*,*x2*,...,*xn*) is a predicate in which *x1, x2, ..., xn* occur as free variables)[2] can be unambiguously abbreviated to:

---

[1] The syntax I use for the tuple calculus in this chapter is defined in reference [3].

[2] An occurrence of a variable *x* in a predicate is free if and only if it isn't bound by a quantifier. For example, the occurrences of *x* are all free in the predicates $x > 3$, EXISTS *y* ($x > 3$), and FORALL *y* ($y > x$). By contrast, the occurrences of *x* are all bound in the predicates EXISTS *x* ($x > 3$) and FORALL *x* ($x > 3$), and *x* occurs both bound and free in the predicate FORALL *x* ($x > 0$) AND $x > 3$.

```
Q1 x1 Q2 x2 ... Qn xn ( q ( x1 , x2 , ... , xn ) )
```

TRANSFORMING PREDICATES

There are many identities, or laws of transformation, that can be used in the process of converting a given predicate into another that's logically equivalent to the given one. Here are a few of them (I've numbered them for purposes of subsequent reference). *Notation:* In what follows, an expression of the form *p* denotes an arbitrary predicate; an expression of the form *p*(*x*) denotes a predicate in which *x* occurs as a free variable.

```
1.   NOT ( NOT ( p ) )        ≡  p

2.   IF ( p ) THEN ( q )      ≡  ( NOT ( p ) ) OR ( q )

3.   FORALL x ( p )           ≡  NOT ( EXISTS x ( NOT ( p ) ) )

4.   ( EXISTS x ( p ) ) OR ( EXISTS x ( q ) )
                              ≡  EXISTS x ( ( p ) OR ( q ) )

5.   EXISTS x ( p ( x ) )     ≡  EXISTS y ( p ( y ) )
```

Note: I'm assuming in Identity No. 5 that the variables *x* and *y* both have the same range.[3]

———♦♦♦♦♦———

Let's look at a more complicated example. Suppose we're given the following predicate:

```
IF ( FORALL x ( x > 3 ) ) THEN ( EXISTS y ( y = 0 ) )
```

(The variables *x* and *y* here range over—let's agree—the set of all integers; in other words, they're of type INTEGER.) Let's see if we can convert this predicate into a PNF equivalent. We can begin by getting rid of the logical implication (IF ... THEN ...), using Identity No. 2. The given predicate becomes:

```
( NOT ( FORALL x ( x > 3 ) ) ) OR ( EXISTS y ( y = 0 ) )
```

Next, we apply Identity No. 3:

```
( NOT ( NOT ( EXISTS x ( NOT ( x > 3 ) ) ) ) )
                                   OR ( EXISTS y ( y = 0 ) )
```

Then Identity No. 1:

```
( EXISTS x ( NOT ( x > 3 ) ) ) OR ( EXISTS y ( y = 0 ) )
```

Identity No. 5 gives:

```
( EXISTS x ( NOT ( x > 3 ) ) ) OR ( EXISTS x ( x = 0 ) )
```

Finally, using Identity No. 4:

```
( EXISTS x ( ( NOT ( x > 3 ) ) OR ( x = 0 ) ) )
```

This formulation is in PNF, but we can simplify it slightly by dropping a few unnecessary parentheses:

```
EXISTS x ( NOT ( x > 3 ) OR x = 0 )
```

---

[3] A logician would say they both range over the same *domain*—but "domain" is a rather loaded word in the database world.

Note: I'm assuming here that NOT and "=" are both of higher precedence than OR. In practice, we make several such assumptions in order to reduce the number of parentheses that would otherwise be needed.

THE PNF CONJECTURE

Now let me get back to the reduction algorithm, and in particular to that first step ("convert the predicate to PNF"). Clearly, there's an assumption here that PNF is always achievable—that is, given an arbitrary predicate *p*, there always exists a predicate *q* that's logically equivalent to *p* and is in PNF. I'll refer to that assumption as *the PNF conjecture*. So the obvious question is: Is that assumption justified? In other words, is the conjecture valid?

Well, let's consider another query on the suppliers-and-parts database—"Get suppliers who supply at least one part or are located in Athens." Here's a tuple calculus formulation:

```
SX WHERE EXISTS SPX ( SPX.S# = SX.S# ) OR SX.CITY = 'Athens'
```

Suppose for the sake of the example that (a) there's just one supplier in Athens, supplier S5, but (b) there are no shipments at all at this time—that is, relvar SP is currently empty. Then the foregoing tuple calculus expression clearly returns just supplier S5 (more precisely, it evaluates to a relation containing just one tuple, viz., the tuple for supplier S5, extracted from the current value of relvar S).

Observe now that the predicate in the WHERE clause in the foregoing example isn't in PNF. Can it be converted into a PNF equivalent? Well, noting that SPX doesn't occur as a free variable in the predicate SX.CITY = 'Athens' (SX does, but not SPX), we can appeal to another logical identity (Identity No. 6):

6. *p* ≡ EXISTS *x* (*p*)

Note: This identity does assume that the variable *x* doesn't occur free in *p*. I'll have more to say about it in the next section. Anyway, using this identity, we can transform the query into the following:

```
SX WHERE EXISTS SPX ( SPX.S# = SX.S# ) OR
         EXISTS SPX ( SX.CITY = 'Athens' )
```

Then using Identity No. 4:

```
SX WHERE EXISTS SPX ( SPX.S# = SX.S# OR SX.CITY = 'Athens' )
```

And the predicate here is in PNF. But the expression overall clearly isn't equivalent to the original! Under the same assumptions as before—just one supplier (S5) in Athens and no shipments at all—the original expression returns just supplier S5 (as previously discussed), but the transformed "equivalent" returns an empty result. (Why? Because there's no value of the range variable that can make the predicate in parentheses evaluate to TRUE.) So the transformation process has broken down. So what exactly is going on?

SHEDDING SOME LIGHT (?)

Now, the fact that the original expression and the transformed version aren't equivalent in the foregoing example doesn't mean the original doesn't have a PNF equivalent—"absence of evidence isn't evidence of absence," as somebody or other once said—but it does at least raise the possibility that the PNF conjecture might not be valid after all, at least in the database context. With that example as motivation, therefore, I began to explore the literature (the literature of logic and database formal methods, I mean). And I found several claims to the effect that the PNF conjecture was true, and several putative proofs of that fact. On investigating further, however, I discovered that those proofs all seemed to rely, either directly or indirectly, on the validity of Identity No. 6, which I spell out again here for convenience (but in prose this time):

If *p* is a predicate in which *x* doesn't occur as a free variable, then *p* is equivalent to EXISTS *x* (*p*); in other words, given such a predicate *p*, we can "harmlessly" make it subject to an existential quantification as indicated.

My first reaction to this discovery was that the alleged identity was simply not valid (in fact, obviously not). After all, consider the extreme case in which *p* is just TRUE (which is certainly a predicate in which *x* doesn't occur as a free variable). The alleged identity becomes:

```
TRUE  ≡  EXISTS x ( TRUE )
```

But suppose now, as we did with the range variable SPX in the example in the previous section, that "there aren't any *x*'s"—i.e., suppose the variable *x* ranges over an empty set. Then EXISTS *x* (*p*) must evaluate to FALSE for all possible predicates *p*, because there's just no value of *x* that can make *p* evaluate to TRUE. In particular, EXISTS *x* (TRUE) is FALSE if there aren't any *x*'s, and the identity reduces to the manifestly absurd form—

```
TRUE  ≡  FALSE
```

—which is in fact a contradiction. (A contradiction in logic is a predicate that's guaranteed to evaluate to FALSE no matter what values are substituted for its free variables.)

Well, to cut a long story short, I gave up on the literature at this point and starting calling various logician friends. And I'm glad to be able to report that one of them, Ron Fagin, resolved the mystery for me:[4]

In logic, it's normal to stipulate that the set over which some given variable ranges not be empty.

Now, this requirement is perhaps reasonable in logic in general, because logic in general is usually *unsorted.* To explain this remark, I first need to explain that *sorted* logic is a form of logic in which the values that are the subject of the logic are divided into "sorts," or what we in the database world would more usually call types. But logic texts generally pay little or no attention to types; instead, they deal with unsorted logic, which effectively means they assume that everything is of the same type. That single type is referred to as *the universe* (or *domain*) *of discourse*—and it wouldn't make much sense for the universe of discourse to be empty, because if it were, then the entire logic would effectively be vacuous.[5]

In strong contrast to the foregoing, in the database world we use sorted logic almost exclusively; in particular, range variables in the tuple calculus—at least in the usual formulation of that calculus—are always of some "sort," where the available "sorts" are defined as follows. Let *DB* be a database. Then:

- If *R* is a relvar in *DB* and *R* is of "sort" (type) RELATION {*H*},[6] then a range variable used in connection with *DB* can be of "sort" (type) TUPLE {*H*}.
- A range variable used in connection with *DB* cannot be of any other "sort" (type).

Moreover, it's perfectly reasonable—in fact, it's not at all unusual—in the database world for the range corresponding to some "sort" to be empty. In the case of suppliers and parts, for example, if we define SPX to be

---

[4] Actually I did subsequently find the solution for myself, but only after doing rather more searching of the literature than it seems to me should have been necessary.

[5] Ron Fagin informs me that the real reason for requiring the universe of discourse to be nonempty isn't that the logic would otherwise be vacuous; rather, it's to guarantee that certain predicates—for example (and in particular), the predicate IF FORALL *x* (*p*(*x*)) THEN EXISTS *x* (*p*(*x*))—are tautologies. (A tautology in logic is a predicate that's guaranteed to evaluate to TRUE no matter what values are substituted for its free variables.)

[6] I adopt the notation of *The Third Manifesto* [3] for definiteness.

a range variable ranging over SP, what we mean is:

- First, SPX is of type TUPLE {*H*}, where {*H*} is the heading of relvar SP. Second, the legal values of SPX at any given time—i.e., the range of that variable at that time—are the tuples (necessarily of type TUPLE {*H*}) appearing in relvar SP at that time.

And as we already know, it's certainly possible that relvar SP might be empty at the time in question.

WHAT DO WE CONCLUDE?

So where does all this leave us? First of all, we've seen that a crucial assumption underlying the PNF conjecture isn't valid in the database world. It follows that the PNF conjecture itself might not be valid in the database world, either; that is, it might not always be possible to replace an arbitrary predicate by a logically equivalent one in PNF. Now, I'm not sure this point matters very much in itself; as I've written elsewhere, PNF is no more logically correct than any other form, though it does tend to become a little easier to write with practice—at least when a PNF version exists, I suppose I should add. But what about formal theorems and the like that rely on the PNF conjecture? Clearly, database researchers concerned with formal methods need to show either (a) that the PNF conjecture is in fact valid after all in the database world or, more probably, (b) that their results don't depend on that conjecture. More specifically, what about Codd's reduction algorithm? Well, I'd be very surprised if Codd's claim to the effect that any expression of the tuple calculus can be converted to an equivalent expression of the algebra turned out not to be valid after all. However, Codd's own proof (or would-be proof, rather) of that fact—viz., the reduction algorithm—appears to be incorrect as stated, because it does rely on the validity of the PNF conjecture in the database world.

> *Aside:* Actually, I believe Codd's reduction algorithm suffers from at least two further defects, both of them also having to do with the possibility of empty ranges. The essence of the matter is this: Let *tcx* be a tuple calculus expression; let the range variables involved in *tcx* be *r1, r2, ..., rn;* and let those variables have ranges *R1, R2, ..., Rn,* respectively. According to my reading of reference [1], then, the reduction algorithm involves forming the cartesian product of those ranges (and, to quote that same reference [1], the result relation is "eventually extracted" from that product). But if any of *R1, R2, ..., Rn* is empty, then that product, and hence the final result, are both empty too. Here are two examples of queries in which such an empty result is definitely incorrect:[7]
>
> 1.
> ```
> SX WHERE EXISTS SPX ( SPX.S# = SX.S# ) OR
>          EXISTS PX ( PX.CITY = SX.CITY )
> ```
>
> Suppose there are no shipments. Then this expression should return suppliers such that there's at least one part in the same city—but the reduction algorithm will yield an empty result.[8]
>
> 2.
> ```
> SX WHERE FORALL PX EXISTS SPX
>                  ( SPX.S# = SX.S# AND SPX.P# = PX.P# )
> ```
>
> Suppose there are no parts. Then this expression should return all suppliers—but again the reduction algorithm will yield an empty result. *End of aside.*

---

[7] You might like to try SQL analogs of these queries on your own favorite SQL product.

[8] Actually I documented this particular flaw some years ago myself in reference [2]. Note that the query discussed earlier in this paper—"Get suppliers who supply at least one part or are located in Athens"—would in fact have been affected by the same error.

ACKNOWLEDGMENTS

I'm grateful to Ron Fagin for a careful review of an earlier draft of this chapter, and in particular for helping me resolve the central issue concerning empty ranges. Thanks too for Hugh Darwen for a helpful suggestion regarding the definition of prenex normal form. Of course, it goes without saying that any remaining errors are my own responsibility.

REFERENCES AND BIBLIOGRAPHY

1. E. F. Codd: "Relational Completeness of Data Base Sublanguages" (presented at Courant Computer Science Symposia Series 6, "Data Base Systems," New York City, N.Y., May 24th-25th, 1971). IBM Research Report RJ987 (March 6th, 1972). Republished in Randall J. Rustin (ed.), *Data Base Systems: Courant Computer Science Symposia Series 6*. Englewood Cliffs, N.J.: Prentice-Hall (1972).

2. C. J. Date: "An Anomaly in Codd's Reduction Algorithm" in C. J. Date and Hugh Darwen, *Relational Database Writings 1989-1991*. Reading, Mass.: Addison-Wesley (1992).

3. C. J. Date: *An Introduction to Database Systems* (8th edition). Boston, Mass.: Addison-Wesley (2004).

4. C. J. Date and Hugh Darwen: *Databases, Types, and the Relational Model: The Third Manifesto* (3rd edition). Boston, Mass.: Addison-Wesley (2006).

Chapter 18

Orthogonal Language Design: How Not to Do It

Simplicity is the unavoidable price which we must pay for reliability.

—C. A. R. Hoare

This brief chapter has to do with the notion of orthogonality. The following remarks are taken from reference [1], though I've reworded them somewhat here:

> Fundamentally, orthogonality means *independence*. The specific application of the term I'm concerned with here originated in the programming languages world, most particularly in the design of the language ALGOL 68 [4]. As we all know, some languages are hard to learn and use and others are easy; well, orthogonality is one of the things that makes the easy ones easy. We say a language is orthogonal if it provides:
>
> a. A comparatively small set of primitive constructs, together with
>
> b. A consistent set of rules for putting those constructs together, and
>
> c. Every possible combination of those constructs is both legal and meaningful (in other words, a deliberate attempt has been made to avoid arbitrary restrictions).
>
> A simple example is provided by numbers in the language PL/I. Numbers in PL/I are represented by numeric expressions, of course, and numeric expressions of arbitrary complexity can be used wherever a numeric value is required—for example, as an array subscript. In other words, the numeric expression and array concepts are clearly independent of one another, and so there should be no special rules regarding the combination of the two, such as (say) a rule to the effect that a numeric expression that specifies a subscript value is allowed to use "+" and "–" but not "*" or "/", or (perhaps less unrealistically) is limited to being a literal and not some more general expression.
>
> A counterexample is provided by numbers in the original version of the SQL standard. Numbers in SQL are (again) represented by numeric expressions, but—prior to SQL:1992, at least—there was at least one context, namely the VALUES clause on INSERT, in which numbers had to be represented by literals instead of by more general expressions.
>
> Here's another counterexample, also taken from SQL. Clearly, the form of the expression that's used to refer to a given column shouldn't depend on the context in which that reference appears; yet (for example) the SALARY column of table EMP is referred to as EMP.SALARY in some contexts, as SALARY (explicitly unqualified) in others, and as an integer, say 3, in still others.
>
> So why is orthogonality important? Orthogonality is desirable because (as can be seen from the examples) the less orthogonal a language is, the more complicated it is and—paradoxically but simultaneously—the less powerful it is. To be more specific:
>
> - The language is more complicated because of the additional rules needed to define and document all of the various exceptions and special cases. And those additional rules make the documentation thicker, the training courses longer, the language harder to teach and learn and describe and remember and use (and so on). In other words, the language gets too big and intellectually unmanageable.
>
> - The language is less powerful because the purpose of those additional rules is precisely to prohibit certain combinations of constructs, and hence (typically, though perhaps not necessarily) to reduce the language's functionality. In other words, there are too many exceptions, special cases, arbitrary restrictions, and surprises (usually of an unpleasant nature).
>
> As reference [3] puts it: "The more orthogonal the design of a language, the fewer exceptions the language

rules require.[1] Fewer exceptions mean a higher degree of regularity in the design, which makes the language easier to learn, read, and understand." And later: "[A] smaller number of primitive constructs and a consistent set of rules for combining them (that is, orthogonality) is much better than simply having a large number of primitives. [The user] can design a solution to a complex problem after learning only a simple set of primitive constructs." Or to quote the ALGOL 68 specification [4]: "Orthogonal design maximizes expressive power while avoiding deleterious superfluities" (this is one of my favorite quotes).

After that preamble, you might care to meditate on the following ... The Microsoft database product SQL Server supports something it calls *indexed views*. *Note:* The remainder of this brief chapter is based on text extracted from (to quote a private email dated March 8th, 2004) "SQL Server Books Online's description of indexed views," and of course it's possible that some of the details have changed since that description was first published. Frankly, however, I don't care if they have; the point of what follows is to describe a situation that should never have been allowed to occur in the first place.

Actually, I hope you're on your guard already: Views are logical, indexes are physical, and the very name of the feature we're talking about should be sufficient to warn us that muddle (or worse) lies ahead. Nor are we disappointed. Here first is the text that introduces the feature:

> Views are also known as virtual tables because the result set returned by the view has the same general form as a table with columns and rows, and views can be referenced the same way as tables in SQL statements. The result set of a standard view is not stored permanently in the database ... If such views are frequently referenced in queries, you can improve performance by creating a unique clustered index on the view. When a unique clustered index is created on a view, the view is executed and the result set is stored in the database in the same way a table with a clustered index is stored ... Creating a clustered index on a view stores the data ...

Now, I could take several pages just deconstructing (not to mention correcting) the foregoing text, but that's not my aim in this chapter.[2] Rather, I just want to focus on "indexed views" as a fairly extreme—though not atypical?—example of lack of orthogonality. The following text is quoted more or less verbatim from the same source as the foregoing introductory extract:

> A view must meet these requirements before you can create a clustered index on it:
>
> - The ANSI_NULLS and QUOTED_IDENTIFIER options must have been set to ON when the CREATE VIEW statement was executed.
> - The ANSI_NULLS option must have been set to ON for the execution of all CREATE TABLE statements that create tables referenced by the view.
> - The view must not reference any other views, only base tables.
> - All base tables referenced by the view must be in the same database as the view and have the same owner as the view.
> - The view must be created with the SCHEMABINDING option. SCHEMABINDING binds the view to the schema of the underlying base tables.
> - User defined functions referenced in the view must have been created with the SCHEMABINDNG option.
> - Tables and user defined functions must be referenced by two-part names. One-part, three-part, and four-part names are not allowed.

---

[1] What reference [3] here calls exceptions to the rules I prefer to regard, rather, as additional rules. Either way, there's more for the user to learn.

[2] Quite apart from anything else, the writing is *dire* (and it gets worse). Some readers might be familiar with an earlier article of mine on this topic, "Good Writing Does Matter" (see reference [2]).

- All functions referenced by expressions in the view must be deterministic.
- The SELECT statement in the view cannot contain these Transact-SQL syntax elements:
    - The select list cannot use the "*" or "table_name.*" syntax to specify columns. Column names must be explicitly stated.
    - A table column name used as a simple expression cannot be specified in more than one view column. A column can be referenced multiple times provided all, or all but one, reference to the column is part of a complex expression or a parameter to a function.
    - A derived table.
    - Rowset functions.
    - UNION operator.
    - Subqueries.
    - Outer or self joins.
    - TOP clause.
    - ORDER BY clause.
    - DISTINCT keyword.
    - COUNT(*) (COUNT_BIG(*) is allowed.)
    - The AVG, MAX, MIN, STDEV, STDEVP, VAR, or VARP aggregate functions.
    - A SUM function that references a nullable expression.
    - The full-text predicates CONTAINS or FREETEXT.
    - COMPUTE or COMPUTE BY clause.
    - If GROUP BY is not specified, the view select list cannot contain aggregate expressions.
    - If GROUP BY is specified, the view select list must contain a COUNT_BIG(*) expression, and the view definition cannot specify HAVING, CUBE, or ROLLUP.
    - A column resulting from an expression that either evaluates to a float value or uses float expressions for its evaluation cannot be a key of an index in an indexed view of a table.

Also:

- The view cannot include text, ntext, or image columns, even if they are not referenced in the CREATE INDEX statement.
- If the SELECT statement in the view definition specifies a GROUP BY clause, the key of the unique clustered index can reference only columns specified in the GROUP BY clause.

I'd like to come up with some snappy conclusion here, but frankly words fail me.

REFERENCES AND BIBLIOGRAPHY

1. C. J. Date: "A Note on Orthogonality," in *Relational Database Writings 1994-1997.* Reading, Mass.: Addison-Wesley (1998).

2. C. J. Date: *Date on Database: Writings 2000-2006.* Berkeley, Calif.: Apress (2006).

3. Robert W. Sebesta: *Concepts of Programming Languages* (6th edition). Boston, Mass.: Addison-Wesley (2004).

4. A. van Wijngaarden et al. (eds.): *Revised Report on the Algorithmic Language ALGOL 68.* New York, NY: Springer-Verlag (1976).

Part III

TYPE INHERITANCE

This part of the book consists of four chapters. Chapter 19 is an updated definition of our inheritance model. Chapter 20 explains the changes we've made to that model—some of which are fairly major—since the version that was published in the *Manifesto* book (i.e., *Databases, Types, and the Relational Model: The Third Manifesto,* 3rd edition, by C. J. Date and Hugh Darwen, Addison-Wesley, 2006). Chapter 21 contains some proposals for extending **Tutorial D** to support the inheritance model. Finally, Chapter 22 presents a detailed examination of certain numeric data types from the point of view of inheritance, and attempts to dispel a few popular misconceptions in this connection.

Chapter 19

The Inheritance Model

Ruinous inheritance

—Gaius: *The Institutes*

This chapter provides a precise and succinct definition of our model of type inheritance. It consists of a heavily revised version of Chapter 13 from our book *Databases, Types, and the Relational Model: The Third Manifesto,* 3rd edition, Addison-Wesley, 2006 ("the *Manifesto* book" for short). Like that chapter, it mostly just states the various *Inheritance Model Prescriptions* (*IM Prescriptions*) that go to make up that model; in other words, it gives very little by way of discussion or further explanation. (It does give some, though—more than would be required if we were aiming at nothing more than an abstract definition.) *Note:* In most respects, our inheritance model is essentially just a logical consequence of our type theory (and that theory in turn is defined in *The Third Manifesto* itself). It follows that support for *The Third Manifesto,* if it's to be complete, must necessarily include support for the inheritance model in particular.

It should be emphasized that there are significant differences between the version of the model defined herein and the version defined in the *Manifesto* book. Reasons for those differences are explained in detail in Chapter 20. Chapter 21 contains a set of proposals, partly but not wholly repeated from the *Manifesto* book, for extending **Tutorial D** to support the model as defined herein.

Terminology: Throughout what follows, we use the symbols *T* and *T′* generically to refer to a pair of types such that *T′* is a subtype of *T* (equivalently, such that *T* is a supertype of *T′*). Keep in mind that types *T* and *T′* aren't limited to being scalar types specifically, barring explicit statements to the contrary. Note too that distinct types have distinct names; in particular, if *T′* is a proper subtype of *T* (see IM Prescription 4), then their names will be distinct, even if that proper subtype *T′* of *T* isn't a proper subset of *T* (see IM Prescription 2). Also, we assume that all of the types under discussion, including the maximal and minimal types discussed in IM Prescriptions 20 and 24, are members of some given set of types *GST;* in particular, the definitions of the terms *root type* and *leaf type* in IM Prescription 6 are to be understood in the context of that set *GST* (though the only explicit mention of that set is in IM Prescription 20, q.v.).

Wherever there's a discrepancy between the present chapter and Chapter 13 of the *Manifesto* book, the present chapter should be taken as superseding.

IM PRESCRIPTIONS

1. *T* and *T′* shall indeed both be types; i.e., each shall be a named, finite set of values.

2. Every value in *T′* shall be a value in *T;* i.e., the set of values constituting *T′* shall be a subset of the set of values constituting *T* (in other words, if a value is of type *T′,* it shall also be of type *T*). *Note:* In the case of scalar types, at least, we would normally expect proper subtypes to be proper subsets (see IM Prescription 4); in other words, we would normally expect there to exist, so long as *T* and *T′* are distinct, at least one value of type *T* that is not of type *T′*. Certain of the prescriptions that follow have been designed on the basis of this expectation; however, they do not formally depend on it.

3. *T* and *T′* shall not necessarily be distinct; i.e., every type shall be both a subtype and a supertype of itself.

4. If and only if types *T* and *T′* are distinct, *T′* shall be a **proper** subtype of *T,* and *T* shall be a **proper** supertype of *T′*.

5. Every subtype of *T′* shall be a subtype of *T*. Every supertype of *T* shall be a supertype of *T′*.

6. If and only if *T′* is a proper subtype of *T* and there is no type that is both a proper supertype of *T′* and a proper subtype of *T,* then *T′* shall be an **immediate** subtype of *T,* and *T* shall be an **immediate** supertype of *T′*. A type that has some maximal type—see IM Prescriptions 20 and 24—as its sole immediate supertype shall be a **root** type; a type that has some minimal type—again, see IM Prescriptions 20 and 24—as its sole immediate subtype shall be a **leaf** type.

7. Types *T1* and *T2* shall be **disjoint** if and only if no value is of both type *T1* and type *T2*. Types *T1* and *T2* shall **overlap** if and only if they are the same type or there exists at least one value that is common to both. Distinct root types shall be disjoint.

8. Let *T1, T2, ..., Tm* ($m \geqslant 0$), *T,* and *T′* be scalar types. Then:

   a. Type *T* shall be a **common supertype** for, or of, types *T1, T2, ..., Tm* if and only if, whenever a given value is of at least one of types *T1, T2, ..., Tm,* it is also of type *T*. Further, that type *T* shall be the **most specific** common supertype for *T1, T2, ..., Tm* if and only if no proper subtype of *T* is also a common supertype for those types.

   b. Type *T′* shall be a **common subtype** for, or of, types *T1, T2, ..., Tm* if and only if, whenever a given value is of type *T′,* it is also of each of types *T1, T2, ..., Tm*. Further, that type *T′* shall be the **least specific** common subtype—also known as the **intersection type** or **intersection subtype**—for *T1, T2, ..., Tm* if and only if no proper supertype of *T′* is also a common subtype for those types.

   Note: Given types *T1, T2, ..., Tm* as defined above, it can be shown (thanks in particular to IM Prescription 20) that a unique most specific common supertype *T* and a unique least specific common subtype *T′* always exist. In the case of that particular common subtype *T′,* moreover, it can also be shown that whenever a given value is of each of types *T1, T2, ..., Tm,* it is also of type *T′* (hence the alternative term *intersection type*). And it can further be shown that every scalar value has both a unique least specific type and a unique most specific type (regarding the latter, see also IM Prescription 9).

9. Let scalar variable *V* be of declared type *T*. Because of value substitutability (see IM Prescription 16), the value *v* assigned to *V* at any given time can have any nonempty subtype *T′* of type *T* as its most specific type. We can therefore model *V* as a named ordered triple of the form <*DT,MST,v*>, where:

   a. The name of the triple is the name of the variable, *V*.

   b. *DT* is the name of the declared type for variable *V*.

   c. *MST* is the name of the **most specific type**—also known as the **current** most specific type—for, or of, variable *V*.

   d. *v* is a value of most specific type *MST*—the **current value** for, or of, variable *V*.

   We use the notation *DT(V)*, *MST(V)*, *v(V)* to refer to the *DT, MST, v* components, respectively, of this model of scalar variable *V*. *Note:* Since *v(V)* uniquely determines *MST(V)*—see IM Prescription 8—the *MST* component of *V* is strictly redundant. We include it for convenience.

   Now let *X* be a scalar expression. By definition, *X* represents an invocation of some scalar operator *Op*. Thus, the notation *DT(V)*, *MST(V)*, *v(V)* just introduced can be extended in an obvious way to refer to the declared type *DT(X)*, the current most specific type *MST(X)*, and the current value *v(X)*, respectively, of *X*—where *DT(X)* is the declared type of the invocation of *Op* in question (see IM Prescription 17) and is known at compile time, and *MST(X)* and *v(X)* refer to the result of evaluating *X* and are therefore not known until run time (in general).

10. Let *T* be a regular type (see IM Prescription 20) and hence, necessarily, a scalar type, and let *T′* be a

nonempty immediate subtype of *T*. Then the definition of *T′* shall specify a **specialization constraint** *SC*, formulated in terms of *T*, such that a value shall be of type *T′* if and only if it is of type *T* and it satisfies constraint *SC*. *Note:* We would normally expect there to exist at least one value of type *T* that does not satisfy constraint *SC* (see IM Prescription 2).

11. Consider the assignment

    ```
    V := X
    ```

    (where *V* is a variable reference and *X* is an expression). *DT*(*X*) shall be a subtype of *DT*(*V*). The assignment shall set *v*(*V*) equal to *v*(*X*), and hence *MST*(*V*) equal to *MST*(*X*) also.

12. Consider the equality comparison

    ```
    Y = X
    ```

    (where *Y* and *X* are expressions). *DT*(*Y*) and *DT*(*X*) shall overlap. The comparison shall return TRUE if *v*(*Y*) is equal to *v*(*X*) (and hence if *MST*(*Y*) is equal to *MST*(*X*) also), and FALSE otherwise.

13. Attributes <*Ax,DTx*> of relation *rx* and <*Ay,DTy*> of relation *ry* shall **correspond** if and only if their names *Ax* and *Ay* are the same, *A* say, and their declared types *DTx* and *DTy* have a common supertype. Then:

    a. It shall be possible to form the **union** of *rx* and *ry* if and only if each attribute of *rx* corresponds to some attribute of *ry* and vice versa. For each pair of corresponding attributes <*A,DTx*> and <*A,DTy*>, the declared type of the corresponding attribute in the result of the union shall be the most specific common supertype of *DTx* and *DTy*. *Note:* In practice, the implementation might want to outlaw, or at least flag, any attempt to form such a union if *DTx* and *DTy* are not subtypes of the same root type.

    b. It shall be possible to form the **intersection** of *rx* and *ry* if and only if each attribute of *rx* corresponds to some attribute of *ry* and vice versa. For each pair of corresponding attributes <*A,DTx*> and <*A,DTy*>, the declared type of the corresponding attribute in the result of the union shall be the least specific common subtype of *DTx* and *DTy*. *Note:* In practice, the implementation might want to outlaw, or at least flag, any attempt to form such an intersection if *DTx* and *DTy* are not supertypes of the same leaf type. Also, intersection is a special case of join; given the prescriptions of paragraph d. below, therefore, the present paragraph is strictly redundant. We include it for convenience.

    c. It shall be possible to form the **difference** between *rx* and *ry*, in that order, if and only if every attribute of *rx* corresponds to some attribute of *ry* and vice versa. For each pair of corresponding attributes <*A,DTx*> and <*A,DTy*>, the declared type of the corresponding attribute in the result of the difference shall be *DTx*. *Note:* In practice, the implementation might want to outlaw, or at least flag, any attempt to form such a difference if *DTx* and *DTy* are not subtypes of the same root type, and possibly also if *DTx* and *DTy* are not supertypes of the same leaf type.

    d. It shall be possible to form the **join** of *rx* and *ry* if and only if no attribute of *rx* that fails to correspond to an attribute of *ry* has the same name as any attribute of *ry* and vice versa. For each pair of corresponding attributes <*A,DTx*> and <*A,DTy*>, the declared type of the corresponding attribute in the result of the join shall be the least specific common subtype of *DTx* and *DTy*. *Note:* In practice, the implementation might want to outlaw, or at least flag, any attempt to form such a join if *DTx* and *DTy* are not supertypes of the same leaf type. Also, intersection is a special case of join; thus, the prescriptions of the present paragraph degenerate to those for intersection in the case where every attribute of *rx* corresponds to some attribute of *ry* and vice versa.

14. Let *X* be an expression, let *T* be a type, and let *DT*(*X*) and *T* overlap. Then an operator of the form

```
TREAT_AS_T ( X )
```

(or logical equivalent thereof) shall be supported. We refer to such operators generically as "TREAT" or "TREAT AS" operators; their semantics are as follows. First, if *v*(*X*) is not of type *T,* then a type error shall occur. Otherwise:

   a. If the TREAT invocation appears in a "source" position—in particular, on the right side of an assignment—then the declared type of that invocation shall be *T,* and the invocation shall yield a result, *r* say, with *v*(*r*) equal to *v*(*X*) (and hence *MST*(*r*) equal to *MST*(*X*) also).

   b. If the TREAT invocation appears in a "target" position—in particular, on the left side of an assignment—then that invocation shall act as a pseudovariable reference, which means it shall designate a pseudovariable *X′* with *DT*(*X′*) equal to *T,* *v*(*X′*) equal to *v*(*X*), and *MST*(*X′*) equal to *MST*(*X*).

15. Let *X* be an expression, let *T* be a type, and let *DT*(*X*) and *T* overlap. Then an operator of the form

```
IS_T ( X )
```

(or logical equivalent thereof) shall be supported. The operator shall return TRUE if *v*(*X*) is of type *T,* FALSE otherwise.

16. Let *Op* be a read-only operator, let *P* be a parameter to *Op,* and let *T* be the declared type of *P*. Then the declared type of the argument expression (and therefore, necessarily, the most specific type of the argument as such) corresponding to *P* in an invocation of *Op* shall be allowed to be **any subtype** *T′* of *T*. In other words, the read-only operator *Op* applies to values of type *T* and therefore, necessarily, to values of type *T′*—*The Principle of* ***(Read-Only) Operator Inheritance***. It follows that such operators are *polymorphic,* since they apply to values of several different types—*The Principle of* ***(Read-Only) Operator Polymorphism***. It further follows that wherever a value of type *T* is permitted, a value of any subtype of *T* shall also be permitted—*The Principle of* ***(Value) Substitutability***.

17. Let *Op* be a read-only operator. Then *Op* shall have exactly one **specification signature,** denoting that operator as perceived by potential users. The specification signature for *Op* shall consist of the operator name and a nonempty set of *invocation signatures*. For definiteness, assume the parameters of *Op* and the argument expressions involved in any given invocation of *Op* each constitute an ordered list of *n* elements ($n \geqslant 0$), such that the *j*th argument expression corresponds to the *j*th parameter (j = 1, 2, ..., *n*). Further, let *PDT* = <*DT1, DT2, ..., DTn*> be the declared types, in sequence, of those *n* parameters, and let *PDT′* = <*DT1′, DT2′, ..., DTn′*> be a sequence of types such that *DTj′* is a nonempty subtype of *DTj* (j = 1, 2, ..., *n*). For each such sequence *PDT′,* there shall exist an **invocation signature** consisting of the operator name and a specification of the declared type of the result of an invocation of *Op* with argument expressions of declared types as specified by *PDT′* (the **declared type** for, or of, such an invocation).

18. Let *Op* be an update operator and let *P* be a parameter to *Op* that is not subject to update. Then *Op* shall behave as a read-only operator as far as *P* is concerned, and all relevant aspects of IM Prescription 16 shall apply, mutatis mutandis.

19. Let *Op* be an update operator, let *P* be a parameter to *Op* that is subject to update, and let *T* be the declared type of *P*. Then it might or might not be the case that the declared type of the argument expression (and therefore, necessarily, the most specific type of the argument as such) corresponding to *P* in an invocation

of *Op* shall be allowed to be some proper subtype *T′* of type *T*. It follows that for each such update operator *Op* and for each parameter *P* to *Op* that is subject to update, it shall be necessary to state explicitly for which proper subtypes *T′* of the declared type *T* of parameter *P* operator *Op* shall be inherited—*The Principle of* ***(Update) Operator Inheritance***. (And if update operator *Op* is not inherited in this way by type *T′*, it shall not be inherited by any proper subtype of type *T′* either.) Update operators shall thus be only conditionally polymorphic—*The Principle of* ***(Update) Operator Polymorphism***. If *Op* is an update operator and *P* is a parameter to *Op* that is subject to update and *T′* is a proper subtype of the declared type *T* of *P* for which *Op* is inherited, then by definition it shall be possible to invoke *Op* with an argument expression corresponding to parameter *P* that is of declared type *T′*—*The Principle of* ***(Variable) Substitutability***.

20. Type *T* shall be a **union type** if and only if it is a scalar type and there exists no value that is of type *T* and not of some immediate subtype of *T* (i.e., there is no value *v* such that *MST*(*v*) is *T*). Moreover:

    a. A type shall be a **dummy type** if and only if either of the following is true:

        1. It is one of the types *alpha* and *omega* (see below).

        2. It is a union type, has no declared representation (and hence no selector), and no regular supertype. *Note:* Type *alpha* in fact satisfies all three of these conditions; type *omega* satisfies the first two only.

        A type shall be a **regular type** if and only if it is a scalar type and not a dummy type.

    b. Conceptually, there shall be a system defined scalar type called *alpha,* the **maximal type** with respect to every scalar type. That type shall have all of the following properties:

        1. It shall contain all scalar values.

        2. It shall have no immediate supertypes.

        3. It shall be an immediate supertype for every scalar root type in the given set of types *GST*.

        No other scalar type shall have any of these properties (unless the given set of types *GST* contains just one regular type—necessarily type **boolean**—in which unlikely case that type will of course satisfy the first property).

    c. Conceptually, there shall be a system defined scalar type called *omega,* the **minimal type** with respect to every scalar type. That type shall have all of the following properties:

        1. It shall contain no values at all. (It follows that, as RM Prescription 1 in fact states, it shall have no example value in particular.)

        2. It shall have no immediate subtypes.

        3. It shall be an immediate subtype for every scalar leaf type in the given set of types *GST*.

        No other scalar type shall have any of these properties.

21. Type *T* shall be an **empty type** if and only if it is either an empty scalar type or an empty tuple type. Scalar type *T* shall be empty if and only if *T* is type *omega*. Tuple type *T* shall be empty if and only if *T* has at least one attribute that is of some empty type. An empty type shall be permitted as the declared type of (a) an attribute of a tuple type or relation type; (b) nothing else.

22. Let *T* and *T′* be both tuple types or both relation types. Then type *T′* shall be a **subtype** of type *T*, and type

T shall be a **supertype** of type *T′*, if and only if (a) *T* and *T′* have the same attribute names *A1, A2, ..., An* and (b) for all *j* (*j* = 1, 2, ..., *n*), the type of attribute *Aj* of *T′* is a subtype of the type of attribute *Aj* of *T*. Tuple *t* shall be of some subtype of tuple type *T* if and only if the heading of *t* is that of some subtype of *T*. Relation *r* shall be of some subtype of relation type *T* if and only if the heading of *r* is that of some subtype of *T* (in which case every tuple in the body of *r* shall necessarily also have a heading that is that of some subtype of *T*).

23. Let *T1, T2, ..., Tm* ($m \geqslant 0$), *T*, and *T′* be all tuple types or all relation types, with headings

```
{ <A1,T11>  , <A2,T12>  , ... , <An,T1n>  }
{ <A1,T21>  , <A2,T22>  , ... , <An,T2n>  }
..................................
{ <A1,Tm1>  , <A2,Tm2>  , ... , <An,Tmn>  }
{ <A1,T01>  , <A2,T02>  , ... , <An,T0n>  }
{ <A1,T01'> , <A2,T02'> , ... , <An,T0n'> }
```

respectively. Further, for all *j* (*j* = 1, 2, ..., *n*), let types *T1j, T2j, ..., Tmj* have a common subtype (and hence a common supertype also). Then:

a. Type *T* shall be a **common supertype** for, or of, types *T1, T2, ..., Tm* if and only if, for all *j* (*j* = 1, 2, ..., *n*), type *T0j* is a common supertype for types *T1j, T2j, ..., Tmj*. Further, that type *T* shall be the **most specific** common supertype for *T1, T2, ..., Tm* if and only if no proper subtype of *T* is also a common supertype for those types.

b. Type *T′* shall be a **common subtype** for, or of, types *T1, T2, ..., Tm* if and only if, for all *j* (*j* = 1, 2, ..., *n*), type *T0j′* is a common subtype for types *T1j, T2j, ..., Tmj*. Further, that type *T′* shall be the **least specific** common subtype—also known as the **intersection type** or **intersection subtype**—for *T1, T2, ..., Tm* if and only if no proper supertype of *T′* is also a common subtype for those types.

Note: Given types *T1, T2, ..., Tm* as defined above, it can be shown (thanks in particular to IM Prescription 24) that a unique most specific common supertype *T* and a unique least specific common subtype *T′* always exist. In the case of that particular common subtype *T′*, moreover, it can also be shown that whenever a given value is of each of types *T1, T2, ..., Tm*, it is also of type *T′* (hence the alternative term *intersection type*)—in which case, for all *j* (*j* = 1, 2, ..., *n*), type *T0j′* is the intersection type for types *T1j, T2j, ..., Tmj*. And it can further be shown that every tuple value and every relation value has both a unique least specific type and a unique most specific type (regarding the latter, see also IM Prescription 25).

24. Let *T, T_alpha,* and *T_omega* be all tuple types or all relation types, with headings

```
{ <A1,T1>        , <A2,T2>        , ... , <An,Tn>        }
{ <A1,T1_alpha> , <A2,T2_alpha> , ... , <An,Tn_alpha> }
{ <A1,T1_omega> , <A2,T2_omega> , ... , <An,Tn_omega> }
```

respectively. Then types *T_alpha* and *T_omega* shall be the **maximal type with respect to type *T*** and the **minimal type with respect to type *T*,** respectively, if and only if, for all *j* (*j* = 1, 2, ..., *n*), type *Tj_alpha* is the maximal type with respect to type *Tj* and type *Tj_omega* is the minimal type with respect to type *Tj*.

25. Let {*H*} be a heading defined as follows:

```
{ <A1,T1> , <A2,T2> , ... , <An,Tn> }
```

Then:

a. If *t* is a tuple of type some subtype of TUPLE {*H*}—meaning *t* is of the form

```
{ <A1,T1',v1> , <A2,T2',v2> , ... , <An,Tn',vn> }
```

where, for all *j* (*j* = 1, 2, ..., *n*), type *Tj'* is a subtype of type *Tj* and *vj* is a value of type *Tj'*—then the **most specific** type of *t* shall be

```
TUPLE { <A1,MST1> , <A2,MST2> , ... , <An,MSTn> }
```

where, for all *j* (*j* = 1, 2, ..., *n*), type *MSTj* is the most specific type of value *vj*.

b. If *r* is a relation of type some subtype of RELATION {*H*}—meaning each tuple in the body of *r* can be regarded without loss of generality as being of the form

```
{ <A1,T1',v1> , <A2,T2',v2> , ... , <An,Tn',vn> }
```

where, for all *j* (*j* = 1, 2, ..., *n*), type *Tj'* is a subtype of type *Tj* and is the most specific type of value *vj* (note that distinct tuples in the body of *r* will be of distinct most specific types, in general; thus, type *Tj'* varies over the tuples in the body of *r*)—then the **most specific** type of *r* shall be

```
RELATION { <A1,MST1> , <A2,MST2> , ... , <An,MSTn> }
```

where, for all *j* (*j* = 1, 2, ..., *n*), type *MSTj* is the most specific common supertype of those most specific types *Tj'*, taken over all tuples in the body of *r*.

26. Let *V* be a tuple variable or relation variable of declared type *T*, and let the heading of *T* have attributes *A1, A2, ..., An*. Then we can model *V* as a named set of named ordered triples of the form *<DTj,MSTj,vj>* (*j* = 1, 2, ..., *n*), where:

a. The name of the set is the name of the variable, *V*.

b. The name of each triple is the name of the corresponding attribute.

c. *DTj* is the name of the declared type of attribute *Aj*.

d. *MSTj* is the name of the **most specific type**—also known as the **current** most specific type—for, or of, attribute *Aj*. (If *V* is a relation variable, then the most specific type of *Aj* is the most specific common supertype of the most specific types of the *m* values in *vj*—see the explanation of *vj* below.)

e. If *V* is a tuple variable, *vj* is a value of most specific type *MSTj*—the **current value** for, or of, attribute *Aj*. If *V* is a relation variable, then let the body of the current value of *V* consist of *m* tuples ($m \geqslant 0$); label those tuples (in some arbitrary sequence) "tuple 1," "tuple 2," ..., "tuple *m*"; then *vj* is a sequence of *m* values (not necessarily all distinct), being the *Aj* values from tuple 1, tuple 2, ..., tuple *m* (in that order). Note that those *Aj* values are all of type *MSTj*.

We use the notation *DT*(*Aj*), *MST*(*Aj*), *v*(*Aj*) to refer to the *DTj, MSTj, vj* components, respectively, of attribute *Aj* of this model of tuple variable or relation variable *V*. We also use the notation *DT*(*V*), *MST*(*V*), *v*(*V*) to refer to the overall declared type, overall current most specific type, and overall current value, respectively, of this model of tuple variable or relation variable *V*.

Now let *X* be a tuple expression or relation expression. By definition, *X* specifies an invocation of some tuple operator or relation operator *Op*. Thus, the notation *DTj*(*V*), *MSTj*(*V*), *vj*(*V*) just introduced can be extended in an obvious way to refer to the declared type *DTj*(*X*), the current most specific type *MSTj*(*X*), and the current value *vj*(*X*), respectively, of the *DTj, MSTj, vj* components, respectively, of attribute *Aj* of tuple expression or relation expression *X*—where *DTj*(*X*) is the declared type of *Aj* for the invocation of *Op* in question (see IM Prescription 17) and is known at compile time, and *MSTj*(*X*) and *vj*(*X*) refer to the result of evaluating *X* and are therefore not known until run time (in general).

Chapter 20

The Inheritance Model: What Was Changed and Why

There's nothing like a confession to make one look mad;
[and] of all confessions a written one is the most detrimental all round.

—Joseph Conrad: *Chance*

If you don't make mistakes you don't make anything.

—19th century proverb

As noted in the previous chapter, there are some significant differences between the inheritance model as defined in that chapter and the earlier version of that model as defined in the *Manifesto* book (i.e., *Databases, Types, and the Relational Model: The Third Manifesto,* 3rd edition, by C. J. Date and Hugh Darwen, Addison-Wesley, 2006). The truth is, we got certain details seriously wrong in that earlier version, and we freely confess as much here—though we hasten to add that we still believe in the big picture as described in that earlier version. But we also believe it can be instructive to examine past mistakes, and we wrote the present chapter for that reason. *Note:* For the rest of the chapter we use the phrase *the previous version* or, more explicitly, *the previous version of the model* to refer to the model as defined in the *Manifesto* book.

Here first is a brief summary of the differences with respect to that previous version:

- IM Prescriptions 21-25 from the previous version are replaced by IM Prescriptions 21-26. IM Prescription 22 from that previous version has been dropped; IM Prescriptions 21 and 23 have been added; and IM Prescriptions 21, 23, 24, and 25 from that previous version are now IM Prescriptions 22, 24, 25, and 26, respectively.

- Major changes have been made to IM Prescriptions 8, 13, 17, 20, and 22 (previously 21).

- Minor revisions (sometimes just cosmetic) have been made to almost all of the others.

We now proceed to describe the changes in detail. In each case, we repeat the pertinent prescription from Chapter 19 and then explain what's changed. We remind you that we use the symbols *T* and *T'* generically, though in this chapter not exclusively, to refer to a pair of types such that *T'* is a subtype of *T* (equivalently, such that *T* is a supertype of *T'*). Keep in mind that types *T* and *T'* aren't limited to being scalar types specifically, barring explicit statements to the contrary. We remind you also that we assume that all of the types under discussion, including the maximal and minimal types discussed in IM Prescriptions 20 and 24, are members of some given set of types *GST;* in particular, the definitions of the terms *root type* and *leaf type* in IM Prescription 6 are to be understood in the context of that set *GST* (though as noted in the previous chapter, the only explicit mention of that set is in IM Prescription 20, q.v.).

IM PRESCRIPTION 1

1. *T* and *T'* shall indeed both be types; i.e., each shall be a named, finite set of values.

The qualifier *finite* has been added, simply in order to bring the prescription into line with RM Prescription 1 (see Chapter 1).

IM PRESCRIPTION 2

2. Every value in *T′* shall be a value in *T;* i.e., the set of values constituting *T′* shall be a subset of the set of values constituting *T* (in other words, if a value is of type *T′,* it shall also be of type *T*). *Note:* In the case of scalar types, at least, we would normally expect proper subtypes to be proper subsets (see IM Prescription 4); in other words, we would normally expect there to exist, so long as *T* and *T′* are distinct, at least one value of type *T* that is not of type *T′*. Certain of the prescriptions that follow have been designed on the basis of this expectation; however, they do not formally depend on it.

The previous version of this prescription required there to be at least one value of type *T* that's not of type *T′*. That requirement was unenforceable, however;[1] moreover, we found that there didn't seem to be any serious problems if it was violated, and we therefore downgraded it (as you can see) to a mere comment.

IM PRESCRIPTION 3

3. *T* and *T′* shall not necessarily be distinct; i.e., every type shall be both a subtype and a supertype of itself.

This prescription remains unchanged.

IM PRESCRIPTION 4

4. If and only if types *T* and *T′* are distinct, *T′* shall be a **proper** subtype of *T,* and *T* shall be a **proper** supertype of *T′*.

This prescription remains unchanged (but see the commentary on IM Prescription 2).

IM PRESCRIPTION 5

5. Every subtype of *T′* shall be a subtype of *T*. Every supertype of *T* shall be a supertype of *T′*.

This prescription remains unchanged.

IM PRESCRIPTION 6

6. If and only if *T′* is a proper subtype of *T* and there is no type that is both a proper supertype of *T′* and a proper subtype of *T,* then *T′* shall be an **immediate** subtype of *T,* and *T* shall be an **immediate** supertype of *T′*. A type that has some maximal type—see IM Prescriptions 20 and 24—as its sole immediate supertype shall be a **root** type; a type that has some minimal type—again, see IM Prescriptions 20 and 24—as its sole immediate subtype shall be a **leaf** type.

It was always the case, even in the previous version of the model, that the concepts of *root type* and *leaf type* were context dependent; for example, if type *T* was a leaf type but then we defined a proper subtype *T′* of *T,* clearly *T* wouldn't be a leaf type any longer. But there was also some question over how the terms *root* and *leaf* should be interpreted if types *alpha* and *omega*—or, rather, maximal and minimal types in general—were taken into account. After due consideration, we've come to the conclusion that (as the foregoing revised definition

---

[1] Well, maybe not; Adrian Hudnott has suggested that in the case of scalar types, at least, we could require the definition of type *T′* to be accompanied by an explicit example of a value of type *T* that's not also a value of type *T′*. (More generally, if *T′* has immediate supertypes *T1, T2, ..., Tn,* it would have to be accompanied by an explicit example of a value of type *T1* that's not a value of type *T′,* an explicit example of a value of type *T2* that's not a value of type *T′,* ..., and an explicit example of a value of type *Tn* that's not a value of type *T′*.) We are actively considering the merits of this suggestion.

makes clear) it makes better sense to define the terms in such a way as to exclude those special types. *Note:* It follows from the foregoing that the type hierarchy and type graph concepts are also context dependent. Of course, those concepts aren't part of our formal inheritance model anyway. But the following points are worth making nevertheless:

- The set of all scalar types including types *alpha* and *omega* is a lattice, with *alpha* and *omega* as upper and lower bound, respectively.
- Let *T* be a tuple type. Then the set of all subtypes and supertypes of *T* is a lattice, with types *T_alpha* and *T_omega* (see IM Prescription 24) as upper and lower bound, respectively.
- Let *T* be a relation type. Then the set of all subtypes and supertypes of *T* is a lattice, with types *T_alpha* and *T_omega* (again, see IM Prescription 24) as upper and lower bound, respectively.
- Let *L1* and *L2* be any two distinct members of the complete set of lattices defined in the previous three paragraphs. Then *L1* and *L2* are disjoint (i.e., no type appears in both of them).

IM PRESCRIPTION 7

7. Types *T1* and *T2* shall be **disjoint** if and only if no value is of both type *T1* and type *T2*. Types *T1* and *T2* shall **overlap** if and only if they are the same type or there exists at least one value that is common to both. Distinct root types shall be disjoint.

This prescription has been reworded, though the general sense hasn't changed. The intent of the revisions is to introduce explicit definitions for (a) the concept of disjoint types in general (not just in connection with root types in particular) and (b) the related concept of overlapping types. Several of the other prescriptions now explicitly appeal to this latter concept. *Note:* It's worth stating for the record that:

- If *T1* and *T2* are distinct scalar types, then they're certainly disjoint if one is type *omega*.[2] *Note:* In particular, it follows from IM Prescription 8 that distinct scalar leaf types are disjoint.
- If *T1* and *T2* are distinct types from the same tuple type lattice (see the remarks above under IM Prescription 6), then they're certainly disjoint if one is the pertinent minimal type (see IM Prescription 25). *Note:* In particular, it follows from IM Prescription 23 that distinct leaf types from the same tuple type lattice are disjoint.
- If *T1* and *T2* are distinct types from the same relation type lattice (again, see the remarks above under IM Prescription 6), then they aren't disjoint, even if one is the pertinent minimal type (again, see IM Prescription 25). For example, let *T1* and *T2* be the relation types RELATION {PF CIRCLE} and RELATION {PF SQUARE}, respectively.[3] These types overlap because they both contain the (empty) relation RELATION {PF *omega*} {}; in fact, every type in the type lattice in question, even the pertinent minimal type RELATION {PF *omega*}, contains that same empty relation as a value. (Note, therefore, that minimal relation types are never empty.) See IM Prescription 24 for further explanation.

---

[2] In fact, the only scalar type that overlaps with *omega* is *omega* itself. Note, however, that *omega* is also disjoint from itself (!).

[3] Here and elsewhere in this chapter we give examples in terms of various geometric types—RECTANGLE, RHOMBUS, SQUARE, ELLIPSE, CIRCLE, and so on—whose semantics we take to be obvious.

IM PRESCRIPTION 8

8. Let *T1, T2, ..., Tm* (*m* ⩾ 0), *T,* and *T′* be scalar types. Then:

   a. Type *T* shall be a **common supertype** for, or of, types *T1, T2, ..., Tm* if and only if, whenever a given value is of at least one of types *T1, T2, ..., Tm,* it is also of type *T.* Further, that type *T* shall be the **most specific** common supertype for *T1, T2, ..., Tm* if and only if no proper subtype of *T* is also a common supertype for those types.

   b. Type *T′* shall be a **common subtype** for, or of, types *T1, T2, ..., Tm* if and only if, whenever a given value is of type *T′,* it is also of each of types *T1, T2, ..., Tm.* Further, that type *T′* shall be the **least specific** common subtype—also known as the **intersection type** or **intersection subtype**—for *T1, T2, ..., Tm* if and only if no proper supertype of *T′* is also a common subtype for those types.

   Note: Given types *T1, T2, ..., Tm* as defined above, it can be shown (thanks in particular to IM Prescription 20) that a unique most specific common supertype *T* and a unique least specific common subtype *T′* always exist. In the case of that particular common subtype *T′,* moreover, it can also be shown that whenever a given value is of each of types *T1, T2, ..., Tm,* it is also of type *T′* (hence the alternative term *intersection type*). And it can further be shown that every scalar value has both a unique least specific type and a unique most specific type (regarding the latter, see also IM Prescription 9).

The previous version of this prescription was much simpler! Here it is:

> Every set of types *T1, T2, ..., Tn* shall have a common subtype *T′* such that a given value is of each of the types *T1, T2, ..., Tn* if and only if it is of type *T′.*

This previous version is still generally valid, but we realized there was a lot more that needed to be said. To be specific:

- We needed to make it clear that the prescription refers to scalar types specifically. Tuple and relation types are covered by the new IM Prescription 23.
- We needed to distinguish between common subtypes in general and intersection subtypes in particular (the latter being an important special case of the former).
- We needed to give common supertypes "equal time," as it were.
- We needed to make it clear that the given set of types *T1, T2, ..., Tm* might itself be empty (see later for further discussion).[4]

In addition, we wanted to spell out certain implications of the prescription that might not be immediately obvious:

- Every set of scalar types has a unique least specific common subtype *T′* and a unique most specific common supertype *T.* Note, however, that there's some asymmetry here, with respect to nomenclature at least: While type *T′* is referred to as the corresponding intersection type, type *T* is *not* referred to as the corresponding union type. That's because *T* is not necessarily a union type as that term is defined within our inheritance model (see IM Prescription 20, later). To be precise, while type *T′* is indeed exactly the intersection of the sets of values that constitute types *T1, T2, ..., Tm,* type *T* by contrast is a *superset*—in

---

[4] The number of types was specified as *n* in the previous version of the prescription but is now given as *m.* Similar changes have been made (in all cases, purely for cosmetic reasons) in certain other prescriptions also.

general, a proper superset—of the union of those sets of values.

- Every scalar value has a unique least specific type and a unique most specific type.

To which we can also add that (as stated under IM Prescription 7):

- Scalar leaf types are disjoint.

Proof that these conclusions are valid can be found in the *Manifesto* book, pages 326-330—though there are some special cases that are worth elaborating on somewhat, and we'll get to those later in this section. Before then, however, there's another issue that merits some discussion. Several critics have questioned the need for most specific types to be unique. Their argument typically goes something like this:

> Suppose an operator *Op* is defined for values of type RECTANGLE and an operator of the same name is defined for values of type RHOMBUS. Then there are two possibilities:
>
> 1. *Op* is defined for both of those types because it's inherited from their common supertype PARALLELOGRAM.
>
> 2. Alternatively, the operator isn't inherited; instead, there are really two distinct operators with the same name.
>
> Now let *X* be an expression that denotes a value that's of both types (i.e., RECTANGLE and RHOMBUS), and consider the expression *Op*(*X*). Then which specific operator is invoked depends on the declared type of *X*, viz., *DT*(*X*):
>
> 1. In Case 1, there's only one operator, so there's no problem. (There might be a problem for the implementation, in that it might have to choose which implementation version to invoke; however, there's no problem for the model, since all such versions are required to implement the same semantics. Indeed, if they don't, then they're not implementations of the same operator anyway, by definition.)
>
> 2. In Case 2, there's no ambiguity because *DT*(*X*) is either RECTANGLE or RHOMBUS, and which operator to invoke is thereby well defined.[5]
>
> So why exactly do we insist on most specific types being unique?

Well, why do we? For simplicity, let's stay with the same example; i.e., let's assume we're given types PARALLELOGRAM, RECTANGLE, and RHOMBUS, where the latter two are immediate subtypes of the first. In terms of this example, then, the question is: Does it make sense to say that some value exists that has two distinct most specific types (viz., RECTANGLE and RHOMBUS)? Suppose the answer to this question is *yes*. We now pursue certain implications of that answer.

First of all, in order for that answer to make sense, it must be the case that there are situations in which the value—*sq,* say—of some expression *re* of declared type RECTANGLE is to be treated as if it were a value of type RHOMBUS (or the other way around, of course). *Note:* We say "it must be the case" because if it isn't, then there's no sense in which it can possibly be of interest to say that *sq* has both types.

This first point, then, implies that the following expression must be legal:

```
TREAT_AS_RHOMBUS ( re )
```

Now, according to IM Prescription 14, this expression is legal only if types RECTANGLE and

---

[5] So the following argument (paraphrased from the *Manifesto* book, page 326) is incorrect: "Suppose some value *v* could be both a rectangle and a rhombus, and suppose type SQUARE (a common subtype of RECTANGLE and RHOMBUS) hasn't yet been defined. Then, if an operator called *Op* has been defined for rectangles and another operator with the same name has been defined for rhombi, an invocation of *Op* with argument *v* would be ambiguous."

RHOMBUS overlap—as indeed they do; but the compiler isn't (and can't be) aware of that fact, because type SQUARE hasn't been defined. So if the compiler is required to allow the expression anyway, the requirement in IM Prescription 14 that "*DT*(*X*) and *T* overlap" becomes essentially meaningless, and it might as well be dropped. Thus, certain compile time checks now become impossible, which in turn raises the possibility of more run time type errors.

In similar fashion, the expression

```
IS_RHOMBUS ( re )
```

must presumably also be legal (it will give TRUE if and only if *sq,* the current value of expression *re,* has RHOMBUS as one of its types). Remarks similar to those in the previous paragraph, regarding IM Prescription 14, thus apply to IM Prescription 15 as well.

Similar remarks apply to equality comparisons as well (IM Prescription 12). But in this case there's a little more that can usefully be said.[6] Consider the following code fragment:

```
VAR RE RECTANGLE ;
VAR RH RHOMBUS ;

IF RH = RE THEN ... ;
```

Clearly, the comparison RH = RE can give TRUE only if RH and RE both contain the same value (*sq,* say), which must be, by definition, a square. What's more, the user will certainly be aware of this fact; that is, type SQUARE must certainly exist in the user's mind, as it were. At least in this context, therefore, there doesn't seem to be any advantage in not requiring type SQUARE to be defined appropriately; at the same time, there do seem to be plenty of advantages in requiring it to be defined. Certainly we haven't seen any cogent arguments to the contrary.

It should be clear without going into details that the arguments of the foregoing paragraph apply to assignment also, mutatis mutandis.

A couple of final observations to close this discussion:

- Parts b. and d. of the revised form of IM Prescription 13 (q.v.) rely, indirectly, on most specific types being unique. Dropping that requirement would thus have a major impact on that prescription if nothing else. (There would probably be other impacts too, though they might be mostly cosmetic in nature. More study is required.)

- It would surely seem a little odd to say—as RM Prescription 1 effectively does—that scalar leaf types have to be disjoint without inheritance and yet don't have to be disjoint with it; in fact, it would represent an incompatibility between the *Manifesto* and the inheritance model. (Without inheritance, of course, all types are leaf types.) And it would make no sense to change RM Prescription 1 in this regard, for that would be to give up on static type checking altogether, contrary to one of the stated aims of the *Manifesto.*

Finally we return as promised to the special cases mentioned in passing earlier in this section. First, suppose the given set of scalar types *T1, T2, ..., Tm* is such that at least two of those types are disjoint. Then the sole—and hence most specific—common supertype will be type *alpha;* likewise, the sole—and hence least specific—common subtype will be type *omega.* (In fact, it's largely to guarantee the validity of IM Prescription 8 in general, even when at least two of the types in question are disjoint, that we insist on the uniqueness of types *alpha* and *omega.* See IM Prescription 20.)

---

[6] Actually, we could have made an argument somewhat analogous to the one that follows in our discussions of IM Prescriptions 14 and 15 also.

Second, suppose $m = 1$; i.e., suppose the given set of scalar types consists of just a single type *T1*. Then the corresponding most specific common supertype and least specific common subtype are clearly both just *T1*.

Third, suppose $m = 0$; i.e., suppose the given set of scalar types *Ti* ($i = 1, 2, ..., m$) is empty. Then:

- A scalar type *T* is a common supertype for a given set of scalar types if and only if, for all types *Ti* in that given set, if value *v* is of type *Ti,* then value *v* is also of type *T*. But if that given set of types is empty (i.e., if there are no such types *Ti*), then the foregoing expression—which is universally quantified, observe—is vacuously true for all scalar types *T*. Hence, the most specific common supertype for the empty set of scalar types is clearly type *omega*.

- A scalar type *T′* is a common subtype for a given set of scalar types if and only if, for all types *Ti* in that given set, if value *v* is of type *T′,* then value *v* is also of type *Ti*. But if that given set of types is empty (i.e., if there are no such types *Ti*), then the foregoing expression—which is universally quantified, observe—is vacuously true for all scalar types *T′*. Hence, the least specific common subtype for the empty set of scalar types is clearly type *alpha*.

IM PRESCRIPTION 9

9. Let scalar variable *V* be of declared type *T*. Because of value substitutability (see IM Prescription 16), the value *v* assigned to *V* at any given time can have any nonempty subtype *T′* of type *T* as its most specific type. We can therefore model *V* as a named ordered triple of the form <*DT,MST,v*>, where:

   a. The name of the triple is the name of the variable, *V*.

   b. *DT* is the name of the declared type for variable *V*.

   c. *MST* is the name of the **most specific type**—also known as the **current** most specific type—for, or of, variable *V*.

   d. *v* is a value of most specific type *MST*—the **current value** for, or of, variable *V*.

   We use the notation *DT*(*V*), *MST*(*V*), *v*(*V*) to refer to the *DT, MST, v* components, respectively, of this model of scalar variable *V*. *Note:* Since *v*(*V*) uniquely determines *MST*(*V*)—see IM Prescription 8—the *MST* component of *V* is strictly redundant. We include it for convenience.

   Now let *X* be a scalar expression. By definition, *X* represents an invocation of some scalar operator *Op*. Thus, the notation *DT*(*V*), *MST*(*V*), *v*(*V*) just introduced can be extended in an obvious way to refer to the declared type *DT*(*X*), the current most specific type *MST*(*X*), and the current value *v*(*X*), respectively, of *X*—where *DT*(*X*) is the declared type of the invocation of *Op* in question (see IM Prescription 17) and is known at compile time, and *MST*(*X*) and *v*(*X*) refer to the result of evaluating *X* and are therefore not known until run time (in general).

We've made a few small changes to this prescription. First, the fact that type *T′* must be nonempty has been spelled out, for clarity (the notion of a value of any kind being of some empty type is, of course, a contradiction in terms).[7] Second, we've added a note to the effect that *MST*(*V*) is strictly redundant. Third, the definition of *DT*(*X*) has been altered slightly to bring it into line with the revised form of IM Prescription 17, q.v. Fourth, we've deleted a remark concerning argument expressions, since it added nothing.

Note: Actually it's possible for a scalar expression *X* not to denote any value at all—for example, if *X* consists of a reference to some attribute *A* and *A* is declared to be of some empty type. For such an expression, of

---

[7] Since we're talking about scalar values here, the sole pertinent empty type is in fact type *omega*.

course, *MST*(*X*) is the applicable empty type and *v*(*X*) is meaningless.

IM PRESCRIPTION 10

10. Let *T* be a regular type (see IM Prescription 20) and hence, necessarily, a scalar type, and let *T′* be a nonempty immediate subtype of *T*. Then the definition of *T′* shall specify a **specialization constraint** *SC*, formulated in terms of *T*, such that a value shall be of type *T′* if and only if it is of type *T* and it satisfies constraint *SC*. *Note:* We would normally expect there to exist at least one value of type *T* that does not satisfy constraint *SC* (see IM Prescription 2).

The first sentence has been changed to make it clear that (a) type *T*, and therefore type *T′* also, are scalar types specifically (the notion of specialization by constraint is relevant to tuple and relation types, but only implicitly), and (b) the prescription doesn't apply if type *T′* is *omega*. The last sentence has been altered to make it consistent with the revision already made to IM Prescription 2, q.v.

Note: As the *Manifesto* book makes clear, IM Prescription 10 has the immediate implication that *specialization by constraint*—S by C for short—must be supported (indeed, that's the real point). But it's worth stating explicitly that we regard S by C as a run time phenomenon; we don't expect it to be done at compile time. For example, let type CIRCLE be a proper subtype of type ELLIPSE; let the applicable specialization constraint be such that an ellipse is a circle if and only if its semiaxes are equal; and let C be a variable of declared type CIRCLE. Then the following assignment—

```
C := ELLIPSE ( LENGTH ( 5 ) /* major semiaxis */ ,
               LENGTH ( 5 ) /* minor semiaxis */ ,
                ... ) ;
```

—will fail at compile time, even though the ELLIPSE selector invocation on the right side will clearly return a circle. Instead, the assignment must be written as follows:

```
C := TREAT_AS_CIRCLE
   ( ELLIPSE ( LENGTH ( 5 ) , LENGTH ( 5 ) , ... ) ) ;
```

Of course, it could also be written thus:

```
C := CIRCLE ( LENGTH ( 5 ) /* radius */ , ... ) ;
```

IM PRESCRIPTION 11

11. Consider the assignment

```
V := X
```

(where *V* is a variable reference and *X* is an expression). *DT*(*X*) shall be a subtype of *DT*(*V*). The assignment shall set *v*(*V*) equal to *v*(*X*), and hence *MST*(*V*) equal to *MST*(*X*) also.

The phrase "*V* is a variable" has been corrected to "*V* is a variable reference." Small cosmetic changes have been made also.

IM PRESCRIPTION 12

12. Consider the equality comparison

```
Y = X
```

(where *Y* and *X* are expressions). *DT*(*Y*) and *DT*(*X*) shall overlap. The comparison shall return TRUE if *v*(*Y*) is equal to *v*(*X*) (and hence if *MST*(*Y*) is equal to *MST*(*X*) also), and FALSE otherwise.

The second sentence has been revised to replace *have a nonempty common subtype* by *overlap*. Other cosmetic changes have been made also.

IM PRESCRIPTION 13

IM Prescription 13 has been totally rewritten. Here first is the previous version:

> Let *rx* and *ry* be relations with a common attribute *A*, and let the declared types of *A* in *rx* and *ry* be *DTx*(*A*) and *DTy*(*A*), respectively. Consider the join of *rx* and *ry* (necessarily over *A*, at least in part). *DTx*(*A*) and *DTy*(*A*) shall have a nonempty common subtype and hence shall also have a most specific common supertype, *T* say. Then the declared type of *A* in the result of the join shall be *T*.
>
> Analogous remarks apply to union, intersection, and difference operators. That is, in each case:
>
> a. Corresponding attributes of the operands shall be such that their declared types have a nonempty common subtype.
>
> b. The declared type of the corresponding attribute of the result shall be the corresponding most specific common supertype.

In order to explain the differences between this version of the prescription and its replacement, it's convenient to begin by considering a simplified example, in which the basic objects we have to deal with are just plain sets instead of, more specifically, relations. It's also convenient to discuss intersection first instead of join, and to abbreviate *declared type* to just *type* until further notice. So: Let SE and SC be, respectively, a set of ellipses and a set of circles, and let SX be the intersection of those two sets. Clearly, then, elements of SX aren't "just ellipses" but are, more specifically, circles. In other words, if SE and SC are of type "set of ellipses" and "set of circles," respectively, we would expect SX to be of type "set of circles" too. Yet IM Prescription 13 as originally defined[8] would say that SX is of type "set of ellipses." Why?

Well, the argument used in the *Manifesto* book to justify this state of affairs was basically as follows (except that we've simplified it here to bring it into line with the foregoing example):

- First of all, it's easy to see (e.g., by means of Venn diagrams) that the expression SE INTERSECT SC is logically equivalent to the expression SE MINUS (SE MINUS SC).
- Let the result of evaluating SE MINUS SC be SD. Then it's clear that (in general) SD will include some ellipses that aren't circles, and so SD must be of type "set of ellipses."
- In the expression SE MINUS SD, therefore, SE and SD are both of type "set of ellipses," and so the result of evaluating that expression must obviously be of type "set of ellipses" also.
- It follows that SE INTERSECT SC, because it's logically equivalent to SE MINUS SD, must be of type "set of ellipses" as well.

What's wrong with this argument? Well, given the limited ability on the part of the system to do type inferencing at compile time, what it really shows is that SE INTERSECT SC is *not* logically equivalent to SE MINUS (SE MINUS SC) after all!—at least, not within the particular formal system we're developing here. Rather, it's logically equivalent to a version of this latter expression that's been "treated" to type "set of circles,"

---

[8] References in this section to IM Prescription 13 as originally defined should be taken where necessary to mean a version of that prescription that has been reformulated to apply to "just plain sets" instead of relations.

perhaps as follows:[9]

```
TREAT_AS_SAME_TYPE_AS ( SC , SE MINUS ( SE MINUS SC ) )
```

This expression and the expression SE INTERSECT SC *are* logically interchangeable; that is, each can be replaced by the other (either by the user or by the system).

What's more, let VSC be a variable of type "set of circles." Under the previous version of IM Prescription 13, then, the assignment

```
VSC := SE INTERSECT SC ;
```

would have been illegal (a TREAT would have been required on the right side). Under the new version, by contrast, that same assignment is perfectly legitimate. (However, the assignment

```
VSC := SE MINUS ( SE MINUS SC ) ;
```

is illegal under both versions, as we've effectively already seen.)

So much for intersection; now let's briefly consider the operators difference, union, and join.

- Difference is straightforward:[10] As we've already seen, with SE and SC as defined above, the result of evaluating SE MINUS SC will include some ellipses that aren't circles (in general), and so we would expect that result to be of type "set of ellipses."

- Now let SNC be a set of ellipses that aren't circles (*noncircles* for short), and let SZ be the union of sets SC and SNC. Clearly, then, elements of SZ are neither all circles nor all noncircles (in general); rather, they're a mixture of the two, or in other words "just ellipses" (again, in general). So we would expect SZ to be of type "set of ellipses." *Note:* The union rule in the previous version of the prescription was simply wrong. To be specific, it required the declared types of corresponding attributes to overlap. But that rule implied that taking the union of a set of circles and a set of noncircles (speaking very loosely, of course) was forbidden!—and the question of the type of the result thus didn't even arise.

- As for join: Intersection is, of course, just a special case of join, and so we would expect the rule for join to be an obvious generalization of that for intersect, and so it is.

Here then is the revised version of IM Prescription 13 (and now we switch back to talking in terms of (a) relations instead of general sets and (b) declared types instead of just types, unqualified):

13. Attributes *<Ax,DTx>* of relation *rx* and *<Ay,DTy>* of relation *ry* shall **correspond** if and only if their names *Ax* and *Ay* are the same, *A* say, and their declared types *DTx* and *DTy* have a common supertype. Then:

    a. It shall be possible to form the **union** of *rx* and *ry* if and only if each attribute of *rx* corresponds to some attribute of *ry* and vice versa. For each pair of corresponding attributes *<A,DTx>* and *<A,DTy>*, the declared type of the corresponding attribute in the result of the union shall be the most specific common supertype of *DTx* and *DTy*. *Note:* In practice, the implementation might

---

[9] See the *Manifesto* book, page 355, for an explanation of the TREAT_AS_SAME_TYPE_AS construct used in this example.

[10] It might be preferable to talk here in terms of semidifference rather than difference, since the former is more general. Here's the definition: The semidifference between relations *r1* and *r2* (in that order), *r1* NOT MATCHING *r2*, is shorthand for *r1* MINUS (*r1* MATCHING *r2*), where *r1* MATCHING *r2* in turn is shorthand for the projection of *r1* JOIN *r2* on all of the attributes of *r1*. From this definition it's easy to see that *r1* NOT MATCHING *r2* degenerates to *r1* MINUS *r2* if *r1* and *r2* are of the same type. However, we stay with difference in the present discussion (and in IM Prescription 13) for reasons of familiarity.

want to outlaw, or at least flag, any attempt to form such a union if *DTx* and *DTy* are not subtypes of the same root type.

b. It shall be possible to form the **intersection** of *rx* and *ry* if and only if each attribute of *rx* corresponds to some attribute of *ry* and vice versa. For each pair of corresponding attributes *<A,DTx>* and *<A,DTy>*, the declared type of the corresponding attribute in the result of the union shall be the least specific common subtype of *DTx* and *DTy*. *Note:* In practice, the implementation might want to outlaw, or at least flag, any attempt to form such an intersection if *DTx* and *DTy* are not supertypes of the same leaf type. Also, intersection is a special case of join; given the prescriptions of paragraph d. below, therefore, the present paragraph is strictly redundant. We include it for convenience.

c. It shall be possible to form the **difference** between *rx* and *ry,* in that order, if and only if every attribute of *rx* corresponds to some attribute of *ry* and vice versa. For each pair of corresponding attributes *<A,DTx>* and *<A,DTy>*, the declared type of the corresponding attribute in the result of the difference shall be *DTx*. *Note:* In practice, the implementation might want to outlaw, or at least flag, any attempt to form such a difference if *DTx* and *DTy* are not subtypes of the same root type, and possibly also if *DTx* and *DTy* are not supertypes of the same leaf type.

d. It shall be possible to form the **join** of *rx* and *ry* if and only if no attribute of *rx* that fails to correspond to an attribute of *ry* has the same name as any attribute of *ry* and vice versa. For each pair of corresponding attributes *<A,DTx>* and *<A,DTy>*, the declared type of the corresponding attribute in the result of the join shall be the least specific common subtype of *DTx* and *DTy*. *Note:* In practice, the implementation might want to outlaw, or at least flag, any attempt to form such a join if *DTx* and *DTy* are not supertypes of the same leaf type. Also, intersection is a special case of join; thus, the prescriptions of the present paragraph degenerate to those for intersection in the case where every attribute of *rx* corresponds to some attribute of *ry* and vice versa.

Certain further points arise from this revised definition. First, note that the concept of "corresponding attributes" is introduced purely for the purposes of this particular prescription, in order to allow us to state the rules regarding operand and result declared types precisely. In fact, we can state the rules—at least for union, difference, and intersection, though not so easily for join—without using the notion of corresponding attributes at all, by appealing to IM Prescriptions 22, 23, and 26.[11] First, for all three operations, *DT*(*rx*) and *DT*(*ry*) must have a common supertype. Then the declared type of the result is as follows:

- *Union:* The most specific common supertype of *DT*(*rx*) and *DT*(*ry*)
- *Difference: DT*(*rx*)
- *Intersection:* The least specific common subtype (i.e., the intersection type) of *DT*(*rx*) and *DT*(*ry*)

Another problem with the previous version of IM Prescription 13 was that it required the declared types of corresponding attributes to have a nonempty common subtype. The idea was to stop the user from trying to join, say, ellipses and rectangles (speaking very loosely once again); in other words, we were trying to "legislate morality." But suppose relations *rx* and *ry* both have just one attribute, A, with declared type some empty type, say *omega,* in both cases; then *rx* and *ry* are certainly equal (i.e., the comparison *rx* = *ry*—which is certainly legal—gives TRUE); and yet the rule under discussion would prevent them from being joined! For such reasons, we decided to drop that rule. At the same time, we wanted to alert people to the problem we had been trying to

---

[11] But those prescriptions hadn't been written when IM Prescription 13 was first formulated.

solve, and that's why we added notes to the effect that the implementation might want to outlaw, or at least flag, any attempt to form certain joins (or unions, intersections, or differences). Such an implementation could at least warn the user that, e.g., an attempt to join ellipses and rectangles might be a mistake.

IM PRESCRIPTION 14

14. Let *X* be an expression, let *T* be a type, and let *DT*(*X*) and *T* overlap. Then an operator of the form

    ```
    TREAT_AS_T ( X )
    ```

    (or logical equivalent thereof) shall be supported. We refer to such operators generically as "TREAT" or "TREAT AS" operators; their semantics are as follows. First, if *v*(*X*) is not of type *T,* then a type error shall occur. Otherwise:

    a. If the TREAT invocation appears in a "source" position—in particular, on the right side of an assignment—then the declared type of that invocation shall be *T,* and the invocation shall yield a result, *r* say, with *v*(*r*) equal to *v*(*X*) (and hence *MST*(*r*) equal to *MST*(*X*) also).

    b. If the TREAT invocation appears in a "target" position—in particular, on the left side of an assignment—then that invocation shall act as a pseudovariable reference, which means it shall designate a pseudovariable *X'* with *DT*(*X'*) equal to *T,* *v*(*X'*) equal to *v*(*X*), and *MST*(*X'*) equal to *MST*(*X*).

In the first sentence, *have a nonempty common subtype* has been replaced by *overlap.* A few cosmetic revisions have been made also.

IM PRESCRIPTION 15

15. Let *X* be an expression, let *T* be a type, and let *DT*(*X*) and *T* overlap. Then an operator of the form

    ```
    IS_T ( X )
    ```

    (or logical equivalent thereof) shall be supported. The operator shall return TRUE if *v*(*X*) is of type *T,* FALSE otherwise.

As with IM Prescription 14, the first sentence here has been revised to replace *have a nonempty common subtype* by *overlap.*

IM PRESCRIPTION 16

16. Let *Op* be a read-only operator, let *P* be a parameter to *Op,* and let *T* be the declared type of *P*. Then the declared type of the argument expression (and therefore, necessarily, the most specific type of the argument as such) corresponding to *P* in an invocation of *Op* shall be allowed to be **any subtype** *T'* of *T.* In other words, the read-only operator *Op* applies to values of type *T* and therefore, necessarily, to values of type *T'*—*The Principle of* ***(Read-Only) Operator Inheritance***. It follows that such operators are *polymorphic,* since they apply to values of several different types—*The Principle of* ***(Read-Only) Operator Polymorphism***. It further follows that wherever a value of type *T* is permitted, a value of any subtype of *T* shall also be permitted—*The Principle of* ***(Value) Substitutability***.

A few cosmetic revisions have been made here. However, it's worth pointing out that the entire prescription is logically redundant, in a sense: All of the principles mentioned are nothing but straightforward logical consequences of the fundamental notion of one type being a subtype of another. Our main reasons for including the prescription nevertheless are twofold:

a. We wanted to introduce explicit names for the three principles.

b. More important, we wanted to draw a sharp distinction between those principles as such and their update counterparts as defined under IM Prescription 19—not least because we've noticed a tendency in the open literature for that distinction to become somewhat blurred.

IM PRESCRIPTION 17

IM Prescription 17 has been totally rewritten. Here's the previous version:

> Any given operator *Op* shall have exactly one **specification signature,** a nonempty set of **version signatures,** and a nonempty set of **invocation signatures**. For definiteness, assume the parameters of *Op* and the arguments appearing in any given invocation of *Op* each constitute an ordered list of *n* elements ($n \geqslant 0$), such that the *i*th argument corresponds to the *i*th parameter. Then:
>
> a. The specification signature shall denote *Op* as perceived by potential users. It shall consist of the operator name *Op,* the declared types (in order) of the parameters to *Op,* and the declared type of the result, if any, of executing *Op*. No two distinct operators shall have specification signatures that differ only in the declared types of their results (if any). Moreover, let *S* be a set of types with a nonempty common subtype. Then no two distinct operators shall have specification signatures that differ only in that, for some *i, j, ..., k,* the declared types of their *i*th parameters are distinct members of *S,* the declared types of their *j*th parameters are distinct members of *S,* ..., and the declared types of their *k*th parameters are distinct members of *S.*
>
> b. There shall be one version signature for each implementation version *V* of *Op*. Each such signature shall consist of the operator name *Op* (and possibly the version name *V*), the declared types (in order) of the parameters to *V,* and the declared type of the result, if any, of executing *V.*
>
> c. There shall be one invocation signature for each possible combination of most specific argument types to an invocation of *Op*. Each such signature shall consist of the operator name *Op* and the pertinent combination of most specific argument types (in order). *Note:* The invocation signatures for *Op* can easily be derived from the corresponding specification signature, but the concepts are logically distinct.
>
> Every version of *Op* shall implement the same semantics.

This version of the prescription was sadly muddled to say the least. To be specific:

- First, all of that talk about implementation versions and version signatures clearly has no place in the definition of a *model!* What's important from the point of view of the model is, obviously, the specification signature.

- Second, the prescription says the specification signature for some operator includes "the" declared type of the result (if any) of executing that operator. But it's perfectly possible for different invocations of the same operator to return results of different types.[12] As a trivial example, consider an operator COPY, defined to return a copy (as it were) of its sole argument. Clearly, if COPY is invoked with a circle, it will return a circle, and if it's invoked with "just an ellipse," it will return "just an ellipse." So it would be nice if we could somehow specify distinct declared result types for distinct argument types (or, more generally, distinct argument type combinations).

- Third, as the previous bullet item clearly indicates, we're primarily concerned here with operators that do

---

[12] Of course, those different types must all be subtypes of a certain common supertype (viz., "the" declared type of the operator in question). Incidentally, it's this fact—the fact, that is, that different invocations of the same operator can return results of different types—that accounts for the phenomenon referred to in the literature, not very aptly, as *result covariance.*

return a result—in other words, with read-only operators specifically.

Now, the *Manifesto* book does already include some text on page 296 that touches on these issues. To quote:

> Now we can explain the remark we made ... to the effect that (a) the fact that the user might like to know which implementation version of a given polymorphic operator *Op* is invoked does not undermine (b) our claim that the user's perception is still that there is really just a single operator. The point is, the semantics of *Op* can—and should—be explained to the user in such a way as to take into account any variations in the most specific types of its arguments (if applicable). For example, the semantics of COPY are simply that it returns a copy of its argument; thus, if it is passed a circle, it returns a circle, and if it is passed "just an ellipse," it returns "just an ellipse."

It follows that, given our usual types ELLIPSE and CIRCLE and the operator MOVE (which returns a result just like its first argument except that it's centered on the center of its second argument, and is defined to have result type ELLIPSE), the user knows the following code will work, because he or she knows that invoking MOVE on a circle will return a circle:

```
VAR CX CIRCLE ;
VAR CY CIRCLE ;
VAR R RECTANGLE ;

CX := TREAT_AS_CIRCLE ( MOVE ( CY , R ) ) ;
```

But wouldn't it be preferable not to have to invoke TREAT at all and write just the following?—

```
CX := MOVE ( CY , R ) ;
```

We believe it would.

Furthermore, the *Manifesto* book also says (on page 300):

> It would be possible to capture more (though still not all) of the "result covariance" property by including parameter names in the specification signature and then allowing the RETURNS specification to refer to those names accordingly. Under such a scheme, the specification signature for MOVE might look like this:
>
> ```
> MOVE ( E ELLIPSE, R RECTANGLE ) RETURNS SAME_TYPE_AS ( E )
> ```
>
> The intent here is that an invocation of MOVE returns a result of the same declared type as that of the argument corresponding to its first ... parameter.

And the text goes on to suggest that such a feature might then indeed allow us to drop the TREAT from the assignment to CX.

Let's look at a slightly more complicated example. Suppose for the sake of discussion that the system has provided INTEGER as a system defined type but hasn't defined the operation of addition on integers (a most unlikely state of affairs, of course, but let's stay with it for the sake of the example). Suppose further that we've defined EVEN and ODD as immediate subtypes of type INTEGER, with the obvious semantics. Then we might define an operator PLUS for adding two integers as follows:

```
OPERATOR PLUS ( A INTEGER , B INTEGER )
   RETURNS CASE WHEN IS_EVEN ( A ) AND IS_EVEN ( B ) THEN EVEN
                WHEN IS_EVEN ( A ) AND IS_ODD  ( B ) THEN ODD
                WHEN IS_ODD  ( A ) AND IS_EVEN ( B ) THEN ODD
                WHEN IS_ODD  ( A ) AND IS_ODD  ( B ) THEN EVEN
           END CASE ;
   RETURN < some expression that computes A + B > ;
END OPERATOR ;
```

The significant point about this example is that the RETURNS clause specifies the declared type of the result for various possible combinations of argument declared types—each individual WHEN/THEN specification effectively defines one *invocation* signature,[13] and there's one such specification for each pertinent argument declared type combination. As a consequence, various TREAT invocations that might otherwise have been needed aren't needed any longer. For example, if EI is a variable of declared type EVEN, we can write

```
EI := PLUS ( ODD ( 3 ) , ODD ( 7 ) ) ;
```

instead of what we would otherwise have had to write:

```
EI := TREAT_AS_EVEN ( PLUS ( ODD ( 3 ) , ODD ( 7 ) ) ) ;
```

(We're assuming here that type ODD has a selector with the same name.)

Note that the foregoing ideas are consistent with the revised version of IM Prescription 13, according to which, for example, the result of an intersection of ellipses and circles has declared type "circles," not "ellipses" (speaking very loosely indeed, of course).

> *Aside:* We should point out, however, that—with reference to the PLUS example in particular—(a) the CASE expression in the RETURNS specification is evaluated at compile time, not run time (to be specific, it's evaluated whenever the compiler processes a PLUS invocation) and hence that (b) the IS_EVEN and IS_ODD operator invocations in that CASE expression are also evaluated at that time, and thus (c) they return TRUE if and only if the corresponding *declared* types are as indicated. In other words, IS_EVEN and IS_ODD here aren't the usual operators of those names, which return TRUE if and only if their operands have the indicated types at *run* time. *End of aside.*

Let's consider one more example. Suppose (a) operator *Op* has a specification signature involving two parameters X and Y, both of declared type ELLIPSE; (b) result declared types are defined (as part of that specification signature) corresponding to the argument declared type combinations ELLIPSE/ELLIPSE, ELLIPSE/CIRCLE, and CIRCLE/ELLIPSE (only); and (c) *Op* is invoked with the argument declared type combination CIRCLE/CIRCLE. That invocation doesn't match any of the specified invocation signatures exactly—so what's its declared type?

The simplest solution to this problem (perhaps not the only one) is to allow the CASE expression that specifies the various invocation signatures to include an appropriate ELSE clause, as here:

```
CASE WHEN IS_ELLIPSE ( X ) AND IS_ELLIPSE ( Y ) THEN ...
     WHEN IS_ELLIPSE ( X ) AND IS_CIRCLE  ( Y ) THEN ...
     WHEN IS_CIRCLE  ( X ) AND IS_ELLIPSE ( Y ) THEN ...
     ELSE ...
END CASE ;
```

With the foregoing discussion and examples by way of motivation, then, here's the revised version of IM Prescription 17:

17. Let *Op* be a read-only operator. Then *Op* shall have exactly one **specification signature,** denoting that operator as perceived by potential users. The specification signature for *Op* shall consist of the operator name and a nonempty set of *invocation signatures*. For definiteness, assume the parameters of *Op* and the

---

[13] The term *invocation signature* as used here and in the revised version of IM Prescription 17 has a meaning different from the one it had in the *Manifesto* book (in the previous version of this prescription in particular). Previously the term referred to the *most specific* types of the arguments to the invocation in question (in other words, it was a run time concept, loosely speaking); now it refers to the *declared* types of the corresponding argument expressions instead (and is thus a compile time concept).

argument expressions involved in any given invocation of *Op* each constitute an ordered list of *n* elements ($n \geqslant 0$), such that the *j*th argument expression corresponds to the *j*th parameter (*j* = 1, 2, ..., *n*). Further, let *PDT* = <*DT1, DT2, ..., DTn*> be the declared types, in sequence, of those *n* parameters, and let *PDT′* = <*DT1′, DT2′, ..., DTn′*> be a sequence of types such that *DTj′* is a nonempty subtype of *DTj* (*j* = 1, 2, ..., *n*). For each such sequence *PDT′*, there shall exist an **invocation signature** consisting of the operator name and a specification of the declared type of the result of an invocation of *Op* with argument expressions of declared types as specified by *PDT′* (the **declared type** for, or of, such an invocation).

IM PRESCRIPTION 18

18. Let *Op* be an update operator and let *P* be a parameter to *Op* that is not subject to update. Then *Op* shall behave as a read-only operator as far as *P* is concerned, and all relevant aspects of IM Prescription 16 shall apply, mutatis mutandis.

This prescription remains essentially unchanged.

IM PRESCRIPTION 19

19. Let *Op* be an update operator, let *P* be a parameter to *Op* that is subject to update, and let *T* be the declared type of *P*. Then it might or might not be the case that the declared type of the argument expression (and therefore, necessarily, the most specific type of the argument as such) corresponding to *P* in an invocation of *Op* shall be allowed to be some proper subtype *T′* of type *T*. It follows that for each such update operator *Op* and for each parameter *P* to *Op* that is subject to update, it shall be necessary to state explicitly for which proper subtypes *T′* of the declared type *T* of parameter *P* operator *Op* shall be inherited—*The Principle of **(Update) Operator Inheritance***. (And if update operator *Op* is not inherited in this way by type *T′*, it shall not be inherited by any proper subtype of type *T′* either.) Update operators shall thus be only conditionally polymorphic—*The Principle of **(Update) Operator Polymorphism***. If *Op* is an update operator and *P* is a parameter to *Op* that is subject to update and *T′* is a proper subtype of the declared type *T* of *P* for which *Op* is inherited, then by definition it shall be possible to invoke *Op* with an argument expression corresponding to parameter *P* that is of declared type *T′*—*The Principle of **(Variable) Substitutability***.

The commentary on IM Prescription 16 above applies here also, mutatis mutandis.

IM PRESCRIPTION 20

IM Prescription 20 has been totally rewritten. Here's the previous version:

> A **union type** is a type *T* such that there exists no value that is of type *T* and not of some immediate subtype of *T* (i.e., there is no value *v* such that *MST*(*v*) is *T*). A **dummy type** is a union type that has no declared possible representation (and hence no selector); a given union type shall be permitted to be a dummy type if and only if it is empty or it has no regular immediate supertype (where a **regular type** is a type that is not a dummy type). Moreover:
>
> a. Conceptually, there is a special scalar dummy type, *alpha,* that contains all scalar values. Type *alpha* is **the maximal type** with respect to every scalar type; by definition, it has no declared possible representation and no immediate supertypes.
>
> b. Conceptually, there is a special scalar dummy type, *omega,* that contains no values at all. Type *omega* is **the minimal type** with respect to every scalar type; by definition, it has no declared possible representation and no immediate subtypes.

The most important difference between this previous version of the prescription and the revised version is as follows: The previous version was supposed to cover tuple and relation types as well as scalar types; the new version is explicitly limited to scalar types only. To repeat: The previous version was supposed to cover tuple and relation types too—but in fact it didn't. To be specific, it defined a dummy type to be a union type with "no declared possible representation (and hence no selector)." But that definition tacitly assumed the type in question was scalar, because:

- Tuple and relation types don't have declared possible representations anyway.
- On the other hand, tuple and relation types do have selectors (except in the very special case, for tuple types only, where the type in question is empty).

In any case, we've come to realize that union, dummy, and regular types, as such, really have to be scalar types anyway—i.e., we believe the concepts make little sense for tuple and relation types—and so we define all such types to be scalar types specifically.

Here then is the revised version of IM Prescription 20:

20. Type *T* shall be a **union type** if and only if it is a scalar type and there exists no value that is of type *T* and not of some immediate subtype of *T* (i.e., there is no value *v* such that *MST*(*v*) is *T*). Moreover:

    a. A type shall be a **dummy type** if and only if either of the following is true:

        1. It is one of the types *alpha* and *omega* (see below).

        2. It is a union type, has no declared representation (and hence no selector), and no regular supertype. *Note:* Type *alpha* in fact satisfies all three of these conditions; type *omega* satisfies the first two only.

        A type shall be a **regular type** if and only if it is a scalar type and not a dummy type.

    b. Conceptually, there shall be a system defined scalar type called *alpha,* the **maximal type** with respect to every scalar type. That type shall have all of the following properties:

        1. It shall contain all scalar values.

        2. It shall have no immediate supertypes.

        3. It shall be an immediate supertype for every scalar root type in the given set of types *GST*.

        No other scalar type shall have any of these properties (unless the given set of types *GST* contains just one regular type—necessarily type **boolean**—in which unlikely case that type will of course satisfy the first property).

    c. Conceptually, there shall be a system defined scalar type called *omega,* the **minimal type** with respect to every scalar type. That type shall have all of the following properties:

        1. It shall contain no values at all. (It follows that, as RM Prescription 1 in fact states, it shall have no example value in particular.)

        2. It shall have no immediate subtypes.

        3. It shall be an immediate subtype for every scalar leaf type in the given set of types *GST*.

        No other scalar type shall have any of these properties.

IM PRESCRIPTION 21

21. Type *T* shall be an **empty type** if and only if it is either an empty scalar type or an empty tuple type. Scalar type *T* shall be empty if and only if *T* is type *omega*. Tuple type *T* shall be empty if and only if *T* has at least one attribute that is of some empty type. An empty type shall be permitted as the declared type of (a) an attribute of a tuple type or relation type; (b) nothing else.

This prescription is new; the intent is to introduce an explicit definition for the concept of an empty type (a concept that, we observe in passing, has given rise to rather more than its fair share of difficulties) and to define exactly where such types are permitted.

First, as the prescription says, there's exactly one empty scalar type: viz., type *omega*. By contrast, there can be any number of empty tuple types (note that the definition of "empty tuple type" is recursive). Here are some examples:

```
TUPLE { E omega }

TUPLE { E ELLIPSE , R omega }

TUPLE { R RECTANGLE , X TUPLE { E omega } }
```

Now let *T* be an arbitrary relation type, with heading {*H*}. By definition, there's always at least one relation of type *T*—viz., the relation with heading {*H*} and body the empty set, or in other words the empty relation of type RELATION {*H*}. It follows that there's no such thing as an empty relation type.

As for the question of where empty types are permitted, let's consider each of the various constructs in turn that have a declared type:

- *Scalar and tuple variables:* An attempt to define a scalar or tuple variable *V* with an empty declared type will fail at run time (if not at compile time) because there's no initialization value that can be assigned to *V*.

- *Relation variables:* A relvar can't be defined with an empty declared type because there aren't any empty relation types.

- *Possible representation ("possrep") components:* An attempt to define a scalar type *T* with a possrep component of some empty declared type will fail at run time (if not at compile time) because there's no example value that can be specified for *T*.

- *Read-only operators:* An attempt to define a read-only operator *Op* with a result of some empty declared type is illegal. If the violation isn't caught at compile time, an invocation of *Op* will certainly fail at run time.

- *Expressions:* By definition, any given expression represents an invocation of some read-only operator. It follows that no expression can have an empty declared type.

- *Parameters:* An attempt to define an operator *Op* with a parameter of some empty declared type is illegal. If the violation isn't caught at compile time, an invocation of *Op* will certainly fail at run time.

- *Attributes:* Attributes of tuple and relation types are allowed to be of some empty declared type. (Note that this observation is true of attributes of minimal types in particular—see IM Prescription 25—but a type doesn't have to be a minimal type in order to have such an attribute.) To say it again, however, if *T* is a tuple type with an attribute of declared type some empty type, then *T* can't be used as the declared type of anything other than, possibly, some attribute of some other tuple type or relation type.

IM PRESCRIPTION 22

IM Prescription 22 (previously IM Prescription 21) has been revised and extended. Here's the new version:

22. Let *T* and *T′* be both tuple types or both relation types. Then type *T′* shall be a **subtype** of type *T*, and type *T* shall be a **supertype** of type *T′*, if and only if (a) *T* and *T′* have the same attribute names *A1, A2, ..., An* and (b) for all *j* (*j* = 1, 2, ..., *n*), the type of attribute *Aj* of *T′* is a subtype of the type of attribute *Aj* of *T*. Tuple *t* shall be of some subtype of tuple type *T* if and only if the heading of *t* is that of some subtype of *T*. Relation *r* shall be of some subtype of relation type *T* if and only if the heading of *r* is that of some subtype of *T* (in which case every tuple in the body of *r* shall necessarily also have a heading that is that of some subtype of *T*).

The revision consists of a tightening up of the definitions. The extensions consist of the last two sentences, which spell out what it means for a tuple or a relation to be of some subtype of a given type. These additions allow us to drop the previous IM Prescription 22—more generally, to drop entirely the notion of a tuple or relation "conforming" to some heading, which was what that previous prescription was all about.

IM PRESCRIPTION 23

23. Let *T1, T2, ..., Tm* (*m* ⩾ 0), *T*, and *T′* be all tuple types or all relation types, with headings

```
{ <A1,T11>  , <A2,T12>  , ... , <An,T1n>  }
{ <A1,T21>  , <A2,T22>  , ... , <An,T2n>  }
.....................................
{ <A1,Tm1>  , <A2,Tm2>  , ... , <An,Tmn>  }

{ <A1,T01 > , <A2,T02 > , ... , <An,T0n > }
{ <A1,T01'> , <A2,T02'> , ... , <An,T0n'> }
```

respectively. Further, for all *j* (*j* = 1, 2, ..., *n*), let types *T1j, T2j, ..., Tmj* have a common subtype (and hence a common supertype also). Then:

a. Type *T* shall be a **common supertype** for, or of, types *T1, T2, ..., Tm* if and only if, for all *j* (*j* = 1, 2, ..., *n*), type *T0j* is a common supertype for types *T1j, T2j, ..., Tmj*. Further, that type *T* shall be the **most specific** common supertype for *T1, T2, ..., Tm* if and only if no proper subtype of *T* is also a common supertype for those types.

b. Type *T′* shall be a **common subtype** for, or of, types *T1, T2, ..., Tm* if and only if, for all *j* (*j* = 1, 2, ..., *n*), type *T0j′* is a common subtype for types *T1j, T2j, ..., Tmj*. Further, that type *T′* shall be the **least specific** common subtype—also known as the **intersection type** or **intersection subtype**—for *T1, T2, ..., Tm* if and only if no proper supertype of *T′* is also a common subtype for those types.

Note: Given types *T1, T2, ..., Tm* as defined above, it can be shown (thanks in particular to IM Prescription 24) that a unique most specific common supertype *T* and a unique least specific common subtype *T′* always exist. In the case of that particular common subtype *T′*, moreover, it can also be shown that whenever a given value is of each of types *T1, T2, ..., Tm*, it is also of type *T′* (hence the alternative term *intersection type*)—in which case, for all *j* (*j* = 1, 2, ..., *n*), type *T0j′* is the intersection type for types *T1j, T2j, ..., Tmj*. And it can further be shown that every tuple value and every relation value has both a unique least specific type and a unique most specific type (regarding the latter, see also IM Prescription 25).

This prescription is new. Its purpose is to do for tuple and relation types what IM Prescription 8 does for scalar types. As we've seen, IM Prescription 8 has been revised too to make it clear that it applies to scalar types only; the previous version of that prescription was meant to cover tuple and relation types as well, but failed to do so adequately. To be specific, it was phrased in terms of an arbitrary set of types *T1, T2, ..., Tm,* and thus failed to take into account that:

- Those types *T1, T2, ..., Tm* were supposed to be all scalar types or all tuple types or all relation types, not a mixture.
- Moreover, if they were all tuple types, then they were supposed all to be from the same type lattice—see the remarks on this topic under IM Prescription 6—and similarly for relation types.

Thus, for example, the prescription apparently required the following set of five types to have some common subtype, which they manifestly don't:

```
INTEGER

TUPLE { E ELLIPSE }

TUPLE { C CIRCLE }

TUPLE { E ELLIPSE , C CIRCLE }

RELATION { R RECTANGLE , X omega }
```

By the way, the prescription makes the claim that (tuple or relation) types *T1, T2, ..., Tm,* if they have a common subtype, also have a unique most specific common supertype. This claim is valid, but perhaps not obviously so; for that reason, we include here an edited version of text from the *Manifesto* book, pages 347-348. Note that in what follows we break for once with our convention that type *T′* is always a subtype of type *T*.

> First of all, let *T* and *T′* be scalar types. Then we assume for present purposes that the most specific common supertype of *T* and *T′* is well defined and well understood. The specifics of this case are comparatively straightforward and can be found in Chapter 15 of the *Manifesto* book.
>
> Second, let *T1, T2, ..., Tn* and *T1′, T2′, ..., Tn′* be two sets of types, where, for all *j* (*j* = 1, 2, ..., *n*), *Tj* and *Tj′* (a) are both scalar types or both tuple types or both relation types, and moreover (b) have a common subtype (i.e., are from the same type lattice). Now:
>
> - Consider tuple types *T* and *T′*, with headings
>
> ```
> { <A1,T1 > , <A2,T2 > , ... , <An,Tn > }
>
> { <A1,T1'> , <A2,T2'> , ... , <An,Tn'> }
> ```
>
> respectively. Then we define the most specific common supertype of types *T* and *T′* to be the unique tuple type with heading
>
> ```
> { <A1,MSC1> , <A2,MSC2> , ... , <An,MSCn> }
> ```
>
> where, for all *j* (*j* = 1, 2, ..., *n*), *MSCj* is the most specific common supertype of *Tj* and *Tj′*.
>
> - Consider relation types *T* and *T′*, with headings
>
> ```
> { <A1,T1 > , <A2,T2 > , ... , <An,Tn > }
>
> { <A1,T1'> , <A2,T2'> , ... , <An,Tn'> }
> ```
>
> respectively. Then we define the most specific common supertype of types *T* and *T′* to be the unique relation type with heading

```
{ <A1,MSC1> , <A2,MSC2> , ..., <An,MSCn> }
```

where, for all j ($j = 1, 2, ..., n$), *MSCj* is the most specific common supertype of *Tj* and *Tj'*.

The definition of most specific common supertype for a set of m types for $m > 2$, where the types are all scalar types or all tuple types or all relation types and all have a common supertype, follows by pairwise application of the foregoing definition to the set in question. But what about $m < 2$?

- The case $m = 1$ is straightforward—the set of types contains just one type, *T* say, and we can define the "most specific common supertype" for that set to be simply *T* itself.

- However, we also need to address the case $m = 0$. In particular, what's the most specific common supertype for the empty set of types corresponding to the empty set of values of some attribute within an empty relation? You probably won't be surprised to learn that the answer to this question is the pertinent minimal type.[14] That is, if the declared type of the attribute in question is some scalar type, then the most specific common supertype is just *omega;* if it's some tuple type or relation type *T,* then the most specific common supertype is *T_omega* (see IM Prescription 24). We remark as an aside that the least specific common subtype of such an empty set of types is the pertinent maximal type (i.e., *alpha* or *T_alpha,* as applicable).

IM PRESCRIPTION 24

24. Let *T, T_alpha,* and *T_omega* be all tuple types or all relation types, with headings

```
{ <A1,T1>       , <A2,T2>       , ... , <An,Tn>       }
{ <A1,T1_alpha> , <A2,T2_alpha> , ... , <An,Tn_alpha> }
{ <A1,T1_omega> , <A2,T2_omega> , ... , <An,Tn_omega> }
```

respectively. Then types *T_alpha* and *T_omega* shall be the **maximal type with respect to type *T*** and the **minimal type with respect to type *T*,** respectively, if and only if, for all i ($i = 1, 2, ..., n$), type *Ti_alpha* is the maximal type with respect to type *Ti* and type *Ti_omega* is the minimal type with respect to type *Ti*.

This prescription was previously IM Prescription 23 but otherwise remains unchanged. However, the following text, extracted and edited from the *Manifesto* book (pages 345-346), gives some illustrative examples and is worth repeating here:

> The minimal type with respect to the tuple type
>
> `TUPLE { E ELLIPSE , R RECTANGLE }`
>
> is the (empty) tuple type TUPLE {E *omega,* R *omega*}. Likewise, the minimal type with respect to the relation type
>
> `RELATION { E ELLIPSE , R RECTANGLE }`
>
> is the (nonempty) relation type RELATION {E *omega,* R *omega*}. In general, the situation with respect to tuple and relation minimal types is as follows: There's exactly one tuple minimal type for each possible tuple type (loosely speaking), and exactly one relation minimal type for each possible relation type (again, loosely speaking). More precisely, if and only if tuple types *TT1* and *TT2* have no common subtype, then the corresponding tuple minimal types are distinct (and analogously for relation types). Also:
>
> - Unlike the scalar minimal type *omega,* the tuple minimal type *TT_omega* corresponding to some tuple type *TT* is not necessarily empty. The particular example shown above—TUPLE {E *omega,* R *omega*}—is empty, of

---

[14] See the final part of the commentary on IM Prescription 8 in the present chapter.

course (there are no tuples of this type). A conceptually important counterexample is as follows: Let *TT* be TUPLE {}. Then *TT_omega* is equal to *TT* (i.e., *TT* is its own minimal type), and it contains exactly one value: namely, the 0-tuple (i.e., the tuple with the empty set of attributes).

- Moreover, the relation minimal type *RT_omega* corresponding to some relation type *RT* is definitely not empty; in fact, as we already know, there's no such thing as an empty relation type (the very phrase is a contradiction in terms). The example shown above—RELATION {E *omega,* R *omega*}—contains exactly one value: namely, the empty relation of that type. Another conceptually important case is as follows: Let *RT* be RELATION {}. Then *RT_omega* is equal to *RT* (i.e., *RT* is its own minimal type), and it contains two values, TABLE_DUM and TABLE_DEE.

Now suppose scalar type ELLIPSE is a dummy type, with immediate regular subtypes CIRCLE and NONCIRCLE, and consider the following types:

- `TUPLE { E ELLIPSE }`

  Since there aren't any values of this type that aren't values of some proper subtype of the type, the type might be implicitly considered a union tuple type, and in fact a dummy tuple type. As already indicated, however, we see little use for such notions, and we don't define them formally.

- `TUPLE { E CIRCLE , X alpha }`

  This one too might be considered a tuple dummy type, if it were thought useful to do so.

- `TUPLE { E omega }`

  This is an example of an empty tuple type. It too might be regarded as a dummy tuple type.

- `TUPLE { X CIRCLE , Y TUPLE { Z omega } }`

  This is a more complicated example of an empty tuple type.

- `RELATION { E ELLIPSE }`

  Here again is the text from the first example above (i.e., for type TUPLE {E ELLIPSE}), except that we've replaced *tuple* by *relation,* twice:

  > Since there aren't any values of this type that aren't values of some proper subtype of the type, the type might be implicitly considered a union relation type, and in fact a dummy relation type. As already indicated, however, we see little use for such notions, and we don't define them formally.

  In fact, however, this text is invalid. Why? And what do you conclude?

- `RELATION { E omega , NC NONCIRCLE }`

  This type is nonempty, even though it has an attribute of an empty type.

- `RELATION { E omega , NC omega }`

  This one too is nonempty. But the interesting thing about it is that it's a proper subtype of the previous type, even though the set of values it contains isn't a proper subset of the set of values contained in the previous one (see the discussion of IM Prescription 2 earlier in this chapter).

IM PRESCRIPTION 25

25. Let {*H*} be a heading defined as follows:

```
{ <A1,T1> , <A2,T2> , ... , <An,Tn> }
```

Then:

a. If *t* is a tuple of type some subtype of TUPLE {*H*}—meaning *t* is of the form

```
{ <A1,T1',v1> , <A2,T2',v2> , ... , <An,Tn',vn> }
```

where, for all *j* (*j* = 1, 2, ..., *n*), type *Tj'* is a subtype of type *Tj* and *vj* is a value of type *Tj'*—then the **most specific** type of *t* shall be

```
TUPLE { <A1,MST1> , <A2,MST2> , ... , <An,MSTn> }
```

where, for all *j* (*j* = 1, 2, ..., *n*), type *MSTj* is the most specific type of value *vj*.

b. If *r* is a relation of type some subtype of RELATION {*H*}—meaning each tuple in the body of *r* can be regarded without loss of generality as being of the form

```
{ <A1,T1',v1> , <A2,T2',v2> , ... , <An,Tn',vn> }
```

where, for all *j* (*j* = 1, 2, ..., *n*), type *Tj'* is a subtype of type *Tj* and is the most specific type of value *vj* (note that distinct tuples in the body of *r* will be of distinct most specific types, in general; thus, type *Tj'* varies over the tuples in the body of *r*)—then the **most specific** type of *r* shall be

```
RELATION { <A1,MST1> , <A2,MST2> , ... , <An,MSTn> }
```

where, for all *j* (*j* = 1, 2, ..., *n*), type *MSTj* is the most specific common supertype of those most specific types *Tj'*, taken over all tuples in the body of *r*.

This prescription was previously IM Prescription 24 but otherwise remains essentially unchanged. But the following text, extracted and edited from the *Manifesto* book (pages 349-351), gives further insight and is worth repeating here. It addresses the question: What exactly is the most specific type of a given value *v* in the case where *v* is a relation?

By way of example, consider the following relation types:

```
RELATION { E ELLIPSE , R RECTANGLE }   /* relation type "ER" */

RELATION { E CIRCLE  , R RECTANGLE }   /* relation type "CR" */

RELATION { E ELLIPSE , R SQUARE    }   /* relation type "ES" */

RELATION { E CIRCLE  , R SQUARE    }   /* relation type "CS" */
```

Let's agree to refer to these types by the names ER, CR, ES, and CS, respectively, as the comments indicate. Then types CR and ES are immediate subtypes of type ER, and type CS is an immediate subtype of both type CR and type ES. Here now are some relations of these various types:

E : ELLIPSE	R : RECTANGLE
E1 : *ellipse*	R1 : *rectangle*
C2 : *circle*	R2 : *rectangle*
E3 : *ellipse*	S3 : *square*
C4 : *circle*	S4 : *square*

E : ELLIPSE	R : RECTANGLE
C4 : *circle*	S4 : *square*

E : CIRCLE	R : RECTANGLE
C2 : *circle*	R2 : *rectangle*
C4 : *circle*	S4 : *square*

E : ELLIPSE	R : SQUARE
E3 : *ellipse*	S3 : *square*
C4 : *circle*	S4 : *square*

E : CIRCLE	R : SQUARE
C4 : *circle*	S4 : *square*

E : *omega*	R : *omega*

Note: We adopt the convention in these pictures that values of the form E*i* are ellipses that aren't circles, values of the form R*i* are rectangles that aren't squares, values of the form C*i* are circles, and values of the form S*i* are squares. The most specific types for all such values are shown in lowercase italics. And the most specific types of these relations are (from top to bottom) types ER, CS, CR, ES, CS again, and ER_*omega,* respectively (where ER_*omega* is the type RELATION {E *omega,* R *omega*}). Note that, e.g., the first (top) relation would still have relation type ER as its most specific type even if we deleted the only tuple—viz., the E1-R1 tuple—that is in fact of *tuple* type ER, as it were. (If we deleted the C2-R2 tuple as well, however, that relation would then have relation type ES as its most specific type.)

Now, you might feel something counterintuitive is going on here, and so it is, in a way. For example, look again at the top relation (call it *TopRel*). For relation *TopRel,* it almost seems as if we've defined the *most* specific type of that relation (viz., relation type ER) to be the *least* specific type of the tuples it contains!—and indeed so we have, in this particular example. So why didn't we define the most specific type of *TopRel* to be relation type CS (the other "extreme" type) instead? The answer is as follows:

- Suppose we had defined that most specific type to be CS instead of ER. Then certain of the attributes in certain of the tuples in *TopRel* would contain values that weren't of the "right" type. The E1-R1 tuple, for example, contains a value of type ELLIPSE (not CIRCLE) and a value of type RECTANGLE (not SQUARE), and is thus certainly not of *tuple* type CS (in fact, it's of tuple type ER).

- But allowing a relation of relation type CS to contain a tuple of tuple type ER would be a contradiction in terms—it would mean, for example, that attribute E of that relation, of type CIRCLE, is allowed to include values that are "just ellipses" and not circles. Indeed, such a state of affairs would be just as bad as allowing a variable of declared type CIRCLE to have a value that's "just an ellipse."

It follows that we must define the most specific type for relation *r* in the way we have: namely, in such a way that the type corresponding to attribute *A* is the most specific common supertype—and not, as might have been expected, the least specific common subtype—of the most specific types of all of the *A* values in *r*.

By way of another example, consider the following set of relations:

PX : PARALLELOGRAM	PY : PARALLELOGRAM
X1 : *rectangle*	Y1 : *rectangle*
X2 : *rhombus*	Y2 : *rectangle*
X3 : *rectangle*	Y3 : *square*
X4 : *square*	Y4 : *square*

PX : PARALLELOGRAM	PY : PARALLELOGRAM
X2 : *rhombus*	Y2 : *rectangle*
X4 : *square*	Y4 : *square*

PX : PARALLELOGRAM	PY : PARALLELOGRAM
X3 : *rectangle*	Y3 : *square*
X4 : *square*	Y4 : *square*

PX : PARALLELOGRAM	PY : PARALLELOGRAM
X4 : *square*	Y4 : *square*

PX : PARALLELOGRAM	PY : PARALLELOGRAM

These relations are all of type RELATION {PX PARALLELOGRAM, PY PARALLELOGRAM}. Their most specific types (from top to bottom) are as follows:

```
RELATION { PX PARALLELOGRAM , PY RECTANGLE }
RELATION { PX RHOMBUS       , PY RECTANGLE }
RELATION { PX RECTANGLE ,     PY SQUARE    }
RELATION { PX SQUARE    ,     PY SQUARE    }
RELATION { PX omega     ,     PY omega     }
```

Note the last one in particular! You might have expected the type in this case to be RELATION {PX *alpha*, PY *alpha*}; if it were, however, then we wouldn't be able to assign the relation in question to a relvar of type, say, RELATION {PX PARALLELOGRAM, PY PARALLELOGRAM}.

IM PRESCRIPTION 26

26. Let *V* be a tuple variable or relation variable of declared type *T*, and let the heading of *T* have attributes *A1*, *A2*, ..., *An*. Then we can model *V* as a named set of named ordered triples of the form <*DTj*,*MSTj*,*vj*> (*j* = 1, 2, ..., *n*), where:

a. The name of the set is the name of the variable, *V*.

b. The name of each triple is the name of the corresponding attribute.

c. *DTj* is the name of the declared type of attribute *Aj*.

d. *MSTj* is the name of the **most specific type**—also known as the **current** most specific type—for, or of, attribute *Aj*. (If *V* is a relation variable, then the most specific type of *Aj* is the most specific common supertype of the most specific types of the *m* values in *vj*—see the explanation of *vj* below.)

e. If *V* is a tuple variable, *vj* is a value of most specific type *MSTj*—the **current value** for, or of, attribute *Aj*. If *V* is a relation variable, then let the body of the current value of *V* consist of *m* tuples ($m \geqslant 0$); label those tuples (in some arbitrary sequence) "tuple 1," "tuple 2," ..., "tuple *m*"; then *vj* is a sequence of *m* values (not necessarily all distinct), being the *Aj* values from tuple 1, tuple 2, ..., tuple *m* (in that order). Note that those *Aj* values are all of type *MSTj*.

We use the notation *DT*(*Aj*), *MST*(*Aj*), *v*(*Aj*) to refer to the *DTj*, *MSTj*, *vj* components, respectively, of attribute *Aj* of this model of tuple variable or relation variable *V*. We also use the notation *DT*(*V*), *MST*(*V*), *v*(*V*) to refer to the overall declared type, overall current most specific type, and overall current value, respectively, of this model of tuple variable or relation variable *V*.

Now let *X* be a tuple expression or relation expression. By definition, *X* specifies an invocation of some tuple operator or relation operator *Op*. Thus, the notation *DTj*(*V*), *MSTj*(*V*), *vj*(*V*) just introduced can be extended in an obvious way to refer to the declared type *DTj*(*X*), the current most specific type *MSTj*(*X*), and the current value *vj*(*X*), respectively, of the *DTj*, *MSTj*, *vj* components, respectively, of attribute *Aj* of tuple expression or relation expression *X*—where *DTj*(*X*) is the declared type of *Aj* for the invocation of *Op* in question (see IM Prescription 17) and is known at compile time, and *MSTj*(*X*) and *vj*(*X*) refer to the result of evaluating *X* and are therefore not known until run time (in general).

This prescription replaces IM Prescription 25 from the previous version of the model. Various cosmetic changes have been made. In addition, paragraph e. has been extended to make it explicit that the value *m* can be zero, and hence that the value *vi* can consist of an empty sequence of *Ai* values. (To be specific, these remarks apply to the case in which *MSTi* is either *omega* or *T_omega* for some tuple type *T*—see IM Prescriptions 20 and 25.) Also, the final sentence has been revised to bring it into line with the revised version of IM Prescription 17 (see earlier in this chapter). Further explanation can be found in the *Manifesto* book, pages 352-353.

CONCLUDING REMARKS

Well, at least there are a few prescriptions from the previous version of the model that haven't changed ... but the fact that we found so much to change is certainly a little embarrassing. On the other hand, as noted in the introduction to this chapter, the big picture is still basically as it was before. What led us to make all of the changes was, in large part, the gratifying degree of interest in our ideas that we found on the part of others—and here we would like to acknowledge the helpful contributions of numerous participants in the *Manifesto* forum (see *www.thethirdmanifesto.com*).

The revisions fall into three main classes: minor clarifications, matters relating to tuple and relation types, and model improvements. We discuss each in turn, briefly.

Minor clarifications: This is the largest class. Examples here include IM Prescription 7, which now includes an explicit definition of the notion of overlapping types, and IM Prescriptions 12-15, all of which include an explicit appeal to that notion.

Tuple and relation types: The changes here consist primarily of corrections necessitated by the fact that certain prescriptions were supposed to cover tuple and relation types as well as scalar types but failed do so adequately. An example here is IM Prescription 8; in this particular case, we've revised the prescription so that it now clearly applies to scalar types only, and we've introduced a new prescription (IM Prescription 23) to serve as the tuple/relation counterpart to that revised IM Prescription 8.

Model improvements: IM Prescriptions 2, 13, 17, 20, and 21 are the relevant ones here:

- IM Prescription 2 has been relaxed to drop the requirement that proper subtypes are proper subsets. This change is a good example of the difference between what might be termed the formal and informal versions of our model. Informally, we believe, and always have believed, that a sensible use of our model would usually abide by that requirement. What's more, we were guided by that belief in the original design of our model. But (a) there seems to be no way to enforce the requirement;[15] (b) dropping it doesn't seem to do any serious harm; and in any case, (c) we've actually found a situation where the requirement doesn't make sense. Hence the revision.

- IM Prescription 13 has been revised to say—among other things, and speaking *very* loosely—that the declared type of the intersection of a set of ellipses and a set of circles is "set of circles" instead of "set of ellipses." This revision clearly brings the model more closely into line with the way the world actually works and for that reason is clearly an improvement. The revision is also closely related to the revisions we've made to IM Prescription 17.

- IM Prescription 17 has been extended (or, rather, corrected) to take proper account of the "result covariance" property—and here we would specifically like to acknowledge the contributions of Adrian Hudnott, whose insights in this area led directly to the current formulation.

- IM Prescription 20 has been revised to clarify the situation with regard to union types, dummy types, and types *alpha* and *omega* (all of which are topics over which a certain amount of confusion has been evident in the past).

---

[15] Except as noted in the footnote to the commentary on IM Prescription 2 earlier in the chapter.

- IM Prescription 21 has been introduced to spell out the details of what an empty type is and where such a type can be used as a declared type.

Chapter 21

Extending Tutorial D to Support the Inheritance Model

I conceive you may use any language you choose
to indulge in, without impropriety

—W. S. Gilbert: *Iolanthe*

In this chapter we offer some proposals for extending **Tutorial D** syntax to support the inheritance model as described in Chapters 19 and 20. Portions of this material originally appeared in the *Manifesto* book (i.e., *Databases, Types, and the Relational Model: The Third Manifesto,* 3rd edition, by C. J. Date and Hugh Darwen, Addison-Wesley, 2006), but they were scattered over several chapters in that book; in any case, there are also several features that are defined here for the first time. *Note:* Examples illustrating most of the ideas can be found in the *Manifesto* book; for that reason, few examples are included in the present chapter.

One general point: **Tutorial D** as defined in Chapter 11 frequently requires some construct to be of some specific declared type. For example, consider scalar variable definitions:

```
<scalar var def>
    ::=   VAR <scalar var name> <scalar type or init value>

<scalar type or init value>
    ::=   <scalar type spec> | INIT ( <scalar exp> )
        | <scalar type spec> INIT ( <scalar exp> )
```

And Chapter 11 goes on to say:

> If *<scalar type spec>* and the INIT specification both appear, the declared type of *<scalar exp>* must be the type specified by *<scalar type spec>*.

With inheritance, however (and with reference to IM Prescription 16, which has to do with value substitutability), this sentence needs to be changed to read:

> If *<scalar type spec>* and the INIT specification both appear, the declared type of *<scalar exp>* must be some subtype of the type specified by *<scalar type spec>*.

Similar changes are required in several places, but we won't bother to spell out the details, letting the foregoing illustration of the point do duty for all.

SELECTORS FOR SYSTEM DEFINED TYPES

We introduce this topic by means of an example. Consider type INTEGER, which (a) is a system defined type in **Tutorial D** and (b) has a system defined synonym, INT (see Chapters 3 and 11). Suppose we decide to define a proper subtype of this type called EVEN, consisting of just the even integers:

```
TYPE EVEN ORDINAL IS { INT CONSTRAINT MOD ( INT , 2 ) = 0 } ... ;
```

MOD ("modulo") here is, we assume, an operator that takes two integer arguments and returns the remainder that results after dividing the first by the second. Now, INT is a system defined type and has no declared possrep. It follows that EVEN has no declared possrep either (at least, let's assume so for the sake of the example, though the issue might require more study in general). And it further follows that EVEN has no literals of its own, other than literals of type INT that happen to denote INT values that are even. According to the *Manifesto* book, therefore, if we wish to assign the value 4 (say) to a variable J of type EVEN, we would have to use a statement of the form

```
J := TREAT_AS_EVEN ( 4 ) ;
```

(because the declared type of the literal 4 is INT, not EVEN). But this state of affairs is certainly clumsy, and might be hard to explain to the user. We therefore propose the following:

- Defining type EVEN causes automatic provision of an operator with the same name and with the following conceptual definition:

  ```
  OPERATOR EVEN ( I INT ) RETURNS EVEN ;
     RETURN ( TREAT_AS_EVEN ( I ) ) ;
  END OPERATOR ;
  ```

  Now the assignment of the value 4 to J can be simplified slightly to just:

  ```
  J := EVEN ( 4 ) ;
  ```

  More generally, the expression EVEN(*x*), where *x* is an expression of type INT, can be regarded as a selector invocation for type EVEN, and it returns an even integer (unless the integer denoted by *x* violates the type constraint for type EVEN, of course). As a consequence, the expressions

  ```
  4

  EVEN ( 4 )

  EVEN ( EVEN ( 4 ) )
  ```

  (and so on) all denote the very same value.

- For consistency, type INT is also automatically provided with an associated selector with the same name INT and with conceptual definition as follows:

  ```
  OPERATOR INT ( I INT ) RETURNS INT ;
     RETURN ( I ) ;
  END OPERATOR ;
  ```

- Since INT is in fact a synonym for the type name INTEGER, the corresponding selector can likewise be referred to as either INT or INTEGER. Thus, all of the following are legitimate integer selector invocations (in fact, they're all integer literals):

  ```
  4

  INT ( 4 )

  INTEGER ( 4 )

  INT ( INT ( 4 ) )

  INT ( EVEN ( 4 ) )
  ```

  (and so on).

  In conclusion, we propose that facilities analogous to the foregoing be provided in connection with all system defined types and all user defined types explicitly defined as proper subtypes of system defined types. Observe in particular that such facilities are fully consistent with RM Prescription 4, part b.

SCALAR TYPE DEFINITIONS

```
<user scalar type def>
    ::=   <user scalar root type def>
        | <user scalar nonroot type def>
```

In Chapter 11, we proposed that the syntax of statements in general should be extended to allow (e.g.) any number of variables, or any number of types, or any number of constraints, all to be defined or destroyed "simultaneously." Even if we choose not to support this idea in its full generality, we will probably at least require the ability to bundle up several *<user scalar type def>*s into a single statement in order to support the definition of union types and their required proper subtypes "simultaneously," as it were.

```
<user scalar root type def>
    ::=   TYPE <user scalar type name>
            [ <ordering> ] [ UNION ] <possrep def list>
              INIT ( <literal> )
```

Let *T* be the scalar root type being defined. UNION must be specified if and only if *T* is a union type. The *<possrep def list>* must be empty if and only if *T* is a dummy type. The INIT specification defines the example value required by RM Prescription 1 (see Chapter 11 for further discussion); the declared type of *<literal>* must be some subtype of *T*. Note that if *T* is a union type, the value denoted by *<literal>* will be of some proper, and necessarily nonunion, subtype of *T*.

```
<user scalar nonroot type def>
    ::=   TYPE <user scalar type name>
            [ <ordering> ] [ UNION ] <is def>
              INIT ( <literal> )
```

Apart from the sentence concerning the *<possrep def list>*, the remarks under *<user scalar root type def>* apply here also, mutatis mutandis.

```
<is def>
    ::=   <single inheritance is def>
        | <multiple inheritance is def>

<single inheritance is def>
    ::=   IS { <scalar type name>
                       <possrep or specialization details> }

<possrep or specialization details>
    ::=   <possrep def list>
        | <additional constraint def> <derived possrep def list>
```

Let *T* be the scalar nonroot type being defined, and let *IST* be the immediate supertype of *T*. The *<possrep def list>* must be specified if *IST* is a dummy type;[1] however, it must be empty if and only if *T* is a dummy type.

---

[1] We remark here that the grammar of *<user scalar nonroot type def>*s in general has been defined on the basis of a certain simplifying assumption: namely, that if type *T* has an immediate supertype *IST* that's a dummy type, then that type *IST* is *T*'s only immediate supertype. However, that assumption (which can be seen as an application of *The Principle of Cautious Design*) does require further study.

The *<additional constraint def>* must be specified if *IST* isn't a dummy type. The *<derived possrep def list>* must be specified (and mustn't be empty) unless *IST* is either a dummy type or a system defined type without a possrep.

```
<additional constraint def>
    ::=    CONSTRAINT <bool exp>
```

Let *T* be the scalar nonroot type being defined, and let *IST* be the immediate supertype of *T*. The *<bool exp>* mustn't mention any variables, but the name of *IST* can be used to denote an arbitrary value of that supertype.

```
<derived possrep def>
    ::=    POSSREP [ <possrep name> ]
                   { <derived possrep component def commalist> }

<derived possrep component def>
    ::=    <possrep component name> = <exp>
```

Let *T* be the scalar nonroot type being defined, and let *IST* be an immediate supertype of *T*. The *<exp>* mustn't mention any variables, but the name of *IST* can be used to denote an arbitrary value of that supertype. *Note:* In practice, we would expect *<exp>* to take the form of a *<THE_ op inv>* (see Chapter 11) in which the argument expression is precisely *IST*. Note, however, that such a *<THE_ op inv>* is evaluated not at run time but at compile time, when the *<derived possrep component def>* is processed by the compiler.

```
<multiple inheritance is def>
    ::=    IS { <scalar type name commalist>
                         <derived possrep def list> }
```

Let *T* be the scalar nonroot type being defined. The *<scalar type name commalist>* must contain at least two *<scalar type name>*s. The *<derived possrep def list>* must be empty if *T* is a dummy type.

OPERATOR DEFINITIONS

```
<user op def>
    ::=    <user read-only op def>
         | <user update op def>

<user read-only op def>
    ::=    OPERATOR <user op name> ( <parameter def commalist> )
              RETURNS <op type spec> ;
                 [ <statement> ]
           END OPERATOR
```

In the absence of inheritance, the RETURNS specification takes the simple form RETURNS *<type spec>*; now, in accordance with IM Prescription 17, it's extended to allow different types to be specified for different combinations of parameter declared types.[2] Every type mentioned in the *<op type spec>* must be a subtype of some common supertype. The *<statement>* can be omitted only if every *<parameter>* in the *<parameter def commalist>* has a dummy type as its declared type.

---

[2] Examples and further discussion can be found in Chapter 20.

```
<op type spec>
    ::=  <type spec> | <type case spec>

<type case spec>
    ::=  CASE <when type list> [ ELSE <op type spec> ] END CASE

<when type>
    ::=  WHEN <parameter type tests> THEN <op type spec>

<parameter type tests>
    ::=  <parameter type test> [ AND <parameter type tests> ]
```

Whether we should extend *<parameter type tests>* to permit NOT, OR, etc., as well as AND is a question that requires more study.

```
<parameter type test>
    ::=  <IS_ op name> ( <parameter name> )
```

Let the *<parameter type test>* IS_*T*(*P*) be specified as part of the *<user op def>* for operator *Op,* and let *OpI* be a *<user op inv>* for *Op* (see Chapter 11). Then the expression IS_*T*(*P*) is evaluated when *OpI* is processed by the compiler, and it returns TRUE—at compile time, not run time—if and only if parameter *P* is of declared type *T*. *Note:* An IS_SAME_TYPE_AS form of *<parameter type test>* should also be supported, along the lines defined for *<type test>*s later in this chapter. We omit the details here for simplicity.

```
<user update op def>
    ::=  OPERATOR <user op name> ( <parameter def commalist> )
            UPDATES { [ ALL BUT ] <parameter spec commalist> } ;
               [ <statement> ]
         END OPERATOR
```

The *<statement>* can be omitted only if every *<parameter>* in the *<parameter def commalist>* has a dummy type as its declared type. *Note:* If the UPDATES specification includes ALL BUT, the *<type spec>* must be omitted from every *<parameter spec>* in the *<parameter spec commalist>* (see the production rule immediately following).

```
<parameter spec>
    ::=  <parameter name> [ <type spec> ]
```

The purpose of *<parameter spec>*s is to satisfy the requirements of IM Prescription 19. Let the parameter *P* identified by the *<parameter name>* be of declared type *T*. If a *<type spec>* is specified, it must denote some subtype *T'* of *T;* omitting the *<type spec>* is equivalent to specifying *T* itself. Then the argument corresponding to *P,* in an invocation of the update operator being defined, can have as its most specific type any type that's both a subtype of *T* and a supertype of *T'*. *Note:* Distinct *<parameter spec>*s in the same *<parameter spec commalist>* can specify the same *<parameter name>*. In terms of our usual example of multiple inheritance (see Chapter 20)—and speaking very loosely—this feature would permit, e.g., an update operator for type PARALLELOGRAM to be inherited for types RECTANGLE and RHOMBUS but not type SQUARE.

TREAT AND RELATED OPERATIONS

Support for the TREAT operator "or some logical equivalent thereof" is required by IM Prescription 14. However, we propose support, not just for TREAT as such, but also for shorthands for certain expressions involving TREAT invocations. *Note:* IM Prescription 14 also discusses the possibility of using TREAT as a pseudovariable. The usefulness of such pseudovariables has been called into question, however; and since pseudovariables are basically just shorthand anyway, we offer no proposals for such support at this time.

```
<treat op inv>
      ::=    <scalar treat op inv>
           | <nonscalar treat op inv>

<scalar treat op inv>
      ::=    <TREAT_AS_ op name> ( <scalar exp> )
           | TREAT_AS_SAME_TYPE_AS ( <scalar exp> , <scalar exp> )
```

A <*scalar treat op inv*> is a new form of <*scalar exp*>. The declared type of the expression TREAT_AS_*T*(*X*) is *T* (*T* and the declared type of *X* must overlap); then, so long as the most specific type of *X* is some subtype of *T*, the expression returns the value of *X*. The expression TREAT_AS_SAME_TYPE_AS(*Y*,*X*) is equivalent to TREAT_AS_*T*(*X*), where *T* is the declared type of *Y*. *Note:* All of the remarks in this paragraph apply to <*nonscalar treat op inv*>s and <*attribute treat op inv*>s as well, mutatis mutandis; we omit the specifics here, since they're tedious but essentially straightforward.

```
<nonscalar treat op inv>
      ::=    <tuple treat op inv>
           | <relation treat op inv>

<tuple treat op inv>
      ::=    TREAT_AS_SAME_TYPE_AS ( <tuple exp> , <tuple exp> )
```

A <*tuple treat op inv*> is a new form of <*tuple exp*>. The declared types of the two <*tuple exp*>s must overlap.

```
<relation treat op inv>
      ::=    TREAT_AS_SAME_TYPE_AS ( <relation exp> ,
                                     <relation exp> )
```

A <*relation treat op inv*> is a new form of <*relation exp*>. The declared types of the two <*relation exp*>s must overlap.

```
<attribute treat op inv>
      ::=    <tuple attribute treat op inv>
           | <relation attribute treat op inv>

<tuple attribute treat op inv>
      ::=    <tuple exp> <TREAT_AS_ op name> ( <attribute ref> )
           | <tuple exp> TREAT_AS_SAME_TYPE_AS
                                     ( <exp> , <attribute ref> )
```

A <*tuple attribute treat op inv*> is a new form of <*tuple exp*>. In the first format, the <*attribute ref*> must denote an attribute of some scalar type; in the second format, the <*exp*> must be a <*scalar exp*>, <*tuple exp*>, or <*relation exp*> according as the <*attribute ref*> denotes an attribute of some scalar, tuple, or relation type.

```
<relation attribute treat op inv>
      ::=    <relation exp> <TREAT_AS_ op name> ( <attribute ref> )
           | <relation exp> TREAT_AS_SAME_TYPE_AS
                                     ( <exp> , <attribute ref> )
```

A <*relation attribute treat op inv*> is a new form of <*relation exp*>. In the first format, the <*attribute ref*> must denote an attribute of some scalar type; in the second format, the <*exp*> must be a <*scalar exp*>, <*tuple exp*>, or <*relation exp*> according as the <*attribute ref*> denotes an attribute of some scalar, tuple, or relation type.

TYPE TESTING AND RELATED OPERATIONS

Support for type testing is required by IM Prescription 15. However, we propose support, not just for type testing as such, but also for shorthands for certain relational expressions involving such testing.

```
<type test>
    ::=     <scalar type test>
          | <nonscalar type test>
```

A <*type test*> is a new form of <*bool exp*>.

```
<scalar type test>
    ::=     <IS_ op name> ( <scalar exp> )
          | IS_SAME_TYPE_AS ( <scalar exp> , <scalar exp> )
```

In the <*scalar type test*> IS_*T*(*X*), the declared type of *X* and the type *T* must overlap; then, so long as the most specific type of *X* is some subtype of *T*, the expression returns TRUE. The <*scalar type test*> IS_SAME_TYPE_AS(*Y*,*X*) is equivalent to the <*scalar type test*> IS_*T*(*X*), where *T* is the declared type of *Y*. *Note:* All of the remarks in this paragraph apply to <*nonscalar type test*>s as well, mutatis mutandis; we omit the specifics here, since they're tedious but essentially straightforward.

```
<nonscalar type test>
    ::=     <tuple type test>
          | <relation type test>

<tuple type test>
    ::=     IS_SAME_TYPE_AS ( <tuple exp> , <tuple exp> )

<relation type test>
    ::=     IS_SAME_TYPE_AS ( <relation exp> , <relation exp> )

<type test restrict>
    ::=     <relation exp> : <IS_ op name> ( <attribute ref> )
          | <relation exp> : IS_SAME_TYPE_AS
                                  ( <exp> , <attribute ref> )
```

A <*type test restrict*> is a new form of <*relation exp*>. In the first format, the <*attribute ref*> must denote an attribute of some scalar type; in the second format, the <*exp*> must be a <*scalar exp*>, <*tuple exp*>, or <*relation exp*> according as the <*attribute ref*> denotes an attribute of some scalar, tuple, or relation type. In the <*type test restrict*> *R*:IS_*T*(*A*), *R* is a relational expression—denoting relation *r*, say—and *A* is an attribute of *r*. The declared type of *A* and the type *T* must overlap. The expression overall denotes a relation with (a) heading the same as that of *r*, except that the declared type of *A* in that heading is *T*, and (b) body consisting of those tuples of *r* in which the *A* value is of type *T*, except that the declared type of *A* in each of those tuples is *T*.

APPENDIX A: UNION TYPES

Several commentators have suggested that the inheritance extensions to **Tutorial D** should allow the definition of a union type to include the names—and further details, perhaps—of the applicable immediate subtypes. The purpose of this appendix is to examine this possibility. Examples to illustrate the discussion are based for definiteness on the type hierarchy shown in Fig. 1. Type ELLIPSE in that figure is a root type and a union type (but regular, not dummy); CIRCLE and NONCIRCLE are nonunion types; and the semantics are meant to be self-evident (in particular, every ellipse is either a circle or a noncircle, and no ellipse is both).

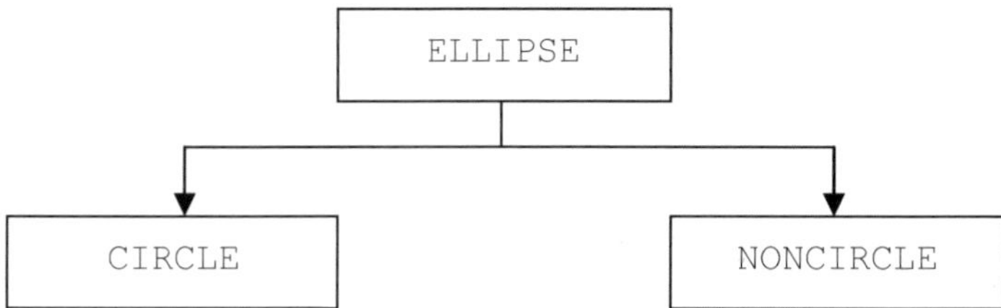

Fig. 1: A simple type hierarchy

Here first is a set of type definitions (consisting of three separate TYPE statements) using the syntax originally proposed in the *Manifesto* book:

```
TYPE ELLIPSE UNION
     POSSREP { A LENGTH , B LENGTH , CTR POINT
               CONSTRAINT A ≥ B } } ;

TYPE CIRCLE
     IS { ELLIPSE
          CONSTRAINT THE_A ( ELLIPSE ) = THE_B ( ELLIPSE )
          POSSREP { R   = THE_A   ( ELLIPSE ) ,
                    CTR = THE_CTR ( ELLIPSE ) } } ;

TYPE NONCIRCLE
     IS { ELLIPSE
          CONSTRAINT THE_A ( ELLIPSE ) > THE_B ( ELLIPSE )
          POSSREP { A   = THE_A   ( ELLIPSE ) ,
                    B   = THE_B   ( ELLIPSE ) ,
                    CTR = THE_CTR ( ELLIPSE ) } } ;
```

Well, since type ELLIPSE can't sensibly be said to exist until types CIRCLE and NONCIRCLE have been defined, it would seem reasonable to require all three type definitions to be bundled up into a single statement, as proposed in the section "Scalar Type Definition" in the body of the chapter. Syntactically speaking, all we need do to achieve such a bundling is to replace the first two semicolons in the foregoing by commas.

So let's assume the foregoing change has been applied. Now we turn to the original question. Suppose we stay, at least for the moment, with the "top down" style of definition, but suppose we want to mention CIRCLE and NONCIRCLE in the definition of ELLIPSE. We might try:

```
TYPE ELLIPSE UNION { CIRCLE , NONCIRCLE }
     POSSREP { A LENGTH , B LENGTH , CTR POINT
               CONSTRAINT A ≥ B } } ...
```

Note, incidentally, that the very fact that it mentions CIRCLE and NONCIRCLE lends further weight to the idea that this ELLIPSE definition needs to be extended to include the CIRCLE and NONCIRCLE definitions as well—for otherwise we're faced with the possibility that a type definition might be allowed to complete execution even if it includes a reference to something that doesn't yet exist, and might never exist. But if we do extend the ELLIPSE definition to include the CIRCLE and NONCIRCLE definitions, then allowing those types to be mentioned as part of the UNION specification doesn't seem to achieve very much.

So what happens if we work bottom up, as it were, and define the subtypes first?—

```
TYPE CIRCLE
     IS { ELLIPSE ...
```

Well, we have to stop right there: Again we have a reference in the definition of one type to a type that hasn't yet been defined, and might never be defined. So that won't work. But perhaps we could define the subtypes first, without mentioning the supertype at all?—

```
TYPE CIRCLE
     POSSREP { R LENGTH , CTR POINT } ;

TYPE NONCIRCLE
     POSSREP { A LENGTH , B LENGTH , CTR POINT
               CONSTRAINT A > B } ;

TYPE ELLIPSE UNION { CIRCLE , NONCIRCLE } ... ;
```

But now what do we do about the possrep for type ELLIPSE? Note that we do want it to have a possrep (it's not a dummy type, and we don't want it to be a dummy type). But if we do specify a possrep, then at best there'll be some kind of redundancy (i.e., repetition of specifications that have already been given—and *must* already have been given—for types CIRCLE and NONCIRCLE); at worst, there'll be some kind of inconsistency (what happens if there's a conflict with or between the specifications already given for types CIRCLE and NONCIRCLE?).

Finally: Even if we can resolve the foregoing issues satisfactorily, it doesn't seem easy (or possible?) to make this "bottom up" style conform to the requirement of IM Prescription 10 that types CIRCLE and NONCIRCLE be defined by constraining type ELLIPSE.

From such considerations, we conclude that there doesn't seem to be an easy way to make the original suggestion work.

Chapter 22

Toward a Better Understanding of Numeric Data Types

God made the natural numbers; all else is the work of Man.

—Leopold Kronecker

This chapter consists of a detailed examination of an example often appealed to in discussions of type inheritance. The example is depicted in Fig. 1 overleaf; it involves a collection of numeric data types—COMPLEX, REAL, RATIONAL, and so on—arranged into a reasonably self-explanatory *type hierarchy*. Intuitively, the types have the following meanings (but it's a large part of the point of this chapter to pin down those meanings, or some of those meanings, rather more precisely):

- COMPLEX: Complex numbers (i.e., numbers of the form $a+bi$, where a and b are real numbers and i is the square root of –1)
- REAL: Real numbers (i.e., complex numbers $a+bi$ for which b is zero); referred to as reals for short
- IMAGINARY: Imaginary numbers (i.e., complex numbers $a+bi$ for which a is zero)[1]
- RATIONAL: Rational numbers (i.e., numbers that can be expressed as the ratio of two integers, like 2/5 or –4/3); referred to as rationals for short
- IRRATIONAL: Irrational numbers (i.e., numbers that can't be expressed as the ratio of two integers, like π or $\sqrt{2}$); referred to as irrationals for short
- INTEGER: Integers (positive, negative, or zero)
- POSITIVE INTEGER: Positive integers (i.e., integers that are strictly greater than zero); sometimes referred to as the natural numbers

Explanation: Each node in the figure represents the type whose name it bears, and there's an arrow from the node for type T to the node for type T' if and only if type T is an immediate supertype of type T'—equivalently, if and only if type T' is an immediate subtype of type T. *Note:* I'll explain the terms *immediate supertype* and *immediate subtype* in detail in a few moments; for now, it's sufficient to know that if type T is an immediate supertype of T', then (a) every value of type T' is a value of type T, but (b) there's at least one value of type T that isn't a value of type T'.[2] For example, type INTEGER is an immediate supertype of type POSITIVE INTEGER; every positive integer is an integer, but some integers aren't positive integers.

[1] Some writers don't require a to be zero and thus treat the term *imaginary number* as synonymous with *complex number*.

[2] But see the discussion of this very point in Chapter 20. The present chapter doesn't rely on the point in any formal sense, however; for simplicity, therefore, I'll just assume it's satisfied, without any further discussion.

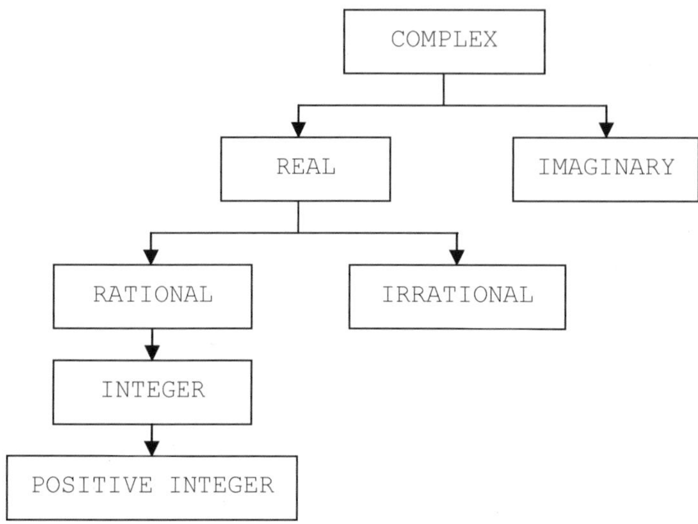

Fig. 1: A hierarchy of numeric types

Incidentally, a point arises in connection with the type hierarchy of Fig. 1 with respect to the types REAL, RATIONAL, and IRRATIONAL in particular. To be specific, every real number is either rational or irrational (and no real number is both), and so it follows that:

1. Types RATIONAL and IRRATIONAL are *disjoint;* i.e., their intersection is empty (they have no values in common).

2. Together, they *partition* type REAL; i.e., their union—which by virtue of the previous point is a disjoint union—is equal to this latter type (every value of type REAL is a value of exactly one of the types RATIONAL and IRRATIONAL).

Note: In practice, of course, computer systems are incapable of accurately representing irrational numbers anyway (and the same is true for most real numbers also, since most real numbers are in fact irrational). However, this state of affairs is irrelevant to the main purpose of the chapter, and I'll ignore it from this point forward.

THE INHERITANCE MODEL

Reference [1] presents a detailed abstract model of types in general, including a model of type inheritance in particular, and that's the model I'm following here. Now, I don't assume you're familiar with that model—I'll explain its salient features as and when I need to appeal to them. However, I do assume you're familiar with the following (I hope noncontroversial) terms and concepts:

1. A *data type* (type for short) is a named set of values. *Examples:* The type named INTEGER is the set of all integers; the type named POSITIVE INTEGER is the set of all positive integers. *Note:* All of the types mentioned in the running example of Fig. 1 are in fact scalar types specifically. For simplicity, I don't propose to discuss nonscalar types in this chapter at all.

2. Every type has an associated *constraint* that effectively defines the set of values that go to make up that type. *Example:* The constraint for type IMAGINARY simply states that an imaginary number is a complex number $a{+}bi$ for which $a = 0$.

3. Every type has a set of *operators* associated with it—where operator *Op* is "associated with" type *T* if and only if at least one of its parameters is of type *T* (more accurately, if the parameter in question is of some supertype of type *T*—see point 10 below). *Example:* The operator RECIPROCAL might be defined to take just one parameter, of type POSITIVE INTEGER (and to produce a result of type RATIONAL), in which case it's "associated with" type INTEGER and also, a fortiori, type POSITIVE INTEGER as well.

4. Type *T′* is a *subtype* of type *T*—equivalently, type *T* is a *supertype* of type *T′*—if and only if every value of type *T′* is also a value of type *T*. Note in particular, therefore, that every type *T* is both a subtype and a supertype of itself. *Examples:* INTEGER and IRRATIONAL are both subtypes of REAL (equivalently, REAL is a supertype of both INTEGER and IRRATIONAL); INTEGER is both a subtype and a supertype of INTEGER.

5. If and only if (a) *T′* is a subtype of *T* and (b) *T′* and *T* are distinct, then *T′* is a *proper* subtype of *T* (equivalently, *T* is a proper supertype of *T′*). *Examples:* INTEGER and IRRATIONAL are both proper subtypes of REAL; POSITIVE INTEGER and IMAGINARY are both proper subtypes of COMPLEX.

6. If *T′* is a proper subtype of *T*, then there must be at least one value of type *T* that's not of type *T′*. *Examples:* There's at least one value of type RATIONAL that's not a value of type POSITIVE INTEGER. More precisely, there's at least one value of type RATIONAL that's not a value of type INTEGER, and there's at least one value of type INTEGER that's not a value of type POSITIVE INTEGER.

7. If and only if (a) *T′* is a proper subtype of *T* and (b) no type exists that's both a proper supertype of *T′* and a proper subtype of *T*, then *T′* is an *immediate* subtype of *T* (equivalently, *T* is an immediate supertype of *T′*). *Examples:* INTEGER is an immediate subtype of RATIONAL; RATIONAL is an immediate supertype of INTEGER.

8. If and only if *T* has no immediate supertype (other than *alpha,* that is—see Chapters 19 and 20), then *T* is a *root* type. *Example:* COMPLEX is the only root type in Fig. 1.

9. If and only if *T* has no immediate subtype (other than *omega,* that is—see Chapters 19 and 20), then *T* is a *leaf* type. *Examples:* POSITIVE INTEGER, IRRATIONAL, and IMAGINARY are all of the leaf types in Fig. 1.

10. If and only if *T′* is a subtype of *T*, then *T* "inherits properties" from type *T*—where the properties in question are, basically, operators and constraints. *Examples:* Every operator that applies to integers in general (e.g., addition, multiplication) applies to positive integers in particular, because positive integers *are* integers. Likewise, the constraint that applies to integers in general to the effect that "there's nothing after the decimal point" (speaking *very* loosely!) also applies to positive integers in particular—again, because positive integers are integers.

11. If value *v* is of type *T* and not of any type that's a proper subtype of type *T*, then *T* is the *most specific* type of *v*. *Example:* Let *n* be a negative integer (e.g., –6). Then *n* is of types INTEGER, RATIONAL, REAL, and COMPLEX (and no others), and INTEGER is its most specific type. Observe, incidentally, that type REAL isn't the most specific type of any value at all (because every real number is necessarily either rational or irrational, as previously noted). In the terminology of reference [1], such a type is called a *union* type (but be aware that various other terms are used in the literature). A union type must always have at least two distinct immediate subtypes (why?). *Note:* It's not as obvious as it might look, but it's true, that—thanks to certain additional features, not discussed here, of the inheritance model of reference [1]—the most specific type of any given value (a) always exists and (b) is unique.

12. In the interest of accuracy, I should mention that the proposals of reference [1] actually divide operators

into two kinds, *read-only* and *update* operators. A read-only operator is one that merely "reads" its arguments (where by *arguments* I mean the values that are substituted for its parameters when the operator is invoked) and doesn't update them; an update operator is one that isn't read-only. For example, the RECIPROCAL operator mentioned earlier is a read-only operator—it reads its sole argument and computes a result, viz., the reciprocal of that argument. By contrast, assignment is an update operator (it updates the variable that's specified as its target). However, the special considerations that apply to update operators aren't important for our purposes here. For simplicity, therefore, I limit my attention elsewhere in this chapter to read-only operators specifically.

Finally, a caveat. Consider, e.g., type RATIONAL. Clearly, values exist that are rational numbers and not integers; an example is 4/3. Equally clearly, the most specific type of such values is just RATIONAL. Likewise, values exist whose most specific type is just COMPLEX (an example is 4+3*i,* which is neither real nor imaginary by my definition), and values exist whose most specific type is just INTEGER (an example is –6). Observe now that none of these types (RATIONAL, COMPLEX, INTEGER) is either a leaf type or a union type. Be careful, therefore, not to fall into the common trap of thinking that the only "nonunion" types are necessarily leaf types, or that values "exist only at the leaves of the tree" (as it were). Although it would be possible, if desired, to set up the type hierarchy in such a way that values did "exist only at the leaves," the inheritance model of reference [1] certainly doesn't require such a discipline.

Aside: To pursue the point a moment longer: Suppose we did want to set up the type hierarchy in our running example in this way. Then we could achieve the desired effect by introducing (a) type NEGATIVE INTEGER OR ZERO (with the obvious semantics) as another immediate subtype of type INTEGER; (b) type RATIONAL AND NOT INTEGER (again with the obvious semantics) as another immediate subtype of type RATIONAL; and (c) type NEITHER REAL NOR IMAGINARY (once again, with the obvious semantics) as another immediate subtype of type COMPLEX. This little thought experiment should be sufficient to suggest why the model of reference [1] doesn't insist on such a discipline. *End of aside.*

I'll close this section by observing that the example of Fig. 1 is of course very simple. But it's easy to find examples in which the supertype/subtype relationships are more complicated than those shown in that figure. For instance, reference [1] gives an example involving geometric figures in which type SQUARE is an immediate subtype of three distinct types—RECTANGLE, RHOMBUS, and RIGHT KITE—and thus has three distinct immediate supertypes.[3] In such a case, of course, a simple hierarchy is inadequate to depict the supertype/subtype relationships; instead, we have to make use of a more general type *graph.*

Examples like the foregoing, in which certain proper subtypes inherit properties from two or more immediate supertypes, display what's usually called *multiple inheritance.* By contrast, examples like that of Fig. 1 in which every proper subtype has, and inherits properties from, exactly one immediate supertype display what's usually called *single* inheritance only. Of course, the latter is just a special case of the former; in fact, single inheritance can be defined as meaning that every proper subtype has exactly one immediate supertype—implying, incidentally, that the type graph consists of a set of disjoint hierarchies, each with exactly one root node—and multiple inheritance is what results if this condition doesn't apply. For present purposes, however, the distinction isn't important, and I'll ignore it from this point forward.

---

[3] A right kite is a quadrilateral ABCD such that sides AB and AD are of the same length, sides BC and DC are of the same length, and angle BAD is a right angle.

INTEGER PAIRS AND RATIONAL NUMBERS

Now I can get to the real point of the chapter (or begin to, at any rate). Note first that the example of Fig. 1 is quite typical, inasmuch as examples of the same general nature are often found in the literature. What's more, the example is intuitively reasonable, too, because "everybody knows" that, e.g., integers in particular are a special case of rational numbers in general. Nevertheless, I'm going to argue that in some respects, at least, the example doesn't really make sense after all. *Now read on ...*

To repeat, "everybody knows" that integers in particular are a special case of rational numbers in general. For example, here's a lightly edited quote from reference [2] (boldface in the original):

> Numbers that are ratios of integers are known as **rational numbers**. Rational numbers can all be written in the form of a ratio a/b where the numerator a may be any integer and the denominator b any positive integer except zero. If $b = 1$, the rational number a/b is an **integer** = a.

Not all writers agree that the denominator must be positive, incidentally, a point I'll come back to in a few moments. More important, note the circularity: Rational numbers are defined in terms of integers, and then integers are defined in terms of rational numbers. Clearly there's something fishy going on! Let's see if we can clarify matters—i.e., let's see if we can formalize the definitions and make them more precise—in such a way as to avoid this problem, among other things.

I'll start by assuming that we're given the (infinite) set **Z** of integers = {..., –2, –1, 0, +1, +2, ...}. I'll also assume that the "+" symbol in +1, +2, etc., can optionally be elided, thus: 1, 2, etc. To formalize the notion of a rational number, then, we might try defining such a number to be an ordered pair of the form $<a,b>$, where a and b are integers and $b \neq 0$. It's easy to see, however, that this simple definition is inadequate in a variety of ways:

- It allows both, e.g., <4,3> and <8,6> as rational numbers; in other words, it fails to guarantee that if p and q are the rational numbers $<a,b>$ and $<c,d>$, respectively, then p and q are equal ("$p = q$") if and only if $a = c$ and $b = d$. *Note:* Here and elsewhere throughout this chapter I assume, reasonably enough but without explicit justification, that this latter property is desirable. After all, it's certainly true that $<a,b> = <c,d>$ if and only if $a = c$ and $b = d$ so long as we regard $<a,b>$ and $<c,d>$ simply as ordered pairs, not as rational numbers as such.

- It allows both, e.g., <–4,3> and <4,–3> as rational numbers; thus it again fails to guarantee that if p and q are the rational numbers $<a,b>$ and $<c,d>$, respectively, then $p = q$ if and only if $a = c$ and $b = d$.

- It allows both, e.g., <4,3> and <–4,–3> as rational numbers; once again, then, it fails to guarantee that if p and q are the rational numbers $<a,b>$ and $<c,d>$, respectively, then $p = q$ if and only if $a = c$ and $b = d$.

- It allows both, e.g., <0,3> and <0,–4> as rational numbers; yet again, then, it fails to guarantee that if p and q are the rational numbers $<a,b>$ and $<c,d>$, respectively, then $p = q$ if and only if $a = c$ and $b = d$. (Note that <0,3> and <0,–4> would both denote zero, under the proposed scheme.)

In order to help fix these problems, let me back off a little (as it were) by taking the foregoing definition to define, not a rational number as such, but merely an *integer pair:*

- **Definition (integer pair):** An integer pair is an ordered pair of the form $<a,b>$ where a and b are arbitrary integers (except that $b \neq 0$).

Note: I don't intend for integer pairs to be seen as a particularly important concept in their own right; I introduce them merely as a stepping stone on the way to the rationals. However, observe in particular that the foregoing definition does at least imply—thanks to the fundamental mathematical notion of what an ordered pair is—that the integer pairs <*a,b*> and <*c,d*> are equal if and only if $a = c$ and $b = d$. Thus, for example, the integer pairs <4,3> and <8,6> are not equal.

Next I define a partial ordering operator ("<") for integer pairs:

- **Definition ("<" for integer pairs):** The integer pair p = <*a,b*> is strictly less than the integer pair q = <*c,d*> ("$p < q$") if and only if $a*d < b*c$. *Note:* The symbols "*" and "<" in this latter expression "$a*d < b*c$" denote the corresponding *integer* operators; observe, therefore, that the definition of integer pair "less than" relies on the definitions of integer multiplication and integer "less than."

I also define the integer pair p to be strictly greater than the integer pair q ("$p > q$") if and only if q is strictly less than p. Observe that, given these definitions and given any two integer pairs p and q, at most one of the following is true: $p < q$, $p = q$, $p > q$. In fact, it's possible that they're all false; consider what happens, for example, if p = <4,3> and q = <8,6>. By contrast, let p = <4,3> and q = <10,12>; then $p < q$ and $p = q$ are both false, but $p > q$ is true.

Next, I define two dyadic operators, "+++" (addition) and "***" (multiplication), whose two operands and single result are all integer pairs in the foregoing sense:[4]

- **Definition (addition of integer pairs):** Given integer pairs p = <*a,b*> and q = <*c,d*>, their sum *p+++q* is the integer pair <*x,y*>, where $x = (a*d)+(b*c)$ and $y = b*d$. *Note:* The symbols "+" and "*" in the definitions of x and y here denote the conventional integer addition and multiplication operators; observe, therefore, that the definition of integer pair addition relies on the definitions of integer addition and integer multiplication.

- **Definition (multiplication of integer pairs):** Given integer pairs p = <*a,b*> and q = <*c,d*>, their product *p***q* is the integer pair <*x,y*>, where $x = a*c$ and $y = b*d$. *Note:* Again, the symbol "*" in the definitions of x and y here denotes the corresponding integer operator; thus, the definition of integer pair multiplication relies on the definition of integer multiplication.

Examples: Let p and q be the integer pairs <4,3> and <10,12>, respectively; then their sum *p+++q* is <78,36> and their product *p***q* is <40,36>. *Note:* From this point forward, I'll assume for simplicity that the integer pair operator "***" is of higher precedence than the integer pair operator "+++", and this latter operator in turn is of higher precedence than the integer pair operators "<", "=", and ">".

Now I can define rational numbers as a special case of integer pairs (so every rational number is an integer pair, but some—actually most—integer pairs aren't rational numbers):[5]

- **Definition (rational number):** Let <*a,b*> be an integer pair as previously defined. Then that integer pair is a rational number, written <<*a,b*>>, if and only if all three of the following conditions are satisfied:[6]

  1. b is positive (i.e., strictly greater than zero).

  2. a and b are coprime, meaning they have no common factor other than unity. *Note:* It follows that, e.g., the integer pair <8,6> isn't a valid rational number according to this definition.

---

[4] I use the symbols "+++" and "***" here to stress the fact that these integer pair operators are logically distinct from the corresponding integer operators "+" and "*".

[5] Note, therefore, that the relationship between integer pairs and rationals is in fact a supertype/subtype relationship. I'll have more to say in connection with this point later in this chapter.

[6] The double angle bracket notation is nonstandard, but I'm not aware of any standard notation in this area—except perhaps for *single* angle brackets, but of course I've already used that notation for integer pairs.

3. If *a* = 0, then (by convention) *b* = 1. *Note:* Actually this third condition can be regarded as a special case of the second, if we agree that, e.g., 0 and 3 have the common factor 3.

It follows immediately from the foregoing definition that:

- The integer pair operators "<", "=", and ">" all apply directly and without change to rational numbers.

- In particular, the rational numbers *<<a,b>>* and *<<c,d>>* are equal if and only if *a* = *c* and *b* = *d.* (In other words, the ordering induced by "<" on the rationals, unlike the one it induces on integer pairs, is total: For any two rationals *p* and *q,* exactly one of *p* < *q, p* = *q,* and *p* > *q* is true.)

Next, I propose an operator *norm* ("normalize") which, given an arbitrary integer pair *<x,y>*, returns the unique rational number *<<a,b>>* such that (*a*/*b*) = (*x*/*y*) according to the usual rules of arithmetic. That rational number *<<a,b>>* can be regarded as the normalized or canonical form of that integer pair *<x,y>*. Note that *norm* is idempotent; that is, *norm*(*norm*(*<x,y>*)) = *norm*(*<x,y>*) for all integer pairs *<x,y>*. Note also that *norm* is explicitly defined to operate on integer pairs as such; no harm is done, however, if we allow it to be applied to rational numbers as well (since rational numbers *are* integer pairs).

Along with the operator *norm* I propose the following definition of equivalence ("≡") for integer pairs: Integer pairs *p* = *<a,b>* and *q* = *<c,d>* are equivalent ("*p* ≡ *q*") if and only if the corresponding normalized forms are equal (i.e., if and only if *norm*(*<a,b>*) = *norm*(*<c,d>*)). Observe that if *p* and *q* are integer pairs and *p* = *q,* then certainly *p* ≡ *q,* but the converse is false; for example, the integer pairs <4,3> and <8,6> are equivalent but not equal. *Note:* I won't actually be making any use of the "≡" operator in what follows; I define it here merely for completeness.

Now, since rational numbers are integer pairs, the integer pair operators "+++" and "***" apply to them directly. However, it's desirable to define specific rational analogs of those operators ("++" and "**") as well:

- **Definition (addition of rationals):** Given rational numbers *p* = *<<a,b>>* and *q* = *<<c,d>>*, their sum *p*++*q* is the rational number *norm*(*<x,y>*), where *<x,y>* = *<a,b>*+++*<c,d>*. *Note:* The symbol "+++" in the definition of *<x,y>* here denotes the corresponding integer pair operator; thus, the definition of rational addition ("++") relies on the definition of integer pair addition (and we already know that this latter definition in turn relies on the definitions of integer addition and integer multiplication).

- **Definition (multiplication of rationals):** Given rational numbers *p* = *<<a,b>>* and *q* = *<<c,d>>*, their product *p****q* is the rational number *norm*(*<x,y>*), where *<x,y>* = *<a,b>*****<c,d>*. *Note:* The symbol "***" in the definition of *<x,y>* here denotes the corresponding integer pair operator; thus, the definition of rational multiplication ("**") relies on the definition of integer pair multiplication (and we already know that this latter definition in turn relies on the definition of integer multiplication).

Examples: Let *p* = <<4,3>> and *q* = <<5,6>>; note that these are the normalized forms of the integer pairs <4,3> and <10,12>, respectively, from the integer pair examples discussed earlier. Consider the sum *p*++*q*. From the definition, we obtain *x* = 24+15 = 39 and *y* = 18; hence *p*++*q* = *norm*(<39,18>) = <<13,6>>. Similarly, for the product *p****q,* we obtain *x* = 4*5 = 20 and *y* = 3*6 = 18; hence *p****q* = *norm*(<20,18>) = <<10,9>>. *Note:* From this point forward, I'll make the same assumptions regarding the rational operators as I did for the corresponding integer pair operators; namely, I'll assume that (a) "**" is of higher precedence than "++" and (b) "++" is of higher precedence than "<", "=", and ">".

Finally, it's easy to see that the operator *norm* distributes over both rational addition ("++") and rational multiplication ("**"). First addition. Let *p* and *q* be rational numbers. Then we have:

```
      norm ( p ) ++ norm ( q )

=     p ++ q
      /* since rationals are normalized by definition */

=     r (say)

=     norm ( r )
      /* since rationals are normalized by definition */

=     norm ( p ++ q )
      /* by definition of r */
```

Thus, *norm* distributes over "++". A precisely analogous argument shows that *norm(p**q)* = *norm(p)**norm(q)*; i.e., *norm* distributes over "**" also.

MORE ON RATIONAL ADDITION AND MULTIPLICATION

I now show that the rational operators "++" and "**" satisfy a number of further desirable properties—to be specific, the properties of closure, commutativity, associativity, and distributivity (of "**" over "++", in this last case).

- *Closure:* For all rationals *p* and *q,* the sum *p++q* and the product *p**q* are both rationals by definition; i.e., the set of rationals is closed under both "++" and "**". *Note:* I'm appealing here, tacitly, to the fact that the integers in turn are closed under the operators of integer "+" and integer "*".

- *Commutativity:* Since their definitions are symmetric in *p* and *q,* it's immediate that "++" and "**" are both commutative; i.e., *p++q* = *q++p* and *p**q* = *q**p.*

- *Associativity:* Let *p, q,* and *r* be the rationals *<<a,b>>*, *<<c,d>>*, and *<<e,f>>*, respectively. Consider the expression *p++(q++r)*. Expanding this expression, we obtain:

```
      << a , b >> ++ ( << c , d >> ++ << e , f >> )

=     norm ( < a , b > +++ norm ( < c , d > +++ < e , f > ) )
      /* by definition of "++" in terms of "+++" */

=     norm ( < a , b > +++ norm ( < c * f + d * e , d * f > ) )
      /* by definition of "+++" */

=     norm ( < a , b > +++ ( < ( c * f + d * e ) / h ,
                                 ( d * f ) / h > ) )
      /* where h = highest common factor of c*f+d*e and d*f */

=     norm ( < ( a * d * f + b * c * f + b * d * e ) / h ,
                                 ( b * d * f ) / h > )
      /* by definition of "+++" */

=     norm ( < ( a * d * f + b * c * f + b * d * e ) ,
                                 ( b * d * f ) > )
      /* multiplying both terms by h */
```

An analogous argument shows that *(p++q)++r* is also equal to this latter expression; hence "++" is associative. A similar argument shows that "**" is associative also.

- *Distributivity:* Again let *p*, *q*, and *r* be the rationals <<*a,b*>>, <<*c,d*>>, and <<*e,f*>>, respectively. Consider the expression *p***(*q*++*r*). Expanding this expression, we obtain:

```
     << a , b >> ** ( << c , d >> ++ << e , f >> )

=    << a , b >> ** norm ( < c * f + d * e , d * f > )

=    << a , b >> ** << ( c * f + d * e ) / h , ( d * f ) / h >>
     /* where h = highest common factor of c*f+d*e and d*f */

=    norm ( < ( a * c * f + a * d * e ) / h , ( b * d * f ) / h > )

=    norm ( < ( a * c * f + a * d * e ) , ( b * d * f ) > )
```

  Now consider the expression (*p****q*)++(*p****r*). Expanding this expression, we obtain:

```
     ( << a , b >> ** << c , d >> )
                 ++ ( << a , b >> ** << e , f >> )

=    norm ( < a * c , b * d > ) ++ norm ( < a * e , b * f > )

=    < ( a * c ) / h , ( b * d ) / h >
                ++ < ( a * e ) / k , ( b * f ) / k >
     /* where h = highest common factor of a*c and b*d */
     /* and   k = highest common factor of a*e and b*f */

=    norm ( < ( a * c * b * f + b * d * a * e ) / ( h * k ) ,
                            ( b * d * b * f ) / ( h * k ) > )

=    norm < ( a * c * f + d * a * e ) , ( b * d * f ) >
```

  which, as we've already seen, is equal to *p***(*q*++*r*); hence "**" distributes over "++".

THE FIELD OF RATIONAL NUMBERS

It follows from everything I've said so far that, together with the operators "++" and "**", the set **Q** of all rational numbers constitutes a *field* in the mathematical sense. (Loosely speaking, a field in mathematics is a formal system in which the operators of addition and multiplication have all of the usual properties that addition and multiplication of real numbers have.) Here are some implications of this fact:

- *Additive identity:* The rational number <<0,1>> serves as the identity with respect to "++"; that is, *p*++<<0,1>> = <<0,1>>++*p* = *p* for all rational numbers *p*.

- *Additive inverse:* Let *p* be any rational number <<*a,b*>>. Then the inverse, –*p*, of *p* with respect to "++" is the rational number <<–*a,b*>>, because <<*a,b*>>++<<–*a,b*>> = <<0,1>> (the additive identity) for all such rational numbers *p*. In other words, subtraction of rationals is well defined. (Note that the symbol "–" in the expression <<–*a,b*>> denotes the corresponding *integer* operator. By contrast, the symbol "–" in the expression –*p* denotes a *rational* operator, and for consistency with "++" I ought by rights to show it as "––"; I didn't do so, however, fearing it might cause confusion if I did.)

- *Multiplicative identity:* The rational number <<1,1>> serves as the identity with respect to "**"; that is, *p***<<1,1>> = <<1,1>>***p* = *p* for all rational numbers *p*.

- *Multiplicative inverse* (sometimes called the *reciprocal*): Let *p* be any rational number <<*a,b*>> other than the additive identity <<0,1>>. Then the inverse, 1/*p*, of *p* with respect to "**" is the rational number *norm*(<*b,a*>), because <<*a,b*>>***norm*(<*b,a*>) = <<1,1>> (the multiplicative identity) for all such rational numbers *p*. In other words, division of rationals is well defined. *Note:* In case you're wondering why the multiplicative inverse of <<*a,b*>> isn't simply <<*b,a*>> instead of *norm*(<*b,a*>), it's because *a* might be negative (in which case the expression <<*b,a*>> wouldn't be well formed).

OVERLOADING AND INCLUSION POLYMORPHISM

Now I return to the subtype/supertype relationships illustrated by the type hierarchy of Fig. 1: in particular, to the relationship illustrated by that portion of the hierarchy that shows INTEGER as an immediate subtype of RATIONAL. First I remind you that the definition of "**" for rationals appeals to the definition of "*" for integers—or, to be more precise, the definition of "**" for rationals appeals to the definition of "***" for integer pairs, and this latter definition in turn appeals to the definition of "*" for integers. In exactly the same kind of way, the definition of "++" for rationals appeals to the definition of "+" for integers (as well as to the definition of "*" for integers).

Now let's concentrate for simplicity—at least until further notice—on the various addition operators specifically ("+" for integers, "++" for rationals, and "+++" for integer pairs). Now, I deliberately gave these operators three different names, or symbols (I use the terms interchangeably), because they're clearly logically distinct. However, I observe now that it would be much more usual in practice to use the same symbol, "+", for all three of them—in which case we could say the symbol "+" is *overloaded:* There's a "+" operator for integers, and there are also "+" operators for rationals and integer pairs. From this point forward, therefore, let's assume for the sake of the discussion that the operators have indeed all been given the same name, "+". *Note:* Let's also agree, for simplicity again, to ignore integer pairs and concentrate on just integers and rationals, at least until further notice.

In general, an operator is said to be overloaded if another operator exists with the same name. To take the most obvious example, equality ("=") is overloaded; there's an "=" operator for integers, and another for character strings, and another for rational numbers, and so on; in fact, there's an "=" operator for every type. In the case of "+" in particular, then, it's clear that what we have is indeed two distinct operators with the same name, one for integers and one for rationals; in other words, we are indeed talking about operator overloading. *Note:* "Operator overloading" is the term that's conventionally used in this context, but it should be clear from the discussion that it's really operator *names* that are overloaded, not operators as such. However, I'll stay with the conventional usage for the purposes of this chapter.

Now, overloading is just one kind of *polymorphism*. Essentially, an operator is said to be polymorphic if its arguments can be of different types on different invocations; again, equality ("=") provides an obvious example. But there's another kind of polymorphism, called *inclusion* polymorphism, that's relevant when we're dealing with type inheritance in particular. To be specific, if *T'* is a proper subtype of *T* and *Op* is an operator that applies to values of type *T,* then *Op* necessarily applies to values of type *T'* also (because values of type *T' are* values of type *T,* by definition). *Op* here is said to be *inherited* by type *T'* from type *T*. Operator *Op* is also said to exhibit inclusion polymorphism: polymorphism, because it certainly permits its arguments to be of different types on different invocations; inclusion, because the set of values constituting type *T'* is (properly) *included* in the set of values constituting type *T*. By way of example, consider the operator "+", which applies to integers—i.e., to integer *values*—and therefore to positive integers as well, by definition; I mean, the very same "+" operator applies to positive integers as well, because positive integers *are* integers (we don't have two different "+" operators, one for integers in general and another for positive integers in particular).

It follows from the foregoing that there's an important logical difference between inclusion and overloading polymorphism, as follows:

- With inclusion polymorphism, as we've just seen, there's really just one operator, logically speaking. While that operator might be supported by several distinct implementation versions under the covers (perhaps one for type *T* and another for type *T′*), the user needn't be aware of that fact—as far as the user is concerned, there's just a single operator (as in the case just mentioned of "+" for both integers and positive integers), and that operator has essentially the same semantics wherever it's applied.

- With overloading polymorphism, by contrast, there are several logically distinct operators. While those operators do all have the same name, the user has to understand that they are in fact logically distinct *and they have distinct semantics* (as in the case previously discussed of "+" for rationals and "+" for integers).[7]

With the foregoing explanations by way of background, let me now repeat, and stress, the fact that in the example at hand (i.e., integers vs. rationals), we are indeed talking about overloading polymorphism as such and not inclusion polymorphism. For example, the rational operator "+" is *defined in terms of* the integer operator of the same name; it's certainly not *inherited* from type INTEGER (which it would have to be if RATIONAL were a subtype of INTEGER), because the two operators have different semantics. In any case, there's obviously no question of RATIONAL being a subtype of INTEGER[8]—most rational numbers simply aren't integers, and there's just no way we could pretend otherwise. *Au contraire,* in fact: I'm building up to a point where, not only is RATIONAL not a subtype of INTEGER, but *INTEGER isn't a subtype of RATIONAL, either* (Fig. 1 notwithstanding).

INTEGERS AREN'T RATIONAL NUMBERS

To pursue the matter a little longer, suppose for a moment that (despite the arguments of the previous section) type INTEGER *were* a subtype of type RATIONAL. Then inclusion polymorphism would have to apply, and in particular the operator "+" for type INTEGER would have to be inherited from type RATIONAL (in other words, there would have to be just one "+" operator, logically speaking). Is this in fact the case?—i.e., is integer addition in fact a special case of rational addition? Do the two operators have the same semantics?

Well, it's hard to see how the answer to any of these questions could possibly be *yes,* given that rational addition is defined in terms of integer addition and not the other way around. But in any case, it's easy to see that INTEGER isn't a subtype of RATIONAL without having to answer these particular questions as such. Consider the following argument:

- Simplifying somewhat, we've seen that a rational number *p* is defined as a pair of the form <<*a*,*b*>>, where *a* and *b* are integers.

- To quote reference [2] again: "Rational numbers are numbers of the form *a*/*b* where *a* and *b* are integers ... If *b* = 1, the number is an integer" (slightly paraphrased). In other words, an integer is a rational number of the form <<*a*,1>>, to use our own notation.

- But if rationals are defined in terms of integers, we certainly can't go on to define integers in terms of rationals! Indeed, the foregoing "definition" of rational numbers would imply that the rational number <<*a*,*b*>> is defined as

---

[7] Distinct semantics, yes, but it's generally a good idea if they can have *similar* semantics, as in the case of "=" for integers and "=" for character strings (and so on).

[8] As noted in an earlier footnote, however, RATIONAL would have been a subtype of the type INTEGER PAIR, if we had bothered to define this latter as an explicit type. Certainly operators that apply to integer pairs apply to rationals (and they would have been explicitly inherited by rationals, if we'd defined that INTEGER PAIR type). For example, the operators *norm,* "+++", and "***", all of which were defined for integer pairs, do necessarily apply to rationals a fortiori, because rationals *are* integer pairs—and the same is true for the integer pair operators "=", "<", and ">". (I did mention this latter fact earlier, but I didn't explicitly point out at the time that we were talking about operator inheritance and inclusion polymorphism.)

```
<< <<a,1>> , <<b,1>> >>
```

which in turn is defined as

```
<< << <<a,1>> , <<1,1>>, >> , << <<b,1>> , <<1,1>> >> >>
```

which in turn is defined as ... (etc., etc.). Clearly, we have an infinite regression on our hands: just one of the many logical absurdities that arise if we try to pretend that INTEGER is a subtype of RATIONAL.

THE TRUE SITUATION

As I've said, the set **Q** of rational numbers, together with its operators "+" and "*", constitutes a mathematical field. (I'm assuming here that "+" and "*" are both overloaded, and I'll continue to do the same for the remainder of this chapter.) A fortiori, therefore, it also constitutes a mathematical *group*. A group in mathematics is like a field, except that:

- Multiplication isn't necessarily defined.
- Addition isn't necessarily commutative. (If it is, the group is said to be a *commutative* or *abelian* group, otherwise it's a *noncommutative* group.)

Consider now the set **J** consisting of all rational numbers of the form <<*a*,1>>; **J** is of course a proper subset of **Q**. Note that the additive identity <<0,1>> and the multiplicative identity <<1,1>> are both elements of **J**, by definition. Now let *p* and *q* denote the rational numbers <<*a*,1>> and <<*b*,1>>, respectively; observe that these rational numbers are also both elements of **J**, again by definition. Then we have:

- The sum *p*+*q* = <<*a*+*b*,1>> and the product *p***q* = <<*a***b*,1>> are clearly both elements of **J**, so **J** is closed under the operations of (rational) "+" and "*".
- Both of these operators are commutative and associative, and "*" distributes over "+", as we already know.
- The rational number <<0,1>> continues to serve as the identity with respect to "+".
- The additive inverse, –*p*, of *p* (i.e., the inverse of *p* with respect to "+") is the rational number <<–*a*,1>>, which is an element of **J**.
- The rational number <<1,1>> continues to serve as the identity with respect to "*".
- However, *most elements of **J** have no multiplicative inverse* (within **J**, that is).[9] For example, the rational number <<2,1>> is an element of **J**, but its multiplicative inverse in **Q** is <<1,2>>, which is not an element of **J**.

It follows that the set **J** of rational numbers of the form <<*a*,1>>, together with its operators "+" and "*", does not constitute a mathematical field. It does, however, constitute a mathematical group—in fact, a *subgroup* of the group consisting of **Q** and the operators "+" and "*". (A subgroup of a group *G* is a subset of the elements of *G* that itself satisfies the definition of a group, under the same "+" and "*" operators as apply to *G*.)

Now, we've already seen that elements of the set **J** are not integers; in other words, **J** is not **Z**, where (as earlier in this chapter) **Z** is the set of integers. However, it's easy to see that the subgroup just defined, consisting of **J** and the rational operators "+" and "*", is *isomorphic* to the group consisting of the set **Z** with the *integer* operators "+" and "*". What this means, loosely, is that each of these groups can be mapped, or transformed, into

---

[9] Why only "most elements"?

the other. Of course, the mapping in question is just about as simple as it could possibly be. Here it is:

```
element <<a,1>> of J     ⇔    element a of Z
<<a,1>> = <<b,1>>        ⇔    a = b
<<a,1>> < <<b,1>>        ⇔    a < b
<<a,1>> + <<b,1>>        ⇔    a + b
<<a,1>> * <<b,1>>        ⇔    a * b
```

To spell this mapping out in detail:

- Every element of **J** has a unique counterpart in **Z** and vice versa; in other words, there's a strict one to one correspondence between the two sets.

- For every expression of the form <<*a*,1>> = <<*b*,1>> (equality comparison between elements of **J**), there's a unique corresponding expression of the form *a* = *b* (equality comparison between elements of **Z**) and vice versa. Moreover, the expression <<*a*,1>> = <<*b*,1>> yields TRUE if and only if the expression *a* = *b* yields TRUE.

- For every expression of the form <<*a*,1>> < <<*b*,1>>[10] ("less than" comparison between elements of **J**), there's a unique corresponding expression of the form *a* < *b* ("less than" comparison between elements of **Z**) and vice versa. Moreover, the expression <<*a*,1>> < <<*b*,1>> yields TRUE if and only if the expression *a* < *b* yields TRUE.

- For every expression of the form <<*a*,1>>+<<*b*,1>> (addition of elements of **J**), there's a unique corresponding expression of the form *a*+*b* (addition of elements of **Z**) and vice versa. Moreover, the expression <<*a*,1>>+<<*b*,1>> yields the result <<*c*,1>> if and only if the expression *a*+*b* yields the result *c*.

- For every expression of the form <<*a*,1>>*<<*b*,1>> (multiplication of elements of **J**), there's a unique corresponding expression of the form *a***b* (multiplication of elements of **Z**) and vice versa. Moreover, the expression <<*a*,1>>*<<*b*,1>> yields the result <<*c*,1>> if and only if the expression *a***b* yields the result *c*.

So the two systems (**J**,+,*) and (**Z**,+,*)—to adopt an obvious shorthand notation—are certainly *isomorphic*. But isomorphic doesn't mean identical! There's a clear logical difference between the two systems. It follows that, as I effectively claimed earlier, the system (**Z**,+,*)—which is basically the type we call INTEGER—is *not* a subtype of the system (**Q**,+,*), which is basically the type we call RATIONAL. Now, we could say, correctly, that type RATIONAL has a proper subtype whose elements are what might be called the "integer-like rationals"; however, it's strictly incorrect to say that it has a proper subtype whose elements are the integers per se. In other words (and contrary to what many people think), the rational number system isn't an "extension" of the integer number system, nor is the integer number system "embedded" in the rational number system.

---

[10] Apologies if this expression is hard to read.

CONCLUSIONS

My purpose in this chapter has been to try to clarify some issues over which there seems to be some confusion in the IT literature. In particular, I've tried to show that types INTEGER and RATIONAL as usually understood are not a good example of a subtype and a supertype, respectively. Please note, however, that I've concentrated on this specific case purely for reasons of definiteness; essentially similar considerations apply to various other pairs of types from the hierarchy in Fig. 1. Consider, for example, the types COMPLEX and REAL. Complex numbers are defined in terms of real numbers (to paraphrase what I said earlier, a complex number is a number of the form $a+bi$, where a and b are real numbers and i is the square root of -1); so how can real numbers then be defined as a special case of complex numbers?[11]

By way of another example, consider the set **Z** of integers as previously defined and the set **N** of natural numbers = {1, 2, ...}. We can say, logically and correctly, that the subset {+1, +2, ...} of **Z** together with its (dyadic) "+" and "*" operators is isomorphic to **N** together with *its* (dyadic) "+" and "*" operators; however, the two systems are certainly not identical. Nor are the natural number 2 and the integer +2 the same object, mathematically speaking; they're equivalent, in a certain well defined sense, but again they're not identical. (By contrast, the integer 2 and the positive integer 2 *are* the same object, mathematically speaking, and the system (**P**,+,*), where **P** is the set of positive integers, *is* a subtype of the system (**N**,+,*); i.e., type POSITIVE INTEGER *is* a subtype of type INTEGER.)

And since I'm on the subject of popular misconceptions, as it were, let me close by mentioning a couple of others:

- Any system in which additive inverses exist supports subtraction. For example, if p and q denote the rational numbers <<*a,b*>> and <<*c,d*>>, respectively, then the expression $p–q$ is defined to be shorthand for the expression $p+(–q)$, which in turn is defined to be equal to the rational number <<*a*d–b*c,b*d*>>. Note, however, that the "–" symbols in the expressions $p–q$ and $p+(–q)$ denote two logically distinct operators—the first is dyadic, and represents subtraction; the second is monadic, and represents the operator "additive inverse of." Of course, the first is defined in terms of the second; however, the fact remains that there's a logical difference between the two. (Incidentally, this example shows why the monadic and dyadic "–" operators have different names, viz., "negative" and "minus," respectively. Thus, "5–2" is pronounced "five minus two," while "–2" is better pronounced "negative two" and *not* "minus two.")

- The "+" symbol in (e.g.) the expression $a+bi$—denoting a certain complex number—represents an operator that's logically distinct from *all* of the addition operators discussed in this chapter prior to this point. Indeed, an argument could be made that it doesn't really represent an operator at all but merely serves as a convenient (?) notation. However, I prefer the alternative argument that says it does in fact represent an operator: namely, an operator that takes a real number and an imaginary number and returns the corresponding complex number (in which case we're dealing with another example of overloading, incidentally). But there certainly isn't any addition going on here in any conventional sense.

ACKNOWLEDGMENTS

I'd like to thank one of my longest standing friends, Bob White, who a little while back wrote me a personal letter on matters closely related to the subject of this chapter and thereby finally spurred me to set down in writing some thoughts I'd been having, off and on, for several years. Thanks also to Hugh Darwen for helpful comments on an

[11] As an exercise, you might try cleaning this case up too, using an approach similar to that adopted in the body of the chapter. *Hint:* Start by defining a complex number as an ordered pair of reals.

earlier draft.

REFERENCES AND BIBLIOGRAPHY

1. C. J. Date and Hugh Darwen: *Databases, Types, and the Relational Model: The Third Manifesto* (3rd edition). Boston, Mass.: Addison-Wesley (2006). See also Chapters 1 and 19 of the present book.

2. Jan Gullberg: *Mathematics: From the Birth of Numbers*. New York, N.Y.: W. W. Norton & Company (1997).

Part IV

MISSING INFORMATION

The "missing information" problem has been with us ever since databases were first invented, and numerous approaches to that problem have been proposed over the years. SQL in particular offers an approach based on the notion of "nulls" and three-valued logic (3VL); that approach has been widely discredited, however. Other writers (the present writer included) have proposed schemes based on default or "special" values; in general these schemes aren't much better than nulls and 3VL (in particular, they all suffer from the general problem of what to do about those special values when they crop up during regular processing), but at least they stay in two-valued logic (2VL), and they can be used successfully in simple situations. Some slightly more ambitious approaches are explored in the first four chapters in this part of the book. To be specific:

- Chapter 23 proposes an approach according to which the database is designed in such a way as to avoid any need for either nulls or special values entirely. (The approach does sometimes require special values to be introduced in the results of queries, but such values aren't recorded in the database and are under the user's complete control.)

- Chapter 24 investigates the possibility of using *multirelations* (in place of relations as such) in order to represent known information explicitly and unknown information implicitly, all in one and the same data structure.

- Chapters 25 and 26 examine what might be seen as disciplined special cases of the special values scheme: Chapter 25 describes a scheme based on the inheritance model from Part III of this book, and Chapter 26 describes an approach based on relation valued attributes.

Please understand that our reason for including the foregoing material in this book isn't necessarily that we advocate any of the schemes described. Rather, it's because we believe it's useful to give them a public hearing, as it were, and perhaps to provide a basis for future debate.

After Chapters 23-26, the next chapter then discusses a specific and important aspect of SQL's 3VL approach; it also offers, in an appendix, a detailed description of exactly how that approach "works." Chapter 28 then responds to a recent criticism of an earlier analysis of our own regarding problems connected with that approach. Finally, Chapter 29 is a bit of light relief; like the preceding chapters, however, it still carries a serious message.

Chapter 23

The Decomposition Approach

Something is better than nothing.

—16th century proverb

This chapter is based on a slide presentation I've been giving annually to undergraduates and others ever since 2003 [4]. In it, I propose an approach to the "missing information" problem that differs drastically from the well known scheme found in SQL [14]. It also differs from others that have been advocated from time to time, especially by Codd in references [1], [2], and [3] (in this latter connection, see also reference [11]). [1] To be specific, the scheme I propose:

- Has no notion of "null" or any other construct that's allowed to appear in place of a value and yet is not itself a value
- Relies exclusively on classical two-valued logic (2VL), instead of some *n*-valued logic (*n*VL) for some $n > 2$
- Abides by Codd's *Information Principle,* in that at all times the database contains relations and nothing but relations
- Is capable of dealing with "missing information" of any number of different kinds

I refer to my proposal as a *decomposition* approach, since it involves decomposing, in a variety of ways, relvars that might appear to require nulls (or something like them) into ones that don't. In other words, the emphasis is on designing the database in such a way as to avoid a perceived need for nulls. However, it's only fair to point out that such a design discipline does lead to certain requirements on the part of the system, and I'll discuss those too, in later sections of the chapter.

Fig. 1 below shows an example I'll use throughout the chapter as a basis for illustrating the approach. The table in that figure—I deliberately don't call it either a relvar or a relation, because the fact that it contains those question marks means it might be neither—is intended to represent a set of suppliers, each of which has an identifying number (S#), a name (SNAME), a status value (STATUS), and a location (CITY). That is to say, the meaning, or *predicate,* for that table looks something like this:

S

S#	SNAME	STATUS	CITY
S1	Smith	20	London
S2	Jones	10	??????
S3	Blake	??????	Paris
S4	Clark	??????	??????

Fig. 1: Table S—sample value

[1] It does, however, have certain points in common with an approach proposed by David McGoveran in reference [15].

- *Supplier S# is named SNAME, has status STATUS, and is located in CITY.*

This predicate is at best approximate, however. It would be appropriate if it weren't for those question marks. After all, the following—obtained from the predicate by substituting values from the row in Fig. 1 for supplier S1—is a meaningful instantiation of it (i.e., a meaningful *proposition*):

- *Supplier S1 is named Smith, has status 20, and is located in London.*

But if we substitute values from the row for, say, supplier S2, we obtain—

- *Supplier S2 is named Jones, has status 10, and is located in ??????.*

—which is *not* a meaningful proposition; in fact, it doesn't make sense at all. (Perhaps I should explain that, in general, *p* is a proposition if and only if the question "Is it the case that *p?*" can be categorically answered either *yes* or *no*. This simple test clearly shows that the example at hand isn't a proposition.)

Another interesting question is: What data types do the various columns of the table—in particular, columns STATUS and CITY—have? (I'm assuming for the sake of the example, and I'll continue to assume throughout the remainder of the chapter, that question marks don't appear, and can't ever appear, in columns S# and SNAME.) In SQL in particular, the question marks in columns STATUS and CITY might indicate the presence of nulls, and the data types of the columns might be INTEGER and VARCHAR(20), respectively. Yet null isn't a value of type INTEGER, nor is it a value of type VARCHAR(20). In fact, of course, null isn't a value at all, of any type; as a consequence, the presence of nulls in a table means among other things that the table in question quite definitely represents neither a relation nor a relvar.

From this preliminary discussion, it should be obvious that what we need to do is get rid of those question marks. I propose using two kinds of decomposition, vertical and horizontal, to achieve this goal.

VERTICAL DECOMPOSITION

First some generalities. Vertical decomposition—"vertical" because the dividing lines in the decomposition are between columns, as it were—is essentially what we do in classical normalization: viz., we decompose by taking projections of the original table.[2] What's more, we can recover the original table by joining those projections together again. (It's crucial, of course, that the decomposition process be nonloss—i.e., no information must be lost in that process—and the fact that we can get the original table back again, using join, guarantees that such is the case.)

Note: For simplicity I'll stay with the terminology of tables, rows, and columns throughout the remainder of this chapter, even though it's not much to my taste. Also, I'll assume you're familiar with the basic ideas of normalization and won't bother to spell out too many of the details here.

Now, vertical decomposition as classically understood is defined in terms of various *levels of normalization,* also known as *normal forms:* Boyce/Codd normal form (BCNF), fifth normal form (5NF), and so on. The ultimate level is sixth normal form, 6NF. Here's a definition:

- **Definition (sixth normal form):** A table is in sixth normal form, 6NF, if and only if it can't be vertically decomposed at all, in a nonloss way, into tables with fewer columns.

Decomposition to 6NF can thus be thought of as *reducing to the simplest possible terms.* A table in 6NF will have no ANDs in its predicate (speaking *very* loosely!), and vertical decomposition can be thought of as a process of removing ANDs, in a sense. (Undoing such a decomposition puts those ANDs back in.) By contrast,

---

[2] But see reference [7].

we'll see later that horizontal decomposition can be thought of as removing ORs.

Before going any further, I should stress the point that the decomposition approach to missing information doesn't actually require tables to be in 6NF. 6NF is often—though not always—a good idea in general, but (to repeat) the approach I'm proposing doesn't rely on it.

To get back to the problem at hand: The first step, then, is to apply vertical decomposition to produce a set of tables with the property that no table ever has more than one "question mark" column. (I use the term *question mark column,* informally, to mean a column in which question marks are allowed to appear.) For the running example, the result of this step is as shown in Fig. 2.

SN

S#	SNAME
S1	Smith
S2	Jones
S3	Blake
S4	Clark

ST

S#	STATUS
S1	20
S2	10
S3	??????
S4	??????

SC

S#	CITY
S1	London
S2	??????
S3	Paris
S4	??????

Fig. 2: Vertically decomposing table S

The meanings or predicates for tables SN, ST, and SC are as follows (and note that they do indeed involve no ANDs):

- SN: *Supplier S# is named SNAME.*
- ST: *Supplier S# has status STATUS.*
- SC: *Supplier S# is located in CITY.*

However, the predicates for ST and SC are still only approximate, because of those question marks—and that's why we need horizontal decomposition, which I'll be discussing in the next section. Before we get to that discussion, however, observe that each of the tables in Fig. 2 has just two columns (in fact, if we ignore the question marks for a moment, they would all be in 6NF). But this state of affairs is a fluke, in a way; it's a direct result of our choice of example. If the example were different—to be specific, if we knew that column STATUS, as well as columns S# and SNAME, could never contain any question marks—then the appropriate vertical decomposition would be as shown in Fig. 3 below (where I've assumed, just for the sake of the revised example, that suppliers S3 and S4 have status 30 and 20, respectively). Table SUT in Fig. 3 isn't in 6NF.

SUT

S#	SNAME	STATUS
S1	Smith	20
S2	Jones	10
S3	Blake	30
S4	Clark	20

SC

S#	CITY
S1	London
S2	??????
S3	Paris
S4	??????

Fig. 3: Vertically decomposing table S, if every supplier has a status

HORIZONTAL DECOMPOSITION

Again I'll begin with some generalities. Horizontal decomposition—"horizontal" because the dividing lines in the decomposition are between rows, as it were—is a process of taking restrictions of the given table. (Again, of course, it's crucial that the decomposition process be nonloss, and in the case of horizontal decomposition we can recover the original table by taking the union of those restrictions.) *Note:* In the interest of accuracy, I should add that the restrictions in question are usually followed by a projection, as we'll soon see.

The basic principle underlying horizontal decomposition is that we shouldn't try to use a table to represent two or more different predicates. By way of example, consider table SC from Fig. 2 (repeated here for convenience):

SC

S#	CITY
S1	London
S2	??????
S3	Paris
S4	??????

In this table, the row for supplier S1 means: *Supplier S1 is located in London.* By contrast, the row for supplier S2 means: *We don't know where supplier S2 is located* (at least, let's agree that's what it means, at least for the time being). So different rows correspond to different predicates, and the predicate I gave before—*Supplier S# is located in CITY*—doesn't really apply to every row.

Now, we might try a different predicate, perhaps like this (note the OR, which I've shown in uppercase bold for emphasis):

- *Supplier S# is located in CITY* ***OR*** *we don't know where supplier S# is located.*

But this predicate doesn't really work either. If we try to instantiate it with values from the row for supplier S2, we get:

- *Supplier S2 is located in ??????* ***OR*** *we don't know where supplier S2 is located.*

And the first half of this sentence ("Supplier S2 is located in ??????") still makes no sense, because ?????? isn't a legitimate city name and can't legitimately be substituted, as an argument, for the CITY parameter in the putative predicate. So what we need to do is separate the two disjuncts[3]—that is, we need to apply horizontal decomposition to table SC, to obtain one table per disjunct. The result of this step is as shown in Fig. 4 opposite.

---

[3] The formal name for logical OR is *disjunction*, and its operands (i.e., the clauses being ORed together, in the example) are called *disjuncts*. Similarly, the formal name for logical AND is *conjunction*, and its operands are called *conjuncts*.

SC

S#	CITY
S1	London
S3	Paris

SUC

S#
S2
S4

Fig. 4: Horizontally decomposing table SC

As you can see, we now have two tables:

- A restricted form of table SC (for which I've kept the name SC), containing just the original SC rows that had no question marks in column CITY
- Another table SUC ("suppliers with an unknown city"), containing just the original SC rows that did have question marks in column CITY—except that the CITY column in that table, if we kept it, would contain nothing but question marks, and so we can project it away without losing anything

The predicates for these tables are as follows (and these, at last, truly are the pertinent predicates, not just approximations):

- SC: *Supplier S# is located in CITY.*
- SUC: *We don't know where supplier S# is located.*

Observe in particular that the predicate for table SC has two parameters, S# and CITY, and that table has two columns accordingly; by contrast, the predicate for table SUC has just one parameter, S#, and that table has just one column accordingly.

Of course, we can and should perform an analogous horizontal decomposition on table ST from Fig. 2. First we show that table again, for convenience:

ST

S#	STATUS
S1	20
S2	10
S3	??????
S4	??????

The result of the decomposition is shown in Fig. 5. The predicates are as follows:

ST

S#	STATUS
S1	20
S2	10

SUT

S#
S3
S4

Fig. 5: Horizontally decomposing table ST

- ST: *Supplier S# has status STATUS.*
- SUT: *We don't know supplier S#'s status.*

What Do the Question Marks Mean?

For simplicity, let's ignore supplier status for the moment and concentrate on supplier cities. So far, then, I've said that question marks in the CITY column mean *we don't know* the applicable supplier city—i.e., the supplier does have a city, but we don't know what it is. But our not knowing is only one of many possible reasons why we might not be able to put an actual city name in some position in that column. For example, it might be that the notion of having a location simply doesn't apply to some suppliers (perhaps because they conduct their business entirely online). If so, then we might say, *very* loosely, that table SC, with those question marks in the CITY column (i.e., table SC as shown in Fig. 2), has a predicate looking something like this:

- *Supplier S# is located in CITY* ***OR*** *we don't know where supplier S# is located* ***OR*** *supplier S# isn't located anywhere.*

Note, therefore, that those question marks now potentially have two distinct interpretations: Some of them mean we don't know the applicable city, others mean the property of having a city doesn't apply. So, again, we apply horizontal decomposition, this time to obtain three tables: SC ("suppliers with a known city"), SUC ("suppliers with an unknown city"), and SNC ("suppliers with no city"). The predicates are:

- SC: *Supplier S# is located in CITY.*
- SUC: *We don't know where supplier S# is located.*
- SNC: *Supplier S# doesn't have a location.*

If we assume for the sake of the example that supplier S2 has an unknown city and supplier S4 doesn't have a city at all, the result of the decomposition is as shown in Fig. 6.

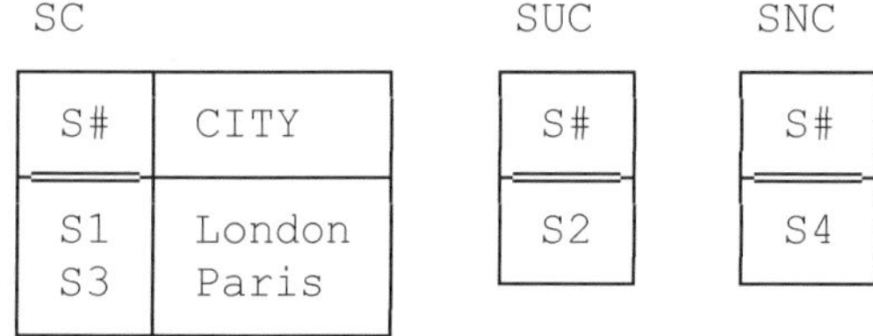

Fig. 6: Horizontally decomposing table SC, allowing for suppliers with no city

In other words, the decomposition approach allows us to represent as many different kinds of "missing information" as we like. To be specific, if there are *n* distinct reasons for supplier cities to be "missing," there'll be *n*+1 tables having to do with suppliers and cities. Two possible objections to the approach thus immediately spring to mind:

1. Aren't some queries going to get awfully complex? For example, suppose we just want to retrieve "everything in the database" that has to do with suppliers—the analog of "SELECT * FROM S" in SQL. Aren't we going to have to do a lot of joins, or (worse) outer joins?
2. Aren't we going to wind up with an awful lot of tables?

I'll come back to the first of these issues in the section "Queries," later. As for the second, well, there are several points I want to make. Let *C* be an SQL column for which "nulls are allowed." Then:

- If the nulls in column *C* all represent the same kind of "missing information," and if the same is true for all such columns *C,* then the number of tables resulting from the decomposition approach is exactly the same as the number resulting from a good relational design. (To paraphrase something I said earlier, the presence of such a column *C* in a table *T* means table *T* is certainly not a *relational* table. Thus, proper relational design requires elimination of such columns.)

- The situation is worse if the nulls in some such column *C* represent two or more distinct kinds of "missing information" but proper decomposition isn't done. In that case, the result will certainly be fewer tables—but the apparent simplicity of that design is spurious: Those tables aren't relational, they don't faithfully reflect the real world, they no longer have a clear predicate, and queries are more susceptible to errors of formulation or errors of interpretation or both.

- There's a tactic we might consider, if we want to reduce the number of tables, which I'll illustrate with reference to Fig. 6. In terms of that example, the tactic would involve combining tables SUC and SNC into a single table with two columns, S# and REASON, where REASON indicates the reason why the applicable supplier has no recorded city:

S#	REASON
S2	*d/k*
S4	*n/a*

  But now we have to define appropriate values, and spell out their interpretations, for column REASON (in the example, I've used *d/k* for "don't know" and *n/a* for "not applicable"). In fact, if the decomposition approach requires *n* "missing information" tables, the combination approach requires *n* "missing information" reasons. So the combination approach is in some respects no less complex than the decomposition approach.

CONSTRAINTS

Let's assume now and for the rest of the chapter that there's just one reason why STATUS values might be missing (we don't know the value) and just two reasons why CITY values might be missing (either we don't know the value or no such value exists). To summarize so far, then, our recommended design looks like the sample tables in Fig. 7 overleaf.

SN

S#	SNAME
S1	Smith
S2	Jones
S3	Blake
S4	Clark

ST

S#	STATUS
S1	20
S2	10

SUT

S#
S3
S4

SC

S#	CITY
S1	London
S3	Paris

SUC

S#
S2

SNC

S#
S4

Fig. 7: Fully decomposing table S

However, this design requires several integrity constraints to hold it together, so to speak. To be specific, the following constraints all need to be stated and enforced:

1. Every table has {S#} as a key.
2. Each row in SN has a matching row in exactly one of ST and SUT (and conversely).
3. Each row in SN has a matching row in exactly one of SC, SUC, and SNC (and conversely).

Of course, Constraint 1 is just a conventional key constraint on each of the tables and can be expressed by means of conventional KEY specifications. As for the other two, they're easily expressed as what reference [6] calls *equality dependencies* (EQDs for short). Here's Constraint 2, for example:

```
CONSTRAINT CX2
   SN { S# } = D_UNION { ST { S# } , SUT { S# } } ;
```

Note that this expression makes use of **Tutorial D**'s D_UNION operator.[4] D_UNION ("disjoint union") is the same as regular relational union, except that it fails if its operands have any tuples (rows) in common. And Constraint 3 is very similar:

```
CONSTRAINT CX3
   SN { S# } = D_UNION { SC { S# } , SUC { S# } , SNC { S# } } ;
```

By the way, you might be thinking that Constraints 2 and 3 involve—or, rather, seem to be a combination of—certain conventional foreign key constraints. For example, the fact that each row in SC has a matching row in SN might be expressed by means of the following specification (part of the definition of table SC):

```
FOREIGN KEY { S# } REFERENCES SN
```

As reference [6] demonstrates, however, conventional FOREIGN KEY syntax isn't very useful when one to one relationships are involved, and one to one relationships are indeed what we're faced with here. For

---

[4] See Chapter 10 regarding the possible undesirability of allowing D_UNION in constraints and for a workaround that avoids it.

example, there's a one to one relationship between the rows of SN and the rows of the (disjoint) union of SC, SUC, and SNC.[5] In such a situation, equality dependencies or EQDs provide a much more succinct, and symmetric, way of formulating the constraints in question.

That said, let me add that interpreting the situation in terms of conventional foreign keys does raise another issue, however. Let's concentrate on tables SN, ST, and SUT, for simplicity. Then every row in table SN has a foreign key value referencing some unique row in either ST or SUT, and every row in either ST or SUT has a foreign key value referencing some unique row in SN. In other words, there's a *referential cycle* here, involving SN on the one hand and the disjoint union of ST and SUT on the other. And referential cycles always lead to questions of how to update the database—which brings us to the next section.

MULTIPLE ASSIGNMENT

An obvious example of a "how to update the database" question is: How can we get started? If, again, we concentrate on tables SN, ST, and SUT for simplicity, then it looks as if we can't insert a row into SN until we've inserted a corresponding row into either ST or SUT, and we can't insert a row into ST or SUT until we've inserted a corresponding row into SN. So what's to be done? *The Third Manifesto* solves this problem by means of a *multiple assignment* operation [12], which (among other things) allows rows to be inserted into two or more tables simultaneously. For example:

```
INSERT INTO SN ( S# , SNAME ) VALUES ( 'S1' , 'Smith' ) ,
INSERT INTO ST ( S# , STATUS ) VALUES ( 'S1' , 20 ) ,
INSERT INTO SC ( S# , CITY ) VALUES ( 'S1' , 'London' ) ;
```

I've shown this update in a hypothetical dialect of SQL rather than **Tutorial D** (which I would normally prefer to use) because of my earlier decision to talk in terms of tables and rows rather than relations and tuples.[6] It's a hypothetical dialect because it allows any number of INSERTs, DELETEs, and UPDATEs to be bundled together into a single statement, using commas as separators and a semicolon (as usual) as terminator. In the example, therefore, the three INSERTs are performed as a single atomic operation, and—this is the important point—no integrity checking is done until all three have been executed and the semicolon is reached.

Now, it's well known that INSERT, DELETE, and UPDATE are each shorthand for a certain assignment operation. The foregoing triple INSERT in particular is shorthand for a triple assignment of the form:

```
SN := ... , ST := ... , SC := ... ;
```

(Hence the term *multiple assignment,* of course.) *Note:* This triple assignment isn't even close to SQL syntax, however, because SQL doesn't currently support an explicit table assignment operator.

As an aside, I remark that (as noted elsewhere in this book) multiple assignment or something like it might be needed just to define the database in the first place. At least, such is likely to be the case if Constraints 2 and 3 from the previous section are formulated as explicit foreign key specifications—but as I've already said, separate (standalone) EQD specifications are probably a better way to go, anyway.

---

[5] Reference [10] shows that the term *one to one relationship,* and others like it, are often used very imprecisely. Here I'm using the term in the following precise sense [8]: A one to one relationship is a correspondence between two sets *s1* and *s2* (not necessarily distinct) such that each element of *s1* corresponds to exactly one element of *s2* and each element of *s2* corresponds to exactly one element of *s1*.

[6] Also, I've assumed for simplicity that columns S# and SNAME are of type character string instead of (as elsewhere in this book) some user defined type.

QUERIES

Now I return to a question I raised earlier: Given a design like that of Fig. 7, aren't some queries going to get awfully complex? In particular, what's involved with that design in doing a query analogous to the "simple" SQL query SELECT * FROM S?

Before I address that issue, let me first point out that some queries—queries, I venture to suggest, that are more likely to be needed in practice than ones like SELECT * FROM S—are actually simpler with the design of Fig. 7. For example, the query "For suppliers for whom CITY is both applicable and known, get supplier numbers and cities" becomes just—

```
SELECT S# , CITY
FROM   SC
```

—instead of:

```
SELECT S# , CITY
FROM   S
WHERE  CITY IS NOT NULL
```

Moreover, the query "Get suppliers for whom CITY is not applicable" is not only simpler with the design of Fig. 7, it can't be done at all with the "design" of Fig. 1. (In other words, not only does the "design" of Fig. 1 not deal with the missing information problem very well, it actually *loses* information!)

Be that as it may, let's now consider the "SELECT * FROM S" question. More precisely, let me show how a respectable version of the table in Fig. 1 can be obtained from those in Fig. 7—where by *respectable,* I mean the table will contain proper and informative data values everywhere (no question marks! no nulls!), as indicated in Fig. 8.

S

S#	SNAME	XSTATUS	XCITY
S1	Smith	20	London
S2	Jones	10	*d/k*
S3	Blake	*d/k*	Paris
S4	Clark	*d/k*	*n/a*

Fig. 8: Revised version of table S

Now, however, I'm going to switch to **Tutorial D** (doing the example in SQL would make it hard to see the forest for the trees); also, I'll now assume explicitly that STATUS values are integers and CITY values are character strings. I'll show the solution a step at a time (using sample values from Fig. 7 to illustrate the result of each step in turn), then bring all the steps together at the end.

1. `WITH ( T1 := EXTEND ST : { XSTATUS := CAST_AS_CHAR ( STATUS ) } ) :`

T1

S#	STATUS	XSTATUS
S1	20	20
S2	10	10

STATUS values are integers; XSTATUS values are character strings

2. `WITH ( T2 := T1 { ALL BUT STATUS } ) :`

T2

S#	XSTATUS
S1	20
S2	10

3. `WITH ( T3 := EXTEND SUT : { XSTATUS := 'd/k' } ) :`

T3

S#	XSTATUS
S3	*d/k*
S4	*d/k*

4. `WITH ( T4 := UNION { T2 , T3 } ) :`

T4

S#	XSTATUS
S1	20
S2	10
S3	*d/k*
S4	*d/k*

5. `WITH ( T5 := SC RENAME { CITY AS XCITY } ) :`

T5

S#	XCITY
S1	London
S3	Paris

6. `WITH ( T6 := EXTEND SUC : { XCITY := 'd/k' } ) :`

T6

S#	XCITY
S2	*d/k*

7. `WITH ( T7 := EXTEND SNC : { XCITY := 'n/a' } ) :`

T7

S#	XCITY
S4	*n/a*

8. `WITH ( T8 := UNION { T5 , T6 , T7 } ) :`

T8

S#	XCITY
S1	London
S2	*d/k*
S3	Paris
S4	*n/a*

9. `WITH ( S := JOIN { SN , T4 , T8 } ) : S`

S

S#	SNAME	XSTATUS	XCITY
S1	Smith	20	London
S2	Jones	10	*d/k*
S3	Blake	*d/k*	Paris
S4	Clark	*d/k*	*n/a*

Putting it altogether and simplifying somewhat:

```
WITH ( T1 := EXTEND ST : { XSTATUS := CAST_AS_CHAR ( STATUS ) } ,
       T2 := T1 { ALL BUT STATUS } ,
       T3 := EXTEND SUT : { XSTATUS := 'd/k' } ,
       T4 := UNION { T2 , T3 } ,
       T5 := SC RENAME { CITY AS XCITY } ,
       T6 := EXTEND SUC : { XCITY := 'd/k' } ,
       T7 := EXTEND SNC : { XCITY := 'n/a' } ,
       T8 := UNION { T5 , T6 , T7 } ,
       S  := JOIN { SN , T4 , T8 } ) :
S
```

Now, it's certainly true that the foregoing expression might look a little complicated (and it would look even more so if I hadn't formulated it a step at a time, using WITH). However:

- Various shorthands could be defined, if desired, that could be used to simplify it. One such shorthand is described in reference [5].
- I frankly doubt whether tables such as that in Fig. 8 would ever be wanted much in practice anyway, except perhaps as the basis for some kind of periodic report.
- In any case, the complexity, such as it is, can always be concealed by making the table a view.

HOW MUCH CAN BE DONE TODAY?

How practical is what I've described in foregoing sections, given the level of today's technology? More specifically, which aspects of the decomposition approach as I've described it can be implemented in SQL systems today? Well:

- *Vertical decomposition:* Can be done.
- *Horizontal decomposition:* Can be done.
- *Key specifications:* Can be done.
- *Equality dependencies:* Can be formulated (though far from elegantly!) using CREATE ASSERTION. For example, Constraint CX2 ("Each row in SN has a matching row in exactly one of ST and SUT and conversely") can be formulated as follows:

```
CREATE ASSERTION CX2 CHECK (
   /* no S# appears in both ST and SUT */
   NOT EXISTS ( SELECT * FROM ST
                WHERE  EXISTS ( SELECT * FROM SUT
                                WHERE  SUT.S# = ST.S# ) )
   AND
   /* no S# appears in ST and not in SN */
   NOT EXISTS ( SELECT * FROM ST
                WHERE  NOT EXISTS ( SELECT * FROM SN
                                    WHERE  SN.S# = ST.S# ) )
   AND
```

```
/* no S# appears in SUT and not in SN */
NOT EXISTS ( SELECT * FROM SUT
             WHERE  NOT EXISTS ( SELECT * FROM SN
                                 WHERE  SN.S# = SUT.S# ) )
AND
/* no S# appears in SN and not in ST or SUT */
NOT EXISTS ( SELECT * FROM SN
             WHERE  NOT EXISTS ( SELECT * FROM ST
                                 WHERE  ST.S# = SN.S# )
             AND    NOT EXISTS ( SELECT * FROM SUT
                                 WHERE  SUT.S# = SN.S# ) ) ) ;
```

Quite apart from the fact that this formulation is clumsy in the extreme—not to mention the fact that it's unlikely to perform well—the sad truth is that today's mainstream SQL products don't support CREATE ASSERTION anyway. (They do allow constraints to be defined as part of a CREATE TABLE statement, but such constraints are typically limited to certain rather simple cases; in SQL terms, they're typically not allowed to contain a subquery.)

- *Multiple assignment:* As noted earlier, the SQL standard doesn't support explicit table assignment at all, and so it certainly doesn't support explicit multiple table assignment. Nor does it allow two or more INSERTs, DELETEs, and UPDATEs to be bundled together into a single statement. The odd thing is, though, the standard does support certain multiple table assignments implicitly, because it supports such things as cascade delete and updating through certain joins. It also supports explicit multiple assignment in some cases (e.g., to assign to two or more SQL variables at the same time). So we might expect to see explicit multiple table assignment in some future version of the standard—but, to repeat, it's not supported at the time of writing.

- *Recomposition:* Deriving the table in Fig. 8 from those in Fig. 7 can be done in SQL today; however, the necessary SQL expression is clumsy and likely to perform badly, given current implementations. But other implementations are possible,[7] and I don't believe bad performance is a necessary characteristic of recomposition (or other "complex") queries.

REFERENCES AND BIBLIOGRAPHY

1. E. F. Codd: *The 25th Anniversary of the Creation of the Relational Model for Database Management* (published by the consulting company Codd & Date Inc. in 1994). *Note:* That company is no longer in existence, and this reference might thus be no longer available.

2. E. F. Codd: *The Relational Model for Database Management Version 2.* Boston, Mass.: Addison-Wesley (1990).

3. E. F. Codd: "Extending the Database Relational Model to Capture More Meaning" (*ACM TODS 4,* No. 4, December 1979).

4. Hugh Darwen: "How to Handle Missing Information Without Using Nulls" (presentation slides), *www.thethirdmanifesto.com* (May 9th, 2003; revised May 16th, 2005).

5. Hugh Darwen: "Outer Join with No Nulls and Fewer Tears," in C. J. Date and Hugh Darwen: *Relational Database Writings 1989-1991.* Reading, Mass.: Addison-Wesley (1992).

---

[7] For example, we might consider representing the original table S from Fig. 1 as a single stored table under the covers, and representing the tables obtained by decomposition in terms of mappings to and from that single stored table.

6. C. J. Date: "Inclusion Dependencies and Foreign Keys" (Chapter 13 of the present book).

7. C. J. Date: "Some Issues in Normalization: An Attempt at Clarification" (Chapter 30 of the present book).

8. C. J. Date: *The Relational Database Dictionary, Extended Edition.* Berkeley, Calif.: Apress (2008).

9. C. J. Date: "The Closed World Assumption," in *Logic and Databases: The Roots of Relational Theory.* Victoria, B.C.: Trafford Publishing (2007). See *www.trafford.com/07-0690*.

10. C. J. Date: "All for One, One for All," in *Logic and Databases: The Roots of Relational Theory.* Victoria, B.C.: Trafford Publishing (2007). See *www.trafford.com/07-0690*.

11. C. J. Date: "Why Three- and Four-Valued Logic Don't Work," in *Date on Database: Writings 2000-2006.* Berkeley, Calif.: Apress (2006).

12. C. J. Date and Hugh Darwen: "Multiple Assignment," in *Date on Database: Writings 2000-2006.* Berkeley, Calif.: Apress (2006).

13. C. J. Date and Hugh Darwen: *A Guide to the SQL Standard* (4th edition). Reading, Mass.: Addison-Wesley (1997).

14. International Organization for Standardization (ISO): *Database Language SQL,* Document ISO/IEC 9075:2008 (2008). *Note:* A detailed overview of the "missing information" features of SQL can be found in Chapter 16 of reference [13]. See also Chapter 27 of the present book.

15. David McGoveran: "Nothing from Nothing" (in four parts), in C. J. Date, Hugh Darwen, and David McGoveran, *Relational Database Writings 1994-1997.* Reading, Mass.: Addison-Wesley (1998).

Chapter 24

The Multirelational Approach

Do I contradict myself?
Very well then I contradict myself,
(I am large, I contain multitudes.)

—Walt Whitman: *Song of Myself*

If we had some ham, we could have ham and eggs,
if we had some eggs.

—Anon.

Quite a few of the various approaches that have been proposed at one time or another to the "missing information" problem involve data structures that look like relations but aren't—they look like relations in that their bodies consist of tuples, but they differ from relations in that tuples in the same body don't all have to have the same heading. The latest such proposal (and the one that prompted the investigations described in this chapter) is in reference [10], where once again the idea is floated that such structures be admitted to the database, subject to certain restrictions I don't need go into here. An earlier proposal can be found in reference [12], by my friend the late Adrian Larner. Larner did discuss his ideas with me at the time, but I failed to understand them properly then and I still fail to understand them fully now.

Fig. 1 overleaf depicts in tabular form a couple of examples of the kinds of structures all such approaches involve (table S represents suppliers and table SP shipments).[1] Please note, however, that the gaps or vacant spaces in the tables in that figure aren't meant to represent SQL-style nulls; nor are they meant to represent blanks or the empty character string. Rather, they're meant to represent *the complete absence* of the attribute in question from the tuple in question—where, of course, the attribute in question is the one whose name appears at the top of the column in which the gap appears, and the tuple in question is the one whose attribute values appear in the row in which the gap appears. Thus, to spell the point out (and to adopt an obvious shorthand notation for tuples), the tuples <S3,Blake,30> and <Smith,20,London>, although they both appear in whatever it is that table S is supposed to represent, have different headings and are therefore of different types. What's more, the heading of the first of these tuples in particular is different from the heading of whatever it is that table S is supposed to represent.

---

[1] If those tables represented relations and those relations were meant to be values of relvars, then I would normally mark certain attributes by double underlining to show they were components of the primary—or at any rate sole—key for the relvar in question. I omit such double underlining in this chapter (except when the table in question really does represent a relation), for reasons to be explained in the discussion of *MR-keys* in the section "Constraints," later in the chapter.

S

S#	SNAME	STATUS	CITY
S1	Smith	20	London
S2	Jones	10	Paris
S3	Blake	30	
S4	Clark		London
S5	Adams	30	Athens
S6			Rome
S7			

SP

S#	P#	QTY
S1	P1	300
S1	P2	200
S2	P1	
S3	P2	200
S4	P4	

Fig. 1: Suppliers and shipments—sample values

At first glance, it would seem that such schemes mean we have to abandon relations, which is why in the past I've tended to reject them out of hand. But the publication of reference [10], an article criticizing some of my own (joint) work, more or less compelled me to produce a detailed justification for those rejections. To do that, I needed to work out in more detail what such a scheme might look like in practice; that exercise, I thought, would clearly expose the flaws in the idea. In thinking about this question, however, it occurred to me that the kind of structure under consideration, though not itself a relation, does in a sense *include* certain relations, and those relations might somehow be extracted from it. And if we did all our real work (as it were) in terms of those extracted relations, then it might be argued that we would have preserved the relational model, and we would have abided by Codd's *Information Principle* (which requires that all information in the database be cast in the form of relations, and nothing but relations).[2] But—and it is a big but—it must still be understood that the kind of object that includes those relations is, to repeat, not itself a relation. With that caveat in mind, I still wished to see where the idea might lead.

It's easy to spot the five nonempty relations included in table S in Fig. 1. One contains the tuples with S# values S1, S2, and S5; each of these three tuples has all four of the attributes S#, SNAME, STATUS, and CITY. The other four relations, which happen to contain just one tuple each, are as follows:

- One contains just the tuple for supplier S3, with attributes S#, SNAME, and STATUS.
- One contains just the tuple for supplier S4, with attributes S#, SNAME, and CITY.
- One contains just the tuple for supplier S6, with attributes S# and CITY.
- And one contains just the tuple for supplier S7, with S# as its sole attribute.

But how many empty relations does that table include in that same sense? And what exactly is that sense? Such questions, and many more, needed to be answered, I thought, before I could begin to think about the operators that might be defined for operating on such objects.

What to call these objects? Because I was expecting my investigations to show why the idea should be rejected, I first considered the somewhat derogatory term *pseudorelation.* As my investigations proceeded, however, I became less convinced that the idea should be rejected out of hand—though I hasten to add that I'm certainly not yet arguing in favor of the idea either—and so I decided to call them *multirelations* instead.

---

[2] As reference [5] points out, this principle might more appropriately be called *The Principle of Uniform Representation*, or even *The Principle of Uniformity of Representation.*

Unfortunately, I then found that this term has been used before, for purposes that are (a) different from the one at hand and (b) multifarious. Because of (b), and also because of my inability to think of any suitable alternative, I decided to stick with *multirelation* for the time being. I do think my use of that term is more appropriate than some others I've found; some people apparently even use it to mean an SQL table, on the grounds that the body of such a table is (in general) a *bag* or, as the SQL international standard has it, a "multiset." See also references [9] and [11], with which I might or might not be significantly at odds.

I've said I'm not currently advocating support for multirelations. In fact, I'd like to emphasize that I don't regard the problem that multirelations address as a previously unsolved one. To be specific, I still stand by the "decomposition" solution presented in reference [1], which is in full conformance with the prescriptions of *The Third Manifesto* [6]. A similar though not identical approach is described by David McGoveran in reference [13] (the two approaches are briefly compared in reference [4]). In addition, Fabian Pascal discusses McGoveran's approach in reference [14] and might possibly be moving toward developing it along lines similar to those of the present chapter, though putting the decomposition under the covers (so to speak). But he doesn't attempt to spell out the details in the way I do here.

Of course, many people have raised psychological objections to these decomposition approaches, though without proposing any alternatives (apart from abandoning relations altogether, as SQL does).[3] The most commonly expressed objections are that they give rise to an excessive number of relvars and an excessive number of associated constraints. I can sympathize with these objections, somewhat. In 1982, the very first customer of Business System 12 (a relational DBMS available at that time to users of IBM's timesharing Bureau Service) was an organization offering information to investors about various companies. Over 300 separate items of information were identified as being of possible interest to investors, but only a very few of those items were available for every company. Under both my proposal [1] and McGoveran's [13], at least 300 separate relvars would be needed, together with a huge number of foreign key and other constraints. So we crammed everything into a single relvar, using "impossible" values such as –9999999.99 to indicate missing information. As we soon learned, however, those "impossible" values gave rise to all sorts of traps for the unwary and led to all sorts of complications in attempts to avoid those traps.

So the crucial question is: Can multirelations solve the "missing information" problem while addressing such objections and avoiding such traps and complications? As a basis for discussing this question, I now present the results of my investigations, without at this time offering much in the way of my own opinion on them. In other words, the chapter should be regarded not as a definitive statement but, rather, as a kind of discussion paper. You're invited to consider the following questions:

1. Are there any fatal flaws in the scheme? (I won't attempt to define exactly what I mean by "fatal flaws" here, but lack of logical soundness would certainly qualify.)

2. Is the scheme too complicated?

3. Does it suffer from too much that is counterintuitive?

4. If the answer to any of the foregoing questions is *yes,* can the scheme be suitably revised? (Presumably not if the answer to the first one is *yes*.)

Finally, the following list of major section headings gives some idea of the scope of the chapter:

- Some relational terminology
- What's a multirelation?

---

[3] Many have raised performance objections also; however, these latter objections invariably assume the approach to implementation found in current SQL DBMSs, which tends to punish decomposition instead of encouraging it.

- Selector operators
- Comparison operators
- Algebraic operators
- Multirelation variables
- Constraints
- Normal forms
- Update operators
- Virtual relvars and multirelvars
- Interpretation
- Potential applications
- Some outstanding questions

SOME RELATIONAL TERMINOLOGY

In this section I define for reference purposes some terms from relational theory that I'll be relying on heavily in the pages to come. The definitions are based for the most part on ones to be found in reference [5].

- **Definition (common attribute):** An attribute that's common to two or more tuples or relations. To be specific, attribute <*A,T*> is (a) a common attribute of relations *r1, r2, ..., rn* ($n > 1$) if and only if each of *r1, r2, ..., rn* has an attribute named *A* of type *T,* and (b) a common attribute of tuples *t1, t2, ..., tn* ($n > 1$) if and only if each of *t1, t2, ..., tn* has an attribute named *A* of type *T.*

- **Definition (joinable):** Relations *r1, r2, ..., rn* ($n \geqslant 0$) are joinable if and only if the set theory union of the headings of those relations is a heading. Tuples *t1, t2, ..., tn* ($n \geqslant 0$) are joinable if and only if the set theory union of those tuples is a tuple. *Note:* The term *joinable* might better be *mutually joinable,* since as we've just seen it's always defined with respect to a given context (viz., a given set of relations or a given set of tuples), and I'll use this latter term occasionally in what follows. Note too that it follows from the definitions that attributes of the relations or tuples in question that have the same name (a) must be of the same type—i.e., must be common attributes—and (b) in the tuple case, must have the same value.

- **Definition (join):** 1. *(Dyadic case)* Let relations *r1* and *r2* be joinable. Then the join of *r1* and *r2, r1* JOIN *r2,* is a relation with heading the set theory union of the headings of *r1* and *r2* and with body the set of all tuples *t* such that *t* is the set theory union of a tuple from *r1* and a tuple from *r2*. 2. *(N-adic case)* Let relations *r1, r2, ..., rn* ($n \geqslant 0$) be joinable. Then the join JOIN {*r1,r2,...,rn*} is defined as follows: If $n = 0$, the result is TABLE_DEE; if $n = 1$, the result is *r1;* otherwise, choose any two distinct relations from the set *r1, r2, ..., rn* and replace them by their dyadic join, and repeat this process until the set consists of just one relation *r,* which is the overall result.

- **Definition (union):** 1. *(Dyadic case)* The union of two relations *r1* and *r2, r1* UNION *r2,* where *r1* and *r2* are of the same type *T,* is a relation of type *T* with body the set of all tuples *t* such that *t* appears in either or both of *r1* and *r2*. 2. *(N-adic case)* The union of *n* relations *r1, r2, ..., rn* ($n \geqslant 0$), UNION {*r1,r2,...,rn*}, where *r1, r2, ..., rn* are all of the same type *T,* is a relation of type *T* with body the set of all tuples *t* such that *t* appears in at least one of *r1, r2, ..., rn*. *Note:* If $n = 0$, (a) some syntactic mechanism, not shown here, is needed to specify the pertinent type *T* and (b) the result is the empty relation of that type.

- **Definition (tuple join):** 1. *(Dyadic case)* Let tuples *t1* and *t2* be joinable. Then the tuple join of *t1* and *t2, t1* UNION *t2,* is the set theory union of *t1* and *t2*. 2. *(N-adic case)* Let tuples *t1, t2, ..., tn* ($n \geqslant 0$) be joinable. Then the tuple join UNION {*t1,t2,...,tn*} is defined as follows: If $n = 0$, the result is the empty tuple; if $n = 1$, the result is *t1;* otherwise, choose any two distinct tuples from the set *t1, t2, ..., tn* and replace them by their dyadic tuple join, and repeat this process until the set consists of just one tuple *t,* which is the overall result. *Note:* Use of the keyword UNION rather than JOIN in the foregoing definition is not a mistake—tuple join could equally well be called tuple union; in fact, for reasons that aren't important here, **Tutorial D** in particular does use the keyword UNION rather than JOIN to denote the tuple join operation.

- **Definition (subtuple):** Tuple *t1* is a subtuple of tuple *t2* if and only if *t1* is a subset of *t2*. *Note:* Since every set is a subset of itself, every tuple is a subtuple of itself.

- **Definition (supertuple):** Tuple *t2* is a supertuple of tuple *t1* if and only if *t2* is a superset of *t1*. *Note:* Since every set is a superset of itself, every tuple is a supertuple of itself.

WHAT'S A MULTIRELATION?

Now I need to pin down precisely what a multirelation is. First of all, observe that I talked earlier in terms of multirelations *including* relations (as subsets), not *containing* them (as elements)—though in fact I think it would be possible to come down on either side of this debate, if debate it is.[4] Indeed, when I get to the multirelational operators later in this chapter, I sometimes give two distinct but equivalent definitions, one based on the inclusion perception and one on the containment perception. A trifle arbitrarily, however, I do tend to favor, if only for definiteness, the inclusion perception, where relations are subsets of the pertinent multirelation instead of being elements of it. *Note:* I'm speaking a little loosely here. It would be more correct to say those included relations have headings that are subsets of the "heading" of the multirelation and bodies that are subsets of the "body" of the multirelation—where "heading" and "body" are in quotes because, as we'll see in a few moments, those relational terms as such don't really apply to multirelations.

Given some multirelation, the included relations are the *participants* in that multirelation. Fig. 2 overleaf shows the same multirelations as Fig. 1, but with the rows in the tables rearranged slightly and with separator lines to show the participants more clearly (and I'll use this style throughout the remainder of this chapter to depict multirelations as opposed to relations). As the figure indicates, the body of a participant with heading *H* consists of those tuples in the pertinent multirelation that have heading *H*.[5] Note, therefore, that (a) no proper subset of a participant body is itself a participant body, and (b) every tuple of a multirelation is contained in exactly one participant body.

Here now are precise definitions:

1. Let *mr* be a multirelation; then *mr* has an *MR-heading* and an *MR-body*.[6] The MR-heading of *mr* (referred to below as *MRH*) is identical in appearance to a relational heading but doesn't mean quite the same thing as such a heading; hence my use of a different term. Similarly, the MR-body of *mr* (referred to below as *MRB*) looks a bit like a relational body—certainly it's a set of tuples—but it differs from such a body in that those tuples don't all have to have the same heading, and so again I use a different term.

---

[4] An analogy that comes to mind is the well known duality principle in quantum theory, according to which the very same phenomenon is interpreted sometimes in terms of particles, sometimes in terms of waves.

[5] Elsewhere—in reference [6] in particular—headings are denoted {*H*} instead of *H*. The simpler notation is more convenient for present purposes, however. An analogous remark applies to bodies also.

[6] I use the prefix "MR" ubiquitously in what follows. It can be pronounced either "emm are" or "mister" according to taste (and perhaps context).

S

S#	SNAME	STATUS	CITY
S1	Smith	20	London
S2	Jones	10	Paris
S5	Adams	30	Athens
....	....	....	....
S3	Blake	30	
....	....	....	....
S4	Clark		London
....	....	....	....
S6			Rome
....	....	....	....
S7			

SP

SP	S#	P#	QTY
	S1	P1	300
	S1	P2	200
	S3	P2	200
	....	....	.....
	S2	P1	
	S4	P4	

Fig. 2: The suppliers and shipments multirelations and their nonempty participants

2. The *degree* of *mr* is the number of attributes in *MRH;* the *cardinality* of *mr* is the number of tuples in *MRB;* and the *type* of *mr* is MULTIRELATION *MRH.* For example, the multirelation S depicted in Figs. 1 and 2 has degree 4 and cardinality 7 and—following the syntactic style of **Tutorial D**—is (let's agree) of the following type:

```
MULTIRELATION { S# S# , SNAME NAME , STATUS INTEGER , CITY CHAR }
```

3. The heading of each tuple in *MRB* is a subset of *MRH.*

4. Relation *p* is a *participant* in *mr* if and only if (a) the heading *PH* of *p* is a subset of *MRH* and (b) the body *PB* of *p* consists of just those tuples of *MRB* that have heading *PH.* It follows that if the degree of *mr* is *n,* then the number of participants in *mr* is 2^n (some of which will be empty, in general; for example, multirelation S from Figs. 1 and 2 has 11 empty participants as well as five nonempty ones). In particular, if the degree of *mr* is 0, then *mr* has exactly one participant (because $2^0 = 1$), and that participant is either TABLE_DEE or TABLE_DUM.[7] Also, since each tuple in *MRB* appears in exactly one participant, the bodies of the nonempty participants form a *partitioning* of *MRB.*

5. Multirelation *mr* is *empty* if and only if *MRB* is empty—equivalently, if and only if every participant in *mr* is empty. Note that emptiness here refers to a lack of tuples, not participants, because (to repeat) a multirelation of degree *n* always has 2^n participants, even if some or all of those participants are themselves empty.

6. If at most one participant in *mr* is nonempty, then the tuples in *MRB* all have the same heading (namely, some specific subset of *MRH*), in which case *MRB* is in fact the body of a relation with heading that subset, and it's tempting to say that *mr is* a relation, to all intents and purposes. Of course, that temptation should be resisted; after all, there's certainly a logical difference between the two concepts. But such

[7] In fact, every multirelation has either TABLE_DEE or TABLE_DUM (and not both) as a participant. For example, the multirelation S depicted in Figs. 1 and 2 has TABLE_DUM as one of its 11 empty participants. If it had TABLE_DEE as a participant instead (a nonempty one, of course), then the tabular representation of that multirelation would have a row of all gaps—i.e., a row with vacant spaces in every attribute position.

multirelations might well have a special role to play if we were to try to define a mapping between relational theory and the theory whose development I sketch in the remainder of this chapter. I therefore define an operator HAMONEP ("has at most one nonempty participant"), as follows: HAMONEP(*mr*) returns TRUE if at most one participant in *mr* is nonempty and FALSE otherwise.

7. When HAMONEP(*mr*) is TRUE, one of the participants in *mr* is called the *prime participant.* That participant is the sole nonempty participant if such exists, otherwise it's the (empty) participant whose heading is *MRH.* For example, if multirelation S contained just the tuple shown for supplier S4 in Figs. 1 and 2, then HAMONEP(S) would be TRUE, and the prime participant in S would be the relation containing just that tuple. As it is, however (i.e., given multirelation S as actually depicted in those figures), HAMONEP(S) is FALSE, and there is no prime participant.

8. I define RELATION(*mr*) to return the prime participant in *mr* if HAMONEP(*mr*) is TRUE and to be undefined otherwise.[8] I also define MULTIRELATION(*r*), where *r* is a relation, to return the multirelation whose MR-heading is the heading of *r* and whose MR-body is the body of *r.* Note that HAMONEP(MULTIRELATION(*r*)) is necessarily TRUE, and *r* itself is the prime participant in MULTIRELATION(*r*) (even if *r* is empty). But note too that it's not the case that MULTIRELATION(RELATION(*mr*)), even if it's defined, is necessarily equal to *mr,* because the heading of the prime participant of *mr* might be a proper subset of the MR-heading of *mr*. By contrast, it is necessarily the case that RELATION(MULTIRELATION(*r*)) is equal to *r,* thanks in part to the definition of "prime participant" in the case where *mr* is empty.

9. It follows from the definitions of *MRH* and *MRB* that if relations *r1* and *r2* are participants in *mr,* then *r1* and *r2* are joinable. Because of this fact, we can use multirelation attribute names in ways very similar to those in which we use relational attribute names in the relational context, as we'll soon see. In particular, we can extend the definition of the term *common attribute* in the obvious way to apply to multirelations as well as relations and tuples.

SELECTOR OPERATORS

The Third Manifesto [6] requires every value to be denotable by some literal, where a literal of type *T* is an invocation of some *selector* operator for type *T* in which each argument to the invocation is itself denoted by a literal in turn. Clearly, just as the relation selector invocation denoting relation *r* needs to specify—either explicitly or implicitly—both the heading and the body of *r,* so the multirelation selector invocation denoting multirelation *mr* needs to specify both the MR-heading and the MR-body of *mr*. So again we can follow the style of **Tutorial D:**

```
MULTIRELATION [ <MR-heading> ] { <tuple exp commalist> }
```

For example:

```
MULTIRELATION { S# S# , SNAME NAME , STATUS INTEGER , CITY CHAR }
  { TUPLE { S# S#('S3') , SNAME NAME('Blake') , STATUS 30 } ,
  { TUPLE { S# S#('S4') , SNAME NAME('Clark') , CITY 'London' } }
```

---

[8] RELATION(*mr*) is used in this chapter for expository purposes only. It couldn't be part of a language like **Tutorial D** that supports static type checking, because—assuming *mr* to be specifiable in such a language by means of an arbitrary multirelation expression—the heading of the prime participant wouldn't be known at compile time (in general). If the user knows that heading, however, then he or she can achieve the effect of RELATION(*mr*) by means of the operator PARTICIPANT FROM (see the section "Algebraic Operators," later).

Note in this example that (a) an explicit MR-heading has been specified, and (b) the specified MR-body contains two tuples with different headings. If no explicit MR-heading is specified, a default MR-heading equal to the set theory union of the headings of the specified tuples is specified implicitly.[9] (By definition, those tuples must be such that the default MR-heading is well defined; that is, they must be such that attributes with the same name are of the same type.) In the foregoing example, therefore, the explicit MR-heading could have been omitted, thus:

```
MULTIRELATION
  { TUPLE { S# S#('S3') , SNAME NAME('Blake') , STATUS 30 } ,
  { TUPLE { S# S#('S4') , SNAME NAME('Clark') , CITY 'London' } }
```

In general, any superset of the default MR-heading would be valid as an explicit MR-heading in a multirelation selector invocation. More generally, in fact, we can observe the following:

> If *MRB* is the MR-body of a multirelation with MR-heading *MRH,* then for every MR-heading MRH^{+} that is a superset of *MRH* there is a multirelation with MR-heading MRH^{+} and MR-body *MRB*. Moreover, if *A* is an attribute of *MRH* but not of the heading of any tuple in *MRB,* then *MRB* is the MR-body of some multirelation with heading MRH^{-}, where MRH^{-} is the set theory difference between *MRH* and {*A*} (in that order).

It follows from these observations that (to spell the point out) distinct nonempty multirelations can have the same MR-body. For example, the MR-body of multirelation S as shown in Figs. 1 and 2 is also a possible MR-body for every multirelation whose MR-heading is a proper superset of the MR-heading of that multirelation S. This state of affairs contrasts sharply with that found in connection with relations, where two nonempty relations can (and do) have the same body only if they're in fact the very same relation.[10] *Note:* You might find this last claim surprising, especially if you're used to SQL; you might be thinking that surely two SQL tables can have the same set of rows and yet be distinct. Well, yes, indeed they can—but that's just another reason why SQL tables aren't relations. To be specific, rows in SQL tables, unlike tuples in relations, don't carry their heading around with them. (In fact, it would be more correct to say that rows in SQL tables, unlike tuples in relations, don't really *have* a heading.) As a consequence, and just by way of illustration, if SQL tables T1 and T2 both have just one column—of type INTEGER, say—but that column is called C1 in T1 but C2 in T2, then their bodies could indeed be equal in SQL, but the bodies of their relational analogs wouldn't be.

Consider now the empty MR-heading {}. There are just two multirelations with that MR-heading (i.e., just two multirelations of type MULTIRELATION {}): one whose MR-body contains exactly one tuple (necessarily the empty tuple), and one whose MR-body contains no tuples at all. I call them MR_DEE and MR_DUM, respectively. In other words, MR_DEE is MULTIRELATION{}{TUPLE {}} and MR_DUM is MULTIRELATION{}{}.

It should be clear that MR_DEE and MR_DUM are multirelational counterparts of TABLE_DEE and TABLE_DUM, respectively. In fact:

- TABLE_DEE is the sole participant, and thus the prime participant, in MR_DEE; so HAMONEP(MR_DEE) is TRUE, and RELATION(MR_DEE) is TABLE_DEE.

---

[9] Except in the case where the specified MR-body is empty, when the desired MR-heading must be specified explicitly.

[10] To state the matter precisely: Let the MR-heading *MRH1* of multirelation *mr1* be a proper subset of the MR-heading *MRH2* of multirelation *mr2*, but let the corresponding MR-bodies *MRB1* and *MRB2* be the same. Then (a) for all tuples *t*, *t* appears in *MRB1* if and only if it appears in *MRB2*; (b) for all relations *r1*, if *r1* is a participant in *mr1*, then *r1* is a participant in *mr2*; but (c) there exist relations *r2* such that *r2* is a participant in *mr2* and not a participant in *mr1* (though all such relations *r2* are empty).

- Likewise, TABLE_DUM is the sole participant, and thus the prime participant, in MR_DUM; so HAMONEP(MR_DUM) is also TRUE, and RELATION(MR_DUM) is TABLE_DUM.

COMPARISON OPERATORS

Let *mr, mr1,* and *mr2* be multirelations with MR-headings *MRH, MRH1,* and *MRH2,* respectively, and MR-bodies *MRB, MRB1,* and *MRB2,* respectively. If every participant in *mr1* is such that its body is a subset of the body of some participant in *mr2,* then *MRB1* is a subset of *MRB2*. Clearly, then, just as in **Tutorial D** we can write "*r1* ⊆ *r2*" (loosely, "*r1* is a subset of *r2*" or "*r1* is included in *r2*"), where *r1* and *r2* are relations, we can also write "*mr1* ⊆ *mr2*" (loosely, "*mr1* is a subset of *mr2*" or "*mr1* is included in *mr2*").

Now, in the relational case, *r1* and *r2* are required to be relations of the same type, but there's no need to impose an analogous rule in the multirelational case (in fact, it would be counterproductive to do so). We might perhaps require *MRH1* and *MRH2* not to be disjoint, but the advantages of doing so seem too slight to warrant such a rule. (If they *are* disjoint, then *mr1* ⊆ *mr2* will be TRUE if and only if *mr1* is empty.)

In the relational case, again, it's easy to see that the comparison operator "⊆" is logically sufficient.[11] But it isn't sufficient for all of the comparisons we might imagine for multirelations. For example, additional operators would be required to support tests such as the following, if there's any need for them:

- Is every tuple in *MRB1* a subtuple of some tuple in *MRB2?*
- Is every tuple of *MRB1* a supertuple of some tuple in *MRB2?*
- Is no tuple of *MRB1* a subtuple of some tuple in *MRB2?*
- Is no tuple of *MRB1* a supertuple of some tuple in *MRB2?*

Seeing no compelling need for such tests, I offer no suggestions for supporting them at this time.

ALGEBRAIC OPERATORS

In this rather lengthy section I define a number of read-only—in fact, algebraic—operators on multirelations, with an eye to what might be needed for practical purposes in a language like **Tutorial D**. However, I do not attempt, here, to develop a formal specification for an algebra of multirelations. Where applicable I do note some interesting algebraic properties, such as commutativity, associativity, and the like, but I make no attempt to identify a minimal or otherwise agreeable set of primitive operators.

Some of the operators have obvious relational counterparts. Where a relational counterpart exists, a concrete syntax might well use the same name for both the relational operator and its multirelational counterpart. I choose not to indulge in such operator name overloading here, however, because I think distinct names are preferable for expository purposes.

Notation: I assume again throughout this section (and I'll continue to make this assumption throughout the rest of the chapter, where appropriate) that *mr, mr1,* and *mr2* are multirelations with MR-headings *MRH, MRH1,* and *MRH2,* respectively, and MR-bodies *MRB, MRB1,* and *MRB2,* respectively. Also, for the sake of examples I take the names S and SP to refer not (as previously) to multirelations but, rather, to *multirelation variables* or multirelvars;[12] thus, for example, the expression "S" is now a *multirelvar reference,* and it denotes the

---

[11] Though for ergonomic reasons **Tutorial D** does also support the operators "⊂" ("is properly included in"), "⊇" ("includes"), "⊃" ("properly includes"), "=" ("equals"), and "≠" ("not equals"). Clearly, we would expect to see multirelation analogs of all of these operators to be supported as well, if multirelations are supported.

[12] Multirelvars are discussed in more detail in a series of sections toward the end of the chapter.

multirelation that's the current value of the multirelvar with that name. As stated earlier (in the section "What's a Multirelation?"), the type of multirelvar S is:

```
MULTIRELATION { S# S# , SNAME NAME , STATUS INTEGER , CITY CHAR }
```

And the type of multirelvar SP is:

```
MULTIRELATION { S# S# , P# P# , QTY QTY }
```

I'll also assume when I show sample results that the current values of these multirelvars are as shown in Figs. 1 and 2 (barring explicit statements to the contrary, of course).

Now I begin my discussion of the operators. The ones described in the two subsections immediately following ("Participant Extraction" and "Multiprojection") each yield a relation as their output; all of the rest yield a multirelation.

Participant Extraction

The PARTICIPANT FROM operator extracts a given participant (specified by means of its heading) from a given multirelation. For example:

```
PARTICIPANT { S# , P# } FROM SP
```

Result (a relation):

S#	P#
S2	P1
S4	P4

- **Definition (participant extraction):** Let *r* = PARTICIPANT {*A1,A2,...,An*} FROM *mr*. Then the heading *RH* of *r* is the subset of *MRH* specified by *A1, A2, ..., An,* and the body *RB* of *r* consists of just those tuples of *MRB* that have heading *RH*. Equivalently, *r* is that participant in *mr* whose heading is the subset of *MRH* specified by *A1, A2, ..., An.*

Note: In **Tutorial D,** wherever a commalist of attribute names can appear, denoting attributes of some relation *r,* that commalist can be preceded by ALL BUT to denote the attributes of *r* other than those mentioned. The same rule can obviously be used here, thereby allowing the example above to be expressed thus:

```
PARTICIPANT { ALL BUT QTY } FROM SP
```

Similar remarks apply, where appropriate, to all of the operators discussed in this chapter.

As noted earlier, if HAMONEP(*mr*) is TRUE and the heading of the prime participant is known, then PARTICIPANT FROM can be used to extract the prime participant from *mr*.

Multiprojection

Multiprojection is just a generalization of relational projection, but for clarity I won't use the relational projection syntax of **Tutorial D;** instead, I'll use a keyword, ONTO (since we often speak of projecting *onto* a given set of attributes). In essence, multiprojection works by first picking out just those tuples that have a specified set of attributes (as well as others, possibly), and then projecting those tuples onto those attributes.[13] For example:

```
S ONTO { S# , SNAME , CITY }
```

Or equivalently:

```
S ONTO { ALL BUT STATUS }
```

Result (a relation):

S#	SNAME	CITY
S1	Smith	London
S2	Jones	Paris
S5	Adams	Athens
S4	Clark	London

- **Definition (multiprojection):** Let *r* = *mr* ONTO {*A1,A2,...,An*}. Then the heading *RH* of *r* is the subset of *MRH* specified by *A1, A2, ..., An,* and the body *RB* of *r* is such that tuple *t* appears in *RB* if and only if *t* has heading *RH* and is a subtuple of some tuple in *MRB*. Equivalently, *RB* is the union of the bodies of the projections onto {*A1,A2,...,An*} of just those participants in *mr* that have heading some superset of *RH*.

Note that if HAMONEP(*mr*) is TRUE, then *mr* ONTO {*A1,A2,...,An*} = (RELATION(*mr*)) {*A1,A2,...,An*} if each of *A1, A2, ..., An* is an attribute of RELATION(*mr*), or an empty relation otherwise.

Now I turn to operators that return multirelations. Most of the operators I describe are multirelational counterparts of some familiar relational operator. I have little to say regarding their possible usefulness; I choose them rather for their teachability, on the grounds that—if multirelations turn out to be useful at all—the operators in question are likely to be as useful in the context of multirelations as their relational counterparts are in the context of relations.

MR-projection

MR-projection (MR_ONTO) applied to multirelation *mr* yields a multirelation *ms* formed by discarding all attributes not specified for retention. For example:

```
S MR_ONTO { STATUS , CITY }
```

Or equivalently:

```
S MR_ONTO { ALL BUT S# , SNAME }
```

Result (a multirelation):

[13] I follow *The Third Manifesto* here [5] here in taking projection to be an operator that can be applied to individual tuples as well as to relations.

STATUS	CITY
20	London
10	Paris
30	Athens
....	....
30	
....	....
	London
	Rome
....	....

By definition, this result has four participants ($4 = 2^2$), all of which happen to be nonempty (though one of them is TABLE_DEE and contains nothing but the empty tuple). It also happens to have the same cardinality as its input, but that's because no two tuples in that input have (a) the same combination of values for attributes STATUS and CITY, or (b) the same value for STATUS and no CITY attribute, or (c) the same value for CITY and no STATUS attribute.

Note: It's perhaps a trifle unfortunate that the operators ONTO and MR_ONTO have such similar names (multiprojection and MR-projection, respectively); it might be desirable to find a better name for at least one of them. At any rate, it's important to be clear over the logical differences between the two:

- First, ONTO ignores tuples that lack one or more of the specified attributes; MR_ONTO doesn't.
- Second, ONTO returns a relation; MR_ONTO returns a multirelation.

Here to illustrate these differences is the result (a relation) returned if we replace MR_ONTO by ONTO in the foregoing example—i.e., the result returned by S ONTO {STATUS, CITY}:

STATUS	CITY
20	London
10	Paris
30	Athens

- **Definition (MR-projection):** Let *ms* = *mr* MR_ONTO {*A1*,*A2*,...,*An*}. Then the MR-heading *MSH* of *ms* is the subset of *MRH* specified by *A1, A2, ..., An,* and the MR-body *MSB* of *ms* is such that tuple *t* appears in *MSB* if and only if *t* has heading some subset of *MSH* and is a subtuple of some tuple in *MRB*.

Note that if HAMONEP(*mr*) is TRUE, then HAMONEP(*ms*) is also TRUE, and RELATION(*ms*) is then some relational projection of RELATION(*mr*). Note too that TABLE_DEE is a participant in *ms* whenever the heading of some nonempty participant in *mr* contains none of the attributes *A1, A2, ..., An*. (This latter point was illustrated in the case of S MR_ONTO {STATUS,CITY}, because the input multirelation included a nonempty participant—namely, that whose MR-body contained just the tuple for supplier S7—whose heading contained neither of the attributes STATUS and CITY.)

MR-join

MR-join is the multirelational counterpart of relational join; it joins every participant in one operand to every participant in the other, and then returns the set theory union of those joins. For example:

```
S MR_JOIN SP
```

Result (a multirelation):

S#	SNAME	STATUS	CITY	P#	QTY
S1	Smith	20	London	P1	300
S1	Smith	20	London	P2	200
....	....	....	....	....	.....
S2	Jones	10	Paris	P1	
....	....	....	....	....	.....
S3	Blake	30		P2	200
....	....	....	....	....	.....
S4	Clark		London	P4	

By the way, you might be thinking that joining every participant to every participant, as MR-join does, has the potential to produce a very large result—a kind of cartesian product of participants, as it were. As the example illustrates, however, it's likely in practice that the majority of those individual joins will yield empty results.

Here now is the definition:

- **Definition (MR-join):** Let *ms* = *mr1* MR_JOIN *mr2*. The MR-headings *MRH1* and *MRH2* must be such that their set theory union is an MR-heading; equivalently, each participant in *mr1* must be joinable with each participant in *mr2*. Then *ms* is the multirelation whose MR-heading *MSH* is the set theory union of *MRH1* and *MRH2* and whose MR-body *MSB* is the set of all tuples *t* such that *t* is the set theory union of a tuple of *MRB1* and a tuple of *MRB2*.

It follows from this definition that (as previously indicated) *p1* JOIN *p2* is a participant in *ms* if and only if *p1* is a participant in *mr1* and *p2* is a participant in *mr2*.

Now, it so happens in the example above that every tuple in the operand multirelations has a value for the sole common attribute (S#, in that example). Here by contrast is an example in which such is not the case:

```
( SP MR_ONTO { S# , QTY } )
  MR_JOIN
( SP MR_ONTO { P# , QTY } )
```

Result (a multirelation):

S#	P#	QTY
S1	P1	300
S1	P2	200
S2	P1	300
S2	P2	200
S3	P2	200
S4	P1	300
S4	P2	200
....	....	.....
S2	P1	
S2	P4	
S4	P1	
S4	P4	

Note that if HAMONEP(*mr1*) and HAMONEP(*mr2*) are both TRUE, then HAMONEP(*ms*) is also TRUE. And if *mr1* and *mr2* have prime participants *p1* and *p2,* respectively, then RELATION(*ms*) = *p1* JOIN *p2.*

Like relational join, MR-join is both commutative and associative. It also has an identity value: viz., MR_DEE. As a consequence, an *n*-adic version of the operator, MR_JOIN {*mr1,mr2,...,mrn*}, can also be defined, thus: If *n* = 0, the result is MR_DEE; if *n* = 1, the result is *mr1;* otherwise, choose any two distinct multirelations from the set *mr1, mr2, ..., mrn* and replace them by their dyadic MR-join, and repeat this process until the set consists of just one multirelation *ms,* which is the overall result.

Unlike relational join, however, MR-join is not idempotent, even though S MR_JOIN S does happen to return its input given the sample values from Figs. 1 and 2. By way of a counterexample, let *mr* be the following multirelation:

```
MULTIRELATION { X INTEGER , Y INTEGER } { TUPLE { X 1 } ,
                                          TUPLE { Y 1 } }
```

Then the MR-body of *mr* MR_JOIN *mr* contains the tuple

```
TUPLE { X 1 , Y 1 }
```

in addition to the two tuples in the MR-body of *mr.*

Note: I considered defining a second kind of multirelation join in which only those participants that actually had values for the common attributes participated (if you see what I mean). But this operation can easily be expressed using MR_WHERE—see later—and MR_JOIN. The following example, a revised version of one of those given above, illustrates the point (the semantics of the "PRESENT{QTY}" construct are explained in the subsection "MR-restriction" but are in any case intuitively obvious):

```
( ( SP MR_ONTO { S# , QTY } ) MR_WHERE PRESENT { QTY } )
  MR_JOIN
( ( SP MR_ONTO { P# , QTY } ) MR_WHERE PRESENT { QTY } )
```

Result (a multirelation):

S#	P#	QTY
S1	P1	300
S1	P2	200
S3	P2	200

(No separator lines are shown because HAMONEP happens to be TRUE for this result.)

MR-union

Relational union requires its operands to be of the same type, but there's no need to impose such a rule on its multirelational counterpart MR_UNION; again, in fact, it would be counterproductive to do so. In other words, MR_UNION is very close to the conventional unfettered union of set theory. (An analogous remark applies to MR_INTERSECT and MR_MINUS also, q.v.) For example:

```
S MR_UNION SP
```

Result (a multirelation):

S#	SNAME	STATUS	CITY	P#	QTY
S1	Smith	20	London		
S2	Jones	10	Paris		
S5	Adams	30	Athens		
....	....	....	....	....	.....
S3	Blake	30			
....	....	....	....	....	.....
S4	Clark		London		
....	....	....	....	....	.....
S6			Rome		
....	....	....	....	....	.....
S7					
....	....	....	....	....	.....
S1				P1	300
S1				P2	200
S3				P2	200
....	....	....	....	....	.....
S2				P1	
S4				P4	

- **Definition (MR-union):** Let *ms* = *mr1* MR_UNION *mr2*. The MR-headings *MRH1* and *MRH2* must be such that their set theory union is an MR-heading. Then *ms* is the multirelation whose MR-heading *MSH* is the set theory union of *MRH1* and *MRH2* and whose MR-body *MSB* is the set theory union of *MRB1* and *MRB2*—i.e., *MSB* is the set of all tuples *t* such that *t* appears in *MRB1* or *MRB2* or both.

It follows from this definition that *p1* UNION *p2* is a participant in *ms* if (but not only if) *p1* is a participant in *mr1*, *p2* is a participant in *mr2*, and *p1* and *p2* are of the same (relation) type. Also, if *p3* is a participant in *mr1* such that no participant in *mr2* is of the same type as *p3,* then *p3* is a participant in *ms;* likewise, if *p4* is a participant in *mr2* such that no participant in *mr1* is of the same type as *p4,* then *p4* is a participant in *ms*. In fact, each participant in *ms* is at least one, and possibly more than one, of the following: a participant in *mr1,* a participant in *mr2,* or the relational union *p1* UNION *p2* of a participant *p1* in *mr1* and a participant *p2* in *mr2*.

Note that if HAMONEP(*mr1*) and HAMONEP(*mr2*) are both TRUE and have prime participants *p1* and *p2,* respectively, then HAMONEP(*ms*) is also TRUE and RELATION(*ms*) = *p1* UNION *p2*.

Like relational union, MR-union is both commutative and associative; it is also, unlike MR-join, idempotent. Also, unlike relational union, it has an identity value: viz., MR_DUM. As with MR-join, therefore, an *n*-adic version of the operator, MR_UNION {*mr1,mr2,...,mrn*}, can be defined, as follows: If *n* = 0, the result is MR_DUM; if *n* = 1, the result is *mr1;* otherwise, choose any two distinct multirelations from the set *mr1, mr2, ..., mrn* and replace them by their dyadic MR-union, and repeat this process until the set consists of just one multirelation *ms,* which is the overall result.[14]

MR-intersection

Relational intersection requires its operands to be of the same type, but MR-intersection does not. For example:

```
S MR_INTERSECT SP
```

Result (a multirelation):

As you can see, this result is empty. But if multirelation SP were to include (say) an additional tuple with S# value S7 and no other attributes, then that tuple would be common to the two multirelation operands and would therefore appear in the result.

- **Definition (MR-intersection):** Let *ms* = *mr1* MR_INTERSECT *mr2*. The MR-headings *MRH1* and *MRH2* must be such that their set theory union is an MR-heading. Then *ms* is the multirelation whose MR-heading *MSH* is the set theory intersection of *MRH1* and *MRH2* and whose MR-body *MSB* is the set theory intersection of *MRB1* and *MRB2*—i.e., *MRB* is the set of all tuples *t* such that *t* appears in both *MRB1* and *MRB2*.

It follows from this definition that *p1* INTERSECT *p2* is a participant in *ms* if and only if *p1* is a participant in *mr1, p2* is a participant in *mr2,* and *p1* and *p2* are of the same (relation) type.

Note that if HAMONEP(*mr1*) and HAMONEP(*mr2*) are both TRUE, then HAMONEP(*ms*) is also TRUE. In fact, HAMONEP(*ms*) is TRUE in several other circumstances as well—e.g., when either *MRB1* and *MRB2* is empty, or more generally when *MRB1* and *MRB2* are disjoint (which they certainly are if one is empty).

Like relational intersection, MR-intersection is commutative, associative, and idempotent; however, whereas relational intersection is a special case of relational join, MR-intersection is not a special case of MR-join. As with MR-join, an *n*-adic version of the operator, MR_INTERSECT {*mr1,mr2,...,mrn*}, can be

---

[14] Of course, we can and do define an *n*-adic version of relational union, too. What we mean when we say relational union has no identity value is this: UNION (unlike MR_UNION) requires its operand relations all to be of the same type; as a consequence, there's no "universal" identity value for relational union in general. But there *is* an identity value for any given relation type—namely, the empty relation of that type.

defined, as follows: If $n = 1$, the result is *mr1;* if $n > 1$, choose any two distinct multirelations from the set *mr1, mr2, ..., mrn* and replace them by their dyadic MR-intersection, and repeat this process until the set consists of just one multirelation *ms,* which is the overall result. Note, however, that the case $n = 0$ is not allowed.[15]

MR-difference

Relational difference requires its operands to be of the same type, but MR-difference does not. For example:

```
S MR_MINUS SP
```

Result (a multirelation):

S#	SNAME	STATUS	CITY
S1	Smith	20	London
S2	Jones	10	Paris
S5	Adams	30	Athens
S3	Blake	30	
S4	Clark		London
S6			Rome
S7			

As you can see, this result is identically equal to the current value of multirelvar S. But if the current value of multirelvar SP were to include (say) an additional tuple with S# value S7 and no other attributes, then that tuple would be common to the two multirelation operands and would therefore not appear in the result.

- **Definition (MR-difference):** Let *ms* = *mr1* MR_MINUS *mr2*. The MR-headings *MRH1* and *MRH2* must be such that their set theory union is an MR-heading. Then *ms* is the multirelation whose MR-heading *MSH* is *MRH1* and whose MR-body *MSB* is the set theory difference between *MRB1* and *MRB2* (in that order)—i.e., *MSB* is the set of all tuples *t* such that *t* appears in *MRB1* and not in *MRB2*.

It follows from this definition that *p1* MINUS *p2* is a participant in *ms* if (but not only if) *p1* is a participant in *mr1, p2* is a participant in *mr2,* and *p1* and *p2* are of the same (relation) type. Also, if *p3* is a participant in *mr1* such that no participant in *mr2* is of the same type as *p3,* then *p3* is a participant in *ms*. In fact, each participant in *ms* is either or both of the following: a participant in *mr1,* or the relational difference *p1* MINUS *p2* between a participant *p1* in *mr1* and a participant *p2* in *mr2* (in that order).

Note that if HAMONEP(*mr1*) is TRUE, then HAMONEP(*ms*) is also TRUE. And if *mr1* has prime participant *p1,* then (a) if *mr2* has a participant *p2* of the same type as *p1,* then RELATION(*ms*) = *p1* MINUS *p2;* (b) otherwise, RELATION(*ms*) = *p1*.

Finally, if *mr1* and *mr2* are multirelations of the same type, then *mr1* MR_MINUS (*mr1* MR_MINUS

---

[15] Alternatively, we might introduce some syntactic mechanism in this case to specify the type of the result, in which case that result would be the universal multirelation of that type—i.e., the multirelation whose MR-body contains all possible tuples with MR-heading some subset of the MR-heading for that multirelation type. Even if we did, however, the implementation might very well want to outlaw (or at least flag) any expression requiring such a multirelation to be materialized.

mr2) is identically equal to *mr1* MR_INTERSECT *mr2*. However, it's easy to see that the same is not true, in general, if *mr1* and *mr2* are of different types.

MR-semijoin

Semijoin (MATCHING, in **Tutorial D**) takes two relational operands and returns those tuples from the first operand that are joinable with at least one tuple in the second, and the multirelational analog does essentially the same thing for multirelations. For example:

```
S MR_MATCHING SP
```

Result (a multirelation):

S#	SNAME	STATUS	CITY
S1	Smith	20	London
S2	Jones	10	Paris
....	....	....	....
S3	Blake	30	
....	....	....	....
S4	Clark		London

- **Definition (MR-semijoin):** Let *ms* = *mr1* MR_MATCHING *mr2*. The MR-headings *MRH1* and *MRH2* must be such that their set theory union is an MR-heading. Then *ms* is the multirelation whose MR-heading *MSH* is *MRH1* and whose MR-body *MSB* is the set of all tuples *t* such that *t* appears in *MRB1* and there exists a tuple in *MRB2* that is joinable with *t*.

It follows from this definition *mr1* MR_MATCHING *mr2* is identically equal to (*mr1* MR_JOIN *mr2*) MR_ONTO {*A1,A2,...,An*}, where *A1, A2, ..., An* are all of the attributes in *MRH1*.

Note that if HAMONEP(*mr1*) is TRUE, then HAMONEP(*ms*) is also TRUE. And if *mr1* has prime participant *p* and *mr2* has participants *p1, p2, ..., pn,* then RELATION(*ms*) = UNION {(*p* MATCHING *p1*),(*p* MATCHING *p2*),...,(*p* MATCHING *pn*)}.

Now, relational intersection is a special case of relational semijoin (i.e., *r1* MATCHING *r2* degenerates to *r1* INTERSECT *r2* if *r1* and *r2* are of the same type). But MR-intersection is not a special case of MR-semijoin (i.e., there exist multirelations *mr1* and *mr2* such that *mr1* MR_INTERSECT *mr2* and *mr1* MR_MATCHING *mr2* are both defined but yield different results, even if *mr1* and *mr2* are of the same type). The reason is that there might be a tuple *t* in *MRB1* that's not also in *MRB2* but is nevertheless joinable with some tuple in *MRB2,* in which case that tuple *t* appears in the result of *mr1* MR_MATCHING *mr2* but not in the result of *mr1* MR_INTERSECT *mr2*.

MR-semidifference

Semidifference (NOT MATCHING, in **Tutorial D**) takes two relational operands and returns those tuples from the first operand that aren't joinable with any tuples at all in the second, and the multirelational analog does essentially the same thing for multirelations. For example:

```
S NOT MR_MATCHING SP
```

Result (a multirelation):

S#	SNAME	STATUS	CITY
S5	Adams	30	Athens
S6			Rome
S7			

- **Definition (MR-semidifference):** Let *ms* = *mr1* NOT MR_MATCHING *mr2*. The MR-headings *MRH1* and *MRH2* must be such that their set theory union is an MR-heading. Then *ms* is the multirelation whose MR-heading *MSH* is *MRH1* and whose MR-body *MSB* is the set of all tuples *t* such that *t* appears in *MRB1* and there does not exist a tuple in *MRB2* that is joinable with *t*.

It follows from this definition that *mr1* NOT MR_MATCHING *mr2* is identically equal to *mr1* MR_MINUS (*mr1* MR_MATCHING *mr2*).

Note that if HAMONEP(*mr1*) is TRUE, then HAMONEP(*ms*) is also TRUE. And if *mr1* has prime participant *p* and *mr2* has participants *p1, p2, ..., pn,* then RELATION(*ms*) = *p* NOT MATCHING *p1* NOT MATCHING *p2* ... NOT MATCHING *pn* (where the NOT MATCHINGs are evaluated in sequence left to right).

Now, relational difference is a special case of relational semidifference (i.e., *r1* NOT MATCHING *r2* degenerates to *r1* MINUS *r2* if *r1* and *r2* are of the same type). But MR-difference is not a special case of MR-semidifference (i.e., there exist multirelations *mr1* and *mr2* such that *mr1* MR_MINUS *mr2* and *mr1* NOT MR_MATCHING *mr2* are both defined but yield different results, even if *mr1* and *mr2* are of the same type). The reason is that there might be a tuple *t* in *MRB1* that's not also in *MRB2* but is nevertheless joinable with some tuple in *MRB2,* in which case that tuple *t* appears in the result of *mr1* MR_MINUS *mr2* but not in the result of *mr1* NOT MR_MATCHING *mr2*.

MR-restriction

Restriction is one of the simplest of the conventional relational operators. In **Tutorial D,** it's expressed as follows:

```
r WHERE cond
```

Here (a) *r* is a relation, represented by a relational expression of arbitrary complexity, and (b) *cond* is a restriction condition on *r*—i.e., it's a boolean expression in which every attribute reference identifies some attribute of *r* and there aren't any relvar references.[16] Each tuple *t* in *r* provides a value for each referenced attribute, thus allowing *cond* to be evaluated for that tuple, and that tuple *t* then appears in the body of the result if and only if the result of that evaluation is TRUE.

By contrast with the foregoing, multirelational restriction is a rather more complicated affair. The reason is that if *mr* is a multirelation, then (in general) some tuples in the MR-body *MRB* of *mr* will lack some of the attributes in the MR-heading *MRH* of *mr*. As a consequence, a simple expression such as

```
S MR_WHERE STATUS > 10
```

---

[16] Like many other languages, **Tutorial D** actually allows WHERE clauses to contain boolean expressions of arbitrary complexity (in particular, it allows them to contain relvar references). But if the boolean expression *cond* isn't of the particular simple form under discussion, then technically speaking the expression *r* WHERE *cond* doesn't represent a relational restriction as such.

will, typically, fail; to be specific, it'll fail at run time if the evaluation process encounters a tuple of S that lacks a STATUS attribute. (Of course, syntax of the even simpler form S WHERE STATUS > 10 would be doubly incorrect, because "S" isn't a relational expression but a multirelational one.)

Now, we could try adopting a rule to the effect that such tuples are simply ignored, but it's easy to see that such a rule quickly leads to worse problems. I'll just point out one such problem here (though there are countless others): The expression

```
S MR_WHERE NOT ( STATUS > 10 )
```

will presumably, in accordance with the hypothetical rule, also have to overlook tuples without a STATUS attribute—with the consequence that such tuples "fall through the cracks," as it were. Indeed, despite the fact that multirelations are quite definitely based on classical two-valued logic, the suggested rule seems to lead directly to just the kinds of difficulties that SQL's three-valued logic gets us into! And if there were no way around *that* problem, then the entire multirelations exercise would become rather pointless.

The most straightforward approach to avoiding such problems—though I feel bound to observe immediately that although the approach might be straightforward, the consequences in practice might not be—is to provide a means of testing, within an "MR_WHERE clause," for the presence of a particular attribute within a particular tuple. For example:

```
S MR_WHERE CASE
              WHEN PRESENT { STATUS } THEN STATUS > 10
              ELSE FALSE
           END CASE
```

Result (a multirelation):

S#	SNAME	STATUS	CITY
S1	Smith	20	London
S5	Adams	30	Athens
....	....	....	....
S3	Blake	30	

Explanation: Imagine the expression following MR_WHERE being evaluated for each tuple of S in turn, in some arbitrary sequence. For such a tuple *t*, PRESENT {STATUS} will evaluate to TRUE if and only if that tuple *t* actually has a STATUS attribute; thus, the CASE expression overall will evaluate to TRUE for just those tuples that do have a STATUS attribute with value greater than 10.

Note, incidentally, that the following syntax does *not* work:

```
S MR_WHERE PRESENT { STATUS } AND STATUS > 10
```

The reason is, of course, that AND is commutative; at run time, therefore, the system might legitimately try to evaluate the expression STATUS > 10 before it determines whether the tuple in question actually has a STATUS attribute. Testing for STATUS > 10 on a tuple with no STATUS attribute will raise an error.[17]

---

[17] Whether the compiler could detect the possibility that some attributes might be absent from some tuples, and could thus perhaps avoid certain run time errors, is an open question. See the section "Constraints" later in this chapter.

- **Partial definition (PRESENT):**[18] Consider the MR-restriction *mr* MR_WHERE *cond*. The construct PRESENT {*A1,A2,...,An*} is allowed to appear within *cond* wherever a boolean expression is allowed to appear, and that construct evaluates to TRUE for tuple *t* in *MRB* if and only if, for all *i* ($1 \leqslant i \leqslant n$), attribute *Ai* is present in *t*.

Note, therefore, that the construct PRESENT {...} is expressly defined in terms of some specific tuple of some specific multirelation. As a consequence, it can't appear in all possible contexts in which boolean expressions in general can appear, but only in certain specific contexts: namely, those in which the pertinent multirelation and pertinent tuple are well defined. (It's precisely for such reasons that I refer to PRESENT {...} as a "construct" and not an expression.[19]) Such contexts include MR_WHERE clauses in MR-restrictions; MR-extractions (see the next subsection); MR_WHERE clauses in DELETE and UPDATE (see the section "Update Operators"; and possibly others, if the need arises.

Now, sometimes we wish to test not for the presence, but rather the absence, of some particular attribute with respect to some tuple. Of course, we might simply use a negated form of PRESENT—for example:

```
S MR_WHERE NOT ( PRESENT { STATUS } )
```

But it's natural to provide a more direct formulation:

```
S MR_WHERE ABSENT { STATUS }
```

Result (a multirelation):[20]

S#	SNAME	STATUS	CITY
S4	Clark		London
S6			Rome
S7			

There are some traps for the unwary here, however. I've implied, in effect (though I didn't say as much explicitly), that PRESENT {*A1,A2,...,An*} is equivalent to

```
PRESENT { A1 } AND PRESENT { A2 } AND ...
                   AND PRESENT { An } AND TRUE
```

It follows that NOT (PRESENT {*A1,A2,...,An*}) is equivalent to

```
NOT ( PRESENT { A1 } ) OR NOT ( PRESENT { A2 } ) OR ...
                          OR NOT ( PRESENT { An } ) OR FALSE
```

So if we define ABSENT {*A1,A2,...,An*} to be equivalent to NOT (PRESENT {*A1,A2,...,An*}), we could run into

---

[18] The definition is partial because PRESENT (and ABSENT, q.v.) can be used in other contexts as well, as we'll see in a moment.

[19] Actually such constructs are expressions, but they're so called *open* expressions, and the unqualified term *expression* is usually taken to mean one that's closed. See Chapter 11 for further explanation.

[20] As you can see, the heading of this result includes an attribute (STATUS) for which no result tuple has a value. To eliminate that attribute—which we would surely want to do in practice—we can use MR_WITH (see the next subsection) in place of MR_WHERE.

some problems. Thus, it seems preferable to define ABSENT {*A1*,*A2*,...,*An*} to be equivalent to

```
ABSENT { A1 } AND ABSENT { A2 } AND ... AND ABSENT { An } AND TRUE
```

Now ABSENT {*A1*,*A2*,...,*An*} is equivalent to NOT (PRESENT {*A1*,*A2*,...,*An*}) only in the special case when n = 1. So we have:

- **Partial definition (ABSENT):** Consider the MR-restriction *mr* MR_WHERE *cond*. The construct ABSENT {*A1*,*A2*,...,*An*} is allowed to appear within *cond* wherever a boolean expression is allowed to appear, and that construct evaluates to TRUE for tuple *t* in *MRB* if and only if, for all i ($1 \leqslant i \leqslant n$), attribute *Ai* is absent from *t*.

Note in particular that, perhaps a little counterintuitively, PRESENT {} and ABSENT {} both evaluate to TRUE for every tuple of every multirelation. By way of explanation, consider first the case of PRESENT {}. This construct does *not* mean no attributes are present; rather, it means the set of no attributes is a subset of the set of attributes that *are* present. Likewise, ABSENT {} means the set of no attributes is a subset of the set of attributes that are absent. Since the empty set is a subset of every set, the result follows.

Here now are some more examples of MR-restriction (syntax only; I leave it to you to work out what the results look like, given our usual sample values):

- ```
  S MR_WHERE S# ≠ S#('S2') AND S# ≠ S#('S4') AND
             CASE
                WHEN PRESENT { STATUS , CITY }
                     THEN STATUS = 20 OR CITY ≠ 'London'
                ELSE FALSE
             END CASE
  ```

- ```
  S MR_WHERE CASE
                WHEN PRESENT { STATUS , CITY } THEN STATUS = 20
                WHEN PRESENT { CITY } THEN CITY = 'London'
                ELSE FALSE
             END CASE
  ```

- ```
  S MR_WHERE CASE
                WHEN PRESENT { CITY } THEN CITY = 'London'
                WHEN PRESENT { STATUS , CITY } THEN STATUS = 30
                ELSE FALSE
             END CASE
  ```

- ```
  S MR_WHERE CASE
                WHEN PRESENT { CITY }
                     THEN CASE
                             WHEN ABSENT { STATUS } THEN TRUE
                             ELSE FALSE
                     END CASE
                WHEN ABSENT { CITY }
                     THEN CASE
                             WHEN ABSENT { SNAME } THEN FALSE
                             ELSE TRUE
                          END CASE
             END CASE
  ```

With all of the foregoing by way of preamble, the following definition of MR-restriction might come as something of an anticlimax:

- **Definition (MR-restriction):** Let *ms* = *mr* MR_WHERE *cond.* Then *ms* is the multirelation whose MR-heading is *MRH* and whose MR-body consists of just those tuples in *MRB* for which *cond* is TRUE.

Note, however, that (to repeat) an error will occur if the evaluation of *cond* on some tuple involves an attempt to reference a nonexistent attribute (unless the reference appears in the context of PRESENT or ABSENT, of course). Note too that if HAMONEP(*mr*) is TRUE, then HAMONEP(*ms*) is also TRUE; and if *mr* has prime participant *p,* then RELATION(*ms*) is some relational restriction of *p*.

MR-extraction

Consider the following example:

```
( S MR_WHERE ABSENT { STATUS } AND PRESENT { CITY } )
                                    MR_ONTO { ALL BUT STATUS }
```

Result (a multirelation):

S#	SNAME	CITY
S4	Clark	London
....	....	....
S6		Rome

As you can see, what's happened here is that multirelation S has been restricted to just those tuples that don't contain a STATUS value but do contain a CITY value, and attribute STATUS has then been "projected away," as it were. Such a combination of operations seems likely to occur quite frequently, and so it seems worth considering a shorthand for it as suggested by the following example:

```
S MR_WITH ABSENT { STATUS } PRESENT { CITY }
```

Recall now the participant extraction operator (PARTICIPANT FROM) discussed earlier in this section, which extracted a specified participant from a specified multirelation. The foregoing MR_WITH expression can also be regarded as performing an extraction operation of a kind, but it extracts not a specified participant but, rather, a specified multirelation. For that reason, I call it *MR-extraction.*

- **Definition (MR-extraction):** Let *ms* = *mr* MR_WITH ABSENT {*A1,A2,...,An*} PRESENT {*B1,B2,...,Bm*}. The sets {*A1,A2,...,An*} and {*B1,B2,...,Bm*} must be disjoint. Then *ms* is defined to be equal to the result of (*mr* MR_WHERE ABSENT {*A1,A2,...,An*} AND PRESENT {*B1,B2,...,Bm*}) MR_ONTO {ALL BUT *A1,A2,...,An*}. Equivalently, let *excl* and *incl* be the attributes specified by *A1, A2, ..., An* and *B1, B2, ..., Bm,* respectively; then the MR-heading *MSH* of *ms* is the set theory difference between *MRH* and *excl* (in that order), and the MR-body *MSB* of *ms* is such that tuple *t* appears in *MSB* if and only if *t* appears in *MRB* and has a heading that is both a superset of *incl* and a subset of *MSH.*

The ABSENT and PRESENT constructs can be specified in either order and need not both appear. Omitting PRESENT is equivalent to specifying PRESENT {}; omitting ABSENT is equivalent to specifying ABSENT {}. A couple of examples:

```
S MR_WITH PRESENT { S# , CITY }
```

Result (a multirelation):

S#	SNAME	STATUS	CITY
S1	Smith	20	London
S2	Jones	10	Paris
S5	Adams	30	Athens
S4	Clark		London
S6			Rome

```
S MR_WITH ABSENT { SNAME , STATUS }
```

Result (a multirelation):

S#	CITY
S6	Rome
S7	

Note that if HAMONEP(*mr*) is TRUE, HAMONEP(*ms*) is also TRUE. HAMONEP(*ms*) is also TRUE whenever the set theory union of *incl* and *excl* is all of the attributes in *MRH* (in which case every tuple in the result certainly has the same heading: namely, the heading that consists of just the attributes of *incl*).

MR-extension

Relational extension is expressed in **Tutorial D** as follows:

```
EXTEND r : { X := exp }
```

Here (a) *r* is a relation, represented by a relational expression of arbitrary complexity; (b) *exp* is an expression in which attribute references identifying attributes of *r* are permitted; (c) *X* is the name of a new attribute;[21] and (d) tuple *t* appears in the result if and only if it's a tuple from *r* extended with a value for *X* that's computed by evaluating *exp* on *t*. Now, elsewhere this book proposes incorporating SUMMARIZE functionality into the relational EXTEND operator. I have not yet investigated the implications of that proposal for the multirelational analog of EXTEND; apart from such considerations, however, that analog is essentially straightforward. Here's an example:

```
MR_EXTEND ( S MR_WHERE PRESENT { STATUS } ) : { NT := STATUS + 10 }
```

Result (a multirelation):

[21] Usually, at any rate. I omit consideration of the case where it isn't for simplicity.

S#	SNAME	STATUS	CITY	NT
S1	Smith	20	London	30
S2	Jones	10	Paris	20
S5	Adams	30	Athens	40
....	....	....	....	....
S3	Blake	30		40

- **Definition (MR-extension):** Let *ms* = MR_EXTEND *mr* : {*X* := *exp*}. Then *ms* is the multirelation whose MR-heading is *MRH* extended with attribute *X* and whose MR-body consists of all tuples *t* such that *t* is a tuple of *MRB* extended with a value for attribute *X* that's computed by evaluating *exp* on that tuple of *r*. *Note:* In fact, this definition is essentially identical to the definition of relational extension, except that *mr* and *ms* are multirelations, not relations. Note too that if attribute *A* is referenced in *exp* but is absent from some tuple of *mr*, then attempting to evaluate *exp* on that tuple will give a run time error.[22]

Note that if HAMONEP(*mr*) is TRUE, then HAMONEP(*ms*) is also TRUE; and if *mr* has prime participant *p*, then RELATION(*ms*) is some relational extension of *p*.

As with relational extension, a multiple form of MR-extension can also be defined, but I omit the details here. An "outer" version might also be defined (see the subsection immediately following).

MR-renaming

At first sight, the multirelational analog of relational renaming appears quite straightforward. Here's an example:

```
S MR_RENAME { S# AS SNO }
```

Result (a multirelation):

SNO	SNAME	STATUS	CITY
S1	Smith	20	London
S2	Jones	10	Paris
S5	Adams	30	Athens
.....	....	....	....
S3	Blake	30	
.....	....	....	....
S4	Clark		London
.....	....	....	....
S6			Rome
.....	....	....	....
S7			

However, one of the most vexing aspects of the whole multirelation idea is trying to decide when

[22] As noted earlier, whether the compiler could detect the possibility that some attributes might be absent from some tuples and thus avoid certain run time errors is an open question.

references to absent attributes (within specific tuples) should be treated as an error and when they should simply be ignored. In the case at hand (viz., MR_RENAME), it might seem harmless on the face of it just to ignore them. If we do, then, e.g., the following expression—

```
S MR_RENAME { STATUS AS XX }
```

—will yield:

S#	SNAME	XX	CITY
S1	Smith	20	London
S2	Jones	10	Paris
S5	Adams	30	Athens
S3	Blake	30	
S4	Clark		London
S6			Rome
S7			

In conventional relational algebra, however, the following identity holds:

```
R RENAME { A AS B }  ≡  ( EXTEND R : { B := A } ) { ALL BUT A }
```

So what about a multirelational counterpart of this identity? More specifically, what happens with the following expression, which ought perhaps to be equivalent to S MR_RENAME {STATUS AS XX}?

```
( MR_EXTEND S : { XX := STATUS } ) MR_ONTO { ALL BUT STATUS }
```

Answer: It fails as soon as a tuple is encountered in S without a STATUS attribute—see the definition of MR-extension in the previous subsection. So perhaps we should reconsider that definition, so that MR_EXTEND simply ignores tuples for which attributes mentioned on the right side of the assignment in braces are absent. If we do, then at least the multirelational counterpart of the foregoing identity will hold. But now consider the following example:

```
S MR_WHERE STATUS + 10 = i
```

(where *i* is some integer). Now, we've already agreed, for very good reasons, that this expression will fail as soon as a tuple is encountered in S without a STATUS attribute (see the subsection "MR-restriction," earlier). But this expression is, or at least ought to be, equivalent to the following one:

```
( MR_EXTEND S : { I := STATUS + 10 } ) MR_WHERE I = i
```

And this expression *doesn't* fail, if MR_EXTEND just ignores tuples as suggested above. So what should we do?

My own strong inclination, in situations like the one under consideration here, is to follow *The Principle of Cautious Design* [3] and to insist, even with MR_RENAME, that references to absent attributes be considered an error. If we take this path, then the example shown earlier—

```
S MR_RENAME { STATUS AS XX }
```

—will have to be rewritten thus:

```
( S MR_WHERE PRESENT { STATUS } ) MR_RENAME { STATUS AS XX }
  MR_UNION
( S MR_WHERE ABSENT { STATUS } )
```

I note in passing, however, that it would be possible to define a shorthand—we might perhaps call it *outer* MR_RENAME—for the foregoing combination of operations. Similarly, we might define "outer" shorthand versions of MR_EXTEND and MR_WHERE, if such operations were thought to be sufficiently useful.

Here then is my preferred definition for MR_RENAME:

- **Definition (MR-renaming):** The expression *mr* MR_RENAME {*A* AS *B*} is equivalent to

```
( MR_EXTEND mr : { B := A } ) MR_ONTO { ALL BUT A }
```

Note that if HAMONEP(*mr*) is TRUE, then HAMONEP(*ms*) is also TRUE; and if *mr* has prime participant *p,* then RELATION(*ms*) is some relational renaming of *p*.

As with relational renaming, a multiple form of MR-renaming can also be defined. I omit the details here.

Internal Join

The multirelation operators I've described in this section so far have all been counterparts of familiar relational operators. By contrast, the operators I describe in this subsection and the next don't have any relational counterpart. The operators in question both have to do with certain *canonical forms* for multirelations, canonical forms that might possibly be of use in connection with database design.

As a basis for illustrating the first of these operators, I'll use a different, and much simpler, value for multirelvar S (see Fig. 3 below). *Note:* Let me point out immediately that this multirelation would be prohibited as a value for S if certain obvious constraints were in effect for that multirelvar. See the section "Constraints," later.

S

S#	SNAME	STATUS	CITY
S1	Smith		London
....	....	....	....
S3	Blake	30	
....	....	....	....
S1		20	
S3		30	
....	....	....	....
S1			London

Fig. 3: Another suppliers multirelation

As you can see, the three tuples for supplier S1 in the multirelation in Fig. 3 are joinable, and so are the two tuples for supplier S3. The *internal join* operation (INTRAJOIN) essentially just performs the corresponding tuple joins; that is, the expression

```
INTRAJOIN S
```

produces the following result (a multirelation):

S#	SNAME	STATUS	CITY
S1	Smith	20	London
S3	Blake	30	

- **Definition (internal join):** Let *ms* = INTRAJOIN (*mr*). Then *ms* is a multirelation with MR-heading *MSH* equal to *MRH* and MR-body *MSB* defined as follows: Let *t1, t2, ..., tn* be a set of tuples within *MRB* such that *t1, t2, ..., tn* are (a) mutually joinable and (b) not joinable with any other tuple in *MRB*. Then *t* is a tuple within *MSB* if and only if it's the join of the tuples in some such set *t1, t2, ..., tn*.

Informally, *mr* and *ms* can be regarded as "information equivalent" (i.e., they effectively both represent the same set of propositions). However, they differ inasmuch as *ms* has the following property: If *t1* and *t2* are distinct tuples of *ms,* then they're not joinable. By contrast, *mr* doesn't necessarily have this property (in fact, if it does, then *mr* = *ms*). As a consequence, *mr* might involve some redundancy (in the case at hand, the fact that supplier S1 is located in London appears twice, and so does the fact that supplier S3 has status 30), while *mr* doesn't exhibit redundancy of this same kind. In other words, one of the effects of INTRAJOIN is to eliminate certain redundancies.

Note that if HAMONEP(*mr*) is TRUE, then HAMONEP(*ms*) is also TRUE; and if *mr* has prime participant *p,* then RELATION(*ms*) is equal to *p*. Note too that TABLE_DEE is a participant—in fact, the sole participant—in *ms* if and only if it's the sole participant in *mr*.

Internal Decomposition

Loosely speaking, internal decomposition (INTRADECOMPOSE) is a kind of inverse of internal join.[23] Here's an example:

```
INTRADECOMPOSE S ON { S# }
```

Suppose S denotes the result of the internal join example from the previous section. Then this expression produces the following result (a multirelation):

S#	SNAME	STATUS	CITY
S1 S3			
S1 S3	Smith Blake		
S1 S3		20 30	
S1			London

[23] In fact, we might reasonably consider calling it "internal projection," and using syntax such as INTRA_ONTO to denote it.

- **Definition (internal decomposition):** Let *ms* = INTRADECOMPOSE *mr* ON {*A1,A2,...,An*}. Then *ms* is a multirelation with MR-heading *MSH* equal to *MRH* and MR-body *MSB* defined as follows: Tuple *t* appears in *MSB* if and only if (a) it's a subtuple of some tuple in *MRB* and (b) its heading includes the attributes *A1, A2, ..., An* and at most one additional attribute.

Note that if *t* appears in *MSB* and has some attribute *B* over and above *A1, A2, ..., An,* then the projection of *t* onto {*A1,A2,...,An*} also appears in *MSB*. Note too that *ms* and *mr* are information equivalent if and only if every tuple of *mr* has all of the attributes *A1, A2, ..., An*. Note finally that HAMONEP(*ms*) is TRUE if and only if *mr* is empty or the only nonempty participant in *mr* is the one whose heading consists precisely of attributes *A1, A2, ..., An*.

Other Operators

Tutorial D supports a variety of other relational operators in addition to the ones mentioned earlier in this section (examples include GROUP, UNGROUP, SUMMARIZE, and TCLOSE). However, I deliberately haven't yet defined multirelational analogs of those operators—but all of those operators except TCLOSE are defined in terms of ones for which I *have* defined multirelational analogs, and so it seems reasonable to assume that multirelation analogs could be defined for those operators as well if desired. I also deliberately haven't yet considered possible multirelation analogs of GROUP and UNGROUP involving multirelation valued attributes in place of relation valued attributes.

MULTIRELATION VARIABLES

The syntax for defining a multirelation variable, or multirelvar, can obviously follow the **Tutorial D** pattern for defining a relvar. Here's an example:

```
VAR S BASE MULTIRELATION
  { S# S# , SNAME NAME , STATUS INTEGER , CITY CHAR }
    MR_KEY { S# } ;
```

The type of this multirelvar is MULTIRELATION {S# S#, SNAME NAME, STATUS INTEGER, CITY CHAR}, but the MR_KEY specification (see the section "Constraints" immediately following) further constrains the values that can be assigned to it, just as a relational KEY specification further constrains the values that can be assigned to a relvar. Note, however, that (as we'll see) whereas every relvar has at least one key, not every multirelvar has an MR-key.

Note: If *MR* is a multirelvar, then its value at any given time (which is a multirelation, of course) has a set of participant relations, one for each subset of the MR-heading of *MR*. It's convenient to extend the "participant" terminology to multirelvars too in the obvious way (just as, in the relational context, we use terminology such as "the body of relvar *R*," by which we really mean the body of the relation that's the current value of *R*).

CONSTRAINTS

Multirelvar constraints of arbitrary complexity can be formulated as boolean expressions with multirelational operands. As in the relational case, however, shorthands to address certain common requirements will probably be desirable in practice. I consider a few possibilities in this connection.

MR_IS_EMPTY

MR_IS_EMPTY(*mr*) is TRUE if and only if *MRB* is empty—in other words, if and only if, for every participant *p* in *mr,* IS_EMPTY(*p*) is TRUE (in which case *mr* has an empty prime participant). In other words, the expression

```
MR_IS_EMPTY ( mr )
```

is shorthand for the following expression:

```
mr MR_ONTO { } = MR_DUM
```

One particularly common application of MR_IS_EMPTY is likely to be in connection with *required attributes*—where an attribute is "required" if and only if it's required to be present in every tuple of the pertinent multirelvar. For example:

```
CONSTRAINT MRC1 MR_IS_EMPTY ( S MR_WHERE ABSENT { S# } ) ;
```

This constraint requires multirelvar S to have as its value at all times a multirelation in which attribute S# is present in every tuple. It might be nice to introduce a further shorthand that expresses the same constraint as part of the definition of the multirelvar in question, perhaps like this:

```
VAR S BASE MULTIRELATION
  { S# S# , SNAME NAME , STATUS INTEGER , CITY CHAR }
    .....
    PRESENT { S# } ;
```

However, this further shorthand is clearly not adequate in itself to express all possible constraints of this same general nature, and additional shorthands based on it might well be desired. For example, suppose certain pairs of attributes are mutually exclusive; suppose, for example, that multirelvar S has an additional attribute, REASON, which has a value if and only the STATUS value is absent and indicates the reason for that absence:

```
CONSTRAINT MRC2 MR_IS_EMPTY
   ( S MR_WHERE PRESENT { STATUS , REASON }
              OR ABSENT { STATUS , REASON } ) ;
```

Observe in particular that MR_WITH isn't particularly helpful with examples like this one—a fact that might raise questions about the usefulness of that operator in general.

By way of a third example, consider the case of a soccer club. It has a fixture list. For each match in the fixture list, the result is eventually entered. So we might imagine a multirelvar, FIXTURE, whose nonempty participants at all times number no more than three: one for those matches that need to be scheduled but have no date assigned yet, one for those that are scheduled but haven't yet been played, and one for those that have been played.[24] Let FIXTURE have attributes GOALS_FOR and GOALS_AGAINST, with the obvious meanings. Clearly, whenever one of these attributes has a value for a particular match, then so must the other:

```
CONSTRAINT MRC3 MR_IS_EMPTY
( FIXTURE MR_WHERE NOT ( PRESENT { GOALS_FOR , GOALS_AGAINST } )
               AND NOT ( ABSENT { GOALS_FOR , GOALS_AGAINST } ) ) ;
```

Clearly, such constraints will get increasingly complex as the number of attributes involved increases—suggesting, again, that further shorthands might be desirable.

MR-keys

I strongly suspect that if multirelvars are to be used at all, then they should always have at least one *MR-key* as a matter of good practice—meaning, to spell the point out, that no two distinct tuples in the same MR-body have the same value for the MR-key in question. (By *multirelvars* here, I mean multirelvars in the database, not necessarily ones that might exist from time to time merely to hold the result of some query.) Here's the

---

[24] Do you see any particular advantages here over a conventional three-relvar design?

definition:

- **Definition (MR-key):** Specifying MR_KEY {*A1,A2,...,An*} for multirelvar *MR* defines an MR-key for *MR*. It's equivalent to imposing the following constraint on *MR:*

```
MR_IS_EMPTY ( MR MR_WHERE NOT ( PRESENT { A1 , A2 , ... , An } ) )
AND COUNT ( MR ONTO { A1 , A2 , ... , An } ) = MR_COUNT ( MR )
```

Note that this definition implies that attributes *A1, A2, ..., An* are all required ones. Also, it's worth pointing out explicitly that the expression *MR* ONTO {*A1,A2,...,An*}—the argument expression in the COUNT invocation on the left side of the equality comparison—returns a relation, not a multirelation. However, the argument expression to the MR_COUNT invocation on the right side is a multirelvar reference (MR_COUNT is, of course, the multirelational analog of COUNT).

Now, I've already indicated that not every multirelvar has an MR-key. By way of example, consider the following multirelation (repeated from the discussion of internal decomposition in the previous section):

S#	SNAME	STATUS	CITY
S1 S3			
S1 S3	Smith Blake		
S1 S3		20 30	
S1			London

Clearly, this multirelation could be the current value of some relvar; equally clearly, it doesn't satisfy any MR-key constraint at all.

In general, an MR-key has the same properties of uniqueness and irreducibility as relational keys do. However, note that "uniqueness" here means "uniqueness across several relations": namely, all of the relations that are participants in the multirelation currently assigned to the multirelvar with the MR-key in question. In the case of multirelvar S, for example, with its MR-key {S#}, no two tuples are ever allowed to have the same S# value, even if the tuples in question would have appeared in distinct participants.

Participant Keys

It seems natural to introduce another kind of key, one that's unique within participants but not necessarily across them, as it were. Here's the definition:

- **Definition (participant key):** Specifying PARTICIPANT KEY {*A1,A2,...,An*} for multirelvar *MR* defines a participant key for *MR*. Such a specification implies that attributes *A1, A2, ..., An* are all required. If *PK* is such a key, then every nonempty participant *p* in *MR* at any given time is such that (a) *PK* is a subset of the heading of *p* and (b) no two distinct tuples in *p* have the same value for *PK*.

Note that if *MK* is an MR-key for *MR,* then *MK* is a participant key for *MR* a fortiori. However, if *PK* is a participant key for *MR,* then *PK* isn't necessarily an MR-key for *MR*.

Foreign MR-keys

The relational concept of foreign keys and, more generally, the relational *inclusion dependency* concept (see Chapter 13 of the present book) will need multirelational counterparts. For example, in the suppliers-and-shipments database (with sample values as shown in Figs. 1 and 2), multirelvars S and SP are subject to the constraint that, at all times, the MR-body of the MR-projection of SP onto {S#} is a subset of the MR-body of the MR-projection of S onto {S#}:

```
SP MR_ONTO { S# } ⊆ S MR_ONTO { S# }
```

Clearly, we might want to define a shorthand according to which a specification of the form

```
FOREIGN MR_KEY { S# } REFERENCES S
```

could appear as part of the definition of multirelvar SP.

MR-DNF

An MR-DNF constraint (DNF = "decomposed normal form"—see the section immediately following) is a constraint on a multirelvar to the effect that the only participants allowed to be nonempty are those whose headings have no more than one attribute in addition to those of a participant key (the same participant key in every such participant).

NORMAL FORMS

As I mentioned a few pages back, there are two obvious canonical forms, or normal forms, that can be defined for multirelvars. I'll call them MR-JNF and MR-DNF, for joined normal form and decomposed normal form, respectively. They aren't mutually exclusive, by the way (i.e., a given multirelvar can be in both at the same time). Their definitions are simple:

- **Definition (MR-JNF):** Multirelvar *MR* is in MR-JNF if and only if it's subject to an MR-key constraint.
- **Definition (MR-DNF):** Multirelvar *MR* is in MR-DNF if and only if it's subject to an MR-DNF constraint.

If multirelvar *MR1* has a participant key *PK,* then its MR-JNF equivalent *MR2,* with MR-key *PK,* can be obtained by the following assignment:

```
MR2 := INTRAJOIN MR1 ;
```

Likewise, its MR-DNF equivalent *MR3* can be obtained by the following assignment:

```
MR3 := INTRADECOMPOSE MR1 ON { PK } ;
```

Both normal forms prevent "accidents" such as the following (an impossible value for multirelvar S, because the two tuples effectively contradict one another):[25]

---

[25] The point is, stating the constraints to prevent such accidents in the case of a multirelvar not in one of the two normal forms is a rather tricky business.

S#	SNAME	STATUS	CITY
S1	Smith		London
....	....	....	....
S1			Paris

With reference to this particular example, enforcing MR-JNF for S prevents the appearance of two or more tuples for the same supplier; enforcing MR-DNF prevents the appearance of two or more CITY values for the same supplier. More generally, the two normal forms both prevent two or more tuples from appearing in the same multirelvar at the same time with the same value for the same MR-key value and with different values for some other attribute. Equivalently, for every pair of participants (*p1* and *p2,* say) in the multirelvar in question, no tuple in *p1* has the same value for the same MR-key value as more than one tuple—or, in the case of MR-JNF, any tuple—in *p2* at any given time.

Note: As you might have realized, there are some interesting parallels to be observed between multirelvars in either of the two normal forms, on the one hand, and relvars obtained by means of the decomposition approach [1] on the other. To be specific, the various constraints (on keys, to be precise) that relvars obtained by means of decomposition are required to satisfy are very similar to the constraints on MR-keys and participant keys that apply when either MR-JNF or MR-DNF is in effect.

Now, it's easy to see that a multirelvar that's in neither MR-JNF nor MR-DNF (such as a single multirelvar constituting the entire database!) would be subject to all sorts of difficulties in connection with update operations. In practice, therefore, I think the only multirelvars (base or virtual) that might not be in one of those two normal forms would be ones used for holding query results. For that reason, at this time I discuss, in the section immediately following, only such update operators as might usefully be defined under the assumption that one of those normal forms is in effect.

UPDATE OPERATORS

Assignment is defined for variables of all types, and multirelvars are no exception; I've already given a couple of examples.[26] As usual, however, certain shorthands are likely to be desirable in practice. The shorthands in question are very similar to the familiar (relational) INSERT, DELETE, and UPDATE shorthands of **Tutorial D**.

MR-INSERT

- **Definition (MR_INSERT):** Let *MR* be a multirelvar and let *mr* be a multirelation with MR-heading some subset of that of *MR*. Then MR_INSERT *MR mr* is equivalent to

```
MR := MR MR_UNION mr ;
```

For example:

[26] Note, however, that whereas relational assignment requires the source relation and target relvar to have the same heading (in other words, to be of the same type), multirelational assignment requires only that the source multirelation have a heading that's some subset of that of the target multirelvar.

```
MR_INSERT S MULTIRELATION { TUPLE { S#    S#('S2')        ,
                                    SNAME NAME('Jones') ,
                                    CITY  'Paris'        } ,
                            { TUPLE { S#    S#('S3')        ,
                                    SNAME NAME('Blake') } ,
                            { TUPLE { S#    S#('S3')        ,
                                    CITY  'Paris'        } } ;
```

Result (assuming for simplicity that multirelvar S was empty before the MR_INSERT):

S#	SNAME	STATUS	CITY
S2	Jones		Paris
S3	Blake		
S3			Paris

This result violates both MR-JNF and MR-DNF. In general, therefore, if the target multirelvar *MR* is required to be in MR-JNF, we will probably want a shorthand for the following:

```
MR := INTRAJOIN ( MR MR_UNION mr ) ;
```

Similarly, if *MR* is required to be in MR-DNF, then we will probably want a shorthand for the following:

```
MR := INTRADECOMPOSE ( MR MR_UNION mr ) ;
```

However, I offer no suggestions for such shorthands at this time.

Other possibilities that might be worth considering include:

- Allowing the *mr* operand to be a relation instead of a multirelation
- Supporting a multirelational analog of **Tutorial D**'s D_INSERT (in which case we'd presumably need a multirelational analog of **Tutorial D**'s D_UNION as well)

MR-DELETE

Note: For completeness, analogs of the first (less commonly used) form of **Tutorial D**'s DELETE, as well as its I_DELETE, might be desirable in addition to the following, but I omit consideration of those possibilities here.

- **Definition (MR_DELETE):** Let *MR* be a multirelvar and let *cond* be a boolean expression. Then MR_DELETE *MR* MR_WHERE *cond* is equivalent to

```
MR := MR MR_WHERE NOT ( cond ) ;
```

For example:

```
MR_DELETE S MR_WHERE CASE
                         WHEN PRESENT { CITY } THEN CITY = 'Paris'
                         ELSE FALSE
                     END CASE ;
```

Note the need to be able to use the PRESENT and ABSENT constructs once again. In the example, the effect is to delete every tuple with an attribute named CITY whose value is Paris (loosely speaking). Tuples without a CITY attribute are *not* deleted.

Here's another example:

```
MR_DELETE S MR_WHERE ABSENT { SNAME , STATUS } ;
```

This MR_DELETE is equivalent to:

```
S := S MR_WHERE NOT ( ABSENT { SNAME , STATUS } ) ;
```

Observe in particular that it's *not* equivalent to:

```
S := S MR_WHERE PRESENT { SNAME , STATUS } ;
```

No special varieties of MR_DELETE are needed for normal form preservation.

MR-UPDATE

I omit a precise definition of MR_UPDATE; the details are tedious, though essentially straightforward, and the effect is (I hope) intuitively obvious.[27] Here's an example:

```
MR_UPDATE ( S MR_WHERE S# = S#('S1') AND PRESENT { STATUS } ) :
                                          { STATUS := 10 } ;
```

No special varieties of MR_UPDATE are needed for normal form preservation.

VIRTUAL RELVARS AND MULTIRELVARS

This subject needs further investigation, but one observation can be made right away. Clearly, if *A1, A2, ..., An* are attributes of multirelvar *MR,* then a virtual relvar—not multirelvar—*PV* can be defined over the participant in *MR* whose heading is just those attributes:

```
VAR PV VIRTUAL ( PARTICIPANT { A1 , A2 , ... , An } FROM MR ) ;
```

Certain updates on *MR* can now be expressed in terms of updates on *PV*. As I more or less suggested earlier (in the section "What's a Multirelation?"), such virtual relvars might thus provide the basis for a mapping from a database design based on multirelvars to a relational design based on the proposals of either reference [1] or reference [13].

INTERPRETATION

Consider the multirelation MSC shown in Fig. 4, which is intended to be a sample value for a multirelvar MSCV of the following multirelation type:

```
MULTIRELATION { S# S# , CITY CHAR }
```

Since MSCV is of degree two, every multirelation (including the one in Fig. 4 in particular) that's a possible value of that multirelvar necessarily has four participants. For the sake of the example—but completely arbitrarily—I've chosen to make each of the participants in the multirelation in the figure nonempty. (One of them is TABLE_DEE, represented in the figure by a row with a vacant space in every attribute position.)

Now let *s#* and *c* be range variables, ranging over the set S# (the underlying type for attribute S#) and the

---

[27] Though we might need an additional form of MR_UPDATE for adding attributes to, and/or removing attributes from, specified tuples (please forgive the loose manner of speaking here). Again I omit the details.

set CHAR (the underlying type for attribute CITY), respectively. I'll consider the four participants one at a time. (You can interpret the discussion that follows in terms of the multirelation in Fig. 4, but of course it's meant to apply to every multirelation that's a possible value for multirelvar MSCV.)

MSC

S#	CITY
S1	London
S2	Paris
....	....
S3	
S4	
....	....
	Athens
....	....

Fig. 4: Multirelation MSC

First of all, the body of the participant with heading {S#,CITY} consists of just those tuples of the form *<s#,c>* that satisfy predicate *p1(s#,c)*, where *p1* is some predicate with parameters *s#* and *c*. (Intuitively, we might expect predicate *p1* to be *Supplier s# is located in city c,* but its exact form is irrelevant here.) So we can say the participant with heading {S#,CITY} is defined by the following domain calculus expression:[28]

```
<s#, c> : p1(s#, c)
```

Similarly, the defining expression for the participant with heading {S#} is

```
<s#>    : p2(s#)
```

for some predicate *p2* with sole parameter *s#*. Likewise, the defining expression for the participant with heading {CITY} is

```
<c>     : p3(c)
```

for some predicate *p3* with sole parameter *c*. And the defining expression for the participant with heading {} is

```
<>      : p4()
```

for some predicate *p4* with no parameters at all (in other words, *p4* is in fact a proposition).

So what's the predicate for multirelvar MSCV overall? Well, let MSCH and MSCB be the MR-heading and current MR-body, respectively, of that multirelvar, and let *t* be a tuple in MSCB. Clearly, *t* has a heading that's some subset of MSCH. Let *H1, H2, H3,* and *H4,* denote the four subsets of MSCH, thus:

```
H1 = { S# , CITY }

H2 = { S# }

H3 = { CITY }
```

---

[28] The domain calculus is slightly better suited to my purpose here than the possibly more familiar tuple calculus.

```
H4 = { }
```

Then we can say that the predicate for MSCV overall—let's call it MSCP—looks something like this:

```
IF heading(t) = H1 THEN p1(t) AND
IF heading(t) = H2 THEN p2(t) AND
IF heading(t) = H3 THEN p3(t) AND
IF heading(t) = H4 THEN p4(t)
```

Observe that:

a. This predicate is a conjunction of implications.

b. For any given tuple *t* with heading *Hi* for some *i* ($1 \leqslant i \leqslant 4$), exactly one of those implications has an antecedent ("the IF part") that evaluates to TRUE.

c. Each of the other three implications has an antecedent that evaluates to FALSE and thus evaluate to TRUE overall.

d. For that tuple *t,* in other words, the predicate reduces to just *pi*(*t*).

Note: We can simplify the formulation of this predicate slightly by introducing the notation *PS*(MSCH) to denote the power set of MSCH:

```
FORALL Hi ∈ PS(MSCH) ( IF heading(t) = Hi THEN pi(t) )
```

A final observation: Consider a conventional relational database *RDB* containing just four relvars *RV1, RV2, RV3,* and *RV4,* with relvar predicates *p1, p2, p3,* and *p4,* respectively. Then what we might call "the database predicate" for database *RDB* will again be essentially just predicate MSCP—which is surely just as we should expect.

POTENTIAL APPLICATIONS

Since the first publication of *The Third Manifesto* in early 1995 [2], we've seen a gratifying amount of interest—and it's still growing—in the idea of providing an interface to existing SQL databases that conforms to the proposals of the *Manifesto* (i.e., is truly relational). Now, the tables shown throughout this chapter, depicting multirelations, could alternatively be understood as depicting SQL tables, with nulls occupying the vacant spaces. It seems, therefore, that there's a straightforward mapping between SQL tables and multirelations. The existence of such a mapping creates an obvious opportunity to provide an alternative language for operating on SQL tables. The operators described in the present chapter are, unlike SQL's operators, based firmly on classical logic and set theory. As a result, they should be significantly easier than SQL's operators to teach, learn, and use, and they should also be capable of serving as a bridge to true relations and *their* operators.

In my opinion, the main application for multirelation operators is likely to be in connection with constraints that would be needed if the database were to contain multirelvars. The usefulness of those operators for query purposes is, I think, somewhat debatable; to be specific, I think their comparative complexity makes them more subject to misinterpretation than their relational counterparts (even though, to repeat, I do think they're simpler than their SQL counterparts).

That said, however, I note that the often perceived requirement for "relational" *outer* operations (especially outer join) can be addressed by means of MR-union in particular. In particular, for a certain kind of report—one commonly required in practice—MR-union might be more suitable than relational join. Such requirements have occasionally given rise to suggestions that "relational" operators might be needed that yield sets of relations instead of just a single relation as their result. Speaking a trifle loosely, the key difference between such suggestions and the multirelation approach seems to be this (though I readily admit the difference in question might be more apparent than real):

- In those suggestions, the result relations are effectively *elements* of those result sets.

- In the multirelation approach, by contrast, relations—that is, participant relations in a multirelation—are *subsets* of that multirelation, not elements of it.

To illustrate, here's what McGoveran has to say regarding such matters in reference [13] (italics and boldface in the original):

> [This discussion] suggests some extensions to the relational algebra to support more general versions of the relational operators. In particular, relational union is a restricted version of the general set union. I propose that the system should automatically create several tables in the output (when appropriate), grouping like rows together by performing the "restrict and project away nulls" operation in the user's behalf ... In effect, such set operations would be many-table-result versions of existing relational operations; they would avoid the need for users to simulate such operations manually, via several SQL statements. Whether many-table *operands* (as opposed to results) should be permitted deserves additional and careful consideration, however. **For the time being, I propose that such many-table values be supported only for output.**

Here's an example of what I mean when I claim that MR-union can be used to address the "outer join" problem. Let S, SP, and SPJ be relvars (not multirelvars) for suppliers, shipments of parts, and shipments of parts to projects, respectively. Relvar S has key {S#}; relvar SP has key {S#,P#}; and relvar SPJ has key {S#,P#,J#}. Now suppose we want a report showing (a) suppliers in supplier number order, each such supplier being followed by (b) a list of parts in part number order, showing parts shipped by that supplier, each such part being followed by (c) a list of projects in project number order showing the projects that supplier supplies that part to. The multirelation denoted by the following expression provides all of the information needed for that report:

```
MR_UNION { MULTIRELATION ( S ) ,
           MULTIRELATION ( SP ) ,
           MULTIRELATION ( SPJ ) }
```

The tuples resulting from evaluation of this expression would have to be processed in a suitable sequence in order to meet McGoveran's requirement of "grouping like rows together." Perhaps that sequence could be specified like this:

```
ORDER ( ASC S# , ASC P# , ASC J# )
```

The semantics of such a specification would have to be defined in such a way that (among other things) each S tuple comes immediately before its first matching SP tuple if any, and each SP tuple comes immediately before its first matching SPJ tuple if any. Of course, if the intuitively obvious foreign key constraints from SPJ to SP and from SP to S don't apply, then the report might display some anomalies.

SOME OUTSTANDING QUESTIONS

As noted near the beginning, this chapter is meant as a kind of discussion paper, not as any kind of definitive statement. Certainly there are quite a few loose ends to be tidied up. And I feel bound to say that, if the scheme overall is seen principally as an approach to the "missing information" problem—a problem to which, I say again, purely relational solutions already exist—then it does seem to involve a degree of complexity out of proportion to the problem it's meant to address. In particular, the possibility that certain attributes might be absent from certain tuples leads to a lot of complexity in connection with MR_WHERE clauses and related matters.

On the other hand, if the approach is felt to be worth pursuing, then there are many topics that need further investigation. Here are some of them (in no particular order):

- Is there a better way of dealing with absent attributes (in MR_WHERE clauses in particular)?
- Do we need additional multirelation comparison operators?
- Do we need additional constraint shorthands?
- What about the possibility of compensatory actions, such as cascade delete?
- What issues are raised by the possibility of defining virtual relvars on multirelvars?
- What about the possibility of virtual multirelvars?
- Can we pin down the specifics of the putative mapping between relations and multirelations in more detail?
- What are the implications for multirelations of the inheritance model as defined in reference [7]—especially with respect to "specialization by constraint"?
- How do aggregation and summarization work with multirelations?
- What's the relationship, if any, between multirelations and support for temporal data as described in reference [8]?
- Can we define a formal multirelation algebra?
- Can the compiler determine when attributes might be absent from one or more tuples in the results of arbitrary multirelational expressions?
- Can the compiler perform any other constraint inferencing—for example, determining that some MR-key constraint applies to the result of some multirelational expression?
- More generally, what problems, if any, can be solved with multirelations that can't be solved without them? (We think: None.)

ACKNOWLEDGMENTS

I'd like to thank Chris Date for his careful review of several earlier drafts of this chapter. Adrian Hudnott also reviewed an earlier draft and gave me useful comments. Dennis Ashley provided me with references [9] and [11], both of which are mathematical treatises that use the term *multirelation* (though it's not clear to me whether their use of the term refers to exactly the same concept, nor how close either of them is to the concept I've defined here).

REFERENCES AND BIBLIOGRAPHY

1. Hugh Darwen: "How to Handle Missing Information Without Using Nulls" (presentation slides), *www.thethirdmanifesto.com* (May 9th, 2003; revised May 16th, 2005). See also Chapter 23 of the present book.

2. Hugh Darwen and C. J. Date: "*The Third Manifesto,*" *ACM SIGMOD Record 24,* No. 1 (March 1995).

3. C. J. Date: "The Principle of Cautious Design," in C. J. Date and Hugh Darwen, *Relational Database Writings 1989-1991.* Reading, Mass.: Addison-Wesley (1992).

4. C. J. Date: "The Closed World Assumption," in *Logic and Databases: The Roots of Relational Theory.* Victoria, B.C.: Trafford Publishing (2007).

5. C. J. Date: *The Relational Database Dictionary, Extended Edition.* Berkeley, Calif.: Apress (2008).

6. C. J. Date and Hugh Darwen: *Databases, Types, and the Relational Model: The Third Manifesto* (3rd edition). Boston, Mass.: Addison-Wesley (2006). See also Chapter 1 of the present book.

7. C. J. Date and Hugh Darwen: "The Inheritance Model" (Chapter 19 of the present book).

8. C. J. Date, Hugh Darwen, and Nikos A. Lorentzos: *Temporal Data and the Relational Model.* San Francisco, Calif.: Morgan Kaufmann (2003).

9. Roland Fraïssé and Norbert Sauer: *Theory of Relations.* New York, N.Y.: Elsevier Science (2000).

10. Maurice Gittens: "On Logical Mistakes and *The Third Manifesto*" (English version of an article that appeared in Dutch in *DB/M Magazine,* No. 2. Array Publications, Netherlands, April 2007). See Chapters 4-9 of the present book (Chapter 9 in particular is relevant to the theme of the present chapter).

11. Wim H. Hesselink: "Multirelations Are Predicate Transformers," *http://www.cs.rug.nl/~wim/pub/ whh318.pdf* (February 23rd, 2004).

12. Adrian Larner: "A New Model of Data," *http://www.btinternet.com/~adrian.larner/ database.htm* (undated).

13. David McGoveran: "Nothing from Nothing" (in four parts), in C. J. Date, Hugh Darwen, and David McGoveran, *Relational Database Writings 1994-1997.* Reading, Mass.: Addison-Wesley (1998).

14. Fabian Pascal: "The Final Null in the Coffin," *http://www.dbdebunk.com/publications.html* (September 2004).

Chapter 25

An Inheritance Approach

Let no one enter here who does not know his geometry.
—inscription at the entrance of Plato's Academy

The following is an edited version of an email [7] from Erwin Smout to *ttm@thethirdmanifesto.com,* the forum that discusses matters related to *The Third Manifesto* [3]:

> The following idea crossed my mind yesterday.
>
> For each and every type xxx, the system automatically provides a proper supertype, called, e.g., POSSIBLYMISSINGxxx. There is precisely one value that is of the supertype but not of the type itself, and that value is the value 'MISSING' (yes, do let me consider it a value for the time being).
>
> All the operators defined for the type apply only to the type xxx itself, and thus not to type POSSIBLYMISSINGxxx. The only operator that does apply to type POSSIBLYMISSINGxxx is, optionally, an operator IS_MISSING() or IS_VALUE(), returning a boolean according to the obvious semantics (having this operator is not strictly necessary because an equality test to the value 'MISSING' does the job too). Type checking thus prevents the invocation of, say, the operator "+" on expressions of type POSSIBLYMISSINGxxx.
>
> Relation attributes can be declared to be of type POSSIBLYMISSINGxxx, or of type xxx. In the case an attribute is declared to be of type POSSIBLYMISSINGxxx, the programmer is forced to first invoke the IS_VALUE() test before invoking a TREAT_AS_xxx (in order to build stable, reliable programs and avoid runtime errors, that is).
>
> There would be one 'MISSING' for each "root" type (which, by creation of the proper supertype, no longer is a "genuine" root type, but that isn't much of a problem, I think). Let's say that type INTEGER = {–32768, ..., 32767}. A proper subtype of INTEGER is EVENINTEGER = {–32768, –32766, ..., 32766}. POSSIBLYMISSINGINTEGER = {–32768, ..., 32767} UNION {MISSINGINTEGER} and POSSIBLYMISSINGEVENINTEGER = {–32768, –32766, ..., 32766} UNION {MISSINGINTEGER}. Thus, if types xxx and yyy do not have a common supertype (*alpha* notwithstanding), then neither do the types POSSIBLYMISSINGxxx and POSSIBLYMISSINGyyy. Likewise, if yyy is a proper sub/supertype of xxx, then POSSIBLYMISSINGyyy is a proper sub/supertype of POSSIBLYMISSINGxxx.
>
> The value 'MISSING' of POSSIBLYMISSINGINTEGER is equal to the value 'MISSING' of POSSIBLYMISSINGEVENINTEGER, with the obvious consequences for join, duplicate elimination in projections, etc., etc.
>
> It looks to me like this is a sound solution for the 'missing information' problem. Does it look like a sensible idea to try and work this out in code?

The answer to Smout's final question here struck me as being *yes,* at least so long as—as Smout clearly intends—the subtype and supertype concepts are as defined in our inheritance model (see references [2] and [5]). I therefore set to work on the examples used to illustrate that model in reference [2], with a view to seeing what would happen to them under Smout's suggestion. In this chapter, I present the results of those investigations and offer some comments on them.

For simplicity, I abbreviate Smout's POSSIBLYMISSING to PM_ (e.g., the "possibly missing" counterpart of type INTEGER is type PM_INTEGER; more generally, the "possibly missing" counterpart of type *T* is type PM_*T*). For that reason, I'll refer to Smout's scheme henceforth as "the PM_ scheme." Also, I don't expect readers to be fully familiar with our inheritance model, and so I'll spell out relevant details of that model (for aspects I'll be relying on) at appropriate points in what follows. Note, however, that one important assumption I'll be making throughout is that all of the types under discussion are scalar types specifically.

THE RUNNING EXAMPLE

Reference [2] uses an example based on ellipses and circles to illustrate the idea of single inheritance, which is the kind of inheritance that applies when no type has more than one immediate supertype (a concept I'll elaborate on in just a moment). The example is based on the rather trivial observation that every circle is an ellipse but some ellipses aren't circles. As a consequence, it seems reasonable to make type CIRCLE an *immediate subtype* of type ELLIPSE: equivalently, to make type ELLIPSE an *immediate supertype* of type CIRCLE. The supertype / subtype relationship between types ELLIPSE and CIRCLE can thus be pictured as a simple type hierarchy (see Fig. 1).

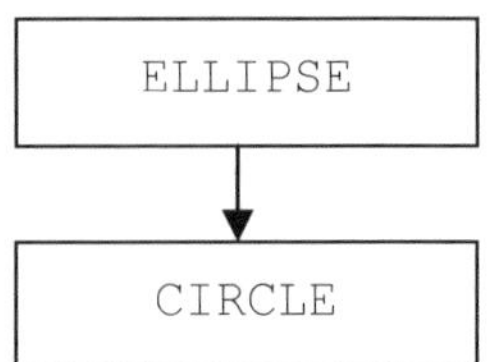

Fig. 1: A simple type hierarchy (ellipses and circles)

Loosely speaking, if type *T* is an immediate supertype of type *T'*, then all properties that apply to values of type *T* also apply to values of type *T'*, but values of type *T'* have certain additional properties of their own. In the case of ellipses and circles, for example, we have the following:

- All ellipses have an area; some ellipses—namely, those that happen to be circles—have a radius as well.
- All ellipses have a major semiaxis *a* and a minor semiaxis *b*, and are subject to the constraint that $a \geqslant b$ (at least, let's assume so for present purposes). For a circle, of course, *a* and *b* coincide in the radius—in fact, we can define a circle to be an ellipse for which $a = b$—and so the constraint is satisfied trivially.

Note: In addition to types ELLIPSE and CIRCLE, reference [2] also makes use of the following additional types from time to time (namely, when ellipses and circles by themselves are insufficient to illustrate some point):

- A type called O_CIRCLE ("O-circles"), which consists of circles whose center is the origin. Type O_CIRCLE is an immediate subtype of type CIRCLE, and hence also a *proper* subtype of both type CIRCLE and type ELLIPSE (see below regarding proper subtypes and supertypes).
- A type called PLANE_FIGURE (plane figures), which serves as the root type for several examples in reference [2] (where a root type is a type with no immediate supertype). In particular, therefore, type PLANE_FIGURE is an immediate supertype of type ELLIPSE. Here, by contrast, I'm ignoring PLANE_FIGURE and assuming for simplicity that ELLIPSE is the root type, at least for the time being.

For completeness, let me add that (a) a leaf type is a type with no immediate subtype (for example, CIRCLE is a leaf type in Fig. 1); (b) every type is both a subtype (but not a proper subtype) of itself and a supertype (but not a proper supertype) of itself.

The supertype / subtype relationships between types ELLIPSE, CIRCLE, and O_CIRCLE are depicted in Fig. 2 opposite. The corresponding type definitions are as follows (repeated from reference [2]): [1]

---

[1] The definitions are expressed in a version of **Tutorial D** that has been extended to support the inheritance model. See references [4] and [6] for further explanation (especially regarding "possreps"). Also, the definition of type ELLIPSE by rights ought to include a constraint to the effect that $a \geqslant b$. I omit that constraint here for simplicity.

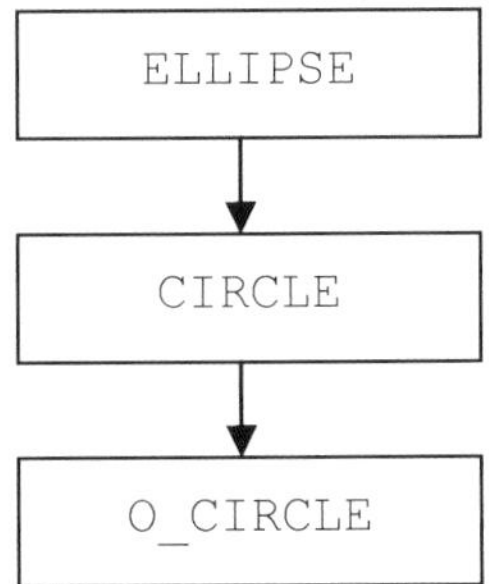

Fig. 2: Type hierarchy for ellipses, circles, and O-circles

```
TYPE ELLIPSE POSSREP { A LENGTH , B LENGTH , CTR POINT } ;

TYPE CIRCLE
     IS { ELLIPSE
          CONSTRAINT THE_A ( ELLIPSE ) = THE_B ( ELLIPSE )
          POSSREP { R   = THE_A   ( ELLIPSE ) ,
                    CTR = THE_CTR ( ELLIPSE ) } } ;

TYPE O_CIRCLE
     IS { CIRCLE
          CONSTRAINT THE_CTR ( CIRCLE ) = POINT ( 0.0 , 0.0 )
          POSSREP { R = THE_R ( CIRCLE ) } } ;
```

I'll refer to such a set of definitions as a *type schema*. Observe in particular that types CIRCLE and O_CIRCLE are defined by "constraining" types ELLIPSE and CIRCLE, respectively; type CIRCLE consists of ellipses that satisfy the constraint that their semiaxes *a* and *b* are equal, and type O_CIRCLE consists of circles that satisfy the constraint that their center is the origin. The definitions of these two types are thus in accordance with IM Prescription 10 ("Inheritance Model Prescription 10") of our inheritance model [2,5], which reads as follows (in outline):

> Let [scalar] type *T* be a regular type ... and let *T′* be a nonempty immediate subtype of *T*. Then the definition of *T′* shall specify a **specialization constraint** *SC*, formulated in terms of *T*, such that a value shall be of type *T′* if and only if it is of type *T* and it satisfies constraint *SC*.

(I'll explain just what that qualifier *regular* in the first line here means in the section "Union and Dummy Types," later.)

INTRODUCING PM_ TYPES

Under the PM_ scheme, we now need to add to the foregoing type schema the following PM_ counterparts of the three types:

- PM_ELLIPSE, consisting of all ellipses plus the value 'MISSING'[2]
- PM_CIRCLE, consisting of all circles plus the value 'MISSING' (the same 'MISSING' value, because there's supposed to be one such value for each root type)

---

[2] 'MISSING' is Smout's term; actually, however, we aren't going to need such a term at all, as we'll see.

- PM_O_CIRCLE, consisting of all O-circles plus the value 'MISSING' (again, the same 'MISSING' value)

Now, it should immediately be clear that:

- Type PM_ELLIPSE is a proper supertype of type ELLIPSE, because every value of type ELLIPSE is an ellipse and thus a value of type PM_ELLIPSE as well.
- Type PM_ELLIPSE is also a proper supertype of type PM_CIRCLE, because every value of type PM_CIRCLE is either 'MISSING' or a circle, and all such values are values of type PM_ELLIPSE as well.

Similarly, type PM_CIRCLE is a proper supertype of types CIRCLE and PM_O_CIRCLE. What's more, in the case of types PM_ELLIPSE and ELLIPSE in particular, there's precisely one value, 'MISSING', that's of the first of these two types and not of the second; as a consequence, it seems reasonable to make type PM_ELLIPSE, not just a proper supertype, but an immediate supertype, of type ELLIPSE.[3] And, of course, a similar remark applies to (a) types PM_CIRCLE and CIRCLE and (b) types PM_O_CIRCLE and O_CIRCLE. So the revised type schema can be depicted as shown in Fig. 3. As you can see, we aren't dealing with a simple hierarchy any longer but, rather, with a more general type *graph*.

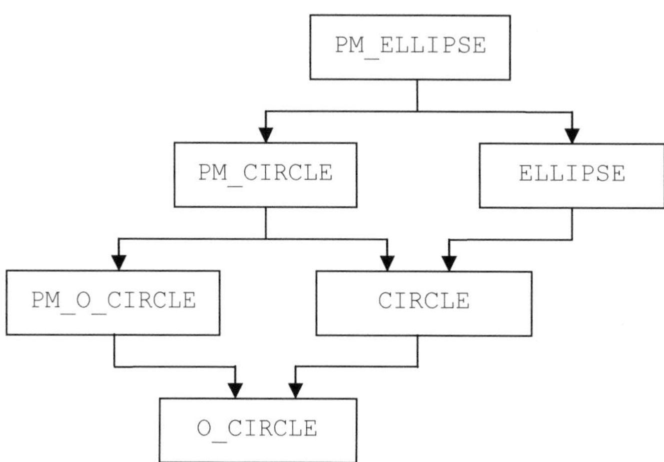

Fig. 3: Adding PM_ types to Fig. 2

As Fig. 3 makes clear, the PM_ idea thus immediately takes us into the realm of multiple inheritance: Types CIRCLE and O_CIRCLE each now have two immediate supertypes, instead of just the one they would have to have under single inheritance (that's why we aren't dealing with a simple type hierarchy any longer). Observe also that each of the three PM_ types contains just the value 'MISSING' in addition to the corresponding set of geometric values. So it seems like a good idea to introduce a new type, M, containing just that 'MISSING' value, and then to make that type a proper subtype of each of the PM_ types. Each of those PM_ types will then consist of the set theory union of M and the corresponding geometric type. Well, in fact, all we really have to do is make type M an immediate subtype of type PM_O_CIRCLE; then it'll automatically be a proper subtype of

---

[3] I say "it seems reasonable" because if type *T* is a supertype of type *T'* and *T* and *T'* are distinct, then we normally expect there to be at least one value that's of type *T* and not of type *T'*. If we follow this discipline, then there's no room (as it were) for another type to exist between types PM_ELLIPSE and ELLIPSE, and so those two types must be, as suggested, an immediate supertype and a corresponding immediate subtype, respectively.

types PM_CIRCLE and PM_ELLIPSE as well, because PM_O_CIRCLE is a proper subtype of PM_CIRCLE and PM_CIRCLE is a proper subtype of PM_ELLIPSE. See Fig. 4.

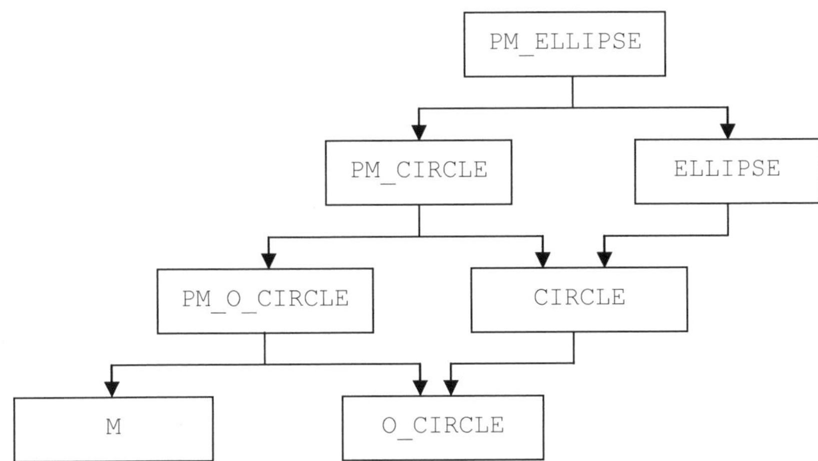

Fig. 4: Adding type M to Fig. 3

UNION AND DUMMY TYPES

I've said that each of the three PM_ types consists of the set theory union of type M and the corresponding geometric type. In our inheritance model, we explicitly refer to such a type—a type, that is, whose set of values is the set theory union of the sets of values constituting two or more other types—as a *union* type, and we explicitly declare it as such in the pertinent type schema. Thus, a union type has the important property that all of its values are in fact values of some proper subtype of the union type in question—there's no value that's just a value of that union type and not of any proper subtype of that union type. To spell the point out, therefore, note that a union type must have proper subtypes, by definition.

> *Aside:* Consider the specific union type PM_ELLIPSE, with its immediate subtypes PM_CIRCLE and ELLIPSE. Observe now that those two subtypes aren't disjoint—they have certain values in common: viz., those ellipses that happen to be circles. Now, it so happens that all of the examples of union types given in reference [2] are such that their immediate subtypes are disjoint; however, there's no requirement that this always be so, and in the case at hand it isn't. *End of aside.*

Since a union type "has no values of its own," as it were, it doesn't have to have a possrep (it's allowed to, but it doesn't have to). But a union type without a possrep isn't just a union type, it's what's called in our inheritance model a *dummy* type. In the example, therefore, we're within our rights to make the various PM_ types not just union types but, more specifically, dummy types. Observe, however, that since a dummy type has no possrep, it also has no selector or THE_ operators, and hence that this state of affairs applies to the various PM_ types in particular.

Incidentally, I can now take care of a small piece of unfinished business: I can explain that a *regular* type is, precisely, a type that's not a dummy type. Regular types do have selector and THE_ operators. Be that as it may, the interesting question is: If the various PM_ types are dummy types and thus have no selector or THE_ operators, then what operators do they have? In order to address this question, I first need to say a little more about type M.

Type M is what we might call a *singleton* type: It contains exactly one value. It's certainly not a dummy type, however (in fact, it's not a union type at all), because it has no proper subtypes; so it has to have a possrep. *But that possrep can, and I suggest should, be empty.* By definition, a type with an empty possrep contains exactly one value and is thus a singleton type, necessarily;[4] moreover, it has no THE_ operators. However, it does have a selector—which I'll assume for simplicity has the same name, M, as the type—and that selector is niladic and so returns the same value on every invocation. Hence, the value previously denoted 'MISSING' can now be denoted by the selector invocation M(). What's more, the IS_MISSING operator required by the PM_ scheme now becomes the IS_M operator required by IM Prescription 15—and that operator is available for use in connection with all of M's proper supertypes, which is to say in connection with all of the PM_ types in the example. Thus, we've conformed to Smout's requirements to the effect that:

> All the operators defined for [type xxx] apply only to ... type xxx itself, and not to type POSSIBLYMISSINGxxx. The only operator that does apply to type POSSIBLYMISSINGxxx is [the] operator IS_MISSING() ...

(Well, sort of conformed; actually, Smout's text overlooks the fact that the operators "=" and ":=" must be defined for *every* type, and PM_ types and type M are no exception, as we'll see in examples later.)

THE COMPLETE TYPE SCHEMA

Here then is the complete type schema, covering all seven types from Fig. 4. I'll elaborate on certain details of this type schema immediately following the definitions—except that I should say immediately that (for reasons of simplicity) I've omitted the various INIT specifications that the proposals of reference [6] would in fact require.

```
TYPE PM_ELLIPSE UNION ,

TYPE PM_CIRCLE UNION IS { PM_ELLIPSE } ,

TYPE ELLIPSE
     IS { PM_ELLIPSE
          POSSREP { A LENGTH , B LENGTH , CTR POINT } } ,

TYPE PM_O_CIRCLE UNION IS { PM_CIRCLE } ,

TYPE CIRCLE IS { PM_CIRCLE , ELLIPSE
                 POSSREP { R = THE_A ( ELLIPSE ) ,
                           CTR = THE_CTR ( ELLIPSE ) } } ,

TYPE O_CIRCLE IS { PM_O_CIRCLE , CIRCLE
                   POSSREP { R = THE_R ( CIRCLE ) } } ,

TYPE M IS { PM_O_CIRCLE POSSREP { } } ;
```

Explanation:

1. Observe first that (in accordance with proposals articulated in reference [4]) each type definition except the last now terminates in a comma instead of a semicolon, thereby converting the entire set of definitions into a single statement. The reason for this state of affairs is that no union type definition is complete until the necessary immediate subtypes have been completely defined as well.

2. Type PM_ELLIPSE is defined to be a union type; moreover, it has no possrep and is thus in fact a dummy type.

---

[4] More precisely, it's a type that contains *at most one* value—but since there aren't any empty user defined types (see RM Prescription 1), it must in fact be a singleton type.

3. Type PM_CIRCLE is also a dummy type and has no possrep, but it's defined to be an immediate subtype of type PM_ELLIPSE.

4. Type ELLIPSE is also an immediate subtype of type PM_ELLIPSE, but it's a regular type, and so it needs a possrep (consisting, as it happens, of the two semiaxes and the center).

5. Type PM_O_CIRCLE is also a dummy type and has no possrep, but it's defined to be an immediate subtype of type PM_CIRCLE.

6. Type CIRCLE is a regular type. It's also the first type (in order of definition) to have two distinct proper supertypes: viz., PM_CIRCLE and ELLIPSE. In fact, it's what references [2] and [5] call the corresponding *intersection* type: A value is a value of type CIRCLE if and only if it's a value of both of those supertypes—and that's what the IS specification says, in effect: A value is a CIRCLE value if and only if it's both a PM_CIRCLE value and an ELLIPSE value. No further constraint is needed, or allowed. However, type CIRCLE, being a regular type, does have to have a possrep, and so it does; to be specific, it has a *derived* possrep, defined in terms of a possrep for one of its supertypes.

7. The definition of type O_CIRCLE follows the same pattern as that for type CIRCLE.

8. Finally, the definition of type M has effectively already been explained.

SOME IMPLICATIONS OF THE FOREGOING

The PM_ scheme and our inheritance model have several additional interactions, or implications for each other, that might merit further investigation, and I'll say a little more about some of them later in this chapter. Before I do, however, I want to examine some of the implications of what we've covered so far for the practical problem of dealing with missing information as such. In order to do so, let me switch to a simpler example: viz., type INT (integers) and its immediate subtypes EVEN and ODD, with the obvious semantics. Fig. 5 shows the type graph (actually a hierarchy) before the introduction of the corresponding PM_ types; Fig. 6 overleaf shows the corresponding type graph after the PM_ types are introduced.

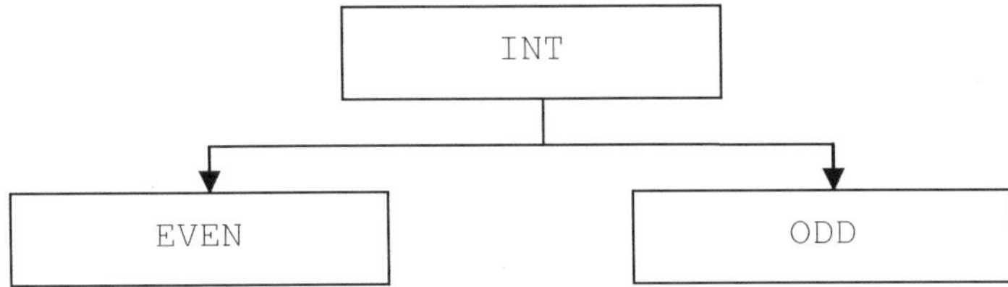

Fig. 5: Type graph for INT, EVEN, and ODD

As you can see, the type graph of Fig. 6 is considerably more complex than the simple type hierarchy of Fig. 5. Observe in particular that type PM_INT has three immediate subtypes, and each distinct pair of those subtypes has its own corresponding intersection type. *Note:* I'm assuming for simplicity that the "missing value" type in this example is still called M; recall, however, that the original idea was to have a distinct "missing value" for each root type (implying that, e.g., the "missing value" for ellipses and the "missing value" for integers would be distinct). I'll come back and revisit this point in the final section of this chapter.

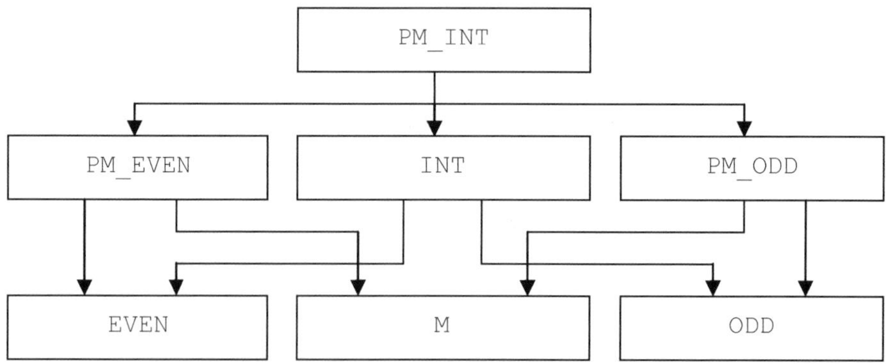

Fig. 6: Type graph for INT, EVEN, ODD and corresponding PM_ types

Now suppose we define scalar variables as follows:

```
VAR I INT ;
VAR E EVEN ;
VAR O ODD ;
VAR PI PM_INT ;
VAR PE PM_EVEN ;
VAR PO PM_ODD ;
```

Now let's consider a series of simple examples involving these variables.

1. *Set PI to the "missing value":*

```
PI := M ( ) ;
```

This assignment is legitimate thanks to *The Principle of Value Substitutability* [2,5]. To be specific, the declared type of the expression on the right side is M; the declared type of the variable on the left side is PM_INT; and the former is a subtype (a proper subtype, in fact, that happens not to be an immediate subtype) of the latter.

2. *Is PI equal to the "missing value"?*

```
IF PI = M ( ) ...
```

Or equivalently:

```
IF IS_M ( PI ) ...
```

3. *Set I to the "missing value":*

```
I := M ( ) ;
```

This assignment fails at compile time—the declared type of the "missing value" M() isn't a subtype of the declared type of the variable I.

4. *Set PI to the value of I:*

```
PI := I ;
```

Again the assignment is legitimate thanks to substitutability. After the assignment, IS_M(PI) will be

FALSE and IS_INT(PI) will be TRUE.

5. *Are the values of PI and I equal?*

```
IF PI = I ...
```

The comparison is legitimate thanks to substitutability.

6. *Is the value of PI greater than that of I?*

```
IF PI > I ...
```

This comparison fails at compile time; the operator ">" isn't available in connection with type PM_INT (the declared type of PI). By contrast, the following is legitimate:

```
CASE
   WHEN IS_INT ( PI ) THEN TREAT_AS_INT ( PI ) > I
   ELSE ...
END CASE
```

However, it's not clear what should appear in the ELSE clause—probably FALSE, I suppose (?).

7. *Set I to the value of PI plus one:*

```
CASE ;
   WHEN IS_INT ( PI ) THEN I := TREAT_AS_INT ( PI ) + 1 ;
   ELSE ... ;
END CASE ;
```

More generally, if *Op* is an operator that (like "+") is defined in terms of an integer parameter, we can't invoke *Op* with PI or PE or PO as the corresponding argument. (However, we can invoke it with I or E or O as that argument.)

8. *Are the values of E and O equal?*

```
IF E = O ...
```

This comparison fails at compile time; types E and O are disjoint, and the compiler is aware of this fact because they have no declared intersection type. The odd thing is, however, that the following comparison is not only legitimate, but could even give TRUE (since, by definition, types PM_EVEN and PM_ODD do have the same "missing value"):

```
IF PE = PO ...
```

Well, these examples do seem to suggest rather strongly that the PM_ scheme has nothing much to offer that makes it significantly superior to the conventional "special values" (or "default values") scheme as described in, e.g., reference [1]. For purposes of comparison, let me show what the examples would look like under this latter scheme. First of all, here are the variable definitions:

```
VAR I INT ;
VAR E EVEN ;
VAR O ODD ;
VAR PI INT_OR_UNK ;
VAR PE EVEN_OR_UNK ;
VAR PO ODD_OR_UNK ;
```

Note: "UNK" stands for *unknown;* thus, e.g., the type INT_OR_UNK consists of all integers plus the "unknown," or "missing," value (which is indeed a value, just as it is in the PM_ scheme, except that there's no notion that the UNK value for one type can or must be equal to the UNK value for another). For simplicity, I'll abbreviate INT_OR_UNK to just INTU below.

1. *Set PI to the "missing value":*

```
PI := UNK ( INTU ) ;
```

The expression UNK(*T*) denotes the unknown value that corresponds to—in fact, is a value of—type *T*.

2. *Is PI equal to the "missing value"?*

```
IF PI = UNK ( INTU ) ...
```

3. *Set I to the "missing value":* Can't be done.

4. *Set PI to the value of I:*

```
PI := CAST_AS_INTU ( I ) ;
```

We're not assuming that INT is a subtype of INTU; thus, substitutability doesn't apply, and explicit CASTs are sometimes needed.

5. *Are the values of PI and I equal?*

```
IF PI = CAST_AS_INTU ( I ) ...
```

6. *Is the value of PI greater than that of I?*

```
CASE
   WHEN IS_INT ( PI ) THEN CAST_AS_INT ( PI ) > I
   ELSE ...
END CASE
```

7. *Set I to the value of PI plus one:*

```
CASE ;
   WHEN IS_INT ( PI ) THEN I := CAST_AS_INT ( PI ) + 1 ;
   ELSE ... ;
END CASE ;
```

8. *Are the values of E and O equal?*

```
IF CAST_AS_INT ( E ) = CAST_AS_INT ( O ) ...
```

This comparison is legitimate but will presumably always give FALSE. (Of course, the comparison E = O will fail at compile time.)

The foregoing "special values" examples serve only to reinforce my feeling that the PM_ approach has little or nothing to offer that makes it obviously better than the special values scheme. What's more, I feel bound to add that:

- First, as already pointed out, the PM_ scheme relies (obviously enough) on support for the inheritance model. The special values scheme doesn't.
- Moreover, the PM_ scheme, at least as I've described it, is limited to dealing with just one kind of missing

information (one kind of "null," as the nulls advocates might put it). The special values scheme isn't.[5]

- In fact, the PM_ scheme overall seems to be excessively elaborate in comparison with the rather limited amount of gain it provides. I'm referring here to the complexity that the scheme introduces into the type schema (and hence into the corresponding type graph, of course). Now, it might be possible to automate some of the definitions and to hide some of that complexity—but the fact remains that the complexity is always there, at least conceptually, and needs to be understood by the user.

Now, please don't misunderstand me here: I'm certainly not arguing in favor of the special values scheme—I'm just trying to show that it appears to be at least as good as the PM_ scheme. That's all.

One final point to close this section: It might be thought that the PM_ scheme is at least well suited to the problem addressed by SQL's definition of referential integrity, according to which—I'm simplifying somewhat—a given referential constraint is regarded as satisfied if (but, of course, not only if) the corresponding foreign key value "is null." Let's investigate. First of all, let relvars DEPT (departments) and EMP (employees) be defined as follows:

```
VAR DEPT BASE RELATION
  { DEPT# DEPT# , DNAME NAME , BUDGET MONEY }
    KEY { DEPT# } ;

VAR EMP BASE RELATION
  { EMP# EMP# , ENAME NAME , DEPT# DEPT# , SALARY MONEY }
    KEY { EMP# }
    FOREIGN KEY { DEPT# } REFERENCES DEPT ;
```

Also, let types DEPT# (department numbers) and EMP# (employee numbers) be conventional—no PM_ types yet. However, assume that type PM_DEPT# does exist (i.e., it's been defined somehow, either explicitly by some human user or perhaps implicitly by the system); and assume now that we want the foreign key constraint to be satisfied for an EMP tuple in which the department number has the "missing value" M(). Clearly, then, we'll have to revise the definition of relvar EMP to change the type of attribute DEPT# to PM_DEPT# in order to allow that attribute to take on that "missing value":

```
VAR EMP BASE RELATION
  { EMP# EMP# , ENAME NAME , DEPT# PM_DEPT# , SALARY MONEY }
    KEY { EMP# }
    FOREIGN KEY { DEPT# } REFERENCES DEPT ;
```

Now the DEPT# attributes in relvars DEPT and EMP, respectively, are (obviously enough) of different types. The comparison between them that's implied by the FOREIGN KEY specification is legitimate nevertheless, because at least it's the case that one of those types is a subtype of the other.[6] However, that comparison will give FALSE for an EMP tuple in which the DEPT# value is M()—and yet the object of the exercise was to get TRUE in this case.

---

[5] It's true, however, that as more and more kinds of missing information are involved, the special values scheme (which is quite ugly to begin with) gets uglier and uglier very quickly; but I venture to guess the same would be true if we tried to extend the PM_ scheme correspondingly.

[6] It follows in particular that the expression EMP JOIN DEPT is still legal.

TENTATIVE CONCLUSIONS

Frankly, I don't think the PM_ scheme is worth pursuing much further. As a matter of fact I did take a look at the other major example from reference [2], the rectangles and rhombuses example,[7] but it didn't lead to any additional insights. For the record, however, I'll just show the corresponding type graph (see Fig. 7).

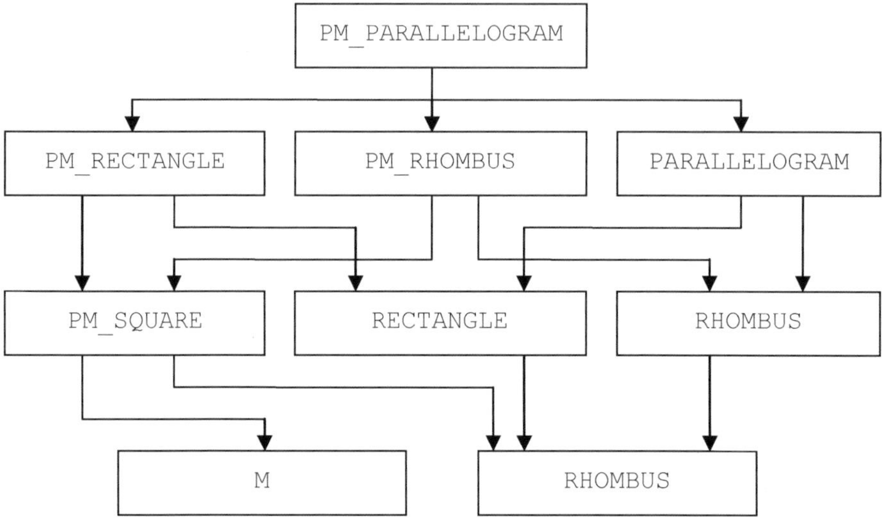

Fig. 7: Type graph for rectangles and rhombuses

Perhaps I should state for the record that:

- A rectangle is a parallelogram with equal angles (actually right angles).
- Some parallelograms aren't rectangles.
- A rhombus is a parallelogram with equal sides.
- Some parallelograms aren't rhombuses.
- A square is a parallelogram that's both a rectangle and a rhombus.
- Some rectangles aren't squares.
- Some rhombuses aren't squares.

Even without the introduction of any PM_ types, therefore, the rectangles and rhombuses example illustrates the concepts of multiple inheritance.

I also took a look at the question of what the PM_ scheme implied for nonscalar types—more specifically, for tuple and relation types—but again I don't think it's worth discussing the details here. I will, however, briefly discuss one further issue that's raised by the PM_ scheme, even if we limit our attention just to scalar types.

---

[7] Yes, I know the usual plural is *rhombi*. I prefer *rhombuses*.

HOW MANY "MISSING VALUES" DO WE NEED?

Recall that the original idea in reference [7] was that there should be a separate PM_ type for each root type, "*alpha* notwithstanding":

> [If] types xxx and yyy do not have a common supertype (*alpha* notwithstanding), then neither do the types POSSIBLYMISSINGxxx and POSSIBLYMISSINGyyy.

Well, it's certainly true that a "PM_*alpha*" type would be a contradiction in terms—by definition, type *alpha* contains all scalar values, so the idea of a type that contains all values in *alpha* plus some additional value (the "missing" value) makes no sense.[8] Indeed, reference [5] states explicitly that type *alpha* "shall have no immediate supertypes."

Now, it would of course be possible to have a distinct "missing value" associated with each type that's an immediate subtype of type *alpha*. However, the sole advantage I see to adopting this idea is that it implies that, e.g., a "missing circle" and a "missing square" will probably be distinct, a state of affairs that I suppose accords well with intuition. But then the idea that a missing circle and a missing square might be equal will show up only on a comparison between values of type PM_CIRCLE and PM_SQUARE, and it's hard to imagine anyone wanting to perform such a comparison anyway. And I think the comparative simplicity of having "the same missing value everywhere" outweighs that small conceptual disadvantage (i.e., that missing circles and missing squares might not be distinct). If the PM_ scheme is adopted, therefore, I would expect there to be just a single "missing value" type M, and I would expect that type to be a proper subtype of type *alpha* and of every PM_ type[9]—in fact, a leaf type.

REFERENCES AND BIBLIOGRAPHY

1. C. J. Date: "Faults and Defaults" (in five parts), in *Relational Database Writings 1994-1997.* Reading, Mass.: Addison-Wesley (1998).

2. C. J. Date and Hugh Darwen: *Databases, Types, and the Relational Model: The Third Manifesto* (3rd edition). Boston, Mass.: Addison-Wesley (2006).

3. C. J. Date and Hugh Darwen: "*The Third Manifesto*" (Chapter 1 of the present book). See also Chapter 4 of reference [2].

4. C. J. Date and Hugh Darwen: "**Tutorial D**" (Chapter 11 of the present book). See also Chapter 5 of reference [2].

5. C. J. Date and Hugh Darwen: "The Inheritance Model" (Chapter 19 of the present book). See also Part IV of reference [2] and Chapter 20 of the present book.

6. C. J. Date and Hugh Darwen: "Extending **Tutorial D** to Support the Inheritance Model" (Chapter 21 of the present book).

---

[8] Unless that "missing" value isn't a scalar value, I suppose. As I've already indicated, however, I don't propose to discuss that possibility here.

[9] And a proper supertype of type *omega,* incidentally. Note that a "PM_*omega*" type would almost certainly be another contradiction in terms, because the only value a variable of that type could have would be the "missing value"!

7. Erwin Smout: "How to Handle Missing Information without Using Nulls," *ttm@thethirdmanifesto.com* (February 20th, 2008).

Chapter 26

An Approach Using Relation Valued Attributes

Empty vessels make the most noise.

—15th century proverb

Over the years it has often been suggested that the fact that some piece of information is missing (for whatever reason) could be represented by means of the empty set—or rather, given that we're operating in a relational context, by means of a suitable empty relation. As far as we know, however, nobody had worked out in detail just what would be needed to implement such an approach, until recently—but now somebody has. To be specific, we now have a database prototype called Muldis Rosetta, with its user language Muldis D, that supports just such a scheme.[1] In this chapter, therefore, we use Muldis D as a basis for considering how certain pertinent ideas from that language might be realized in **Tutorial D**. We also consider, briefly, some shorthands and other possible extensions that might be incorporated into **Tutorial D** in support of the approach.

THE RUNNING EXAMPLE

Fig. 1 overleaf shows some sample values for our usual relvars S ("suppliers") and SP ("shipments"). The figure is basically a repeat of Fig. 1 from Chapter 24; however, its meaning here is different. It's true that the blank cells in the tables still denote "missing information," as they did in Chapter 24, and it's therefore also true as it was in Chapter 24 that those tables don't denote relations—at least, not in the usual way. But while this latter observation in particular was true of Fig. 1 in Chapter 24 as well, it was true for very different reasons (refer to that chapter for the specifics).

By way of example, consider the blank STATUS cell in Fig. 1 in the row in table S for supplier S4. If we're to think of that cell as containing an empty relation, *e* say, then every other STATUS cell must also contain a relation, and furthermore all of those relations must be of the same type as that empty relation *e*—because it's of the essence of what a relation is that the values of any given attribute must all be of the same type. In other words, the declared type of attribute STATUS must be, not just INTEGER (or INT) as it usually is, but rather some relation type *RT,* where that relation type *RT* has just one attribute and that attribute in turn *is* of declared type INTEGER (or INT). And then the value of that attribute, in any given tuple, will be a relation of type *RT,* and that relation will be of cardinality either zero, if "the status value is missing," or one otherwise (in which case the sole tuple in the relation will contain the pertinent status value). And, of course, similar remarks apply to every attribute for which "blank cells" (missing values) are allowed—i.e., to attributes SNAME, STATUS, CITY, and QTY, in our running example.

---

[1] Darren Duncan: "Muldis Rosetta," *http://www.muldis.com.*

S

S#	SNAME	STATUS	CITY
S1	Smith	20	London
S2	Jones	10	Paris
S3	Blake	30	
S4	Clark		London
S5	Adams	30	Athens
S6			Rome
S7			

SP

S#	P#	QTY
S1	P1	300
S1	P2	200
S2	P1	
S3	P2	200
S4	P4	

Fig. 1: Suppliers and shipments—sample values

Now, it's clear that the scheme under discussion is going to involve lots of unary relations of cardinality either one or zero.[2] Thus, it's useful to have a distinguishing name for relations that satisfy this description, at least for present purposes. We can take the time later to come up with a better term, if we think the approach worth pursuing; for now, however, we propose to use the term "ZOO relation"—ZOO for "cardinality Zero or One, degree One." And in keeping with this terminology, we'll refer to the approach overall as "the ZOO approach" from this point forward.

Back to the example. As already indicated, we're going to replace attributes SNAME, STATUS, CITY, and QTY by certain relation valued attributes. To avoid confusion, let's call those relation valued attributes Z_SNAME, Z_STATUS, Z_CITY, and Z_QTY, respectively. Let's also agree to call the suppliers and shipments relvars, with their "Z attributes," ZS and ZSP, respectively. Then the **Tutorial D** definitions for these relvars might look like this:

```
VAR ZS BASE RELATION
  { S# S# ,
    Z_SNAME  RELATION { SNAME  NAME } ,
    Z_STATUS RELATION { STATUS INT  } ,
    Z_CITY   RELATION { CITY   CHAR } }
    KEY { S# } ;

VAR ZSP BASE RELATION
  { S# S# , P# P# , Z_QTY RELATION { QTY INT }
    KEY { S# , P# } ;
```

We've adopted the convention that each "Z attribute" is of declared type RELATION {*A T*}, where *A* is the name of the corresponding attribute in our usual relvar S or SP (as applicable) and *T* is the declared type of that attribute *A*. Thus, e.g., attributes Z_STATUS and Z_QTY are of declared types RELATION {STATUS INT} and RELATION {QTY INT}, respectively.[3] Fig. 2 opposite shows a sample value for relvar ZSP corresponding to the shipments sample value from Fig. 1 (we omit relvar ZS for reasons of space).

---

[2] Therefore the only key constraint they satisfy is that denoted by KEY { }, which explains the absence of double underlining in our tabular pictures of such relations.

[3] Elsewhere in this book quantities are defined to be of type QTY. We've changed the type to INT here purely in order to simplify some of the examples later in the chapter.

ZSP

S#	P#	Z_QTY
S1	P1	QTY 300
S1	P2	QTY 200
S2	P1	QTY
S3	P2	QTY 200
S4	P4	QTY

Fig. 2: Shipments with "missing quantities"

However, the foregoing definitions are inadequate as they stand—certain cardinality constraints are needed as well, in order to guarantee that every value of every Z attribute is indeed a ZOO relation (i.e., a relation of degree one—which of course it is, by definition—and cardinality at most one). For example, we clearly mustn't allow a supplier to have more than one name or a shipment to have more than one quantity. Note that such constraints are enforced trivially in the case of our usual relvars S and SP (because {S#} is a key for S and {S#,P#} is a key for SP), but for our revised relvars ZS and ZSP we need to be more explicit:

```
CONSTRAINT AT_MOST_ONE_NAME_PER_SUPPLIER
   IS_EMPTY ( ZS WHERE COUNT ( Z_SNAME ) > 1 ) ;

CONSTRAINT AT_MOST_ONE_STATUS_PER_SUPPLIER
   IS_EMPTY ( ZS WHERE COUNT ( Z_STATUS > 1 ) ;

CONSTRAINT AT_MOST_ONE_CITY_PER_SUPPLIER
   IS_EMPTY ( ZS WHERE COUNT ( Z_CITY ) > 1 ) ;

CONSTRAINT AT_MOST_ONE_QTY_PER_SHIPMENT
   IS_EMPTY ( ZSP WHERE COUNT ( Z_QTY ) > 1 ) ;
```

We now proceed to consider what queries, updates, and constraints might look like given the foregoing design.

QUERIES

First a general point: Given that supplier status values are now represented by relations instead of integers, even a simple application program request to retrieve, say, supplier S1's status requires either (a) a target variable within the application that's a relation variable specifically, or (b) a target variable that's an integer variable, plus a slightly complicated piece of processing to extract the desired status value from the pertinent relation before assigning it to that integer variable. And in case (b), we also have to worry about the possibility that supplier S1 might not have a status value, anyway.

Be that as it may, we turn now our attention to some more complicated query examples. We assume where it makes any difference that relvars ZS and ZSP have values corresponding to tables S and SP as shown in Fig. 1. We also assume the availability of support for certain extensions to **Tutorial D** (specifically, image relations and enhanced aggregate operator invocations) as described in Chapter 16.

Example 1: Get shipments having quantities greater than 200.

```
( ZSP UNGROUP ( Z_QTY ) ) WHERE QTY > 200
```

Result:

S#	P#	QTY
S1	P1	300

The effect of the UNGROUP, broadly speaking, is (a) to eliminate ZSP tuples where the Z_QTY value is empty and (b) to derive, from each remaining ZSP tuple, a tuple obtained by replacing the Z_QTY relation within that ZSP tuple by the QTY value contained in that Z_QTY relation.

Here's an alternative formulation, avoiding the use of UNGROUP:

```
( EXTEND ZSP WHERE IS_NOT_EMPTY ( Z_QTY ) :
       { QTY := QTY FROM TUPLE FROM Z_QTY } )
             WHERE QTY > 200 ) { ALL BUT Z_QTY }
```

Example 2: For each city in which there is at least one supplier, get the average status of suppliers in that city.

The problem here is that some cities might have suppliers with no status (Rome/S6 and London/S4 are cases in point, given our specified sample values). If we just want to ignore such city/supplier combinations, a suitable formulation is:

```
WITH ( T1 := ( ZS UNGROUP ( Z_CITY ) ) UNGROUP ( Z_STATUS ) ) :
     EXTEND T1 { CITY } :
          { AVG_STATUS := AVG ( !!T1 , STATUS ) }
```

Observe that (a) if T1 is nonempty, the expression AVG(!!T1,STATUS) is guaranteed to have a nonempty relation argument, and (b) if T1 *is* empty, that expression will never be evaluated anyway. Thus, the result of the expression overall is:

CITY	AVG_STATUS
London	20
Paris	10
Athens	30

On the other hand, we might want to treat suppliers with no status as having a status of zero:

```
WITH ( T1 := ZS UNGROUP ( Z_CITY ) ) :
     EXTEND T1 { CITY } :
          { AVG_STATUS := AVG ( !!T1 , SUM ( Z_STATUS ) ) }
```

Given that, within any given tuple of T1, the Z_STATUS value is a relation of cardinality either one or zero, the expression SUM(Z_STATUS) will return either the sole STATUS value contained in that relation or zero, respectively. The result of the expression overall is:

CITY	AVG_STATUS
London	20
Paris	10
Athens	30
Rome	0

Example 3: Get details of suppliers for whom all possible information is available.

```
( ( ZS UNGROUP ( Z_SNAME ) )
               UNGROUP ( Z_STATUS ) )
                       UNGROUP ( Z_CITY )
```

Result:

S#	SNAME	STATUS	CITY
S1	Smith	20	London
S2	Jones	10	Paris

Example 4: Get supplier numbers for suppliers for whom we have no names.

```
( ZS WHERE IS_EMPTY ( Z_SNAME ) ) { S# }
```

Result:

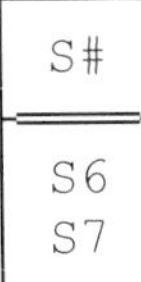

S#
S6
S7

CONSTRAINTS

Example 5: Let relvar CC have attributes CITY and COUNTRY, giving for each city the country in which it is located. Define a "foreign key" constraint to the effect that all CITY values appearing (indirectly) in ZS must appear as CITY values in CC.

For interest we show two distinct formulations:

```
CONSTRAINT FK_CITY
   AND ( ZS , IS_EMPTY ( Z_CITY NOT MATCHING CC ) ) ;

CONSTRAINT FK_CITY
 ( ZS UNGROUP ( Z_CITY ) ) { CITY } ⊆ CC { CITY } ;
```

UPDATES

Example 6: Assuming that supplier S1 is represented in relvar ZS, set that supplier's status to 30.

```
UPDATE ZS WHERE S# = S#('S1') :
     { Z_STATUS := RELATION { TUPLE { STATUS 30 } } } ;
```

Example 7: Add 10 to the status of every supplier in Paris who currently has a status.

```
UPDATE ZS WHERE IS_NOT_EMPTY ( Z_CITY WHERE CITY = 'Paris' ) :
   { UPDATE Z_STATUS : { STATUS := STATUS + 10 } } ;
```

We remark that the IS_NOT_EMPTY invocation in the WHERE clause here could be replaced by either of the following boolean expressions:

```
PM_CITY = RELATION { TUPLE { CITY 'Paris' } }

{ TUPLE { CITY 'Paris' } } ∈ PM_CITY
```

Example 8: Set every supplier's status to "missing."

```
UPDATE ZS : { DELETE Z_STATUS } ;
```

SOME POSSIBLE SHORTHANDS

In this section, we investigate the possibility of introducing certain shorthands into **Tutorial D** that might help simplify the formulation of examples like the ones discussed in previous sections. Please note, however, that the suggestions that follow should not be taken too seriously at this time; indeed, the whole of this chapter—like others in this part of the book—is offered only as a preliminary investigation, nothing more. (On the other hand, we've tried to design the shorthands in such a way as to make at least some of them worthwhile for other purposes too, even if we reject the ZOO approach as such.)

Z Attribute Definition

Let's assume we wish to continue to adhere to the "Z attribute" naming convention we've been using throughout the chapter so far. In other words (and speaking rather loosely), if relvar *R* has an attribute *A* for which values might be "missing," and attribute *A* is of declared type *T*, then we will replace *R* by a relvar in which the corresponding attribute is called Z_*A* and is of declared type RELATION {*A T*}. Let's also assume for simplicity that no other attributes (i.e., no attributes that aren't "Z attributes") have names of this form. Then we could allow an abbreviated form of definition for such attributes as in this example (part of the definition of relvar ZSP):

```
Z_ATTR ( QTY INT )
```

This construct would be defined to be shorthand for:

```
Z_QTY RELATION { QTY INT }
```

In fact, we might make such a shorthand work even harder for us. Recall the following cardinality constraint ("no shipment has more than one quantity"):

```
CONSTRAINT AT_MOST_ONE_QTY_PER_SHIPMENT
   IS_EMPTY ( ZSP WHERE COUNT ( Z_QTY ) > 1 ) ;
```

In other words, no relation that's the value of attribute Z_QTY has more than one tuple. Now, if we want to constrain some *relvar* never to have more than one tuple, we can do so very easily by specifying the empty set as a key for that relvar.[4] Well, if we're allowed to include a KEY specification as part of a relvar definition, then perhaps we might reasonably be allowed to include a KEY specification as part of the definition of a relation valued attribute, as here—

```
Z_QTY RELATION { QTY INT } KEY { }
```

—with the obvious (?) interpretation. And then we might define this entire construct to be the longhand form of the proposed Z attribute definition

```
Z_ATTR ( QTY INT )
```

(thereby obviating the need for an explicit cardinality constraint).[5]

In fact, however, including a KEY specification as part of the definition of a relation valued attribute is explicitly *not* allowed by the *Manifesto* book (i.e., *Databases, Types, and the Relational Model: The Third Manifesto,* 3rd edition, by C. J. Date and Hugh Darwen, Addison-Wesley, 2006), for reasons explained therein. But even if such remains the case, we could perhaps still consider the Z attribute definition Z_ATTR(*A T*) to be shorthand for the attribute definition Z_*A* RELATION{*A T*} together with an appropriate constraint definition of the form IS_EMPTY(*R* WHERE COUNT(*A*) > 1), where *R* is the pertinent relvar.

Relation Selector Invocations

To recap, a ZOO relation is a unary relation of cardinality either one or zero, and the ZOO approach involves lots of such relations (though obviously they can occur in other contexts as well). As a direct consequence, the ZOO approach in particular will often have a need for relation selector invocations that denote such relations. For example, consider the following extended definition for relvar ZSP, in which we've included an INIT specification to initialize the relvar to the value shown in Fig. 2. (Note that we're making use of the Z attribute definition shorthand introduced in the previous subsection.)

---

[4] In case you're not familiar with this trick, see Hugh Darwen's paper "The Nullologist in Relationland," in C. J. Date and Hugh Darwen, *Relational Database Writings 1989-1991* (Addison-Wesley, 1992).

[5] On the other hand, it might be a little risky to have Z_ATTR imply the corresponding constraint. **Tutorial D** allows the declared type of a variable to be implied by the corresponding INIT specification (assuming such a specification is present, of course). But specifying the declared type for a relvar implicitly in this way could mean the loss of some constraints, if that relvar involves any Z attributes.

```
VAR ZSP BASE RELATION
  { S# S# , P# P# , Z_QTY ( QTY INT ) }
  INIT ( RELATION
  { TUPLE { S# S#('S1') , P# P#('P1') ,
                          Z_QTY RELATION { TUPLE { QTY 300 } } } ,
    TUPLE { S# S#('S1') , P# P#('P2') ,
                          Z_QTY RELATION { TUPLE { QTY 200 } } } ,
    TUPLE { S# S#('S2') , P# P#('P1') ,
                          Z_QTY RELATION { QTY INT } { } } } ,
    TUPLE { S# S#('S3') , P# P#('P2') ,
                          Z_QTY RELATION { TUPLE { QTY 200 } } } ,
    TUPLE { S# S#('S4') , P# P#('P4') ,
                          Z_QTY RELATION { QTY INT } { } } } )
  KEY { S# , P# } ;
```

As you can see, this definition involves unary relation selector invocations of two basic forms, of which the following are exemplars:

```
RELATION { TUPLE { QTY 300 } }    /* cardinality one */

RELATION { QTY INT } { }          /* cardinality zero */
```

(If the relation in question is empty, **Tutorial D** requires us to specify the heading. If it's not empty, specification of the heading is optional.)

Given the frequency with which such relation selector invocations will be needed—not just in the context under discussion—the possibility of introducing more shorthands seems worth investigating. So let's agree to define the expression

```
Z_REL ( A x )
```

to be shorthand for

```
RELATION { TUPLE { A x } }
```

Likewise, let's agree to define the expression

```
Z_REL { H } ( )
```

to be shorthand for

```
RELATION { H } { }
```

(We note in passing that this latter shorthand would work for empty relations of arbitrary degree, not just for empty relations of degree one.) Then we can simplify the foregoing definition for relvar ZSP slightly as follows:

```
VAR ZSP BASE RELATION
  { S# S# , P# P# , Z_QTY ( QTY INT ) }
  INIT ( RELATION
    { TUPLE { S# S#('S1') , P# P#('P1') ,
                            Z_QTY Z_REL ( QTY 300 ) } ,
      TUPLE { S# S#('S1') , P# P#('P2') ,
                            Z_QTY Z_REL ( QTY 200 ) } ,
      TUPLE { S# S#('S2') , P# P#('P1') ,
                            Z_QTY Z_REL { QTY INT } ( ) ,
      TUPLE { S# S#('S3') , P# P#('P2') ,
                            Z_QTY Z_REL ( 200 ) } ,
      TUPLE { S# S#('S4') , P# P#('P4') ,
                            Z_QTY Z_REL { QTY INT } ( ) } } )
  KEY { S# , P# } ;
```

Likewise, the formulation we gave earlier for Example 6 could be simplified slightly too:

```
UPDATE ZS WHERE S# = S#('S1') :
     { Z_STATUS := Z_REL ( STATUS 30 ) } ;
```

Attribute Value Extraction

Our second formulation for Example 2 made use of the following aggregate operator invocation:

```
SUM ( Z_STATUS )
```

If the relation denoted by Z_STATUS contains just a single tuple (containing in turn a single status value), the effect of this expression is to return that status value. But this use of SUM is slightly obscure, and really little more than a trick, in a sense. Indeed, it's strange that we have operators that can directly "aggregate" the values of some attribute of some relation, but no operator that can simply and directly return the value of some attribute of some relation, in the special case where there's just one such value. Rather, the best we can currently do by way of such an operator is something like the following:

```
STATUS FROM ( TUPLE FROM ( Z_STATUS ) )
```

(The parentheses here are unnecessary but are included for clarity.)

Not only is this kind of expression slightly longwinded, but we also have to know the name (STATUS, in the example) of the sole attribute of the tuple from which the value is being extracted (observe that we *don't* need to know such names with operators like SUM—at least, not always). So let's invent a new operator, patterned after SUM, called XVF ("extract value from"), with syntax as follows:

```
XVF ( <relation exp> [ , <exp> ] )
```

The semantics are as follows: Let the relation denoted by *<relation exp>* be *r*. If *r* is of cardinality one, then *<exp>* is evaluated on the sole tuple of *r* and its value is returned; otherwise an exception is raised. The *<exp>* can be omitted if and only if *r* is of degree one.

Given the availability of this operator, our second formulation for Example 1 could be reformulated thus:

```
( EXTEND ZSP WHERE IS_NOT_EMPTY ( Z_QTY ) :
       { QTY := XVF ( Z_QTY ) } )
            WHERE QTY > 200 ) { ALL BUT Z_QTY }
```

To return to Example 2 and the expression SUM(Z_STATUS): Of course, part of the point of using SUM in that example was to obtain a zero if the relation denoted by Z_STATUS happened to be empty, and the XVF operator as defined above doesn't help with this problem—in fact, the expression XVF(Z_STATUS) will raise an exception in this case. But why not extend the definition of that operator to take care of the empty case as well? The following syntax should work:

```
XVF ( <relation exp> [ , <exp> ] [ : <alt exp> ] )
```

Now if the relation denoted by *<relation exp>* is empty, the XVF invocation returns the value of *<alt exp>*. Using this extended version of XVF, our second formulation for Example 2 can be revised thus:

```
WITH ( T1 := ZS UNGROUP ( Z_CITY ) ) :
     EXTEND T1 { CITY } :
          { AVG_STATUS := AVG ( !!T1 , XVF ( Z_STATUS : 0 ) ) }
```

A Note on Aggregate Operators

OO Prescription 6 of *The Third Manifesto* (see Chapter 1 of the present book) states that if an aggregate operator is applied to an empty relation and no appropriate identity value exists, then the result of the aggregation is undefined. But we could extend the device introduced in connection with XVF in the preceding subsection to apply to such aggregate operators, too. For example, the expression

```
AVG ( S , STATUS : 0 )
```

could be defined to return zero if relvar S is currently empty.

COULD SUBTYPING HELP?

Recall our proposal that, e.g., the attribute definition

```
Z_ATTR ( QTY INT )
```

might be taken as shorthand for

```
Z_QTY RELATION { QTY INT }
```

together with a certain constraint definition (perhaps an explicit KEY specification, perhaps a separate CONSTRAINT statement). Muldis D, however, adopts a rather different approach to the constraint part of this issue. In our terms, the type of the implied attribute Z_QTY in Muldis D wouldn't just be RELATION {QTY INT}; rather, it would be a certain subtype of that type—namely, the subtype consisting of all relations of type RELATION {QTY INT} that have cardinality either zero or one (in other words, all ZOO relations of that type). Thus, the required constraint on Z_QTY values would be implied by their type, and no additional constraint is needed.

Now, this idea is in keeping with our inheritance model inasmuch as we do at least define subtypes in general by constraining supertypes—see Chapter 19 of this book, IM Prescription 10—and that's basically what Muldis D is doing here. However, in the case of a relation type in particular (*RT,* say), the only subtypes our model recognizes are those that arise, implicitly and necessarily, from the existence of subtypes of the types of the attributes in terms of which *RT* is defined (again see Chapter 19, IM Prescription 22). We provide no explicit means of defining relation subtypes in any other way. One important reason why we exclude other ways has to do with relation type names and relation type inferencing; another has to do with the complications that would arise from the interactions between subtypes that implicitly and necessarily exist and those that were explicitly defined (if this latter were possible). It follows that if we were to adopt the Muldis D scheme, we would have to make certain changes or extensions to our inheritance model. Thus, while that scheme might eventually prove to be sound and useful, and while those changes or extensions might likewise prove sound and useful, we feel more study is needed at this time.

RECORDING REASONS FOR INFORMATION BEING MISSING

Information can be missing for many different reasons. The ZOO approach as so far described does not cater for the recording of such reasons, however, and nor does Muldis D's approach. Here we offer just a preliminary thought as to how the ZOO approach might be extended to include such recording.

Consider relvar ZSP, where quantity information is allowed to be missing. If we want to be able to record the reason why, the obvious approach is simply to add an appropriate attribute:

```
VAR ZSP BASE RELATION
  { S# S# , P# P# , Z_ATTR ( QTY INT ) , REASON_QTY CHAR }
    KEY { S# , P# } ;
```

(Of course, in relvar ZS we would need three such attributes: REASON_SNAME, REASON_STATUS, and REASON_CITY.)

Now, a REASON_QTY value will clearly be required if and only if "the corresponding QTY value is missing" (i.e., the corresponding Z_QTY relation is empty); if a QTY value is present, the corresponding REASON_QTY value must somehow be absent. Perhaps the empty character string could stand for an absent reason; but in the spirit of the ZOO approach we should surely be representing "missing" reasons by an empty relation. So the declared type for REASON_QTY should really be RELATION {REASON_QTY CHAR}, and its attribute name should really be Z_REASON_QTY. What's more, we will need the following additional constraint:

```
CONSTRAINT REASON_QTY_PRESENT_IFF_QTY_ABSENT
   AND ( ZSP , IS_EMPTY ( Z_QTY ) XOR IS_EMPTY ( Z_REASON_QTY ) ) ;
```

Perhaps another shorthand could be provided for use when we want to record reasons. For example, perhaps the definition of relvar ZSP could be reduced to something like this:

```
VAR ZSP BASE RELATION
  { S# S# , P# P# , Z_ATTR_WITH_REASON ( QTY INT ) }
    KEY { S# , P# } ;
```

The idea is that the addition of _WITH_REASON to a Z_ATTR specification implies the definition of a systematically named reason attribute and the constraint that goes with it.

CONCLUDING REMARKS

We have shown how an approach to missing information using relation valued attributes ("the ZOO approach") can be made to work within the confines of the relational model as defined in Chapter 1. Thus, it could be adopted in, e.g., **Tutorial D** without any additions to the language. If it *is* adopted, however, then certain shorthands, along the lines of those we have tentatively suggested, will probably be desired. A further small improvement might also be obtained if subtyping is supported; however, this latter possibility requires further investigation.

One final thought: The ZOO approach works for attributes of any type. That means it works for relation valued attributes in particular. And that means it "works" for Z attributes! The reader might (or might not) care to ponder the possible uses—or lack thereof—for attributes such as Z_Z_STATUS and Z_Z_Z_QTY.

Chapter 27

Is SQL's Three-Valued Logic Truth Functionally Complete?

The answer is maybe (what else?)

This chapter consists of a major revision and expansion of a paper I originally wrote in the early 1990s [5]. As its title suggests, my aim is to investigate whether SQL, considered as a logical system, is truth functionally complete; in other words, does SQL support, directly or indirectly, all possible logical connectives? It turns out that the answer to this question is *maybe* ... It's definitely *yes* if (a) the BOOLEAN data type as defined in the SQL standard [12] is supported and (b) that support can be considered to include support for what's called the Slupecki T-function [15]; otherwise it seems to be *no*.

Now, SQL is based, as is well known, on three-valued logic (3VL for short); the claim is that 3VL provides a good basis for addressing the so called "missing information" problem. As you'll know if you've read any of my writings on this subject (see, e.g., references [2-4], [6], and [8]), I don't agree with this claim at all. But in any case my aim in this chapter is not so much to discuss the "missing information" problem as such; rather, what I want to do, as I've already said, is conduct an investigation into the precise nature of SQL's logical underpinnings in general. That's all.

First of all, then, as noted in the first paragraph above, the SQL standard does support an explicit BOOLEAN data type;[1] what's more, under a slightly charitable interpretation of that standard, that support does include support for the Slupecki T-function. Thus, it might be possible to say that the standard as such is truth functionally complete. Whether the same can be said of specific SQL implementations is another matter, however; partly because of this state of affairs, therefore, all references to SQL in the remainder of this chapter must be understood as referring to the standard dialect of that language, barring explicit statements to the contrary.

Why is truth functional completeness desirable? Well, to quote reference [14]:

> The connectives [supported by] the query language should suffice to express every connective definable by means of some truth table [*that is, the language should be truth functionally complete*]. In other words, for every possible fact in the universe of discourse, there should be a truth valued expression that determines whether that fact is represented in or can be derived from the database.

I remark that the phrase "possible fact" here might better be "proposition"—facts are usually taken to be true by definition, but propositions can be either true or false [9]. Be that as it may, here's another quote, from reference [13] this time:

> Truth functional completeness is an extremely important property; a logical system that didn't satisfy it would be like a system of arithmetic that had no support for certain operations, say the operation of addition.[2]

Suppose SQL were not truth functionally complete. Then there would exist a nonempty set of connectives

---

[1] Though I'm not aware of any commercial product that does, at the time of writing.

[2] Following up on this point, incidentally, reference [14] has this to say (slightly edited here): "Contrary to Codd's position on this issue as articulated in reference [2], the number of distinct logical connectives in a truth functionally complete logic isn't analogous to the infinite number of distinct arithmetic functions that can be defined in ordinary arithmetic. Instead, it's analogous to the number of distinct operations (e.g., addition and multiplication) that are needed to *define* that infinite number of arithmetic functions. For arithmetic, that number is very small."

(NOT, OR, AND, and so on) that it did support and another nonempty set that it didn't. *But it would be very hard to know which connectives were in which set.* For example, what about the one defined by the following truth table (which I pick more or less at random)? *Note:* Here and throughout this chapter I use *t, u,* and *f* in truth tables to denote the truth values TRUE, UNKNOWN, and FALSE, respectively, of three-valued logic.

	t	u	f
t	t	u	u
u	f	u	f
f	f	t	u

The essence of the matter is that if the system is truth functionally complete, then the user has to learn and remember only a very small number of connectives. Moreover, that user also knows without having to think about the matter any further that

a. All possible connectives are available,

and hence (paraphrasing that earlier quote from reference [14]) that

b. For every possible proposition that can be formulated within the universe of discourse, there's a query that will determine whether that proposition is a true one, in the sense that it's represented, either explicitly or implicitly, in the database.

Without truth functional completeness, however, the user will have to learn and remember just which connectives are available and which not, and will have to deal with the fact that certain queries (which ones?) can't be expressed.

SQL'S THREE-VALUED LOGIC

I turn now to SQL per se. To say it again, SQL is based on three-valued logic (3VL for short). This section contains a brief, slightly formal, and somewhat idealized explanation of this fact. (It's idealized in the sense that in some respects, at least, it describes the way SQL ought to work—or the way it might be thought it ought to work—rather than the way it actually does. Appendix A has more to say regarding the way SQL's 3VL is actually defined.)

Our starting point is the BOOLEAN data type, which, because the logic is three-valued, contains exactly three distinct values, known generically as truth values or boolean values—throughout this chapter, I use these terms interchangeably—and denoted by the literals TRUE, UNKNOWN, and FALSE, respectively. SQL variables and columns can be declared to be of this type. (Since this chapter is explicitly concerned with SQL per se, I use the SQL terminology of tables, rows, and columns throughout instead of the relational terminology of relations, tuples, and attributes, which I much prefer.) For example:

```
DECLARE B BOOLEAN ;     /* SQL variable   */

CREATE TABLE T          /* SQL base table */
     (  ... ,
       C BOOLEAN ,      /* SQL column     */
        ... ) ;
```

Next, several familiar operators, including among others the well known comparison operators "=", "<", and ">", are defined to be of type BOOLEAN, meaning the result they return when invoked is a truth value. And those comparison operators in particular are defined to return UNKNOWN if either of the comparands is null; so before I can go any further, I need to digress for a moment and say something about SQL's "null" construct.

Null can be thought of as the absence of a value (or, a little more precisely, the absence of all possible values). For example, if we say "*x* is null," what we mean is that *x* actually has no value at all; in other words, none of the values that *x* might possibly assume is present. And the intended interpretation of "*x* having no value" is that, actually, *x* does have a value—in the real world, as it were—*but we don't know what that value is*. (For example, suppose we don't know employee Joe's salary; in the tuple for Joe in the database, then, we can't enter a real salary value, precisely because we don't know what that value should be, and so we "put a null" in the relevant position instead.) And it's that intended interpretation that's the justification—such as it is—for the fact that $x = y$ returns UNKNOWN if either comparand is null. Note, moreover, that such a comparison returns UNKNOWN even in the special case where the comparands are *both* null, not (as might have been expected) TRUE. Even the comparison $x = x$ returns UNKNOWN, if *x* is null.[3]

So two nulls aren't equal—but neither are they unequal; the expressions NULL ≠ NULL and NOT (NULL = NULL) both also return UNKNOWN, not (as might have been expected) FALSE.[4] Likewise, for data types for which the operators "<" and ">" are defined, the expressions $x < y$ and $x > y$ both return UNKNOWN if either *x* or *y* is null. Note, moreover, that such comparisons return UNKNOWN even in the special case where the comparands are *both* null, not (as might have been expected) FALSE. Even the comparisons $x \neq x$, $x < x$, and $x > x$ return UNKNOWN, if *x* is null.

This marks the end of the digression regarding nulls. Now you can more or less forget about them, until we get to Appendix A.

Here then is a grammar for SQL boolean expressions, referred to in this chapter as *<bool exp>*s. (I choose to depart from the terminology and nomenclature of the SQL standard [12] when I find the latter not very apt, and boolean expressions are a case in point—the official term for the construct is *<search condition>*, which strikes me as wildly inappropriate.)

```
<bool exp>
    ::=   <bool term>
        | <bool exp> OR <bool term>

<bool term>
    ::=   <bool factor>
        | <bool term> AND <bool factor>

<bool factor>
    ::=   [ NOT ] <bool test>

<bool test>
    ::=   <bool primary> [ IS [ NOT ] ] <bool literal>

<bool primary>
    ::=   <bool literal>
        | <bool var ref>
        | <bool column ref>
        | <condition>
        | ( <bool exp> )
```

---

[3] That intended interpretation is also the "justification" for the fact that scalar expressions in general all return null if any of their operands is null. The claim is that, e.g., adding an unknown value to anything must surely produce an unknown result (?). Note in particular, therefore, that even an expression such as $x - x$ returns null, not (as might have been expected) zero, if *x* is null.

[4] I use uppercase (NULL) when I'm referring to the SQL keyword, lowercase (null) when I'm referring to the concept. That said, I also have to add that in fact NULL ≠ NULL and NOT (NULL = NULL) aren't syntactically legal in SQL anyway! Sorry about that.

```
<bool literal>
    ::=   TRUE | UNKNOWN | FALSE
```

I won't go into details regarding the syntactic category *<condition>* here; suffice it to say that it certainly includes simple scalar comparisons, existence tests (i.e., EXISTS operator invocations), and other such truth valued expressions.

SQL'S CONNECTIVES

Every logic includes certain *connectives,* which are operators that take either one truth value or two as operand(s) and produce another as a result. (The operands can, of course, be denoted by arbitrarily complex truth valued expressions.) Familiar examples include the monadic connective NOT and the dyadic connectives OR and AND, where *monadic* means the connective in question takes just one operand and *dyadic* means it takes two. A logic is truth functionally complete if and only if it supports, directly or indirectly, all of the monadic and dyadic connectives that can possibly be defined within that logic. For example, in conventional two-valued logic (2VL), exactly four monadic and 16 dyadic connectives can be defined, as the following tables indicate:

```
monadics:                      dyadics:
          │                              │ t  f
     ─────┼──────────              ──────┼───────
        t │ t t f f                    t │ r1 r2
        f │ t f t f                    f │ r3 r4
```

Explanation: First let's take a look at the monadics table. In that table:

- The leftmost column shows the two possible operands.
- Each of the other columns corresponds to one possible monadic connective and shows, for each possible operand, what the corresponding result is. Since there are exactly four possible result combinations, there are exactly four monadic connectives; reading from left to right, the first maps both TRUE and FALSE to TRUE, the second leaves them unchanged (that's the *identity* connective), the third interchanges them (that's NOT), and the fourth maps them both to FALSE.

Turning to the dyadics table, the leftmost column and the top row in that table together show the four possible operand combinations, and the body of the table shows the possible result combinations for each operand combination. Since each of *r1, r2, r3,* and *r4* can be either TRUE or FALSE, it follows that there are exactly 16 dyadic connectives. By way of example, if *r1* is TRUE and *r2, r3,* and *r4* are all FALSE, the connective is AND.

Now, it's easy to prove—see, e.g., reference [9]—that, in 2VL, all 20 (= 4 + 16) monadic and dyadic connectives can be expressed in terms of NOT and either OR or AND. Thus, a 2VL system that directly supports NOT, OR, and AND is certainly truth functionally complete. (In fact we don't need both OR and AND, because OR can be defined in terms of NOT and AND; alternatively, AND can be defined in terms of NOT and OR. The set {NOT,OR,AND} is thus not a *primitive,* or minimal, set—but of course it's very convenient in practice to have direct support for both OR and AND.)

So what about 3VL? Well, in 3VL, there are 27 (= 3 to the power 3) monadic connectives and 19,683 (= 3 to the power 3^2) dyadic connectives [14]. In order to show that a 3VL system is truth functionally complete, therefore, it's necessary to show that all 19,710 (= 27 + 19,683) monadic and dyadic connectives can be expressed in terms of whatever connectives that system does directly support. Thus, to show that SQL in particular is truth functionally complete, we need to show that all of those 19,710 possible connectives can be expressed in terms of those connectives that SQL directly supports.

So which connectives does SQL directly support? From the grammar in the previous section, we can see that it does at least support certain dyadic connectives directly: namely, those that it chooses to call OR and AND. It also supports equality comparisons on boolean values, and thus "=" too can be regarded as a dyadic connective (since the result of such a comparison is certainly a truth value). It also supports certain monadic connectives directly: namely, those that it calls NOT, IS [NOT] TRUE, IS [NOT] UNKNOWN, and IS [NOT] FALSE. Here then are the corresponding truth tables:

NOT	
t	*f*
u	*u*
f	*t*

OR	*t*	*u*	*f*
t	*t*	*t*	*t*
u	*t*	*u*	*u*
f	*t*	*u*	*f*

AND	*t*	*u*	*f*
t	*t*	*u*	*f*
u	*u*	*u*	*f*
f	*f*	*f*	*f*

=	*t*	*u*	*f*
t	*t*	*u*	*f*
u	*u*	*u*	*u*
f	*f*	*u*	*t*

IS TRUE	
t	*t*
u	*f*
f	*f*

IS UNKNOWN	
t	*f*
u	*t*
f	*f*

IS FALSE	
t	*f*
u	*f*
f	*t*

IS NOT TRUE	
t	*f*
u	*t*
f	*t*

IS NOT UNKNOWN	
t	*t*
u	*f*
f	*t*

IS NOT FALSE	
t	*t*
u	*t*
f	*f*

Now let *x* be a boolean expression. Clearly, then, *x* IS NOT TRUE is logically equivalent to NOT (*x* IS TRUE), and similarly for *x* IS NOT UNKNOWN and *x* IS NOT FALSE—indeed, that's how those "IS NOT" connectives are defined. It follows that the connectives directly supported by SQL certainly don't constitute a primitive set. *Note:* I remark in passing that IS UNKNOWN is essentially identical to the MAYBE connective of reference [3]; similarly, IS NOT FALSE is essentially identical to the TRUE_OR_MAYBE connective of that same reference.

In addition to the foregoing, there are certain connectives that SQL supports "almost" directly. Again let *x* be a boolean expression. Then, using "≡" to mean "is logically equivalent to" or "can be defined as," we can say, a trifle charitably, that SQL additionally supports the following monadic connectives:

```
IDENTITY ( x )   ≡  ( x )

TRUE ( x )       ≡  ( ( ( x ) IS TRUE ) OR
                      ( ( x ) IS UNKNOWN ) OR
                      ( ( x ) IS FALSE ) )

UNKNOWN ( x )    ≡  ( ( x ) = UNKNOWN )

FALSE ( x )      ≡  ( ( ( x ) IS TRUE ) AND
                      ( ( x ) IS UNKNOWN ) AND
                      ( ( x ) IS FALSE ) )
```

As you can see, IDENTITY(*x*) returns the truth value of its input; TRUE(*x*) always returns TRUE; UNKNOWN(*x*) always returns UNKNOWN; and FALSE(*x*) always returns FALSE. In other words, the truth tables look like this:

IDENTITY	
t	*t*
u	*u*
f	*f*

TRUE	
t	*t*
u	*t*
f	*t*

UNKNOWN	
t	*u*
u	*u*
f	*u*

FALSE	
t	*f*
u	*f*
f	*f*

I remark in passing that:

- IDENTITY(*x*) is equivalent to NOT(NOT(*x*)). Also, of course, it reduces to simply *x* (as the definition indicates).
- TRUE(*x*) is equivalent to (*x* IS *lit*) IS NOT UNKNOWN, where *lit* is any of the literals TRUE, UNKNOWN, and FALSE. More conveniently, it reduces to the literal TRUE.
- UNKNOWN(*x*) reduces to the literal UNKNOWN. (Incidentally, it's precisely this connective that's meant by that rather daunting phrase "the Slupecki T-function.")
- FALSE(*x*) could in fact be defined as the AND of any two of *x* IS TRUE, *x* IS UNKNOWN, and *x* IS FALSE; I defined it as the AND of all three purely (and harmlessly) for reasons of symmetry. It's also equivalent to (*x* IS *lit*) IS UNKNOWN, where *lit* is any of the literals TRUE, UNKNOWN, and FALSE. More conveniently, it reduces to the literal FALSE.

Finally, note that my definitions of TRUE(*x*) and FALSE(*x*) in particular rely on the well known fact that OR and AND are both commutative and associative. *Commutative* means that, for all boolean values *x* and *y*,

```
x OR y    ≡   y OR x
```

and

```
x AND y   ≡   y AND x
```

And *associative* means that, for all boolean values *x*, *y*, and *z*,

```
x OR ( y OR z )     ≡   ( x OR y ) OR z     ≡   x OR y OR z
```

and

```
x AND ( y AND z )   ≡   ( x AND y ) AND z   ≡   x AND y AND z
```

SQL'S MONADICS

From the previous section, we see that SQL provides reasonably direct support for eleven monadic connectives (monadics for short). In what follows, I'll abbreviate the names of those connectives as follows. Note the abbreviation IF in particular!—don't confuse it with the conventional IF keyword, which is sometimes used in logic to denote the connective known as material implication (see later).

```
IDENTITY             I
TRUE                 T
UNKNOWN              U
FALSE                F
NOT                  N
IS TRUE              IT
IS UNKNOWN           IU
IS FALSE             IF
IS NOT TRUE          INT
IS NOT UNKNOWN       INU
IS NOT FALSE         INF
```

I'll refer to these connectives henceforth as "the original eleven." Also, I'll assume for simplicity that they're expressed using conventional functional notation, thereby writing, e.g., INU(*x*) instead of—as SQL would actually require—*x* IS NOT UNKNOWN.

The following table summarizes the situation so far (specifically, it indicates by their abbreviated names the eleven monadics that are supported "directly" in SQL):

	T		INF			I	INU		IT					U					INT		IU	N			IF		F
t	*t*	*t*	*t*	*t*	*t*	*t*	*t*	*t*	*t*	*u*	*u*	*u*	*u*	*u*	*u*	*u*	*u*	*u*	*f*	*f*	*f*	*f*	*f*	*f*	*f*	*f*	*f*
u	*t*	*t*	*t*	*u*	*u*	*u*	*f*	*f*	*f*	*t*	*t*	*t*	*u*	*u*	*u*	*f*	*f*	*f*	*t*	*t*	*t*	*u*	*u*	*u*	*f*	*f*	*f*
f	*t*	*u*	*f*	*t*	*u*	*f*	*t*	*u*	*f*	*t*	*u*	*f*	*t*	*u*	*f*	*t*	*u*	*f*	*t*	*u*	*f*	*t*	*u*	*f*	*t*	*u*	*f*

There are thus 16 monadics that SQL does *not* directly support. They can conveniently be labeled by the initial letters of the truth values to which they map the truth values TRUE, UNKNOWN, and FALSE (in that order), respectively, as follows:

```
TTU       UTT       UUF       FTU
TUT       UTU       UFT       FUU
TUU       UTF       UFU       FUF
TFU       UUT       UFF       FFU
```

To show that SQL is truth functionally complete, then, we need to show among other things that these 16 monadics can all be expressed in terms of the original eleven or the directly supported dyadics OR and AND (or a mixture). In what follows, I'll limit my attention to this specific issue—i.e., I'll limit my attention to the monadics—until further notice. More specifically, I'll show that the answer to the question "Does SQL support the remaining 16 monadics?" is *yes*. *Note:* Reference [5] effectively showed the same thing, but it omitted the detailed analysis, leading to that conclusion, that follows in the next two sections.

Now, there are two ways in which two monadics can be combined to form another: They can be *composed*—that is, they can be applied in sequence, one after the other; for example, we can construct an expression of the form N(IT(*x*)). Or they can be *disjoined* or *conjoined*—that is, they can be ORed or ANDed together; for example, we can construct an expression of the form IT(*x*) OR IU(*x*).[5] I'll examine compositions in the section immediately following and disjunctions and conjunctions in the one after that.

---

[5] They can also be combined using the "=" connective, but I have no need to make use of that connective in the analysis that follows.

COMPOSITIONS OF THE MONADICS

In this section I consider all possible compositions of two of the original eleven monadics. Let me first give an example to illustrate the method. Suppose we wish to examine the composition of INT and IU (meaning first apply IU, then apply INT). The following truth table shows that composition to be equivalent to INU, because the final column is identical to the defining column in the truth table for INU. In symbols, then, we can say that INT(IU) ≡ INU, where again "≡" means "is logically equivalent to."

x	IU(x)	INT(IU(x))
t	f	t
u	t	f
f	f	t

Examining all possible compositions is tedious but essentially straightforward; I'll leave the details as an exercise for the reader, and simply summarize the results in the form of a matrix:

	I	T	U	F	N	IT	IU	IF	INT	INU	INF
I	I	T	U	F	N	IT	IU	IF	INT	INU	INF
T	T	T	T	T	T	T	T	T	T	T	T
U	U	U	U	U	U	U	U	U	U	U	U
F	F	F	F	F	F	F	F	F	F	F	F
N	N	F	U	T	I	INT	INU	INF	IT	IU	IF
IT	IT	T	F	F	IF	IT	IU	IF	INT	INU	INF
IU	IU	F	T	F	IU	F	F	F	F	F	F
IF	IF	F	F	T	IT	INT	INU	INF	IT	IU	IF
INT	INT	F	T	T	INF	INT	INU	INF	IT	IU	IF
INU	INU	T	F	T	INU	T	T	T	T	T	T
INF	INF	T	T	F	INT	IT	IU	IF	INT	INU	INF

The matrix is meant to be understood as follows: The connective corresponding to column *j* is applied first, followed by the connective corresponding to row *i*, and the entry at position [*i,j*] in the body of the matrix shows what that particular composition is equivalent to. Inspection of the matrix shows that every possible composition of two monadics from the original eleven is equivalent to one of those eleven. It follows that none of the other 16 connectives can be expressed in terms of the original eleven using composition alone.

DISJUNCTIONS AND CONJUNCTIONS OF THE MONADICS

The next step is to consider the effects of ORing any two of the original eleven monadics together. Again I'll begin by giving an example to illustrate the method. Suppose we wish to examine the disjunction (i.e., OR) of IT and IU. The following truth table shows that disjunction to be equivalent to INF (as is indeed intuitively obvious), because the final column is identical to the column in the truth table that defines INF; in symbols, IT OR IU ≡ INF.

x	IT(x)	IU(x)	IT(x) OR IU(x)
t	*t*	*f*	*t*
u	*f*	*t*	*t*
f	*f*	*f*	*f*

Examining all possible disjunctions is again tedious but essentially straightforward, so again I'll leave the details to the reader, and simply present a summary matrix here. Note that the matrix is symmetric (because OR is commutative).

OR	I	T	U	F	N	IT	IU	IF	INT	INU	INF
I	I	T	**TUU**	I	**TUT**	I	INF	**TUT**	T	**TUT**	INF
T	T	T	T	T	T	T	T	T	T	T	T
U	**TUU**	T	U	U	**UUT**	**TUU**	**UTU**	**UUT**	**UTT**	**TUT**	**TTU**
F	I	T	U	F	N	IT	IU	IF	INT	INU	INF
N	**TUT**	T	**UUT**	N	N	**TUT**	INT	N	INT	**TUT**	T
IT	I	T	**TUU**	IT	**TUT**	IT	INF	INU	T	INU	INF
IU	INF	T	**UTU**	IU	INT	INF	IU	INT	INT	T	INF
IF	**TUT**	T	**UUT**	IF	N	INU	INT	IF	INT	INU	T
INT	T	T	**UTT**	INT	INT	T	INT	INT	INT	T	T
INU	**TUT**	T	**TUT**	INU	**TUT**	INU	T	INU	T	INU	T
INF	INF	T	**TTU**	INF	T	INF	INF	T	T	T	INF

And here's the matrix (also symmetric) for AND:

AND	I	T	U	F	N	IT	IU	IF	INT	INU	INF
I	I	I	**UUF**	F	**FUF**	IT	**FUF**	F	**FUF**	IT	I
T	I	T	U	F	N	IT	IU	IF	INT	INU	INF
U	**UUF**	U	U	F	**FUU**	**UFF**	**FUF**	**FFU**	**FUU**	**UFU**	**UUF**
F	F	F	F	F	F	F	F	F	F	F	F
N	**FUF**	N	**FUU**	F	N	F	**FUF**	IF	N	IF	**FUF**
IT	IT	IT	**UFF**	F	F	IT	F	F	F	IT	IT
IU	**FUF**	IU	**FUF**	F	**FUF**	F	IU	F	IU	F	IU
IF	F	IF	**FFU**	F	IF	F	F	IF	IF	IF	F
INT	**FUF**	INT	**FUU**	F	N	F	IU	IF	INT	IF	IU
INU	IT	INU	**UFU**	F	IF	IT	F	IF	IF	INU	IT
INF	I	INF	**UUF**	F	**FUF**	IT	IU	F	IU	IT	INF

As you can see, both of these matrices include certain entries (shown in **bold**) that aren't just the shorthand names for one of the original eleven monadics. In the matrix for OR, for example, the entry for I OR U is **TUU**. To review briefly, the meaning of that entry is that the corresponding truth table looks like this:

x	I(x)	U(x)	I(x) OR U(x)
t	*t*	*u*	*t*
u	*u*	*u*	*u*
f	*f*	*u*	*u*

That is, the final (defining) column reads, vertically, *t-u-u*. And the connective TUU defined by this truth table is *not* one of the original eleven.

Inspection of the matrices for OR and AND together shows that all of the following are connectives that (a) can be obtained by forming disjunctions or conjunctions of connectives from the original eleven and (b) aren't themselves included in that original eleven:

```
TTU    UUF
TUT    UFU
TUU    UFF
UTT    FUU
UTU    FUF
UUT    FFU
```

So we see now that SQL does support at least 12 of the "missing" 16 connectives. That leaves four to be accounted for, which (by inspection, and using the same notation) are as follows:

```
TFU
UTF
UFT
FTU
```

However, it's fairly easy to see that these connectives too can be expressed in terms of ones we already know are supported. Possible definitions (not necessarily unique) are as follows:

- TFU ≡ INU AND TTU
- UTF ≡ INF AND UTU
- UFT ≡ INU AND UUT
- FTU ≡ INT AND UTU

For example, the following truth table spells out the details for TFU (I'll leave the others as an exercise):

x	INU(x)	TTU(x)	INU(x) AND TTU(x)
t	*t*	*t*	*t*
u	*f*	*t*	*f*
f	*t*	*u*	*u*

Conclusion: SQL does support, directly or indirectly, all 27 monadic connectives of 3VL.

♦♦♦♦♦

For the record, I give below a summary definition of all of the 27 monadics in terms of the original eleven:

```
TTT  ≡  T
TTU  ≡  U OR INF
TTF  ≡  INF
TUT  ≡  I OR N
TUU  ≡  I OR U
TUF  ≡  I
TFT  ≡  INU
TFU  ≡  INU AND ( U OR INF )
TFF  ≡  IT
UTT  ≡  U OR INT
UTU  ≡  U OR IU
UTF  ≡  INF AND ( U OR IU )
UUT  ≡  U OR N
UUU  ≡  U
UUF  ≡  I AND U
UFT  ≡  INU AND ( U OR N )
UFU  ≡  U AND INU
UFF  ≡  U AND IT
FTT  ≡  INT
FTU  ≡  INT AND ( U OR IU )
FTF  ≡  IU
FUT  ≡  N
FUU  ≡  U AND N
FUF  ≡  I AND N
FFT  ≡  IF
FFU  ≡  U AND IF
FFF  ≡  F
```

SQL'S DYADICS

I've shown that SQL does support all 27 monadics. But this fact alone is obviously not sufficient to show that SQL is truth functionally complete; to do that, we would need to show that SQL supports all 19,683 dyadics as well. Now, I'm clearly not going to carry out the same kind of brute force investigation here as I did for the monadics. However, it turns out I don't have to. Consider the dyadic δ, defined by the following truth table:

δ	*t*	*u*	*f*
t	*f*	*f*	*f*
u	*f*	*t*	*t*
f	*f*	*t*	*u*

According to reference [15], δ is a *generating operator* for the whole of 3VL, meaning that all possible 3VL connectives can be expressed in terms of δ alone—just as (as reference [9] shows) NOR is a generating operator for 2VL, meaning that all possible 2VL connectives can be expressed in terms of NOR alone.[6] Thus, if I can show that SQL does support δ, I will have shown it's truth functionally complete. (Of course, knowing one connective suffices isn't the same as knowing how any given connective can be expressed in terms of it!)

> *Aside:* The 2VL dyadic connective NOR (also known as the *Peirce arrow* and sometimes written as a down arrow, "↓") is defined as follows: The expression *x* NOR *y* is equivalent to NOT (*x* OR *y*); thus, it evaluates to TRUE if and only if *x* and *y* both evaluate to FALSE. It can be read as "neither *x* nor *y* is true." *End of aside.*

> In fact, SQL does support δ. To be specific, $\delta(x,y)$ is equivalent to the following:

```
INT ( x ) AND INT ( y ) AND ( INF ( x ) OR INF ( y ) OR U )
```

Observe that this definition is symmetric in *x* and *y* (as in fact must be the case, because the corresponding truth table is symmetric in *x* and *y* also). To see that the definition is valid, let $p \equiv$ INT(x) AND INT(y) and let $q \equiv$ INF(x) OR INF(y) OR U, and consider the following truth tables. First *p* (which, let me point out, will give FALSE if either *x* or *y* is TRUE, and TRUE otherwise):

p	t	u	f
t	f	f	f
u	f	t	t
f	f	t	t

Next *q* (which will give UNKNOWN if *x* and *y* are both FALSE, and TRUE otherwise):

q	t	u	f
t	t	t	t
u	t	t	t
f	t	t	u

Putting the foregoing together, we have:

x	y	p	q	p AND q
t	t	f	t	f
t	u	f	t	f
t	f	f	t	f
u	t	f	t	f
u	u	t	t	t
u	f	t	t	t
f	t	f	t	f
f	u	t	t	t
f	f	t	u	u

[6] Here's the pertinent text from reference [15] (lightly edited): "D. Webb has shown that all possible connectives for an *n*-valued logic can be defined using one single connective ... See D. L. Webb, 'Generation of Any *n*-Valued Logic by One Binary Operation,' *Proceedings of the National Academy of Sciences,* vol. 21 (1935), pp. 252-254. M. Wajsberg has made this finding in the 1920s. See ..." (and the text goes on to give more detailed references).

The final (defining) column in this truth table is the defining column for δ; so SQL does support δ and is thus truth functionally complete.[7] And if I had demonstrated this fact previously, without going through that detailed analysis of the monadics in earlier sections, I would have saved myself a lot of trouble! However:

- That detailed analysis did at least show exactly *how* SQL supports all of those monadics. It might thus prove more useful than a mere demonstration of the fact that such support must logically exist.

- Perhaps more to the point, observe that my definition of δ in SQL terms, and hence my proof that SQL is truth functionally complete, both rely crucially on the assumption that SQL supports the U connective, *aka* the Slupecki T-function. (By the way, I can now explain the name "T-function": The T stands for *tertium,* which is Latin for third, and UNKNOWN is "the third truth value.")

Note: Reference [5] also "proved" that SQL is truth functionally complete, but not by demonstrating SQL's support for the δ connective. Instead, it relied on the fact that, according to reference [15], any 3VL system that supports all three of the following—

- The conventional NOT connective of 3VL

- The Slupecki T-function

- The connective known as *Łukasiewicz implication* (see below)

—is indeed truth functionally complete. Now, SQL obviously supports the NOT connective directly, and I've shown that it effectively supports the Slupecki T-function also. As for Łukasiewicz implication, here first is the truth table for that connective:

	t	u	f
t	t	u	f
u	t	t	u
f	t	t	t

Aside: As you can see from this truth table, Łukasiewicz implication differs from the more familiar *material* implication, which is defined to be equivalent to NOT(x) OR (y). To be specific, it differs just in the case where x and y are both UNKNOWN—material implication gives UNKNOWN in this case, while Łukasiewicz implication gives TRUE. *End of aside.*

Let the Łukasiewicz implication connective be denoted by α. Then it's easy to see that $\alpha(x,y)$ is equivalent to the following:

```
NOT ( x ) OR ( y ) OR ( IU ( x ) AND IU ( y ) )
```

It follows that—assuming once again that SQL does support the U connective—SQL is truth functionally complete.

[7] As you can see, the style of this particular truth table differs from the style I've used previously in this chapter for dyadic operators. In practice different styles are useful for different purposes, and it's customary to use whichever style is most convenient for the purpose at hand.

A REMARK ON CODD'S THREE-VALUED LOGIC

SQL's 3VL is widely considered to be based on a 3VL defined—well, sketched—by Codd in reference [1]. (I say "sketched," because almost all Codd actually did in this connection in reference [1] was to define truth tables, identical to their SQL counterparts, for NOT, OR, and AND.) It follows that all of the results concerning SQL in the present chapter also apply, mutatis mutandis, to Codd's 3VL as well.

ACKNOWLEDGMENTS

I'd like to thank Hugh Darwen and Jim Melton for assistance with certain technical questions regarding the SQL standard, and Hugh Darwen and David McGoveran for reviewing earlier drafts of this chapter.

REFERENCES AND BIBLIOGRAPHY

1. E. F. Codd: "Extending the Database Relational Model to Capture More Meaning," *ACM TODS 4,* No. 4 (December 1979).

2. E. F. Codd and C. J. Date: "Much Ado About Nothing," in C. J. Date, *Relational Database Writings 1991-1994.* Reading, Mass.: Addison-Wesley (1995).

3. C. J. Date: "NOT Is Not 'Not'! (Notes on Three-Valued Logic and Related Matters)," in *Relational Database Writings 1985-1989.* Reading, Mass.: Addison-Wesley (1990).

4. C. J. Date: "EXISTS Is Not 'Exists'! (Some Logical Flaws in SQL)," in *Relational Database Writings 1985-1989.* Reading, Mass.: Addison-Wesley (1990).

5. C. J. Date: "A Note on the Logical Operators of SQL," in *Relational Database Writings 1991-1994.* Reading, Mass.: Addison-Wesley (1995).

6. C. J. Date: "Missing Information," in *An Introduction to Database Systems* (8th edition). Boston, Mass.: Addison-Wesley (2004).

7. C. J. Date: "Why We Need Type BOOLEAN," in *Date on Database: Writings 2000-2006.* Berkeley, Calif.: Apress (2006).

8. C. J. Date: "Why Three- and Four-Valued Logic Don't Work," in *Date on Database: Writings 2000-2006.* Berkeley, Calif.: Apress (2006).

9. C. J. Date: "The Building Blocks of Logic," in *Logic and Databases: The Roots of Relational Theory.* Victoria, B.C.: Trafford Publishing (2007). See *www.trafford.com/07-0690.*

10. C. J. Date and Hugh Darwen: *A Guide to the SQL Standard* (4th edition). Reading, Mass.: Addison-Wesley (1997).

11. C. J. Date and Hugh Darwen: *Databases, Types, and the Relational Model: The Third Manifesto* (3rd edition). Boston, Mass.: Addison-Wesley (2006).

12. International Organization for Standardization (ISO): *Database Language SQL,* Document ISO/IEC 9075:2008 (2008).

13. David McGoveran (with C. J. Date): "Why Relational DBMSs Are Based on Logic," in *Logic and Databases: The Roots of Relational Theory.* Victoria, B.C.: Trafford Publishing (2007). See *www.trafford.com/07-0690.*

14. David McGoveran (with C. J. Date): "Why Relational DBMS Logic Must Not Be Many-Valued," in *Logic and Databases: The Roots of Relational Theory.* Victoria, B.C.: Trafford Publishing (2007). See *www.trafford.com/07-0690.*

15. Nicholas Rescher: *Many-Valued Logic.* New York, N.Y.: McGraw-Hill (1969).

APPENDIX A: SQL'S 3VL, WARTS AND ALL

You may be consistent or inconsistent,
but you shouldn't switch all the time between the two.

—Anon.

Note: Portions of what follows are based on material previously published in reference [6]. However, there's quite a lot of new material as well.

The description of SQL given in the section "SQL's Three-Valued Logic" in the body of the chapter was, as stated in that section, somewhat idealized (*economical with the truth* might be a better way to put it). The purpose of this appendix is to set the record straight, as it were, by correcting some of the "idealized"—in other words, false—statements made earlier. Thus, where there are discrepancies between statements in the body of the chapter and statements in this appendix, the latter should be regarded as superseding. (It's my belief, however, that the existence of such discrepancies in no way invalidates my overall message.)

Before getting into details, I remind you that while the SQL standard does support an explicit BOOLEAN data type,[8] current SQL products typically—perhaps universally—don't. Nevertheless, the dialect of SQL supported in those products might still be truth functionally complete. To be specific:

- The connectives NOT, OR, and AND have been part of SQL from the very beginning and thus certainly will be supported. *Note:* The SQL standard appears to have no formal counterpart to the term *connectives,* but it does use the term *boolean operators* informally.

- The connectives IS [NOT] TRUE, IS [NOT] UNKNOWN, and IS [NOT] FALSE were introduced into the standard in 1992—i.e., several years before the BOOLEAN data type itself was introduced—and support for them might thus be a little more likely than it is for the BOOLEAN data type itself. (In practice, however, current products typically—perhaps universally—don't support them, any more than they support the BOOLEAN data type itself.)

  Aside: I've already said that SQL doesn't actually refer to NOT, OR, and AND as connectives (it calls them boolean operators instead). As for IS [NOT] TRUE, IS [NOT] UNKNOWN, and IS [NOT] FALSE, it doesn't even regard these operators as logically distinct! Instead, it defines another boolean operator that it calls IS, and then it defines, one by one, the semantics of each of the various possible invocations of that operator (x IS TRUE, x IS UNKNOWN, and x IS FALSE; note that the right comparand in each case must be a boolean literal specifically).[9] It also defines x IS NOT *lit,* where *lit* is any of the literals TRUE, UNKNOWN, and FALSE, to be equivalent to NOT (x IS *lit*). *End of aside.*

- Boolean variables (or references to such variables, rather) can be simulated by means of boolean expressions. For example, a reference to a hypothetical boolean variable x might be simulated by means of an expression of the form ($a = b$), where a and b are variables of the same type (INTEGER, say)—in which case we could say the hypothetical variable x would have the value TRUE if and only if the expression ($a = b$) IS TRUE evaluates to TRUE, the value UNKNOWN if and only if the expression ($a = b$) IS UNKNOWN evaluates to TRUE, and the value FALSE if and only if the expression ($a = b$) IS FALSE evaluates to TRUE.

---

[8] I note in passing that this data type has the property that TRUE is regarded as being greater than FALSE—i.e., the comparison TRUE > FALSE returns TRUE. By contrast, the comparisons TRUE ⩾ UNKNOWN and UNKNOWN ⩾ FALSE, which might have been expected to return TRUE also, both return UNKNOWN.

[9] It's very tempting to add, therefore, that (as somebody or other once said) it really does all depend on what the meaning of IS is.

- The literal TRUE and the connective TRUE(x) can both be simulated by means of an expression of the form (0 = 0), say.
- The literal UNKNOWN and the connective UNKNOWN(x)—i.e., the Slupecki T-function—can both be simulated by means of an expression of the form ($a = b$), say, where at least one of a and b is null.
- The literal FALSE and the connective FALSE(x) can both be simulated by means of an expression of the form (0 = 1), say.
- Finally, the connective IDENTITY(x) is logically equivalent to x; it can thus be simulated by means of whatever expression is being used to simulate x itself.

Of course, the foregoing discussion does rely on the fact that SQL products, even if they don't support the BOOLEAN data type as such, nevertheless do support certain limited boolean expressions that can be used in certain limited contexts: for example, in constraint definitions, and CASE expressions, and WHERE, ON, and HAVING clauses. But I can't resist pointing out that the dialects of SQL supported by such products thereby exhibit a very strange property—namely, they support expressions that are of an unknown data type![10] (By *an unknown data type,* I mean, of course, a data type that's not known in the language.) In particular, they don't permit boolean variables, they don't permit SQL tables with boolean columns, and they don't permit boolean expressions in a SELECT clause (this list of prohibitions isn't meant to be exhaustive). Such a curious state of affairs surely violates some very fundamental principles of good language design [7]. (In fact, of course, the same criticisms applied to the SQL standard itself prior to 1999, when the BOOLEAN data type was introduced.)

I should also point out, before getting into SQL's 3VL support per se, that in a certain trivial sense the answer to the question "Is SQL truth functionally complete?" is *obviously* yes. That's because SQL does support CASE expressions of the following form—

```
CASE <when clause list> END
```

—where a *<when clause>* in turn takes the form:

```
WHEN <bool exp> THEN <exp>
```

So let x and y be arbitrary *<bool exp>*s. Then the CASE expression

```
CASE
   WHEN ( x ) IS TRUE    AND ( y ) IS TRUE    THEN r1
   WHEN ( x ) IS TRUE    AND ( y ) IS UNKNOWN THEN r2
   WHEN ( x ) IS TRUE    AND ( y ) IS FALSE   THEN r3
   WHEN ( x ) IS UNKNOWN AND ( y ) IS TRUE    THEN r4
   WHEN ( x ) IS UNKNOWN AND ( y ) IS UNKNOWN THEN r5
   WHEN ( x ) IS UNKNOWN AND ( y ) IS FALSE   THEN r6
   WHEN ( x ) IS FALSE   AND ( y ) IS TRUE    THEN r7
   WHEN ( x ) IS FALSE   AND ( y ) IS UNKNOWN THEN r8
   WHEN ( x ) IS FALSE   AND ( y ) IS FALSE   THEN r9
END
```

(where each of *r1, r2, ..., r9* is either TRUE, UNKNOWN, or FALSE) clearly represents an application of that particular dyadic connective whose definition is given by the truth table shown below:

---

[10] How very *à propos.*

	t	u	f
t	r1	r2	r3
u	r4	r5	r6
f	r7	r8	r9

Also, we already know that SQL supports all 27 monadic connectives; so the desired result follows. However, we would obviously prefer not to have to write out the full definition of each dyadic connective every time we need to use it (and the same goes for those monadics that SQL fails to support directly—which is most of them, of course).

♦♦♦♦♦

Now I turn to SQL's 3VL per se. First a caveat: As is well known, SQL's 3VL is highly intertwined with its notion of nulls. And nulls in SQL are widely recognized to be nonsense; indeed, as I've written elsewhere (see, e.g., reference [8]), a fully coherent explanation of them is logically impossible. It follows that a fully coherent explanation of SQL's 3VL is logically impossible as well! So I apologize if the material that follows doesn't entirely make sense; if such is the case, however, I refuse to accept full responsibility. I'm doing my best.

Onward. Now, it's certainly true that SQL does support the boolean literals TRUE, UNKNOWN, and FALSE, corresponding to the three truth values of 3VL—though I can't resist immediately pointing out another little oddity here. The keywords TRUE, UNKNOWN, and FALSE were introduced (in the context of the connectives IS TRUE, IS NOT TRUE, and so on) in 1992; the BOOLEAN data type was introduced in 1999. For the years 1992-1999, therefore, those keywords *weren't* literals, because literals denote values by definition and there weren't any values for them to denote! (I mean, the values in question weren't supported at that time.) Indeed, the standard version of the grammar that I showed earlier in the body of the chapter for *<bool exp>*s still refers to those keywords not (as I did) as *<bool literal>*s but as *<truth value>*s—thereby managing to introduce yet another confusion into the mix: to be specific, a confusion over the logical difference between values as such and the symbols (i.e., literals) used to denote them.

Be that as it may, it's important to understand (though I deliberately didn't stress the point in the body of the chapter) that there's a logical difference between null and UNKNOWN—UNKNOWN is a value, but null isn't a value at all. (As I said in the body of the chapter, it can be thought of as the absence of a value.) To be more specific, let *x* be a variable of type BOOLEAN. In principle, then,[11] *x* must have one of the values TRUE, UNKNOWN, or FALSE. So when we say "*x* has the value UNKNOWN," we mean the value of *x* is *known to be* "the third truth value," viz., UNKNOWN. By contrast, when we say "*x* is null," we mean *x has no value at all*. *Note:* I remind you that the intended interpretation of "*x* is null" isn't that *x* has no value at all, but rather that we don't know what the value of *x* is. However, this interpretation, though it might be helpful from an intuitive point of view, is necessarily informal; the formal position, to repeat, is that "*x* is null" means *x* has no value at all.

Incidentally, since null isn't a value, it follows that the keyword NULL—unlike the keywords TRUE, UNKNOWN, and FALSE—can't sensibly be regarded as a literal, since literals denote values by definition.[12] Here's what the standard [12] has to say on the matter:

> [The] **null value (null)** [is a] special value, or mark, that is used to indicate the absence of any data value ... There is no <literal> for a null value, although the keyword NULL is used in some places to indicate that a null value is

---

[11] I regret that here, as so often, the phrase "in principle" might best be interpreted as "what I'm about to tell you is not entirely true." To be specific, assertions to the effect that the value of some boolean variable *x* is "the third truth value," UNKNOWN, don't really make much sense in SQL, as we'll soon see.

[12] What this observation implies for the literal UNKNOWN is beyond me, however, since (as we'll see in a few moments) there *is* no value for it to denote. I'll return to this point in a footnote on the next page.

desired.[13]

Actually, it would be more accurate to say that, since NULL is not a valid literal, it's certainly not a valid expression. Thus, just because an expression is allowed to appear in some given context, it certainly doesn't follow that NULL is allowed to appear in that same context. (Sometimes it is so allowed, but only when there's a special syntax rule to that effect—it's *not* because the keyword NULL is being regarded as a literal or expression in the context in question. For example, there are special rules to the effect that an INSERT of the form INSERT INTO T (C) VALUES (NULL) [*sic!*] and an UPDATE of the form UPDATE T SET C = NULL are both syntactically legal.) And yet ... given that, for example, the expression $x = y$ is legal but the expression x = NULL is not, how can we coherently explain what happens with that expression $x = y$ in the case where "y is null"?

To repeat, there's a logical difference between null and UNKNOWN. It follows that to confuse the two is a serious logical mistake. Indeed, to use null instead of UNKNOWN to represent "the third truth value" would be exactly as serious a mistake as it would be to use null instead of 0 to represent zero! And, unfortunately, SQL manages to make exactly this mistake[14] ... That is, SQL's BOOLEAN data type—contrary to what was stated in the body of the chapter—does *not* contain "exactly three distinct values"; instead, it contains just the two denoted by the literals TRUE and FALSE, and the UNKNOWN truth value is represented not by a value at all but by null. In other words, there simply *is* no "third truth value" in SQL—despite the fact that SQL is explicitly supposed to be based (as we know) on three-valued logic! Here are some immediate consequences of this serious logical mistake:

- Any expression that ought logically to evaluate to UNKNOWN is instead considered to "evaluate" to null ("evaluate" in quotes because in fact any expression that "is null" denotes no value and so can't sensibly be said to evaluate to anything at all). Note, however, that (as previously stated) the literal UNKNOWN is supported, even though the corresponding truth value is not! But specifying that literal is always effectively equivalent to specifying NULL[15]—except that, in the context of an expression of the form x IS [NOT] UNKNOWN, it really does mean UNKNOWN (and the same goes for expressions of the form x AND UNKNOWN and x OR UNKNOWN—see the final bullet item in the present list). Note also that, the foregoing state of affairs notwithstanding, the keyword NULL is not a boolean literal; in fact, as we saw earlier, it isn't technically a literal of any kind at all.

- As a consequence of the previous point, assigning UNKNOWN—either directly by means of the UNKNOWN literal or by means of some more general expression that "ought to" evaluate to UNKNOWN, such as $a = b$ if a or b happens to be null—to a variable x of type BOOLEAN actually sets that variable x to null.

- After the foregoing assignment, the comparison x = UNKNOWN "evaluates" to null, not TRUE.

- The comparison x = NULL (not meant to be valid SQL syntax) always "evaluates" to null, regardless of the value of x. In particular, it "evaluates" to null, not TRUE, even in the case where UNKNOWN was what was most recently assigned to x. *Note:* I can't say "UNKNOWN was the *value* most recently

---

[13] The phrase "null value" is clearly a contradiction in terms. However, that same phrase appears ubiquitously throughout reference [12], and indeed throughout SQL publications in general.

[14] Sadly, so does Codd. To quote reference [1]: "[What] is the truth value of $x = y$ if x or y or both are null? An appropriate result in each of these cases is the unknown truth value ... We use the same symbol [as we did for null] to denote the unknown truth value, because truth values can be stored in databases and we want the treatment of all unknown or null values [*sic*] to be uniform."

[15] In other words, a good way to think about the literal UNKNOWN is as shorthand for the expression CAST (NULL AS BOOLEAN) (thanks to Hugh Darwen for this observation).

assigned to *x*," because SQL doesn't support the truth *value* UNKNOWN.

- One final oddity: Let boolean variables *x* and *y* have values TRUE and UNKNOWN (i.e., null), respectively, and consider the expression *x* OR *y*. Now, expressions in SQL where one of the operands is null are generally defined to "evaluate to null." In this particular case, however, SQL understands that the null in question actually represents the truth value UNKNOWN, and the expression therefore evaluates to TRUE, not null. (In other words, SQL is breaking its own rules here.) Similarly, if *x* and *y* have values FALSE and UNKNOWN (null), respectively, the expression *x* AND *y* evaluates to FALSE, not null.

Next, SQL provides two special comparison operators, IS NULL and IS NOT NULL, to test for the presence or absence of nulls. The syntax is:

```
r IS [ NOT ] NULL
```

where *r* denotes an SQL row. Points arising:

- The rationale behind the provision of these operators is that, since nothing (not even null) is equal to null, expressions of the form x = NULL make no sense and therefore must be, and are, outlawed. (Of course, the same goes for expressions of the form $x \neq$ NULL, $x <$ NULL, and $x >$ NULL as well.) At the same time, there has to be a way of determining whether something "is null"; hence the operators under discussion.

- Note that the operators under discussion (viz., IS NULL and IS NOT NULL) are not logical connectives: Although they're truth valued—i.e., they do return truth values—their operands aren't necessarily truth values (in practice, in fact, they're usually not).

- In saying these operators "test for the presence or absence of nulls," I choose my words carefully ... If null is defined as the absence of a value, then the presence of null is the absence of a value, and the absence of null is the absence of the absence (and hence the presence) of a value.

- As you would probably expect, an SQL row, like (e.g.) an SQL variable of type INTEGER, can be null. For example, if R is an SQL variable of some row type, the assignment SET R = NULL will cause R to contain a null row, and the expression R IS NULL will then return TRUE (and the expression R IS NOT NULL will return FALSE). But R IS NULL can also return TRUE even if R doesn't contain a null row!—as the next few bullet items explain.

- First of all, let *r* denote a row of degree one, and let that row *r* not be a null row. Then SQL treats *r*, rather questionably, as if it actually denoted the single value[16] contained in that row instead of that row as such; in other words, it implicitly converts, or *coerces*, *r* to the single value it contains. Let *x* be the single value contained in *r*. (The SQL syntax for such a row *r* is (*x*), but the parentheses are optional;[17] thus, the expression *x* is taken to refer sometimes to a row as such and sometimes to something that appears, or could appear, in a row.) In this case, then, (a) *r* IS NULL reduces to *x* IS NULL, and it evaluates to TRUE if *x* is null and FALSE otherwise, and (b) *r* IS NOT NULL reduces to *x* IS NOT NULL, and it evaluates to TRUE if *x* is not null and FALSE otherwise. To say it again in different words: If *r* is of degree one and isn't null, then *r* IS NULL will still return TRUE if *r contains* a null; likewise, *r* IS NOT NULL will return FALSE if *r* contains a null.

---

[16] I'm being sloppy: The phrase "the single value," here and in similar contexts elsewhere, ought by rights to be "the single value or single null," of course. But life is too short.

[17] The syntax ROW(*x*) is also supported, but in this case the parentheses are required.

- Now let *r* denote a nonnull row of degree greater than one.[18] In this case, SQL treats *r* as denoting that row as such, and (a) *r* IS NULL returns TRUE if and only if, for every component *x* in *r, x* IS NULL returns TRUE (otherwise *r* IS NULL returns FALSE); (b) *r* IS NOT NULL returns TRUE if and only if, for every component *x* in *r, x* IS NOT NULL returns TRUE (otherwise *r* IS NOT NULL returns FALSE). Note, therefore, that if *r* is a row with (say) two components *x* and *y,* then the expressions *r* IS NOT NULL and NOT (*r* IS NULL) aren't equivalent!—the first is equivalent to *x* IS NOT NULL AND *y* IS NOT NULL, and the second is equivalent to *x* IS NOT NULL OR *y* IS NOT NULL.

- Another strange consequence of the foregoing state of affairs is that if some components of *r* are null and some are not null, then *r* itself is considered to be neither null nor not null!—that is, *r* IS NULL and *r* IS NOT NULL both return FALSE. In such a case, I suppose we might say that *r* is not null but not NOT null. As I've had occasion to remark elsewhere [3], in SQL, NOT is not not.

- So if row *r* has at least one component that's null and at least one that isn't, then (as we've just seen) the expression *r* IS NULL gives FALSE; yet the comparison *r* = *r* gives UNKNOWN (or rather null) in such a case! In SQL, therefore, if ((*r* = *r*) IS UNKNOWN) is TRUE, the most we can say is that *r* has at least one null component; in particular, we can't necessarily say that *r* IS NULL is TRUE (!).

- In theory, of course, there's a logical difference—or, rather, there ought to be a logical difference—between (a) *r* itself being null and (b) *r* having at least one null component. (If you're having difficulty with this observation, the following analogy might help: Clearly, there's a logical difference between some set *s* being empty and that set *s* having at least one empty element.) In fact, *r* itself ought not necessarily to be regarded as null even if all of its components are null—though in fact such a row *is* regarded as null in SQL, as we've already seen.

——— ♦♦♦♦♦ ———

Another trap for the unwary arises in connection with the SQL EXISTS operator. Without going into a lot of detail, let me just say that the SQL EXISTS operator isn't a faithful representation of the existential quantifier of 3VL, because it always evaluates to TRUE or FALSE, never to UNKNOWN, even when UNKNOWN is the logically correct answer. (Note too that both cases are possible—sometimes EXISTS in SQL incorrectly returns TRUE, sometimes it incorrectly returns FALSE.) See reference [4] for further discussion.

A related error occurs in connection with the SQL ANY and ALL operators, each of which takes as its sole operand a column of boolean values; ANY (which can alternatively be spelled SOME) returns TRUE if any of those values is TRUE, and ALL returns TRUE if all of those values are TRUE. Thus, if the argument column is empty, ANY and ALL ought to return FALSE and TRUE, respectively; in SQL, however, they both return null.

SQL also supports an operator called UNIQUE, which allows a table to be tested to see whether it contains any duplicate rows. (Tables that contain duplicate rows are prohibited in the relational model, of course, but they're permitted in SQL.) This operator too has a trap for the unwary. To be specific, the expression UNIQUE (*<table exp>*) returns TRUE if the table denoted by *<table exp>* contains no two distinct rows,[19] *r1* and *r2* say, such that the comparison *r1* = *r2* gives TRUE; otherwise it returns FALSE. Thus, UNIQUE sometimes returns TRUE when UNKNOWN is the logically correct answer.

---

[18] SQL doesn't allow it to denote a row of degree less than one—rows in SQL are always required to contain at least one component (possibly null, of course).

[19] Incidentally, it's an educational exercise to try to pin down, both in the context under discussion and possibly in other SQL contexts also, precisely what it means for two rows to be distinct. In particular, does it have anything to do with the SQL DISTINCT operator (which I'll be discussing in just a moment)? If so, what?

Next, I've said that two nulls aren't considered to be equal. But sometimes they have to be! Such is the case, in effect, in connection with the well known business of "duplicate row elimination," which is required, in SQL terms, when the DISTINCT operator is invoked (either explicitly or implicitly). That operator can be defined as follows. Let *a* and *b* be rows of the same degree, *n* say. Let the *i*th components ($i = 1, 2, ..., n$) of *a* and *b* be *ai* and *bi,* respectively. (There's no such thing as the *i*th component of a row in the relational model, of course, but there is in SQL.) Components *ai* and *bi* must be such that the comparison *ai* = *bi* is valid.[20] Then *a* and *b* are duplicates of each other if and only if, for all *i,* either (a) *ai* = *bi* returns TRUE or (b) *ai* and *bi* are both null; otherwise the rows are distinct.

The question of whether or not two nulls are equal also arises (as might be expected) in connection with keys. Let column *C* be a component of key *K* of table *T.* If *K* is defined to be the *primary* key for *T,* SQL will not allow *C* to contain any nulls; otherwise it will allow *C* to contain any number of nulls, just so long as no two rows contain the same value for *K*—which clearly raises the question of what the phrase "the same value" might mean, in SQL ... In this connection, you might like to meditate on the following lightly edited extract from reference [10]:[21]

> Let *k2* be a new value for *K* that some user is attempting to introduce via an INSERT or UPDATE operation. That INSERT or UPDATE will be rejected if *k2* is the same as some value for *K, k1* say, that already exists in the table. What then does it mean for the two values *k1* and *k2* to be the same? It turns out that no two of the following three statements are equivalent:
>
> 1. *k1* and *k2* are the same for the purposes of comparison (e.g., in a WHERE clause).
>
> 2. *k1* and *k2* are the same for the purposes of key uniqueness.
>
> 3. *k1* and *k2* are the same for the purposes of duplicate elimination.
>
> Number 1 is defined in accordance with the rules of 3VL; Number 2 is defined in accordance with the rules for the UNIQUE operator; and Number 3 is defined in accordance with the definition of duplicates [*see the discussion of DISTINCT above*]. In particular, if *k1* and *k2* are both null, then Number 1 gives UNKNOWN, Number 2 gives FALSE, and Number 3 gives TRUE.

To the foregoing let me now add that the rules defining what it means, in the presence of nulls, for a given foreign key value to "match" some key value in the referenced table are very complex indeed: much too complex, in fact, to be spelled out in detail here.

Finally, I pointed out in the body of the chapter that nulls aren't considered to be either less than or greater than genuine values. But sometimes they have to be! Such is the case, in effect, in connection with the ORDER BY operator. ORDER BY is used in SQL to impose an ordering on the rows resulting from the execution of some query (more precisely, from evaluation of the table expression in some cursor definition). So the obvious question arises: What is the relative ordering for *a* and *b* if *a* is null or *b* is null or both? In SQL, the answer is as follows:

1. For ordering purposes, as well as for certain other purposes already discussed (but not for all purposes), nulls are considered to be equal to one another.

2. For ordering purposes (but no others), nulls are considered either to be greater than all genuine values or less than all genuine values (it is implementation defined which).

——— ♦♦♦♦♦ ———

[20] Note that, in SQL, the comparison *ai* = *bi* can be valid even if *ai* and *bi* are of different types (because SQL performs certain type conversions implicitly).

[21] Throughout the extract in question, I fear the term "value" has to be understood as including the possibility that the "value" in question might be null.

I'll close this appendix (and this chapter) by summarizing some of what I've been saying in tabular form. Let X be an SQL variable of declared type BOOLEAN:

```
DECLARE X BOOLEAN ;
```

Consider the following possible initializations for X:

- Case 1: `SET X = TRUE ;`
- Case 2: `SET X = UNKNOWN ;`
- Case 3: `SET X = FALSE ;`
- Case 4: `SET X = NULL ;`

Also, let Y be another SQL variable of declared type BOOLEAN, and let Y be initialized to null. Then the table opposite shows, for each of the foregoing cases, what the value of a certain boolean expression ("*exp*") involving X is defined to be according to the standard (perhaps I should say, rather, according to my own understanding of the standard). *Note:* Please be aware that UNKNOWN in the notes following the table denotes "the third truth value," not the SQL literal of the same name.

exp	Case 1	Case 2	Case 3	Case 4
X	TRUE	*Note 3*	FALSE	null
NOT X	FALSE	*Note 3*	TRUE	null
X IS TRUE	TRUE	FALSE	FALSE	*Note 4*
X IS NOT TRUE	FALSE	TRUE	TRUE	*Note 2*
X = TRUE	TRUE	*Note 5*	FALSE	*Note 3*
X IS UNKNOWN	FALSE	TRUE	FALSE	*Note 2*
X IS NOT UNKNOWN	TRUE	FALSE	TRUE	*Note 4*
X = UNKNOWN	*Note 5*	*Note 1*	*Note 5*	*Note 3*
X IS FALSE	FALSE	FALSE	TRUE	*Note 4*
X IS NOT FALSE	TRUE	TRUE	FALSE	*Note 2*
X = FALSE	FALSE	*Note 5*	TRUE	*Note 3*
X IS NULL	FALSE	*Note 2*	FALSE	TRUE
X IS NOT NULL	TRUE	*Note 4*	TRUE	FALSE
X = Y	*Note 3*	*Note 3*	*Note 3*	*Note 3*

Notes:

1. Should be TRUE, but SQL gives null
2. Should be UNKNOWN, but SQL gives TRUE
3. Should be UNKNOWN, but SQL gives null
4. Should be UNKNOWN, but SQL gives FALSE
5. Should be FALSE, but SQL gives null

It seems appropriate to remind you one more time of that dictum of Wittgenstein's that Hugh Darwen and I have appealed to so many times (throughout reference [11] in particular):

All logical differences are big differences.

Chapter 28

A Critique of *Nulls, Three-Valued Logic, and Ambiguity in SQL:* *Critiquing Date's Critique*

To be criticized is not always to be wrong.

—Anthony Eden

I'd like to thank Claude Rubinson for his thoughtful critique [3] of my remarks in reference [1] on nulls and three-valued logic (3VL). Clearly we're in agreement on the major issues; as Rubinson says, "I agree with Date that three-valued logic is incompatible with database management systems." We also agree that null isn't a value; as Rubinson says, "SQL defines null not as a value but a flag" (though in fact SQL isn't completely clear on the matter—sometimes it regards null as a value, sometimes it doesn't). However, I'd like to comment on three specific issues arising from Rubinson's article. *Note:* All otherwise unattributed quotes are from that article. Note too that I follow Rubinson for the most part in using the SQL terminology of tables, columns, and rows.

THE ORIGINAL EXAMPLE

The database I used as a basis for my examples in reference [1] looked like this (S = suppliers, P = parts):

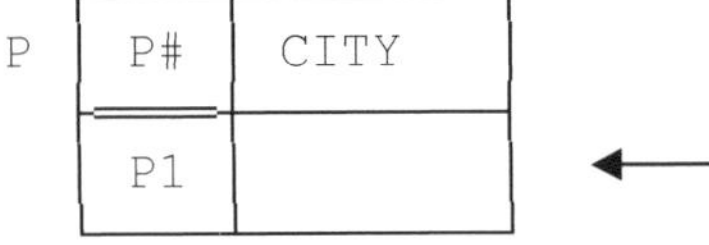

In this database, "the CITY is null" for part P1. What's more (as I said in reference [1]):

> Note carefully that the empty space in [the] figure, in the place where the CITY value for part P1 ought to be, stands for *nothing at all;* conceptually, there's nothing—not even a string of blanks or an empty string—in that position (which means the "tuple" for part P1 isn't really a tuple, a point I'll come back to [later]).

I then posed the query "Get S#-P# pairs where either the supplier and part cities are different or the part city isn't Paris (or both)," and offered the following as "the obvious SQL formulation of this query":

```
SELECT S.S# , P.P#
FROM   S , P
WHERE  S.CITY <> P.CITY
OR     P.CITY <> 'Paris'
```

I then showed that, given the sample database, the result produced by this SQL expression differed from the result that the user would expect from the original formulation (i.e., the natural language version) of the query. But Rubinson says:

> The problem [with Date's example] is not that SQL's results disagree with reality but, rather, that Date poorly formulated his original query ... The formulated SQL statement does not, in fact, correspond to [the natural language] query; in fact, Date's query cannot properly be translated into SQL.

But that was exactly my point! I agree that "the formulated SQL statement" (or expression, rather) doesn't properly correspond to the natural language query; of course it doesn't, because it produces different results. In particular, *pace* Rubinson, I most certainly didn't claim that this state of affairs "indicates a flaw in SQL's logic." SQL's logic as such isn't flawed (at least, let's assume not for the sake of this discussion). Rather, what I did claim was that "SQL's logic" is different from the logic we normally use "in the real world." That's all.

In any case (and regardless of whether Rubinson agrees with me here or whether we simply agree to disagree), I really don't think it's worth wasting a lot of time on this particular example, nor on others like it. The real question is: How are we supposed to interpret the tables in the database? Which brings me to my next point.

THE ISSUE OF INTERPRETATION

Now, in reference [1], I deliberately did not spell out in detail how tables S and P were meant to be interpreted. That's because I knew that if I did so carefully enough, the fact that nulls are nonsense would have been completely obvious (implying among other things that there wouldn't really be much point in discussing the sample query at all). The trouble is, the argument based on interpretation is a little esoteric and might, for some readers, be a little hard to follow; rightly or wrongly, therefore, I gave an argument that I thought would be intuitively easier to understand ("more accessible," as Rubinson puts it). However, let me give that argument based on interpretation now.

First of all, in case readers aren't familiar with the terminology I'll be using, let me explain that:

1. Each table *t* is supposed to correspond to some predicate *pred.*
2. If table *t* has *n* columns, then predicate *pred* has *n* parameters.
3. Each row *r* in table *t* contains *n* column values. Further, each such row is supposed to correspond to some proposition *prop:* namely, a proposition obtained from predicate *pred* by using the *n* column values from *r* as arguments to replace the *n* parameters in *pred* (each such proposition is thus an *instantiation* of the predicate *pred*).
4. Each proposition *prop* so obtained—i.e., each such instantiation of predicate *pred*—is one that we believe, or know, to be true [2].

Now, Rubinson appears to be arguing in reference [3] that it's the logical difference between (a) something being true, and (b) our knowing it's true, that lies at the heart of our difficulties with 3VL. In fact, however, we have to pay attention to that difference even without nulls and 3VL (see point 4 above), though it's certainly the case in practice that we often don't. Thus, I think Rubinson's argument here is something of a red herring. What's more, as I show in reference [2], we can still get "don't know" answers, even out of a database without nulls and without using 3VL—but that's a red herring too, perhaps. Let me get back to the issue at hand.

Consider table P. That table has two columns, P# and CITY, and so whatever predicate it represents must have two parameters. What is that predicate? Well, the obvious candidate is: *Part P# is stored in city CITY.* But we need to be more precise than that. In fact, in accordance with the remarks in the previous paragraph, a more reasonable candidate is: *We know that part P# is stored in city CITY.*

But now suppose we *don't* know where part P1 is stored. Then a true proposition of the form *We know that part P1 is stored in city CITY* simply doesn't exist!—it simply isn't the case that we know, for any specific value of *CITY* whatsoever, that part P1 is stored in city *CITY*. (*Note:* Presumably we do know it's stored somewhere, because all parts are stored somewhere, but *We know that part P1 is stored somewhere* is a completely different proposition. Observe in particular that it's an instantiation of a monadic predicate—i.e., a predicate that takes just one parameter—whereas *We know that part P# is stored in city CITY* is dyadic and takes two.)

Since no true proposition of the pertinent form exists, it follows that no corresponding row exists, either. And so no row for part P1 can appear in the table.

All right, then: Accepting for the moment that a row for part P1 (with a "null city") does in fact appear in the table after all, we must have the predicate wrong. Perhaps it should be:

> *Exactly one of the following is true: (a) we know that part P# is stored in city CITY; (b) we don't know the city for part P#.*

(Note that there must be an exclusive, not inclusive, OR connecting the two pieces of this predicate. We can't allow the same part to have both a known and an unknown city.)

Observe now, however, that the first piece of this predicate has two parameters (P# and CITY), while the second piece has just one (P#). It follows that rows representing true instantiations of the first piece have two column values and rows representing true instantiations of the second piece have just one. It further follows that these two kinds of rows can't logically both appear in the same table.[1] Thus, to talk of some row *r* in some table *t* as "containing a null" is, as I said before, nonsense—or at least, and this is really a better way to put it, it's a contradiction in terms. (Incidentally, note the implications here for outer join!)

Perhaps I should add that a design that does faithfully represent the situation—and doesn't involve nulls, of course—would have two separate tables: (a) table P, with columns P# and CITY and predicate *We know that part P# is stored in city CITY,* and (b) table P', say, with a single column P# and predicate *We don't know the city for part P#.*

DO NULLS VIOLATE THE RELATIONAL MODEL?

Although he agrees with me that nulls and 3VL are undesirable, Rubinson says he's "not convinced that three-valued logic violates the relational model." But it does! The arguments of the previous section, as well as others not articulated here, clearly demonstrate that a table that "contains a null" doesn't correspond to a relation in the relational model sense, because it fails to satisfy the basic relational requirement that every row in that table contains a value for every column. Thus, the fundamental object in a system that supports nulls isn't a relational table (I don't know what it is, but it isn't a relational table). As I said in reference [1] (and now I revert to traditional relational terminology):

- A "type" that contains a null isn't a type (because types contain *values*).
- A "tuple" that contains a null isn't a tuple (because tuples too contain *values*).
- A "relation" that contains a null isn't a relation (because relations contain *tuples,* and tuples don't contain nulls).

Taken all in all, therefore, I believe this short discussion serves to bolster the claim I made in reference [1] to the effect that, if nulls are present, then we're certainly not talking about the relational model. In other words, I stand by my claim that nulls (and 3VL) and the relational model are mutually incompatible.

---

[1] What it might mean if (nevertheless) both kinds are allowed to appear "in the same table" is explored in detail in Chapter 24.

REFERENCES AND BIBLIOGRAPHY

1. C. J. Date: *Database in Depth: Relational Theory for Practitioners*. Sebastopol, Calif.: O'Reilly Media, Inc. (2005). *Note:* This book has since been superseded by the book *SQL and Relational Theory: How to Write Accurate SQL Code*. Sebastopol, Calif.: O'Reilly Media, Inc. (2009).

2. C. J. Date: "The Closed World Assumption," in *Logic and Databases: The Roots of Relational Theory*. Victoria, B.C.: Trafford Publishing (2007). See *www.trafford.com/07-0690*.

3. Claude Rubinson: "Nulls, Three-Valued Logic, and Ambiguity in SQL: Critiquing Date's Critique," *ACM SIGMOD Record 36*, No. 4, December 2007.

Chapter 29

Nothing to Worry About

A parable for the database community

"So what's this thing here?"

The salesman smiled broadly. "Well spotted!" he cried. "I can see you're very observant." I don't like car salesmen at the best of times. "You'll *really* like this! That's a top of the line function on this model; we call it the **NULL** control. NULL stands for *No Unpleasant Lifting or Logic*. It's a special feature."

"So what does it do?" I wanted an automatic, with the two basic controls, brake and accelerator, which I like to think of as stop and go, respectively—nice and two-valued, in other words. I'm a great believer in simple user interfaces. "What does it do?"

"Oh, you're going to love this. Trust me! What does it do? Well—imagine you're driving and you find yourself in some situation where normally you'd have to do some quick—but careful and accurate!—thinking ... or action ... or judgment ... or tact and finesse—anything like that. Say the lights have just gone to amber, and you have to decide, quickly, whether to slow down or speed up. Or the gate's beginning to come down at the railroad crossing, and a train's coming—same deal: Do you slow down or speed up? Or some junk has just fallen off a truck or something and appeared in front of you on the freeway: Do you veer to the left or the right? Or the gas gauge is on empty, and you don't know whether to drive a mile or two off the freeway to get gas or try to get home where you have some spare gas in a can. EASY—all you do is hit the null control, and the system does the rest. You don't have to think about it. The null feature makes the decision for you and acts on it, instantly!"

"Hmmm ... I think I see. But now you mention it, it seems to me I've heard about this thing before—in fact, I think I've heard some consumer advocates arguing against it. What's going on, exactly?"

"Oh, you don't want to listen to those kooks. All they're interested in is decrying all the latest technologies! Look—do you think the SQL Motor Corporation would build and market a car that was *unsafe?*"

Oops. He shouldn't have said that. He knew it, too. Unsafe? A loaded word to inject into our conversation at this point! "What do you mean, unsafe?"

"Oh, nothing ... nothing. Nothing to worry about. Nothing at all. Look! Look at all these other bright and shiny features!—real *faux* leatherette upholstery, five million radio channels, electronic sliding star roof, special circular bike rack ..." He was on a roll now, but I interrupted him. "No, no, no, wait a bit, wait a bit ... What do you mean, *unsafe?*"

"Well ..."—he looked a little shifty—"well, all right. If you must. I mean, if you really have to be pushy about it ..." He stopped and looked over his shoulder. "Look—come into my office a minute." We moved off the showroom floor and into a small cubicle at the side, with a glass door. He shut the door, rather carefully I thought, and pulled down the blind. "Front desk—please hold all calls. Thanks." We sat down, and he turned to look at me.

"See, it's like this. I wouldn't tell everyone this, but I like the look of you, see. That null thing? Well, it does do everything I said. I mean, it's really great, you know! In fact, it's just amazing!" He began to wax enthusiastic again: Pavlovian reaction, I suppose. Then he remembered what he was about. "Yes, but ... The thing is, sometimes it just causes the most horrendous ... well, *failures*. I mean ... er, that is ... I mean, what I'm trying to say is, sometimes you just ... Well, sometimes you just crash."

"WHAT?"

"Listen, I'm trying to tell you. Most of the time that old null thing works just fine! Usually you get away with it! But, like I said, sometimes it just fails, dramatically ... and then you crash."

"I see." I didn't know how to respond. I mean, it was so unexpected! After a few moments, I said: "Can you tell *when* it's going to crash? I mean, is there some warning? Is there something that causes it? Is there a way you can make sure it doesn't happen?"

He sighed, and for a moment—for a salesman—he looked almost haunted. "No sir. I don't know. If I knew I'd tell you. The fact is, it seems to be completely unpredictable. Random." He looked over his shoulder again. He took a gulp from the glass of water sitting on his desk. He seemed suddenly at a loss for words. I felt I had to say something.

"OK. Well, I suppose I have to thank you for making things so clear. For being so honest, I mean." He looked as if he was going to cry. For a moment I almost felt sorry for him. "But—well, you know, in the circumstances there's no way I'm going to buy this thing! I mean: Would you? You'd have to be crazy!"

He heaved a deep sigh again. "Yes, you're right. OK, OK. When you're right, you're right. That's why we usually just don't mention the problem. But you more or less forced me to ..." He looked very unhappy. "I wasn't always a car salesman, you know! I used to have a respectable job. I used to be a database application developer! But then they sent my job overseas, and I was downsized out, and one thing led to another, and, well, here I am ... I still try to be as honest as the job will let me—I mean, I do my best—but sometimes it's really hard." He pulled out a handkerchief and dabbed at his eyes for a moment. "But ... I guess I should thank *you*. You don't know what a relief this has been for me, to talk to you like this! None of the other guys want to talk about it at all. I don't think most of them even understand the problem, they just think that old null thing is so wonderful. They're so ... oh, I don't know." More than ever, I thought he was going to burst into tears.

"OK," I said, patting his arm. "I won't tell anyone you've been honest. Your reputation is safe with me. But, like I say, I couldn't possibly buy this thing ... and in fact I feel obliged now to tell everyone else not to buy one, either! The way I see it, even if I decided never to use that null thing myself, somebody else might drive my car and use it. Right? How could I stop that? Hell, the only safe thing to do is never use it at all, right? It ought to be called the *Never Use, Leave aLone* control! Why on earth would anybody design something like that?"

"Ah," he said, brightening again, "I can answer that one!" I made an excuse and left.

——— ♦♦♦♦♦ ———

A note about the author: C. J. Date is a database specialist who believes that nulls should indeed be left alone and never used. He can prove conclusively, with a little lifting and logic, that they can lead to disastrous errors. Thus, he thinks it's incumbent on anyone who thinks they're a good idea to prove equally conclusively that their own use of them cannot.

Part V

MISCELLANEOUS TOPICS

This part of the book consists of just two chapters. Chapter 30 discusses a variety of issues that arise in connection with further normalization. Chapter 31 offers some observations on the state of the database industry today; more specifically, it proposes a distinction between what it calls database *professionals* and database *practitioners*.

Chapter 30

Some Normalization Issues: An Attempt at Clarification

How often misused words generate misleading thoughts.

—Herbert Spencer

I've claimed on many occasions and in many places—for example, in reference [3]—that a failure to distinguish properly between relation values (relations for short) and relation variables (relvars for short) has historically led to confusion. One area in which that confusion has manifested itself, and continues to do so, is that of normalization. The purpose of this chapter is to identify some of the confusions in this particular area and try to shed some light on them.

THE RUNNING EXAMPLE

Let S ("suppliers") be the relation shown in Fig. 1, with attributes S#, STATUS, and CITY. *Note:* The suppliers example usually includes an SNAME attribute as well, but I'm ignoring that attribute here for simplicity. Also, the status for supplier S2 is usually shown as 10, but I've changed it to 30 here in order to conform to the functional dependency to be discussed in just a moment.

S

S#	STATUS	CITY
S1	20	London
S2	30	Paris
S3	30	Paris
S4	20	London
S5	30	Athens

Fig. 1: Relation S

Observe in particular that relation S is indeed a relation and not a relvar. Observe too that it satisfies the functional dependency (FD)

```
{ CITY } → { STATUS }
```

Now let me remind you of Heath's Theorem, which I deliberately state here exactly as Heath gave it in his original paper (reference [10]):

<u>Theorem</u> A relation R(A,B,C), where A determines B, is the natural join J of R[A,B] and R[A,C].

(Note: R[A,B] means the projection of R on fields A and B.)

As you can see, Heath uses "field" to mean what we would now call an attribute. He also uses "A determines B" to mean the relation under consideration satisfies the FD {A} → {B}. What's more, he also goes on to show that his theorem holds even if A, B, and C aren't just individual fields (or attributes) but, rather, arbitrary combinations of fields (or attributes). But these terminological issues aren't important; what's important is that the theorem is a theorem about relations, not relvars, as his proof makes quite clear. I'll give that proof here for interest—it's quite short, as well as simple—but I won't comment further on either the notation or the terminology, except to say that the expression R(a,b,c) simply means that tuple (a,b,c) appears in relation R, and similarly for other expressions of that same general form:

Proof	R(a,b,c)	⇒	R[A,B](a,b) & R[A,C](a,c) ⇒ J(a,b,c)
	and J(a,b,c)	⇒	R[A,B](a,b) & R[A,C](a,c)
		⇒	R(a,b,c') & R(a,b',c) for some b' and c'
		⇒	R(a,b,c), since b'=b by A determines B.

Thus, R(a,b,c) iff J(a,b,c), which completes the proof.

Applying Heath's Theorem to the example of Fig. 1—taking A as CITY, B as STATUS, and C as S#—we see that relation S is equal to the join of its projections on {CITY,STATUS} and {CITY,S#}, or as we would "more naturally" tend to write them, interchanging the two projections and specifying the attributes in a "more natural" order, on {S#,CITY} and {CITY,STATUS}. See Fig. 2 below, where I've labeled the two projections SC and CT, respectively.[1] And we use this fact to justify a common decomposition we perform in normalization. To be specific:

- Let SV be a relvar (not a relation) with those same attributes S#, STATUS, and CITY. Fig. 1 can be thought of as showing a sample value for that relvar (and I'll assume that specific sample value throughout what follows, for simplicity).

- Let the FD {CITY} → {STATUS} apply to SV. In other words, let that FD not just happen to be satisfied by the particular relation shown in Fig. 1; instead, let it be an integrity constraint that must be satisfied by all possible values of relvar SV.

- Then we appeal to Heath's Theorem as justification for decomposing relvar SV into its two projections—I'll call them SCV and CTV—on {S#,CITY} and {CITY,STATUS}, respectively. If relvar SV has the value shown as relation S in Fig. 1, then relvars SCV and CTV have the values shown as relations SC and CT, respectively, in Fig. 2. *Note:* I'll come back in the next section but one ("The Second Issue") to explain just what I mean when I talk about a projection of a relvar, as opposed to a projection of a relation as such.

SC

S#	CITY
S1	London
S2	Paris
S3	Paris
S4	London
S5	Athens

CT

CITY	STATUS
Athens	30
London	20
Paris	30

Fig. 2: Projections SC = S{S#,CITY} and CT = S{CITY,STATUS}

[1] S for S#, C for CITY, and T for STATUS, of course (I use T rather than the more obvious S for STATUS, here and throughout this chapter, in order to distinguish more clearly between distinct relation and/or relvar names).

THE FIRST ISSUE

So far, so good; this is all very familiar stuff. But now I want to raise a question concerning predicates.[2] Let's get back to relations as such, for the moment. Let's assume that relation S from Fig. 1 corresponds to the following predicate:

Supplier S# is under contract, has status STATUS, and is located in city CITY.

By "corresponds to" here, of course, I mean the tuples in the body of relation S represent all and only those instantiations of this predicate that evaluate to TRUE; in other words, relation S represents the *extension* of this predicate.

Now consider the projection CT of relation S on {CITY,STATUS} (again, see Fig. 2). That projection too is "just a relation," not a relvar; but what's its predicate? Well, I've gone to great lengths in numerous previous writings to explain that it's as follows:

There exists a supplier S# such that supplier S# is under contract, has status STATUS, and is located in city CITY.

In other words, removing attribute S# from the relation, through projection, causes the introduction of an existential quantifier—"there exists a supplier S# such that"—into the predicate. And it's easy to see from Figs. 1 and 2 that relation CT does indeed contain a given tuple if and only if the tuple in question does satisfy this latter, quantified predicate.

But now let's switch back to relvars and normalization. First, let's agree, not unreasonably, that the predicate I gave above for relation S is in fact the *relvar* predicate—i.e., the meaning, or intended interpretation—for relvar SV:

Supplier S# is under contract, has status STATUS, and is located in city CITY.

Now we do some normalization on relvar SV to obtain, among other things, a relvar CTV that's the projection of relvar SV on {CITY,STATUS}. As mentioned previously, relation CT in Fig. 2 can be taken as a sample value for that relvar CTV. However, we surely wouldn't say the predicate I gave for *relation* CT—

There exists a supplier S# such that supplier S# is under contract, has status STATUS, and is located in city CITY.

—is the predicate for *relvar* CTV, would we? Rather, we would surely say, more simply, that it's just:

City CITY has status STATUS.

So what's happened to the quantification? More generally, how do we explain the discrepancy between the two predicates? *Now read on ...*

THE SECOND ISSUE

Let's consider relvar CTV, one of the two "projection" relvars produced by the foregoing normalization, in a little more detail. That relvar is indeed a relvar—I mean, it's a variable—and so we can update it, perhaps as follows:

```
INSERT CTV RELATION { TUPLE { CITY 'Rome' , STATUS 10 } } ;
```

But after this update, relvar CTV contains a tuple—viz., <Rome,10>, to adopt an obvious shorthand

---

[2] The specific confusion identified in the present section manifests itself, I fear, in certain writings of my own—in particular, in the section titled "Relvar Predicates" in reference [7].

notation—that has no counterpart in relvar SV (nor in relvar SCV, come to that). Indeed, such a possibility is often used—in fact, Codd used it himself in his original normalization papers [1,2]—as an argument in favor of doing the normalization in the first place: The normalized, two-relvar design is capable of representing certain information that the original one-relvar design isn't. (In the case at hand, it can represent information regarding cities that currently have no supplier located in them.) But that same fact also means that the two designs aren't really equivalent after all, and moreover that relvar CTV isn't exactly a "projection" of relvar SV after all—it contains a tuple that isn't a projection of, or otherwise derived from, any tuple in relvar SV.

So what do we mean by the phrase "a projection of relvar SV," anyway? Well, here's an edited extract from reference [6]:

> By definition, the operators projection, join, and so on apply to relation values specifically. In particular, of course, they apply to the values that happen to be the current values of relvars. It thus clearly makes sense to talk about, e.g., the projection of relvar SV on attributes {CITY,STATUS}, meaning the relation that results from taking the projection on those attributes of the relation that's the current value of that relvar SV. In some contexts, however (normalization, for example), it turns out to be convenient to use expressions like "the projection of relvar SV on attributes {CITY,STATUS}" in a slightly different sense.[3] To be specific, we might say, loosely but very conveniently, that some *relvar,* CTV, is the projection of relvar SV on attributes {CITY,STATUS}—meaning, more precisely, that the value of relvar CTV at all times is the projection on those attributes of the value of relvar SV at the time in question. In a sense, therefore, we can talk in terms of projections of relvars per se, rather than just in terms of projections of current values of relvars. Analogous remarks apply to all of the relational operations.

But in the example, as we've seen, the value of CTV at the time in question *isn't* a projection of the value of SV at that time,[4] and so we really shouldn't be saying things like "CTV is a projection of SV" after all.

Now, this state of affairs does at least provide an answer to the question from the previous section: The predicate for relvar CTV certainly isn't *There exists a supplier S# such that supplier S# is under contract, has status STATUS, and is located in city CITY;* rather, it's the much simpler *City CITY has status STATUS.* And we can see, now, why the quantification disappears, as it were. But now we're faced with some further questions:

- If we can't validly say things like "relvar CTV is a projection of relvar SV," then how can we say that normalization is a process of taking projections or, equivalently, that the decomposition operator used in normalization is relational projection?

- If Heath's Theorem applies to relations, not relvars, then how can we appeal to it, or other theorems of a similar nature, as a formal basis for the normalization process?[5]

Well, here's my own take on these questions, for what it's worth. It seems to me that if it's possible for relvar CTV to contain a tuple such as <Rome,10> that has no counterpart in relvar SV, then the original design, consisting just of relvar SV, was simply wrong. That is, if it's possible for a true instantiation to exist of the predicate *City CITY has status STATUS* without there existing—at the same time and with the same CITY value—a true instantiation of the predicate *Supplier S# is under contract, has status STATUS, and is located in city CITY,* then a design consisting just of relvar SV doesn't faithfully reflect the state of affairs in the real world. To put it another way, if that design did faithfully reflect that state of affairs, then the "projection" relvars SCV and CTV would have to satisfy the following constraint ("Every city in SCV also appears in CTV and vice versa"):

---

[3] *Slightly* might not be the mot juste here. All logical differences are big differences!

[4] Perhaps more to the point, it isn't a projection of the value of SCV JOIN CTV at that time either, and so that join "loses information," in a sense.

[5] Please note that I'll have quite a lot more to say regarding that phrase *the normalization process* later in this chapter (see the section "How to Do Normalization (?)").

```
SCV { CITY } = CTV { CITY }
```

But this constraint—which is an example of what reference [5] calls an *equality dependency*—manifestly isn't satisfied in the example under discussion. (By contrast, the *inclusion* dependency SCV{CITY} ⊆ CTV{CITY} is satisfied, as we would probably want it to be.[6] That is, we probably wouldn't want to allow relvar SCV to contain any tuple that has no counterpart in relvar CTV.)

Given the foregoing, it seems to me in general that (a) normalization is *not* exactly a process of taking projections after all, and moreover that (b) theorems like Heath's Theorem do *not* in fact fully apply in the normalization context. Rather:

a. Normalization is a process of decomposing relvars in such a way as to be reminiscent of, but not quite the same as, what we do when we take projections of relations.

b. Theorems like Heath's Theorem can be used to guide us in our choice of what "projections" to take when we do perform such decompositions. However, they aren't quite the formal basis for normalization they're usually taken to be.

THE THIRD ISSUE

Despite the conclusions of the previous section, it's convenient to continue to refer to the relvars obtained by normalization as "projections" of the pertinent original relvar. In fact, I'll drop those annoying quotation marks from this point forward; however, you should think of them as still being there in some virtual kind of sense.

Consider the same example once again, in which relvar SV is decomposed into its projections SCV and CTV. Even if relvars SCV and CTV aren't true projections, we can at least say the following:

> If we join the current values of those projection relvars back together, then, even if relvar CTV does contain some tuples with no counterparts in relvar SCV, we do at least get back a legitimate value for relvar SV (i.e., a value that satisfies the FD {CITY} → {STATUS}, which I'm assuming is still supposed to apply to that relvar).

In other words, we can apparently still regard relational join as the *re*composition operator (with respect to the normalization process as usually understood). But now I'd like to consider a different example.

Let the FD {S#} → {STATUS} apply to relvar SV (as indeed it normally does; in fact, {S#} is a key for SV). Then, taking A as S#, B as STATUS, and C as CITY, we can appeal to Heath's Theorem again—inasmuch as such an appeal makes sense!—to decompose SV into its projections STV, on {S#,STATUS}, and SCV, on {S#,CITY}. Fig. 3 overleaf gives sample values corresponding to the sample value shown for relvar SV in Fig. 1 (the labels ST and SC in Fig. 3 denote the relations that are the current values of relvars STV and SCV, respectively; of course, relation SC is the same as it was in Fig. 2).

Before going any further, I need to point out that, in practice, if we're trying to do normalization as conventionally understood, then we probably wouldn't perform this particular decomposition, precisely because the FD on which it's based, {S#} → {STATUS}, is "an FD out of a key." But there's nothing in Heath's Theorem that tells us not to; in other words, the decomposition is at least formally plausible, and what I'm trying to show (among other things) is that Heath's Theorem, while it might be useful, is by no means a complete guide in these matters.

---

[6] Equivalently, we can say that {CITY} in relvar SCV is a foreign key, referencing the key {CITY} of relvar CTV ("Every city in SCV also appears in CTV").

ST

S#	STATUS
S1	20
S2	30
S3	30
S4	20
S5	30

SC

S#	CITY
S1	London
S2	Paris
S3	Paris
S4	London
S5	Athens

Fig. 3: Projections ST = S{S#,STATUS} and SC = S{S#,CITY}

Suppose we now perform the following update on relvar SCV:

```
UPDATE SCV WHERE S# = S#('S1') : { CITY := 'Paris' } ;
```

Now if we join the current values of STV and SCV, we obtain the relation S' shown in Fig. 4, and that relation is *not* a legal value for relvar SV (because it violates the FD {CITY} → {STATUS}, which I remind you is still supposed to apply to relvar SV). In this example, therefore, not only are relvars STV and SCV not really projections of relvar SV, but relvar SV isn't the join of those projections either. In general, then, how can we say that the recomposition operator used in normalization is relational join?

S'

S#	STATUS	CITY
S1	20	Paris
S2	30	Paris
S3	30	Paris
S4	20	London
S5	30	Athens

Fig. 4: Relation S'

Of course, the foregoing example shows why, when we do normalization, we're usually advised to *preserve dependencies* wherever possible, or in other words to decompose into "independent projections" (see reference [11]). The foregoing decomposition is contraindicated precisely because it fails to preserve the dependency {CITY} → {STATUS}, with the consequence that joining the projections together isn't guaranteed to take us back to where we started.[7] But the decomposition has certainly been done in accordance with Heath's Theorem; and yet the fact remains that, as we've seen, the result of the decomposition can't validly be claimed to

---

[7] Of course, I'm assuming for the sake of the discussion that no analog of the FD in question is being enforced, either (not by the system and not by the user either) in the decomposed design. Note that any such analog will be a "multi-relvar constraint" (i.e., a constraint that spans relvars). It might be stated thus: COUNT ((STV JOIN SCV) {CITY,STATUS}) = COUNT ((STV JOIN SCV) {CITY}). Equivalently, we might just say, following reference [8], that (STV JOIN SCV) {CITY,STATUS} is subject to the key constraint KEY {CITY}.

satisfy the property that the original relvar is equal to the join of those projections.[8] Thus, the example illustrates very clearly the point that Heath's Theorem does not, in general, apply to relvars as opposed to relations.

BUT WHAT ABOUT REDUNDANCY?

Near the end of the section "The Second Issue," I said that if it's possible for a true instantiation to exist of the predicate *City CITY has status STATUS* without there existing—at the same time and with the same CITY value—a true instantiation of the predicate *Supplier S# is under contract, has status STATUS, and is located in city CITY,* then a design consisting of just relvar SV is simply wrong. But suppose now that it *isn't* possible; in other words, suppose that every city that has some status is the location for some supplier. In this case the original design, consisting just of relvar SV, is no longer logically incorrect. But it does involve some *redundancy;* to be specific, it states *n* times, for any city it mentions, that the city in question has a given status, where *n* is always greater than zero and often greater than one. And, of course, normalization—i.e., decomposition of relvar SV into relvars SCV and CTV—can be used to eliminate this redundancy, as is well known. Observe, however, that this decomposition satisfies the following integrity constraint:

```
CTV = SV { CITY , STATUS }
```

(which is another example of an equality dependency, incidentally).[9] In other words, relvar CTV now truly is a projection of relvar SV, in the sense that the relation that's the value of relvar CTV at any given time truly is the projection on {CITY,STATUS} of the relation that's the value of relvar SV at the time in question. What's more, the relation that's the value of relvar SV at any given time is equal to the relation that's the join of the relations that are the values of relvars SCV and CTV at the time in question. Thus, the predicate for relvar CTV in particular now does include the quantification:

> *There exists a supplier S# such that supplier S# is under contract, has status STATUS, and is located in city CITY.*

And the INSERT example I gave earlier—

```
INSERT CTV RELATION { TUPLE { CITY 'Rome' , STATUS 10 } } ;
```

—will now definitely fail.[10]

---

[8] In other words, the decomposition isn't nonloss. For the record, here's a definition (based on one given in reference [6] but refined somewhat here): Nonloss decomposition is a process in which a relvar *R* is replaced by projections *R1, R2, ..., Rn* in such a way that (a) at any given time, the join of the values of *R1, R2, ..., Rn* at that time is guaranteed to be equal to the value of *R* at that time, and usually also that (b) each of *R1, R2, ..., Rn* is needed in order to provide that guarantee (i.e., none of those projections is redundant in the join). In the case at hand, we could make the decomposition nonloss only by enforcing the constraint discussed in the previous footnote—but then the design would involve some explicit redundancy (see the section immediately following).

[9] Of course, if we really have performed the decomposition into projections SCV and CTV, then relvar SV no longer exists; thus, this constraint, and the subsequent explanations, have to be understood as referring to a hypothetical state of affairs in which relvar SV does still exist, living redundantly (as it were) alongside the two projections.

[10] To be specific, it will fail because it violates the constraint CTV{CITY} = SCV{CITY}, which needs to be stated and enforced precisely because the predicate for CTV requires every city to be the location for some supplier. (At least, it will fail unless some suitable compensatory action has been defined [4]—but in the case at hand, it's hard to see what an appropriate compensatory action might be.)

MORE ON PRESERVING DEPENDENCIES

In the section "The Third Issue," I said we're generally advised to do normalization in such a way as to preserve dependencies, if possible.[11] The example I used to illustrate the point involved relvar SV and the FDs {S#} → {CITY} and {CITY} → {STATUS} (and hence, by transitivity, {S#} → {STATUS}). To be specific, I showed that:

a. Replacing SV by its projections STV (on {S#,STATUS}) and SCV (on {S#,CITY}) was contraindicated because it failed to preserve the FD {CITY} → {STATUS},

and hence that

b. The original decomposition—i.e., replacing SV by its projections SCV (on {S#,CITY}) and CTV (on {CITY,STATUS}), as discussed in earlier sections of this chapter—was preferable, precisely because it did preserve that FD.

Preserving FDs is desirable in general because it has the at least psychological advantage that it makes the pertinent constraints easier to state, and probably easier to enforce, than they would be otherwise. Moreover, given the level of technology found in today's commercial products, it might even make the difference between system enforcement and user enforcement. It might also have performance implications; if it does, however, I have no wish to be seen as condoning such a state of affairs, and I certainly don't advance it as my principal argument in favor of preserving FDs.[12]

Recall now the familiar notions of second normal form (2NF) and third normal form (3NF). Just to remind you, here are definitions of these concepts (paraphrased somewhat from reference [6]). It's convenient to begin by defining a number of auxiliary terms:

- **Definition (superkey):** Let *X* be a subset of the heading of relvar *R;* then *X* is a superkey for *R* if and only if no possible value for *R* contains two distinct tuples with the same value for *X*. A *proper* superkey is a superkey that isn't a key.

- **Definition (subkey):** Let *X* be a subset of the heading of relvar *R;* then *X* is a subkey for *R* if and only if there exists some key *K* for *R* such that *K* is a superset of *X*. A *proper* subkey is a subkey that isn't a key.

- **Definition (key attribute):** An attribute of relvar *R* that's part of at least one key of *R*.

- **Definition (nonkey attribute):** An attribute of relvar *R* that isn't part of any key of *R*.

- **Definition (nontrivial FD):** An FD is trivial if and only if it can't possibly be violated, and nontrivial if and only if it's not trivial. *Note:* The FD $X \rightarrow Y$ is trivial if and only if *Y* is a subset of *X* (i.e., $Y \subseteq X$).

- **Definition (irreducibly dependent):** Let *X* and *Y* be subsets of the heading of relvar *R*. Then *Y* is irreducibly dependent on *X* if and only if it's functionally dependent on *X* and not on any proper subset of

---

[11] Note, however, that it isn't always possible. For example, let relvar *R* have attributes *A, B,* and *C,* and let it satisfy the FDs {*A,B*} → {*C*} and {*C*} → {*B*}. Then *R* suffers from redundancy; but if we eliminate that redundancy (by decomposing into the projections on {*C,B*} and {*C,A*}), we lose the FD {*A,B*} → {*C*}. For further discussion, see reference [9].

[12] As I pointed out in a footnote earlier in the chapter, *not* preserving (i.e., losing) an FD really means replacing a certain single-relvar constraint by a certain multi-relvar constraint. In a sense, therefore, preserving FDs is considered desirable precisely because it avoids the need for certain multi-relvar constraints. Given this state of affairs, it's a trifle ironic that, as we saw in the section "The Second Issue," normalization in general explicitly introduces certain multi-relvar constraints (typically certain inclusion dependencies or foreign key constraints)! The fact remains, however, that preserving FDs is indeed generally desirable.

X.

- **Definition (second normal form):** Relvar *R* is in second normal form, 2NF, if and only if every subset *X* of the heading of *R* is irreducibly dependent on every key of *R*.

- **Definition (third normal form):** Relvar *R* is in third normal form, 3NF, if and only if, for every nontrivial FD *X* → *Y* satisfied by *R, X* is a superkey or *Y* is a subkey.

Examples to illustrate these definitions are left as an exercise. Observe, however, that relvar SV is in 2NF and not in 3NF, while the projection relvars STV, SCV, and CTV are all in 3NF. Hence, it might be thought—and has been thought, by some—that dependency preservation is relevant only to the step in the normalization process that takes us from second normal form to third.[13] Such is not the case, however. Consider the following extended version of the example. We're given a relvar SPCTQV with attributes S#, P#, CITY, STATUS, and QTY and predicate as follows:

> *Supplier S# is under contract, has status STATUS, is located in city CITY, and supplies part P# in quantity QTY.*

Let the following FDs apply (not unreasonably) to this relvar:

```
{ S# }        → { CITY }
{ CITY }      → { STATUS }
{ S# , P# } → { QTY }
```

It's easy to see that certain additional FDs also hold. First, the FD {S#} → {STATUS} holds by transitivity. Then, given that {S#} → {STATUS} and {S#,P#} → {QTY} both hold, it follows straightforwardly that {S#,P#} → {STATUS,QTY} holds as well; in fact, {S#,P#} is a key for SPCTQV.

Now, the first step in conventional normalization is generally to look for FDs of the form A → B such that A is a proper subkey (on the grounds that such an FD means the relvar is in 1NF and not 2NF). In the case at hand, {S#} → {CITY} is such an FD. Applying Heath's Theorem, therefore (taking A as S# and B as CITY), we obtain the following as a decomposition of relvar SPCTQV:

```
SCV   { S# , CITY }
SPTQV { S# , P# , STATUS , QTY }
```

So relvar SPCTQV is "only" in 1NF (it fails to satisfy the definition of 2NF, because neither {STATUS} nor {CITY} is irreducibly dependent on the key {S#,P#}). Relvar SCV, by contrast, is in 2NF (and 3NF as well, as it happens). But the second of the original three FDs—viz., the FD {CITY} → {STATUS}—has been lost in the decomposition. The example thus demonstrates the point that dependency preservation can indeed be relevant to steps in the normalization process other than the one that takes us from second normal form to third.

> *Aside:* As a matter of fact relvar SPTQV too is "only" in 1NF. We can apply Heath's Theorem again to decompose it into its projections on {S#,STATUS} and {S#,P#,QTY}, both of which are in 2NF (and in fact 3NF); however, the damage has already been done, as it were—the FD {CITY} → {STATUS} has already been lost. *End of aside.*

To return to the original relvar SPCTQV for a moment: It should be clear that, in that example, it would have been better to use the FD {CITY} → {STATUS} as the basis for the first normalization step. That way, we

---

[13] It might also be thought that reference [9] supports this position, since it uses essentially the same example to illustrate the problem. In fact, however, that reference explicitly states, in connection with the normalization process, that "the process of taking projections *at each step* must be done ... in a dependency preserving way" (page 391, italics added).

would eventually have wound up with projections on {S#,P#,QTY}, {S#,CITY}, and {CITY,STATUS}, and no FDs would have been lost. But that FD {CITY} → {STATUS} isn't a projection out of a proper subkey; as a consequence, it typically wouldn't have been considered during that first decomposition step. See the section "How to Do Normalization (?)" later in this chapter for further discussion.

... AND A LITTLE MORE

There's another point to be made in connection with dependency preservation. Consider the following example (taken from reference [8]). Suppose suppliers are partitioned into classes, so that our usual suppliers relvar SV is extended to include an additional attribute CLASS. Suppose also that (a) each class has just one associated status; (b) each city has just one associated status as well; (c) suppliers are subject to the constraint that, for any given supplier, the class status and the city status are one and the same; but (d) classes and cities are otherwise quite independent of each other. Then the predicate for this extended version of SV is:

> *Supplier S# is under contract, is part of class CLASS, has status STATUS, and is located in city CITY.*

And the relvar satisfies the following FDs (among others):

```
{ CITY }  → { STATUS }
{ CLASS } → { STATUS }
```

Observe, therefore, that the relvar is in 2NF but not 3NF (just like the version of SV used to introduce the idea of FD preservation earlier in this chapter, in fact, in the section "The Third Issue"). Observe further that the FD {CITY} → {STATUS} is not an FD out of a key, and hence that we could (and typically would) use it as a basis for decomposing the relvar, in accordance with Heath's Theorem, into projections as follows:

```
SLCV { S# , CLASS , CITY }
CTV  { CITY , STATUS }
```

These two projections are both in 3NF (the keys are {S#} and {CITY}, respectively); but the decomposition loses the FD {CLASS} → {STATUS}.[14]

Consider now a revised version of the example in which suppliers are again partitioned into classes, but each class is associated with just one city (where each city in turn has just one associated status, as before). The predicate for this version of relvar SV is:

> *Supplier S# is under contract and is part of class CLASS, which is associated with city CITY, which has status STATUS.*

And the relvar now satisfies the following FDs (among others):

```
{ S# }    → { CLASS }
{ CLASS } → { CITY }
{ CITY }  → { STATUS }
```

Again the relvar is in 2NF but not 3NF, and again it's the case that two of the given FDs aren't FDs out of keys. Once again, therefore, we would typically use one of those FDs as a basis for the first decomposition step; but this time it makes a difference as to which FD we choose as a basis for that first step. If we choose the FD

---

[14] Of course, if we had decomposed on the basis of the FD {CLASS} → {STATUS} instead, we would have lost "the other" FD {CITY} → {STATUS}. One or other of these FDs is also lost if we decompose on the basis of either {S#} → {CLASS} or {S#} → {CITY}. In fact, what we have here is an example of the situation, mentioned in an earlier footnote, in which the objectives of full normalization and FD preservation are in conflict with one another.

{CLASS} → {CITY}, we obtain:

```
LCV  { CLASS , CITY }
SLTV { S# , CLASS , STATUS }
```

Now we can go on to decompose relvar SLTV on the basis of the FD {CLASS} → {STATUS}, but the damage has been done: The FD {CITY} → {STATUS} has been lost in the first step. By contrast, if we go back to the original relvar and use the other FD {CITY} → {STATUS} first, we obtain:

```
CTV  { CITY , STATUS }
SLCV { S# , CLASS , CITY }
```

And now we can decompose relvar SLCV on the basis of the FD {CLASS} → {CITY}:

```
SLV { S# , CLASS }
LCV { CLASS , CITY }
```

No FDs are lost in this decomposition.

So now we've seen four examples of decompositions in which FDs are or might be lost. How do they differ? Well:

- In the first example (in the section "The Third Issue"), relvar SV (with attributes S#, CITY, and STATUS) was decomposed on the basis of the FD {S#} → {STATUS}. But that FD was a *transitive* FD, implied by the pair of FDs {S#} → {CITY} and {CITY} → {STATUS}. And it would not be usual in practice, when doing normalization, to use such an FD as a basis for decomposition. That example was thus somewhat unrealistic; indeed, it was intended merely to illustrate the basic idea of FD loss vs. FD preservation.

- In the second example (relvar SPCTQV, in the previous section), the decomposition was done on the basis of the FD {S#} → {CITY}. That example was therefore more realistic—a little less contrived—than the first example, because decomposing on the basis of an FD that's an FD out of a proper subkey (which is what that FD was) is exactly what we're told to do in practice, in the normalization process, when we go from 1NF to 2NF. As the example showed, however, what we're told to do in practice can sometimes cause an FD to be lost.

- In the third example (the first of the two involving a CLASS attribute), the decomposition was done on the basis of the FD {CITY} → {STATUS}. That example too was more realistic—less contrived—than the first example, because decomposing on the basis of an FD that's out of some nonkey attribute (which is what that particular FD was) is exactly what we're told to do in practice in the normalization process when we go from 2NF to 3NF. As the example showed, however, what we're told to do in practice can again cause an FD to be lost; in the particular example under consideration, in fact, an FD definitely will be lost if we want to avoid redundancy and normalization is the only tool available to us for achieving that goal.

- Finally, the fourth example (the second of the two involving a CLASS attribute) was, like the third, an example of going from 2NF to 3NF. This time, however, we had a choice: There were two different FDs, both of them out of some nonkey attribute, and the example showed that which one we chose as a basis for the first decomposition step meant the difference between losing and not losing an FD.

Taken together, then, the examples show among other things (a) that FD preservation can be relevant even when the decomposition seems reasonable, in the sense that it's being done on the basis of an FD that's not an FD out of a key, and also (b) that it can be relevant to steps in the normalization process other than the one that goes from 2NF to 3NF.

... AND STILL MORE

There's still another point to be made on this topic. Consider again the first of the two examples in which suppliers are partitioned into classes. I said before that, for any given supplier, the class status and the city status were one and the same; and precisely for that reason, I was able to get away with including just one STATUS attribute in relvar SV. For clarity, however, let's replace that attribute by two separate attributes, CLASS_STATUS and CITY_STATUS. Then the fact that the two status values are equal for any given supplier needs to be stated as a separate constraint, perhaps like this:

```
IS_EMPTY ( SV WHERE CLASS_STATUS ≠ CITY_STATUS )
```

This constraint is not an FD, of course; however, it is a single-relvar constraint, applying as it does just to relvar SV.[15]

Now, conventional normalization on relvar SV would lead to the following three projections:

```
SLCV { S# , CLASS , CITY }
LTV  { CLASS , CLASS_STATUS }
CTV  { CITY , CITY_STATUS }
```

And the fact that the two status values must be equal (for any given supplier) has now become a multi-relvar constraint, spanning all three of these relvars:

```
IS_EMPTY ( JOIN { SLCV , LTV , CTV }
           WHERE CLASS_STATUS ≠ CITY_STATUS )
```

In other words, the original single-relvar constraint has been lost, in a sense.

The message here is simply that the whole business of losing or preserving FDs in particular is really just a special case of a more general phenomenon. In fact, it should be obvious that, in general, if we start with some database design *DBD1* and map it into some logically equivalent design *DBD2,* then that mapping process will necessarily involve some restructuring of constraints as well as of relvars.

HOW TO DO NORMALIZATION (?)

I've used phrases such as *the normalization process* (or procedure), and *conventional normalization,* and *normalization as usually understood,* several times in this chapter. But such phrases all tend to imply there's some consensus as to what "the normalization procedure" might consist of, which isn't really the case. In particular, what might be called the classical procedure, which is widely documented and taught (e.g., in schools and universities), fails to deal satisfactorily with examples like those discussed in this chapter. To be specific:

- That procedure has little or nothing to say regarding which FD to choose as a basis for the next step, when such a choice needs to be made.

- It also overlooks the fact that FD preservation can be relevant to steps other than the one that takes us from 3NF to Boyce/Codd normal form (BCNF).

- But the major problem with that procedure is its insistence on a particular step-at-a-time sequence. That is, the procedure effectively assumes that the best fully normalized design can always be achieved by stepping

---

[15] In fact, it's an example of what's sometimes called a *tuple* constraint, on the grounds that it can be checked for a given tuple by examining just that tuple in isolation. An alternative formulation is AND(SV,CLASS_STATUS = CITY_STATUS). *Note:* AND here is an aggregate operator. See Chapter 11 of the present book (section titled "Recent Changes").

sequentially from 1NF to 2NF to 3NF (and so on). However, examples in this chapter have shown that this assumption can lead to problems, because it can prevent certain design possibilities from being considered at all. An argument could even be made that the nomenclature of "first normal form," "second normal form," "third normal form" (and so on) is misleading in itself, inasmuch as it does tend to suggest that normalization should be done in accordance with that particular step-at-a-time sequence.

Clearly, what we need is a procedure that doesn't suffer from such deficiencies. And such a procedure does exist; indeed, the foregoing deficiencies have long been recognized, and several texts (see, e.g., reference [12]) give a procedure that's guaranteed always to yield relvars in 3NF without losing any FDs. The procedure in question can be stated as follows. First, let *R* be the given relvar, and let *I* be an irreducible cover for the FDs that hold in *R*. Then:

1. Let *D* be an empty set.
2. Let *X* be the left side of some FD *X* → *Y* in *I;* let the complete set of FDs in *I* with left side *X* be *X* → *Y1, X* → *Y2, ... X* → *Yn;* and let the union of *Y1, Y2, ..., Yn* be *Z*. Add the union of *X* and *Z* to *D*.
3. Repeat Step 2 for each distinct *X*.
4. If the set *U* of attributes of *R* not included in any element of *D* is nonempty, add *U* to *D*.
5. If no element of *D* is a superkey for *R,* add *K* to *D,* where *K* is some key of *R*.

At the conclusion of this procedure, the elements of *D* are precisely the headings of a set of 3NF projections into which the original relvar *R* can be decomposed.

As you can see, this procedure relies on the concept of an irreducible cover (for a set of FDs). This isn't the place for a complete explanation of that concept (such an explanation can be found in, e.g., reference [9]); I content myself here with just a brief sketch.

First of well, it's well known that some FDs imply others (I gave several illustrations of this point earlier in the chapter). Given a set *S* of FDs, then, a *cover* for that set is a set *C* of FDs such that every FD in *S* is implied by the FDs in *C*. The significance of this concept is that it's sufficient to enforce the FDs in the (typically small) set *C* in order to enforce the FDs in the (typically large) set *S*.

Second, a cover *C* for a set *S* of FDs is *irreducible*[16] if and only if the following three properties hold:

1. (*Singleton right side*) The right side of every FD in *C* involves just a single attribute.
2. (*Irreducible left side*) The left side of every FD in *C* is irreducible in turn—i.e., no attribute can be discarded from that left side without destroying the property that *C* is a cover for *S*.
3. (*No redundant FDs*) No FD in *C* can be discarded without destroying the property that *C* is a cover for *S*.

For example, consider relvar SV from the very first section in this chapter, with its attributes S#, CITY, and STATUS. The following FDs (among many others) hold in that relvar:

```
{ S# }    → { STATUS , CITY }
{ CITY } → { STATUS }
```

Call this set of two FDs *S*. Then the following set *C* is an irreducible cover for *S:*

---

[16] This is the term used in reference [9]. Most of the literature uses the term *minimal* instead. I remark in passing that a given set of FDs can have more than one irreducible cover.

```
{ S# }    → { CITY }
{ CITY } → { STATUS }
```

Explanation: The set *S* is not itself an irreducible cover; for one thing, the right side of the FD {S#} → {STATUS,CITY} isn't irreducible. We can replace that FD by the pair of FDs {S#} → {STATUS} and {S#} → {CITY}; but then we see that the FD {S#} → {STATUS} is implied by the pair of FDs {S#} → {CITY} and {CITY} → {STATUS}, and so we can discard it. What's left is an irreducible cover for *S*.

Now I can explain the normalization procedure introduced on the previous page:

- Step 1 is just an initialization step.

- Step 2 combines all FDs in the irreducible cover that have the same left sides into a single FD *X* → *Z* and then adds a heading to *D* that's the union of *X* and *Z*.

- Step 3 simply repeats Step 2 until all possible *X*'s have been dealt with.

- As for Step 4, consider the case of a relvar SCPV with attributes S#, CITY, and P#, with irreducible cover the set consisting of the single FD {S#} → {CITY}. In this example, Step 4 will cause {P#} to be added to *D*.[17]

- As for Step 5, again consider relvar SCPV. The sole key for that relvar is {S#,P#}, but none of the steps in the procedure so far will have produced a projection on (any superset of) that key; so we add {S#,P#} to *D*.

It's instructive to see how this procedure deals with certain of the examples from earlier in the chapter. Consider first relvar SPCTQV from the section "More on Preserving Dependencies," with its attributes S#, P#, CITY, STATUS, and QTY. The following FDs hold in that relvar:

```
{ S# }       → { CITY }
{ CITY }     → { STATUS }
{ S# , P# } → { QTY }
```

This set of FDs is already irreducible, and so the procedure yields projections as follows:

```
SCV   { S# , CITY }
CTV   { CITY , STATUS }
SPQV { S# , P# , QTY }
```

Observe in particular that the FD {CITY} → {STATUS} is preserved in this decomposition (contrast what happened earlier in the chapter, when we used the FD {S#} → {CITY} as a basis for the step from 1NF to 2NF).

By way of another example, consider the first of the examples involving a CLASS attribute (from the section "... And a Little More"). That relvar had attributes S#, CLASS, CITY, and STATUS, and the following FDs held:

```
{ S# }      → { CLASS , CITY }
{ CLASS } → { STATUS }
{ CITY }   → { STATUS }
```

An irreducible cover is the same, except that the FD {S#} → {CLASS,CITY} is split into two:

---

[17] Note, however, that in this example Step 5 will cause {S#,P#} to be added to *D* as well. The example thus illustrates the point that 3NF projections produced by the procedure overall aren't necessarily all needed to reconstruct the original relvar (in the case at hand, the 3NF projection {P#} is redundant).

```
{ S# }     → { CLASS }
{ S# }     → { CITY }
{ CLASS } → { STATUS }
{ CITY }   → { STATUS }
```

The normalization procedure will then recombine those two FDs, and we obtain the following projections:

```
SLCV { S# , CLASS , CITY }
LTV  { CLASS , STATUS }
CTV  { CITY , STATUS }
```

Note in particular that projections LTV and CTV both have a STATUS attribute; thus, no FDs are lost, but the design does involve some redundancy, and a constraint is therefore needed in order to ensure that the redundancy in question doesn't give rise to any update anomalies (see the section "... And Still More").

Incidentally, if we add the following Step 6 to the normalization procedure as defined above, we obtain a decomposition into BCNF projections (see, e.g., reference [9]). This further decomposition isn't guaranteed to preserve FDs, but any FDs lost are ones that can't be preserved without violating BCNF.

6. For each nonBCNF projection *T* produced by Steps 1-4 and for each FD $X \rightarrow Y$ satisfied by *T* where *X* is not a superkey for *T*, replace *T* by (a) its projection over the union of *X* and *Y* and (b) its projection over all of its attributes except those in *Y*. (Note that this replacement is an application of Heath's Theorem.)

ACKNOWLEDGMENTS

I'm grateful to Hugh Darwen for helpful comments on several earlier drafts of this chapter and much technical discussion. In particular, it was Hugh who made me realize the importance of distinguishing carefully between (a) normalization as a technique for fixing a logically incorrect design and (b) normalization as a technique for reducing redundancy in an otherwise logically correct design.

REFERENCES AND BIBLIOGRAPHY

1. E. F. Codd: "Normalized Data Base Structure: A Brief Tutorial," Proc. 1971 ACM SIGFIDET Workshop on Data Description, Access, and Control, San Diego, Calif. (November 11th-12th, 1971).

2. E. F. Codd: "Further Normalization of the Data Base Relational Model," in Randall J. Rustin (ed.), *Data Base Systems: Courant Computer Science Symposia Series 6*. Englewood Cliffs, N.J.: Prentice-Hall (1972).

3. C. J. Date: *SQL and Relational Theory: How to Write Accurate SQL Code*. Sebastopol, Calif.: O'Reilly Media Inc. (2009).

4. C. J. Date: "How to Update Views" (Chapter 10 of the present book).

5. C. J. Date: "Foreign Keys and Inclusion Dependencies" (Chapter 13 of the present book).

6. C. J. Date: *The Relational Database Dictionary, Extended Edition*. Berkeley, Calif.: Apress (2008).

7. C. J. Date: "Frequently Asked Questions," in *Logic and Databases: The Roots of Relational Theory*. Victoria, B.C.: Trafford Publishing (2007). See *www.trafford.com/07-0690*.

8. C. J. Date: "Data Redundancy and Database Design," in *Date on Database: Writings 2000-2006*. Berkeley, CA: Apress (2006).

9. C. J. Date: *An Introduction to Database Systems* (8th edition). Boston, Mass.: Addison-Wesley (2004).

10. I. J. Heath: "Unacceptable File Operations in a Relational Database," Proc. 1971 ACM SIGFIDET Workshop on Data Description, Access, and Control, San Diego, Calif. (November 1971).

11. Jorma Rissanen: "Independent Components of Relations," *ACM TODS 2,* No. 4 (December 1977).

12. Jeffrey D. Ullman: *Principles of Database Systems* (1st edition). Rockville, Md.: Computer Science Press (1980).

Chapter 31

Professionals or Practitioners? Some Reflections on the State of the Database Industry

There is no royal road to geometry.

—Euclid

For the past several months I've been working on a book—which I'll refer to in this short essay as "the subject book"—with the title *SQL and Relational Theory: How to Write Accurate SQL Code*.[1] My aims in that book are twofold:

1. To show how SQL can be used relationally, so that, as the book's subtitle suggests, users can be confident the SQL code they write is correct
2. As a prerequisite to that first objective, to explain what it means to use SQL relationally; in other words, to teach the underlying theory (viz., the relational model in particular, and certain additional aspects of relational theory in general) on which SQL systems and SQL practice are supposed to be based

But one reviewer of the manuscript—I'll call him Reviewer A—commented as follows:[2]

> [Your] target audience is not sufficiently clearly defined. Having worked and moved in both the academic and commercial spheres of the database world for rather a long time, I can say with confidence that these two worlds are quite distinct. Your text is unambiguously academic in tone, and I am constantly asking myself how relevant are the points you are making to the jobbing database developer ... I am concerned that the jobbing database worker is being taken far beyond the point he or she needs to go to understand the relational model ... If [your audience] is the academic community, fine. But I don't think that helps. The task ... is to steer the users of database systems towards the benefits of the RDBMS. Frankly, the academics are irrelevant.

Well, Reviewer A might have a point here, I thought. Certainly his remarks caused me to examine my own thoughts on the matter more carefully; in fact, they led me to write the present essay, in which I offer those thoughts for public consumption, as it were.

I'll begin by quoting (with some very minor editing) the response I gave to Reviewer A at the time:

> The extent to which the academic and commercial spheres are distinct is, I think, a large part of the problem. It's precisely because the commercial people don't understand or appreciate the "academic" aspects of their field—by the way, I reject the term "academic" here, which (again I think this is part of the problem) is seen or meant by

[1] This chapter was originally written in late 2008. The book in question was completed and published in early 2009 by O'Reilly Media, Inc.

[2] Reviewer A's comments are taken from private communications dated July-August, 2008. They're quoted here by permission.

commercial people as a pejorative[3]—that we have failures in the commercial sphere. The subject book is meant to help bridge that gap! In fact, it's heavily based on an earlier book with the explicit subtitle *Relational Theory for Practitioners*. As for how relevant the points I'm making are to practitioners: I'm offering concrete advice and recommendations on the use of SQL; that seems highly relevant to me. Moreover, that advice and those recommendations stem directly from the underlying theory. If your "jobbers" want to understand what they're supposed to be doing, rather than just blindly follow a recipe, then they need to know about that theory.[4] I have no interest in writing a mere cookbook.

As already noted, however, I realized on further reflection that there was quite a lot more I wanted to say on the matter; hence this essay, which can be seen as an elaboration on my response just quoted.

SQL USERS

One point I need to get out of the way up front. As well as raising the issue of what I'm going to call "the academic / commercial divide," Reviewer A actually had considerably more to say (in a separate communication) regarding database professionals:

> You describe your book as being for "the database professional." But that broad description describes a myriad of specialisms. For example, the DBA is undoubtedly a database professional who uses SQL, but that job is embedded deep in the physical implementation of the system. It's a far distance from the logical systems you are describing. The DBA may use SQL, but often it is in the form of "cookbook" scripts provided by the vendor to achieve certain results (new users, setting privileges, backups, patches, new versions, etc.). The DBA does NOT build SQL scripts to interrogate a production database—that is not their role. They may have an out-of-hours interest in the content of this book—but do you really consider them as part of your target audience? Many will not have had the benefits of tertiary education, let alone any exposure to mathematics. They probably came into their work as "hackers" with an interest in technology. Perhaps they started lifting disk drives in and out of enclosures, or changing tapes. They are not and should not be regarded as part of your target audience, even though they merit in full the description "database professionals."
>
> Just to make this point again. I passed two chapters (1 and 10) to a good friend ... He is an Oracle DBA of many years experience with a worldwide reputation, much sought by conferences etc. He liked what you were laying out in Chapter 1, but expressed himself extremely disappointed in Chapter 10, which he described as "impenetrable." More to the point, he said there was no way he could recommend this book, on the evidence of that chapter, to his junior DBAs.
>
> Consider the librarian, or the similar data manager, charged with looking after the database (therefore a database professional). Such people probably don't get anywhere near SQL, but rather use a succession of programs and perhaps scripts to meet their day to day responsibilities. They understand their data in great detail, they make intimate use of database technology to meet their daily job requirements, but again ... they have no place in your target audience.
>
> All I am suggesting is that you define more particularly who you are targeting and who you are not ... I have by no means exhausted the list of "database professionals" in my discussion ... Further, you should state what you expect the educational background of your readers to be. Not to mention mathematics (and even logic) might be unfortunate. Indeed, should your readers have a tertiary education that has included mathematics? We need to know

---

[3] To quote *The Complete Plain Words,* by Ernest Gowers (Harmondsworth, England: Pelican Books, 1962, reprinted 1978): "Sometimes words appear to have changed their meanings when the real change is in the popular estimate of the value of the ideas they stand for ... [In particular,] *academic* has suffered a ... debasement owing to the waning of love of learning for its own sake and the growth of mistrust of intellectual activities that have no immediate utilitarian results. It is frequently used to mean *irrelevant, theoretical,* or *impractical.* In music, according to the music critic of *The* [*London*] *Times,* the word 'has descended from the imputation of high esteem to being a withering term of polite abuse,' in spite of Stanford's attempt to stop the rot by defining the word as 'a term of opprobrium applied by those who do not know their business to those who do.'"

[4] I've said that *academic* is often perceived as a pejorative—but so is *jobber!* To quote *Chambers Twentieth Century Dictionary:* **jobber** ... one who turns official actions to private advantage: one who engages in a mean lucrative affair.

> the answer to this question.
>
> This is not to deny the value of education, it is to be realistic in determining who is best able to take advantage of that education. There is no point in teaching airline pilots cosmology, even though they spend half their life flying on the edges of the cosmos.

I've quoted this passage at length because I think it raises a number of pertinent issues. For the moment, the most important one is: What *do* we mean, in general, by the term "database professional"? I'll give a working definition here of what I mean by the term (but note immediately that I plan to refine that definition later in this essay). Until further notice, then, for the purposes of both this essay and the subject book, I take a database professional to be *anyone who has to use, or has to be familiar with, SQL in order to carry out any part of his or her job*. Note that this definition thus certainly includes (but is not limited to):

- Database application developers
- Database administrators
- Computer science professors specializing in database matters
- DBMS designers and implementers
- Persons involved in database standards activities
- Independent database consultants
- Persons responsible for DBMS product evaluation and acquisition

To a lesser extent, perhaps, it also includes database designers. What's more, since my own work certainly requires me to be familiar with SQL (even though I don't write SQL code for a living), it also includes me! Be that as it may, I think the reference to SQL in the title of the subject book not only makes it clear that the foregoing categories are all included, it also rules out many of the "nonSQL" job descriptions mentioned by Reviewer A. (Regarding DBAs in particular, however, I certainly do intend them to be part of my target audience; that is, I definitely do believe that DBAs need to know the material. After all, one of the things DBAs are supposed to be able to do is teach and give advice to other people on how to use the system. In fact, I would estimate that, in the U.S. at any rate, at least 50 percent of the attendees at my live seminars are DBAs.)

As for the educational background required, I don't believe it's either necessary or desirable to state any particular expectations explicitly. The educational background required is the educational background required to understand and use SQL, and *that* goes without saying. Of course, the phrase "the educational background required to understand and use SQL" certainly raises a few questions in its turn ... but I'll get to those later (in the section "Concluding Remarks" in particular).

One last point to close this section: I really don't think much of Reviewer A's "cosmology and airline pilots" analogy. It's certainly true that professionals in any discipline need to know the foundations of their field. Precisely for that reason, database professionals need to know relational theory—it's directly relevant to their daily job, and that's why I wrote the subject book. By contrast, airline pilots don't need to know cosmology to do their job. What they do need to know is something about aeronautics! Which brings me to the next section.

KNOWING THE FOUNDATIONS

I say again: Professionals in any discipline need to know the foundations of their field. We surely wouldn't tolerate an electronics engineer who didn't understand Ohm's Law, or a chemist who didn't understand the periodic table, and we surely wouldn't want to fly in a plane with a pilot who didn't understand aeronautics. Yet, in the database field, we seem to be quite content to put up with professionals who don't *and apparently can't* understand the theory on which their practice is based. That's what I find so disturbing about Reviewer A's remarks concerning the Oracle DBA who found Chapter 10 of the subject book "impenetrable." Chapter 10 is titled "SQL and Logic," and this is what it does:

- First, it explains some basic ideas from elementary logic: propositions, connectives (AND, OR, etc.), truth tables, predicates, and quantification (EXISTS, FORALL, etc.). All of this material is not only directly relevant to SQL, *it should already be familiar to SQL users*—at least in concept, though some of the notation and terminology might possibly be novel.

- Second, it explains how certain aspects of relational theory—to be specific, the so called "tuple relational calculus" and various related matters—are based directly on those ideas from logic, and it shows how those tuple relational calculus ideas then map directly to certain constructs in SQL.

In other words, the chapter elucidates the SQL constructs in question by relating them to, and explaining them in terms of, their fundamental logical underpinnings. That's all. So for "an Oracle DBA of many years experience with a worldwide reputation" to find the material "impenetrable" is, frankly, rather shocking. But it is, perhaps, merely symptomatic of a much bigger problem.

THE REAL PROBLEM

All through the exchanges between Reviewer A and myself I had a nagging feeling of *déjà vu*. We've been here before ... Eventually I realized (or remembered) what it was that was in the back of my mind: viz., SQL is a programming language; writing SQL code is programming; *and programming is hard*. (I state this last observation as a matter of fact, but it would be more honest to say it's my opinion. But I'm not alone in holding that opinion, as I'll soon demonstrate.)

First let me bolster my claim that there seem to be database "professionals" who don't and can't understand the theory on which their practice is based. In fact, the Internet is replete with evidence to this effect. I've quoted a variety of awful examples in numerous other writings, but I'll give a few more here for good measure. They're chosen almost at random, but they're by no means atypical. They're reproduced absolutely verbatim, typos (?) and all, except that I've added some distinguishing labels in italics to the first one:

1. *Question:* The query "SELECT * FROM myTable WHERE color!='2'" does not return rows when color is NULL.

   That's about the dumbest thing I've ever heard of. What's up?

   First answer: i think NULL means the value has not yet been set, thus although it is not equal to 2 in one sense it also has no value at all so it is also not not equal to 2 as well (eg NULL isn't zero, you aren't comparing like with like)

   ... heck, this sounds like a stupid answer, but i know what i mean.

   Second answer, quoting from MySQL documentation: In SQL, the NULL value is never true in comparison to any other value, even NULL.

2. I guess I'm a slob. I would say that 3rd normal form is about as high as I usually go, but there's always a few bits of 1st normal form hanging around to accomodate some bit of slop where cleanly modelling the real world becomes unweildy. So I consider the DB 1st normal form. Anything higher is nice if you can get it. Anything lower is probably unacceptable.

   In my pragmatic little world, anyways.

3. "DKNF" is 6NF, "Domain key Normal Form," which says that all the data decisions are defined by the domains of the relation, and the programs won't need to make any logical decisions, they'll all be defined by the data.

The persons responsible for these gems (including—perhaps especially including—the author of the text quoted from the MySQL documentation) are presumably all database professionals as I've defined them. Which is a pretty worrisome thought ... and one I'll come back to at the end, in the section "Concluding Remarks." Here

I'll just remark that, given the level of (in)competence attested to by such quotes, it's hardly surprising that software products in general, and database products in particular, are so bad.

Now I'd like to offer a series of "good" quotes (I mean, ones whose sense I strongly agree with) in support of the various positions I want to argue in this essay. Unless otherwise noted, they're all due to Edsger Dijkstra (1930-2002), though I've made a few tiny cosmetic changes here and there.[5] Here's the first:

> When, in the late 1960s, it became abundantly clear that we did not know how to program well enough, people concerned with programming methodology tried to figure out what a competent programmer's education should encompass. As a result of that effort, programming emerged as a tough engineering discipline with a strong mathematical flavor. This conclusion has never been refuted. Many, however, have refused to draw it because of the unattractiveness of its implications, such as
>
> 1. Good programming is probably beyond the intellectual abilities of today's "average programmer."
> 2. To do the job well with today's army of practitioners, many of whom have been lured into a profession beyond their intellectual abilities, is an insoluble problem.
> 3. Our only hope is that, by revealing the intellectual contents of programming, we will make the subject attractive to the type of students it deserves, so that a next generation of better qualified programmers may gradually replace the current one.
>
> The above implications are certainly unattractive: Their social implications are severe, and the absence of a quick solution is disappointing to the impatient. Opposition to and rejection of the findings ... are therefore only too understandable. We should remember that the conclusion about the intrinsically mathematical nature of the programming task has been made on technical grounds, and that its rejection is always on political or emotional ones.

As you can see, the foregoing quote strongly supports my position that programming is hard. More specifically, it claims that programming is "a tough engineering discipline with a strong mathematical flavor," and further that this claim "has never been refuted." Of course, it also observes that these facts are somewhat unpalatable and politically unacceptable; however, lack of acceptability isn't going to make them go away.

The next quote is short, but it follows on logically from the previous one:

> Any attempt to teach programming while disguising its intrinsic mathematical nature is doomed to failure.

I'll pick up on this particular point in later sections. Meanwhile, here's Dijkstra again:

> Don't blame me for the fact that competent programming, as I view it as an intellectual possibility, will be too difficult for "the average programmer"—you mustn't fall into the trap of rejecting a surgical technique because it's beyond the capabilities of the barber in his shop around the corner.

And here he is again (in this one he's complaining about the kind of computer science teaching that's all too prevalent these days, even in universities, which limits itself to teaching "facts about [current products, releases,] systems, machines, languages, etc." instead of principles:

> This form of teaching computing science is very common. How else can we explain the often voiced opinion that the halflife of a computer science student is about five years? What else is this than saying that the student has been taught trash and tripe? ... The trouble is that these facts (regarding products, etc.) represent about 10 percent of what is to be taught; the remaining 90 percent is problem solving and how to avoid unmastered complexity. In short, it is the teaching of thinking, no more and no less. The explicit teaching of thinking is no trivial task, but who said that the teaching of programming is?

And elsewhere:

---

[5] All Dijkstra quotes in this essay are taken from Edsger W. Dijkstra: *Selected Writings on Computing: A Personal Perspective* (New York, N.Y.: Springer-Verlag, 1982).

> Universities are seen less as seats of learning and centres of intellectual innovation and more as schools preparing students for well paid jobs. If industry and government ask for the wrong type of people—students brainwashed by COBOL and FORTRAN—then that is what they get.[6]

So what exactly is "the real problem," as I called it above? The real problem, it seems to me, is simply that the world of programming in general, and the world of SQL programming in particular, have grown too fast for their own good (and for ours, I suppose I should add). Almost from Day 1, in fact, the demand for programmers has far exceeded the supply. As a consequence, there has been, and continues to be, a significant financial incentive to lure would-be programmers into the fold, with the effects already described—including, in particular, the fact that we seem to be surrounded by practitioners of somewhat questionable competence and software products of such poor quality.

On a personal note—lest I should be seeming to put myself above the crowd and claiming that I, at least, am one of the competent ones—let me state for the record that I am now and always was very bad at programming. Programming *is* hard! I started my computing career as a programmer but moved after a while into the field of computer education, and subsequently into language design and database theory. (So I'm sure some of my readers are now going to point a finger ... "Hah! Who does he think he is? He admits he's no good at programming himself, yet he goes round criticizing other people who do it for a living. How dare he? Etc., etc., etc." Well, guilty as charged; but you don't have to be a competent carpenter to criticize a piece of furniture as badly made, and you don't have to be a good mathematics student to come up with a dramatically new theory of the universe. In fact, I believe quite strongly that experience in teaching can be highly useful in areas such as language design and database research. Teachability is always a good test. Indeed, if only the people responsible for the SQL standard had tried the experiment of teaching other people the results of their deliberations before casting them in concrete, as it were, we might have had a much better standard. But I digress.)

THE ACADEMIC / COMMERCIAL DIVIDE

Now I want to turn my attention to the specific issue of "the academic / commercial divide." Clearly, Reviewer A is right in saying such a divide exists. As I indicated in my initial response, however, I believe the academic / commercial divide is a large part of the problem; more specifically, I believe it lies at the root of what in the previous section I called the *real* problem (emphasis added). Let me elaborate.

First of all, the academics are concerned with principles, not products—or at least, they're supposed to be; but I've already mentioned Dijkstra's criticism of the academic world in this regard, at least with respect to the kind of teaching it does ("facts about current products, releases, systems, machines, languages, etc., instead of principles"). Here's another pertinent quote, from Christopher Strachey this time:

> I am quite convinced that in fact computing will become a very important science. But at the moment we are in a very primitive state of development; we don't know the basic principles yet and we must learn them first. If universities spend their time teaching the state of the art, they will not discover these principles and that, surely, is what academics should be doing.

Strachey wrote this in 1969, but I think it's still relevant today.

Anyway, let's agree for the sake of the argument that the academics are indeed concerned with principles, or in other words with the underlying theory.[7] By contrast, the commercial world is concerned with practice (of course it is, that's its job). *But practice without theory is doomed to fail.* Here's another quote:

---

[6] The notion of "the average programmer" is sometimes invoked—rather curiously, when you come to think about it—as a justification for this state of affairs (i.e., for not setting educational sights and standards too high). Dijkstra again: "[I'm often asked:] But what about the education of the average programmer? ... [My answer is] the counter question: What about the education of the average mathematician?"

[7] Indeed, to the extent that this is not the case, we have another part of the root of "the real problem."

> Those who are enamored of practice without theory are like a pilot who goes into a ship without rudder or compass and never has any certainty where he is going. Practice should always be based upon a sound knowledge of theory.

This one is due to Leonardo da Vinci (1452-1519) and is thus some 500 years old!—but I believe it sums up the situation admirably. To repeat something I said earlier, professionals in any discipline need to know the foundations of their field. It follows that database professionals in particular need to know relational theory, since that theory is the foundation of the database field. In fact, I want to go further: I want to say that a professional—or "professional" in quotes, rather—who is ignorant of the foundations of his or her own field is, frankly, nothing but a charlatan. (See my earlier remarks regarding chemists, pilots, and electronics engineers.) Which brings me to my promised revised definition of the term *database professional* ... Earlier, I gave the following as a working definition:

- A database professional is anyone who has to use, or has to be familiar with, SQL in order to carry out any part of his or her job.

However, I now propose that anyone who fits this definition, but nothing more, be called merely a database *practitioner*. And I'll (re)define the term *database professional* as follows:

- A database professional is a database practitioner *who is familiar with relational theory.*[8]

So let *A* and *B* be, respectively, the set of all database practitioners and the set of all database professionals, according to these definitions. Ideally, then, the sets *A* and *B* would be equal. But we already know they're not. Again, that's why I wrote the subject book; I wanted to bridge the gap between the professionals and the mere practitioners, with a view to converting the latter into the former.

Aside: The following quote from Tony Hoare is, perhaps, off topic (but if it is, it's only slightly so):

> There are few engineering disciplines in which the successful pursuit of academic ideals can pay higher material dividends than in computer science.

Hoare is speaking here of computer science in general, but I think his remarks are applicable to database management in particular. *End of aside.*

Anyway, Reviewer A was clearly right in this respect: I should have defined my target audience as practitioners rather than professionals (and I will—at the time of writing, the book still exists only in manuscript form, and the manuscript is easily corrected). But one thing I definitely won't do is "dumb down" the style of presentation. *Pace* Reviewer A's comment, quoted earlier, to the effect that the text is "unambiguously academic in tone," I think that if you're not prepared to invest a little effort in learning how to do your job properly, you don't deserve to be called a professional. I'm not prepared to compromise on this issue. Of course, I *am* prepared to do my best to teach and explain the theory as simply, clearly, and accurately as I can—but, to repeat, I'm not prepared to dumb the material down. Here I stand. I can do no other.

---

[8] One reviewer objected to the fact that these proposed definitions are framed in terms of SQL specifically (albeit implicitly, in the second case): "Is Date saying that [e.g.] *Rel* users are not practicing database usage? I think 'SQL' should be replaced with 'a relational language or SQL.'" I'm sympathetic, somewhat, to the sense of this criticism. But I didn't say *Rel* users weren't practitioners; I only said those who used SQL and knew nothing more *were* practitioners. What's more, it seems to me that if you do know some truly relational system like *Rel*, then you'll effectively be familiar with relational theory anyway, and so you'll automatically be not just a practitioner but a professional, by my definition.

CONCLUDING REMARKS

I have a couple of pieces of unfinished business to attend to. First, I said earlier that the phrase "the educational background required to understand and use SQL" raises a few questions. Well, I hope by now I've given some idea of what my own answers to those questions might be, even though I never came out and stated the questions themselves explicitly. In order to use SQL successfully, I believe you need to understand relational theory; and in order to understand that theory properly, you must have some training in, or at least some aptitude for, abstract logical thinking. And as I'm sure you'll be expecting by now, Dijkstra has some words on this issue too:

> Programming in the sense of thinking, or thinking in the sense of programming, can indeed be taught. Not all your students will learn it, but in that respect it is no different from any other subject.

Second, I said earlier that it was "a worrisome thought" that the authors of those dreadful Internet quotes were "presumably database professionals" as I had defined them at that point in the essay. Well, I'd say now, rather, that they were practitioners but probably not professionals, given my extended definition of this latter term. And yet again Dijkstra has a relevant observation:

> From experience I have learned that ... an excellent mastery of their native tongue is an absolute requirement for all [programmers]. A programmer that talks sloppily is just a disaster. Excellent mastery of his native tongue is my first selection criterion for a prospective programmer; good taste in mathematics is the second important criterion. (As luck will have it, they often go hand in hand.)

APPENDIX A: THE STATE OF DATABASE TECHNOLOGY

I've quoted Dijkstra extensively in this short essay in support of my opinions, but it would be very wrong of me to give the impression that he would have agreed with everything I've said about databases in particular. Indeed, what evidence there is suggests he probably wouldn't, since, in the early days at least, he was hardly a fan of database technology as a respectable academic discipline. In a trip report on a conference he attended, he wrote the following:

> I learned a few things about databases. I learned—or, had my tentative impression confirmed—that the term "database technology," although sometimes used, is immature, for there is hardly any underlying "science" that could justify the use of the term "technology." I even have my doubts when I am asked to believe that "database technology is still in its infancy," for that strikes me as being asked to regard the quacks at the fairs as the infancy of medical science. The point is that the way the database management experts tackle the problems seems to be so grossly inadequate. They seem to form an inbred crowd with very little knowledge of computing science in general, who tackle their problems primarily politically instead of scientifically. (In this respect the panel discussion was very revealing: At least half the time was devoted to problems related to standardization! From the history of programming language development they should have learned to what disasters that premature concern about standardization may lead.) Often they seem to be mentally trapped by the intricacies of early, rather ad hoc solutions to rather accidental problems; as soon as such a technique has received a name, it becomes "a database concept." And [they display] a totally inadequate use of language, sharpening their pencils with a blunt axe.[9]

Now, the conference in question was held, and Dijkstra's comments were written, in 1976, when "database technology" was still a pretty young field.[10] The products IMS, IDMS, and TOTAL (perhaps one or two others as well)—all of them nonrelational, of course—accounted for most if not all of the installed base. Codd's original

---

[9] A reference to an aphorism of Dijkstra's own: "About the use of language: It is impossible to sharpen a pencil with a blunt axe. It is equally vain to try to do it with ten blunt axes instead."

[10] It's immodest but not irrelevant to mention that the first edition of my textbook *An Introduction to Database Systems* was published only one year previously, in early 1975.

papers on the relational model were written only a comparatively short time before, and his ideas were still a long way from being universally accepted. (They definitely weren't accepted by the majority of the participants on the panel that Dijkstra mentions, to my own certain knowledge.) There were no relational—or "relational"—products (there were a few prototypes, but they were very new). SQL had only recently been defined and was still comparatively unknown. And so on.

Of course, the real question is: Has our field matured since that time? Well, in some respects, the answer is obviously yes; for example, we now have a much better appreciation of the significance and relevance of predicate logic, we have a clearer understanding of the nature of both data and transactions, we have a better scientific handle on the question of database design (though much remains to be done in this regard), we know a lot more about optimization and other techniques for efficient implementation, and so on. On the other hand, I believe many of Dijkstra's strictures are still applicable. For one thing, I can certainly point to cases where the database community has failed to learn from other disciplines but has instead invented "solutions" for itself, solutions that have subsequently been found lacking. And then there's SQL ... Considered as a programming language (which, I repeat, is what it is), do you think SQL has been designed in accordance with well known and widely accepted principles of good language design? If your answer is *yes,* I think you should examine your reasons rather carefully. And if it's *no,* what does that say about the database field?

Index

For alphabetization purposes, (a) differences in fonts and case are ignored; (b) quotation marks are ignored; (c) punctuation symbols—hyphens, underscores, parentheses, etc.—are treated as blanks; (d) numerals precede letters; (e) blanks precede everything else.